Views from Abroad

The Spectator Book of Travel Writing

Edited by Philip Marsden-Smedley
and Jeffrey Klinke

PALADIN
GRAFTON BOOKS
A Division of the Collins Publishing Group

LONDON GLASGOW
TORONTO SYDNEY AUCKLAND

Paladin
Grafton Books
A Division of the Collins Publishing Group
8 Grafton Street, London W1X 3LA

Published in Paladin Books 1989

First published in Great Britain by
Grafton Books 1988

A CIP catalogue record for this book is available
from the British Library

ISBN 0-586-08896-2

Printed and bound in Great Britain by
Collins, Glasgow

Set in Trump Mediaeval

CONTENTS

2 WESTERN EUROPE

3 EASTERN EUROPE

4   AFRICA

5 THE MIDDLE EAST

6   THE FAR EAST AND AUSTRALIA

7   NORTH AMERICA

8   CENTRAL AND SOUTH AMERICA

FOREWORD

by Colin Thubron

'I do not expect to see many travel books in the near future,' wrote Evelyn Waugh in 1946, lamenting that the past six years had reduced Western civilisation to a desert of displaced persons and authoritarian control. His contemporaries would never have travelled in such innocence, he felt, if they had known that 'all that seeming-solid, patiently built, gorgeously ornamented structure of Western life was to melt overnight like an ice-castle, leaving only a puddle of mud.'

But the forty years embraced by this anthology testify to his mistake, and to the speed with which travel-writing adapted to new circumstances. The changes which Waugh considered so destructive seem only to have offered wider and sharper perspectives, different challenges, new butts for ridicule.

At first, it is true, an uncharacteristic national humility appears. Peter Fleming, in 1951, laments that the British – almost stripped of empire – are out of touch as never before. A year later an article attacks the phrase-books designed for the British abroad – all written for a time when they could afford to dispense with popularity – and prescribes, instead, a humorous list of emollient phrases more suited to the national decline. Soon afterwards Kingsley Amis intimates that travel-writing is now dead, and that its place can be decently usurped by fiction.

But the sheer flexibility of the genre rendered all announcements of its death premature, and by 1964 James Morris is expressing his delight in the fading of travel snobberies and prejudice. There follows such a flood of articles from distinguished writers – ranging from the anecdotal to the synoptic – that one wonders what contemporary magazine could have attracted a comparable breadth of talent.

The Spectator travel format (if anything so loose qualifies as a format) invited articles at once compact, apparently leisurely, and politically alert. The study of the past – the classical or biblical antiquity which obsessed an earlier age – has become extinct. The only true subject is contemporary people. The format lends itself not only to the vignettes which illumine national character (sometimes, unwittingly, the writer's own) but also to a pithy density which the more expansive form of the travel book generally inhibits. So, notably, Peter Ackroyd digs out the heart (or heartlessness) of Finland, Paris, Texas; Patrick Marnham interprets Spain; Shiva Naipaul describes the lost destiny of Portugal.

The anthology's opening sections alone display a diversity of subject which engages three generations and twenty different tones of voice. Browsing at random, the reader may pass from Freya Stark's inimitable philosophy of travel to Simon Raven's cameo of a homosexual ball in Hanover, discover the mandarin nostalgia of Harold Nicolson, or Patrick Leigh Fermor on a serpent-cult in the Abruzzi; find Evelyn Waugh himself dyspeptically en route for Africa; Rose Macaulay, John Betjeman, Nancy Mitford or Alice Thomas Ellis.

But the marshalling of these forty years' travelling by continent or region exposes, too, a gradual darkening. The early American articles of Kenneth Tynan or William Golding read like fairy-tales beside the ghastly blankness diagnosed by Peter Ackroyd. The Middle East sinks under a resurgent Islam. Attitudes to Africa become fraught with ambivalence, and slowly shed the 'tolerance' which Shiva Naipaul saw as the white man's ultimate act of condescension – the refusal to blame a people for their own chaos.

In fact, if there is one voice which permeates this anthology, it is Naipaul's. With unsentimental outspokenness he dared to say things which a native-born Briton scarcely could. Like his brother V. S. Naipaul, he was at once repelled and fascinated by the so-called Third World, and brought to his reportage a similar fastidiousness and intelligence – whether he was confronting Kenya or indicting the pre-revolutionary vulgarity of Iran.

With writing of this order, travel reportage begins to shed its age-old disengagement. 'Abroad' ceases to be purely pantomime or pleasure. It becomes closer, more urgent.

The many voices of this selection – echoing, enriching and occasionally contradicting one another – reflect the changes at home as well as abroad. The old traveller's delight, it seems, has waned a little, and a new unease has surfaced. It is hard, of course, to know which has deepened – the malaise in the spectacle or the sensitivity in the spectator; but that is the perennial fascination of the traveller's voice – which is the sound of one civilisation reporting on another.

ACKNOWLEDGEMENTS

The editors wish to thank Freya Stark and all the other authors who agreed to have their work reprinted in this volume.

'In Spain and Portugal' by Rose Macaulay is reproduced by permission of A. D. Peters & Co. Ltd.

'My Voyage Round Reagan's America' by John Mortimer is reproduced by permission of Advanpress Ltd.

'City and Suburban' articles by John Betjeman, reprinted by permission of the Literary Executors of the Estate of the late Sir John Betjeman.

EDITOR'S PREFACE

All the articles in this book first appeared in *The Spectator* between 1950 and 1987. They were selected, from some 2,000 issues, for their diversity – of place, date and experience – and also for the quality of writing.

The period chosen, loosely termed 'post-war', has meant that a broad range of writers could be included. Some of them, like Freya Stark, Rose Macaulay, Evelyn Waugh and others, had done their formative travelling during the 1920s and 1930s. Set their accounts against the younger generation of writers, like Shiva Naipaul, Colin Thubron or Patrick Marnham, and two distinct camps emerge with different experiences and very different styles of writing. The post-war years have also seen changes in the nature of travel itself. The younger generation has had to wrestle with the distinction between travel and tourism. This has meant, as Thubron himself has pointed out, a new emphasis on writers who travel rather than, as their predecessors tended to be, travellers who wrote. The predominance of the former in this selection reflects how much more good travel writing there has been in recent issues of *The Spectator*. From the 1950s it was much harder to find material that was sufficiently well-written to qualify.

What is travel writing, and how does it differ from foreign reporting? Most of the pieces that appear in *The Spectator* under a foreign dateline are concerned with presenting a picture of a country, or an aspect of it, and concentrating on political or historical observations. Those that qualified did so more for their emphasis on the personal experience of 'being abroad' with all its ironies and afforded wisdoms (in this way travel writing is much closer to fiction than to journalism, not least because it does not date so quickly).

The material appears as it was first published – without cuts. The exceptions are Evelyn Waugh's 'Tourist in Africa' and Nancy Mitford's 'A French Revolution Diary'. The extracts are taken from series of articles too long to republish in total, but too good to leave out altogether.

Philip Marsden-Smedley
January 1988

1 TRAVEL AND TRAVELLERS

Freya Stark

THE PHILOSOPHY OF TRAVEL

It is usually assumed that the traveller who prefers lonely places, the desert traveller so to say, is one who wishes to escape from his world and his fellows. The popular conception gives to his wanderings a touch of misanthropy. To him the gentle things of every day make no appeal; the intercourse of humanity – that fragile house of cards built with such delicate and assiduous labour through millenniums of time, threatened by every cataclysm, and which yet stands because of the mere fact that every card leans up against the others – this finite and infinite structure of civilisation is supposed to be the object of his aversion, the atmosphere from which he turns away.

I should like to offer a far less negative interpretation of the longing which leads men out into the wastes. The Lord Byrons of this world,

> 'Tired of home, of wife, of children tired,
> The restless spirit is driven abroad to roam,'

are rather bogus spirits more often than not. I have a suspicion that Lord Byron himself might easily have settled into a domesticated middle age if his fates had not cut the thread so soon. The discontented are the least capable of all people to live with themselves for very long; and the same goad which has driven them out into the wilderness will prick them home again.

The true wanderer, whose travels are happiness, goes out not to shun, but to seek. Like the painter standing at his easel, he moves constantly to get his perspective right, and feels, though half a country may be spread out to a far horizon in his view, that he is too close to his picture and must get away now and then to look at it with an eye of distance. This necessity keeps him for ever on his feet. He touches and retouches the tones of his world as he sees them; and it is to make the proportions more accurate that he travels away from them, to come back with a more seeing and a rested eye.

It is, of course, absurd to think that one gets away from the world by moving into lonely places. All that happens is that one reaches a simplified world, with few personal attachments of one's own. The human figure itself takes on immense majesty when you meet it solitary in a landscape that scarcely speaks of humanity at all – where no fields, no walls, no hedges, no milestones, telegraph poles and unnaturally straight lines of road make the single human being seem less important by adding continuity to the image of humanity as a whole. Ruins go well with deserts for this reason; the human continuity is visibly broken by them, and the rare human figures you may meet among them stand doubly isolated in space and time. Even without ruins or deserts, the sea or the mountains can create the same impression, of dignity and gallantry, round the fisherman's boat aslant in the trough of the waves, or the shepherd with his flock, alone on pastoral edges where the high rocks come down. The smallness and the weakness of the human creature is there made unmistakably apparent, and yet at the same time you feel in yourself the elation of victory, the knowledge that the solitary puny being is the master of his immense horizon; and if you yourself are sharing the life of solitude and hardship, you feel that you too have a part in the victory which you see.

This is a true feeling, presenting humanity as it is, amid the antiquity, the size and grandeur of earth. It is worth a long hard journey to attain it, for it is scarcely to be found in towns or easy places, where men triumph so habitually one over the other that their more cosmic victories are difficult to distinguish. For every victory of man over man has in itself a taste of defeat, a flavour of death; there is no essential difference between the various human groups, creatures whose bones and brains and members are the same; and every damage we do there is a form of mutilation, as if the fingers of the left hand were to be cut off by the right; there is no pleasure in it, nor any deep sense of achievement or peace.

We like the country, and even more so the comparatively desert places, because there we can take pleasure in watching with far less interruption the progress and the triumphs of mankind. The countryman is not, I imagine, nobler than his fellows, nor is the sympathy that we, travellers in Arabia, feel for the rough bedouin a result of any marked superiority of theirs over other men. Their violence, their crimes against their own kind and therefore against themselves, are, if anything, greater than the average that our civilisation allows; and yet we are happy because we can see behind these crimes a background of real and vast achievement, the primitive vanquished background of earth. The courtesy of the desert Arab who stands in his poor tent to receive the stranger is not greater necessarily than that of the diplomat at the head of his staircase; yet a difference is made by the darkness of the surrounding hills, by the stony hardness of their paths, by the scarcity of food and water. Even the smallest crumb of grace or virtue is a triumph when the whole darkness of earth and time lies around it; and we are constantly comforted even for the worst crimes in those lands of treachery and murder by the sight of a victory immeasurably greater than these defeats, wrested by the whole of humanity out of the 'fell clutch of circumstance.'

This is, I believe, the obscure reason which has lured not only explorers, but hermits, saints and philosophers into their solitudes. They are not anxious to leave the paths of their fellows, but they do seek out the less frequented stretches, where – free from obstructions – they can comfort themselves with the certainty that the path does go uphill and not down. It is, of course, not impossible to make sure of the same fact in other surroundings. More discrimination and more imagination are required, and also a mind less sensitive, less alert to the impact of what surrounds it, so that it may keep the essential truth in sight through all the contradictions of times and men. Socrates loved the market-place, and his sense of proportion was not impaired; but perhaps he is not a fair example, for the light of Attica is a very clear light and preferable to most deserts even now. The artist, too, if he is sufficiently in earnest, can follow his vision in a crowd, and is made happy perpetually by the victory of the human spirit, in which he has the delight of taking an active part; and of the scientist, pursuing knowledge for its own sake, the same may be said. But to most even of these, and to many of lesser calibre, it is a help and a rest to get away for a while to where the pattern of mankind is traced in less complicated lines, so that background and direction show clearly beyond the tangle of our self-inflicted sorrows.

I have often noticed that the eyes of sailors and hillmen are free and quiet. Countrymen, too, when they walk among their fields, and women who surround themselves with love in their homes and think rather little of what lies beyond, old men contented with the end of their journey, and painters, carpenters and all makers, when happy in their jobs – these and many others, men and women who have found their true vocations, share the same atmosphere of certainty and peace. I have noticed, too, that the business of these people is never such that it makes them consciously share in the wounding of their fellows, whether through rivalries, or vanities, greed or envy; not only are they free of such impulses in themselves, but the happiness of their condition is such that they are largely exempted from watching this strife in others, either through the solitude of their lives or through the absorbing interest of what they care for. For it is to be hoped, and I think believed, that the worried look visible on so many city faces is more due to the constant witnessing than to the constant infliction of pain – though both must take their share in a competitive life. Those who are so happily free from this affliction have no need to travel; they can sit quietly and continue to be philosophers at home.

To the rest of us the roads lie open and lead to a true and happy panorama of our world. We will avoid mere sightseeing and the rush of trains, or cars, or liners, where the suicidal tendencies of mankind are just as visible as in a street of bankers; and will confine ourselves to two sorts of landscape, each of which can give us what we need by different means. We may go to some quiet land, not over-populated, where there is enough natural propriety for contentment, enough leisure for beauty, enough poverty for kindness, and enough labour for health – some mountain land like the Dolomites, where the harvests are sufficient to feed the villages, and the families go in summer to cut their hay and live in their wooden chalets high up amid their pastures in the sun. Here one need not search to pick out one man in many hundred with the look of contentment in his eyes; one meets it, clear as the current of the mountain streams, in the glance of almost every passer-by; and that is the human comfort of the hills.

Or one may go to the wilderness where there is no consolation of human peace, but where the magnitude of Nature is so apparent, the reality of her obstacles so visible, that the smallness of our achievements matters no longer. The fierce and tiny tribes can tear and lacerate each other; we see that this is a mere incident in the colossal triumph achieved by man in his mere existence, with whatever small measure of order, courtesy and goodness he has managed to collect. And we are comforted because we know in our hearts that the city and the desert background are the same, and the noise of our machines is not much louder than the tribal battle-cry, and is just as temporary against our tremendous background in space and time.

24 March, 1950

Peter Fleming

THE MAN FROM RANGOON

As the audience flowed out through the foyer at the end of the play I caught the tail-end of an invitation which a well-dressed, middle-aged, rather purposeful lady was addressing to a tall, serious young man.

'Next Tuesday,' she was saying, 'any time after six. Henry's bringing a friend of his who is just back from Rangoon. Do come if you can.'

'Thanks awfully,' said the young man. 'I should love to.' And I heard no more.

It may be, of course, that the lady knew, or supposed, that the young man had a particular interest in Rangoon; but he looked too young to have been there in the war (when in any case Rangoon was not a place where soldiers grew social or sentimental roots, as some did in Cairo or in Athens) and he had not at all the air of a youth who was on the point of setting out to seek his fortune in Burma. As I walked away from the theatre reflection failed to invalidate my first impression: which was that in England today a man who has just come back from Rangoon is a rare and a potentially interesting phenomenon, a purveyor of exotic information, a sort of little austerity lion.

It need not, of course, have been Rangoon. A dozen other place-names would have done as well. Names which were once large, uninviting milestones on the beaten track, places where big firms had their head offices and European communities were in general too preoccupied with suburban protocol to be well-informed or even curious about the hinterlands behind them. You felt rather sorry for the people who were obliged to live in such banal, unrewarding places. You spoke of them as being 'stuck' in (for example) Rangoon, and when they came home on leave you were not surprised to hear them say that they were terribly out of touch with things. If you travelled through the countries in whose capitals or seaports they lived they were wonderfully kind to you. They envied you your mobility and the chance it gave you of visiting places in the interior which they had never seen; and when you came back from the interior they asked you many questions and listened, rather wistfully, as you tried to answer them. ˙

All this has changed considerably in the last few years. Rangoon, and many places like it, have become 'the interior'. How interesting it would be, when one comes to think of it, to meet a man with recent first-hand experience of Poona. How unimaginable is the life of the foreigner (if there are any foreigners) in Hankow, how exciting it would be to visit Simla. The horizons of the British have been sharply contracted. The whole of China is out of bounds. Persia would hardly attract the casual traveller. The Indian peninsula, though still accessible, is no longer dotted with a dependable network of Government Houses and Residencies and dak bungalows, hill-stations and cantonments, between which residents and visitors formerly drifted almost without effort. French Indo-China is a battlefield.

I remember in the '30s, spending a morning in an ante-room of the

Legation in Moscow of the Outer Mongolian Peoples' Republic, the first, and in those days the only, satellite of the USSR. I was on my way to Manchuria and hoped – not at all confidently – to get a visa from the Outer Mongolians which would enable me to leave the Trans-Siberian express at a place called Verkhne Udinsk and travel south-east by a motor road which led to Urga, the Outer Mongolian capital. It was a wasted morning. If there were any Outer Mongolians in the consulate, which had an uninhabited air, they were not interested in me; and the uncommunicative Russian who took my card, though he came back once or twice to scrutinise me in a rather bewildered way, could throw no light on my prospects of an interview. Eventually I gave it up and wandered out into the early autumn sunshine.

I was not in the least surprised by my failure to make the slightest impression on what we should nowadays call the Iron Curtain, but I remember feeling mildly aggrieved that travellers should be arbitrarily excluded from a little-known territory with an area of a million square miles; it seemed wrong and unnatural. Today embargoes of that sort, affecting not one but many millions of square miles, do not seem in the least unnatural. We accept them as an almost axiomatic feature of the world we live in, and they combine with the contraction of our Empire on the one hand and our incomes on the other to reduce very considerably our knowledge – as a nation – of the world. With the rather shallow civilisation of Africa we have indeed increased our contacts; and the number of Britons with first-hand experience of Malaya and Korea is, fortuitously, far higher than it ever was before. But it must be true that, generally speaking, the British at the moment are more out of touch with the rest of the world than they have been for several generations.

One used to take very much for granted the far-flung but well-established contacts which linked these islands with remote parts of our planet. At one stage of the last war a plan was being made for the recapture of the Andaman Islands from the Japanese. At the end of a long day's work I remember one officer on the planning staff saying wearily to another: 'I suppose these blasted islands really *are* important?' 'Important?' said the other. 'Of course they are. Only place I ever made a century.' The point that struck me about this remark – which was quite true, incidentally – was that, though in a way it was surprising, it was also very typical. The world was until recently a place in almost every corner of which the speaker's contemporaries had done enterprising or incongruous things. The atlas was dotted with *points d'appui.* 'Who's consul there now?'. . . 'My brother-in-law'll put you up if he's not on tour.'. . . 'There's sure to be someone in our Tientsin office who knows the form on that. I'll send them a cable.'. . . 'I should ask the missionaries when you get there.'

Some people, of course, derived a more direct advantage than others from this sort of cosmic version of the 'old boy net'; but even if we had no contact with it as individuals, it did, I think, perceptibly flavour the background of our national life. 'Muriel says Lashio's much better for the children than Mergui.' . . . 'It's only pewter, but it's a nice shape, isn't it? My son had it made when he was in Swatow.' . . . Remote, romantic place-names became domesticated in English households, the ends of the earth were pasted into snapshot albums, grandmothers headed for Asia in the autumn.

Perhaps it didn't all mean very much. It is not essential to the well-being of fifty million people that one of them should have made a century while playing cricket in the Andaman Islands. But our horizons have shrunk, and look like continuing to shrink. 'What's it like there now?' we more and more often find ourselves asking; in the next generation the question will be 'What sort of a place is that?' Sooner or later, no doubt, some new historical trend will reverse the process and the age of rediscovery will dawn. Publishers will announce titles like *Poona Unveiled*, *My Three Weeks in Tsingtao* and *Forbidden Mandalay*, and it will hardly occur to anyone to say 'This is where my great-great-grandfather came in.'

5 *October, 1951*

E. Arnot Robertson

GAMBITS FOR TRAVELLERS

All the foreign phrase books in this country date from the time when the British abroad could afford to dispense with popularity: having prestige and money to back them, they needed to know only the vernacular for 'These sheets are not clean. This window will not open. Bring me some hot water. Where is the manager?' Nothing ingratiating.

Now that we require to be liked as never before, to offset the decline in our spending power, travel agents should supply a list of the key words and phrases which open local hearts in various countries, however unprofitable the tourist. Here is the beginning of my own invaluable private compilation, much of it gathered the hard way – by watching people who found these keys before me getting away with the berth, the ticket or the meal which I thought I had secured. Then I began, nervously at first, to rely on them. Popularity, I find, can practically be guaranteed by their right use in the right place.

Cyprus. 'Thembirazi' (it doesn't matter in the least) and 'Siga-siga' (slowly-slowly or gently-gently). I can't be sure of the spelling, but in demotic Greek that is the pronunciation. 'Siga-siga,' particularly, produces a beam of incredulous delight on Cypriot faces when it accompanies a request of any kind. You don't get whatever you want any slower, because you weren't going to get it quickly, anyway. Cyprus may be physically in the Mediterranean, but in spirit, especially where time is concerned, it is much further east. You will get it eventually, though, with lots of jolly goodwill thrown in. One of my vividest memories of the island is of an American striding through the foyer of the Dome Hotel at Kyrenia, saying: 'Now, look, I'm in a hurry — ' when the place seemed unusually full of porters and waiters leaning up against pillars, and before the sentence ended there was nobody there at all but the two of us.

With 'Thembirazi,' though this can be very effective too, care should be taken over Easter. An over-courteous friend learnt the word from me and used it freely while sightseeing on the Sunday morning, under the impression that the talkative crowds in the streets were apologising for jostling her. (As if they would.) This is the day when people assure one another in conversational tones that Christ has risen. To be told that it didn't matter in the least was not endearing. 'Siga-siga' would have been much better. It is, in fact, infallible. This is as well, because Cypriots at home cannot be cajoled by ordinary compliments, however sincere. They tend to outdo yours at once by one of their own, also directed to themselves. When I told a man who was just getting married that I thought his bride very pretty, 'Yes,' he said, 'and she has a nice character, too, although for all-round purposes I prefer my own.'

Holland. 'Your sense of humour is so like ours.' I can't imagine why the Dutch should respond so readily to this idea, but over and over again in Holland since the war I have heard the same phrase, said always with the same over-modest pride: 'The Germans hated us, you know, when they were here because we have the same sense of humour as the British.' The Germans had far better reasons for hating them than that, the Dutch being the toughest resisters in all Europe. And it is not even a true, if insignificant, claim. Whatever sense of humour these stalwarts have, it isn't in the least British. I have only seen it functioning once. By some strange misunderstanding, an English trick cycling team was sent to Walcheren Island when there was a *Kermesse* at Middelburg. In Walcheren the whole populace moves everywhere on wheels: a builder cycles past you in the morning with a ladder balanced over one shoulder, two planks propped on one foot and his smallest child standing on the other, clinging to his thigh, being taken to school. A slightly older child sits on the handlebars, while the eldest, on the carrier behind, holds the cycle on which all three will ride home after school, if their return doesn't coincide with Pap's. The Dutch audience sat in dead silence, watching the English Performers, balancing in ballet positions on one wheel, pedalling with their hands, riding five machines at once, and stolidly they waited for the show to begin. It was one of the most embarrassing spectacles I have ever seen. As the only other English person present, I tried clapping what seemed to me the more wildly spectacular feats, but at once all heads turned wonderingly in my direction, and the lonely noise made the situation feel worse, so I stopped. Then the cyclists, piled in a pyramid, rode mournfully out of the arena. After another long silence the Dutch realised that this was the performance, and it was over. How they laughed, rolling around in their seats. Their enormous, tear-compelling merriment went on and on and on. It couldn't have been less British, but the similarity of our senses of humour is an article of faith which they are charmed that you should share.

Italy. 'Tell me, when you were with the *Partigiani* — '

Norway. 'How nice to be back again among people who don't care about making money.' This is the only one of the keys I can use with my whole heart. It is always delightful. Never shall I forget the *bel canto* distress of the Scala Opera Company from Milan, travelling on the wagon-lit train which leaves Oslo at seven every evening and reaches Trondheim at eight the next morning, when they discovered that not only was there no dining car, but the Norwegians could not be bothered to come down to the many intermediate stations to sell the hard-boiled eggs, gelati, and so on, that would have been forthcoming, of course, in Italy, at a price. They raged along the corridors – such lack of civilisation! Was it possible, when they were hungry, hungry, ready to pay anything? And every night it must be the same! Meanwhile, the Norwegians and the British aboard, made kin at once by Latin outbursts, sidled up to one another, muttering, 'Got a biscuit in my compartment. If you'd care — ?'

Iceland. 'I had no idea you were still a tall and golden-haired people.' No one else has either, I think, except the Icelanders. It is a long while since they were Vikings, and in the interval the whole world has grown noticeably swarthier. The majority of the Icelanders are small, dark runts, just like the majority of the British, but there never was a people who cherished more myths about themselves, and this is the favourite.

Canadians and Americans. 'Someone told me you were a Canadian' (or American), 'but I knew at once that you were an American' (or Canadian). I have never known who is the more put out by a mistake, nor does it seem to matter.

On second thoughts, this is too important a line of research to be left to travel agents and phrase book publishers: the Foreign Office should pursue it, if we are to be allowed to travel at all.

2 October, 1953

Kingsley Amis

IS THE TRAVEL-BOOK DEAD?

The vogue for the highbrow travel-book shows no immediate signs of abating. At any rate, here are two more endeavours in that field.* The usual characteristics of such books are, first, a leaning towards the more elaborate and unfashionable graces of prose – rightly unfashionable they seem to me, if I may show my hand thus early – and, secondly, a desire to get away from the exhausted sterilities of Western civilisation so feelingly alluded to from time to time by Mr Priestley. In themselves, these two things may be all very well, though I judge it unlikely; in practice, however, the stylistic graces degenerate briskly into an empty and indecent poeticism, apparently based on a desire to get into the next edition of *The Oxford Book of English Prose*, while the escape-motive is only with difficulty to be distinguished from the feeling that the other fellow's grass is greener, that the really good time, or good life, is going on somewhere else. The two tendencies, in these degraded forms, find remarkably unhallowed expression in Mr Laurie Lee's volume.

The experienced reader will know what to do with a book whose blurb announces, as if in recommendation, its author's claim to 'the enchanted eye . . . of a true poet,' but the reviewer must act differently. His part is to soldier grimly on, trying not to mind too much the absence of a verb in the opening sentence, the incessant din of adjective and poeticality ('the scarred and crumpled valleys,' 'the oil-blue waters'), the full close of the first paragraph, mannered as any Ciceronian *esse videatur*:

> And from a steep hillside rose a column of smoke, cool as marble, pungent as pine, which hung like a signal over the landscape, obscure, imperative and motionless.

*A Rose for Winter. By Laurie Lee. (Hogarth Press). *The Narrow Smile*. By Peter Mayne. (John Murray)

(The effect is a little marred through having been anticipated, three sentences earlier, by a cadential 'raw, sleeping and savage.') Another item on the list of things to try not to mind too much is the prevalence of lists – cf. Mr Auden's *Spain*, which Mr Lee has perhaps been cf.-ing too – like 'the bright façades . . . the beggars . . . the vivid shapely girls . . . the tiny delicate-stepping donkeys,' and so on; and yet another one is the 'striking' image – 'fragrant as water' – which at first sight seems to mean almost nothing, and upon reflection and reconsideration is seen to mean almost nothing. One way of summing up this book would be to call it a string of failed poems – failed not-very-good poems too, for whoever said that bad poetry is much more like poetry than good poetry is, was in the right of it there.

This kind of objection, however, though compulsory for the reader of almost any highbrow travel-book, is here purely trifling. The really telling strictures emerge from a mulling-over of what Mr Lee actually reveals to us about Andalusia. The figure of the narrator himself, having terrific fun with a drum in a wedding procession, carrying *two* guitars 'everywhere,' carefully recording every pass made at his wife, drinking like mad at a party in a telephone exchange while the switchboard lights 'twinkled unheeded' (not too good for people who wanted to ring the doctor) – can safely be left on one side. One might even haul to the other side the bull-fighting question, although the author's taste for 'the sharp mystery of blood' will remain unshared in some quarters, where, in addition, the use of the phrase 'the moment of truth' will appear a little worse than *naïf*, and to upbraid a bull for having no grace or honour or 'vocation for martyrdom' will appear a lot worse; if we enjoined these duties upon a bull, he would not understand us. But the least attractive part of Mr Lee's portrayal of Spain is his portrayal of Spaniards, so far as this can be debarnacled from rhetoric, generalisation and rhapsody. The effect is not what he evidently intends; where he seeks to show us gaiety, mere instability or hooliganism emerges, unselfconsciousness is detectable as coxcombry or self-pity, while the gift attributed to Andalusians of greeting others' misfortune with a shrug or a grin is neither mature nor admirable. I am sure these people are not as bad as all that, just as I am sure that they are not in touch with the 'pure sources of feeling' and the 'real flavours' of life, whatever these entities may be; Coleridge put Wordsworth right on peasants a long time ago. Perhaps too many people in England do watch television, or do they watch it too much of the time? Anyway, *nostalgie de la boue* is not the answer; it is silly to sleep on straw in the inn yard if you can get hold of a bed; and while it is no doubt better to be gay and have sores than to be un-gay and not have sores, it is better still to be fairly gay and not have sores.

Turning from Mr Lee's vulgar and sensational little book to Mr Peter Mayne's straightforward account of the Pathans is a relief not to be lightly underestimated. At first sight, admittedly, there are points in common, notably this business of the escape-motive, the desire for a simpler, more elemental existence, but *The Narrow Smile* does at any rate propound a less lethally familiar solution to this problem, and propounds it without egotism or complacency – indeed, without much conviction, which is sympathetic if nothing else. And this kind of honesty is reflected in the style: despite a few echoes of the Graham Greene of *The Lawless Roads*, Mr Mayne is agreeably unliterary, nor is he the kind of travel-writer who feels obliged to demonstrate his sensitivity at every turn. Much of his book, in fact, is sober reporting of political and social conditions among the Pathans, who, in case you don't know, live on either side of West Pakistan's frontier with Afghanistan. The hillmen on the Pakistani side of the frontier having had perforce to abandon the local tradition of exercising our Indian Army, are now engaged in exercising, on a more tranquil level, the administrative officials of that area – a proceeding viewed with enjoyment in Kabul, where a Pathan separatist movement is being encouraged. Oddly enough, the proposed independent Pathan State, though taking in a good deal of non-Pathan Pakistan, includes no Afghan territory whatever.

Now although I quite liked being told about all this, I did feel at times that, to adapt the old gag, I was being given more information on the subject than I cared to have. Most readers, I think, will be more interested in the author's other theme, the character of the Pathan tribesman and the difficulties and rewards awaiting the European who tries to get to know him. The Pathan, as depicted here, is certainly different from ourselves, and simpler, and in a way more free, but whether he is more admirable is very doubtful, and whether he can provide any answer to any spiritual escape problem is a speculation few will feel moved to undertake. I for one cannot share Mr Mayne's thesis that violence tends to become morally neutral when pursued openly, in a picturesque tribal costume, under conditions of physical discomfort, and against a background of boulders and precipices. Loyalty, genuine dignity, high spirits and independence are all valuable qualities, but they ought to shed their glamour when accompanied by arrogance, cruelty and bloodthirstiness; and the Pathan avenger with his rifle and knife is as contemptible, however much more impressive looking, as our own species of gangster with his razor or bicycle chain.

It is a measure of Mr Mayne's candour and unpretentiousness that he can provoke this kind of disagreement without at any time forfeiting sympathy. His other virtues are no less attractive: he can readily give the feel of a terrain or a conversation, his eye for character remains unclouded by the similarity of most of the types he draws, and he can be very funny – most of all in his portrait of a certain Said Akbar, the most endearing snob I can remember ever having come across. The main weakness of his book lies in its form, which, as you will have gathered by now, is that of the travelogue. This means that the encounters he describes are for the most part indecisive, and the factual thread on which he strings them is inadequate to bear their weight; there is no principle of selection or emphasis. Short of epic or sonnet-sequence, the only way of introducing such a principle, of imposing order on the discursive, is to write the thing as a novel. I have little space, and no inclination, to start discussing the kinds of truth which writing can embody, and it may be enough to rely upon a bare mention of *A Passage to India* in order to propose that fiction is the mode in which the kind of issues that interest Mr Mayne – and Mr Lee – can best be worked out. This is not a conclusion of unparalleled novelty, but it is one which travel-writers, good and bad, might do well to ponder.

17 June, 1955

James Morris

HOME AND AWAY

'Abroad is unutterably bloody,' Miss Mitford's Uncle Matthew thought, and only the other day Mr Ian Fleming endearingly remarked about a journey round the world: 'What fun it all was! What fun "abroad" will always be!' The frontiers, though, are distinctly fading; where once the first nigger ingratiatingly awaited your arrival at Calais, today it is becoming increasingly difficult to feel abroad at all. The comfortable old stereotypes of travel have been scoffed into oblivion; the Italian no longer has waxed moustaches, the German no longer clicks his heels, the American has abandoned horn-rimmed spectacles, and even the Englishman no longer habitually turns to the personal column of *The Times*, as he gingerly nibbles his *croûton* beside the boulevard. There is little in contemporary travel that is altogether unfamiliar; partly because television has taken us everywhere already, but partly because the human race is, rather late in the day, discovering its own unity.

There is often something priggish in our present preoccupation with international good works (charity begins in Calcutta). From all the welter of sanctimonious initials, though, from the easy way out of the Oxfam Christmas card, from our lofty condemnation of racialists in far stickier positions than we are ever likely to endure – from our present mood of ostentatious holier-than-thou, there has incidentally emerged an altogether more agreeable approach to the techniques of travel. Sickly it may sometimes be, to pretend that we are all brothers under the skin; but how much pleasanter it has made the world, how exhilarating it is to feel that no ineradicable old barriers of race, creed or nationality divide us from the gendarme, the banana-sorter or even the wild fakir. We have been released! Travel for our forebears, as any Victorian memoir will confirm, was girded about with wretched prejudices, restraining the free impulses even of the Kinglakes, the Bakers or the Richard Burtons. We are much luckier. We start from scratch. For us, a man can be a man again, and even the shadows of the heathens, wogs and natives have vanished into parody.

In a way frontiers have always been most artificial for the British, for wherever we go in the world we have a stake. When we wander across Europe, we are never really in foreign parts, so close is the mesh of history, and so patent is it – *pace* de Gaulle and his fuzzy islanders – that we are Europeans too. When we go to the United States, we have to try hard to be foreigners, in a country where almost everything, from the Constitution to the current Broadway presentations, still has an English smack to it. In Egypt or India, Jamaica or Hong Kong, Australia or the Argentine – in all of them we may legitimately feel half at home, and know that were it not for earlier British travellers the face of the land would not be quite the same.

Within a hundred yards of the remotest kraal or most uncompromising *pissoir*, somebody is almost sure to speak at least a few words of our language. The wandering scholars of the Middle Ages were never lonely, they say, because as they staggered from Bologna to Oxford, and back to the philosophical disputations of the Sorbonne, everywhere they lived among men who spoke Latin. Today, as it luckily happens, the language of tourism as of scholarship, of show business as of aviation, is pre-eminently English. We can still, like those learned vagrants, argue with foreign sages the composition of angelic substance; but more to our present point, wherever we go we can confidently order a scotch-and-soda in our own language, or even inquire after the political fortunes of President Nasser without taking a preliminary course in what diplomats still love to call 'the Arabic'. Indeed, it has often seemed to me, at convivial moments of a peripatetic life, that there cannot be more than four or five young people in the world whose ambition is *not* to perfect their English by practising their irregular verbs on me.

There are those who deplore all this, who grumble about sameness, Americanisation and the impossibility of getting away from the tourists. I am not among them. It seems to me that the abolition of unnecessary differences clears the deck for a merrier kind of mélange: not the old chequer-board of black and white, Christian and pagan, Froggies and Wops, their lingo and ours, Us and Them, but the much happier hodge-podge of individual variety. Abroad is not so abroad as it used to be, but now that the *categories* of travel are dissolving, we can see all the better how marvellously mixed is mankind itself, how overwhelmingly the interest of travel lies in the particular rather than the general, in what you do rather than where you are.

The doctrines and snobberies of travel have lost their point, thank God, and it does not mean much nowadays to boast that you are just back from Barcelona or Bangkok. We are travelling lighter, fresher, kindlier – and we are finding that familiarity does not kill surprise. For more than twenty years I loathed, with an ingrained spleen, the idea of Clovelly. How splodged and saccharine it used to look on the biscuit tins – so stagy, so over-painted, so appallingly picturesque. Last autumn, however, I actually went there, for the first time in my life – and I found it to be, of all the tourist marvels I have ever visited, among the most genuinely astonishing. The moment I set eyes on the place, it sprang out of a pigeon-hole into a pleasure: and so, to our fortunate generation, can all the world around us, as the old structure of prejudices collapses, and we are left to make a fresh start.

'Going abroad this year?' they always ask. Certainly: abroad to Singapore or Aberystwyth, abroad down the High Street or up to the Bronx, abroad on the Red Sea, the Volga or the Grand Union Canal – abroad wherever we go, among those blackguards, bores and charmers, the rest of us.

24 January, 1964

Simon Raven

TRAVEL: A MORAL PRIMER

Since life is short and the world is wide, the sooner you start exploring it the better. Soon enough the time will come when you are too tired to move farther than the terrace of the best hotel. *Go now*.

No need, you may say, to tell us that. But what I do need to tell you is that you will meet with a surprising amount of opposition and frustration the moment you try to set out. Rubbish, you will reply: more people go abroad nowadays than ever before; never has travel, particularly among the young, been more strongly encouraged, never has there been so much in the way of organised tours and educational visits, of international exchanges and cultural fraternisation. Perhaps not; but none of this, my dear young friends, is travel. Travel is not going on a round coach trip for £67 all in, or spending ten days at a provincial university just over the Channel simpering out platitudes about student values. *Travel* is when you assess your money and resources and then set out, alone or with chosen friends, to make an unhurried journey to a distant and desiderated goal, repudiating official supervision, leaving only a post restante address (if that), and giving no date for your return.

Real travel, then, is independence in action, and as such is detested by the authorities. They don't mind your going (say) in a school party to Athens, because they know just where you are and when you'll be back, and they can therefore permit you the illusion of freedom (thus winning your future good will) without for one second letting you beyond their control. But what they cannot bear is that you should launch off over the horizon as the spirit happens to move you, for then you are no longer to be found in the neat little slot assigned to you, all ready to be bullied and interfered with. You (and perhaps your taxes) have escaped them; their files on you rapidly become irrelevant and out of date; there is a danger that you might actually become *your own man*.

So in order to see that it doesn't happen, the authorities (socialist authorities in particular) do their best with forms and regulations, above all with spiteful restrictions about money, to keep you, if not permanently at home, at any rate confined to voyaging within the smallest pos-

sible compass for the shortest possible period – and even this niggardly
licence is made out to be a gracious concession. 'Few ordinary people,' the
dreary cry goes up, 'can afford more than £50 to travel with, so let us limit
everyone to that.' Never mind about whether the Government's excuse is
good or bad; the point is that from now on and for ever an excuse there
will always be, because it suits the authorities to keep us all mewed up.

And yet, my friends, I have good news. It is still just possible to get
going and stay clear, provided you proceed somewhat as follows;

1. Put money in thy purse. Earn it, save it or borrow it (perhaps
you have a sporting bachelor uncle or a weak-minded grandmother?),
wheedle it, scrounge it or extort it, but make sure you have a sum of cash
commensurate with the probable duration of your journey. Although
beachcombing sounds so romantic, it rots both body and soul. And don't
think you can live on your wits, for better men than you have tried and
failed. You don't want to end up selling yourself. Therefore, put money in
thy purse.

2. Keep very close about the extent of your resources, even in the privacy of your own home. Parental interference can be quite as virulent as
the bureaucratic kind, for much the same reasons.

3. Courtesy requires that your parents should be told you are actually
going, but you should imply that it is a brief, safe trip of the familiar and
sponsored type. Keep your real route and destination strictly to yourself.
In no case take dons, schoolteachers, family doctors or priests into your
confidence, for these days such people are quite as officious as the public
servants to whom they liken themselves. Always remember this: if anyone at all suspects that you intend really to *travel*, bloodymindedness will
blaze forth all about you.

4. Leave unobtrusively, with the minimum of luggage and the maximum of prepaid tickets (always secure a line of retreat).

5. Currency. Let us suppose you have the nous to collect between two
and three hundred pounds. Now, although there *are* legal ways of taking
more than £50 with you, most of these (health or business allowances,
etc etc) apply only to your elders or else presuppose that you are going on
some official or educational tour, which is just what you are not doing.
Your best bet is therefore to take yourself and your money direct to the
sterling area nearest where you want to be (e.g. Cyprus for Greece or Turkey) and arrange matters there, which will not be difficult. As for the
morality, well, bad laws invite disobedience.

6. On arrival at (say) Boulogne, you are now your own master for up to
three months. Do not abuse the privilege. Behave with modesty (especially if you are very young) lest you arouse curiosity. Send frequent
friendly postcards to your parents to forestall anxiety; but do not give too

definite an impression of enjoying yourself, as this causes more irritation than anything else in the world.

7. Return before the beginning of term or whatever. You have, after all, your career to make.

So much for techniques. Now a little more about behaviour and attitudes, this to ensure your independence (see 6), to increase your pleasure, and to maintain the repute abroad of yourself and your fellow-Englishmen.

If you enter a foreign country, you do so of your own free will, and this must mean that you are prepared, while you are there, to tolerate if not to approve the political regime which obtains. Do not, therefore, make childish remarks either about General Franco on the one hand or Chairman Mao on the other. If you do, you will be locked up, and serve you right.

Certain peoples (e.g. the Greeks) are peculiarly courteous to strangers, receiving them all, without distinction, as 'guests'. Do not take advantage of this. Young persons of a certain type have recently taken to exploiting the hospitality of the Greeks and then boasting that they have been over the entire country without spending a penny. Such behaviour is unkind to the Greeks, who are poor, and unworthy of an Englishman. It would also detract from your enjoyment, as dependence on one's hosts can be very incommoding. (Another excellent reason for paying attention to (1) above.)

Remember at all times that you are British. This is nothing to be ashamed of, nor, as things are, to be very proud of. But you are what you are, and if you start pretending to be something else you will become nobody at all. I have a dear friend who once lived much in Italy and flattered himself that he was always taken as an Italian because he was small and dark and spoke the language fluently. Why, I once asked, do you wish to appear Italian? Because, he said, I find Italians more sympathetic than Englishmen. What my friend did not know was that no one in Italy ever thought he was an Italian; they thought that he was what he was – a Jew. This story has several morals, but the main one is that a man should know his identity and stick to it.

Knowing your identity, and therefore your nationality, you should not affect to feel, on this account, either inferiority or the reverse. We are all different (thank God) and that is all there is to it. So when you go among foreign people, relish what is pleasurable or excellent, and also take note of what is not. You will never be able to make their everyday habits truly your own, but you can share in them, for the time, and you can understand them. That is enough. The same, of course, goes for their moral customs: accept them while there, understand them, imitate them if you wish. But be sure that it can only be imitation, and that you cannot bring alien customs back to England, except for purposes of private pleasure or reference. In public they do not fit here. The more's the pity, you may say. I cannot agree: we are all (thank God) different.

This simple fact will come out most clearly should you penetrate to countries where the people are coloured. You are not superior to such people; you are merely much richer (or you would not be there) and probably much better educated from the western point of view. They have their own traditions (read Laurens van der Post on this subject) and you have yours; in so far, then, as they aspire to partake in your way of life, they must for some generations be at a grave disadvantage. This is nothing for you to sneer about or for them to resent; it is simply so. If you should not sneer, neither should you patronise; and you should never be misled, by sentimentality, into refusing to accept menial services from them on the ground that these 'insult their human dignity.' They need the money; and if you just give it to them, you insult them far more than if you insist on a definite service in exchange. For while it is doubtless unpleasant to clean another man's shoes for a small coin, this is far less humiliating than to receive the coin as a mere dole. Shoeshine boys have ended up as presidents of republics; beggars have always remained beggars.

9 August, 1968

Alexander Chancellor
pays tribute to an exceptional writer

SHIVA NAIPAUL

If, like me, one has never been to Trinidad, and perhaps even if one has, it is extremely difficult to imagine the circumstances in which Shiva Naipaul grew up. He has described them often enough, and with great eloquence, but his story still has about it the quality of a fairy tale. Most of the Indians in Trinidad before the first world war had come there as 'indentured labourers', arbitrarily transferred from one end of the British Empire to the other to work in the sugar plantations. Shiva's grandfather was one of them. His father, however, contrived to escape from this wretched environment. He became a journalist (working for the *Trinidad*

Guardian), married into a family of Indian landowners, and settled eventually in the Trinidadian capital, Port of Spain, where Shiva was born, one of seven children, on 25 February, 1945.

Three years ago, Shiva returned to Trinidad to make a television programme for the BBC. In it he described the life that might have been his:

> My father's family lived in darkest Caroni, Trinidad's Indian heartland. They worked on the sugar estates, lived in mud huts, kept cows and goats and chickens; men and women with rough hands, who smelled of dust and sugar-cane and – all too often – of rum: an authentic peasantry whose existences were very different from my own and yet, ancestrally, so close. Only a kind of magic separated me from them; a kind of luck I could not understand. It was out of this background that my father emerged, managed somehow to get an education – English was a language he had to acquire – and eventually was able to turn himself into a journalist and writer of short stories. Looking back, it seems a miraculous achievement.
>
> I could so easily have been exactly like my country cousins: labouring in the canefields and ricelands, taking cows out to pasture, bringing bundles of firewood home at dusk. I could, I suppose, have been married off at 17 or 18; become father to a child or two by the time I was 20. I might have drunk away the wages of the sugar harvest in the local rum shop and regularly beaten my wife. My childish ears picked up rumours of all these horrors. As it was, I lived in Port of Spain. I was a town boy, having a reasonably good education drummed into me, driven by quite other impulses and ambitions.

Among the bright Indian boys of Port of Spain, these impulses and ambitions had a single objective: escape. For the poor among them, who included Shiva, the only possible escape route was to Oxford University through one of the four 'island scholarships' awarded each year. His elder brother, V. S. Naipaul, had already achieved this dazzling goal. He was in London, working for the BBC, becoming a writer. Now it was Shiva's turn. 'Education under these circumstances,' said Shiva, 'became a barely controlled form of frenzy shared by parents and offspring alike.' It was a conventional English education imposed with the ruler and the leather strap. At one time the misery was so great that Shiva played truant for a month, roaming the slums around Central Market. At another time, against his own inclinations and aptitudes, his parents decided he should be a doctor – the most prestigious career open to a Trinidadian Indian – and put him into the science stream of his school, with near-disastrous consequences. But, returning to the more 'humane' branches of study, he finally obtained his 'island scholarship' and, at the age of 18, triumphantly boarded the banana boat for Avonmouth and Oxford, leaving an island he had found tawdry, confining and alien.

'Trinidad calls itself a nation,' Shiva has said. 'But Trinidadians have no geniunely collective existence. We are merely a random collection of different races thrown together by outside forces for purposes quite alien to our well-being.'

It was to be a voyage of no return, or at least of no permanent return. 'Having to return to Trinidad – to St James [Shiva's home district of Port of Spain] – nearly always fills me with alarm. It brings on this nightmare – that, having once arrived there, I may never be able to get out again. I imagine myself trapped there for ever,' he wrote in a long autobiographical essay published last year in the *New Yorker* and reprinted in his last book, a collection of stories and pieces called *Beyond the Dragon's Mouth* (Hamish Hamilton, £12.50). For most of the next 22 years, until the tragedy of his sudden death last week, he was to live in England. But he was never to regard England as home. He was by now convinced that he was incapable of allegiance to any community, or indeed of any normal social existence. He had left Trinidad, so he wrote, 'haphazardly cobbled together from bits and pieces taken from everywhere and anywhere'. Lacking, so he believed, any coherent identity, he felt obliged to 're-invent' himself every day. Oxford, which had been the miraculous fulfilment of a great dream, did nothing to change this idea he had of himself. 'The magic of Oxford had not rubbed off on me,' he wrote in an article for the *Sunday Telegraph* seven years ago. 'I had no splendid conversations that went on all night, no intellectual or spiritual revelations. The University cannot be blamed for this. It belonged to a tradition, a civilisation, concerning which I had only the most primitive notions.' When he left Oxford, with a degree in Chinese and a young English wife, it was in a very gloomy state of mind. 'I had no vision of myself: I would have to start afresh; to discover, unaided, my human possibility. In my meagre baggage was the beginning of a novel, the outlines of which had occurred to me one bilious and despairing afternoon as, sick in mind and body, I gazed at the mossy apple tree that grew in the unkempt garden of the flat I had been renting. It wasn't much to be taking away after four years, but it was better than nothing: it gave me, however unreliably, a reason to go on living.'

The portrait of Shiva that emerges from his own writings is one of a remarkable, exceptionally gifted man, but possibly of a man one would not care to know, of a solitary, gloomy, self-obsessed person, lacking the gift of companionship. It is a portrait in this last respect so misleading that it fairly takes the breath away.

What keeps coming back to me at the moment is his laugh: high, rasping and infectious. Writing may have been his main 'reason to go on living' – indeed, I believe that it was – but he was one of the most companionable people I have ever met. The headline over Martin Amis's appreciation of him in last Sunday's *Observer* was 'A talent for warmth'. It was exactly the right headline, because it was – to those who did not know him – the most improbable of Shiva's qualities.

I first met him about ten years ago after he had already written two prize winning novels, both set in Trinidad: *Fireflies* (1970), and *The Chip-Chip Gatherers* (1973). I had read neither of them. Indeed, I knew very little about him. I had just been appointed editor of *The Spectator* and had advertised for a secretary. I interviewed about 30 candidates, but one was quite obviously much better qualified, much more intelligent, and very much nicer than any others. She turned out to be Shiva's wife, Jenny. Jenny quickly became far more than a secretary, though she was brilliant in that role. She became (and still is) an indispensable member of the editorial staff, the person with whom our contributors most liked to communicate. I was sometimes quite jealous of her in this respect. I was even more jealous of Shiva. However petty his needs might have seemed in comparison with mine, he always came first. Working for an 'island scholarship' is clearly a full-time occupation. So far as I could tell, Shiva had failed to master even the most elementary of practical skills. He couldn't boil an egg or mend a fuse. If a tap was dripping, so to speak, he would telephone Jenny at the office and she would rush home immediately to deal with it. She would deal with everything. He couldn't possibly have coped without her. If, in his literary persona, he tended to ignore her existence, his dependence on her was nevertheless absolute.

One of the things Jenny did was to introduce Shiva to *The Spectator*. More than half the non-fictional pieces in *Beyond the Dragon's Mouth* were first published in this paper, as were parts of his 1978 African travel book *North of South*. These articles were, without exception, excellent. As a writer dedicated to his craft, he devoted much more time to them than most journalists do. He refused to be rushed. He would only deliver his pieces when he felt they were right. He brought to them not only his rare skills as a writer and his novelist's powers of observation, but an independence of mind which came from his own sense of belonging nowhere. One might be tempted to call it detachment, but that would not be right. He minded very much about things and about people. What he minded most of all was the way in which fools and bigots would misrepresent reality. He was a genuine seeker after truth.

But the main thing now is to recall those qualities which he seemed not to realise he possessed – warmth, good humour, and an exceptional capacity for friendship. He was much too obsessed with his lack of 'a collective consciousness'. It made him think he was much unhappier than he was. I believe he had recently become quite happy, with his large and comfortable new flat in Hampstead, with his growing success as an author, with his circle of devoted friends – not to mention his extraordinary good fortune in his wife and son, Tarun. Had he lived, he would not only have written more marvellous books; he would soon have been ready to call England his home. Or so I believe. His death was an appalling tragedy. His loss is even harder to understand than his extraordinary life.

24 August, 1985

PILGRIM SEEKING DANGER

A profile of Freya Stark, indestructible explorer

In her autobiography, Freya Stark has written that she became a traveller at the age of four, when she set out one morning from home with a macintosh over one arm, walking down the road towards Plymouth to find a ship and go to sea. Yet for one whose mind was made up so young the true departure was almost indefinitely postponed: it was not until 1927, when she was 34, unmarried, a short, somewhat stout figure of admirable self-discipline, who had learnt Arabic from a Capuchin monk who bred Angora rabbits in San Remo, that she at last set sail with Lloyd Triestino for Beirut, and, as she recorded later, 'my travels in the East began'.

After that, however, there was never an end to them. Ninety-two last January, living in the mountain village of Asolo, at the foot of the Dolomites, that she made her home in the Twenties, she continues to travel, retaining a preference for rough places, an almost complete disregard for comfort or safety, and a sense of mild despair about what tourism has done to the landscapes she knew so well. Consistently well reviewed and much honoured – she was made a Dame in 1972 – since the publication in 1932 of her first book, *Baghdad Sketches*, the recent cult of travel writers has brought her greater popularity and more readers than ever before.

Freya Stark's first stop was the village of Brummana in Lebanon, where she discovered deserts, practised her Arabic and realised that in the Middle East she had found a style of life that suited her in a way that the Devonshire of her childhood or the adopted Italy of her mother never could. Later came more exacting journeys across Persia to the then unidentified castles of the Assassins, to the distant villages of Persia's western frontier, and to discover the collecting point for frankincense and the lost city of Shabwa in South Arabia. As the blank spaces on the map were rapidly being filled in, she continued to search out still uncharted pockets and, if she was seldom the first explorer in any place, she was certainly the first European woman in many.

More than that, she brought to these journeys from the first something particularly her own: a vision of landscape, people and history that seemed to make them accountable for one another. Because she bothered to add Kurdish and Persian to her Arabic (and French, German and Italian) and because long illnesses and a Victorian upbringing had instilled in her a sense of the importance of not rushing, she was well received by those among whom she travelled. By the day she talked with the men; the nights she spent in the harems, complaining sometimes that the gossip was as boring as any Dartmoor village.

Delightful with friends, she is not always easy or charitable with all travelling companions, setting for them as well as for herself almost impossible goals, and feeling and showing contempt for those, particularly women, whom she considers too feeble, too frivolous, too vacillating or too self-important. All forms of inefficiency appal her.

She herself never complains. 'She is,' says an old friend, 'indestructibly brave.' When in her seventies she saw off a gang of youths come to burgle her remote house by firing a pistol just over their heads, she explained that she had to fire or they would never have taken her seriously.

The early journeys were recorded not in diaries, but in letters, first to her mother and later to a growing band of correspondents – Field-Marshal Wavell, Sir Sydney Cockerell, Bernard Berenson – which became, as her publisher Jock Murray puts it, 'the grindstone of her style'. These gave substance to more than 20 travel books, four volumes of autobiography, and, in the late Seventies, formed the basis of eight volumes of collected letters.

They are not, as one reviewer has pointed out, great letters, in the vein of Byron or Oscar Wilde, but they are funny, descriptive and alive. Possibly more than the books, which are distanced by memory, they show how lordly, how fearless she was; they prove too that she was as capable as any traveller of fear and hunger and irritation.

Public recognition came first in the mid-Thirties with a Royal Geographical Society grant, invitations to speak on the radio and address the Royal Central Asian Society and the presentation of the Burton Medal. She was the first woman to receive it. With them came meetings with other travellers and orientalists, and new friends, as well as new clothes, of an expensive kind. Extra money, and much that should have gone on bills, has always gone to the little *haute couture* frock. 'There are few sorrows through which a new dress or hat will not send a little gleam of pleasure however fugitive,' she once wrote.

When the war came, the British authorities turned to her for help in an area perfectly suited to her regard for the Arab world and her enthusiasm for British empire, just as they had once turned to Gertrude Bell. First in Aden, later in Cairo and Baghdad, she spent the war years using her colloquial Arabic and by then many acquaintances to counter Axis propaganda, to set up the Brotherhood of Freedom, a network of people – gossip centres, her critics called them – committed to the cause of British political interests. Under her direction people, mainly women, chatted. Field-Marshal Wavell was later to say that the Brotherhood had done much to lessen sabotage against the Allies in Egypt.

Her friends have bestowed on her many godchildren. These, particularly the young men, she has taken on journeys down the coast of Turkey, giving to them something of her love of wild places, while acting as mentor to a new generation of travel writers. Colin Thubron, who met her in the Sixties, speaks of the influence she exercised over his style: 'I was absolutely fascinated by her use of words, the way she could make certain words shine. She seemed to make them move again.'

Her house in Asolo, the gatehouse next to the villa where Robert Browning used to stay, and particularly its English garden of lawns and herbaceous borders, became a meeting place for Arabists, young travellers, scholars, diplomats. It was the perfect traveller's home: bathrooms of oriental splendour in carved marble, passages hung with Arab cloth, cabinets full of treasures, a library with a rosewood desk and shelves designed by herself. Well into her seventies, she rode a Vespa, to the extreme unease of local inhabitants, for she never learnt either to corner or to switch the motor off and would arrive at dinner parties, her diamonds and Arab dresses in disarray from several tosses.

In 1947 Freya Stark married a colleague from Aden days, Stewart Perowne, but the relationship did not last. Friendships, however, have been immensely well tended, though she has always preferred the company of men. On her 70th birthday Jock Murray invited 17 of her closest friends to dinner: they were all men. 'She has one of those extremely rare natures,' explains one life-long friend, a little wryly, 'that makes of those who love her willing slaves.'

Her manner is precise, elegant; she speaks the best old-fashioned English. It can also be demanding. Friends are expected to be educated and to have something to say. With those she despises she can be merciless.

Freya Stark's distinction comes, say those who rank her as the greatest woman traveller of her age, not from the places she has visited, nor from her insights as historian, but from her qualities of mind: the powers of observation, her vision of morality and history that allows her to set what she describes in the context of a large screen of time and knowledge. 'She is a bigger figure even than her writing,' observes a friend. 'The audacity is something extraordinary.'

Over the stone lintel of Montoria, the marble and stone house she built outside Asolo when she was 70, are engraved the words: 'We are pilgrims, as you are.' The word pilgrim appears often in her work. 'I like,' she wrote in a letter in 1950, 'to feel a pilgrim and mere sojourner in this world.' It fits in with her desire to observe and not to organise, to learn and not to dictate, and above all, perhaps, with her wish to progress, with courage, towards the end. She once explained to a friend that the reason she travelled was to seek danger, 'for I remember wishing often to find what might silence fear, and to reach the end of my days free from that mortal weakness'.

31 August, 1985

AN EXTRAVAGANCE OF CURIOSITY

A profile of Patrick Leigh Fermor, soldier, writer and architect

Patrick Leigh Fermor is something of a phenomenon – the kind of man that English society tips out of its curious nest once in a hundred years. Most living legends fade as time blunts the blade of action; here the years have tempered the steel. In 1984, his 70th year, he matched the impassioned strokes of young Leander by swimming across the Hellespont, as much out of curiosity as for the experience. As with most of his achievements this bold and energetic feat is passed off as a divertissement, the dolphin at play. He is termed the avatar of Byron and yet he is twice Byron's age at his death and possessed of an energy that leaves contemporaries breathless.

This zest propelled him, aged 18, across the continent with five pounds a month, a headful of classics and a charm that cut swathes through European aristocracy and peasantry alike. As a putteed footslogging gallant he turned the weariest, most bitter continental winter walk into a decorative confection of brilliant language, mulled with history, flavoured with encounter and anecdote, that evolved into his glorious book *A Time of Gifts*. It was culled years later from his densely inscribed journals and the colossal multilingual memory which serves him as an unparalleled source for quotation, genealogy and literature.

Each of his travel books from *The Traveller's Tree* to *Mani* and *Roumeli* have enjoyed long confinements – often three typescripts, myriad alterations, inversions, additions, subtractions, interpolations and supplements. And beside it all there is his pursuit of a thousand scholarly and linguistic diversions. 'He has that element of the Irish in him – he's fascinated by everything – you know he's never the first to leave a party,' observes Jock Murray. Every phrase is turned, each word weighed, his ideas are fashioned, the arguments are polished and all components analysed – above all he is a philologian.

In heady pre-war days his meandering path took him into Romania and Moldavia where he was drawn into the life of the Cantacuzene family, forming an affection for that noble house which is characteristic of his fascination for the aristocratic clans of central Europe, with their elegant idiosyncrasies. But the Balkans beckoned and the Pindus and Rhodope mountains lured him east and south so that by the age of 20 he was riding with the Greek cavalry during a rebellion, and five years later he was in Albania with a future Greek prime minister, Kanellopoulos, as a comrade-in-arms, pushing back the Italian army.

That taste of Greece and the Greeks at war sowed the seeds of his philhellenic passion – later he ran the resistance movement in German-occupied Crete, gilding his extraordinary career as a Guards officer by capturing and evacuating to Cairo the German commander, General Kreipe, in 1944. That episode earned him a DSO as well as becoming the subject of Stanley Moss's book, and later film, *Ill Met by Moonlight*. Other frequent chilling encounters with the Germans in the White Mountains and the adventurous spirit amongst the SOE fraternity in Cairo created a lasting camaraderie, above all with author, traveller and colleague Xan Fielding, who detailed their harrowing life in *Hide and Seek*.

The post-war years saw the fulfilment of delayed pleasure. Carousing vied with conversation, and the nightlife of artistic cafés filled the early hours across Europe from the Athens of Katsimbalis and Seferis to the Paris of Diana Cooper and the London of Philip Toynbee, Ann Fleming and Andrew Cavendish, now Duke of Devonshire. This appetite for society played havoc with creative production sometimes, for instance during their sojourn in Poros, as the artist John Craxton records, where the daylight hours seemed too brief for his painting and the night time too abbreviated for Paddy's writing. Paddy occasionally dived into monastic retreat, from the deep peace of which he drew his book *A Time to Keep Silence*.

But stronger and more lasting intoxication than the ouzo at the British

Institute in Athens came in the renewed acquaintance he made with Joan Eyres Monsell who became companion, wife and the steadying hand on the tiller of his fast barque. 'She has given a line to his life – the discipline he needed sometimes.' She has had to manoeuvre him away from the ceaseless crowds that cross their threshold for an hour of conversation with the man whose writing has been called 'the despair of all future autobiographers' by C. M. Woodhouse.

Throughout Greece he is a celebrated figure and the draughts of retsina that have been sunk to confirm that country's welcome to him are unnumbered. That some unseen political enemy blew up his car – causing him no injury fortunately – merely reinforces the impact he has had on the Greeks.

In company he is a firework, colourful, flamboyant and dazzling. A dinner party in his presence is hardly complete if his companions are not regaled with recitations of Homeric Greek, the Eton Boating Song in Hebrew or the folk songs of Cretan bandits, and these are the merest tincture of his melodic and folkloric range. The artist Ghika records him singing wildly in New York, Lawrence Durrell describes him entrancing Cypriot peasants with his tunes, Peter Quennell reports Paddy leaping from rock to rock chanting wild Greek songs and Rudolf Fischer admits to correcting the odd word in the lyrics of Paddy's remembered Hungarian gypsy songs. Then there are Romanian couplets, Sarakatsan odes, French calypsos, Gregorian chants and opera, all expressed with the genial ebullience of a buffo operatic star whose voice is wrought with laughter, and whose face is cast with smiles.

One of Paddy's companions during arduous mountain treks, Renée Fedden, describes how 'he turned every evening during our expeditions into a cocktail party. We would all be exhausted, weary from the day's journey and as soon as we were in the tent the evening would be transformed into a celebration.' On a trip to the Andes, Paddy describes his role as that of tending the primus stove but from that he evolves into jester and storyteller as well as an acute diarist. His enthusiasms sometimes lead to the most enjoyable explosions in the starchiest of places. Once aboard the Niarchos yacht at dinner, a *premier cru*, a great classic vintage claret, pre-phylloxera, was being poured out by white-coated waiters with infinite caution for the sacred nectar. Paddy having sensed its nose, eyed its colour and allowed the precious wine to caress his palate cried out: 'Let's have beakers of this wine!' as the stunned fellow diners took on the features usually seen in an H. E. Bateman caricature.

An occasion he now savours with wry reflection was when he was invited to stay with Somerset Maugham after winning the Heinemann Foundation Prize for Literature. He arrived loaded with luggage, expecting a pleasant stay. Feeling surprisingly unequal to the task of managing dinner on the first evening he fortified himself with a couple of drinks before meeting the Master. As the meal progressed more wine flowed and inhibition gave way until Paddy told a malapropos story about the College of Heralds, the enactment of which required the imitation of a stutter. Maugham's Achilles heel had been touched. Towards midnight he proffered Paddy a cup of coffee; stirring it lightly, he bent towards him and said: 'I'll wish you good night, Mr Leigh Fermor, and goodbye – since you'll be gone by the time I get up in the morning.' Thus dismissed, Paddy hauled off his weighty baggage to a nearby hotel.

Paddy enjoys a global knowledge of architectural styles and the personal design and construction of his home in the Peloponnese reflects much of his character. On a rocky promontory amidst patrician cypress trees and dark olives, above the sea and set in a delightful terraced garden stands a substantial house. Roman villa, Pelion manor house, Pasha's summer residence – the house defies classification. 'It highlights so much of Paddy – the refinement, the timbered detail, the shady arcades, the geometric pebbled mosaic – it merges with the landscape,' John Craxton says. To Ghika, its essence is Hellenistic,with fractured local masonry inserted into stone walls giving the place an air of history and completing an architectural delight.

Here, and earlier on Hydra, constellations of literary figures have gathered to imbibe the spirit and catch the warmth of the intellectual fire which emanates from his inquiring mind.

The Duke of Devonshire notes the comfort of the villa and reports with pleasure how each meal is eaten at a different part of the house or garden. This migration is geared to defeat the blinding heat of the Messenian sun and allows for the maximum consolation of seasonal breezes and shade. From his writer's sanctum, a pavilion separate from the main house, he composes his long letters. Here he creates an almost annual greeting to his correspondents in the form of a special *oeuvre* – translations of German poetry or the latest travelogue of his ventures into Peru, the Pindus or Himalayan peaks. Here too he has mulled over the language of the Quecha Indians and the bizarre speech of the Malani in their remote Indo-Himalayan outpost.

Paddy's strength – the extravagance of his curiosity – leads to a density of style, saturated with references and rich language; as one acquaintance says, he does 'overcharge his rifts with ore – but such ore!' Another friend describes Paddy at Chatsworth devising joke titles for those library doors masquerading as bookshelves. Peter Quennell singles Paddy out as a most intrepid horseman. 'He once asked to be put up on a hunter and insisted on trying every jump at the Towcester races. His hostess Kisty Hesketh watched him through fieldglasses crashing through the jumps and falling off, remounting and continuing the whole way round. The whole course had to be rebuilt.'

That determination is balanced by great loyalty to his friends and generosity to all. In turn he is much loved and in Greece he has been made a Visiting Member of the Athens Academy. One of his proposers to that body describes Paddy as a great civilising influence.

A taste of his qualities is to be had in his most recent book, which has just reached the publishers. *Between the Woods and the Water*, recording the second part of his walk across Europe, getting as far as the Iron Gates, will be published by John Murray in early 1986. For those addicted to his style this delay may seem long, but the work will be worth waiting for. The third part of his journey, bringing him to Istanbul itself, is still being pieced together, without any dimming of memory or dulling of immediacy, though he is taking the trouble to return to Bulgaria over 50 years after his first visit.

7 September, 1985

HIS PICNICS HOLD THEIR HORRORS

A profile of Eric Newby, brilliant survivor of mishaps

If, instead of finding ourselves in our usual seat on the Clapham omnibus, we armchair travellers were to be placed upon yaks riding into the Karakorams, with a Hunza porter, two months' provisions, and instructions to make for Yarkand, no companion upon a neighbouring yak would be greeted with more delighted relief than the stalwart and eager figure of Eric Newby. 'Everyman, I will go with thee and be thy guide': to no travel writer's works is the epigraph of the Everyman Library a better fit.

For there is nothing in Eric Newby (as he projects his personality in his books) of that lonely, craggy singularity which is the repellent, if awe-inspiring, characteristic of 'the great traveller'. Newby will not, we feel, keep striding ahead to reconnoitre mountain-tops, keep pushing us beyond our limit, keep pointing sternly to a further horizon for today's march than we can hope to attain. He seems to possess no specialised skills. Tough as he must be, it appears to be the kind of resilience which

enables him to recover from mishap, rather than the horniness of carapace which is impervious to the ill-usage of hard travel. If he drinks water
from a Persian brook, he is as ill as the rest of us would be, his toughness
not preserving him from harm but enabling him to stagger onwards,
though seriously harmed. The impression we have of a journey made in
his company is not of an expedition, but of a picnic overtaken by misfortune. It is this expectation he has of enjoying himself – the vigorous
good-humour of his voice as we hear it in his narrative – his evident good-
fellowship – which makes him a companion to be chosen above any traveller, past or present, if a real journey were to be made with any writer of
books of travel.

The two books that first made his name, *The Last Grain Race* and *A
Short Walk in the Hindu Kush* – one the account of a voyage in a square-
rigger undertaken at 19, the other a journey into Nuristan made at 37 –
are the narratives of two remarkable adventures. Still, there have been
adventures equally stirring recorded in books of travel: Newby's genius,
above other travellers, is to select and delineate both his incidents and his
dramatis personae so that each character and each event shapes and
advances his narrative in so artistic a fashion that the satisfactory symmetry of fiction seems to be added to the vigour of truth. Take Hugh
Carless, his companion in the Hindu Kush. Mr Carless is the very man a
novelist might hope to invent to inflict upon Mr Newby in wild lands if
an amusing book were to result. His precision, his experience, his wari-
ness, his preparations, all contrast wonderfully with Newby's slapdash
methods. No caricature out of *Stiff Upper Lip*, he is yet very easily
recognisable by Everyman as a diplomat, which enables us to flesh him
out in our own minds, and imagine his responses even when they are not
recorded. Dialogue between Carless and Newby never fails to distinguish
the character of each more clearly, so that the contrasts and frictions of
their relationship develop alongside the narrative. Newby asks:
' "What's a kro?" Carless: "One kro equals half an Iranian farsak." It was
some time before I was able to pluck up courage to ask what an Iranian
farsak was. "The distance a man travels over flat ground in an hour. And,
quite frankly, I think you should have made more progress with your Persian by now." '

The dialogue – the art – is faultless. Or take an exchange in a cave in the
Apennines between Newby and another escaped PoW, which refers to
Newby's cough. ' "You should try to control yourself," he said severely
one day when he was thoroughly exasperated. "I do try," I said. "Do you
think I enjoy it?" "I don't know," he said, and I felt like striking him.' It is
scenes so human as these, where the landscape and the circumstances
have squeezed the people together, which are a rarity in books of travel.

Dialogue in a book of travels (unless the writer has the total recall which Mr Newby specifically disclaims) must surely be art. With equal art Mr Newby makes sure that his actors – the fo'c'sle full of seamen in *The Last Grain Race* for example – do not outgrow the role required of them by dramatic narrative. He creates no Frankenstein's monster which will hog the stage. The Captain of the *Moshulu*, like the seamen, is all he should be – all we half-remember from reading Marryat or Dana – but neither he nor anyone else in Mr Newby's books is so excessively original a 'character' as to unbalance the narrative or to distract our attention from our chief interest in it, which is to listen to Mr Newby's account of his adventures and to watch our hero's character displayed in action. For it is always Newby we want more of – Newby we sympathise with – Newby's cough, or feet, or dashed hopes, with which we suffer. Without one word of vanity in all his books, he emerges effortlessly as the hero of them all.

As leading lady his wife, Wanda, plays a beautifully orchestrated part too. An individual of magnetism and resolution from her first appearance in *Love and War in the Apennines*, her progress towards a co-starring role is steady throughout successive books; in *A Short Walk in the Hindu Kush* taken only as far as Tehran, she completes the voyage (though constantly threatening to 'go back to my country and my people') in *Slowly Down the Ganges*, and is, in *On The Shores of the Mediterranean*, the writer's indispensable companion, their inseparability understood and admired by us quite as if we knew them as a 'devoted couple' of our acquaintance.

This, of course, we do not. To make us believe, through his books, that we have the privilege of his friendship – that he, who has stood 150 feet above the deck of a square-rigger in a gale in the Southern Ocean, is here sitting by us on the sofa – is the illusion produced by the charm of his writing. The style, the exuberantly humorous tone, is wonderfully beguiling. But literary art which includes only what is relevant to the narrative of a journey must exclude as irrelevancies all the traveller leaves behind him at home. Of day-to-day life *chez* Newby we know nothing. Of the hopes and fears, even of the spirit behind that handsome, full-blooded face turned eagerly towards adventure we know little. The traveller's life, driven by restlessness, is fitful and episodic. 'Prayer' (he decided during the war) 'is at most . . . a reminder that there has been a past and might be a future.' What we must wish for, in short, is that the episodes be linked. *A Traveller's Life*, which might not be thought his 'best' or 'most amusing' book, does however convey by its very faults the impression of an episodic and restless existence, and so perhaps tells us, more truly than does the narrative of a single journey, what inroads of uncertainty and fragmentation a passion for travel and adventure may make in a man's life.

Certainly the war, coming when he was 20, would have drawn him into adventures, but nothing is more bizarre than the inspiration of his travels according to his own account of it. 'Diving in Starehole Bay, I saw what remained of the 4-masted Finnish sailing barque . . . which had crashed into the Ham Stone with a cargo of grain . . . And on the way back to London . . . I wrote a letter to the owner . . . asking him for a place in one of his grain ships.'

A wrecked ship is a dark reason for going to sea, yet connection might be made between his diver's view of the foundered sailing ship, which inspired him to take a place in one like her, and his view of 19th-century Constantinople, as it appeared to him in the depths of Bartlett and Allom's dream-like engravings, and inspired in him a craving to travel into that vanished Eastern world. The gusto with which he dwells upon the horrors of bowstring and sack in old Stamboul might be linked to the attractions which the doomed ship held for him. The true traveller is not content without dangers and terrors, however lightheartedly he may afterwards relate them. We realise with alarm that our picnicking friend Mr Newby had more about him after all of that grim, fierce spirit of the old travellers than he allows to appear. As he lets fall at the end of a chapter describing 19th-century Constantinople, 'I was born 100 years too late.'

Perhaps it is fear of being 'too late' which is the mainspring of the traveller's energy. When he is young, the vanished world which beguiles him – City of the Sultan or sunken barque – appears to be just within grasp, if he goes at once this minute, in quest of it. Hence *A Short Walk in the Hindu Kush* and *The Last Grain Race*, those two spirited forays into the 19th century. Later in life it seems that the desired world withdraws beyond reach, and, when the traveller can persuade himself that what he wanted of it has gone forever, he may retire. Ending *A Traveller's Life* Newby seems to say that he is tired of travelling in a world spoiled by 'tourism'. Perhaps he meant that eight years as travel editor of the *Observer* had satiated his meaner desires as a traveller – the desire merely to rush about and see places with minimum trouble and no expense – or perhaps he meant, more gravely, that he could no longer find the energy or appetite for turning back the clock with sufficient force to overcome the mishap of being born 100 years too late.

Eric Newby now lives in a manor house on the Isle of Purbeck, its large garden well-stocked with statues and obelisks, the spare elegance of its rooms ready to welcome his two children and his grandchildren. The size of the place – its permanence – the obduracy of such a possession – does not weigh him down. He and Wanda live there, as they do everything, for the fun of the thing. Asked (by a country neighbour) who would look after the garden while they were away for some months in Italy, he turns to Wanda with genuine surprise: 'Yes, who *will* look after the garden when we're away?' Will the many trees he has planted, as well as the weight of the statues and obelisks he has erected, anchor him at last to the spot? Dorset neighbours would be amazingly fortunate if he 'settled down'. For everyone acquainted with the man, in person or through his books, will have reflected, when reading the famous story of his meeting with Wilfrid Thesiger in the Hindu Kush, on an unrecorded aspect of the encounter: what a stroke of luck for Thesiger to run into Eric Newby, of all Englishmen, on an Afghan slope at dusk.

If he doesn't recover the energy to push back the clock and resume his adventures, remaining instead in his Dorset manor, he may yet please his readers in another form. In the preface to *Love and War in the Apennines* he lists the inadequacies of his experiences as an escaped PoW and comments: 'Scarcely a help in producing an exciting book. I let the whole thing drop.' He let it drop from 1945 until 1971. Those 25 years of reflection turned what might only have been 'an exciting book' into (some would say) his masterpiece to date. The elapse of time, too, must have encouraged him to take those liberties with exact truth also mentioned in his preface – 'It is not true/And if it were it would not do' – which are the liberties of the novelist. Having entertained us with journeys as vividly recounted as any of James Morier's, Mr Newby alone of modern travel writers is equipped to rival Morier's feat in producing a novel as entertaining as *Haji Baba*.

21 September, 1985

Noel Malcolm

THE LOST ART OF TRAVEL WRITING

What has happened to travel books? One thing which has happened in the last five years or so is that they have suddenly become popular. All bookshops now have sections devoted to them; some shops have opened which deal in nothing else; and the reprint publishers are scouring the libraries for Victorian classics in need of rediscovery. Ten years ago I opened a dusty copy of Captain Burnaby's *A Ride to Khiva* and found that the bookmark used by the previous reader was a postcard dated 1936. Now my nearest bookshop has two different works by Burnaby in paperback. And alongside them the shelves are groaning with recent contributions to the genre; every publisher or literary agent with an author at a loose end seems to be telling him to go East, young man, and write a travel book.

It is the strange contrast between these different generations of authors which makes me think about what has changed during the last hundred years or so. Many of the recent 'classics' are based on some sort of stunt, an exercise in journey-making which can replace the countries visited as the real focus of interest; thus Dervla Murphy cycles from France to India, or Gavin Young travels in small boats from Greece to China. Long journeys by train have produced a genre of their own, with Eric Newby's *The Big Red Train Ride* and Paul Theroux's *The Great Railway Bazaar* and *The Old Patagonian Express*. Trains do have a fascination of their own, of course, and long-distance travel by rail presents its own practical difficulties. Theroux (unlike Newby) sometimes has to change trains or buy a new ticket; occasionally the lavatory will not flush, or fellow passengers ask him to stop smoking his pipe. It is hard to imagine a Victorian traveller writing a book about a train journey. (The nearest thing, J. R. Pearson's *Railways and Scenery*, came out in 1932.) Where the Victorians tackled the Empty Quarter, Mr Theroux takes on the Full Compartment. Occasionally, to be fair, a note of wry self-ironising breaks through. 'Jujuy looked peaceful and damp. The rain on the blossom perfumed the dark air and a fresh breeze blew from the river. It seemed idyllic, and yet later I heard that Jujuy was so badly flooded that thousands of people had to be evacuated from their houses. It is not possible to see everything from a train.'

Of course it would be wrong to chide all the modern travellers for their lack of difficulty or danger. Administrative obstacles can be worse now than they ever were, and the risk of being knifed for one's money becomes stronger all the time as the codes of hospitality in traditional societies are gradually eroded. Some dangers have not changed. After only nine pages Dervla Murphy is attacked by wolves; one is already hanging from her shoulder by its teeth when she coolly pulls a pistol out of her pocket and shoots it through the skull. Gavin Young comes close to being murdered by pirates but bluffs his way through, unnerving them by keeping up a constant smile. (The 1872 edition of Francis Galton's *The Art of Travel* includes this advice under the heading 'Management of Savages': 'A frank, joking, but determined manner, joined with an air of showing more confidence in the good faith of the natives than you really feel, is the best.') But it is almost as if the modern writers cannot believe in the seriousness of their predicaments. Dervla Murphy dismisses the incident as if a friend's labrador had misbehaved, and Gavin Young can only conjure up a sense of danger by connecting episodes in his journey to memories of 'real' dangers he experienced as a war correspondent.

Modern travel writing has somehow ceased to believe in itself. The closer it comes to old-fashioned exploration of unknown or hostile territory, the more it takes refuge in self-deflating humour. Two of the best travel books written since the war are Eric Newby's *A Short Walk in the Hindu Kush* and Redmond O'Hanlon's *Into the Heart of Borneo*; both are brilliantly funny, and much of the humour depends on the contrast between the self-consciously bungling author and the severe shadow of his Victorian predecessors. This is the style of travel-writing which seems to have been invented by Peter Fleming in the 1930s. His emphasis was not so much on his own lack of competence as on his lack of the mental attitudes which distinguished the great 19th-century travellers. Not that he had many attitudes of his own to put in their place. Humour is one refuge, and relativism is another: a determination to avoid the appearance of prejudice, not by refusing to pre-judge but by failing to judge at all.

The attitudes we have lost were a paradoxical mixture of assimilation and criticism. The greatest 19th-century travellers, men such as C. M. Doughty, steeped themselves in the societies they visited, learning their languages, their customs and their beliefs. There is a sort of receptivity and openness here on a scale which is almost extinct among modern travellers; Wilfred Thesiger, the last great writer of this kind, is the exception that proves the rule. One wonders how many modern travellers could go to Mecca disguised as an Arab. (How far would Jonathan Raban get?) Arminius Vambery visited the cities of Central Asia in the guise of a Turkish dervish, and afterwards wrote: 'When a man travels as I did, and when he has as thoroughly and completely adapted himself to the Tartar mode of life, it is no wonder if, in the end, he turns half Tartar himself.' And yet it is striking how often the very men who were most receptive to the life of their hosts – Doughty among the Bedouin or Borrow among the gipsies – were almost the most unyielding upholders of certain moral axioms of their own. Borrow might equivocate but he would not lie. Vambery could not bring himself to kill, at an ideal opportunity, the man who was trying to bring about his certain death by exposing him as an impostor. And Doughty, the most inflexible of all, declared in the strongholds of Muslim fanaticism: 'Friends, I have said, I am come to you in no disguises; I have hidden nothing from you; I have always acknowledged myself a Nasrany, which was a name infamous among you.'

These moral principles were not just reserved for private use as scruples of conscience. The travellers may have learned to understand strange moral codes from the inside; but this did not prevent them from criticising individuals or whole societies for their habits of dishonesty, cruelty, procrastination or cowardice. When Doughty describes the strict justice of the Bedouin but observes that they operate it only among themselves, he suggests that this limitation of the practice implies a flaw in the principle. He is able to criticise a moral code precisely because he understands what it is like to believe in it; where values are concerned, understanding and criticism go hand in hand. The notion that understanding must be 'objective', detached and free of value judgments is a modern dogma, sheltering behind the pseudo-scientific claims of anthropology.

I am not trying to suggest that anthropology is to blame for the decline and fall of the traveller. But I am suggesting that the most recent study of modern travel-writing (Paul Fussell's *Abroad: British Literary Travelling between the Wars*) is completely wrong when it picks on Evelyn Waugh's critical attitudes to his subject-matter and identifies them as a major symptom of the malaise. (Fussell, incidentally, writes as if he has read none of the great 19th-century travellers, and his whole book is a suppressed hymn of hatred towards everything he cannot understand about the English character.) Waugh, we are told, was a devotee of the norm', poking fun at everything that was not normal and English. Fussell has to admit that it was Waugh himself who declared: 'Criticism only becomes useful when it can show people where their own principles are in conflict.' What makes Waugh's travel-writing sparkle is his sense of how a society's values conflict when it has lost many of its own principles and gained in their place nothing but an assortment of half-understood principles derived from the West.

Humour is perhaps the best response to this mongrelising of values, and the more the world becomes mongrelised, the less room there will be for classic travel-writing of the same stature as Doughty's *Arabia Deserta*. But there is a difference between critical humour and the comedy of self-deflation. We read travel books in order to be given a better sense of what is strange in the world; but the best qualification for understanding and describing the values of others is that the writer should have some values of his own.

25 January, 1986

John Casey

A PLACE IN THE SHADE

Waugh's Gilbert Pinfold abhorred plastics, Picasso, sunbathing and jazz. In due course plastics will become obsolete, an appreciation of jazz will be confined to antiquarians, and Picasso will be relegated to that very respectable status of a talent who was not a Master. But sunbathing? It is possible that future social historians will find it difficult to convince their readers that such a bizarre practice ever existed. Future generations may find the thought that the numerous ruined structures which they encounter over hundreds of miles of coastline were built purely in order that people could get their skin to turn brown no more intelligible than that the Great Pyramid was built to contain the remains of one Pharaoh.

On the other hand, this may not happen at all. The investment in the modern mass holiday, of which sunbathing is the *raison d'être*, is so huge that what ought to have been simply an amusing upper-class fad with a natural lifespan of about 20 years, may be with us for ever.

Sea bathing began to be popular in England at the beginning of the Victorian period, or a little before, for reasons of 'health'. As one might expect, the evidence for its healthiness was hard to come by. Yet popular health fads are nearly always based on something other than medical facts. What the Victorians really felt was that to plunge into the sea for a few minutes was to go back to Nature. It was because it was so unquestionably natural that the sea was felt to be health-giving. That all the imaginary benefits that used to be attached to taking the water in the civilised, 'artificial' surroundings of a spa were transferred wholesale to sea bathing was a legacy of the Romantic movement.

Sunbathing was simply the next step. It was invented by Germans, early in this century as part of an ideology which included fresh air, tea-drinking, nudism and the international youth movement. In Germany all these ideas were taken very seriously as a 'philosophy' and had an influence on artists, architects and politicians. (The jollifications of the Hitler Youth summer camps were the purest expression of it.) The English, with their incapacity for speculative thought, settled for a stolid and faithful belief in the healthy properties of sunbathing. But to call any of these activities 'healthy' is not really to express a serious belief, but to employ one of the most common terms of commendation in the modern world. It is the equivalent of Sancho Panza's saying of a wine he had particularly relished, 'Oh whoreson rogue! How *Catholic* it is!'

But why should an amusing Twenties idea that a tanned skin is chic have transformed the coasts of the world and resulted in millions of people spending hours every day grimly acquiring a sun-tan, convinced that they are benefiting from it?

The word has much to with it. 'Sunbathing' was a brilliant coinage, more alluring if less descriptive than the Australian 'sunbaking'. It retains the promise of health that the Victorians found in sea bathing and insinuates that ignoble sloth may really be the active pursuit of well-being and beauty. The sun has taken the place of the sea as the mystic source of health. (The sun-mysticism of some of D. H. Lawrence's writings must have had some influence.) After thousands of years during which human beings have regarded direct sunlight as unpleasant and harmful, people now seek it out in the conviction that the 20th century has discovered something new and good in it that had previously been undetected.

A curious thing that I have noticed when I tediously challenge people to name even one benefit to health that comes from exposure to the sun, is that they nearly all say that it cures rickets. Rickets must be remote from the experience of most adult English people under about 70, and yet this folk-belief seems to be at the back of everyone's mind. It is not entirely baseless: but a reasonable diet is incomparably more effective. Tropical Africa is full of children with rickets. What is unfortunately certain is that prolonged sunbathing can cause wrinkles, keratosis and malignant melanomas.

It is quite probable that the most effective way of making sunbathing unpopular would be to convince people that it gives you skin cancer. Yet this would be a pity – it would just be using one current health obsession to remove another, calling on Satan to drive out Beelzebub. Besides, the mythology of the sun is so deeply rooted that the medical evidence may simply be ignored; or more powerful protective creams will be invented. The real case against sunbathing is not medical but *aesthetic*. A tanned skin is not beautiful at all, especially in a woman. A slightly weather-beaten look can suit a man by suggesting that he leads an active, adventurous life. But a deep tan indicates merely an unmanly narcissism. It is one thing that a woman with a poor skin should welcome the equality that a sun-tan imposes upon beautiful and plain alike for a few weeks each year. It is quite another when the flower of English womanhood – including alas! the Princess of Wales herself – should forget that delicacy of skin-tone is part of European female beauty. A sun-tanned skin loses most of its expressiveness and all of its sensuality.

People do not understand this because they have largely forgotten how to *see* the human body, and respond instead to signs. The sun-tan is a sign of 'sexiness' and so people think that it *looks* sensual, which it doesn't. It stands for other things as well – health, one's money's-worth on a holiday, conspicuous leisure. And sunbathing has its semiotic heroes. President Kennedy made sure of a hideously deep tan all year round as a sign of his youth and vitality. I remember him, as President-elect, moving through thousands of hysterically excited students, who looked as though they were about to crush him to death, across a snow-covered Harvard Yard in mid-winter, looking just like a chocolate-coloured tailor's dummy. Another memorable sight was Idi Amin – as black as a man could be – determinedly sunning himself by a pool in Jedda while his favourite wife applied the sun-tan lotion.

It might be best to think of it all as yet another secularisation of the religious sense. Like mediaeval peasants longing to go on a pilgrimage and gain indulgences, people now gather at the great Mediterranean sun-shrines to acquire a merit which will last them through the winter. Even if the grounds of their faith were to dissolve, and everybody realised that, far from being healthy, sunbathing is positively harmful, the devotional practices would probably continue. For the whole idea of the modern mass-holiday depends upon them. It was a brilliant notion to decant millions of workers upon the coasts, persuade them to lie in the sun for two weeks, and then bring them back tanned and happy, convinced that they have been doing themselves good, recharged and ready to face another working year. If they were to realise that all this is merely a ridiculous superstition, that sunbathing is worthless from the point of view of health, and that a sunburnt skin is boring and ugly, that nearly all sea coasts are depressing wastelands which human beings would do well to avoid, then morosity and despair might set in. Even worse, they might mend their ways and decide to force their unwelcome company upon the readers of *The Spectator* – who of course do *not* sunbathe – in Tuscany and the Dordogne.

23 August, 1986

Alice Thomas Ellis

PHRASE AND FABLE

Phrase books seem to be a universal and eternal source of hilarity and I think I know why. Their authors go mad in the course of compiling them. If you know how to do something – for instance speak your own language – you can go crazy trying to put across the basics to a load of idiots. I once wrote a book about how to feed babies – how long to boil their wee eggs for them, etc – and time and again I found myself addressing my imagined reader in tones of impatience and hostility: 'Oh go and ask your mother how not to burn water, you silly thing.' I had grown to picture my reader as dreadfully unhygienic and monumentally stupid, forgetting that I myself had once not known the rules about poaching and boiling and roasting and had in my time done some jolly weird things to some perfectly good food.

This, however, is beside the point. What I was saying was in connection with the phrase book I bought in order to bone up on my Arabic. The author's pre-occupations, prejudices and thought processes are perfectly fascinating. Opening the book at random one finds the useful phrase: 'My friend whom you saw the other day died last night.' This is followed by the logical 'What happened to him?' To which the answer comes: 'A drunken soldier killed him in front of my house.' Then, I think, the author went off for a glass of mint tea because he changes tack and goes into millinery: 'Is she willing to buy this hat?' 'Why is she not willing to sell it?', and then back to more significant matters: 'She was groping in the darkness.' 'I wish to live and die with you.' There is quite a lot of sex and violence here as you riffle through. 'He advised me not to take her by force.' 'I hit him because he did not tell the truth.' 'If he does this another time I shall beat him.' 'He has torn my clothes and spoilt my work. Please prevent him (from) doing this again.'

I personally found Alexandria not quiet (every vehicle has at least two horns in case one conks out) but remarkably pacific and unthreatening. We roamed round the streets and up and down the Corniche in the middle of the night and so, apparently, did everybody else, all good-naturedly, sucking sugar cane or eating roasted corn cobs, or mango ices.

I wouldn't idle round Camden Town in the middle of the night, I can tell you; so I don't know why my phrase-book man is so paranoid. He's nervous about health too: 'I feel pain in my tummy when I touch it.' 'It is nothing.' 'I think you are wrong.'

Some lines further on we have the reassuring 'Help yourself to a piece of bread and butter,' and 'Good people go to Heaven when they die.' I can't really imagine having occasion to make that last remark. Would one utter it in a reflective fashion, as though it had just occurred to one, or does it conceal a veiled threat? It is preceded by 'She can not cross the street alone,' which certainly applies to me. Substitute 'I' for 'She' and I was yelling that phrase every time we left the house. Crossing the road in Egypt is like trying to cross the M1 and thoughts of death were constantly on my mind. We are also offered 'You must drive in the middle of the street,' and I can't figure that one out. Everyone drives in the middle of everything and there aren't any rules at all. How about: 'She was wearing her new hat and riding her old car.' 'Never mind.' Can anyone follow the sequence of thought there?

The following is simpler: 'What is the colour of your horse?' 'It is white.' 'Give me a small bottle of red ink.' You can see the madness beginning to take hold. The author is going to throw red ink all over that boring old horse. He's going to be rude to the cook too: 'Who is this ugly woman?' 'She is our cook.' 'I cannot look at her face.' He really hates the cook. 'The cook has burnt the cooking.' 'A fly has fell [sic] in my coffee.' This last sentence is of course indispensable if you want to make jokes, only I can't find the Arabic for 'Waiter, waiter!' or 'Soup'.

I keep getting side-tracked. I am now utterly riveted by the end of page 15: 'Do you like it on the first or second floor?' 'We have a big one in the upper storey.' 'We like to have one downstairs.' 'What happens to your trousers?' I think I can follow his train of thought here only perhaps I'd better not. He is ostensibly speaking of bedrooms which is tricky to start with. Let us leave him in his more philosophic vein: 'We can often (many times; frequently) dispel (drive away) gloom (grief; sorrow) by laughter (or laughing).' How very true.

18 October, 1986

V. S. Naipaul

MY BROTHER'S TRAGIC SENSE

*This address was delivered at the meeting
held in memory of the life and work of
Shiva Naipaul on 6 December 1985*

I left home in 1950, to go to Oxford and to become a writer. Writing was a
family ambition. It was something both my brother and I inherited from
our father; many of our ideas of nobility and honour were bound up with
it.

I was nearly 18 when I left home. My brother Shiva was five and a half.
Up to that time I had seen him, been aware of him, every day. For the next
six years I never saw him, never heard his voice. Travel in those days
often meant that kind of separation.

Two years after I left home, my father fell ill. He became an invalid and
lost his job; it was the beginning of a bad time for our family. The first letter I have from my brother comes from the year of our father's illness.
Shiva was eight; his letter to me was full of childish rage. I was not there
when I was needed. This letter, when I looked at it the other day, caused
me even more pain than when I first read it in Oxford in 1953. I was 20
then; full of doubt, far from home, and with the burden of the family
ambition. I had fallen – like so many young men of that age – into a mor-
bid depression. To my brother I was an adult; in fact, at that period, and
for some time afterwards, there was helplessness on both sides. Four or
five months after that letter, our father died. The event marked my
brother, more than I knew; but, far away, I was obsessed with my own
grief, and became even more useless to my family at that critical moment.

It was three years before I felt I had done something and could go back
home. I went by ship. At home on the afternoon of my arrival, in a quiet
time after the family welcome, Shiva came to me upstairs. He had after all
been waiting for me to come back home. And he had something to show
me; a piece of writing he had done, a story. Easily, as if it was the most natural thing, he lay down beside me, and we read his story together. This
moment with Shiva, then 11, this welcome and affection from someone
who was like a new person to me, remains one of the sweetest and purest

moments of my life. But I could not stay. After six weeks or so I had to go back to London, to that writing career.

When, in the next year, my publishing career began – when proofs could be sent home and printed books began to appear and I could write to him about what I was writing – my brother was full of enthusiasm and encouragement – doing for me, when he was 12, what I, at the same age, had done for our father 14 years or so before. The writing ambition bound us all together. And the effect of my own books on Shiva was to make him write, in his letters, as a writer. And from the very start his tone, and his material, were his own.

This is how, in December 1957, when he was nearly 13, he ended one letter – about some neighbours of ours: 'Rita and Lalsingh the jeweller are having regular quarrels. He squeezes her throat, chases her with a cutlass and threatens to strangle her. Recently, he and his son Gurcharan had a fight. He nearly stabbed his father. A merry Christmas to you all.'

But, in spite of letters, we had been separated; circumstances had separated us. The closeness of those years – younger brother to older brother, child to adult – couldn't last. My brother, growing into adolescence and early manhood, was on his own, facing his own kind of problems.

Twelve and a half years separated us. But we grew up in different worlds. I had felt swallowed up by our extended Hindu family, a family close to India in some ways; but that family had given me a very bright idea of who I was. My brother was without this cultural support. By the time he was growing up, our extended family had disintegrated. Our own family unit, with the early death of our father, was impoverished and full of stresses and strains. My brother was very much on his own.

There was something else. I had grown up towards the end of the colonial period. This was a time of law and optimism. My brother's adolescence coincided with the rise of colonial politics – racial politics. One of my brother's early letters, in 1956, is about going to one of Eric Williams's mass meetings in central Port of Spain – then a place for taking walks in, today a dangerous, criminal wasteland. That mass meeting of 1956 would have been frightening for an Indian boy of 11. Because, whatever was said on the platform, or was printed in the papers, everyone knew that the politics were racial, with more than a hint of African millenarianism; and that chaos was coming.

This is the background to my brother's work. This explains the tragic sense, the sense of a dissolving world, and at times the quietism, which were the other side of his wonderful comic gift.

There is a way currently in vogue of writing about degraded and corrupt countries. This is the way of fantasy and extravagance. It dodges all the issues; it is safe.

I find the way empty, morally and intellectually; it makes writing, literature, the opposite of what it should be; it makes writing an aspect of the corruption of the countries out of which it issues. I find my brother's tragic sense, his insistence on rationality and the intellect, and his high artistic conscience, more exhilarating.

The feeling of solitude that overcame me in the middle of the morning on the day my brother died – some hours before I heard he had died – that feeling will probably never leave me now. It is like something at the tips of my fingers; something of which I am reminded by the very act of composition, the family vocation we shared.

But there is his work. That revivifies. It is a large body of work and it will hold its own: the record of a growing knowledge of the world, an ever-deepening response to the world, and of a skill developing to match knowledge and response. My brother aimed high; the better he became the higher he aimed. What an instrument his prose became. And consider the astonishing completeness of his Jonestown book. What a labour he imposed on himself there, finding a narrative – which was also an analysis – to link the now congruent, now complementary, corruptions of black Guyana and sunny California. He could so easily have got away with less.

His development in the last eight or nine years was prodigious. This was more or less the period of his association with *The Spectator*. The welcome and freedom and fellowship he found on the paper answered his need; and he flourished. The manifold elegance of the paper is not a matter of literary style alone. It is also an elegance of mind, an expression of a high civilisation.

Men cannot do more for other men than to express fellowship with them. This meeting is an expression of fellowship; it is very moving.

24 January, 1987

Digby Anderson

RUINED BY THE HOLIDAY WRITERS

The Englishman was a northerner. They all are in Sorrento. He was sitting with his wife in a horse-drawn trap – a tourist trap – and smiling in a contorted way. It was the same smile worn by the rest of his holidaymaking countrymen. It said, 'I assure you I do want to be up here. I chose to be up here. I was not had by the trap man. I like it. Very nice – well, of course, it's partly to please the wife.' In three days in Sorrento (the things one does for *Spectator* readers), I did not see a genuine smile on a sober English face, all were twisted with trepidation or defiance or apology or excuse. But I admit I did not venture into the 'English pub with video'. No doubt they were happy in there. Instead I escaped in the evenings, my observations done, to the delights of Naples; St Januarius, zuppa di pesce and many genuine smiles but no English, that one would notice, at all.

I blame the journalists who write about holidays. Their aim seems to be to get as many people as possible sitting in traps and smiling. They may not agree with the travel agents as to *which* resort is best for it, but they share the assumption that the populace should be encouraged to go abroad on holiday. They are delighted at the trend towards longer and second holidays and talk of the numbers going abroad as if they were a personal success. They persistently keep up an inviting tone about both the different places and types of holiday and are at pains to reassure readers that anyone can do it. There is something for everyone – 'Have you ever considered a boat-holiday on the Canal du Midi? No, I know you have never managed a boat. Nor had I. But you quickly get the hang of it. A few false starts on day one, but then that's part of the holiday fun. By the end of a fortnight, you'll feel strange on dry land.' The canal-boaters are, to be sure, a different class from the trap-smilers and less likely to let their discomfort show, but watching them trying to moor in the small town ports along the Etang de Thau as the Mistral blows, you can still see the smile, broken at the ends to give hissed instructions to a wife so the locals can't hear: 'I said "push" not "pull", dear, quick.'

It is surely no mystery that travel firms encourage as many people as possible to go on these holidays, but why should travel journalists? Why should they devote themselves to finding new delights, reassuring potential holidaymakers about imagined difficulties of language or food or boats, and in general encouraging as many people as possible to go? What is needed is the reverse – Imperative holiday writing. Imperative holiday writing is negative, its object to make readers think twice before going, to protect them from the temptations of the travel firms, to undermine rather than inflate their self-confidence, indeed to reduce those going to that minimum which will really enjoy it.

Imperative holiday writing would certainly involve being rude about particular places: 'All the French Mediterranean is horrid in August. Don't go.' 'Taormina may have been pleasant once; it isn't now.' And the blunter, the better. Lots of precious holiday weeks and money are wasted because no one will be blunt. But, in fact, being rude about places is not what is really required. To some extent, in a mealy-mouthed way, the journalists do this already. What they cannot bring themselves to be is rude about people. There are two groups of people they should insult. First, those associated with the destination. Indeed it is these who account for much of the apparent unpleasantness of the places. Taormina is unpleasant *because* it's stuffed full of loud, boring Germans. The French Mediterranean is ruined by campers trying to do it on the cheap, ugly people who mistakenly want to be looked at and British primary school teachers who block all roads with their cornflake-laden caravans. Caravanners are overdue for abuse. No one can claim to be a holiday journalist rooting in his readers' interests until he has carried out a sustained campaign of vilification against caravanners, especially those from the middle classes, who should know better.

Into this category also come the persons one might have to travel with. There seems little point in going to destinations such as Lanzarote, which are still enjoyable, if the outward and, worse, the return journeys are stuffed with drunken persons in vests being treated to the latest football results on the plane's address system. Of course, those who pay mass prices must be prepared to put up with mass vulgarity but they should be warned first about the particular unpleasant forms it takes and where.

It is important that the distinction between awful places and awful people be maintained. There are places which are awful by themselves: Dunkirk, one imagines, has always been less than entrancing, at least since the war. It needed no help in this from the day trippers who now visit it. Other, otherwise harmless places are rendered temporarily uninhabitable by seasonal holidaymakers. In yet others the duration of the season or the extreme awfulness of the holidaymakers has permanently ruined the place. It should be the responsible travel journalist's task to keep us up to date on which is which. In so doing he should follow, not attempt to correct, his various readers' prejudices. If we don't like holidaying with lots of noisy, nude Germans, it is his job to tell us where they are so we can avoid them, not to reform our prejudices. If we don't like being approached by Italian waiters offering cups of tea, he should tell us where the influx of proletarian northerners (English) has had such a sustained effect that the understandably market-oriented Italians have comprehensively bowed to it. It is not his job to teach lessons about tolerance. However virtuous tolerance may be, there is no reason why one should be tolerant of, let alone friendly with, persons on holiday whom one would not mix with at home. And this goes in both directions. Surely the tea-drinking pony-trappers and naked Germans need to be warned of the places in which they will encounter snobs, Blimps and middle-class warriors in navy-blue woollen trunks. It can't be a help, when you are struggling to keep your radiant equanimity on a pony and trap in Sorrento High Street, to have some chap in a Panama stop and lean his head back so he can look down his nose at you. The fact that we have different prejudices, far from being a reason for less rudeness on the journalist's part, is clearly a justification for much more, enough to cater for each of the prejudices.

When the Imperative holiday writer has finished being rude about the people you'll find at the destination or on the way, he has only just started. His real task is to be rude about you, the potential holidaymaker. No more of this 'Anyone can do it' business. You want to go to Calabria? Why? You heard it was nice from a friend. Have you taken any trouble to find out about it? Come back when you have. In fact it is splendid. Good food, good religion, good sun and highly entertaining people. But what about you? Are you good enough for it? You aren't interested in the spotlighted gladioli-resplendent cult of the Sacred Heart. You don't mind pasta once or twice with a heavy sauce, but don't fancy it every day, plain with a little aubergine or a few chillies and garlic followed by grilled bream. You are uncomfortable without a menu. You are not prepared to negotiate for meals. You expected it to be more like France. You are disconcerted that your hotel room shower doesn't work. You usually have two showers a day on holiday. You are upset by what you call slums and can't see the point of all those barbers. You don't expect so much noise from the traffic or the people and you aren't moved by bursts of Rossini played badly by a band of what look like waiters on the sea front. You like your coffee white.

Then don't go. You're not up to it. Oh, yes, it will accommodate to you. They will come, eventually, and mend the shower (though the lavatory cistern will break in response). They will fish out an old and irrelevant menu for you. And happily pipe milk into your coffee. But why? Why bother? You won't really enjoy it.

The holiday writers would be doing us a favour if they made us think twice before we booked, but it's more than that. They need to remind us that pleasure demands effort and is improved by knowledge and taste. It is unusual, except among the loony Left, to deny this about literature, music or painting. Why should it be any less true of travel and holiday? What is needed is more genuine and far fewer smiles.

31 January, 1987

Charles Moore

NOTEBOOK

Bruce Chatwin's new book, *The Songlines*, which I have not read, apparently introduces us to a system by which Aborigines find their way about. From songs, they learn the routes by which they can navigate thousands of miles. Some irreverent spirits have suggested that the Abos have hoodwinked us and that they are doing nothing more than humming 'Waltzing Matilda' in return for government grants. The truth of the matter must be very hard to discover without going on a guided tour of the Songlines oneself. But what is interesting is the romance and importance with which these lines are invested. Mr Chatwin imagines Songlines reaching back to the 'isolated pocket in the African savannah' where man was first conscious of his own existence. Why is it that such things are only considered exciting and cosmically significant when they concern primitive man? However remarkable the Aboriginal Songlines may be, they are nothing like as extraordinary as the Songlines of civilisation. How miraculous and strange it is, for example, that a supermarket can contain fresh food from thousands of miles away, that we trust the system of food supply so much that we will eat this food, that because we hand over bits of paper and metal in return for this food the growers, shippers and retailers all make a living, and that the whole chain is established without a single presiding intelligence. How wonderful it is that we have developed a language capable of expressing not just material wants and basic desires but ideas, histories, moralities, scientific information, jokes, complex feelings, scenes imagined and remembered; and that this language communicates not just in speech and song, but through writing, printing, radio, television and computer. Mr Chatwin, I gather, attributes the authorship of civilisation to nomads. Even if he is right, the flower seems to me infinitely more fascinating than the root. The dullest London street tells us far richer things about humanity than everything primitive peoples have ever done. The Ordnance Survey is a more beautiful achievement than the Aboriginal Songline.

18 July, 1987

Digby Anderson

IMPERATIVE COOKING: THE AIRBORNE PICNIC

Somewhere over the Atlantic

The Englishman had parked by the side of a main road near Brive. There he was, at 8 a.m., one foot gingerly placed on French soil, the other on the step to his vile caravan. In his left hand, he held a bowl, in his right a packet of cornflakes which he was discharging into the bowl.

If I were a Dutchman I might have been just as embarrassed by what I saw once on the autoroute near Avignon. A Dutch family had parked their caravan by the service station of the north-bound side – they were presumably returning to the dykes. I could not see what they were eating inside but on the table was a jar of their pickled cucumbers and some brown bread in a packet with Dutch writing on. They had brought enough of both to last their holiday. The Dutch are renowned in France for this sort of tasteless and discourteous behaviour. Behind Montpellier, there is a whole village of émigré Nederlanders victualled by a grocer's van which arrives weekly from Amsterdam.

Even worse are the Dutch or the English who don't stay. Throughout the summer, the French have to put up with a stream of Nordic foreigners driving through their country, spending nothing, holding up the traffic with their absurd caravans and leaving a trail of cornflake packets, pickled cucumber jars and sawdust sausage skins as they edge towards a 'site' in Spain.

Spectator readers are unlikely to behave like this. Indeed, the worry is that in their keenness not to they may go to the opposite extreme and imagine that one should never eat on the move, that one should always eat what a host country has to offer. This is certainly not advisable in Germany or Sweden: Berlin appears to receive gravy through a pipeline from the East which it pours over a daily compulsory dose of carrots, and the lumpy mashed potato and nationalised non-alcoholic beer in Stockholm during homosexual week in September are pleasures best, but with difficulty, forgotten. Readers would be wise to take their own supplies with them if they have to visit either place.

But I was thinking of supplies to eat on the move, for while it is daft to eat cornflakes in caravans in France when a good restaurant beckons, there is one occasion when 'self-catering' is essential: on long aeroplane flights. Obviously one can't eat the unpleasant things provided.

Young fogeys, new and fresh to the battle against modern 'standards', will want to go the whole hog and take a full six-course dinner in a wicker hamper. First, a challenging *hors d'oeuvres* such as oysters; a dozen or two packed in damp seaweed and opened just before serving (don't forget the oyster knife, the stewardesses never have one). Later, perhaps a nourishing mutton *daube* with anchovies (piping hot from a thermos). Why not end with walnuts? Since one object of the exercise is to shame the airline, noisy and smelly dishes are a good idea.

We older fogeys who are slightly battle-weary can make do with something simpler: it goes without saying that one takes a napkin, plate, knife, fork and glass. Inexpensive ones are best, then you can leave them on the plane. Try starting with a variation on salade niçoise – it's one of the few salads which improve if dressed some time before serving and is easy to carry, serve and eat. I use potatoes, tomatoes, tuna, anchovies, eggs, onions and olives. Instead you could have one of the cold soups, gazpacho, or a selection of charcuterie. The important thing with the main course, if it is to be cold, is to avoid the depressing English devotion to cold joints. Serve dishes which are better cold than hot or only ever served cold: salmon or halibut with mayonnaise, vitella tomato, steak tartare, game pie, soused mackerel, sprats or herrings, or, best of all, a stuffed goose neck (more of this another week).

End with a very large selection of cheese and celery, then perhaps a *tarte*. You can safely use the salt they give you on the plane for the celery but you should grind pepper at home and take it with you, unless you can acquire a miniature portable grinder. The enterprising Lord Harris of High Cross has the only one I have seen. Coffee is unfortunately impossible, unless you, as I do, like *caffe freddo*. Don't forget the bread and toothpicks.

All this is equally possible on long-distance trains or, I imagine, coaches. But one last note; if you do discard your crockery and cutlery at the end of the journey, don't just leave them on the seat. Hand them to the stewardess on leaving and ask where she would like you to put them. It's polite and, what is more, draws attention to them. Who knows – a resourceful airline may collect them and start using them itself.

23 March, 1985

2 WESTERN EUROPE

Peter Mayne

YOU SEE ME OLD AND FAT . . .

'The journey will be long,' the driver said, staring ahead through his windscreen at the mountains of Thrace and the track that dipped and disappeared and then appeared again in the distance. In the south, but far away, the dark Aegean glistened. The Turkish border lay somewhere behind us. 'It will take an hour and a half, more even,' he said, nodding.

We were three people sharing the hired car: a young Greek couple and myself. The driver was fat, fiftyish; nearer sixty, I dare say; and though Greek he did not look as if he had come from these northern lands.

'Perhaps you would like it if I told you the story of my life,' he was saying to the girl. 'To lighten this long journey for you. It is a very simple story.'

'Tell it to me,' she said.

He settled down behind his steering-wheel, but it was some moments before he began his story. He wanted to compose his thoughts, I expect. After this pause, he began:

'You see me old and fat, but I too was beautiful; and I had many loves – the lady must forgive me mentioning this, but girls – it was easy for me because of my beauty, you see. Yet each time it proved but dust and ashes. So one day, it was a Monday, I said to myself, "I shall go out in search of a wife." I was still a soldier, it was after the war with the Turks, 1922 it was, and I was wearing my uniform. All this took place here in Thrace, you understand, and I saw a girl drawing water from a well. I could not see her face as she drew up her water, only her back, but from the clothes she wore I could tell that she was from Eastern Thrace and also that she must be in needy circumstances. So I waited patiently until she had drawn up the water and then quietly I followed behind her at a distance and when she came to a small shack I saw that her family were certainly refugees from the Turks, for only refugees could be living in such sad poverty. So I waited a little, not wishing to frighten her, and then I knocked at the door of the shack and it was opened to me by a woman and I guessed that this woman must be the mother of the girl. But as soon as this older woman saw me she stepped back in alarm. My uniform, you see. The people were scared of any uniform at that time. So I quickly said to her:

' "Do not be scared of me, *kyria*, for I come to this house as a suitor."

' "As a *suitor* . . . ?" she asked me, bringing her hands to her face in an astonished manner. "But . . ."

'And I broke into the thread of her sentence and asked in my turn:

' "Are you *not*, then, the mother of the girl I have seen drawing up water from the well near by, the girl who has this moment returned to this house?"

'And the mother said: "Yes, I am."

'And I said: "Well, I am come as a suitor for the hand of your daughter."

'And at this the woman became confused, perhaps because this was the first good circumstance that had befallen the family for a long time, you understand, my coming to her as a suitor for the hand of her daughter in this way.

'Finally she said: "I am a widow, sir. I must first seek the approval of my two sons."

'And I said: "First you may seek the approval of your daughter herself, and thereafter I shall arrange myself with her two brothers."

'So she called to the girl and the girl came out and stood before me with her eyes lowered: but she had seen me and she nodded to her mother, saying: "I approve of this man . . ." and then, what a strange thing! When I was brought before her two brothers, one of these two men had been my companion-in-arms throughout a year of bloody fighting against the Turks and indeed we were already as brothers. So I took this girl and married her and we came to love each other and throughout these years she has been a satisfactory wife to me and she has borne me two sons and one daughter, and though it has pleased God to take our dear daughter from us, yet our two sons have been spared to us, and the little reward that I have gained and set aside from my work suffices for me and my wife and for our two sons, and that is how my life has been spent.'

The driver had slowed down the car a little and turned in his seat so that he could look into the faces of his passengers and see the reaction to his story. The car stopped.

'But you are crying!' he said to the girl: and then to her young husband: 'Tell her not to cry, the little child. There is nothing sad in my life, that she should cry.' And the young husband stroked her gently and said: 'Do not cry. Why are you crying, my little bird?'

'I do not know,' she whispered, her face hidden in her husband's shoulder.

The driver sat looking at her. A new and faint surprise had come into his expression, and perhaps this was because his life, which had taken fifty, sixty years of living, had yet been compressible into two little minutes of this long journey to Komotini, and the long journey had scarcely even started.

23 January, 1959

John Betjeman

CITY AND SUBURBAN

I do not like going abroad, and am ashamed to say I have never been to Venice. But so many cultivated people have talked to me about it that I have accepted an invitation to stay with friends there next week. My inferiority about not having been to Venice has been so great that I have even pretended to 'art historians' that I have been there in order to avoid further conversation about it. The problem is, what to wear. I'm told this is the height of the season. Some of the nicest people in Europe will be lying on the Lido. I went to an off-the-peg shop and asked for the right clothes and they advised white evening dress with a red cummerbund. I went to another and they suggested a grey tropical suit such as hot clergymen wear. I'm going dressed as an American by way of compromise.

19 August, 1955

Harold Nicolson

MARGINAL COMMENT

We are always assured that Paris is at her loveliest when the chestnuts are in flower and the weeping willows planted below the quays stretch their tendrils towards the passing Seine. The month of May does certainly emphasise and embellish the panoramic aspect of the great city, but not its intimacy. I prefer the early winter evenings when the sky is red behind what was once the Trocadero and the windows of the cafes glimmer through a haze of steam. For me the smell of chestnuts roasting evokes more private memories than any aroused by the candelabra of spring. Yet Paris in the rain, as I last saw it, is in truth a saddening sight. The pavements seem to become and to remain wetter than in any other city, with the possible exception of Oxford; the awnings drip terribly; and the long perspectives of street lamps, each reflected in its own splashed puddle, seem all directed to a glum and aqueous end. 'It rains in my heart,' as Verlaine observed, 'as it rains on the town.' On a night last month, as I motored out of Paris onto the rain-soaked Ile de France, my eye was caught by a single yellow leaf sticking among the rain-drops to the glass. The screen-wiper hummed backwards and forwards with the regularity of a metronome, but the leaf was thin enough, adhesive enough, to permit the rubber to pass over it; the rain-drops disappeared and then appeared again; the leaf was always there. Depressed as I was by the wet streets and awnings, depressed by the water which descended from above or splashed below, I found myself regarding that leaf as a symbol or portent of decay. It seemed so irremovable; it adhered. Could it be true, I asked myself, that the French, with their passion for living rapidly, had exhausted their vitality, that the amazing resilience which had marked their history had at last lost its sap, and that they had even forsaken that gaiety *'qui faisait croire à leur génie'*?

27 October, 1950

Never so long as I live and my brain retains even one per cent of its activity shall I cease to be filled with wonder at the supreme moment of sleeping-car experience: the moment when one unhooks the blind from its small stud, allows it to creep up the window, and lies back to see a wholly new landscape sliding past one's angle of vision. Those who share with me the ecstasy of this sudden experience will understand better than others when I say that short sharp journeys to the Continent provide a stimulus more intense than the ordinary prolonged visit. One may have driven the night before through wet and shining streets to the Gare de Lyon, observing how the crowds on the boulevards will cluster under dripping café awnings, waiting for the storm to pass. One may have heard the rain clattering upon the glass roof of the station and observed the wet leather capes of the policemen escorting the mail trolleys towards the train. As night descends, the large panes of the corridor windows are slashed diagonally by lit streaks of water; the train shakes and rumbles onwards through the dripping night. And next morning, when one wakes, when that wonderful encounter occurs with the blind and its small stud, there suddenly is a rushing landscape, lit with a light such as (were the quotation not so wearied) one might describe as unusual on sea or land. For surely that first fall of sunshine upon the Provence landscape is among the most miraculous of unnatural phenomena, appearing to be as artificial as the rose-madder glow that illuminates the small panorama boxes in the windows of travel agencies. Black and wet was the world but a few hours before; and now pink, golden and blue. Yet within a morning these colours will have lost their magic: by the same afternoon one will glance at the Mediterranean scene without surprise.

15 June, 1951

What I enjoy so much about the Greek scene is the abruptness with which it changes. A lime-stone gorge, with cistus and sage tangled above the torrent, will stop suddenly and be followed by a vast plain, the limit of which, where it reaches the next range of mountains, is as straight as a horizon. The sea, which until a few moments ago was glistening to the east, its light blue scudded with dark blue squalls, its white horses dancing sharply under a sharp morning sun, is swept from our sight by the sudden lunge of a promontory: almost immediately a quite different sea glides into our vision from the west, calm as a lagoon. The rocks that soar above the Vale of Tempe (through which I am at this moment passing) are jagged, bare and flecked with snow; far below them hurries the amber river, past the big plane trees on the bank, past the willows already green; around grow terebinth and myrtle, clematis and jasmine, and clumps of euphorbia lush and yellow in the gorge's shade. The mind is filled with visions of giants assaulting Olympus, with Pelion and Ossa as their siege-engines; of Poseidon cleaving the range with a faint touch of his trident; of Apollo descending with serene eyes to calm such savage legends; of Cicero even, bidding the slaves rest his litter beside this running water, welcoming the stream of *frigida Tempe* after the fierce heat of the journey from Larissa. Two Greek engineers in my compartment, who until now have been discussing with bitter stridency some hydro-electric scheme in the Vardar valley, stop talking suddenly and start to play backgammon. They rattle the neatest little dice and slowly, between brown finger and broken thumb, they move pieces from one section of the board to another. The click of ivory accompanies me across the Thessalian plain. It will be dark before we pass the lion of Chaeronea or enter the defiles of Cithaeron, where Pentheus was murdered, and the ladies of the Court of Thebes dipped into the wine that Dionysus gave them the resin of the pine-cones on their wands.

The differences that delight me when I return to Greece are partly due to the fact that I have had the good fortune to visit the country at different seasons of the year. In summer even the children wear enormous sun-spectacles, the pepper trees that fringe the boulevards of Athens hang their pods in dusty despair, and the Ilissus – never one of Europe's mightiest rivers – ceases even to be a trickle seeping in an open drain. It is then that the unvintaged sea really comes into its own. In autumn, the morning and evening air is golden, and at sunset Hymettus glows above the Acropolis and the town with incomparable radiations of pink and amethyst and purple. I have never quite seen why Aristophanes, who could himself be sentimental enough, should have jeered at Pindar for calling Athens 'violet-crowned'; or why later scholars have insisted that the epithet did not apply to Hymettus at sunset, but to the practice, at the time of the vernal Dionysia, of twining the wands with violet sprays. Hymettus, in a clear October sunset, is enough to set even a Theban heart aflame. But perhaps the best of all seasons is the month of March, when the snow rests upon the lower mountains also, when the poplars are just beginning to be tinged with green, and when the anemones, the grape hyacinths, the scillas, the tulips, the dwarf irises and the scented nar-cissus cluster in companies together around the drifts of pink cyclamen. Around them splash the rivulets released by the quick-melting snow.

There is, however, one natural element in Greece which always surprises me with its immutability: the Greek national character. No nation on earth has, within the last half century, endured such terrible calamities. Since 1897 the Greeks have experienced six major wars, four foreign invasions, two civil wars – the first distracting, the second fiercely destructive – all manner of *coups d'etat* and *pronunciamientos*, several revolts, three serious revolutions, and a succession of economic catastro-phes such as would have shattered any weaker breed. Their villages have been burnt and their children kidnapped; the most frightful murders have been committed; yet here they are, their railways working splen-didly, their roads repaired, their merchant navy almost restored to its pre-war prosperity, starting to argue passionately again whether more might not be done with American aid to canalise the waters of the Vardar. We all know that the Greeks are very brave; we all know that they are highly intelligent; but it is their astonishing resilience that, more than any other quality, compels my deep respect. Along the line that runs from Salonika to Athens a few block-houses and military posts still remain from the civil war. The soldiers have amused themselves in their spare moments by marking out in white-washed stones the battle-honours of their regi-ments. Victories against the Bulgarians in Macedonia, victories against the Turks in Thrace, victories against the Albanians in Illyria, victories against the Italians in Northern Epirus; but these lists, scarring the mountain-side with the motto 'Long live the King!' always begin with three lapidary names: – 'Marathon,' 'Salamis,' 'Plataea.' No, I am certain that I could not really like anybody who did not really like the Greeks.

How insatiable, how Socratic, is their curiosity! The two men in my compartment finished their backgammon and began all over again to get angry with each other about the Vardar valley. The light tinkle of the luncheon-bell prevented a conflict. They seated themselves amicably at my table in the restaurant-car. Was I English or French? Was I married? Did I still live with my wife? Had I any children? Had they entered a profession? Was I rich or poor? What was the amount of my yearly income? Did I, like most Englishmen, suffer from weak kidneys? What did I think of Marshal Papagos? Did I know that Amphikleia was the source of the Cephisus? What had I been scribbling while they were playing backgammon? Would I read it aloud to them in French when we got back to the compartment? And (if I did not mind their asking so personal a question) did I like Greece?

21 March, 1952

The Dunkirk ferry that night, throbbing gently, wafted me back to England; the bottle of Evian in my sleeper tinkled a different tune when we became sea-borne. In the morning the orchards smiled gaily in the sunshine, being freed from the apprehension of May frosts. The silence of London, after all that conversation and all those motor horns and whistles, engulfed me soothingly. What a stimulus, what an excitement, it is to go for three days to Paris! What a relaxation to get home!

30 May, 1952

Patrick Leigh Fermor

THE SERPENTS OF THE ABRUZZI

Leaving the gentle, Italian-primitive landscape of Umbria for the blank sierras of the Abruzzi was as complete a change as a journey to a different planet. Indeed, these wild grey peaks have an almost lunar remoteness, and the little village of Cocullo, a grey honeycomb of houses at the end of a blind alley of the mountains a dozen miles from Ovid's birthplace at Sulmona, must usually seem a desolate habitation. The sun beats down from a blazing sky, but in the labyrinthine shadows of the lanes there is a chill bite in the air from the towering snows of the Gran Sasso.

But once a year, in the first week of May, this planetary silence is broken, and the village population, normally only a few hundred souls – shepherds and small cultivators to a man – swells to several thousands. Pilgrims, last month, swarmed from all the neighbouring villages, and, as this is one of the few parts of Italy where regional costumes survive, the streets were a kaleidoscope of different colours and fashions. A bearded shepherd, playing an ear-splitting pibroch on a bagpipe made of a patched inner tube, wore raw-hide moccasins, and his legs were cross-gartered with thick leather thongs, like those of a Saxon thane.

The religious occasion was also the pretext for a rustic fair, and the market was full of trussed poultry and squealing pigs. Pedlars carried trays of rosaries, medals, little tin motor-cars, celluloid thumbs-ups and dried acorn-cups. There were 'lucky' hunch-backs, crippled beggars, hucksters with fortune-telling canaries and a wandering hypnotist. Less usual was the presence, wherever one turned, of snakes, slung over brown forearms or twisting like bracelets, lying in loose tangles among the funnel-topped bottles in the wine-shops, or held in clusters of four with their unwinking heads all gathered in the palm between the laden fingers of both hands, their long forked tongues sliding in and out of their jaws. Some were nearly two yards in length, and all of them looked alarmingly dangerous.

Most of the *serpari*, or snake catchers, are under twenty. For weeks past they had been hunting them in the mountains, where they abound. Capturing them while they are still dazed with their winter-sleep, they disarm the poisonous ones by giving them the hem of a garment to bite, which, when snatched away, breaks off their teeth and drains their poison. Then, stored in jars or sewn into goatskins, they are put by until the great day comes round. There were now several hundred of them in the streets of Cocullo – black, grey, greenish, speckled and striped, all hissing and knotting together and impotently darting and biting with their harmless jaws.

The floor of the baroque, and surprisingly large, church was deep in crumbs and bundles and débris, for hundreds of visiting peasants, finding the village overflowing, had slept there all night. Queues waited their turn at the confessional, and, under a pink and blue baldachin, relays of priests administered the sacrament. In the north transept a bell clanked almost unceasingly as peasant after peasant, taking a metal ring between his teeth, tugged at a chain that rang the clapper of a bell that had once belonged to St Dominic, to draw his notice to their petition. On waiting trays the crumpled fifty *lire* mounted up. From behind the altar precious lumps of rubble – from the ruins, it is said, of one of St Dominic's foundations – were carried off to be sprinkled over the fields and ensure a good harvest, and rid the fields of rats.

A young priest applied a battered silver reliquary to the arms and shoulders of an interminable succession of kneeling pilgrims, or to the upheld crusts of bread they would later feed to their livestock to ward off rabies. Inside the cylindrical casket swung and rattled a wonder-working tooth of St Dominic; now, after a thousand years, a chipped and discoloured fang. Then the devotees moved on to the effigy of St Dominic himself, a lifesize, wooden figure in black Benedictine habit with a horseshoe in one hand and in the other a crosier. Embracing him with a hungry and possessive veneration, they rubbed little bundles of coloured wool – sovereign thenceforward, when applied to the spot, against toothache and snakebite and hydrophobia – down the grooves of his skirt, or lifted their children to kissing distance of the worn and numinous flanks. Silver exvotos hung round his neck, and pink ribbons, on which were pinned sheaves of offered banknotes, fluttered from his shoulders. St Dominic of Sora, or 'the Abbot' – he has nothing to do with the great founder of the Order of Preachers – was a Benedictine of Umbrian origin, born in 951. He was eremitical and peripatetic by turns, and his countless miracles during his lifetime, and, the Abruzzesi relate, through the agency of his relic ever since, were nearly all connected with the foiling of the bears and wolves, and, especially, of the snakes.

By the time High Mass began, there was no room to move in the crowded church. Yet a passage was cleared and two young women advanced with large baskets balancing unsupported on their heads, each of them containing great hoop-like loaves; both baskets were draped in pink and white silk and decked with carnations and wild cyclamen. The girls stood like caryatids on either side of the high altar until, at the end of the service, the image of the saint was hoisted shoulder-high and borne swaying into the sunlight before the church door. There, while the compact multitude clapped and cheered and the bells broke into a jubilant peal, the *serpari* clustered round the lowered float. Snakes began flying over the tonsured head like lassos. Parish elders arranged them featherboa-like, about his shoulders, twisted them round his crosier and wound them over his arms and through the horseshoe and at random all over his body until the image and its pedestal were a squirming tangle. Many fell off or wriggled free, and one over-active reptile was given a sharp crack over the head. It was raised shoulder high once more like a drowned figurehead salvaged from the Sargasso Sea. A small pink banner, pinned all over with notes, and a large green one, were unwieldily hoisted. Village girls intoned a hymn in Abruzzi dialect in St Dominic's honour; then the clergy, one of them bearing the cylinder with its swinging tooth, formed a phalanx.

Then came the two girls with their peculiar baskets. A brass band struck up the triumphal march from *Aida*, and the Saint, twisting and coiling with the activity of the bewildered snakes and bristling with hissing and tongue-darting heads, rocked insecurely forward and across the square. The innumerable peasants, the conjurors and pedlars and quacks, fell into step; the wine-shops emptied; pigs and poultry were abandoned in their pens, and the whole immense concourse, now itself forming a gigantic many-coloured serpent, wound slowly along the rising and falling streets. Every few steps the effigy came to a halt while fallen snakes were replaced or yet more banknotes, which floated down from the upper windows, were pinned to the fluttering ribbons. Boys on all sides brandished tangled armfuls of redundant snakes, and looking up at the bright mid-day sky, I saw girls on the rooftops waving the now familiar reptiles in either hand.

At last the saint was back at the church door, and there, like a disentangling of cold macaroni, the de-snaking began. It was as if they had frozen to their perch. When Saint Dominic was in his chapel once again, a strange haggling and chattering began over the carcasses of his denizens. For snakes are eagerly sought by pedlars; they display them as a reinforcement to their patter, attract a crowd, and then slily open their suitcases of combs or medals or celluloid toys. There was even a patent-medicine manufacturer all the way from Bologna, who boils them down to make an ointment against rheumatism. The back of his little car was soon aswarm.

It is tempting to seek a link between these strange doings and some possible pre-Christian worship of Aesculapius. But there was no Aesculapian temple in the area, though Apollo and Jupiter were worshipped at Sulmona. It is known, however, that the warlike Marsi from whom these Abruzzesi descend were snake-worshippers and snake-charmers, and there is no reason why these things should have died out by St Dominic's day. Antiquarians also find certain affinities between the Cocullan customs and the fertility rites of the Agathos Daimon. Be that as it may, the strange cult in honour of St Dominic the Abbot shows no signs of dying out. If anything, it grows more popular and more deeply felt as time goes on.

With every mile of the return journey next day, through the twisting

Sabine gorges and down into Campagna with the dome of St Peter's growing larger on the skyline,the proceedings at Cocullo seemed odder and
more remote. It was only when I touched my coat-pocket and felt a
responsive uneasy wriggle through the tweed, that it seemed real at all.
For, by paying a few hundred *lire*, I had become a snake-owner. It was a
fine grey animal over a yard long with clever little black eyes; very active,
letting slip no chance of nipping my hand with its unarmed (I hope)
gums. But, when I reached my destination in Rome, it had vanished. It
must have slid gently away to freedom in the train between the city-walls
and the Piazza di Spagna. Perhaps, after a panic in the train, it was put out
of the way. But perhaps it is still rattling its way unobserved round the
Seven Hills; or it may be curled up among the pillars of the Forum, or, last
of all, basking sleepily on a warm and grassy ledge of the Colosseum,
beyond the reach of all harm.

5 June, 1953

Rose Macaulay

IN SPAIN AND PORTUGAL

The Iberian peninsula is foreign, in a sense in which France, Italy, Germany and Scandinavia are not. These are the houses and gardens next
door, inhabited by familiar neighbours with whom we have always talked
over the wall. Iberia is remote, not in distance but in spirit; to travel there
is a foreign adventure, and not all the recent popularity of its coasts can
make it anything but exotic. Enter Spain, meet the Spanish; in them you
meet Africa, Gothia, Islam, Carthage, Greece, and behind them all the
dark indigenous Iberians, who were there before history began. The startling magnificence of Spain is partly in its shape and colour, the stark,
formidable beauty of its scenes; more in the wrecked civilisations that
stand about it, broken but undefeated, unexpelled, still indomitably
asserting their continued existence in the fabric of country and people.
Rome ruled here, and does not allow you to forget it; her broken walls,
arches, aqueducts and bridges bestride the craggy, tawny land. Africa
ruled here; and still less can you forget this; her descendants and her heritage, the stately fantastic glories of Islam, the delicate, massive Arab
dreams in stone, the Moorish fabric of society, lie round about the medi-

aeval structure like palm-grown desert sands. The feudal Middle Ages ruled here; they still do. Here are the great dark Romanesque-Gothic churches, the walled hill cities, the shattered feudal castles, the storming ghosts of princes and bishops at war, the huge Benedictine monasteries, assaulted and demolished down the ages by anti-clericalist Spanish raging, but still superbly standing high on their mountains, dominating and guarding the lands once theirs, the blue bays and fishing ports that were their markets. The Counter-Reformation once ruled here; it still does. Here are the graceful, florid, pillared, ochre façades, enturbed with lively angels, saints and gods, enwreathed with carved fruits and flowers, adorning Romanesque churches and seignorial palaces with their baroque elegance. All about Spain, and more about Portugal, you will find baroque, exploding here and there into wedding-cake churrigueresque. In Portugal you find something stranger – the marine manueline that has carved ropes and shells and anchors everywhere, and the glazed china azulejos that deliciously plaster churches, walls and town halls.

In Spain the cities stand in fabulous splendour – Toledo, Avila, Cordoba, Granada, Salamanca, Santiago, Tarragona, Ronda, Gerona, Seville, Burgos, Pampeluna, Pals, Zaragoza, Huesca, Lerida, Lorca, Cadiz, Jerez, Ciudad Rodrigo, Orihuela, Guadix and a hundred more. The landscape, baked, rocky, arid and bleak, has a hard beauty which makes other lands seem soft and lush: the sea has driven deep indentations and gulfs into its shores. The modern parts of the cities are execrably hideous; visit Madrid only for the Prado and if you have a passion for capitals. The modern restoration and interior décor of churches and cathedrals are worse than anything in Britain; it has a superbly Latin bad taste. The people are delightful to talk to. Avoid gypsies, flamenco dancing, bull-fights and Easter in Seville; all these are commercialised and wearying.

Portugal is on an altogether smaller and softer and less grand scale, as George Borrow found. It has no cities in the Spanish class; Lisbon is very beautiful, with its mixed mediaeval and Pombaline streets and magnificent poise above the Tagus; about half its population have an African look. This is not so in the north, where the peasants are beautiful and Latin. Oporto is grandly placed on its cliffs and on the Douro, and is a noble city; the mountain wine country round it is romantically superb. Ride a horse or a mule about the Minho and Tras-os-Montes; stand on the quays and watch the ships in Viana port, the cradle of the port wine trade; visit Braganza, Guimaraes, the mountain homes of Portuguese revolutions.

Travel south, by Coimbra on its hill, the Mondego running round it, by the Gothic beauties of Alcobaça and Batalha, by the desolate Alemtejo, the Roman Evora, the great cork forests of Montalegre; you pass a thousand delicate beauties of architecture and small cities on the way. Reach the Algarve, with its chain of small sea ports and its African shrubs, its scarlet flowers on white walls, its tiled churches and its formidable, desolate cape that is Europe's end. Portugal is an odd mixture of wildness and elegance, bijouterie and grandeur; it seems a land made for happiness. Its people, talking their softened and curtailed Galician, smile.

22 February, 1957

Simon Raven

ROUGH ISLAND STORY

The Isle of Hydra is some three hours' sail from the Piraeus. In winter there is only one boat a day, but in summer there are many more because this tiny island is now one of the most celebrated tourist-traps in the Near East. With good reason: it is rocky and dramatic in appearance, it has an archetypically cute harbour, there are no roads and therefore no cars; highly coloured representatives of the arts abound, what is more, and the fisher-boys are notoriously co-operative. The food is a nightmare, but even this is an added attraction to those who want to feel they are off the beaten track. In fact, of course, they are nothing of the kind – you can get by very well without a word of Greek. But all tourist resorts have their own particular confidence trick; and Hydra's is the false appearance of being (my dear) remote. Not but what other attractions are genuine enough: there are occasional scenes of pagan licence in the 'best' *taverna*, during which (with these eyes I have seen it) people positively take their clothes off; and there was a much-discussed sermon by a local bishop which was devoted in its entirety to the iniquities of a bar which opened – and closed – last summer. But in the main Hydra as seen by travellers is phoney; it is a *trompe-l'oeil* island sticking out of a painted sea: until, that is, one starts inquiring into the real habits of the real inhabitants – into what goes on when winter comes, when the last epicene giggle has hovered and died in the October air.

For in winter Hydra is a great deal odder than the casual summer visitor could conceive. Not because it has changed, but because the wrappings and trappings have been removed (to be carefully stored until next April), and because there is now room to see. There is room to see a barren island with a handful of lean and savage occupants, whose only livelihood comes from the sea and from a few grudging patches of earth which have been cleared, with something near heroism, of flint and rock. There is leisure to observe that the demeanour of the people, so bright and hospitable when there were tourists to be cosseted and cheated, is now bleak and cheerless, that their eyes, which promised so much during the dog days, are now suspicious and cruel. 'What is he doing, this stranger, lingering on into the winter? Cannot he see he has outstayed his welcome? There is nothing left here for him. Though meanwhile, of course, we can continue to take his money . . .'

This hostility, so unexpected and upsetting to anyone who has been told from his infancy that the Greeks regard *xenos* as a sacred word, has its roots in the island's history. For the Hydriots (Albanians by origin) were, and in spirit remain, pirates. They chopped down their fine trees to build ships, they sailed the Aegean and then all of the Eastern Mediterranean; they were brave, cunning and ferocious; and if the merchants wanted their fleets to ride safely home – to Venice, to Heraclion, to Acre – then they must pay the Hydriots and wear a smile. By the end of the eighteenth century all sea-trade from Corcyra to Alexandria to the Bosphorus was under Hydriot control. The little island grew rich. The islanders built strong and graceful houses, some of which survive. But they did not grow soft; their swift ships continued to put out at dawn, to return at evening laden with money and goods. Their power and wealth, however, did not endear them either to the Turks or their Greek subjects. Hydra was getting much too big for its boots. Attempts were made to teach a lesson to the insufferable Hydriots – attempts which were answered by cannon from the harbour mouth. Nor was it an island – it could not be – to welcome strangers. It was Hydra *contra mundum*.

It is well known that the only way of uniting the Greeks is to sound the trumpet of war. Then all Greeks, however fractious, make common cause without question and without stint. And so, when the War of Independence began, even the inhabitants of Hydra turned patriot. More so, indeed, than many others. They stripped their island of its last trees, built more ships, sent these and the splendid fleets they had already to sweep away the Turks. They pursued the cause of freedom with single-minded passion. Freedom was duly won but by this time the wealth of the Hydriots – their money, their trees, their ships – was spent.

To the new government in Athens, wary and jealous, this was far from inconvenient. Petitions for compensation from the once proud island were turned aside. Hydra began to starve. Popular outcry at length compelled the authorities to do something for the gallant Hydriots; but it was too little and too late. The population of 35,000 (today it is only 2,000) was already shrinking daily, while the noble houses of the admirals began to tumble down the hill towards the harbour. There was bitterness and decay. The islanders were now hostile for a different reason: strangers, once warned away lest they should pry on wealth, were now hated because they came to mock at poverty. There was, in any case, nothing for them to eat. Until within living memory no stranger could set foot on Hydra. But at last, as communications improved and manners softened, the first trickle of travellers came – bringing money. There had not been any money on the island for a long time and it was to be had for a little politeness. A little island *esprit*, the Hydriots found, went a long way. So they put aside their grimness, and the trickle of travellers grew to a stream, and the stream to a rushing torrent, a torrent washing down gold.

So in the summer all is merry and bright. The privateers, in a fashion, sail once more. But in the winter the old distrust, the old fear that strangers are there either to pry or mock, returns as the days shorten. For there is much that the Hydriots would sooner went unobserved – which, in the confusion of summer, does go unobserved. But in the bare winter the harsh outlines of island life are not easily concealed. It becomes plain, for example, that the local women are still kept more or less in purdah – a proceeding not uncommon in the islands and provinces of Greece, but here carried to a vicious extreme. Pre-pubescent girls and aging widows you will sometimes see on the quayside, marriageable virgins and young wives almost never. Women stay in the house to cook and clean and breed. They do not even do the marketing – their men do that. A woman may get as far as the nearest pump or water-tank and there meet other women in like case. Further than this her social life does not extend. The men, married or unmarried, go out in the evening accompanied only by male friends; and since they are deprived, from adolescence until marriage, of female company, homosexuality and incest are both common, the former at least being regarded only as a subject for mild gossip. In the summer, if they are lucky, the young men might find foreign women, but these are seldom in their first youth. In the winter they must pursue their homosexual courtships in the alleys and the taverns, while the married men (habit dies hard) take a genial and even active part in the proceedings. Fights are frequent, exhibitionism of the crudest kind a commonplace.

Nor would the Hydriots wish it known how very near to starvation they still exist. Not all of them see much of the tourists' money. For those that do not, winter will bring little more than olives and bread, perhaps some rancid white cheese. It will bring long, idle days – it is often too rough to fish – spent crouching, without refreshment, in the cafés (for it is of course obligatory to leave the women in the cold houses to shift for and amuse themselves). Life is hard and even shameful: not something for strangers to be privy to. Small wonder that resentment grows and there are ugly incidents: the children of a foreign couple beaten up by local toughs, the windows of the American painter smashed as he sits at dinner. For the island is showing its evil nature – its hatred, its envy, its bitterness at lost fortune and presently enforced servility.

And so it is that the spirit of the old pirates still shows in Hydra – but a maimed spirit now, thwarted and driven in upon itself. There are no longer wide seas to sail and rich prizes to bring home. The spirit of piracy must now be confined to the exploitation of summer customers; or, in the winter, to the sly, dangerous hatred, formerly turned on strangers who coveted Hydra's wealth, now reserved for foreigners who stay too long on the island – those who are still there after the Hydriots have put away their summer charade and started to inspect their empty cupboards.

27 May,1960

Evelyn Waugh

TOURIST IN AFRICA

December 28, 1958. On the third day after Christmas we commemorate the massacre of the Holy Innocents. Few candid fathers, I suppose, can regard that central figure of slate in Breughel's painting in Antwerp without being touched by sympathy. After the holly and sticky sweetmeats, cold steel.

I declare smugly that at fifty-five I am at the time of life when I have to winter abroad, but in truth I reached that age thirty years ago. Even when I thought I enjoyed fox-hunting my enthusiasm waned by Christmas. I have endured few English Februaries since I became self-supporting. February, 1940, found me a probationary temporary second-lieutenant in an asbestos chalet on the English Channel; never again, I resolved. February, 1941, was far from luxurious, but it was warm, in a densely crowded troopship steaming through the tropics on the great detour to Egypt; but in 1942 I was in a Nissen hut on a Scottish moor; never again. In those days the politicians had a lot to say about our Freedom. They met – few will now recall – and guaranteed everyone Freedom from Fear. Did they

also guarantee Freedom from Religion? Something of the sort, I think. All
I asked in that horrible camp was freedom to travel. That, I should like to
claim, is what I fought for, but I did far too little actual fighting to make
that boast effective.

Then when the war was over the politicians did what they could to
keep us all wired in; but I escaped regularly. Nowadays, I suppose, if such
things were still required, I could get a doctor to certify that I needed to go
abroad for my health. I begin to stiffen early in December. Stooping, turning, kneeling, climbing in and out of modern motor-cars, which are
constructed solely for contortionists, become increasingly painful. By
Christmas I look out on the bare trees with something near melancholia.

Childermas is the Sabbath of *cafard*. I have just looked up this popular
word in the dictionary and have learned, as no doubt the reader already
knows, that its roots come from 'hypocrisy' and 'cant.' It is therefore
peculiarly apt for the emotions with which the father of a family per-
forms the jollities of Christmastide. It is at Childermas, as a rule, that I
begin to make plans for my escape, for, oddly enough, this regularly
recurrent fit of claustrophobia always takes me by surprise as, I am told,
the pains of childbirth often surprise mothers. Writing now in high summer (for this is not the diary as I kept it. I am trying to make a book from
the notes I took abroad) it seems hardly conceivable that I shall ever want
to leave my agreeable house and family. But I *shall*, next Christmas, and
no doubt I shall once more find myself with no plans made.

It is not so easy as it was thirty years ago to find a retreat. Tourism and
politics have laid waste everywhere. Nor is fifty-five the best age for
travel; too old for the jungle, too young for the beaches, one must seek
refreshment in the spectacle of other people at work, leading lives quite
different from one's own. There are few more fatiguing experiences than
to mingle with the holidaymakers of the Jamaican North Shore, all older,
fatter, richer, idler and more ugly than oneself. India is full of splendours
that must be seen now or perhaps never, but can a man of fifty-five long
endure a regime where wine is prohibited?

I have worked for eighteen months on the biography of a remarkable
but rather low-spirited friend many years older than myself. I have read
nothing and met no one except to further my work. Old letters, old dons,
old clergymen – charming companions, but a lowering diet when prolonged. Last year I went to Central Africa but saw nothing. I flew there
and back and spent a month in purely English circumstances cross-
examining authorities on the book I was writing. Africa again without
preoccupations, with eyes reopened to the exotic. That's the ticket.

January, 1959. Ticket? Not altogether easy. This is the season when the ships are fullest. The wise man sails before Christmas. A visit to the Union Castle office in London. They are able to offer a cabin in the Rhodesia Castle at the end of the month. She is a one-class ship sailing on the eastward route through the Suez Canal, stopping at several places I knew in other days and will gladly revisit, and reaching Dar-es-Salaam on February 20. On March 27 their new flag-ship, the Pendennis Castle, leaves Cape Town on her fast return voyage to England. That leaves me exactly five weeks in which to wander down by land.

I am told I shall need an inoculation against yellow fever and that under the new medical organisation this cannot be given by one's own doctor. Instead one must visit a city. In London a nurse was giving, it seemed, some thirty shots an hour at a guinea a time. I purchased my certificate there. In the course of my journey I crossed many frontiers but no government official ever asked to see it. The only person to show any concern for my health was the ticket clerk at a tiny airfield in Tanganyika.

Medical authorities seem to have grown tamer lately. I remember great annoyance at the hands of the captain of a Belgian lake steamer crossing to the Congo in 1931: he sent me ashore under a blazing sun to find a doctor on a golf links who, as the hooter was sounding for departure, certified my immunity from a variety of contagious diseases. As for the nineteenth century, which is popularly supposed to have been so free, readers of Charles Waterton may remember that in 1841 he was shipwrecked on a voyage from Civita Vecchia to Leghorn and with his fellow passengers obliged to transfer to the ship with which they had collided. When they reached Leghorn they were refused permission to land by the quarantine authorities on the grounds that their original bill of health had gone down with their ship. Only the impassioned intervention of Prince Charles Napoleon saved them from twenty days' incarceration. It is wrong to represent bureaucracy as an evil contrived solely by socialists. It is one of the evidences of original sin. The great alluring false promise of the socialists is that the State will wither away.

When I tell people of my movements they say either: 'Not a very pleasant time to be going. Everything will be very disturbed after the Accra Conference,' or 'A very interesting time to be going. Everything will be full of life after the Accra Conference.' No one, when one is going to Paris, warns one of the dangers from Algerian terrorists or envies one the excitements of UNESCO. As a defence I pretend to have an interest in archaeology. 'I want to have a look at the Persian vestiges in the off-shore islands.' I like showy ruins and am moderately knowledgeable about European architecture, but I can't distinguish periods or races in Mohammedan building. I mean to go to some of these 'off-shore islands' (what is an in-shore island?) if I can. I am grateful to them for turning many conversations from the 'colour problem' and African nationalism.

January 27. A friend in London gave a dinner party to wish me a good journey and kindly assembled people she thought I should like to see. I was put in mind of Swift's observation: 'When we are old our friends find it difficult to please us, and are less concern'd whether we be pleas'd or no.'

An odious and graceless thought; a wintry thought; high time to be off.

January 28. It is satisfactory to leave for the tropics in bitter, dingy weather. Sometimes I have left in sun and new snow and felt sorry to be off. I am taking the train to Genoa and boarding my ship there . . . .

January 29. Genoa shortly before eight. I have a friend whom I have more than once attempted to portray in fiction under the name of 'Mrs Stitch'. Mrs Stitch was wintering in Rome and I had told her I was coming to Genoa on the remote chance that she might join me. The main reason for my anxiety to get into the Rome Express was that I should be at the hotel at the time I had told her. Just as I finished shaving after my bath she turned up with four hats, six changes of clothes and a list of complicated chores for her friends, for whom she habitually recovers lost property, books, tickets, and collects peculiar articles of commerce.

Her first business was at the railway station which, for a reason that was never clear to me, was harbouring a coat of unlovely squalor abandoned somewhere by one of her more irresponsible cronies. Without authority or means of identification Mrs Stitch cajoled a series of beaming officials and possessed herself of the sordid garment. 'How different from the French,' Mrs Stitch said, 'they would never have let me have it.' I sometimes suspect that one of the reasons she gets on so badly with the French is that she speaks their language well. In Italy she has to rely purely on her looks and always gets her way without argument.

Breakfast in the station. The one perennial dissension between Mrs Stitch and me is that I like to eat in marble halls under lofty chandeliers while Mrs Stitch insists on candlelit garrets and cellars. She thinks my preference hopelessly middle-class and tells me I am like Arnold Bennett. Mrs Stitch's greatest difficulty in Italy is that there are singularly few quiet, murky restaurants; the smaller they are, the noisier and the more brilliantly lighted. The railway station at Genoa provided a happy compromise. For luncheon we found what Mrs Stitch wanted at Olivo's on the old quay. At dinner at Pichin in the new quarter the cooking was admirable but the light blinding. On the second day we drove out to a gay little beach restaurant at Nervi. I was never able to get her into the restaurant of our hotel and wistfully caught only an occasional glimpse of its sumptuous Victor-Emmanuel trappings. The cooking of Genoa, like its architecture, is mild-flavoured and wholesome.

From this generalisation I exclude the Campo Santo which for the amateur of cemeteries is one of the wonders of the modern world. We went there at once and emerged after two hours dazed by its preposterous splendours. When the Genoese lost their independence, the energies that had once taken them on piratical hazards into unknown waters and the remains of their accumulated wealth were devoted to the private commemoration of their dead.

We are accustomed to the grandiose tombs of monarchs and national heroes. In Genoa for more than a hundred years professional and mercantile families competed in raising purely domestic temples. They stand round two great quadrangles and extend along the terraced hillside beginning with the strong echo of Canova and ending in a whisper of Mestrovie and Epstein. They are of marble and bronze, massively and intricately contrived. Draped and half-draped figures symbolic of mourning and hope stand in unembarrassed intimacy with portrait sculptures of uncanny realism. There stand the dead in the changing fashions of a century, the men whiskered, frock-coated, bespectacled, the women in bustles and lace shawls and feathered bonnets, every button and bootlace precisely reproduced, and over all has drifted the fine grey dust of a neighbouring quarry. 'He's taken silk all right,' said Mrs Stitch before a gowned barrister, and indeed that is precisely the effect of the dust that has settled in the hollows of the polished white marble. All appear to be lined, flesh and clothing alike, in grey shot-silk.

There are *tableaux* almost *vivants* in which marble angels of consolation emerge from bronze gates to whisper to the kneeling bereaved. In one group there is a double illusion; a marble mother lifts her child to kiss the marble bust of his father. In the 1880s the hand of *art nouveau* softens the sharp chiselling. There is nothing built after 1918 to interest the connoisseur. It is as a museum of mid-nineteenth-century bourgeois art in the full, true sense, that the Campo Santo of Genoa stands supreme. If Père la Chaise and the Albert Memorial were obliterated the loss would be negligible as long as this great repository survives.

Fortunately it was untouched, or apparently so, in the bombardments of the Second World War. It was reported in 1944 that the city was 'flat'. Some fine buildings were irreparably lost but today, apart from an unexploded British naval shell that is gratefully exhibited in the Cathedral, there is little evidence of damage. I remember, when Italy declared war on us in 1940, a politician exultantly proclaiming on the wireless that we should soon add notably to the ruins for which that country was so justly famous. (It is worth recalling that before the surrender of Rome the English wished to destroy it and we were prevented only by our American allies.) He did not take account of the Italians' genius for restoration. They do not, as do those in authority in England, regard the destruction of a good building as a welcome opportunity to erect something really ugly in its place. They set to work patiently exercising the arts of their ancestors. The palaces and churches of Genoa were, it seems, in ruins in 1945. Now, walking the streets with Augustus Hare's guide book of 1875, Mrs Stitch and I could see almost all that he saw, as he saw it.

I did not know Genoa before the war. I went through by owl-light countless times but the train runs underground and one gets no glimpse of the city's beauties. It is a place much neglected by English and American sightseers who hurry through on their way to Rome and Florence and Venice. Genoa cannot be compared with these. It has no stupendous works of art and is haunted by few illustrious ghosts. It is stately and rather prosaic and passes almost unnoticed in the incomparable riches of Italy. In another country it would be the focus of aesthetic excitement.

All that is interesting, apart from the Campo Santo, lies in the little triangle between the two railway stations and the water-front. There one may see two streets of palaces and some thirty churches displaying every phase of architecture from early mediaeval to late rococo. The palaces are all, I think, in public hands or divided into offices and flats. The shipping agency, where I went to verify my sailing, is housed in a delicate eighteenth-century building whose gates lead into a *cortile* with beyond it, through the further arch, a hanging garden rising into the sunlight on elaborately sculptured terraces. The two important streets, the Via Balbi and the Via Nuova, unpleasantly renamed Via Garibaldi, are narrow and deeply shaded except on the roofs and upper storeys where at dawn and sunset the pediments and cornices reveal their strength. The doorways are immense and through them beyond the quadrangles and open staircases there is often a bright view, on one side of the sea, on the other of the mountains. Steep populous alleys lead down to the harbour, but they are clean and sweet. The people are as polite as Romans. There are no child-beggars, only the traditional, black-robed, bead-telling old people on the steps of the churches. The Genoese of the old city go to bed early. After dinner one can promenade the empty streets, finding at every corner a lamp-lit shrine and meeting few motor-cars.

The chief hotel in Genoa stands near the railway station. Luggage is carried there through a tunnel under the traffic which during the day is thick and fast. It is as good an hotel as I have found anywhere. As I have said, I was not allowed to try the cooking; everything I did try was first-class, in particular the two concierges. When one is travelling one's comfort depends more on concierges than on cooks or managers or head waiters. These functionaries are getting rather rare in England and are quite unknown in America. Outside Europe they tend to be rascals. There is in England a Corps of Commissionaires, who have their own burial ground at Brookwood. They are uniformed and be-medalled touts who, as far as I have ever seen, do nothing except collect tips. But concierges have to be polyglot, omniscient, imperturbable as croupiers, patient as nuns, and endowed with memories as deep and accurate as librarians. Mrs Stitch has some of the requisite qualities, but not all. I should be the worst possible man for the job. The concierges of Genoa romantically assumed that my meeting with Mrs Stitch was clandestine and showed exquisite tact in defending our privacy and concealing our identities from an inquirer whom they took for a private detective. I should like to believe that there is an international corps of concierges, a Sovereign Order like the Knights of Malta, and a splendid cemetery where they can all lie together at the end, but I am told they never resort together and mostly retire quite young and rather rich and blandly fatten ducks in remote soft valleys.

Mrs Stitch and I took our sight-seeing easy. One night in a wagon-lit did not work in me any miracle of rejuvenation. I was not yet good for more than two miles a day nor could I eat more than a spoonful or two of the delicious confections of fish that were put before us. I was the same seedy old man who had groaned up to Paddington. But my eyes were opening. For months they had ceased to see; I had moved like a blind man through the lanes and hamlets of Somerset and the familiar little area of London that lies between the London Library and the Hyde Park Hotel. I needed a strong draught to quicken my faculty and I found it in the Counter-Reformation extravagance of the Gesu. That picked me up and I was ready for the subtler beauties of the Cathedral.

My hope, not I trust wholly presumptuous, in publishing this diary is that the things which amused and interested me on my little tour, may amuse and interest some others. I do not attempt to guide them by enumerating all the objects to be seen, nor even all I saw. E. V. Lucas's 'Wanderer' series of descriptions of famous towns, which give so beguiling an air of leisure, of the sensitive eye freely roaming, of mature meditation, of unhurried feet pottering, of the mind richly stored with history and anecdote, were in fact, his daughter has revealed, the fruit of break-neck speed and frantic jottings of the kind most ridiculed in less adroit tourists. During these two days in Genoa I hobbled along beside Mrs Stitch, popped into places that looked interesting, sat down as often as possible and stared hard; and my vision cleared. I was not to see much of architectural beauty during my tour but I brought to other spectacles eyes sharpened on the stones of Italy.

One little puzzle I met which has 'often exercised me since. For centuries the most illustrious relic in the very rich treasury of San Lorenzo (it claims also the ashes of St John the Baptist and has furnished them with superb vehicles for exposition and procession) was the Sacro Catino. It is a large dish of green glass, broken and put together with a small piece missing, and handsomely mounted. It is displayed in the treasury still but the sacristan makes no claims for its authenticity. It has an old history. In 1101 Genoese and Pisan crusaders sacked Caesarea. The loot was enormous but the Genoese happily surrendered all their share in exchange for this dish which local pundits assured them was used by Our Lord at the Last Supper for washing the apostles' feet. More than this, it was cut from a single prodigious emerald which Solomon had given to the Queen of Sheba.

The Genoese bore it back in triumph, enshrined it and protected it as the greatest possession of the republic. Twelve knights were appointed to the high honour of holding the key of its casket for a month each, year after year. In 1476 a law was passed making it a capital offence to try alchemical experiments with it. So it was guarded and venerated until the Revolution. In 1809 French free-thinkers captured the city and bore the Sacro Catino off to Paris with other treasures. In 1815 it was restored, but on the road between Turin and Genoa someone dropped it and broke it and plainly revealed that it was made of glass. By an inexplicable process of human reason the Genoese at once decided that it was totally spurious. If it was not the Queen of Sheba's emerald it was not Our Lord's basin. No knights guard it now. It is displayed to profane eyes as an *objet de vertu* among the silver altar fronts and the Byzantine reliquaries, all beautifully arranged and lighted as though in the Victoria and Albert Museum.

After luncheon on the second day I covered my suitcases with the gummy labels of the steamship line and lay down to read. After half an hour I was disturbed by a series of strange noises, cracklings and rustlings. Every one of the labels, whether attached to leather or canvas, was detaching itself and rolling up into a little cylinder. Rum.

Farewell Mrs Stitch. She returned to Rome with the gruesome coat on her elegant arm.

15 July, 1960

Simon Raven

SPECIAL OCCASION

Some six years ago, when I was in Germany, my friend Edward told me that there was to be a special dance in Hanover the following Saturday. A *special* dance? Yes, undeniably special; only . . . er . . . gentlemen would attend it; the occasion might well be curious, and would I care to come with him? Further inquiry revealed that this frolic was to be held under the auspices of the Hanover branch of a network of 'gentlemen's' clubs which ramified all over the north of free Germany. It didn't ramify with much success in the south, Edward said, because the Catholics weren't keen about it. The legal position was tricky, but the police had been notified and had given a qualified and sort of semi-official blessing: a 'gentlemen's' agreement had been reached.

So the following Saturday we took rooms in a hotel near Hanover station, and after dinner Edward went to put on his costume, for fancy dress, although not mandatory, was encouraged by the organisers, and my friend felt one should enter into the proper spirit. Myself, I was not disposed to commit myself too far, being still at that time in the Army, and I remained dressed in the discreet dark suit I always wore when asked to dinner by brother officers' wives. As ill luck would have it, Edward (an English student of advancing years) had fixed himself up with a parody of my own regiment's uniform. Since the regiment was well known in the area this was rather tasteless of him; but I was eventually able to persuade him to demote himself from lieutenant-colonel to private ('more democratic') and to refrain from actually wearing our badge in his hat. After this we set off in a taxi, Edward sulking somewhat at the loss of his temporary rank, but then cheering up at the thought of a Hanoverian bus-conductor who had promised to meet him at the ball. ('After all, Simon, a German bus-conductor might have been rather *scared* by a colonel.')

We drove into one of the sections of Hanover which had been badly bombed and had not, at that time, been rebuilt. Indeed, from the taxi it seemed as if in the whole region there was only one building still standing . . . a bizarre and much-turreted Charles Addams affair. 'Back entrance for us,' cried Edward, who was getting over-excited, and scampered over three heaps of broken bricks to what looked like a kitchen entrance. But inside and sitting behind a cash-box there was a grim old woman in black, who, having asked to see some document which Edward duly produced, took five marks from each of us and then pointed with evident disapproval towards a winding stairway which led up one of the towers I had noticed from the taxi.

Apart from the woman in black, whom I was in any case inclined to regard as a witch, there was no sign whatever of human occupancy. It was, therefore, with relief and almost with delight that I found myself, after passing through a low door half-way up the tower, in an ample hall which was crammed to the rafters with chattering, smirking, screeching, dancing and attitudinising hordes of fancifully dressed men. But I could see that the dance was in fact very well arranged. At the far end of the room was a long bar, behind which several late-adolescents got up as barmaids were efficiently selling everything from Steinhäger to French champagne. Half-way up the left-hand wall, raised on a three-foot dais, was a six-piece band: all its members were dressed roughly like the Greek Royal Guard, a style susceptible of various subtle adjustments and therefore comprehending and no doubt gratifying a wide range of tastes. Over to the right and under the windows were several little nooks and bays, these being filled with chairs and tables occupied mostly by the more elderly revellers who, like myself, had tended to eschew fancy dress. There was no doubt about it; this was no impromptu homosexual scrimmage of the kind that is sometimes seen in London flats and clubs on New Year's Eve; it was a proper and well-controlled dance, organised with all the foresight and care that should go to such an undertaking, but with the one anomalous condition that it must cater for an attendance which was entirely male.

The essential orderliness of the occasion was reflected in the conduct of those present. For all the noise and movement that had overwhelmed me on arrival, it was soon apparent that on the whole the guests were simply making good-humoured and well-mannered use of the amenities provided. They were behaving just like people at any other dance. True, some of the costumes were a trifle embarrassing, especially in the (rather rare) cases where transvestitism had been attempted; but, though frequently indecorous, they were seldom indecent and never obscene. The dancing itself was affectionate but not often immodest: there was no 'heavy necking' on the floor, whatever might be going on under the windows . . . and even here no one was going further, *mutatis mutandis*, than they would have done at an averagely uninhibited heterosexual dance. There was, too, a certain discrimination: a man would tend to dance with the same partner most of the time, only abandoning him to a friend, as he might have abandoned his wife or girl, for an occasional isolated dance. No doubt, as at all dances, a number of people were out for a quick pick-up; but the rule of catch as catch can was not the general rule. In all, one can say, this was in no sense an orgy or a riot, but a definite social event which had its own clearly defined precedents and examples.

Ages seemed to vary from seventeen to seventy. The social classes, as far as I could tell, were entirely intermixed. Edward's bus-conductor (who had appeared as soon as we arrived) was a good-natured plebeian with the slightly inflated sense of standing which, in Germany, such minor officials commonly enjoy. On the other hand, there were assured-looking men of middle age who might have been university professors or ex-officers. Most of these were buying drinks for younger men (artisans, shopwalkers, an occasional student), who treated them with a kind of gay deference, without irony, without ill-will and – this was very significant – apparently without that sly intent to exploit or defraud which is so common among young homosexuals, particularly those of the working class, in England. In short, everyone, whatever his social status, seemed to be there in an amateur capacity – for enjoyment. Remembering comparable circles in England, I was surprised and pleased. But I was also anxious for an explanation; and since Edward was now dancing enthusiastically with the conductor, I accepted an invitation, given by a grey-suited and distinguished-looking man of about sixty, to join him for a drink.

After listening for some minutes to praise of England and the Lake District, where my acquaintance, who was something or other academic, had spent a happy pre-war summer with Professor X of Oxbridge, I inquired after the social standing of the company.

'We are of all classes, but we are careful not to admit young men who ask for money.'

'It is all very pleasantly arranged,' I conceded.

'You must remember we are German. We take care to find out all who are of our way of thinking. We give thought to these entertainments and we participate with our whole hearts.'

'So I see. But there is discipline?'

'How else?' said my academic companion. 'To have pleasure you must first have order. The Greeks knew that.' He thought for a moment. Then he said:

'In Germany we are very serious about . . . these matters. In England you are casual or hysterical or immoral or even sometimes passionate, but whatever you are you are never properly serious. It is because you have no corporate sense. Here, we regard ourselves as a brotherhood – a German brotherhood. We are honoured to see you, an Englishman, as our guest, but we do not forget that we are really a sodality of German fellowmen, all of whom wish to aid the same cause. You follow me?'

'More or less,' I said.

'And so we must be careful. We cannot be dishonoured by the presence of male prostitutes. We do not much like to see men who also like women. We are liberal – we must be – in matters of class. In other things we are more strict.'

'In what things are you more strict?'

'Look about you, my friend. You will see many Germans, some Englishmen, even a few Americans. But you will not see anyone who is . . . alien to you or me in blood. You will see nobody who is too dark and nobody who is too sallow. If you look all night,' he said with a long, cool look, 'you will see nobody who is even by the sixteenth part a Jew.'

25 November,1960

Elizabeth David

PLUM PUDDING AND PICKLES

A white cube of a house, two box-like rooms and a nice large bare kitchen. No bath. No plumbing. A well and a fig tree outside the front door and five yards away the Aegean. On the horizon a half-circle of the islands of the Cyclades. In the village, about three dozen houses, two churches (one Orthodox, one Roman Catholic), one provision shop. Down on the shore one shack of a tavern, and in the village street a more important one, stacked with barrels and furnished with stout wooden tables. Christo, the owner of this second tavern, was one of the grandees of the village. He operated, in addition to the tavern, a small market garden, and sold his produce in the island's capital seven miles away. He also had a brother-in-law, called Yannaki. Yannaki was that stock Greek village character, the traveller come home after experiencing glamorous doings and glorious events in far-off places. True to type, he spoke a little Anglo-American and, unusually, a little French; he was always on hand to help out if foreigners came to the village. He seemed a kind and cheerful man, rich too; at any rate, he owned a spare donkey and was prepared to lend me this animal, along with a boy to talk to it, so that I could ride into the town when I needed to stock up with fresh supplies of beans and oil, bottled wine, cheese, dried fruit, and boxes of the delicious Turkish Delight which was – still is – a speciality of the island.

Before long it transpired that the greatest favour I could bestow upon Yannaki in return for the loan of his transport would be some tomato soup in tins and perhaps also a jar or two of English 'picklies.'

Handing over to one of the brothers who owned the hotel and the Turkish Delight factory in the capital a bundle of drachmae which would have kept me in wine and cheese for a month I got in return four tins, vintage, of the required soup. Of English piccalilli, which I took it was what Yannaki meant by 'picklies,' there was no sign nor sniff, and very relieved I was. Many more such exotic luxuries, and it would be cheaper for me to leave my seashore village for Athens and a suite at the Grande-Bretagne.

The tomato soup gave Yannaki and Christo and their families a great deal of pleasure. It was the real thing, no mistaking it. In return I was offered baskets of eggs, lemons, oranges, freshly-dug vegetables and salads, glass after glass of wine in the tavern. And, then, next time the picklies? I *was* English, wasn't I?

For days I scanned the horizon for sight of an English yacht. I could, in my turn, have bartered fresh vegetables and fruit for the jars of mustard pickles which I knew must grace the table of any English lordos grand enough to be roaming the Aegean seas. It was late in the season. That way no yacht came.

Anybody who has experience of the stubborn determination, courteous but quite unrelenting, of an Aegean islander when he has made up his mind about something will understand why, in the end, I was obliged to set to and make those confounded pickles myself.

Into the town then for mustard, vinegar, spices. Long mornings I spent cutting up cauliflower and onions, carrots and cucumbers. Afternoons, I squatted in my kitchen fanning the charcoal fires into a blaze brisk enough to boil the brew. The jars, the only ones I could find, which I had bought to pack the stuff in were of one oke capacity. Three pounds, near enough. Also they were rough earthenware, unglazed, and exceptionally porous. Before I could even give the filled jars away they were half-empty again, the liquid all soaked up by that sponge-like clay. Every one had to be replenished with a fresh batch of pickle. To me the mixture seemed fairly odd, but with my village friends it was successful enough. In fact, on the barter system, I could have lived for nothing so long as I was prepared to dedicate my life to my pickle-making. Before long, though, it was getting on for December, and references to 'Christmas pudding' began to crop up in the tavern talk. By now I had learned a little more about these kindly village tyrants. If Christmas pudding they wanted, Christmas pudding I should have to give them. But not, so help me, made on the improvised happy-go-lucky system I'd used for the mustard pickles. Once more then into the town (I never could stay five seconds on a horse or a mule or even a bicycle, but by that time I had at least found out how to sit on a donkey and get the animal moving over stony paths and up and down steep hills) to telegraph home for a recipe.

Now, all you with your fine talk of the glories of old English fare, have you ever actually made Christmas pudding, in large quantities, by old English methods? Have you, for instance, ever tried cleaning and skinning, flouring, shredding, chopping beef kidney suet straight off the hoof? Have you ever stoned bunch after bunch of raisins hardly yet dry on the stalk and each one as sticky as a piece of warm toffee? Come to that, what would you make of an attempt to boil, and to keep on the boil for nine to ten hours on two charcoal fires let into holes in the wall, some dozen large puddings? Well, I had nothing much else to do at the time and quite enjoyed all the work, but I'd certainly never let myself in for such an undertaking again. Nor, indeed, would I again attempt to explain the principles of a hay-box and the reasons for making one to peasants of whose language I had such a scanty knowledge and who are in any case notoriously unreceptive to the idea of having hot food, or for that matter hot water or hot coffee, hotter than tepid.

All these things considered, my puddings turned out quite nicely. The ones which emerged from the hay-box were at just about the right temperature – luke-warm. They were sweet and dark and rich. But my village friends weren't as enthusiastic as they had been about the mustard pickles. What with so many of the company having participated in the construction of the hay-box, my assurances that the raisins and the currants grown and dried there on the spot in the Greek sun were richer and more juicy than the artificially dried, hygienically treated and much travelled variety we got at home, my observations on the incomparable island-made candied citron and orange peel (that was fun to cut up too) given me by my neighbours, and the memorable scent of violets and brilliantine given to the puddings by Athenian brandy, a lot of the English mystery had disappeared from our great national festive dish.

That *le plum-pudding n'est pas anglais* was a startling discovery made by a French chef, Philéas Gilbert, round about the turn of the century. No, not English indeed. In this case *le plum-pudding* had been almost Greek. What I wish I'd known at the time was the rest of Gilbert's story. It seems that with a passing nod to a Breton concoction called *le far*, 'obviously the ancestor of the English pudding,' an earlier French historian, Bourdeau by name, unable or perhaps unwilling to claim plum pudding for France, says that it is precisely described by Athenaeus in a report of the wedding feast of Caranus, an Argive prince. The pudding was called *strepte*, and in origin was entirely Greek.

24 November, 1961

Nancy Mitford

SELECTIONS FROM 'A REVOLUTION DIARY'

France, May and June 1968

16 May. We have heard the young leaders on TV for three quarters of an hour. It was very tiring. There is a fat boy whose name I didn't hear; the other two are suitably named Sauvageot and Cohn-Bandit. People's names are so often suitable: Montgomery, Alexander, de Gaulle, Wilson, Brown and so on. Sauvageot apes Robespierre, cold and quiet, hoping to be creepy no doubt and not quite succeeding. Bandit very reminiscent of Esmond Romilly – a bounding, energetic little anarchist, giggling from time to time but not making jokes which one might have liked. The fat boy seems the most human of the three.

Having said how much they despised everything in life, especially money, they keenly gave the numbers of their postal accounts so that we could hurry out and send them some. There was a great deal of wailing about their treatment by the police. I despise them for it. They were out for a rough-up and they got it. Nobody was killed and now they are behaving like babies who have been slapped. It's not very dignified.

The postman has made our blood run cold by saying 'tout va changer'. He comes an hour late and dumps the neighbour's letters, and I must say mine, in my box. Madame Pines said to Marie, my old servant, 'What is the General waiting for? As soon as he has gone everything will be all right.' I told Marie to remember that this lady is a most fearful idiot. She is the only person I know down here* who is against the General. But then to be quite honest she is the only real have-not that I know. Even so her little flat is adorable and with her work and her late husband's pension she is absolutely comfortable . . . .

*Nancy Mitford (Mrs Peter Rodd) lived about a mile from Versailles.

19 May. General strike so as I haven't got a car I am stuck here. Very good for work. The wireless has been taken over and the announcers who used to seem such dears have suddenly become extremely frightening. They rattle out bad news like machine guns. The French seem to have turned into Gadarene swine.

I've got a great friend in the town who is a workman at Renault's where the strike began. I have dined with him and his wife and they have dined here. I went along to see them. Both very Gaullist. According to them nobody wants to strike, but what can one do? *They* say one has got to, and that's that. It seems Renault are having trouble keeping up the pickets because the workmen, who have all got cars, want to go away for the weekend.

20 May. . . . The wireless is terrifying. If the BBC were not always so utterly wrong about French affairs I would listen to it, but what is the good? They understand nothing. The *Figaro* still appears, screaming 'do something' to the government like a hysterical woman whose house is on fire.

Marie tells her beads whenever there's nothing else to do. I am afraid that I think like Frederick the Great that God exists but leaves us pretty well alone to make our muddles while we are here. No good bothering Him, I'm afraid. 'Mrs Rodd is on the line again, Almighty.' 'Tell her to get on with her work.' . . .

23 May. . . . The new Archbishop of Paris speaks of much misery. It's so strange – where is this misery? One sentence recurs among all my modest friends here: '*La France a été trop heureuse.*' My impression for several years now has been that France is almost entirely bourgeoise. Marie's father was a very poor peasant and his children were brought up almost hungry. But her nephews and nieces are more than well off. All with motor-cars and little weekend houses. . . .

24 May. More trouble with the students last night. Cohn-Bandit is not being allowed back from Germany. A move which seems to me fatal but is wildly applauded by everybody here. I can just imagine the fun he'll have getting in – which of course he will. Lovely cloak and dagger stuff, and then how will they ever dig him out of the Sorbonne?

All night a pitched battle raged around Jean de Gaigmeron's house. I hope he's gone away. These battles are a nightmare for those in nearby houses because of the tear gas which seeps in and can't be got out for ages. Marie says all these young people seem very *mal élevé*. Tony Gandarillas rang. He says Jean had an awful night and the streets are still full of gas.

Went to the market. Never saw so much food. Bought chicory for
Marie who can't find it here and craves it. How can she? Things seem a
shade more hopeful, I should say.

25 May. The General was perfect last night. After the flood of words
we've been treated to of late, it was a relief to hear something short, sharp
and to the point. But I've got a feeling that he is fed up. Though he will do
his duty of course for as long as he can.

I've just turned on the wireless. It seems they had another sick night in
Paris. Fouchet made a statement. He says the *pègres* have crept out from
under the stones. I remember Bodley once talking to a French friend
about the Commune and saying, 'What can have happened to all those
savages who, such a little time ago, set fire to everything and skinned live
horses in the streets?' 'They are still there,' he replied. The men of General Leclerc's division have issued a statement to say that they didn't liberate Paris in order to see it destroyed from within and are ready at any
time to come and keep order. Mendès-France, gloating over the riots from
a balcony, said the police have got an unfair advantage. Thank God.
Bertrand says the problem is democratic. There are too many young
people and they are turning against the old everywhere . . .

26 May. Léon Zitrone reappeared on the television last night smiling and
pimpant. But this morning all the RTF journalists are on strike, saying
the news they have to give is not objective. That beats me – there has been
a running river of communist propaganda for a week. Perhaps they want
to keep Pompidou off the air.

The General told the new American ambassador that the future
belongs to God, but the Archbishop who broadcast last night never mentioned God. He only spoke of material things like wages. Though at the
end he said that Christians could pray. Marie didn't notice the oddity of
this and I didn't point it out. Madame Saclay says it's the new style in the
Church. The accent is no longer on God but on living conditions. I got
her on her own and asked if Suzanne (the daughter) had been surprised
by the revolt of her fellow students. She says Suzanne is deeply religious
and takes everything calmly but she has been saying for a long time now
that the boys – though not the girls – have been spoiling for a fight.
Madame Saclay, like many people here, thinks the unrest comes from a
physical desire for violence. Young friends of ours from the Argentine
who until recently had been living in the *Cité des Arts*, an annexe of the
university, and who still go about with students, told Bodley that so far
from foreseeing events they were astounded by them. They had a horrid

frightening time when lunatics surged into their street and set fire to the dustbins. Our faithful dustman still comes, by the way.

Marie dreamed all night of the General. She worries about him. I wonder if he knows how much people like her love him . . . .:

What a volcano this country is ! Of course one knows it may erupt at any moment; but as with real volcanoes the soil is so rich and so fertile in every way that having once lived here any alternative seems unthinkable.

27 May. Today I gave the whole thing a rest and only listened to the news at dinner-time. The strikers have not accepted the government's protocol. They say if they do, in a few months the country will be ruined and they will be blamed. Good joke – but where do we go from here? The students are upset because they have lost the limelight, reminding one of a little girl I could name who has to be the centre of attention or else. The fat boy has resigned from the students' union to devote himself to politics. We certainly need more like him in public life.

It now seems they think that everybody over thirty ought to be dead. Marie Antoinette, when she became Queen, said she didn't know how people over thirty dared show their faces at court. She called them *les siècles*. Poor dear, she was soon over thirty herself and didn't end too well. The political associates of the Sorbonne gerontophobes are Waldeck-Rocher, who looks like the father of Yul Brynner, Mendès-France, aged sixty-one, and the *taureau de la Nièvre* (Mitterrand), who at fifty-two is no lad. Perhaps they count as being in the second childhood.

The chemists in Paris are out of stock but tons of medicaments are said to have been squirrelled away at the Sorbonne. I do hope our future rulers are not a bunch of hypochondriacs.

28 May. . . . The French wireless has asked anybody who knows of a full petrol pump to report it. I am fairly public-spirited but if I knew of a full petrol pump I should tell my friends and not the French wireless in its present mood.

Went to the town and bought a few things to hoard, a practice to which so far I have not lent myself, but I only took as much as I could carry and only things abhorred by the French like Quaker Oats. . . .

On my way home from the park two boys on a motor-bike pretended they were trying to kill me, following me up on to the wide footpath; but I must say when I laughed so did they, and went away with friendly waves. I do hope the over-thirties are going to be killed mercifully and quickly and not starved to death in camps.

Mitterrand on the tele – Marie kept up a running commentary and I was laughing so much at it that perhaps I didn't get his message correctly, but the impression was that he is claiming a *coup d'état*. Then we had Pompidou, whose calm reasonable manner inspires optimism every time that he appears. He asked for a secret ballot in the factories. What a hope! I also heard William Pickles from London, who said that Mendès-France is every Englishman's favourite French prime minister, but not every Frenchman's. This is true. I wish the BBC correspondents here were as well informed as Mr Pickles – but they seem to hate France and predict a worst for which they long. The worst will probably occur but one can't be certain that it will.

29 May. . . . I hear that the Embassy Rolls-Royce has been all round Paris delivering cards for the garden party – that's the spirit – up the old land.

At luncheon-time the wireless announced that the General has left for Colombey. Marie and I looked at each other in terror and despair, but it seems he has only gone to ponder and will be back tomorrow. There is now a rush of politicians to the microphones – all kindly say they are ready to take over. God preserve us from any of them: even the students might be better than those old hacks. What do the students really want? We know so little about them; when they appeared on the tele their only cry was 'Down with everything.' Fouchet said rather impatiently the other day they've got ideals – everybody has at that age, but what ideals! People over thirty must go, nobody need learn anything or pass any exams (as an autodidact myself I see the point – though as a taxpayer I can't quite see in that case what the schools and universities are for). People who don't agree with them must keep their mouths shut. They enjoy lighting fires and desecrating war memorials. They have also said down with concrete – hear hear, but where will everybody live? In tents? None of this constitutes a positive programme. They now say they will go from house to house and explain their policy. I can't wait. Marie thinks if we let them in they will be laying plans for future burglary. Never mind, I must see them.

In the grocer's shop a woman said, 'Is the post office open?' 'Of course it is, it's occupied.' General laughter.

30 May. I hadn't quite realised what a hermit I am by nature – the days go by and I have no desire to move from my house and garden. I haven't done so for three weeks now. Of course one is virtually kept going by the excitement. We live in a thrilling serial story and the next instalment will be the General's statement this afternoon. (*Later.*) I waited for it feeling quite sick but as soon as he opened his mouth one knew everything would be all right. France is not going to be handed over like a parcel to a regime which she may or may not want without being allowed to say 'Yes' or 'No.'

I went to the market and thought the shoppers in the streets were looking more cheerful already. Then the demonstration in the Champs Elysées, reported in full and with enthusiasm on the wireless, showed that the General has not lost his magic. I'd have given anything to leave my house and garden for that.

The eight o'clock news on television was a real muddle . . . But we were shown a lovely photograph of Mendès-France and Mitterrand looking like two vampires who had seen a piece of garlic.

31 May. Woke up feeling as though I had come out of a nightmare. People who went to the Étoile yesterday say it was like the Liberation. The General's ADC, hearing the noise from the Elysée, said, 'That's all for you, mon Général.' To which de Gaulle replied, 'If it were only me.' The Parisians have been bottled up for about a fortnight but it seemed much longer and the sky looked black indeed. Now they have exploded.

Some hours after the demonstration the *taureau de la Nièvre* was caught between two groups of students, Gaullists and anti-Gaullists, in the Boulevard Saint-Germain. They stopped arguing with each other and all rounded on him and a corrida began from which the poor old bull, puffing and blowing, had to be rescued by those very police about whom he has been so insulting.

The BBC, at it again, says it is evident that the ORTF is back in the hands of the General because no opposition reaction to his speech has been broadcast. Untrue. We have had statements in all the news bulletins from every leader except Mendès-France, who has so far refused to comment. As a matter of fact, a child of six could have written these statements – they are so predictable and so dull.

I wonder if habitués of the television find the lack of it as much relief as I find the lack of letters? I used to think I lived for the post, now I don't know how I shall bear the sight of it. The joy of letters from various cherished correspondents is outweighed by all the requests, demands and statements from strangers. Plans to remember, forms to fill in, and so on, which often occupy my whole morning. I haven't got a secretary and wouldn't care for the physical presence of one. I see that the post office workers are on their way back, so I am doubtless enjoying a last few days of peace. . . .

1 June. I took the local bus and went over to Orsay. This little bus, which has been faithfully running all through the troubles, is very symptomatic of the modern world. As every soul in this country except me has got a motor-car it only caters for Arabs and children. I have never seen a fellow-bourgeois in it. The journey is most beautiful, through Jouy-en-Josas which, buried in deep woods and composed of seventeenth century cottages, must look almost exactly as it did when the Duc de Luynes saw Louis XV galloping quite alone down the village street, having lost the hunt. Then one goes through the woods on to a great plain of cornfields and huge farmhouses – the atomic centre in the middle of it is not ugly or out of scale and is discreetly hidden by poplar trees. Down again into the valley of the Chevreuse and here the spoiling begins. Orsay, which used to be such a dear little market town, is now part of the Sorbonne, covered with university buildings in the modern taste. The inhabitants are furious with the students – they say everything has been done for them – huge swimming pools and sports grounds, free holidays in the mountains and so on, and this is how they show their gratitude.

I got hold of some English papers of the last week or two. My goodness, they were alarming – no wonder people rang up from London offering blankets and tea. One felt frightened here, but it was for the future – the possible ruin of this beautiful land. The bang on the door and the commissaire telling one to pack up a change of linen and go. There was a letter in one of the papers from a woman whose hedgehog speaks to her – I am jealous. My hedgehogs never address a word to me and I am rather anxious to know their demographic plan.

2 June. . . . Lucy is yearning over the students again. She says they are out in the streets again this morning, beautiful and polite, collecting money for the old – to give a Molotov cocktail party for them, I expect, said I. 'Oh Nancy, you're so cynical.' The fact is these students are like a chicken whose head has been cut off – they are running round in circles with nobody paying much attention to them and with nothing to do. They held a demonstration yesterday, but instead of the hundreds of thousands of a week ago they mustered only about 20,000 people.

Cohn-Bandit's locks are now dyed black – he'll soon look very odd unless he forks out £4 to a hairdresser to have them retinted.

3 June. . . . I went to see my friend from Renault's. He spoke as if everything had already returned to normal, though in fact the strike is still going on: '*Oh là, on a eu chaud.*' That's what they always say when France has seemed to be losing a big football match and then wins it. But what will happen to us when *Le Grand* has gone? I said, 'France explodes like this about once in a generation. Thank God this blow-up happened while the General is still here to cope with it. With any luck at all you and I won't be alive to see the next time.'

31 May and 7 June, 1968

Sam White

STILL A WONDERFUL TOWN

Paris

There was a time when to speak ill of Paris was to brand oneself as a barbarian. Times have changed. Today, from the Glenda Slaggs and the Lunchtime O'Boozes to the highest reaches of the British intelligentsia the cry goes up that Paris is both a clip joint and a cultural desert, an architectural eyesore and a gastronomic poor relation to Soho. 'Paris,' a prominent British intellectual told me the other day, 'is in danger of pricing itself out of civilisation.' Shades of: 'Storm in Channel – Continent Isolated.'

From all these views I beg to differ. For me Paris is easily the most agreeable capital in the world to live in. I would define it simply as a city where a civilised man can still lead a civilised life against a civilised background and consider it not as a feat of escapism but as something amounting to total immersion. It still remains a city manageable in size, easy to get about in and easy to get out of, with each area retaining an individual character. And it still remains lived in for the greater part by the people who actually work in it. This of course makes an enormous difference to life as compared to cities like London and New York which each day gorge and disgorge millions of commuters leaving only a desolation of office blocks behind them. Nothing like this needless to say happens in Paris and this is particularly noticeable at weekends when London becomes a graveyard and Paris a playground.

All this of course I realise is old hat but it still continues to make an inestimable difference to the quality of life between Paris and London. There is one other European city which might rival Paris both in beauty and in its closely-knit character and that is Rome; but Rome is essentially a provincial city which has lost its provincial charm. With its noise and its traffic problems, it is now scarcely habitable. It has a further handicap: it is not big enough to absorb its expatriate population, especially the

Americans. These latter are of an exceptionally mediocre and pretentious quality with the result that one tends to meet more bores in bars in Rome in the course of an evening out than one would meet anywhere else in a month. Away with Rome then as with Berlin and Vienna, both of which have lost their status as great capitals.

Having said all this I now realise that I stand exposed to the full counterblast of the Paris detractors. They will talk of the architectural horrors perpetrated in Paris in recent years, such as the Montparnasse skyscraper and the complex of skyscrapers to the west of Paris looming over the Arc de Triomphe, to say nothing of the desolation created when the central markets of Les Halles were uprooted and moved out of the city centre. That these protests should be particularly vociferous across the Channel is probably an indication of our own uneasy conscience over the much vaster vandalism perpetrated in London. The vandalism in Paris has been limited in extent and has at any rate spared the centre of the city and its historic and architectural sites.

Here the Seine continues to flow past the same landmarks and under the same bridges. It still remains impossible for building promoters to lay their hands on such delectable pieces of real estate as the unused Gare d'Orsay. In short, anyone who was visiting Paris for the first time in say fifty years and planted himself in the middle of the Concorde bridge would see to right and left in front and behind him the same unspoilt magnificent views. As for the Montparnasse tower, admittedly it does not please me and would please me even less if I had a flat, say, overlooking the Luxembourg Gardens, but at least it does not dominate the city like for example the even more hideous Post Office Tower in Soho. As for the other object for protest and outcry, the skyscraper complex at La Défense, here not only does it not disturb me but I approve of it wholeheartedly. It is situated well away from the centre of the city and is in itself an interesting and rather beautiful architectural creation.

On the question of Les Halles and the uprooting of its famous pavilions suddenly discovered to be notable works of art, here I have even less sympathy for foreign critics than over the affaire of La Défense. Once it was decided to end Les Halles' role as Paris's central food market, then it seems to me there was no point in keeping the pavilions on the site. There is a large element of hypocrisy in the whole debate over Les Halles: for decades the very existence of this market in the heart of Paris was considered evidence of French backwardness, but once the decision was taken to remove it and put the space to new and largely non-commercial use there was this huge outcry. It would seem that in the eyes of foreign critics Paris can't win: if it modernises itself it is guilty of vandalism and if it doesn't, of backwardness. For those nostalgiques for the days of

Hemingway and 'A Moveable Feast' it should be pointed out that the cost of maintaining Paris as a city for foreign expatriates to live in was precisely to keep France as a backward and basically agricultural country.

Despite the enormous changes of the last twenty years the essential human quality of Paris still remains. It still remains, as I pointed out earlier, a lived-in city, a city of Parisians while London is ceasing to be a city of Londoners and New York has long ceased to be a city of New Yorkers. It still remains too an 'open' city where a citizen's rights include those of being able to get a meal or a drink at any hour of the day or night and as the whim takes him. All this too in a city with a still solidly implanted tradition of good food and service. All this adds up for me to my idea of what a city should be: where a civilised man can partake of civilised pleasures in a civilised manner and in a civilised setting.

I must admit – and it remains a constant regret with me – that I am the least qualified of men to get the most out of Paris. My French remains incorrigibly bad, my taste in food and wine does not rise much above the standards of La Coupole and my feeling for the French cultural scene is exceedingly feeble. Yet I like it here and carry my self-inflicted frustrations lightly. None of the awful misadventures which befall colleagues when they visit Paris seem to befall me despite my give-away accent or at least not with anything like the same regularity. So much so that I cannot recall the last time I was cheated by a taxi-driver. I hear dark tales of Paris's cultural decline but I notice that at the moment sixty-eight theatres are playing to full houses and that two new Jean Anouilh plays are running. I note too something like twenty times more books are sold in Paris than in London and that a learned political essay by President Giscard has sold well over a million copies. I note too that so many art shows are listed that it would take one a fortnight working an eight-hour day to take them all in. All this makes me puzzled at the current Francophobia that reigns in London. Could it be bafflement and bewilderment at the fact that the French have made a better fist of running their country since the war than we have? Could it be resentment at our relative decline in relation to the French?

1 January, 1977

Taki Theodoracopulos

TAX-EXILE GRAND PRIX

Monte Carlo

Penned to the water's edge by the Alps behind it, huddled around the polluted grey harbour and scrambling upward for extra space, the concentrated form of Monaco burst at the seams last Sunday. The 368-acre plot of Ruritanian real estate took the form of Noah's Ark for the huddled masses, the rich and the tax exiles.

First the huddled masses. More than 300,000 of them – mostly Italian and French – poured across Monaco's undefended borders in motorised columns of small cars with souped-up engines. With them came tents, camping equipment, baby carriages, rubber dinghies, model aeroplanes, bicycles, picnic baskets and the rest of the accoutrements needed to survive a weekend among the idle rich. The invading army wore sandals, net shirts, blue jeans and paper hats. After paralysing the streets of the Principality they pitched their tents in every available square foot.

The dispossessed were less obvious in arriving. The winds of political change had already blown them out of Beirut's seaside resorts, Rome's Via Veneto, and Estoril's casinos. Silently they had infiltrated Monaco through Barclays, Lloyds and First National. The very rich did not have to come in. They were already part of Monaco, whose main and only industry consists of parting the rich from their money. The tax exiles were nowhere to be seen. Some of them, like Bjorn Borg, were playing tennis in America, others hiding behind false beards or in the bowels of rented yachts from roving bands of gossip columnists.

The Principality has a population of 20,422, only 2,696 of whom are Monegasques. Fortunately some of the invading humanity spilled over to Cannes. Hundreds of gossip columnists, ordered by their editors to get both stories or else, tried to commute between the Monte Carlo Grand Prix and the Cannes Film Festival. But as the roads clogged up, overloaded telephone lines broke down and helicopters for hire were grounded due to overuse.

The overspill and the mass suicide of the gossip vendors, however, made it possible for the Monaco police to find room in Ruritania for the drivers to practise. Dressed like Ronald Colman in Prisoner of Zenda uniforms, they baton-charged the multitudes and eventually blocked off the streets for the Grand Prix. Cries of 'Fascist pigs' and 'Power to the people' were heard, for the first time in the Principality. Italian anarchists wearing Gucci shoes flung their Cartier watches at the police. Realising the danger, Prince Rainier and Princess Grace decided to mollify the people by throwing a party. On Friday night they invited 200 guests to dinner in the Palace. Among them were the King of Sweden and his Queen, David Niven, Baron Heiny Thyssen – a recent Monaco arrival from war-torn Switzerland, Jackie Stewart, James Hunt, some Spanish princesses of unknown quality, and Philip Junot, Princess Caroline's plebeian fiancé. Nigel Dempster was later discovered trying to crash the party, and was unceremoniously thrown out.

While the royal party was taking place, uninvited jet-setters tried to drown – or sniff away – their embarrassment at Regine's, the local pub. At £75 the bottle, the champagne flowed throughout the night. Police reinforcements had to be called to stop German tycoons from breaking down the doors of the place once it was filled to the rafters, and then again when the lines in front of the pub's lavatories got unruly over the time people would take in the loo. As one jet setter said: 'These rich Germans have no manners. They take ten minutes to have a sniff of coke. What are we supposed to do? Sniff in public?' Across the road from Regine's the Rococo Casino was also doing overflow business. Milanese tycoons – wearing masks because of the recent kidnappings in Italy – gambled away millions; Arab potentates went on dining while dispatching flunkies to bet thousands of dollars on a single roulette number. Thirty-two brave Englishmen were arrested and roughed up when they foolishly tried to change their pounds for chips.

On Saturday, the Cossack-like police force once again went to work. This time they ordered all the yachts to move away from the northern side of the harbour in case a racing car got out of control. The yacht set resented it but eventually complied. The time trials were under way.

Monte Carlo is essentially a road circuit, a true driver's course, unlike the high speed ovals of Monza or Indianapolis where engine performance comes first and driving ability second. The course has all the natural hazards of the road – manhole covers, adverse cambers, rough patches and bumps. It goes up past ornamental balustrades, shop windows, the Hotel de Paris, the Casino, dips down past night clubs and new luxury hotels, curves around a tunnel into the harbour, and winds around finally reaching the 'Place d'honneur' where the Rainiers sit out the two-hour spectacle.

The circuit measures 1.97 miles to the lap and there are seventy seven laps. It requires 1,500 gear changes and 160 miles are covered in less than two hours. Due to the circuit's narrowness only twenty cars take part. Thus, the time trials not only determine who will take part but also decide pretty much who has a real chance of winning. Once behind, it is impossible to get past and the smart drivers press the leaders hoping to force them into committing a fault. The type of man who used to race disappeared. It used to be an esoteric event with a few dare-devils, some rich, others noble, all of them romantically inclined towards danger and death. For little or no money they would throw down a last glass of champagne, kiss some actress goodbye and roar off. There were no guard rails, no wire fences, no haystacks, fire marshals and fireproof suits. They could all be seen celebrating the night before, and after, at the Tip-Top or the Hotel de Paris.

Not any more. Professional and businesslike drivers such as Niki Lauda, Jody Scheckter and James Hunt, living as tax exiles and constantly conferring with their business managers, cannot afford such lightheartedness.

The drivers are now walking billboards. Everything they wear, drink or do is for commercial gain. They are extensions of the outdoor advertising industry. They are required to be at least 50 per cent engineers. On Sunday afternoon, precisely at 3.30, the race got under way. Round and round they hurtled, twenty figures unrecognisable except for the cigarette and petrol advertisements on their cars, as distinguishable from each other as astronauts bouncing about the moon – the Italian anarchists screamed for Ferrari and Lauda (even anarchists are chauvinistic in Italy), cursed him as he failed to overtake the South African, Jody Scheckter, who won by half a second.

Sunday night Monte Carlo – in the words of playboy Gunther Sachs – reminded him of a Cuban whorehouse during Batista's days. The French and Italian invaders began the long retreat by gunning their motors, and hooting their horns. Young Arabs revved up their fathers' Rolls-Royces while their impassive mothers sat eating their dates. The Germans, their ham-like faces exploding after a weekend of rich Provençal food, wine and sun, roared off in unison in their Mercedeses for the four-star restaurant closest to Monaco. The Arabs moved their yachts to Cannes for heavier gambling. The Greeks flew their private planes back to more cosmopolitan settings, while the English began to thumb rides back up to the frozen north. And Nigel Dempster was off to St Tropez, following Princess Caroline.

28 May, 1977

Jan Morris

ON REVISITING VENICE

Venice

The saddest things in Venice now are unquestionably the two remaining horses on the façade of the Basilica. They are mourning their two colleagues, who have never been separated from them before during the thousand-odd years of their existence, and who are presently hidden away somewhere in the hands of the metallurgists – one of them is pictured hideously decapitated, for science's sake, on the cover of the new UNESCO report on the Saving of Venice.

When the horses of St Mark's were bridled, the Genoese used to say, Venice would be conquered, and visitors to the old place last month, contemplating that shattered companionship of the Golden Four, might have thought the worst had indeed come to the worst: for as it happens the remaining animals could be seen forlornly reflected in the high tidal water which has lately flooded the Piazza itself, and seeped once again into ground floors, crypts and alcoves all over the city.

Aghast, the autumn tourists stared at that anguished façade, from their dry refuge under the arcades, while the pigeons clustered for the feeding on islands among the puddles, and the long line of shoppers picked its way across makeshift causeways to the Merceria. It was just what they had been told. Venice was failing before their eyes, and they were only just in time . . .

In fact these have been the first high tides for several years: while the two golden horses, wrenched so tragically from their stables beneath the mosaics, have I am assured nothing much wrong with them at all, and could easily stay up there for another few centuries without noticeable decay. Like so much of the Venetian emergency, it is all in the mind: or if not in the mind, in the museum.

For the Awfulness of it all has been self-generating, and the necessary restoration of some things has led to frenzied re-appraisals of everything else. The horses, it is now confidently forecast, will be replaced up there by fibre-glass replicas, while the magnificent originals will be *re*-capitated, scientifically treated and expensively illuminated in a museum. But they are victims only of the experts.

Actually, though those first impressions may have been depressing, Venice has been great fun this autumn. The *aqua alta*, though obviously miserable for those whose premises got flooded, did not disconcert anyone else for long. Grand ladies were conveyed cheerfully through pools clumped like sacks on porters' trolleys. Adorable children sploshed meditatively about in gumboots, or zoomed here and there on bicycles in plumes of spray. The keeper of the Campanile was to be seen confidently brushing the ocean away from his Loggia with a broom, like Dame Partington faced with another tide. The weather was lovely; business seemed good.

I loved it, but then I enjoy the place largely for Philistine reasons. I rejoice to see the tankers still treading gigantically past the city, despite the dread suggestion that one might explode and destroy it all at a blow (has any tanker, by the way, *ever* spontaneously exploded?). I love to hear the jets sweeping down to Marco Polo airport across the lagoon, and see the unchanging rich wary over their scampis in Harry's Bar.

All in all, I found things reassuringly as usual; and not least the fraternity of conservationists, the UNESCO functionaries, the representatives of the National Committees, the spokesmen of the Superintendent of Monuments, the exponents of the Special Law, the advisers to the Procurators of St Mark's – not least that lively guild, now so much a part of the Venetian matter, seemed to be in excellent form, surrounded by triplicated documents and veiled in controversy.

Some nice small things have happened. How lovely to see the Dogana's gilded ball resplendently gilded again! How reassuring for the mighty Colleoni, to feel the base of his statue renovated beneath his hoofs! How suitable that the Empress of Iran should be taking a personal interest in the future of the Arsenal!

But on a grander plane, the condition of Venice remains as suitably obscure as ever. Still nobody seems to know what has happened to all that official money, though it is now said that inflation would have made it totally inadequate anyway. Successive government committees, I gather, have rejected *all* the several ingenious schemes for the closure of the Lido entrances. All the enthusiastic private committees, Swedes to Australians, have in ten years spent only £2 million between them on the salvation of their beloved. The city has been touched up here and there: but fortunately for those of my tastes, it preserves still most of its patina of age, dignity and honest wear, the crumble that testifies to its sad destiny, the blend of tristesse and opportunism that speaks of a majestic history long ago.

Time, tide and preservationists have not destroyed it yet: and if its true lovers scoff loudly and angrily enough, perhaps even the Golden Horses may yet be unbridled again, to be restored to the splendour of their ancient fellowship, and corrode nobly down the centuries above their incomparable Piazza.

6 January, 1979

Peter Ackroyd

'AND GOD GAVE US THE ROCKS...'

Helsinki

Each Nordic country is cold in its own way; in Oslo, it is a rural cold, the cold of surrounding landscape. An urban cold rises from Stockholm, from the streets and public buildings. In Helsinki it is an elemental cold, a cold which invades the body and leaves it stunned. At midday you gaze at the sun without blinking; all things turn to ice. It is like the coldness of God. To travel here from Sweden is to move from light sleep to a harsh and sudden consciousness.

'We are doomed to be eternal sentinels,' one Finnish poet wrote of his race, 'our periods of rest have not been long'. There is, at first glance, a certain hardness, a reserve, in their features. It has been calculated that, over the last seven centuries, the Finns have been engaged in warfare for one year in every seven. They suffered the indignities of colonisation, Swedish and then Russian, for 700 years. Their border with Russia is over 700 miles long. Finland is at the end of the West. 'Europeans speak of communism and we speak of communism,' a Finnish publisher said to me, 'but it is the difference between the young speaking of death, and the old'. Outside, in the wind from the Baltic, the face becomes numb. It is difficult to breathe.

And yet the cold has not entered the souls of the Finns; out of privation and menace have sprung a vivacity and a huge good humour. I was sitting in a discothèque, which was really just a small upstairs room with tables and chairs. I expected the familiar beat but, from the start, the music was quite distinctive. The recorded sound of a waltz came through the modern, stereophonic speakers – and each couple, as if at a ball, swirled madly around the small, wooden floor. Elderly waitresses served beer. The waltz was followed by a polka, and these disco champions danced a kind of rural measure, clapping their hands to the music. Each man then escorted his partner off the floor. Polite courtesies were exchanged. Some minutes later, the conventional high notes of the Bee Gees and the Jacksons rose into the air; here, at last, was the discotheque. But, later, the waltz and the polka were played again. By now most of the men were drunk and yet they executed the formal, rapid steps of these dances with as much relish as if they had been invented yesterday. If we contemplate this odd collaboration – the polka alongside the disco, the men drunkenly high-spirited and yet still observing the rituals of the old dance – we may come a little way toward understanding this most paradoxical of European nations.

There is, however, a Byzantine complexity about its social customs and arrangements that makes it almost impenetrable to an outsider. The municipal theatre at Turku was to perform a dramatised version of *Darkness At Noon*, Arthur Koestler's anti-Stalinist tract, but a Communist politician objected; the play was banned. In recompense, Brecht's adaptation of Gorki's *Mother* was also banned. When Harold Macmillan appeared recently on Finnish television, his remarks about 'Soviet expansionism' were deleted. The list is extraordinary; a 'Cantata in memory of Jan Palak' could not be performed, a Swedish broadcast of *One Day in the Life of Ivan Denisovich* was jammed, a BBC documentary on the relations between Finland and Russia was also banned. Nothing must disturb the delicate equilibrium which exists between Finland and its large neighbour. The process is known as 'self-censorship'; it represents a caution and a deliberate obliquity which seem, in any case, to spring naturally from the Finnish character.

This is, after all, the most highly politicised nation outside the Communist bloc. Civil servants can work for political parties; politicians can become civil servants. Most public bodies, from the national television service down to the local hospital, come under the scrutiny of politically appointed 'supervisory boards'. The small manoeuvrings and bickerings between parties reach downwards into every area of social life. But these are not the politics of inertia. A civil war wrecked Finland just 60 years ago; Finland has a treaty of 'friendship, co-operation and mutual assistance' with the Russians which is the same as that of Afghanistan's. Politics here are a busy, protective carapace – a combination of self-discipline and defensiveness. The English expression, 'don't rock the boat', is used here in an exemplary and not a pejorative sense. I imagine it has many Finnish equivalents, since that notion of perilous balance, of the menacing waves within sight, is at the centre of the Finnish experience.

It was really what one MP meant when he indicated to me that 'no politician is acceptable here unless he is an expert on foreign policy'. 'Foreign policy' is longhand for 'Russia', and to be 'an expert on Russia' is to be able to anticipate its moods and its demands. The Finns are dependent upon the Soviet Union for their oil; a third of Finland's armaments come from Russia. There have been Communists in all recent Finnish governments: the Conservatives have been consistently excluded from power for fear of antagonising the Politburo. Russia has pledged itself to come 'to the aid of' Finland if it should be threatened by Germany or Germany's allies.

And yet this is by no means a satellite state. Finland's mixed economy is prosperous and highly productive. And although many Finnish politicians are over-cautious in their dealings with the Soviet Union ('They try to be more papal than the Pope,' according to one newspaper editor), there is a stubbornness and independence here which have been formed under duress and nurtured in isolation. In Helsinki, still, are the massive and brooding remnants of Russian imperial architecture; but, beside them, are the soaring spires and the clean, white lines of contemporary Finnish design. These buildings seem weightless, as if they might rise into the air. They suggest the simplicity and the affirmation of the Finnish spirit. There is, I think, a longing to be free.

And yet this simple affirmation has become entangled in the facts of geography and history: never has so independent a race been so thoroughly betrayed by the circumstances of its history. Their culture has been dominated by their Swedish conquerors. They are bound, helplessly, to their Russian neighbours. And so, now, a series of compromises has been established – a deep reserve characterises their dealings with the world, just as it marks the faces of these people. In conversations with public figures here, there is a constant ambiguity, a circuitous moving away from the point: 'The Russians cannot be aggressive towards us. It is theoretically impossible because of the friendship treaty . . . in Finland, the press has traditionally been more loyal to the government . . . ' The understandable desire not to offend the Russians, and the elaborate politicisation of Finnish life, have created a form of double-talk. A bland and mannered obliquity hovers over official pronouncements; 20 words are used where one might do.

It has, I suppose, become a kind of neurosis. A young Finnish writer, Dan Steinbock, suggested a convenient analogy. 'When Freud described certain symptoms as sexual, he caused great offence. If he had simply said "emotional", everyone would have understood him and agreed. It is dangerous here to touch upon the Finns' subconscious.' He himself had been, in speeches, attacking the Russian invasion of Afghanistan, and abusing Brezhnev. 'I talk about things which the Finns believe, but cannot bring themselves to say. There has been no serious liberal tradition here since the late Sixties. Now I get threatening phone calls. I got a black eye in the street, from some Stalinists.'

Stalinism; censorship; obliquity. It all sounds ominous, as though Finland were the last act of some Expressionist drama. And yet, when I turned on the television, there was a concert of what looked like the equivalent of punk rock. Helsinki itself has adopted the more elegant aspects of Western commercialism while retaining its specific identity. I was sitting in a bar, when a young Social Democratic MP was introduced to me. I was from *The Spectator*? 'Ah, the honourable schoolboy.' It was his birthday. His wife had bought him a cashmere scarf, from London. 'And,' she said, 'I could have got two St Laurent scarves for the same price.' We were talking in a city where the Russians are known, jocularly, as 'the men from headquarters': a few hundred miles away, an anti-Stalinist play has been banned. The polka and the Bee Gees are played together in the discothèque. Opposites co-exist; contradictions are resolved or accepted with equanimity. These people have their roots in the East, and their allegiances in the West. Their language is a strange variant of Hungarian which nobody else understands: a whole English sentence seems to emerge in one long, forbidding Finnish word. The Finns baffle foreigners, and they enjoy doing so. They relish their special position. They live with contradictions, with paradoxes, with double-talk, because they are certain of their identity.

In the art gallery in Helsinki, the major works are figurative. The individual stares out, reserved, but not cold or melancholy. The faces are stubborn, wily, good-humoured – although the landscape is harsh, the dwelling in the left-hand corner dilapidated. There is a faithfulness to specific facts, to facts of individual temperament, which disclaims generalities. A colonel in the Finnish army was explaining to me the country's defences; although the standing army was small, 700,000 men could be mobilised, instantly, to fight in the mountains or among the forests and lakes. We went on to discuss Cruise missiles. And then he said, suddenly, 'And God gave us the rocks'. He was talking about nuclear shelters. But there was an echo here of an older wisdom. The rocks epitomise that stubborn faith which the Finns have in their own geography – and they represent, too, the hardness of temperament which will survive the compromises and constrictions of present circumstances. If God has created the rocks, he has created also a race of sentinels.

8 March, 1980

Patrick Marnham

SOME PROGRESS

Andalusia, Spain

The house stands on the village street, in a line of white-washed walls
and heavy wooden doors. It is designed to repel the long summer heat.
During the short winter the house is bitterly cold inside and no longer
cheap to run. It seems slightly larger than most of its neighbours but one
would have little idea of its splendour from the outside. Once past the
front door, with its grilled peephole, you walk through several rooms to
reach the only one that is heated in January. Here are the television and
the *camilla*, a round table with a charcoal or electric fire set in its base and
a heavy cloth reaching to the floor to trap all the heat. To warm yourself
you take a seat by the table and lift the cloth. The family who live here,
descendants of the landowners who built this house and who once
employed many of their neighbours, are now considering ways in which
to sell it. The land around is irrigated by the Guadalquivir. It is more productive than ever, producing oranges, and maize and wheat. But to profit
from the land no longer means that one can live in the area in the old
comfort.

Beyond the house, completely enclosed by the village and by the river,
there is a large garden. It contains tall palms, ornamental fruit trees, a
sweet lemon, cypresses, roses, jasmine, lawns, a vegetable patch and an
irrigation tank large enough to swim in. The garden is still beautiful but
the family say that it is a shadow of its true self. The man who made this
garden and who filled the house with his treasures died some years ago.
His wife preferred Seville. He preferred his garden, and his terrace overlooking the Guadalquivir, and his music. He had a machine of antique
English design for playing cylinders which operated a keyboard. He collected a library of theological books. He made a family shrine to the Virgin in one of the colder corridors, and cut niches into the walls of other
rooms for statues of the saints. He set aside a room by the garden for the
regular visits of his spiritual director. He slowly filled the house with furniture and paintings and probably lived for most of the time in a world of
his own creation, waiting with such patience as he could muster to satisfy his curiosity about the world to come. With his departure accom-

plished and his curiosity at an end the house and the garden linger on. The trees grow ragged, the books gather dust, the furniture is chipped. His heirs slowly come to terms with the fact that though they love the house they cannot continue with it. It died when he did.

All over Spain the same decision must be looming. A country which seems to have largely avoided the 19th century, and to have accepted the 20th century on a very selective basis for its first 60 years, is now trying to catch up all at once. As a result the visible changes which have taken place in only two years are remarkable. Public manners are now only slightly more formal than they are elsewhere. Women are regularly insulted and attacked in the city streets while crowds pass unheedingly by. Children are starting to enjoy the freedom to destroy private and public property. The *tapas* bars which abound everywhere are now coming into competition with 'burger bars' and have provided their customers with electronic fruit machines in self defence. Spanish football hooligans are learning the international system of grunts and moans. Fifteen years of fundamental change behind the heavy closed doors of the Spanish home have suddenly worked their way out onto the street.

Twenty years ago the convents in Seville inculcated discipline and self denial by methods that would have interested Dickens. The girls were not allowed to drink water, even during the summer, except with meals. Every Christmas there was a play that was one of the social highlights of the school year. But while it was performed the nuns sat at the back of the hall watching the play. The girls stood in front of them with their backs to the stage, watching the nuns. They were told that this was politer. The point was that none of them questioned any of this. They look back on it now with amazement, but also say it was not an unhappy period in their lives. The changes that they worked so hard for, on leaving school, have come about. Now they are beginning to notice some of the disadvantages.

Wherever the foreigner travels in Spain he must sense this anxious desire for European normality. Are we modern enough, people seem to be asking: are we considerate enough, predictable enough, silly enough, boring enough, to be one of you?

The answer is, 'No you are not'. There remains far too much evidence of a higher culture in Spain. Quite unimportant people retain a capacity to think for themselves. Even today the country is notably marked by a living religious faith, and by potentially violent disagreements over ideas. Many people work seriously at two jobs. Family life is flourishing. Prosperity is still a novelty which has to be fought for. Men still derive a sense of individual dignity based on their own character and behaviour rather than on their income or professional status.

One can see why the Spanish yearn for the Common Market. For far too long they have suffered from the fulfilment of the old curse, 'May you live in interesting times'. Nothing could be more boring than the culture of the new Europe; nothing could be less lethal than protracted bickering over the price of fish. But they have some way to go before they are the good little Europeans we have come to expect. Somehow one just can't see them taking the burning moral issues, such as the annual Canadian seal cull, at all seriously.

10 January, 1981

John Stewart Collis

THE VOLCANO

My first impression was of harmony. As I approached the vicinity of Mount Etna (erupting in 1928) it seemed to me that harmony had been established between Man and Nature. Every rock and all the stones, every cliff and cleft, each yard of soil, had joined with Man in the making of vineyards. On the level and the perpendicular, the slant and the crisscross, grape-vines were succoured by Nature and supported by Man. And sometimes high crags turned into castles, and on many a ledge or shoulder single houses clung like flowers.

I reached the famous mountain citadel of Taormina, separated by several ridges from Mount Etna. Looking south from my hotel window I could see the mountain domed with snow. And there also, even up to the snow, vines were laced. The eruption did not burst out dramatically from the top, but from half-way down the mountain. At this distance it looked in the daytime like a big bonfire, trailing smokingly down to the sea. At night it was a waterfall of fire.

I determined to do two things: to reach the scene of the eruption, and to find what was left of the village of Mascali which was reported to be overwhelmed by the lava. At first I tried to do this on my own, but completely failed to get anywhere near the right spot to start climbing towards the volcano. Then I fell in with a German journalist with a car and guides who knew the right place to go – and I joined them. We drove at a dangerous speed along terrible roads, and through un-motorconscious mountain villages, until the track stopped even our driver.

We went along a path with walls on each side, and the walls, and the groves, ended. In fact they were buried under what looked to me like a huge railway embankment composed of charcoal. I climbed onto it. It did not burn my shoes. This was my first experience of lava. I could see it stretching up the mountain and down towards the sea.

The next thing to do was to follow it up to its source. After climbing by the side of this 'embankment' for some distance I tried walking on the lava again. This was less comfortable now, for I was in danger of scorching my shoes, and smoke got into my eyes. The width of this lava-stream was roughly that of the Thames at Charing Cross. I say stream, for I discerned that the centre of it was *slowly moving*. My part on the edge was steady, though a little hot. In the centre it was moving down. Its red heat could be seen even in the sunlight. I was interested also in its silence, its quantity, and its power.

At this point the guides said it would be dangerous to climb any higher, and the German journalist concurred. So I parted from them and pursued my way alone.

It was not long before I actually did reach the source from which the lava flowed. I could see very little through the smoke which now began to affect my throat, so sticking a handkerchief into my mouth I advanced. I was near the pit. I dimly saw a stream of grey boiling fluid rising from a kind of cave in the mountain. I approached nearer; and now I heard a noise as of men pouring gravel down a shaft into a ship's hold – sounds of men at work where no men could be at work. I retired through the sulphurous air, catching sight while doing so of the chill, fresh snow above. I was satisfied with this.

Now to find Mascali. I ran down by the side of the lava, hoping to see what had happened to the village. It was the same scene all the way down; walls, roads and groves suddenly ending, and the embankment of charcoal in their place, obliterating everything. Sometimes a farmhouse would be half-submerged, or standing on the fringe quite untouched with a tree at the door, while another tree a few yards further out was bent down under the weight of the edge of the lava, whereas the tree in front of it was scarcely visible at all. I even saw, what one hears of so often, a Madonna and Child placed in a nook in a wall, just escaping destruction. Nothing seemed to be burnt. This tree would be overthrown, the one a yard away not even singed: this house destroyed – its neighbour intact, though pathetically deserted.

As I ran down I could see a long expanse of lava now, a kind of desolate moor, so wide had the 'river' become. If a moor is desolate, what of this? – here no living thing would ever lodge. I saw again that the middle part was slowly moving. Near the bottom, I had heard, it advanced a few hundred yards a day. Before it reached a house the inhabitants could remove the windows and doors for future use. Then entering in, creeping slowly, creeping surely, the monster would deposit itself upon that house, and *bury* it.

Darkness was coming on and still I could not find Mascali. I got back to a road and met some people who said that all the village had been destroyed, nothing of it could be seen. Not believing this, I continued descending by the side of the lava. It made an eerie search. I met no one: the silence, the solitude and the dusk were principalities making ghostly the strange 'river' on my right, the suddenly ending walls, the half-buried farms, the orchards turned to stone. Waterfalls of fire flowed in the gathering dark, and high above at the source flames flapped out from the belching shaft. I looked round once more for signs of Mascali – and still in vain. But now I saw a man afar off coming towards me. And so to him I could address my question – where is Mascali, *'Dov'é Mascali?'* He pointed to the ground on which we stood. *'Ecco,'* he replied. Mascali was beneath my feet.

28 March, 1981

Peter Ackroyd

GLARE BUT NOT GLOIRE

Paris

'The late *run* to the French capitol may have undeceived my countrymen in very many particulars, on which distance, the illusions of imagination, and the *glare* the French have the address to throw round every object, may have led them to form very erroneous opinions'. *A Few Days in Paris* (published 1802).

I found myself in the middle of a great plain; large tower blocks, reflecting the light from each other, would have dazzled Christian and led him astray from his Progress. They receded into the distance like a modernist, more bewildering, version of de Chirico. A painted grotto and a marble hill rose in the middle distance; behind them, placed as the vanishing point in this ever diminishing perspective, was the Arc de Triomphe. The only noises were those of the escalators, running up and down with no people – for this was Sunday morning – to disturb their even motion. Bright electronic messages circulated above my head, one of them announcing a new film, *La Terreur des Zombies*. A sculpture of Miro's, like a great bone painted in bright primary colours, gleamed; it was the presiding deity of the place. It was elegant, perhaps a little chilling. The 19th century traveller had got it right: not *gloire*, but *glare*.

When I retreated underground, into a Metro station as large as a cathedral, I recognised the shining halls. The area is called La Défense, a modern precinct set carefully apart from the old Paris, and it was here that the opening sequences of a recent picture, *Buffet Froid*, had been filmed. In this film Gérard Depardieu had wandered in a Paris so empty of human beings that it resembled a crystal vessel, and had become involved in 'crimes de passion' without sequence and without sentiment. The film had been elegant, perhaps a little chilling.

Later that day I found myself sitting in the Café de Flore. Quite without warning a middle-aged man, a few tables in front of me, let out a loud and sinister rattle, like that of a crank being turned too quickly, and fell backwards upon the floor. He may have been having a seizure; he may have been dying. The elegant middle-aged lady in front of me put up a hand to shield her eyes from the sight, looking at me for sympathy in her predicament. Some smart young men and women, immediately behind the now supine man, paused momentarily to take in the spectacle and then resumed their conversation. An elderly man to my right kept on reading his *livre de poche*. Within a few seconds the manager of the café, and two of its waiters, surrounded the man, as if shielding him from the censorious gaze of their clients, and propped him back in his chair.

He seemed, fortunately, to be recovering when a police van drew up outside the café; three policemen hurried up and, apparently against the man's will and despite his protestations, took him away. Perhaps they were about to take him to hospital – it was, after all, unlikely that he was being arrested for falling ill in public. But it would have been impossible to ask anyone sitting around me since – with the exception of the manager whose dignity seemed in some way to have been impaired – they went on talking and reading, taking not the slightest interest in proceedings. They were all very well-dressed, very chic. If the furs around the middle-aged lady's shoulders had come suddenly to life and started eating her face, they would no doubt have remained calm and called for a policeman.

The Pompidou Centre is a miracle of lucidity; it resembles one of those fashionable watches with a transparent back, through which every detail of the mechanism can be seen working in unison. Transparent, tubular passageways hang from it like stalactites. It is so constructed and designed that one knows exactly where one is – both in relation to the building and to the rest of the city – exactly what material it is constructed out of, exactly how it has all been arranged. One gets the same sensation with the Grand Palais which housed the Exhibition of 1900, and with the Eiffel Tower – when the rays of the sun strike the metal girders of the Tower, it is like looking into the mind of the engineer. Everything exists in a clear and even light.

And then inside the Pompidou Centre, within a section marked 'La Galérie Retrospective du Centre de Création Industrielle', the history of technological civilisation was marked out as if it were also part of some majestic *son et lumière*. Seven separate screens glowed, severally or together, creating a symphony of information and enlightenment. Reading contemporary French literature affords a similar experience – the screens of the sentences and paragraphs glow and fade and glow again, and the world is transformed into a number of discrete theorems placed in careful relation to each other. You are continually invited to marvel at how it is being done, rather than what is being said. Outside the Centre, the travellers are propelled up and down the transparent tubes, like specimens waiting to be anatomised within some future galérie.

It is impossible to overestimate the effect of architecture upon manners. In Paris, it is something to live up to rather than in. The pavement cafés are places where people go to sit and watch, and be watched in turn. It is almost as if the French had invented glass, that medium which imparts brightness but not necessarily heat. The clearness, the unambiguity, the lucidity are everywhere: the relentless clarity of French realism, the lucid structures of French philosophical thought, the sometimes comic obviousness of French fashion. In such a place, the world itself is transformed into spectacle. The main function of Paris is its appearance; the subways look like museums, and the museums like theatres. When certain French radicals, in the early Sixties, defined capitalism as 'the society of the spectacle' they were in reality talking about themselves.

The election campaign was noticeable for its posters. There were several images of M. Chirac – to the untrained eye, they might all have looked the same but there were subtle differences. One proclaimed 'Il nous faut un homme de coeur': M. Chirac is wearing a grey suit and a blue shirt. Another, 'Il nous faut un homme de nouveau': M. Chirac is wearing a pullover and an open-necked shirt. Yet another: 'Il nous faut un homme de parole': M. Chirac is wearing a dark suit with a white shirt, the cuffs peeping through. Grey for the heart, black for the truth.

Everything is to be seen to be believed. The waiters of this city look more like waiters than anywhere else in the world, and as a result they have never found any necessity to change their behaviour. The traveller of 1802 had champagne poured in his ear by one of them: 'We were attended by an impudent French waiter. He did everything but attend civily on us. I never took a greater aversion to a man in my life'. The workmen look more workmanlike than anywhere else as if they had stepped out of a film starring Jean Gabin. The tramps who lurk in the Metro – relegated, as it were, beneath ground, beneath the level of elegant discourse – more gnarled and twisted than their counterparts elsewhere, as though they had modelled themselves on Charles Laughton's performance in *The Hunchback of Nôtre Dame*. The elegant young men and women are stridently, ferociously elegant. *Glare*, not *gloire*.

But this attention to, or absorption in, appearance is a great virtue. It leads to a certain vivacity and a genuine freedom of spirit, a wit unattached to questions of 'purpose' or 'meaning'. Only a very clever, or at least quick-witted, people understand the virtue and importance of appearance. Walking through the streets of Paris is like being trapped forever in the first 15 minutes of *Les Enfants du Paradis*. And so it was before, in 1802: 'They are a century behind us in the common conveniences of life, carriages etc; but their great quickness and versatility of talent is visible in everything'. The important word, again, is 'visible'.

Some things, of course, have changed. 'Why Paris?' Ezra Pound wrote in 1921, 'Paris is the center of the world!' And, indeed, so for a while it seemed – Joyce, Picasso, Apollinaire, Ravel, Stravinsky; now all that is left of them, and of those Americans and Englishmen who joined them, are the photographs affixed in the walls of small bookshops. Those Englishmen and Americans I met complain now of the dullness of the place, of the tide of prosperity which has submerged everything else. Prosperity is not conducive to an exciting life; it creates elegance, perhaps, but not value.

Americans still come. I met a young man from California who expatiated on the wonders of Paris. 'It is,' he said, 'just as beautiful as San Francisco.' I suggested that there were more palaces here, more buildings of note, perhaps even more culture. 'But we've got music and movies,' he said. 'Music and movies are universal.' There is still, as in the Twenties, a 'lost generation' of Americans – only the present one does not know that it is lost.

Of course there is beauty here. All cities are impressive in their way, because they represent the aspiration of men to lead a common life; those people who wish to live agreeable lives, and in constant intercourse with one another, will build a city as beautiful as Paris. Those whose relations are founded principally upon commerce and upon the ferocious claims of domestic privacy will build a city as ugly and as unwieldy as London. It is the law of life.

The tomb of Oscar Wilde, at the Père Lachaise cemetery, is covered with marks and graffiti – the only sepulchre in that city of the dead which still attracts the living: 'Oscar Nostro', 'Love For Life', 'I Love You' and then, less plaintively, scratched upon the white stone in large letters 'Sex Pistols' and then, less plaintively still, 'You Old Fruit'. There is no peace for Oscar Wilde even in death. A car zoomed down the path beside his grave (it would be ironic, I thought, to be killed in a cemetery – it would fit the peculiar French sense of propriety). But he would not have minded; at least here – with Bellini and Bernhardt, Piaf and Molière, Proust and Bizet, Balzac and Ingres, Héloïse and Abelard – he would have been in good company. Oscar Wilde, like the French whom he fled to, knew the importance of appearances, the values of the surface.

And it is perhaps the evident truth of this which makes the modernist complex of La Défense, with its Miro and its painted grotto, at once so astounding and so chilling. Everything here is designed to be seen and, once seen, admired. The eye wanders across the buildings as it would wander over the surface of a dead planet thrown into sharp relief by the light of a distant galaxy. The truth is precisely this: there are only appearances. It is foolish to look for any other reality, any other meaning, as the spectacle moves on. The appearance *is* reality. *Glare*, in the end, is *gloire*.

9 *May*, 1981

Shiva Naipaul

LEGACY OF A REVOLUTION

Lisbon

Poised atop his tall, traffic-besieged column, companioned by a lion, the Marques de Pombal, 18th-century strong man of Portugal, gazes southward down the elegantly graded slope of the Avenida da Liberdade – the imposing thoroughfare slicing through the heart of central Lisbon – to the broad, glinting Tagus framed, on its farther shore, by a line of misty hills. He is looking towards his own creation, the Baixa or lower quarter of the city, a dour, militaristic grid of streets adorned with a regimented architecture of precise, virtually prefabricated symmetry: the new Lisbon he had planned – following the disastrous earthquake and tidal wave which had struck the city on All Saints Day 1755 – to give expression to the rigorous rationalism of the Enlightenment then flourishing in the more advanced lands across the Pyrenees. It has been estimated that between 15 and 20 thousand people were killed in the Lisbon earthquake; many of them, on so sacred a day, trapped in the city's crowded churches. Voltaire was not slow in providing an ironic commentary on the event: his ingenuous Candide happens to be in Lisbon when the catastrophe strikes.

Pombal had spent many years abroad. He had been Portuguese ambassador in London and Vienna. During his travels, he had absorbed many of the more advanced ideas and hostilities of his day. In 1750 he was recalled home and appointed a Minister. The earthquake was, in a sense, his great opportunity. When the king asked him what was to be done, his reply was brusque. 'Bury the dead and feed the living,' he replied. Pombal buried the dead, fed the living and razed the ravaged city. In the affected area he levelled even those buildings which had remained intact: he would start anew. The ruthless energy he displayed secured his ascendancy.

From then on for roughly the next 25 years it was Pombal who ruled Portugal; who, seizing his chance, used it to impose his visions of 'progress' on Western Europe's most fallen, most backward society. The reconstruction of Lisbon was only the most visible aspect of his programme. Suspicious of their power and, in particular, of their near-monopoly on education, he expelled the Jesuits – a move that was to encourage the eventual dissolution of the Order; he humiliated the feudal aristocracy, setting up a royal depotism which modelled itself on the practices of Europe's more 'progressive' monarchs; he subverted the powers of the Inquisition; he reorganised the University of Coimbra, sweeping away the traditional pietistic curriculum, founding instead schools of mathematics and natural science; he abolished slavery – though not, let it be said, in Brazil; he sought – without great success – to promote an industrial revolution and to weaken the commercial stranglehold of the long-settled English merchants.

He was one of the great figures of the period, an embodiment of its impatience and its optimism. His type remains familiar in our own century – the intolerant moderniser seeking to rescue his country from dereliction and decay. It seemed appropriate that, on his pedestal, he should be escorted by a lion and look towards the Baixa – that Enlightenment dream of order, of rationality, of unclouded light; of a new dawn. Pombal was, in some ways, the exact opposite of his 20th-century successor – the reclusive Dr Antonio de Oliveira Salazar – whose distrust of international influence was so deep-seated that he even discouraged the formation of a Boy Scout movement in Portugal. The Marques struggled to kick and drag his society into the world of the late 18th century. Salazar locked the doors against the ideological incursions of the 20th and did his best, with the help of his secret police, to lose the key.

To the east of the Baixa rises the Alfama, Lisbon's mediaeval Moorish quarter. Strangely, it was unharmed by the earthquake; and survived the subsequent tidal inundation. Nor was it affected by Pombal's city-planning. What he can see of it today from the summit of his column is probably much the same as he would have seen 200 years ago. Only the television aerials might puzzle him. Westward, in the direction of the open sea, Lisbon sprawls along the northern shore of the Tagus. A vertiginous suspension bridge looms triumphantly over the river. When it was opened in 1966, a grateful nation dedicated it to Dr Salazar. But then times changed. Portugal decided it wasn't so grateful to its dictator after all. Now it is dedicated to the Revolution of 1974 which overthrew all that Dr Salazar had ever symbolised. With the Portuguese fondness for dates it was rechristened Ponte 25 Abril, commemorating the day despotism was said to have ended for ever. On the distant side of the bridge, dimmed by the haze, robed arms spanned out like some prodigious bird of prey, rears the giant effigy of Christ the King. Beyond the Ponte 25 Abril – the sun-bleached splendours of Belem, imbued with evocations, ancient and modern, of vanished grandeur, of Empires gained and lost . . . Belem with its rattling commuter trains, its slogan-daubed walls, its dreary suburban slopes climbing away from the water. Further along the shoreline, the Tagus by now lost in the Atlantic ocean, are the resort towns of Estoril and Cascais, Lisbon's Sunday retreats. Along this shoreline, turquoise waves hiss and foam among the rocks; sand-dunes drift across the highway. In high summer, the pine groves and windblown grass smoulder. Ash spreads like a greyish snowfall up the barren slopes yellow with gorse. Along the roadside, stalls offer for sale sheepskins, blankets, all kinds of trinkets. The wind slices off the sea. At Cabo da Roca, Eurasia's western-most projection, tourists buzz about the gift-shop. 'Portugal Is For Lovers' say the tote-bags and T-shirts. The stele marking the site strikes a more poetic note. It is inscribed with a quotation plucked from the work of Luis de Camoes, 'Aqui . . . Onde a Terra se Acaba . . . E O Mar Comeca . . .' Here the earth ends . . . here the ocean begins . . . The wind scythes through the grass. Buffeted tourists flee to the warmth of the shop.

Pombal gazes south. Northwards, behind his back, towards the airport, wide avenues sweep between featureless banks of apartment blocks, circle round bleak housing estates that have sprung up within the last 20 years; and pass within the shadow of shanty towns, promontories of rural restlessness trespassing close to the heart of the city. Maize grows in gardens; chickens scuttle along muddy lanes; bare-footed girls fill water buckets at a communal pipe; peasant faces stare from windows and ramshackle verandas.

But Pombal and his lion see nothing of this.

Lisbon, I had been told, was sometimes compared with San Francisco. It had not occurred to me to compare the two places – despite the fact that I knew San Francisco fairly well, having once spent several months there. The similarities were listed: the proximity to the ocean; the Ponte 25 Abril – an admittedly somewhat less elegant replica of the Golden Gate; the fog or mist that now and again creeps over the water; the survival of trams; the hilliness – Lisbon, like Rome, is alleged to have been built on seven hills; the abiding fear of earthquakes. Even the increasing prevalence of homosexuality had been cited. After that catalogue, I could appreciate the temptation to draw the parallel. But the similarities having been listed, there, so to speak, all similarity ended. At bottom, the coincidences were no more than arresting curiosities, offered up as a kind of joke at Lisbon's expense.

'You have come to the Third World,' an acquaintance had remarked sourly. It was a point of view prompted by exasperation. But there was also truth in the statement. Portugal remains, despite everything, the poorest country in Europe. It tends to be either at or near the bottom of just about every index of 'development' – agricultural yield, industrial production, per capita income, etc, etc. As late as 1960, for instance, only about 35 per cent of the population had received a primary education. Under the Salazar regime, university education was the preserve of the wealthy, the state offering virtually no scholarships or any kind of assistance to those who were not well-off. In 1967 this elite made up less than 0.5 per cent of the population. One in every four or five Portuguese was probably an illiterate. The situation has improved since then, but Portugal must harbour among its population the highest proportion of illiterates in Western Europe. Exactly what that proportion is remains a matter of dispute. There are those who would claim – on grounds more emotional than factual – that the problem has been eradicated. When one reflects on all of this, San Francisco seems very far away.

Portugal, when the Revolution arrived in 1974, was 'European' merely in a geographical sense; an essentially agrarian society governed by feudal attitudes, riven to its foundations by class privilege, vaingloriously battling to preserve her 'overseas provinces' in Africa and maintain the long outmoded doctrine of her 'civilising mission'. 'Authority and liberty,' Salazar had said, 'are two incompatible ideas . . . Liberty diminishes in proportion as man progresses and becomes civilised.' The atmosphere on the eve of the Revolution must have been surreal.

Symptoms of backwardness are to be found in the beggars who frequent the open-air cafés of Lisbon, in the cripples seeking alms near church entrances, in the roughly typed hard-luck stories which, occasionally, are flourished in one's face (the same technique of drawing attention to personal suffering is used in India), in the shanty towns teeming with refugees from the countryside, in the thousands who transform themselves into 'guest workers' and take themselves off to France and Germany in search of work. As happens all over the Third World, you get nowhere without 'influence', without knowing the 'right people' and being able to exploit a system of relationships based on family ties, on favours given in the expectation that, in due course, some return will be made. He who naively confronts the Portuguese bureaucracy is, they say, doomed to futile expenditures of energy. A Sisyphean labour can ensue.

Portugal, in 1974, resembled, to a certain extent, a country that had just been granted an unexpected and dubious Independence: panic-stricken, skill and capital immediately fled abroad to more congenial havens – chiefly Brazil. And, after seven years of turbulent democracy, the rich remain anxious and fearful of further change. Some, when they let themselves go, assume the outraged demeanour of expatriates complaining about the spoiled natives. 'You know,' one affluent woman said to me, 'nobody wants to work any more. You cannot fire anybody any more.' Her lovely face contracted with indignation. 'Why,' she exclaimed, 'after these women have their babies, they have to be given so many hours off for each breast.' I looked flabbergasted. 'It is true,' she cried. 'It is there in the labour regulations. For each breast, so many hours. That is what we have come to in Portugal.' I could have been in almost any newly independent African state listening in to vulgar Club conversation.

VOTA APU . . . SOCIALISMO EM LIBERDADE . . . CONTRA D'FASCISMO, CONTRA A MISERIA . . . REPRESSA NAO! VIVA REFORMA AGRARIA . . . The charged atmosphere of the 1974 Revolution lives on, to some extent, in the slogans defacing the walls of Lisbon. These slogans are one of the first things to draw the attention of the freshly arrived visitor. Daubed on virtually every available surface, they assume, after a while, the appearance of a disfiguring lichenous growth. The Left makes most of the running in this wall war. Apart from the occasional swastika, I saw few overtly 'fascist' proclamations and symbols: these in fact, are a much commoner sight in London. The Communists seem to be the masters of the art. Some of their efforts are quite elaborate pictorial compositions, showing the 'people' – the *povo* – heroically advancing towards lurid skylines serrated by the roofs of factories and smoking chimneys.

In the euphorically blurred period that had followed the stirring events of April 1974, the Communists had swiftly shown themselves to be the best organised political party in the country – virtually the *only* party. Throughout the years of suppression the Party, though invisible, had managed to maintain itself and preserve a coherent identity. It was a seed frozen into impotence by the Salazarian ice-age but with its capacity for germination still intact. The Communists emerged from their hibernation united around their exiled leader Alvaro Cunhal: who, on his return home, was given a hero's welcome by an ecstatic Lisbon. He was even made a Minister. For a while, it was not entirely inconceivable that the country might fall into the Party's waiting, well-prepared hands. Anything seemed possible in a Portugal suddenly loosed from its leading strings, suddenly on course for the previously unutterable and unthinkable – voluntary relinquishment of its cherished 'overseas provinces' in Africa and the long martyrdom they had entailed.

Angola, Mozambique and Guinea were indeed surrendered one by one. After 500 years, the Portuguese Empire was dead. But the Communists did not seize power. Cunhal's hero's welcome did not signal love of his doctrines. It was a celebration; a festa. He was a symbol, not a saviour. In the seven years that have since gone by the Party has declined steadily in popularity: in the last elections they received a modest 13 per cent of the vote. The Revolution's novelty, its excitement, has, inevitably, been dulled with the passage of time. Portugal, meandering through a succession of ephemeral coalitions, has gradually drifted rightward, towards what one might describe as the conservative-centre. 'The revolution is screwed,' lamented a Canadian folksinger of unspecified leftist persuasion and a long-time resident. 'If tomorrow Salazar should be raised from the dead, these people would fall at his feet. They don't care for freedom any more.' That is too bitter and uncharitable a judgement. There is no evidence that surviving Salazarist nostalgia is anything more than idle fantasy. Too much has happened in Portugal, too much has been overturned, for so naive a reversion to occur.

Whatever the discontents, the fruits of democracy remain real. One Saturday evening I went out to Belem to have a look at a lavish festa sponsored by the Communist Party: the colourful posters advertising the event – to be held over three days – were freely displayed all over Lisbon. It seemed at a glance that the whole city was wending its way to the fairground. The nearby streets were jammed with cars, buses, trams. Serpentine queues fermented about the turnstiles. It was a long time since I had seen such swarms of people. On distant stages bands performed. Red, blue, yellow and green flags fluttered from tall poles. Scattered loudspeakers broadcast snatches of music and exhortation. Dust rose from the beaten earth, fogging the noisy, fluorescent night. Young men and women danced among the eddying multitudes, holding aloft flags adorned with the hammer and sickle.

'Sixty Years of Struggle' proclaimed the banners. I wandered in and out of booths – the Communist Party of Cape Verde sent fraternal greetings to their Portuguese comrades; so did the Angolans, the Poles, the Cubans, the Italians; so too did *Pravda*. Militant internationalism scented the Lisbon air that evening. By no means all – or even a majority – of these people were Communists. For most, no doubt, it was a night out, one unmarred by ideological commitment. Yet, whatever their motives, each, by his mere presence, was an emblem of the new Portugal. Salazar ('We are opposed to all forms of internationalism, Communism, Socialism, syndicalism . . .' he had once proudly declared) . . . Salazar, so apprehensive of the Boy Scout movement, had been well and truly buried.

Nevertheless, those who mourn the past, who suffer from acute withdrawal symptoms, are not necessarily wicked men hellbent on destroying the achievements of the last seven years and restoring dictatorship. That is an unjust assumption. The lunatics aside, most will concede that such a restoration is not possible. Their sense of loss, their *saudade* (a visceral Portuguese concept, not easy to render into English, combining the notions of nostalgia, yearning, deprivation: it finds its purest expression in the *fado*, those sombre love-songs which, over the last 200 years, have become the distinctive folk music of Portugal), is less rooted in a feeling, cloudy but none the less real, that the country has lost its 'soul'; that it no longer has a reason to be. 'We have lost our way,' a former ambassador mourned. 'We Portuguese have lost our sense of ourselves. We no longer know why we exist.'

The Revolution of 1974, he went on, had gone even deeper, had been, in its special way, even more devastating than the French and Russian revolutions. Those revolutions might have changed profoundly the structure of their societies but they did not harm their essence. The upheavals in France and Russia, he argued, had enhanced their national destinies: France, under Napoleon, dominated Europe; Russia, under the Communists, had transformed itself into the standard-bearer of a new idea of civilisation – one, it went without saying, he abhorred . . . but that was not the point.

In Portugal it had not been like that. Their Revolution had severed the ties linking them to their past. What was Portugal without its African territories? Where now was its 'civilising mission'? It was nothing! A cork floating aimlessly on the ocean of history! Overnight, it had shrunk into marginality; a poor, small, shabby country on the fringes of Europe, whose highest ambition was entry into the consumer paradise of the Common Market. Theirs, he concluded, was a tragic fate.

In Belem, a bluish mist hangs over the river. The tide is out, stranding its 16th-century watch-tower, exposing its mossy barnacled base. Seaweed drapes the rocks. I make the pilgrimage to its summit and look down on the Tagus. The Ponte 25 Abril rises dreamily out of the blue mist. Christ the King is barely visible in the milky haze obscuring the far shore.

Along these shores Portugal had embarked on its great maritime adventure – when, in 1415, crusading piety fusing with the desire for gold, the armada was assembled that would seize Ceuta in North Africa from the Moors. The success of this expedition would give birth to the 'civilising mission', to the lust for overseas expansion and the conquest of the new worlds. In the far south of Portugal, on the windy promontory of Sagres, that dour and obsessed prince, Henry the Navigator, would, in the years to come, brood over his charts, collating rumours of unknown lands, enticing to his presence the most knowledgeable and skilled mariners and navigators of the time.

Under his guidance Madeira was discovered and settled; as were the Azores and Canary Islands. It was at his instigation that frail Portuguese ships began their explorations of the African coast and initiated the European trade in slaves. When he died in 1460, the Cape of Good Hope was still to be rounded, the sea-route to India and the Far East yet to be revealed. But the momentum had been established. Within 40 years of his death, Vasco da Gama would be dropping anchor off Calicut – the voyage transmuted into legend in Os Lusiadas (the Lusiads), the national epic composed by Portugal's most celebrated poet, Luis de Camoes.

On his return from India, da Gama had offered prayers of thanks in Belem, at the Church of Our Lady. King Manuel, carried away by the scale of the discoveries, conferred on himself the title of 'Lord of the Conquest, Navigation and Commerce of Ethiopia, Arabia, Persia and India'. In 1502, on the Belem beach where da Gama had embarked on his voyage, he ordered the erection of what was to become one of the masterpieces of Portuguese architecture – the Jeronimos Monastery. Nothing better reflects the self-assurance and magnificent optimism of Portugal's heroic age. Half a millennium later it stands there, facing the river, its greying, ivoried facade glowing in the white heat of noon.

Not far away is the modern monument raised to the pioneering glories of the Navigator Prince. He holds himself erect at the stylised prow of a ship, gazing out across the water. Angled behind him, faces lifted to the sky, are some of those he had gathered about him at Sagres. Etched into the brick pavement of the surrounding plaza is a map of the world. Meticulously, it charts the explorations of the Portuguese along the coasts of the continents. How small Portugal! How immense the scope of its endeavour!

I stare at the Jeronimos Monastery glowing in the sunshine. Gone were the lords of Ethiopia, Arabia, Persia, India . . . Africa. REPRESSA NAO! proclaimed the walls of Belem . . . VIVA REFORMA AGRARIA! The commuter trains sweep past. Below me, the muddy fringes of the Tagus nuzzle the mossy rocks and stir the tentacles of blackened seaweed.

22 May, 1982

Jeffrey Bernard

CRUISE NEWS

I couldn't address you last week because I was stuck in a Norwegian fjord aboard a luxury cruise liner and the radio signals that transmit the telex couldn't get through the mountains and cliffs surrounding the said fjords. I was there aboard the ship on a freebie press trip. Right. Let's get rid of the plugs and moans to begin with. SAS – Scandinavian Airlines – who flew me to join the ship at Oslo are without doubt the best airline I've ever flown with. Their First Business Class was excellent. The grub was good, the drinks kept coming and the staff seemed to be aware of the fact that they were mere waiters and waitresses in the sky and not showbusiness entrepreneurs. A very good airline indeed. Secondly, Royal Viking run a good, clean ship and a happy ship. If cruising is your cup of tea then Royal Viking are the people to get in touch with. Now, as it happens, press trips aren't my cup of tea but on this trip the press happened to be delightful, with one exception: a girl who works – I won't say writes – for a Fleet Street daily. She contrived to last six days without buying one single round of drinks. Think about it. Six days. Wages. Expenses. Six days without a sortie to the bar. Granted she didn't wear her sunglasses on top of her head but six days without making contact with a barman has to be a record of some sort. As Charlie in the Coach and Horses would say, this one could peel an orange in her pocket. Come the first class lounge in Copenhagen before the SAS flight home where the booze was free she bought me two drinks. Have these hackettes no shame?

And what of Norway and a ship of fools in the shape of 500 or so geriatric American women with arthritic fingers festooned with diamond rings? Well, it was a rum do and a close thing, as the victor of Waterloo might have said. For the most part the scenery is pretty monotonous and a little like Snowdonia on a bigger scale. Rocks and more rocks. There was a spectacular fjord at Geiranger and I actually sat on deck at 3 a.m. well inside the Arctic Circle nursing a drink in sunlight but, for the most part, the views were pretty dull. I assume that Norwegians live for most of the year in darkness, feed on roll mops, read Ibsen and then blow their brains out. The whole thing was like a series of postcards and reminded me of the time I suggested to Francis Bacon that he live in Switzerland for tax reasons. 'What?' he screamed. 'All those fucking *views*.' Quite.

Anyway, the first shipboard acquaintance I made was an attorney from Washington with the splendid name of Wally Schubert. He was okay at first but then he drifted into the habit of saying 'What would you have done without us?' I told him, 'The same as we did between 1914 and 1917 and the same as we did between 1939 and 1941, you prick.' Americans, I discovered on the cruise, are completely unaware of anything whatsoever that goes on outside America. Amazingly isolated. Then Mr Schubert, a real wally, began to tell me what a great man President Reagan was. He then showered praise on Mrs Thatcher, told me that he was going to spend a night in the Sheraton Hotel in Knightsbridge and asked if they would know what a dry martini was. I told him that we in England know what a dry martini is and that furthermore we have electric light, running hot and cold water, telephones, automobiles and that we invented the law he practises round about AD 1215, 300 years or so before his country was discovered. He made me want to scream and the Fleet Street hackette walked around with a notebook and biro taking notes. I only once used a notebook and a biro, the uniform of a journalist, and that was on the very first job I went on. I had to interview an actress and I was a bit pissed for a change. I suddenly cast the notebook aside and said, 'I can't interview you. All I'm doing is sitting here and thinking how much I'd like to fuck you.' She said, 'Well, why don't you, you silly boy?' A splendid lady.

But, to the cruise. The food aboard the *Royal Viking Sky* was pretty good and there was masses of it too, which you could order and get at any time of night or day. The Americans on board ate like pigs and all had horribly fat arses. The only exceptions were a delightful grandmother accompanied by three grand-daughters, one of whom was and is one of the most nourishing girls I've met for years. But that's another story. The only really bad night on the ship was the night I discovered the casino. There was a lady croupier from Milton Keynes who kept turning her 14s into 21s with monotonous regularity and it hurt. There was also a croupier from Southport and a barman from Bournemouth. My favourite barman was a Swiss-German called Rikki and in spite of the ghastly combination of Swiss and German he turned out to be a pretty good chap. I don't remember the first night on board because I was pretty smashed, but the next day, first man in the bar at 10 a.m., he looked at me and said, rather casually, 'The usual sir?' and proceeded to pour me a vodka, lime, ice and soda.

What happened the first night? Most of the people aboard were surprisingly un-drinky and I fear I stood out like some kind of sore thumb. There's not a lot to do on a ship except drink unless you happen to be into deck quoits or jogging and I'm not. It struck me that all you need on a cruise is a friend of the opposite sex – if you happen to be heterosexual – and a good barman who pours whoppers like Rikki did. You wouldn't want to look at a fjord on your own and all those wretched rocks need company. I didn't go on any of the shore excursions although I had a pleasant wander around Bergen one morning and saw a superb tall ship. A drink in that town I was told costs £3.50. No wonder the Vikings came here and no wonder the suicide rate in Scandinavia is so high.

There was only one suicide lacking that would have made the cruise perfection. Instead of throwing herself and her notebook at almost every man in sight because of her insecurity, the girl should have thrown herself overboard. Six days without buying a round! I ask you. Even Norman buys me a drink once a week in the Coach, Richard Ingrams smiles at me once a week so I suppose that my cup runneth over anyway. Yes, it's good to be home again. Last night I took my doctor from the Middlesex out for a drink and she told me I'd end up with a leg off – the one I try to get over – if I don't stop smoking. It's been a wonderful life – so far.

7 July, 1984

Jeffrey Bernard

TRAVELLER'S TALE

Seville was very much all right. Cordoba with its wonderful mosque was fractionally marred by the presence of a party of American lesbians in my hotel but I shall never forget that amazing building and the surrounding gardens. Further up the river that runs through Andalucia, the Guadalquivir, I came to Andujar, where I was a little disappointed. I was disappointed because as so often in the past I had taken too much notice of what I had read in a travel book. Never again. Travel books I now think are like cookery books and recipes. Lovely bedtime reading but when you've read them you should go your own way. I had read that Andujar was 'exquisite', 'full of flowers', so much so that they grew in the streets and 'dripped from window-boxes'. Ah well, the imagination can rage on a damp, cold day in London. Anyway, Spain always beckons and, of course, Andujar is pretty nice really. So many people have got Spain all wrong. They rush to the various Costas, pack themselves on to the beaches, get sick on brandy and survive on egg and chips and peel hideously. Away from those beaches there's a different country. The landscape along the Guadalquivir valley is stunning, rich and fertile and the food it produces is dazzling in a way. I can stand and stare at the heaps of it in those marvellous markets in Spain that combine every sort of food and to sit under an orange tree eating tapas and sipping wine by the Alcazar gardens has got feeding flies with Ambre Solaire on a beach outside Malaga well beaten.

One thing the guide books did have right was that the rather dilapidated quarter of Trania is the right place to stay in Seville. It is lively, cheap and happily far beneath the noses of Hilton-minded people. It reminded me of the backwaters of the Ramblas in Barcelona. I spent most of my first afternoon there sitting by the river with some wine and eating delicious grilled sardines which a man kept giving me while they prepared the dinner proper. The fact that he looked vaguely like Norman couldn't even spoil it. That night I stayed in a nearby hotel which charged £4 a night. So it didn't have its own bathroom but it was fine for a couple of days. The next day I made the startling discovery that the coffee was so

strong I'd have to stick to wine or the beer which is a sort of yellow mineral water. Still, it's cold. And I soon again got to quite like the wine as
cold as they serve it. Why are so many things okay abroad which aren't at
home? I wouldn't dream of drinking chilled red wine here. Neither would
I think of scoffing lumps of dry bread without butter, eating cold omelettes and having simple oil and vinegar poured over a salad, as opposed
to something more contrived with Dijon etc. I relished all that standing
at a bar. It seemed right and civilised. Perhaps I was cut out for the simple
life which is why I've never wanted a trip to Gstaad. But I can see it now
that farmhouse of mine on the banks of the Guadalquivir. A garden with
lots of flowers, orange and olive trees, meals outside, a few chickens, a
lovely white Spanish horse and the odd day at the local bull fights. Yes, I
know. I would go stark, raving mad after a month. I did, for a start, miss
hearing the English language quite soon but it's probably quite good for
one to shut up almost completely for a few days. Maybe I wouldn't like
the Spanish so much if I could understand what they were saying. On the
way back and stopping over in Cordoba again I heard the lesbians still
yacking away. I knew it was time to come home and leave the strumming
guitars for the ring of Norman's till.

4 May, 1985

John Ralston Saul

THE BEACH EMBRACE

St Tropez

It has become increasingly common over the last decade to see women on
beaches wearing a single postage stamp, which used to be limited to the
professional stage under the name of the 'G-string'. Sometimes they wear
nothing at all. As for men, most of them conceal their parts within what
is called a bikini, which consists of one half the material needed to make
a narrow tie, narrow ties being in fashion this year. Some do not hide at
all.

All of this, on the basis of what I see, is to be applauded in the name of
gravity (Newton's law of) if nothing else. The average human, when fully
dressed, is able to disguise a good part of his or her physical imperfec-
tions, but once the protective layers are peeled off the flaws appear. The

effect of an old-fashioned bathing suit, which covered much of the body
with one layer of constricting material, was to emphasise these flaws;
elastic and stretch nylon have a cruel way of drawing attention to protruding stomachs, cellulite, flabby backsides and sagging or uneven
breasts. What this means is that the more perfect the body, the better it
looks covered up.

Today's flowering of visible flesh on the beach has created the sort of
unexpected myth that belongs in the category of the big joke. Nudity, it
would seem, is the result of increased blindness and not of a relaxation in
the details of daily prudery. Put another way, no matter what is standing
before you on the sand, you must act as if the world is as it has always
been.

A perfect example of this is the social embrace. All across the beaches
of Europe in the months of July and August, from Marbella with its rich
Moors reconquering Spain, through the cheap-holiday-makers of the
various Costas to out beyond St Tropez where the golden sands of Tahiti
and Pampelonne are covered by the flaccid glitz of Parisians who can't
swim but lie in neat, tight rows, and on past the sweating, dusty
suburbanites at St Maxime and the swollen-bellied property developers
at Cannes and Nice to the neat little social packages of Italians eating and
smoking and talking on the sand north and south of Porto Ercole, and
further south the large-breasted, black-haired, black-suited Mommas on
the other side of Rome . . . on and on through the Greek islands covered
by ephemeral Vikings with their sturdier, interesting women or by
assorted flocks of homosexuals or lesbians, each dominating their rocks
. . . everywhere, everywhere you will find people greeting each other
with the standard social embraces, as if they were arriving at a Paris dinner or an opera in Milan: two kisses for the middle classes and above;
three for the lower-middle; four for the working class. All of this, however, is complicated by the risk of direct skin contact.

A greeting, which in town usually involves a hug and some show of
affection, is suddenly transformed into a spectacle of tortured acrobatics.
Last week, on a secluded beach, I saw men and women approach each
other with a smile of friendship. Their eyes met; in fact, their eyes locked
as if they were trying to stare each other down. To allow the gaze to wander would have been lewd. The bodies halted at a distance one from the
other that varied anywhere between 50 centimetres and one metre. Both
sets of feet were spread to the side in search of greater balance. Backsides
were arched to the rear to avoid any contact of pubic hair. If both
embraces were integrally nude, this arch risked throwing out the spine.
The shoulders were then squared and stretched back to avoid loose and
uncontrollable breasts from touching male pectorals, firm or slack.

Finally, the necks were bent forward into a hunchbacked position and each body curved towards the other from the point of the unmoving toes until a pair of lips touched a cheek.

At such an angle, the chances of actually falling over are high and when this happens, the result is a tangle of naked, horizontal bodies writhing with a confusion which can be mistaken for the gropings of nascent sex. The female often prevents such a collapse by raising her right hand and placing it on the male's left shoulder. After two, three, or four kisses, the eyes dart away towards the sea or the umbrellas and a non-related comment is made – 'Calm day' or 'Il y a du monde, hein.'

Equally peculiar is the beach handshake between two naked men, during which invisible briefcases suddenly seem to dangle from the free hands. Yet even this pales before the kissing of hands, often witnessed in the Parc de Saint-Tropez or on Cap Ferrat or at Porto Ercole. Loyalty to the *ancien régime* involves a panoply of dangers. For example, if the male is short with a noble nose and the woman is older and plump, the odds are high that his nostrils will pass between her breasts. On the other hand, if the man is tall and the woman raising her hand is short – keeping in mind that the eyes are locked into a self-limiting stare and not paying attention to what the rest of the body is doing – she may well grasp the wrong thing.

All myths, like this one, pretend to be true. Some will inspire armies to defend their truth. Others are more transparent. These people on the sand, for example, are clearly not dining in Milan. The proof: no one in Milan wears Estée Lauder sun block after sunset. What's more, they clearly are semi- or entirely nude. Besides, they do know each other and there does not seem to be anything wrong with their sight.

To attack a real myth is gratuitous and facile, but it is impossible to avoid the reflection here that modern man is missing an opportunity to stare reality in the face. If he doesn't want to stare, then he ought to limit himself and herself to the distant Anglo-Saxon greeting that involves vague nodding from distances of two to three yards. But why not deal with reality? Why not define a code for the ethics of beach greeting?

For example, why shouldn't you take a good look at what you are about to embrace? You are going to look later anyway, when the other person isn't. And why not comment on what you see? In town you are expected to say, 'I love that dress', or 'You look a bit tired'. Why not say, 'What nice nipples' or 'You're about ready for a lift.'

Here also is an opportunity to use the distance between facing toes as a measure of friendship. For example, the touching of nipples to pectorals might mean friendship; the pressing of breasts against chest, good friends. And a hug could be limited to very good friends. The implication

of friendship, after all, is that had circumstances been different, you
might have gone to bed together. You may already have done so and you
certainly wouldn't be averse to the idea. That would be an insult; which
perhaps explains the hesitancy of all those people standing around awk-
wardly on the sand searching for a gesture which falls neatly between
open suggestion and unnecessary indifference.

17 August, 1985

Dhiren Bhagat

WAITING FOR THE BOMBS

Cannes

At the Colombe d'Or in St Paul-de-Vence my copy of Patrick Howarth's
book caught the head waiter's eye. 'The Riviera that was Ours' – he
repeated the book's title with deliberate incredulity – 'cheeky!' (But he
seemed genuinely taken by the reproduction of Churchill's 'Riviera
Landscape' on the front cover, less so by the photograph on the back
cover, Queen Victoria taking tea at Nice in 1895, attended by two Indian
servants.)

Cheeky, but true. The Riviera was a British invention, in time became
almost a British possession. In 1765 Smollett began the fashion of bathing in the sea in Nice; by 1822 the Revd Lewis Way had constructed the
Promenade des Anglais and opened an Anglican church in the town. In
1835 the Lord Chancellor, Henry, Lord Brougham, unable to proceed to
Nice on account of an epidemic of cholera that had broken out in
Provence, bought a plot of land in the fishing village of Cannes; four
years later the Italianate Villa Eleonore was completed. Brougham's
friendship with King Louis Philippe – who entertained the Englishman
with his imitations of Danton and Robespierre – proved beneficial to the
people of Cannes. He made a personal application to the King for the
funds to build a harbour and 995,000 francs were promptly made available. (The annual budget of the municipality of Cannes was 29,600
francs.) The gardens of the Villa Eleonore were laid out with turf brought
by boat from England and in time Brougham's gardener, a Suffolk man
called John Taylor, found himself a new profession by finding properties
for Brougham's English friends. (His descendant, Mrs Montagu, carries
on the estate agency John Taylor's in the Place de la Croisette.)

It was a neighbour of Brougham's who worried about the spiritual welfare of the English in Cannes. In 1847 Thomas Woolfield built a chapel in
his grounds. Holding a Protestant service was not as easy. On the very
first attempt, as the minister called out the numbers of the hymns the
local commissioner of police aided by two gendarmes dissolved the
'unlawful assembly'. After a successful appeal Woolfield was able to hold
English services in his drawing room every Sunday afternoon.

'If only there was an English church at Cannes we should not run away
from you,' Woolfield recorded the English visitors as saying. In 1885 he
therefore petitioned the French government for permission to build an
Anglican church and later that year the corner stone of Christ Church,
Cannes was laid. By the end of the century there were three other
Anglican churches, St George's, St Paul's and Holy Trinity and weekly
Bible classes were held in Cannes for the benefit of English domestic
servants.

To find the English, I decided, I would have to go to their churches.
Easier said than done. Christ Church and St Paul's, I was informed, have
ceased to exist; St George's was recently sold to the Catholics (though an
ecumenical service is held every Christmas in which the Anglicans participate). Holy Trinity (1884) survives, but it was pulled down in the early
Seventies and rebuilt in raw brown concrete as part of a block of flats
with underground parking.

The Revd Ian Watts and his wife Dorothy live in one of the flats. It was
just past eight in the evening when I rang their bell and they were in the
middle of their spaghetti bolognaise which they cheerfully invited me to
share. We sat at the refectory table. 'Pot luck. It's always open house, it's
an open church . . . there are always lots of things happening here, a sort
of community centre which is nice but the community aspect is not separate from the church . . . '

During the chaplaincy of his predecessor, it had been a small congregation, no more than 15 on a Sunday. But things had picked up of late; last
Sunday there had been 142 in the congregation and 'most of them are regulars'. Fifteen years ago it was an old congregation, now the old ones don't
know anyone. No, no yachting types, 'it's difficult to pull in the boat
people', but lots of young executives and people who've retired young.
'Even the older people here are extremely active and agile . . . Lady Young
is 93 and planning a holiday to Pakistan.'

After supper I went down to the vestry with a calculator and examined
the Marriage and Death records. The Register of Burials begins with an
entry for 17 April 1878; for the next five years the average age at which
the English expatriates died was a mere 42. Things have changed. In the
six years that Revd Watts has been in the job he has performed 88 burials

and the average age for this period works out at over 76. I suppose young executives don't die, they just go on driving their Volvos.

In 1961, IBM decided to move its operations from Paris to La Gaude near Nice. The next year Bill Youdale left his job in Barclays to join them. A few years later the younger brother of his boss at IBM, Pierre Lafitte, decided to create Sophia Antipolis, a landscaped Silicon Valley only miles from Cannes where over 60 international firms are engaged in 'clean' industry. After the library at Holy Trinity on Friday, Bill Youdale drove me through the complex. 'There are about two or three hundred English families here, very intelligent and a good many of them come to church. They've brought a new life to the church.'

A new life perhaps, but as Youdale admits, Cannes is no longer a 'British' town. The French began coming to the Riviera in hordes exactly 50 years ago in 1936, the year the Socialist Front Populaire instituted paid holidays, the Congés Payés. Youdale was at the Lycée Massena in Nice then, his father the manager of Cook's at Monte Carlo. 'Most of them came camping,' he recalls, 'couldn't afford hotels.' In December 1936 the government announced there would be 11 daily trains from Paris to Nice and that for the next four months passengers on certain days would be allowed to travel at half fare. A month later the French air ministry approved the proposal to build an airport at Nice.

Since the war the English have mostly left the coast. They now live in the country on the hill slopes. Money is one reason, gardens another. Besides, the coast towns have become far too crowded and brash. Though themselves repsonsible for starting the trend, the English have never liked the invasion of the Riviera. In 1863 the first trains chugged into Cannes and, as Patrick Howarth tells us, the villa-owning British residents found the prospect 'most unwelcome'.

Of course the trains attracted the brash sort and helped convert the Riviera into a gambling den. In a poem in the *Menton and Monte Carlo News* in1920 Anon complained:

> Once again to Montikarlo comes the awful Profiteera
> With the lurid Maridorta from his Palace in Baisworta.

It was around that time that Katherine Mansfield, in the Riviera searching for a cure for consumption, wrote of the 'continual procession of whores, pimps, governesses in thread gloves – Jews – old, old, hags, ancient men, stiff and greyish, panting as they climb, rich fat capitalists, little girls tricked out to look like babies.'

Some came for the sin, but most for the sun. Teddy Fouracres was born in 1897 in a colonial family ('a hundred years' service to the Empire'). 'Signed up for the first war, was wounded in France, asked them if I could study Hindu or whatever at the School for Oriental Studies, they said sorry, no places for Hindu. Put me in Arabic instead. Served 40 years in the Sudan Political Service. Came here after that. Needed the sun.' I met him at the Hotel Molière in a tiny room he has moved to since his wife died. 'They're throwing me out next week, need rooms for the Film Festival. Lucky I've got a room in the Anglo-American Hospital.' His face was covered with shingles, he could barely see.

Perhaps it's best not to look. There are joggers on the Promenade, in the shops International Arab Vulgarity – pendants, shiny shirts – and on the streets Hush Puppy Casual. The English Bookshop is owned by Australians, the Swan pub – which boasts a darts team – by a Frenchman. The gardens of the Villa Eleonore have been divided into little plots on which 'villas' with names like Mediterranée and Chantazur stand. But Teddy Fouracres still comes to church in a waistcoat.

I suppose they'll soon start making nostalgia movies about the Riviera. I went back to Holy Trinity last Friday for the library (six helpers, two borrowers). The thick-set Mr Watts (also from the Sudan Political Service) took me aside. 'May I have a word with you?' He sat me down. 'After you left that night we began to doubt your credentials. I don't mean it badly, but we rang the editor of *The Spectator* in London to check if you're really from *The Spectator*. You see, only three and a half hours before you came round a French policeman was over warning us that someone would very likely come round asking us questions about the British community. Just the questions you asked. You see, it's the Cannes Film Festival next week and it's that and the Olympics, there'll be three thousand journalists in Cannes . . . They fear a terrorist attack on the British community . . .'

'So you mean all the time I was in the vestry looking at the Burial register you thought I might be a terrorist . . . ' 'We thought, maybe, maybe he's looking for a place to plant a bomb.'

10 May, 1986

P. J. Kavanagh

KISS OF BABEL

Years ago, climbing the marble steps of the Acropolis, a companion raised his camera to his eye and when the Parthenon came into view he snapped it, before, as it were, he had seen it. This seemed to me the placing of a barrier between himself and experience.

Now, after a drive across Europe to Italy, and back again, when I try to make sense of the expensive pile of impressions slurping about, I wonder if that is all that our minds are capable of accumulating when we travel – unrelated snapshots. Why, for instance, when I examine the pile, is the first image that of a petrol-pump attendant outside Como taking a lighted cigarette out of his mouth and resting it on top of the petrol-pump while he filled us up? And in France there was a man in a quiet midday bar in the Champagne district who was drinking beer through his nose. He had a tube attached to it by tape.

Surely I can do better than that . . . Well, I am always struck by the visual good-taste of the Italians. Santa Maria del Carmine in Florence is being restored, and is lined inside with the neatest possible wooden boarding, top to bottom, a house within a house. The noble Masaccio frescoes are being cleaned there, and the scaffolding is painted matt-black, its links painted gold, very beautiful and appropriate to the beauty of the frescoes. (Incidentally in Florence we visited the library of the British Institute, a haven of peace, with tables poised above the Arno; recommended.)

Perhaps the uneasiness at the discontinuous nature of the impressions, the inability to make them a whole, comes from being English, for there is no doubt that England – Britain – is more different from countries on the Continent than they are from each other. Do people abroad enjoy themselves more, know better how to live? Impossible to be sure because most travellers have lost the use of their ears. I have passable French, bazaar Italian, bazaar Spanish (the last two sometimes become confused with each other, which makes them bizarre) so I cannot hear whether the groups animatedly talking are happy or not, interesting or not. I am cut off, reduced to my eyes only. But in Mantua, the square of what the guide books call, deliciously, the herb market (*herb* market!) is filled at evening with crowds of young people grouped closely together, talking, some astride motorbikes or bicycles, some not, drinking (an occasional ice-cream to be seen), just talking, enjoying the company of each other, and the noise is of an enormous open-air cocktail-party in the arcaded thirteenth-century square.

George d'Almeida, an American painter who lives all the year round in the Tuscan hills, is amazed at people's eagerness to travel: 'I'm blown out of my mind just by crossing this valley!' The suggestion is that there are two sorts of people, those who go seeking impressions, and those, George and I among them, who have to stay long in a place before they can really see it, before, in Blake's words, a tree ceases to be 'a green thing in the way'.

George turns himself round and round in his patch. With the aid of old military maps, and frequent reconnaisances, he has found a way of walking into Siena, 20 miles away, 'without setting foot on asphalt'. On the walk he hardly saw a soul, an indication of the state of Tuscan agriculture. Recently in Chianti the beautiful terraces were bulldozed and intensive grape-planting was encouraged. Now many vineyards are neglected and it is an offence even to plant a vine. The reason for this confusion, apparently, is the word, darkly muttered, 'Brussels!' George plans a similar walk north, to Florence, and we try a stretch, bombarded by butterflies the size of wrens. The neglected places are becoming paradisal for wildlife.

He reminds me about the Portuguese poet, Fernando Pessoa, who discovered himself suddenly writing poems in a different voice, so he gave this new poet a different name: then came a third voice, then a fourth; four poets in one. Perhaps this is the way to put scattered impressions in order, by allotting them to different selves: urban-ironic; rural-pathetic; sophisticatedly innocent; wistfully autumnal. None of us is any of these things all the time. I shall read Pessoa, all four of him, irritated that it will have to be in English.

13 September, 1986

Barry Humphries

DIARY

We climbed Mount Epameo, the volcano which dominates – which I suppose really is – Ischia. To 'climb' it with two children means a 40-minute taxi trip and then donkey rides to the summit. The volcano's topmost vent is now stopped by a 'cork' of pumice fashioned rather like a fanciful Gaudi turret. The caves and tunnels which perforate this strange eyrie once accommodated monks and hermits but now house a small hotel with a terrace, affording sublime views of the whole island. We set out on this 'climb' a bit too late in the day, however; I wanted to see the famous 'green moment' just after sunset, when everything, presumably, turns green. We were also keenly anticipating the 'hunter's rabbit', an Ischian speciality which we were assured by our hotel concierge would be abundantly available at the summit restaurant. However, dusk was gathering fast as we mounted our donkeys and tackled the last precipitous path to the top. It was very beautiful up there, even if what I supposed to be white orchids nestling in the boscage turned out to be broken polystyrene cups. 'It isn't green every night,' the waiter said to me (in German) when we finally arrived at the restaurant and gazed out at the grubby horizon. There were signs saying: 'Deutsche Bier' and 'Probien Sie Unsere Schinken' and the management furnished us with blankets against the nippy updraught. The rabbit was 'off' that night as well, but we had a fortifying 'red moment' eating *spaghetti a pomodoro* on the terrace in the dark on top of a volcano. 'Is that all there is?' said my jaded son Oscar.

22 August, 1987

3 EASTERN EUROPE

Cyril Ray

MOSCOW NIGHT OUT

Nowadays, as the tourists bustle hither and back, under the kindly eye of Mr Khrushchev, when people say, 'But didn't you actually *live* in Moscow, Ray?' I reply, 'Ah, but that was in *Stalin's* time,' and try to give the impression, without actually lying, of long sufferings, silently borne. All I really suffered was a sort of bang-your-head-against-a-feather-wall neurosis that was born on my first night out in Moscow, seven winters ago.

I had just arrived, the only British correspondent in the city, except for the *Daily Worker* man, but there were three or four Americans, all married to Russian girls and tied, therefore, to the Soviet Union, for in those days there was no getting exit visas for their wives. It was one of these Americans, Genry (there is no letter 'h' in the Russian alphabet, and we called him what the Russians called him), who asked me to a party some four days after my arrival. So far, I had spent the evenings in my hotel, composing a brilliant first despatch, describing my journey from Leningrad in a train old-fashioned enough to have been the one that Anna Karenina had flung herself under – a despatch that still lies, as far as I know, in the Moscow censor's pending tray. In triplicate. After four evenings in the Metropole Hotel, it was high time that I went to a party, and I walked blithely out into the icy, glittering cold of Theatre Square to pick up a taxi.

Unsure of my few words of Russian, and my accent, I showed the driver Genry's address written down by Genry himself, in Russian characters. The driver nodded comprehension, and we swung past the Bolshoi Theatre, out of the clean, dry centre of the city, which is always kept clear of snow, into the narrow, snowy streets where people live.

The taxi pulled up. I stepped out into the snow, paid my fare and watched the taxi drive off into the darkness. I put on my fur gloves again, against the cold; looked at the block of flats we had stopped at; looked up at the name on the wall – it was the wrong building and the wrong street. For all I knew, it was quite the wrong part of Moscow. (I got used, eventually, to the fact that Moscow taxi-drivers never knew the way to anywhere except the most prominent public buildings and – true peasants –

would never admit their ignorance. In those security-mad days there was no guide-book to the city and no town plan, any more than there was a telephone directory.)

There wasn't a soul in sight; it was bitterly cold; all was hushed under the snow. I was lost in a strange and slightly hostile city, where I couldn't speak the language, where Western Europeans were almost unknown, and where any ordinary citizen would regard me with puzzlement heavily laced with suspicion. So I heaved a typically English sigh of relief as a uniformed policeman came round the corner, for to my English eyes nothing could have been more reassuring – even if he did wear a pistol at his belt. Up I went to him, a trusting smile on my face, and my piece of paper in my hand: where was this street I was looking for, please? He looked at me, and he looked at the piece of paper, and he looked at me again, and he said, 'Documenti.' Where were my papers?

What a silly question. I had no *documenti*, and for a perfectly good reason. In those days, when you arrived in Moscow, you gave up your passport whilst they made out a foreigner's residence permit for you. So far, they had my passport, but had not yet got around to issuing the permit. As a foreign journalist, I should have had a press card, too. I had applied for it on arrival, had rung up for it daily, and it still hadn't turned up. So I hadn't a press card, and I hadn't a residence permit, and I hadn't a passport, and it wasn't my fault: Soviet officialdom takes its time. And how could I explain this to a stony-faced policeman when I didn't know more than a couple of words of his language?

I explained it all in English and I explained it all in French. I mimed the party I was bound for. And all the policeman did was to put a whistle to his lips and blow a piercing blast to summon up a comrade – not to help in the language difficulty, but so that the two of them could escort me to the nearest police station. I stand five foot two and a bit in my socks, and one policeman would have been enough, even without his pistol, but I was marched off, between the two beefy, armed bobbies, to the station, where one watched me and the other telephoned for a security officer.

One uniformed security policeman stood guard while two plain-clothes men questioned me, across a table with a telephone between us. They would let me get as far as picking up the receiver – after all, I could clear it up in five minutes if only I could speak to the Embassy or to Genry – but then they would smile and say 'Nyet' and take it out of my hand and put it back on its rest. Suspects, according to their book, were not allowed access to the telephone. Not that they were able to interrogate me; nobody had arranged for an official who could speak English or French. If the rules said that a suspect should first be questioned by an officer of such-and-such a rank, and then by such-and-such – that was the way it was done. If the suspect couldn't understand the questions, and the officer couldn't understand the suspect – *nitchevo*.

So they telephoned the next highest plain-clothes man, and this was one who didn't smile as he took the telephone away. He frowned as I pointed to the hours that had slid around the face of my watch; scowled when I pantomimed my story that a friend was awaiting me with drinks (a lift of my elbow and a gurgling noise); that there would be girls (my hands made curves in the air); and that there might be dancing (a Chaplinesque shuffle). This was a man who refused my proffered cigarettes and immediately took out one of his own; waved away my lighter and struck his own match. Till now it had been exasperating, but somehow funny. Now it began to look disagreeable. I had been held incommunicado for five hours or so; the new interrogator was obviously of high rank and equally obviously hostile.

Perhaps, in the cold-war atmosphere of the time (there was a hot war raging in Korea), it was understandable that my captors – as I had begun to think of them – wouldn't telephone the British Embassy on my behalf. A spy-mad bureaucrat would say to himself, 'Pah! His accomplices!' The *Daily Worker* man had, in fact, just published a pamphlet about the spy-ring at the Embassy. But why didn't they ring Genry, I thought, who could assure them that I hadn't just been dropped by parachute to write rude words on the Kremlin wall?

Not until the next day did I realise that while the men facing me had been telephoning their superiors a man in another room had been putting in a lot of work on Genry's number. Long after my policemen had at last got through to a Kremlin official senior enough to say that I could be let loose with a warning, Genry was told by his Russian cook that his telephone had rung three times that night, between eight o'clock and one in the morning, and that three times there had been a typically Russian conversation:

'Who are you?' asked the policeman.

'Who are *you*?' asked the cook.

'Never you mind who *I* am,' said the policeman: 'who are *you*?'

'Don't be impudent,' said the cook: 'if you've rung this number, you know who *we* are. I want to know who *you* are.'

'Impudent yourself,' said the policeman: 'who *are* you?'

'What sauce!' said the cook, and banged down the receiver.

Muscovites had got into the habit of being careful, in Stalin's time, and when Genry's cook told him, next day, about the three mysterious telephone calls she said triumphantly, 'They didn't get anything out of *me*: I never told 'em nothing.'

10 January, 1958

J. B. S. Haldane

GUIDE FOR TRAVELLERS

SIR, – General Hilton has, apparently, found it difficult to escape the attentions of secret police in Eastern Europe. I have found the following technique adequate in several countries. Mount a tram, noting that no one mounts with you. Get off where no following vehicle is in sight. Repeat the process several times. Unless the secret police have cloaks of darkness, the method is effective. – Yours faithfully, J. B. S. HALDANE.

University College, London, Department of Biometry, Gower Street, W.C.1.

14 December, 1951

John Betjeman

CITY AND SUBURBAN

Are you going to Albania for your summer holidays this year? Though my passport entitles me to go to all countries in Europe, including the USSR, it does not apparently include Albania. The A-K part of my telephone directory is 1949 and mentions an Albanian Consul-General on Finsbury pavement. Alas, he has disappeared. Why did he go? Is he back in Albania or has he joined King Zog? (Forgive my bringing politics into this travel talk.) I telephoned to the Foreign Office and said I wanted to go to Albania, and a lady there told me shortly and definitely that we had no diplomatic relations with that country. I asked the Passport Office for its Albanian section, and a very charming lady told me I should have to apply for a visa through the Albanian Embassy in Paris. She did not know what had become of the Albanian Consul-General. Thomas Cook and Son told me they could book me to Kotor in Yugoslavia or to Brindisi, but they knew of no boats crossing to Albania. So now I shall never know whether there are tramcars in Durazzo nor whether there is electric light in the capital, called Tirana, nor what Orthodox monasteries still have monks, mosaics and frescoes among those mysterious mountains. I shall never know unless, like Waring, I give you all the slip. Perhaps Strix would like to visit Albania?

17 May, 1957

Tim Garton Ash

ALBANIA'S THEATRE OF THE ABSURD

Tirana

Albania is the longest-running farce in the Western World. Since Edward Lear visited it in 1851, the country has been touched with nonsense. Ten years ago Albanians would tell you that the population of their tiny land was 702 million (the other 700 million being Chinese). Now that this 'eternal' friendship has ended in tears, China's righteously indignant Balkan protégée seems set on resuming her old ways. These are the ways of Stalinism. The *reductio ad absurdum* of Stalinism – Stalinism as opera bouffe – continues after a short intermission.

All the old familiars are here. The cult of the personality as well parodied in the treatment of Enver Hoxha (pronounced Hodger, and not to be confused with his rival of the nineteen-forties, the unspeakable Xoxe). The ubiquitous, larger than life posters of Comrade Enver must be caricatures of the curious icons which most socialist countries seem to produce of their leaders. Dressed in a slightly shabby and very old-fashioned three piece suit, and bearing a tired bouquet of cut flowers from an invisible admirer, he looks for all the world like a character from a Twenties newsreel – forty years on.

Alongside 'democratic centralism' and the 'dictatorship of the proletariat' we find another totalitarian favourite, the 'election'. At the October 1974 election, we are told, 1,248,528 persons out of an electorate of 1,248,530 voted for the Albanian Democratic Front. There were two spoiled ballot papers.

Rampant bureaucracy, too, is amusingly represented by the police in the capital Tirana (another name from Edward Lear). The boulevards around the main square are wider than Haussmann's. There is no traffic in the square. But there are four traffic policemen. They occupy themselves by controlling the pedestrians, and above all the tourists; or sometimes the single tourist. More doubtful is the taste of the official party newspaper in its treatment of bureaucracy. When asked why the Ministry of Agriculture continually requested useless information, after a slight hesitation (reports *Zeri i Popullit*) an old specialist said, 'If one abolished unnecessary forms, many employees of the ministry would be idle'. This may be an attempt to introduce a Brechtian 'alienation effect' into the situation – by telling the truth. I personally still prefer the old-fashioned iron curtain theatre, and the traditional suspension of disbelief.

The metaphors used to describe the classical Stalinist purges are startling. The most recent of these occurred in 1974–5. Several of Hoxha's closest associates were the victims: 'The Party and the Dictatorship of the Proletariat hit them with an iron fist,' explained Hoxha, 'and threw them into the dustbin'. Mehmet Shehu, a surviving henchman, outdid his leader. The 'gang' had been 'cleaned up', he declared, with an 'iron broom'.

Whom do such euphemisms deceive? Certainly not, you might think, the foreign visitor. You would be wrong. Rather, they support an audience's willing suspension of disbelief – its wilful self-deception. This audience, too, is in the best Stalinist tradition. Your fellow traveller here is almost certainly a fellow-traveller. And, this being Albania, the chances are that he will be a caricature. A Dane joined me as I looked out across the Albano-Yugoslav border which bisects Lake Ohrid. He pointed out that the water was much bluer this side. This, he adds, was because over here we were building socialism. I looked for a hint of irony in his blue eyes, but found only bovine earnestness. I muttered something about the Yugoslav waters being muddied by revisionism. We joined an Albanian girl who had just completed a month's compulsory labour, building a railway to the port of Vlora. 'Vlora? Ah yes,' enthused the leader of a Belgian 'friendship group', 'it's very beautiful there!' (Siberia? Ah yes, the *grandeur* of the steppe.)

These 'friendship groups' practise self-censorship by day and unison singing by night. Some of these songs are in praise of Stalin. One evening a Scandinavian journalist, full of whisky and indignation at these goings-on, blew his cover by rising unsteadily to his feet and declaiming – albeit indistinctly and in Serbo-Croat – a long poem in praise of Tito. He was severely admonished: such an offence would normally be punished by instant expulsion. However, it is typical of Albania that he quite redeemed himself the next morning by delivering an equally long encomium to the fifteenth-century national hero, Skanderbeg.

These fellow-travellers are not old men in search of their God. They are a new generation, freshly minted from the universities of Western Europe. Particularly in evidence are students from the two nations which occupied the country during the last war. The Italians are to be seen on the terrace of the 'A' class Hotel Adriatika – built by order of Mussolini – where they sit drinking away, each evening, an Albanian's average weekly wage, and singing 'Liberta! Liberta!' But of whose liberty do they sing? The (West) Germans are to be found grouped around a guitarist on the beach. Here, as the sun sets behind the mountains, they sing of the *Volk* and the *Heimat*: 'Our love we give to the party/to the fatherland, life' is their refrain. Nationalism in West Germany equals Fascism. Nationalism in Albania/Russia/China/ equals Socialism. It is a symptom of the thirty years old German crisis of national identity that these highly educated Germans – most of them under thirty – have to come to Albania to find their fatherland. Indeed both groups testify to the problems of historical identification which seem to afflict the youth of all the Axis powers. Some, of course, have found worse solutions than adopting Albanian nationality.

By contrast Britain sends only the odd charabanc of misfits. One sample reveals a clutch of teachers; a few representatives of the Communist Party of Great Britain; an ex-Catholic pacifist who cleaves to Albania for its militant atheism; and a former policeman called Mr Godsave who believes that Hitler 'had the right idea' because the Jews in Palestine 'didn't play the game', and who is here to 'get to know the enemy'. (No, there are no Jews in Albania. We mean the *communists* of course.) Yet in its way, in its diversity and mutual tolerance, even this group is a better advertisement for liberal democracy than its fellow travellers. At least, to a man, it derides the humbug which the postgraduate student of Soviet politics from Frankfurt swallows so earnestly.

But only the euphemisms are funny, and there are no euphemisms for the labour camps in the North East of the country. Nor is the frenetic pursuit of forced industrialisation for the defence of Socialism so entertaining. Nor the violent substitution of a crude blend of Marxism-Leninism, Hoxha worship, and nationalism for the protestant, Catholic, and Islamic faiths. Nor the desiccation of a rich folk culture. Nor the crippling of intellectual life. The similarities with the Soviet past are uncanny, and perhaps they give cause for hope – that this people, too, has been drugged rather than lobotomised.

But anyone who can think for himself is given few opportunities to recognise these parallels. The past has been rewritten to serve the present. A student of English at the university showed me his textbook on English history. Of the Second World War he reads that, 'From its very beginning the English government did not take the war against Germany very seriously . . . the Anglo-French and American imperialists aimed at channelling Hitler's aggression towards the East. But the correct policy followed by Stalin turned all the diabolic plans of the imperialist warmongers to ashes.' So he knows that Stalin's policy was 'correct', but not what it was. He had not heard of the Hitler-Stalin pact. He had heard, vaguely, of the Zogist (monarchist) *Legalitet* resistance movement, and even of a Reactionary called Amery – but they have been consigned to the dustbin of history. Soviet help in foiling Anglo-American 'destabilisation' attempts in the early Fifties is acknowledged although the role of Kim Philby in tipping off the Russians is not. In accounting for the 1960/1 split with Russia, Khrushchev is the great bogey-man. He is the subject of authorised 'jokes'. A teacher told me the one about the Soviet leader saying in 1958 that the Soviet Union consumed more grain in a day than Albania could produce in a year ('But we have proved him wrong,' my informant added). What Khrushchev had said about Stalinism he did not know. This is obviously too close to home and not in his curriculum.

Russia today is again seeking Albania's hand – and her strategically important port of Vlora. At the moment she has not responded favourably to these advances – although Stalin himself has set a precedent for allying with yesterday's devil. If she ever did, then Brezhnev would find himself embracing the Ghost of Times Past. This would be a suitably improbable next act. And there is an obvious candidate for the part of Soviet ambassador – the country's erstwhile saviour, Kim Philby.

30 September, 1978

Alistair Horne

A FEW DAYS IN DRESDEN

I always wanted to visit Dresden to see the fabulous treasures which that remarkable baroque monarch, Augustus the Strong, had collected there (plus 354 bastards), much of which has miraculously survived the day of shame of February 1945. Last month, accompanying two West Germans, who were to provide some useful counter-points, I set off through the Berlin Wall.

Each time one sees that sinister corral, the Wall still shocks. It is, I am told – with the possible exception of that other monument to man's beastliness, the line of trenches of World War I – about the only creation of the twentieth century that could be seen from another planet. Certainly it is aggressively visible to all incoming aircraft, its minefields and beaten death-zone snaking endlessly into the distance. When I first saw it, East German industry had triumphantly capped it with sewer-piping just to prevent any would-be escaper, who actually reached it, from getting his hands over. With typical West Berlin humour, wooden towers had been erected for tourists to stare back in derision at the 'Vopos' in their machine gun turrets a few yards away across the Wall, and hundreds of rabbits had insouciantly turned the death strip into a *Watership Down*. Now the 'Vopos' have been replaced by robot guns (a 22-year-old escapee was shot down shortly before we crossed over), and even the poor bunnies seem to have been dispatched.

The true face of Communism, of which the Boat People are but another profile, the Wall somehow conditions all entry into the DDR. It makes it at once more ominous and trying to visit than any other East Bloc country I know. From observation, it seems consciously to be made even more irksome for West Germans to enter than for lesser breeds; despite the fact that the millions of hard-currency DMs they bring in at an absurd rate of exchange must virtually keep the DDR's rickety economy afloat. First of all, four pages of bossy instructions dictate what you may *not* import: 'calendars, almanacs and diaries, stamps and stamp catalogues'; records ('unless works of the cultural heritage', whatever that may mean); newspapers ('unless on the postal list of the DDR'); books 'whose content is aimed against the preservation of peace'; children's toys 'of a military character'; films 'whose content is hostile to the Socialist State' (by some amazing attempt at augury, this also includes *unexposed* film). Meanwhile the copious list of banned exports revealingly covered most foodstuffs and textiles.

So much for the Spirit of Helsinki and *Ostpolitik*. Subserviently we left our *Vogues* and *Country Lifes* in a locker in West Berlin airport. At the frontier we waited an hour (apparently, a very good day), submitting to various checks and form-filling, while a disembodied hand (possibly female) grabbed our passports through a slot in a wooden box. A perfect Le Carré setting, I was thinking when – as we sat in that grim No-Man's-Land – my travelling companion inquired sweetly and with superlative timing: 'tell me, were you ever a spy?' The question being, strangely, not on the declaration form, I expected the alarms to ring and robot guns to start firing at us through that wooden slot. But, mysteriously we were waved through, and into the Socialist paradise.

We stopped first at Potsdam, and *Sans Souci*. The railings were rusting away unchecked, the lawns looked as if they hadn't been mown since the death of Frederick the Great, and birch trees were growing out of the roof of the New Palace. For 45 minutes we queued to get in; allegedly because of a shortage of felt *Pantoffeln* for walking on the parquet, but, more likely, I was to reflect later, because queuing is – apart from skiing – *the* national sport in a country which offers precious few other distractions. At Potsdam, and everywhere else, there are hordes of khaki-clad Russian troops, photographing each other. We note how they and the East German soldiery in *Feldgrau* give each other a wide berth, like rival gangs at school. At Wittenberg alone, we were told that, 'protecting' this town the size of Haywards Heath where Luther nailed up his 95 protests, there were 40,000 Soviet 'allies' – or three times the total British troops in Ulster. Unlike Poland, the Russians make no effort to keep a low profile; here, one has the sense of the conqueror still flaunting himself – 35 years on.

The next shock comes with the first sight of Dresden. It didn't feel good to be English. Even now the traces of that one night of February 1945, when 35,000 were killed, show up worse than one had ever imagined. How little seems to have been restored in 35 years, and how appallingly shoddy is the new! The fire-blackened towers of Augustus's Schloss still gape open at the top, resembling obscene skulls from a cartoon by George Grosz. Our hotel stands at the top of the pride of 'new' Dresden, the Pragerstrasse. No GLC architect could have done worse. Where the old medieval heart of Dresden once stood, rise acres of uniform square blocks with balconies of corrugated plastic stitched on, such as you see on the poorest outskirts of Paris. Down below on a long parvis with checkered squares, broken up by a few undistinguished fountains, drab figures move aimlessly as if motivated by hidden magnets. We rechristened it Lowry Allee. It is infinitely depressing; an encapsulation of the combined horrors of our century – senseless destruction and soulless reconstruction.

The state of unrestored Dresden takes me back to my memories of Berlin and Cologne when I first went to West Germany in the early Fifties; the same gaunt ruins, the same weed-covered empty spaces. And the people: the same sallow faces stamped with undernourishment and overstress; the dung-coloured clothes of inferior material. The sparse traffic, too, belongs to that unreconstructed West Germany of a generation ago; the put-putting tatty two-stroke cars, incrementing a pollution problem obviously gigantic by western standards, and equally tinted in sallow shades of grey to ochre.

Down in the Hotel Neva (note the name) a friendly native points out warningly the closed circuit TV cameras; 'but the rooms aren't bugged!' A big plus-mark; everybody is incredibly friendly – embarrassingly so, considering that the DDR is celebrating its 30th birthday by introducing new laws to impose up to 12 years jail on any citizens passing disparaging information to Westerners, even if no secrets are involved.

Stories had a certain consistency. In a long queue at a miserably provisioned supermarket, shoppers complained loud about the worsening economic crisis and soaring prices. They were queuing for a few dispirited tomatoes, and already resignedly anticipated no fresh vegetables this coming winter. Yet, all agreed that 'at least we're the best off materially of the East Bloc countries.' Looking at the shop windows of Lowry Allee, it was hard to credit. By the absurdly artificial rate of exchange which puts the DDR mark at par with the DM, consumer goods seem to cost roughly the same as in the Federal Republic, though of far inferior quality, while equivalent wages might be perhaps only a quarter as high. What was most missing, then? Why, freedom of course. One Dresdener defined it in words that Ernie Bevin might have used; 'to get in a train and go anywhere you please, not just to Rumania or Bulgaria.' As a young man he had travelled widely (presumably with the *Wehrmacht*); but his children could go nowhere, except Rumania and Bulgaria (and the former, now, presumably only by bicycle).

That night I heard on Leipzig radio a nauseatingly treacly voice sing: '. . . on a Sunday in Avignon, there is all loneliness gone, . . . so come with me to Avignon.' But how? My Dresdener was additionally unlucky; he could not even receive TV from the West, though 80 per cent of the DDR can. A friendly Wittenberger, born under Nazism and grown up in Marxism, told me with glistening eyes how he had lived for each instalment of the West German version of *Upstairs, Downstairs*.

How could this seemingly listless populace ever be sparked into winning all those Olympic medals, all those engineering contracts in the Third World? By endless exhortation, I concluded. Everywhere the slogans and propaganda shout at you. One restaurant displayed a kindergarten-like chart giving each waitress good conduct marks; at another a photo of Rosa Kleb beamed out over the inscription 'This Month's Best Co-worker.' In the museums they never miss the big-bass-drum about the wicked Anglo-Americans blasting Dresden and the culture-loving Russians saving and restoring all those pictures (which, indeed, *have* been superbly restored, as has the partly destroyed Zwinger – one of Europe's baroque marvels). At Meissen a magnificent set of 1740 porcelain bears the 'social' explanation – 'Many had to work hard so that the select few could enjoy pleasure at table.'

As we rattled back over neglected roads to leave the rich and beautiful life, thinking that the TUC should be invited to hold their next annual conference here, my companion remarked glumly 'these aren't Germans – they've partly gone Russian.' And yet, despite the Wall, to the outsider those blood ties still seem awfully strong. One could not help wondering what would happen should any remote reversal in the Heartland ever cause those khaki hordes round Potsdam and Wittenberg to decamp and go home.

Back in Berlin, our car was waved away at Check-Point Charlie; no West German number plates. On to the Heinrich Heine crossing point; car OK, but no British passports. So I am dumped back to cross Check-Point Charlie on foot, feeling uncomfortably like the Spy-who-was-not-coming-in-out-of-the-Cold. A surly 'Vopo' lieutenant growled at me, 'but where's your car? It's written down in your papers.' That was too much; I lost my temper and bellowed back like a true Prussian. To my amazement the Wall parted and I was out. An hour later my companions picked me up, the petrol tank having been searched for an escaping dwarf. They had also found nowhere to change their worthless remaining East Marks; instead of the 1:1 they had paid, they were forced to accept 1:5 in West Berlin. The Wall had exacted one last toll.

18 August, 1979

Frederick French

EASTER IN MOSCOW

Outside the Church of the Nativity of Christ on the Lenin Hills the barricades are up. Hundreds of red-armbanded part-time police line the crush barriers while dozens of grey-uniformed regular police, and an unknown number of the other sort of police, mingle with the crowd.

Arrowhead flames of Easter candles, flickering in the cold spring night, illuminate the small green-and-white church. The midnight procession round the church, the *khrestny khod*, symbolising the search by Mary Magdalene and others for Christ's body in the sepulchre, is soon to begin. A British traveller of a century ago, Sir Donald Mackenzie Wallace, described the crowd at a Moscow Easter mass:

An immense number of people had assembled . . . The crowd was of the most mixed kind. There stood the patient bearded muzhik in his

well-worn sheepskin; the big, burly self-satisfied merchant in his long
black glossy *kaftan*; the noble with fashionable greatcoat and
umbrella; thinly clad old women shivering in the cold, and bright-
eyed young damsels with their warm cloaks drawn closely round
them; old men with long beard, wallet, and pilgrim's staff; and mis-
chievous urchins with faces for the moment preternaturally demure
... All stood patiently waiting for the announcement of the glad
tidings: 'He is Risen!'

A century later, there are no bearded muzhiks, no self-satisfied merchants, no fashionably-dressed nobles, no sheepskins (all exported now),
no *kaftans*, no pilgrims' staffs. There are old women, however – nowadays
properly dressed against the cold. But they do not stand outside – their
place is inside the church, and they testily push their way through the
waiting crowd, apparently resenting its uncommitted curiosity. There
are bright-eyed young 'damsels' also, mostly dressed in woollen bobble
hats, heavy overcoats and Soviet jeans rolled up to the calves to reveal
high boots. There are also very many young men, dressed mainly in
anoraks.

Most of these young men and girls are students from the huge Moscow
State University looming across the road: not believers, just curious
agnostics. A sexy film is being shown at the University as a counter-
attraction but still these students have come to the church for a glimpse
of its rich pageantry. They mingle with the rich assortment of police
without.

Some of the uniformed of the latter, doubtlessly obeying orders, put
themselves about. One experienced policeman (you can tell he has done
this sort of thing before) approaches a group of smoking young men and
says something to them: I catch 'I advise you . . . '. They answer flip-
pantly, not at all cowed. He replies, as casually, 'No, no, simply advice.'
One of the young men insolently flicks away his still-smouldering cigarette.

The police are sauntering up and down the crowded pavement, every
now and then putting a walkie-talkie to mouth or ear. One tough-looking
cop suddenly points very decisively into a group by the barriers at a
young man holding a transistor radio that until a moment ago was blaring forth pop music. The policeman's finger signals, 'Come here.' The
young man, a stout boy with puffy red mouth, hands his radio to a friend
and leaves the group. The policeman takes him by the elbow and leads
him further away, to the outer edge of the pavement, where three policemen have a quiet word with him. Finally they let him rejoin his group,
and he thanks them profusely for being so kind as not to arrest him or

beat him up. The tough cop now puts on the manner of a benevolent village bobby, saying something like, 'That's all right, son.' The stout young man dives back into his group.

I had arrived early, but not early enough either to get a place inside the church before the procession or to get a place against the barriers, which is the best place to view the procession. So I settled for a slightly elevated position on a mound of hard snow by a tree on the outside of the pavement by the church.

A side-door of the church opens. From my vantage, only the top half of the doorway is visible; the icons and banners dip to pass under it, then straighten and float on upright. I can see painted crosses on gilded poles, banners of Christ the Saviour and the Virgin and Child and the tops of icons in curved and wrought covers, silver, gold, covered with phrases and names in old Church Slavonic, but I cannot see the bearded priests in gilded robes, the deacons, the choir or the parishioners.

The procession is supposed to circle the church three times before re-entering the building to celebrate the Resurrection, singing as it goes, but it seems to go round once only and then re-enters the church by a door on the other side. Soon afterwards there is a slow steady stream of smartly dressed youngsters emerging from the church, some still carrying their small red candles bought inside, all of them relaxed and casual. At first this seems proof that the Russian Orthodox Church is no longer attracting mainly old women, when I realise they are all foreigners, probably diplomats' families.

The foreigners having seen part of the Mass in comfort, the believers are now let in. So many of the curious students also press forward to go in that the line of police is breached, and they all surge forward. Some police stand in the entrance pathway behind their colleagues for the purpose of intimidation. In one case the intimidation becomes crude, when they stop two young men and say, 'And where do you think you are going?'; they usher them to the side. But the rest of us pile in shoulder to shoulder, unable to turn. I am lucky, for I have just squeezed in when someone shouts, 'Enough, Kolya!' and Kolya shuts the heavy wooden door behind us. We stand jammed inside. I am about to take off my hat when an old woman snatches it off my head for me.

I edge forward until I can see a little of what is going on. Forests of candles emblazon the church and illuminate numerous icons, some of which are encased in silver or gold. A big picture of Christ on the cross is draped with silver cloth. In orange lights overhead are the words 'Christ is Risen' in Church Slavonic. At the altar the heavily bearded priest is swinging a smoking censer. The church is filled with the cloying smell of burning incense. The choir chants the repetitive litany. In the brief pauses between the chants is heard the quiet crackling of the candles burning in front of the icons. Every now and then the priest intones, 'Christ is Risen' four times, and the believers murmur after him, 'Truly He is Risen,' crossing themselves with the two-fingered, right-to-left Russian Orthodox gesture.

Many are holding the small red candles bought at the back of the church, with pieces of paper acting as a guard against the hot wax dripping onto the hand. Those wishing to buy a candle have to push and fight their way through. On the candle counter stands a coin box with a sign in Russian and English, 'For church restoration.' Some are buying a candle and then passing it forward with whispered instructions as to which icon the candle should be lit at, the candle and instructions being passed on by many people, exactly as money and tickets are passed along in crowded Moscow buses.

Smelly waves of sweat, incense smoke and steam hover over the crowd. The flaming tongues of the big candles in front of the icons crack faintly and sway and give off threads of smoke that drift upwards. I fight my way out. Outside, the green church domes are silhouetted against the moon. The whitewashed walls flicker in the candlelight. I put on my hat. No onlookers are standing outside now. Only uniformed and auxiliary police remain, bored and cold, and a few believers. One man goes up to another and says, 'Christ is Risen.' The other answers, 'Truly He is Risen.' They kiss three times on alternate cheeks. A policeman looks on sceptically.

18 April, 1981

Gavin Stamp

LEARNING FROM LENINGRAD

Leningrad

Behind the old barracks of Tsarskoe Selo, way off the Intourist track, we found what we were looking for: a ruined Neo-Classical church, four-square with four Greek Doric porticoes and a low dome, standing forlorn in a muddy expanse of waste ground. A shabbily dressed native, picking through the rubbish, came up to us; amongst an incomprehensible stream of Russian we recognised one word – Kameron – which is to say

Charles Cameron, the British architect imported along with other Western artists by Catherine the Great. The equivalent in Britain is hard to imagine with any conviction: a tramp outside, say, the Lyceum in Liverpool – "'tis by Thomas 'arrison, sir. Can yer spare the price of a cup of tea . . .'

In Britain, war-damaged buildings seldom survived long as ruins; the sites were too valuable, the planners too eager. Thirty years after the Blitz, the proud shell of Wren's Christ Church, Newgate Street, suffered the indignity of being half demolished for a road. But it is typical of Russia that the cathedral of St Sophia, battle-scarred and crumbling, still stands awaiting restoration and, when the builders and craftsmen have finished the remaining rooms in Rastrelli's Baroque palace and completed the rebuilding of Cameron's Chinese village, doubtless they will turn their attention to his church.

The remarkable restorations of the palaces of the Tsars by the Russians are rightly famous. Peterhof, Tsarskoe Selo and Pavlovsk were all left smashed and gutted after the Germans retreated from Leningrad in 1944. Repairs began almost immediately and still continue. Original drawings and documents were acquired and studied; craftsmen sent to Italy to be trained. The result is a series of magnificent, scholarly and costly recreations of rooms which make the care of country houses by our own National Trust seem amateur.

All this is well known; the great surprise of a visit to Leningrad is that the whole centre of the city is intact and beautifully preserved. Yet from September 1941, Leningrad was besieged by the Germans for almost 900 days; a million died – over half from starvation – and the city was constantly bombed and shelled. Apart from memorials and appalling mass cemeteries, there is nothing to show for this today. The streets are intact, the public buildings and palaces all extant. Not a single modern building breaks the delicate skyline and dares challenge the dome of St Isaac's Cathedral or the gilded spires of the Admiralty and the Peter and Paul Fortress. A comparison with London – a city which suffered less and where very few of the Wren City churches have been really well restored – is inevitable and, for an English visitor, painful.

The citizens of Leningrad evidently care deeply about their buildings – as well they might. Although the first buildings raised by Peter the Great after the foundation of the city in 1703 and by his daughter Elizabeth are Baroque, the real character of St Petersburg-Petrograd-Leningrad was created between the reigns of Catherine and her grandson Nicholas I – 1762 to 1856 – and it is now quite simply the finest Neo-Classical city in the world. Western architects – Cameron, the Italians Rossi and Quarenghi, the Frenchman de Thomon – brought a new style to the banks of the Neva which took root and was then developed with native brilliance by Russian architects – Zacharov, Voronikhin, Stasov. That a style which emulated the severe purity of the Antique, sharply modelled in the Mediterranean sun, should have flourished so healthily in the cold north of Europe is a strange paradox, but Edinburgh, Berlin, Helsinki and St Petersburg still stand to show that Neo-Classicism was more concerned with republican or revolutionary ideals (even *pace* Washington).

The city most like St Petersburg was Berlin. Both cities were created in barren, flat wastes by military autocrats; both were cities of stucco, without much good building stone; both were cities of Neo-Classical buildings standing by water, whether the Neva, the Spree, or canals. But there were differences. The monuments of the Hohenzollerns, the buildings of Schinkel, were austere, grey and sometimes forbidding; but in St Petersburg, Neo-Classicism became Russian, more decorative and colourful – the stucco is still gaily painted ochre, green or red. Zacharov's Admiralty in the centre of the city is a quarter of a mile long, but with its sculpture, its several porticoes and its fanciful steeple, it is almost a friendly building: in Leningrad it is the distances and the spaces which are forbidding. Ironic, therefore, that it should have been the Germans who shelled St Petersburg and the Russians who completed the destruction of Berlin.

Much of Berlin remains in ruins, but in 1945 Leningrad was evidently determined to recreate the beauty of the city and its palaces. The fact that it was built by and for the Tsars did not worry them – the buildings were made by (on the whole) Russian craftsmen and belonged to the Russian people, and it is touching to find at Pavlovsk a room devoted to the architects, painters and craftsmen who have restored the palace since the war. This is an attitude to the national heritage which contrasts markedly with that manifested by city authorities in Britain since 1945, both Labour and Conservative. Councils in Newcastle, Manchester and elsewhere seemed determined to remove all trace of the wicked capitalist past – but there was one Socialist politician who should be remembered with honour: Attlee, who used his casting vote in Cabinet to save the war-worn Nash terraces in Regent's Park (whereas Macmillan, ostensibly a Conservative, personally permitted the Euston Arch and the Clarendon Hotel, Oxford, to be demolished).

Perhaps we are too old a nation, perhaps we have been too confident and complacent, to need to keep our historic buildings and cities as visible expressions and symbols of national identity – but we have certainly recognised that necessity in others. 'Bomber' Harris struck a blow at German cultural pride when he ordered the RAF to destroy the old mediaeval Hanseatic cities of Lübeck and Rostock in 1941. The Germans, furious, swiftly retaliated with the 'Baedeker' raids, but the city authorities of

Exeter, Canterbury and elsewhere did not try to recreate their scarred cities after the war. Instead, architects and planners almost welcomed the Blitz as an opportunity for modernisation and many damaged buildings which could have been repaired were pulled down. Even worse, of course, has sometimes been the fate of those historic towns which did not enjoy the attentions of the Luftwaffe: foreign tourists often assume today that the horrible redevelopments in, say Worcester and Gloucester are the result of bombing, when they are nothing of the kind.

Not that the Russians are incapable of calculated vandalism: pride in national monuments can work in reverse. In the march into Germany, the Soviet armies destroyed Königsberg, the birthplace of Kant and the ancient capital of East Prussia, expelled its German population and renamed it Kaliningrad. Similarly, since 1945 a policy of cultural imperialism has been pursued in the Islamic parts of the Soviet Empire, where the narrow streets, bazaars and mosques of old Muslim cities have been replaced by modern Western-style redevelopments in a deliberate attempt to undermine a culture by destroying its context. Nor should the large number of churches and other old buildings destroyed by Stalin in Moscow be forgotten.

It is, no doubt, wrong to attribute the remarkable architectural integrity of Leningrad to communist government: indeed, most of the good things in Russia seem to survive in spite of it. Of course, as the city was created by a ruthless autocracy, so, perhaps, it needs a dictatorship to maintain it just as it needs one to maintain vast public expenditure on the armed forces. But the preservation of old buildings must be truly popular in Leningrad: certainly it is not done just for tourists (the chief argument used for preservation in Britain); ironically, the only modern buildings which spoil the city centre are two hotels for Western tourists.

The Classical tradition in Leningrad must be seen as an expression both of strong nationalism and of civic pride. The city was founded on Baltic territory newly seized from the Swedes in a bid to make Russia a European nation. The transfer of the capital back to cruel, half-Asiatic Moscow by the Bolsheviks in 1918 can be interpreted as a return to Russian insularity. But Leningrad remained loyal to its history and its European image. Unlike Moscow, nothing was destroyed; Constructivism never took root there and in the Thirties large monumental housing schemes in the Classical style were erected (similar, in fact, to what modern Western architects like Leon Krier and Ricardo Bofill propose today). As late as the Fifties a Metro line was constructed, with marble-lined, chandelier-lit stations worthy of Ledoux. Then, in 1955, came Khrushchev's condemnation of architectural 'excesses' and the advocacy of industrialised system building (which was not without influence on our own architects in the LCC). The result is vast acres of high-rise housing even more depressing than those in the Gorbals or the Piggeries, and which, sadly, is still being built and is still officially approved of (our bus to Peterhof made a detour through this estate expressly to elicit the admiration of Westerners).

The centre of Leningrad nevertheless remains a dream. The oppressiveness and sheer awfulness of Soviet Communism is still there to be seen and felt, of course; the queues, the absence of any pleasant places to eat or drink, the slogans. It seemed most like *1984* on the day of unpaid labour, the *corvée* in honour of Lenin, when 'Music While You Work' blared from loudspeakers all over the city and even in the gardens at Pavlovsk. But, to the Western visitor, there can be compensations in addition to the completeness of the architecture: few cars and a cheap, efficient public transport, the absence of advertisements (apart from the absurd ikons of Communist saints) and of offensive pornography.

Although it was not Communism which has made the Czechs preserve the unspoiled beauty of Prague, which inspired the Poles to reconstruct Warsaw and Danzig as they were, and which moved the women of Dresden to start repairing the Zwinger within weeks of the fire-bomb attack, it is true that the dampening effect of Soviet rule has saved Eastern Europe from many of the mistakes of the West. If the Iron Curtain ever lifts, Europe will still be divided in two physically; in the one half historic cities rebuilt and preserved, in the other cities ruined by a combination of foolish utopianism and sheer greed.

The great beauty of Leningrad, an authoritarian city built largely with forced labour, can be profoundly disturbing for a British visitor, for it highlights a strange paradox: that Soviet Russia, officially wedded to a determinist, progressive view of history, is in fact very conservative and preserves its Tsarist past at great expense; while, in theoretically free and individualistic Britain, where any intelligent sensitive person is acutely conscious of cultural decline, intellectuals have for decades felt that tradition must surrender to the supposed demands of a dominating idea of progress – in architecture as in other spheres. Just look at modern Bath.

16 May, 1981

Richard Bassett

CEAUSESCU'S MADNESS

Bucharest

It is an increasingly popular speculation that Romania's leader, the aging Nicolai Ceausescu, is rapidly approaching a mental state which even by the lax standards of modern psychiatry can be diagnosed as certifiable. Last month he dismissed his foreign minister for daring to disagree with him twice in one morning. Two weeks before that, he had ordered his architects to demolish blocks of flats constructed only six months earlier because they might overlook the site of the future republic's palace. Earlier this year, he gave instructions to mine a mountain known for centuries to contain not a single mineral of value.

At first glance some of the conducator's mad schemes seem to be quite sensible. He is, for example, said to be passionately fond of shipping all old pensioners out of Bucharest and resettling them in the Transylvanian foothills. This is a commendable idea. Realised in Vienna where old ladies wield a power comparable to that enjoyed by any one of Seyss-Inquart's gauleiters, this plan would at a stroke liberate that city from octogenarian tyranny.

There is also something perhaps to be said for the soft lighting – the country's energy crisis has plunged the once garishly lit streets of Bucharest into darkness. It is a novel if unnerving experience to be able to land at a fog-bound airport at night and realise that the only lights for miles are those of the runway. But however entertaining this most Tintinesque of eastern European capitals is to visitors, the Romanians who have to live there this winter are facing the greatest test of their powers of survival since the Balkan wars.

Heating, electricity, food, petrol are all strictly rationed. In an hour's stroll around Bucharest, it is possible to count queues for these essentials in which the numbers even reach four figures. At one petrol station, hundreds of cars, many abandoned, formed a queue which I was assured would remain virtually unchanged for weeks.

If these shortages are not demoralising enough, Mr Ceausescu in an effort to leave his mark on Bucharest is creating what his strictly censored press calls 'the first socialist capital for the new socialist man'. No

one, with the exception of the conducator, quite knows what this is
supposed to mean but it involves building a vast avenue called the
'Boulevard of Socialist Victory' and bulldozing every building which
stands in its way. Of the 9,000 houses which were in the path of this
socialist victory, none survives. Eighteenth-century villas, neo-classical
palais, a dozen mediaeval churches and two complete monasteries all
gone in a little more than a year.

The hideous blocks whose designs are personally supervised by the
Romanian leader and which will rise in the place of these picturesque
buildings are expected to house 90 to 95 per cent of the inhabitants of
Bucharest. They will be a 'model' for other cities in Romania.

In the face of these outrages, it is remarkable that the Romanians still
remain the most civilised and charming people of all eastern Europe. It is
still possible even during the energy crisis to visit the well-lit neo-classical Athenaeum and hear an orchestra play with more musicianship than
anywhere else in the Balkans, and see an audience which exceeds in its
elegance and attentiveness anything to be found on either side of the iron
curtain. That they can retain such style with a crush bar that is permanently closed and a foyer which for all its charm maintains a temperature
of about zero degrees is impressive. The Romanian women glimpsed here
seemed to have stepped straight out of the pages of Olivia Manning. In
contrast to nearly every other example of eastern Europe's fairer sex, they
rest engagingly easily on the eye while their gestures (as a secret treatise
on Balkan affairs published in 1910 for the exclusive use of the Austrian
general staff observed) are indeed the most beautiful in Europe.

Inside the Athenaeum, music and audience combine to banish the
chaos Mr Ceausescu has created outside. But when the concert ends,
there is no more pitiable sight than this dignified audience sloping off to
their unlit and unheated homes to prepare themselves for the next day's
battle of bribes with those who hold the coupons for food and petrol.

In the remarkably well stocked national gallery where the works of
Theodore Amman show that Romanian art at the turn of the century was
superior to almost anything else produced in eastern Europe, there are
more disturbing contrasts. Amman's paintings evoke a world where
Western cultural values once flourished in an essentially oriental environment. His intimate gardens, sunlit drawing rooms and coffee houses
are inhabited by elegant Romanians who clearly know what coffee and
cigarettes are. The gallery is virtually empty, lights switched off, attendants in heavy winter coats. It is hard to imagine a group of
schoolchildren recognising even for a moment that the comforts
depicted in these paintings might actually have existed in Romania.

Upstairs where the old masters hang, there is a little more light and the staccato accompaniment of water dropping from a leaking roof. Buckets have been placed at strategic intervals to catch it; eight in front of the Rubens portraits, six in front of the El Greco and two near some Brueghels.

An out of breath gentleman emerging from the stairs in a hurry manages to knock one of the buckets over as he enters the room devoted to Neapolitan baroque. His rather sullen face has with its dark glasses been a familiar sight in Bucharest over the last few days. At the Athenee Palace hotel, he seemed to be having difficulty lighting a cigarette in the dark ten-volt-bulb lit corridor outside my room. Since then, he has turned up lighting cigarettes in a lot of places. Possibly frustrated by the no-smoking regulations of the gallery, he loses himself in thought gazing at a Gianbologna statue of the rape of the Sabine women. Discreetly heading off towards the Flemish room after a feint aimed at giving the impression of a lingering interest in Poussin, I was about to congratulate myself on the skill with which this ruse had been executed when the sound of another bucket colliding with someone's boot in the room next door revealed that the gentleman touchingly shared my interest in Brueghel.

There are, it is said, more people employed in the Romanian secret police than in any other country in Europe. Certainly at night, there seem to be a lot of people hanging around in front of various houses just watching windows. It is pointed out with relief by those who live in Bucharest that unlike East German secret police, the Romanians are at least corruptible. In Ceausescu's Romania, everyone has his price, not least because the official currency is worthless for any transactions involving food, petrol, accommodation or any number of goods which most housewives would deem essential. For these, Kent (and only Kent) cigarettes will suffice and he who enters Romania without these is doomed to service which in Baedeker's words is 'always extortionate and frequently offensive'.

The debilitating effects of this, coupled with a widespread feeling that no one can be trusted, can be easily imagined. As essential supplies become fewer, the mind is forced to concentrate on a fight for survival. Morality and even friendships are costly luxuries.

There is no tradition of public revolt among Romanians. A state of affairs which would ignite a popular rising in any other European country against the dictator responsible for such chaos is unimaginable. The army has been purged and Mr Ceausescu has successfully installed no fewer than 17 members of his family on the Central Committee of the Party.

But if there is no tradition of revolt, there is one, fostered under Turkish rule, of survival. As the paranoia of Europe's last Stalinist dictator becomes worse, the Romanians will have to draw on the last reserves of this hereditary quality. In the post-Ceausescu era, it will take years of stability and trust to erase the evil this one man has inflicted on a most civilised country.

4 January, 1986

Denis Hills

POLAND STRANGELY CHANGED

Forty-five years had passed since Hitler's panzers severed my connection with Poland – where I had been working in Polish journalism in the Corridor and later as a teacher – and I walked over a footbridge across the Dniestr into Romania from Polish Galicia. All I had salvaged was a fibre suitcase with a few scraps of holiday clothing. The German army was already deep in Poland and there were rumours that the Red Army was mobilising along the eastern border. The Polish frontier policeman who stamped my passport gave me a memorable goodbye. 'Panie profesorze,' he said, 'when you return to Poland come back in a bomber.'

Now, after those many years, I was on my way back, not in a bomber but in an old camping van that had been lying out in a field near Henley-in-Arden. With my store of romantic but rusty memories I was prepared for an emotional experience. That first sight of cobblestones, tumbledown villages and plodding farm carts across the Oder. The endless beet fields. Flaking churches, flower-strewn graveyards, unpronounceable names. Like Rip Van Winkle I would find much that was barely recognisable: rebuilt city centres, new ideologies and war memorials. Forewarned about Iron Curtain shortages I took care to stock up in the supermarkets of Brunswick with provisions.

My passage through the Iron Curtain at Frankfurt-an-der-Oder seemed ominous: a two-hour search by a German customs officer of everything in my van, from tea-bags and tobacco pouch to books. The Polish official was also unhelpful. 'Where is the *mleko* (milk)?' he insisted, 'How many kilos?' 'I have no *mleko*,' I said. 'Only enough for my tea.' Perhaps there was a smuggling racket in powdered milk. It was long after midnight before I was allowed to drive off into the welcoming darkness of the Polish countryside and find a gap in a wood for a night's rest.

When I stopped for a morning meal in a small restaurant I was joined by the local photographer. One of the first things he said to me was, 'Why did Churchill and Roosevelt sell Poland to Stalin?' It was a question I was to hear again in Poland. I also learned about the black market. A taxi pulled up while I was resting in a lay-by near Poznan and a smart girl hurried out. 'Are you a Hollander?' she asked. 'Where is your woman? Have you dollars?'

In Warsaw I parked my van in a tourist camp. The camp was used by Poles with tiny caravan-trailers like boxes, school parties and their teachers, a few foreigners and gypsies. I found the capital greatly changed. Tower blocks and new apartment buildings had shot up everywhere – those in the outskirts ugly conglomerations of prefabricated sections housing thousands of families in small crowded rooms. Streets were much wider. The city centre had been transformed by gouging out a great empty space for the huge Palace of Culture, Soviet Russia's gift to the Polish nation.

The restoration of ancient landmarks from war-time rubble has also been done on a massive scale. Churches, their baroque interiors gleaming with gilt, have been rebuilt, the old Market Square with its painted and carved gables meticulously resurrected, broken statues have been pieced together or remade and new war memorials have sprung up. In public places and at street corners tablets to commemorate the dead heroes hang like tear-drops.

The parks and public places were much as before, crowded with pensioners sitting on benches in the sun, young mothers with prams, children (very clean and beautifully dressed), people walking their dogs, pigeons, a few drunks. But the queues waiting outside shops, perhaps in the rain, and the ubiquitous police waving down motorists, watching the crowds at traffic lights, sitting in trucks near public buildings, were something new. And there were no Jews. There were none in the cinemas, the surgeries or lawyers' chambers The orthodox Jews – unmistakable in the old days with their ringlets, their long gaberdines and Russian boots – and the ghetto streets had vanished: with them the cavalry officers bowling along in cabs or bagging the girls in the night clubs. One missed their cloaks, their smart breeches and riding boots and handsome profiles. The old night life is dead. People stay in after dark. They entertain their friends at home or watch the television screen.

One of the first things I did was to go to my old address in Hoza Street where I had lived in 1939. Alas, the building had been destroyed during the uprising and a new apartment block stood in its place. The landlady, a greyhaired woman who had been brought up in Moscow, used to talk

Russian with me. Over my bed hung a picture of the Tsar's mounted Cossacks slashing at a crowd with sabres.

Not far away were Lazienki Gardens where I used to sit with a book near Chopin's statue. The statue, destroyed by the Germans, has been replaced. I joined the Sunday morning crowd seated round the pedestal listening to an open-air piano recital of Chopin's music. The music seemed to have cast a spell on them. Many had their eyes closed. No one coughed. No one smoked. Chopin's head is half-turned as though listening to the music of a willow tree. After the recital I spoke to two Polish women who were sharing my bench. 'The Germans feared Chopin,' they said. 'His music was a symbol of Polish patriotism, the sound of the Polish heart.' When I told them that I had sat there before the war they looked at me as though I were an antique

I went to Father Popieluszko's church where, before he was murdered by police agents, he used to spread his rebellious message to a rapt congregation. The church has been turned into a place of pilgrimage and his grave, lit by guttering candles and swamped with flowers, has become more widely known and honoured among Poles than the Unknown Soldier's Tomb in Warsaw's Victory Square. Inside the church is a gallery of photographs showing Father Popieluszko at various stages of his life as he treads the road to Calvary. As a young man, laughing with children and youths. As a sportsman, bare to the waist, sun-tanned, sitting in a boat on a lake. Preaching. Saying Mass. The final photograph shows a car with smashed windows and flat tyres. In the open boot and back seat two dummy infants have been placed with outstretched arms – dead. The grisly pathos of this exhibit and a picture of the dark dam where the priest's body was dumped are calculated to perpetuate anger and a desire to avenge.

People come and go all day and long after dark. Their faces show deep piety. The church itself is full of banners and bric-a-brac. Hanging in the yard I counted 50 Solidarnosc posters – the inscriptions turned inwards, not facing the street. One wonders if it is right to build up the murdered man into such a hero, a sort of Hollywood star, to be ready to canonise him?

But the Poles worship their heroes, their warriors and their poets, even though the cause they fought for was often lost, a victory in defeat. (I sometimes think that the only thing they really envy the English for is the charge of the Light Brigade!) One of Poland's best known and admired paintings is Matejko's battle scene where the Poles and their allies destroyed the Teutonic Knights at Grunwald in 1410. As one looks at these huge men, the Knights on their chargers, the Poles and Lithuanians fighting mostly on foot, one can almost hear the grunts and screams and the thud of steel on crushed bone. All schoolchildren are taken to see the picture. A diagram identifies the warriors: Jan Zyska, enormously strong, one-eyed, bare-headed, is slashing away at the Knights like a man felling trees. The Grand Master is shown at the moment of being slain.

The present Jewish synagogue in Grzybowski Square was built after the war. The site of the old synagogue, which was destroyed, has brought bad luck to the builders of the new tower block that now stands on it. The block has been condemned as unsafe, a huge white elephant, conspicuously empty. The caretaker gave me a paper skull-cap and took me inside the synagogue. He told me the number of Jews in Warsaw was about 500. There were some 30 regular worshippers. Near the synagogue is the Jewish theatre and newspaper office. An old Jew came and spoke to me. 'Are you a Catholic or a Protestant?' he asked. 'Protestant.' 'Protestants are good,' he said.

From the synagogue I went to the Jewish cemetery in Okopowa. The most recent section of tombs – the dates go up as far as 1940 – is in fairly good condition. Many are elaborately carved with roofs and railings and costly marble slabs. The inscriptions are bilingual (Hebrew and Polish). But the older burial ground (the cemetery is large) is a dark, wild place where one can lose one's way in a jungle of undergrowth. The gravestones are rotting, choked by bushes and brambles, the slabs lie at random as though felled by a typhoon, the ground is thick with humus. The inscriptions here are in Hebrew only. All the familiar names are to be found: Feigenblatt, Strumpfmann, Szpacenkopf. Relatives have added fresh names and words to some of the gravestones in the new section: 'Family burnt in Treblinka'; 'In memory of the victim of German bestiality'; 'Tortured to death'.

The attendant, who has an office near the gate, told me there had been no serious vandalism – 'nothing to complain of – just a few youths, louts, not Germans'. But the proper upkeep of the cemetery, he explained, was beyond the resources of the Jewish community in Warsaw. 'We are poor. Most of the Jews are old, living lonely lives in small rooms with a few tins and bits of furniture. Having survived for so long they are determined to go on to the bitter end.'

Through my old teaching contacts I got to know a number of Polish lecturers and their friends at the university linguistics department. Like all Polish intellectuals they combined realism – the acceptance of the hard facts of life in a poor country under political pressures – with romantic escapism and cynical wit. Their parties were never dull. There

was always something to eat, vodka and Balkan wine. With them I went
to films and plays, art exhibitions, concerts and a *dacha*.

One artist had hung his paintings in a derelict factory that used to
make gun barrels. We had to climb over rusty machinery to view them.
All but one of the paintings showed the violent martyrdom of St Peter,
his great muscular body twisted in agony. The exception was the sombre
painting of a dead working man. The symbolism was obvious. Two mar-
tyrs: the murdered Father Popieluszko and an industrial worker shot by
police – the Church and Solidarity. The bizarre setting too – a grimy factory workshop – made its point. To avoid embarrassment with the
authorities the exhibition had not been advertised. There were about 50
private guests, and glasses of cheap vermouth.

The Soviet film week was a flop. I saw three of the films – they were not
overtly propagandist – but few people came to watch them. At one performance I visited there were only four of us in the cinema: myself and a
friend, a youth, and a man who dropped off to sleep. The Red cavalry
commander Budyonny, in the person of a Cossack actor, was whirling his
sabre to virtually empty houses.

Claude Lanzmann's nine-hour film *Shoah* received special approval
from General Jaruzelski to be performed for a week. It was shown in three
separate parts to audiences of about 50. The film was admired but considered controversial. No one wanted to be reminded of the anti-semitic
feelings that have been endemic in eastern Europe wherever history
shows a pale of Jewish settlement. It was thought that Lanzmann's
shrewd interrogation methods had put Polish villagers, who had lived
near the death camps, in a poor light. There was, of course, no love lost
between the Jews and their Polish neighbours. Their cultures, community lives and occupations were too different. Neither expected to be
loved by the other; and they neither gave to each other nor received much
love. After the Russian Cossack film and Lanzmann's epic, the British
Council film *The Shooting Party* (James Mason) seemed tame and contrived.

This morning I talked to a priest on a bench outside the War Museum.
'You will notice great changes,' he remarked. 'Yes, Warsaw is bigger and
much busier,' I said cautiously. 'I don't mean that,' he said. 'We are not
satisfied.' 'You mean economic problems?' 'They're not important either'.
He raised his voice. 'We are not free. *Nie ma wolnosci!*' He got up, a big
cross swinging over his breast. 'Poland is not free!' he repeated and hurried away. He was wearing a beret, and his black shoes twinkled under his
robe.

I thought of the priest's words when I visited the Red Army cemetery near my camp. A tablet at the foot of the memorial obelisk bears the words, 'In honour of the heroes who fought for the independence of Poland and the liberation of our capital'. Poles don't go there except to read the newspaper or stroll with girls. There are two separate burial sections, one for Russian officers, who have plaques and are named, and one for other ranks, who have no plaques and are not named. Under the five-pointed Soviet stars that marked the burial plots there was no equality even in death.

From Warsaw I drove to the death camps at Majdanek, Oswiecim (Auschwitz) and Treblinka, watched the unveiling of the Black Goddess at Czestochowa, and heard the great resonant voices of the choir at the Russian Orthodox church at Bialystok. Majdanek: soggy beet-fields fertilised by human ash at the end of Lublin's Street of the Tormented. Oswiecim: huts full of human hair, battered shoes and suitcases. It was here that Rudolf Hoess gassed his 'best loved prisoners', the gypsies. They were 'undisciplined' and some fought like wild cats to avoid being driven into the black chambers. Treblinka: sleeping now in quiet woods, where villagers pick mushrooms. It took the guards less than half an hour to unload a freight train of families, coax them up the Road to Heaven through the birch trees, strip, shave the women's heads and annihilate them.

A mile or two from the Russian border, east of Bialystok, I visited the last Jewish cemetery I was to see, at Krynki. It was a bleak, windy mound with a horse tethered to a gravestone. New village houses are encroaching on it. In the vale below it the Orthodox cemetery was strewn with fresh flowers and candles. I would have gone on to the nearby Tatar village of Kruszyniany but it began to snow. Warsaw, when I got back, had turned into a grey wintry city. People were queuing up for warm boots and wearing padded jackets like lumberjacks. I parked my van under a tree in Zbawiciela Square and went indoors.

14 June, 1986

Rowlinson Carter

WHAT A RUSSIAN GIRL WANTS

Moscow

One of the social adjustments brought about by Mr Gorbachev's clampdown on drinking is that appointments for lunch, which used to be early, are now postponed until 1.45, time enough to be settled at a table for the opening of the bar at 2.00. The bar does not then close in mid-afternoon, so there is no compulsion to rush. I was surprised and slightly embarrassed to be singled out for preferential treatment from the inevitable queue outside a restaurant admitting locals, although those left behind showed no signs of resentment. I was shown to a table already occupied by two elderly women. They looked up amiably but spoke no English. I was resigning myself to a mute meal and turning the pages of a book when a pretty girl in her early twenties materialised from nowhere to take the spare place opposite. Her eyes fastened on the book and the notebook next to it. 'I believe you are a correspondent,' she said, a statement rather than a question. My visa said nothing of the sort and I hoped to keep quiet about it, but I muttered a vague confession. The few words were enough to give her a fix on the accent. 'English, not American.' Another statement.

Her eyes, slightly distanced by the glasses she was wearing, seemed apart from the rest of her face, which was open and smiling. A mismatch, I thought; a mistake with the upper and lower halves of different 'Identikit' drawings. Something that goes with a journalist's job, especially in a country like Russia which is, and makes visitors feel, paranoid about informers, is the fantasy of being cornered by a Mata Hari, in which case one was resolved to string the poor thing along until she discovered, too late, that the prisoner in her arms was for all official purposes useless. Did the KGB keep a female task force tucked away in restaurants to spring on mildly suspicious strangers? Was I looking at my KGB temptress?

She said she was an interpreter, but not for the government. Her English was excellent and she was remarkably well-informed about Britain. One of her first questions was whether Murdoch would win at Wapping. Moscow has about as many daily newspapers as London and I asked how many she took. 'Five.' Most impressive; she *did* mean every day? 'Per year!' She could not pick up the BBC World Service on her radio, but a friend sometimes did and passed the word along. Her job gave her access to foreign newspapers. The topic of Chernobyl arose. 'In Russia,' she said, 'no news is bad news.' Did I know, she asked, leaning forward, that a second reactor had gone up? (Wrong.) The drift of the conversation brought to mind some advice from an old American hand in a part of South-East Asia where the KGB were hyperactive. Beware of Russians, he had said, when they start telling you how terrible things are at home.

And what should one make of a stranger in a restaurant who quoted at some length from Horace, in Latin? She had just come across Evelyn Waugh and on finishing *Decline and Fall* would immediately read it all over again. Could I recommend a couple of more recent writers? I suggest the two Naipauls and Amis Junior.

We had been talking about everything under the sun when she tossed in a question as an apparent afterthought: 'Are you staying at the embassy?' I said that HMG did not customarily provide bed and breakfast for hacks; I was staying at the Intourist Hotel. She was watching the reply searchingly. Her eyes seemed to re-adjust behind the glasses and her face relaxed; the bits of the 'Identikit' fitted.

'Good – let's get some wine!' It sounded like an invitation to a party. 'We are the perfect combination. I'll tell the waiter you're an important visitor and I'm your official interpreter. He'll give us the best.' A bottle of tasty Georgian red was duly produced. 'May I offer some to my mother?' Her mother? Where? The woman next to her, who all along had been looking pleasantly our way but remained silent. 'Your mother, really? Of course.' They must have arrived before me, and the daughter was probably in the lavatory or somewhere when I turned up. I ought to have picked up the resemblance earlier. Not even the KGB could conceivably go to the trouble of maintaining mother and daughter duos at tables in restaurants which foreigners did not frequent. I suppose it was time for my face to relax. Pity about the temptress: welcome anyway to some cracking and uncomplicated company.

She was pleased that I noticed she spoke 'English', rather than 'American'. I said Russian foreign broadcasts usually employed American voices. 'Them!' she remarked derisively. She wanted the latest slang, so I did my best with a mixture of *Private Eye* and *Minder*'s Cockney rhymes. The expressions were soon coming back to me. She was experimenting, determined to get the nuance spot on. 'D & D' was specifically a matter negotiated with a magistrate in Bow Street, as opposed to 'tired and emotional'. She asked about Ireland – 'that's not what they say about it here' –

and Arthur Scargill. She found the joke about the fat, round and unloved pound coin being a Scargill – and 50 pence thus logically 'Arfa Scargill' – so rollicking funny that even her mother joined in. An impossible translation, surely?

'Did you enjoy the wine?' Indeed. 'Georgian brandy is good, too.' We must have some. It seemed silly to stop the party; would she like dinner? She said she would, in a way I thought was intended to hide from her mother what was going on. 'Be outside your hotel at seven exactly. Please don't be late, that is most important.' She did not, then, say why.

I was horrified to wake from a snooze to discover that I was already five minutes late. She was nowhere to be seen outside. I was still kicking myself when she emerged from the middle of a knot of passing pedestrians. Was she also late? No, it was her second pass; now we must move away quickly. Too early for dinner, she would show me some of the sights. It was unwise, she explained as we walked among people making their way to Red Square, to linger outside tourist hotels. She was less concerned about being mistaken for one of the whores, who flaunted themselves unmistakably on the highest of heels, than catching the attention of the pimps among the men permanently gathered around the entrance. Not ordinary pimps, she said, the KGB.

Moscow is not a good city for walking. The bland uniformity of the streets is caused in part by the absence of the colour and variety of small shops. A couple of Knightsbridge window-dressers could transform the face of Moscow without upsetting the collective system. The typical window display is a symmetrical mountain of tins, say pilchards. It is as if the state enterprises were calling out: 'Look at all these pilchards, comrades! So many! Isn't the revolution working well?' Restaurants, naturally, are not owned or run by individuals. Many of them are where they were before the Revolution, in magnificent rooms (frescoes and chandeliers, occasionally a fountain) where the food is rarely a match for the surroundings. The menus are hang-overs too, page after page of delicious promises. Reality means skipping items that are not priced and hoping that the restaurant has not run out of the restricted choice from the rest.

The restaurant she chose for dinner was a rarity, a neighbourhood establishment in a residential area. I was still curious about the cloak-and-dagger activity outside the hotel. The street girls would take their customers elsewhere, she said, because they were not allowed into tourist hotels, nor were Russian women with impeccable credentials. Could she explain then, how it was that in the plush hotels reserved for businessmen in Russia by state invitation the bars were crawling with a higher class of tart who was well-dressed and often exceedingly easy on the eye. I was right, she said, a higher class of tart. 'They're inside the hotels because they pay the KGB or work for them, usually both.'

Her account of corruption in the KGB, of protection rackets and trafficking in girls and foreign currency – 'everything, just like the Mafia' – was to be endorsed if not confirmed by subsequent conversations. The lower class of tart, the streetwalkers, had a lesser measure of protection: sufficient, however, to parade with impunity under the noses of uniformed police.

I was later to meet a girl who once managed to slip past the doorman, planning to wait in the foyer while her fiancé, a foreigner, nipped up to his room to collect something. She was instantly taken away by plainclothes police and held for seven hours. In contrast, a girl who was on the game and under no threat in the bar of the same hotel was telling an old 'friend', a regular business visitor who recounted the tale, how much she was looking forward to her departure the following day to join her new husband in Switzerland. She interrupted herself on spotting a randy Japanese pacing about. 'Excuse me.' She returned half an hour later and $100 richer. 'But . . . ' her old pal started incredulously. 'Don't be silly, darling, how else could I buy my dear husband some duty frees.' The doormen, it was explained, were in no doubt as to a girl's level of influence inside the KGB.

Dinner with the interpreter passed pleasantly. She said she admired Mrs Thatcher enormously and was taken aback when I said that Mrs Thatcher, and the Tories in general, out of necessity and in fact appealed to a broad section of the working class. 'Now I know something about her I don't like.' Her family had been dispossessed by the Bolsheviks and it was obvious where her atavistic class loyalties lay. She was also a loyal Muscovite, resenting the shuffling around of the population by the state that brought in a flood of 'foreigners'. 'They bring them in to work in things like cement factories. Moscow doesn't need any more cement factories, and it definitely doesn't need any more of *them*.'

She was not, and never would be, a member of the party, although both her mother (a flashback to the restaurant at lunchtime) and father had been members since their youth. 'Joining the party can get things done, but the people who join are usually those who are not good at their jobs – or anything really – and would not get on.' She thought that what frightened the party was not democracy but meritocracy, which would sweep the membership into the nearest national dustbin.

When the waiter decided it was too late for a brandy, she said she had a bottle at home. I wondered about the logistics of getting back to my hotel after the metro closed. Where were we and where did she live? 'Around the corner, two minutes.' As we passed through an archway into her square – her parents had given her the flat and moved themselves into communal housing – we came face to face with a policeman, a bobby on a neighbourhood beat. She spun on her heel and tugged me away. 'Was that really necessary?' I asked when we were out of hearing. 'Please, you must not speak English here. Wait until we are inside. I'm going to see about the neighbours; I'll come back for you.' The policeman had moved on and I was alone in the square. The lights were still on in a few flats but there wasn't a sound.

Her flat was in darkness. She would not switch on a light because, she said, she did not want me to see the mess. I could make out planks propped against a wall. The internal partitions were gone, leaving pipes and wiring in mid-air. She was waiting for building materials to complete an ambitious renovation that would put the flat closer to Sloane Square than the intentions of the man who built it, Stalin. She would exploit the high ceiling to build a minstrel's gallery for her bed. In the meantime, the bed was the only place to sit and it was next to a curtainless window overlooking, and overlooked by, the square. I thought, uncharitably, that we were sitting ducks for any photographer with an image intensifier.

She turned on music, a Western group I had never heard of, and poured out a brandy. Was she not having one? No, there wasn't much and I must have it. We talked away the night while I stretched out the drinks. It was after she had turned another of her phrases – 'in Britain the unemployed are victims, in Russia criminals' – that I asked what had given her the idea that I might be staying at the embassy.

'I didn't think you were, I hoped you weren't, but I had to ask. I don't want anything to do with that kind of thing, you know?' I believed I did.

'I wondered about you, too.'

'I know.'

The conversation, for the first time, lapsed. She had drawn her legs up and was resting her head on the window. She looked different, a vulnerable child. She was still staring into the square when she broke the silence. 'Can I ask you . . . anything?' Of course. 'I want you to find me a husband.'

Silence again, and I needed it. 'I can't believe you couldn't manage on your own.' A foreign husband, an Englishman perhaps, and a passport. Was it a matter of getting out of Russia at any price? Did many women of her generation feel that way? 'Only half of them.' I don't think she meant it literally.

She was not in any substantial sense a political dissident. Her love of Russia was the most powerful emotion in her body. She would hesitate to leave without an assurance that she could return as often as she liked, one day for ever. She wanted to talk and travel and to see things. What else could I tell about England? What was France like, and Holland? At dinner in London, what did we talk about? Would people in England not like her, because she was Russian? What emerged above all was that in a country that stretches across 11 time zones she was suffering from claustrophobia.

If I could find her a husband and she were given a work permit, she would be self-sufficient, neither expecting, nor asking for, money. She then said something softly in Russian. Sorry? She would settle for either kind of marriage. Either kind? 'Sex or no sex.' I said I was sure hers would have sex. She allowed herself the faintest of smiles. Was she a virgin? No, but only one man.

'Is there anything a Russian girl should know about it?'

'What, marriage to an Englishman?'

'Sex with an Englishman.'

We next met at the Bolshoi. A tenor came bounding on stage, having trouble with his wrists and generally mincing about. She leant over to whisper: 'Can you say, if he's ginger, that he's also interested in Ugandan affairs?' I whispered back that I should have to consult higher authorities in London. 'But the other business must come first.' I was struck by the realisation that she was no longer experimenting with the language: she was rehearsing.

28 June, 1986

4 AFRICA

Hugo Charteris

VESPER FOR A COMMANDANT

Senegal

The pink haze of fire spreads in the dark sky, to left and right in front. Now, suddenly, there is a patch behind.

New explosions deafen and shake the ground; a figure is outlined, running, in the distance – with the speed of frantic intention.

The haze becomes a glare, still without source, and the silhouettes of the beehive huts have the regularity of things turned out of one mould.

Shouting starts again – but is drowned at once in a clattering rhythmic volley.

The near fence which seemed to screen nothing but desertion suddenly coughs attentively. The next explosion is so close that an old reflex waits for the cry 'Stretcher-bearers' – but instead there is another volley and then roars of laughter – for this is a wedding in Senegal.

The bridegroom's sisters are slowly taking the bride to her new bed – with a pause at each junction of paths for song, clapping, dance and salute from home-made one-inch-bore guns. The single carbide lamp, slung high on a crook, is not enough, so grass has been lit all round the village perimeter.

Somewhere the local ruler and sole resident European is sitting unshaved in a kimono, drinking iced beer, reading *Paris Match* after a hard day. Tonight he gave permission for '*tamtam jusqu' à onze heures.*'

Renewed laughter of women and inspired clapping, as instantly *tutti* as a section of demonstration Vickers machine-guns, means a new dancer has pitted her feet against the hands of the chief drummer.

Bowed slightly forward, she looks at them objectively to see how they're doing. They are invisible with speed – but above the waist she is loose as a weed in a stream and her arms swing slowly. The drummer's face gleams with sweat and he comes closer, arches over her, browbeating and straining, but her face reflects nothing but the calm of concentration. Excited laughter sounds above the syncopated clapping and a brilliant scarf arrives on her shoulder.

But at eleven the lonely, feverish hum dies suddenly down. The lights go out. Then the big queen termites bundle their impossible bodies up the sides of the oil-lamps and in the distance the clapping drums and laughter go on like the noise of the sea after a running tap. *Paris Match* is put away. *Le Monde* was never unfolded.

Said one young *adjoint-administrateur:* 'Folles nuits d'Afrique – don't you believe it. I'm a bachelor – and one isn't a monk. All the women can be bought. But they're like planks. Partly because of excision.'

Something, however, has not been excised and if the nights aren't *folles*, they are *troublantes* – full of remote gaiety that is nostalgic, like something lost for good.

1 March, 1957

Evelyn Waugh

TOURIST IN AFRICA

February 13. The city of Mombasa has grown enormously since I last saw it and now covers the whole island. There is a large, brand-new 'inter-racial' hotel. 'Inter-racial' in practice means mainly Indian, for few Africans can afford it and the Europeans foregather in their houses or at the club. There is an impressive Muslim Institute, erected by the Aga Khan and the Sultan of Zanzibar and other pious benefactors for the technical education of East African Mohammedans. (The Government of Kenya provide the staff and the running expenses.) They were unusually fortunate in their architect, Captain G. N. Beaumont, an engineer amateur of Mohammedan art who is splendidly uncorrupted by the influence of Corbusier which pervades the modern East. Dome, minaret, arcade, fretted and crenellated parapets, carved doors, tiled walls and pools stand happily disposed in acres of garden, whispering hints of the Alhambra, of Mena House, of the Anglican Cathedral at Gibraltar, of Brighton, but never the harsh tones of UN.

These two buildings are the chief architectural additions to the city. There is evidence of what seems to be the universal process of offices becoming larger and private houses smaller. For the first time in Africa I heard complaints of the scarcity and expense of domestic servants. The population of the island is more than ever heterogeneous. There are now poor whites in quite formidable numbers – a thing unknown thirty years ago. There is also in the main street a notorious dancing-bar, part brothel, part thieves' kitchen: everyone spoke of it with awe. When at length, after many invitations, I found a companion to go there, I found it the genuine thing; not at all the tourists' apache cafe but something which awoke nostalgic memories of the Vieux Port of Marseilles. All races and all vices were catered for. I have never been in a tougher or more lively joint anywhere. Gentle readers should keep clear.

I have here run away from my diary and given the impressions of several days. On the day I am ostensibly chronicling I spent a restful afternoon on the club verandah with the intention of reading the news I had missed since leaving England. The club is unchanged since I was last here, a spacious, old-fashioned building designed to catch every breath of air. The monsoon was blowing. It was deliciously cool, but it is not easy to read the *Times* India paper edition in deep shade and a brisk wind. Have the editors, I wonder, considered what a high proportion of their copies are perused under fans?

Opposite the club stands one of the most notable buildings in East Africa, Fort Jesus, built by the Portuguese at the end of the sixteenth century and still bearing the royal escutcheon on its walls. Its base is cut from the rock; its upper stories are faced with hard, coral stucco which changes colour as the sun moves over it, mottled, sometimes dun, sometimes rose-red. It is a massive little castle sited for defence on all fronts, battlemented, pierced by slits, approached by a single narrow flight of steep enfiladed steps. Until lately it was used as a prison and all the visitor could see of it were its noble elevations. He could smell it, when the wind was in the wrong quarter, from the club verandah. Now, by means of a grant from the Gulbenkian Foundation, it is being cleaned and restored. By the time that these words appear it will be open to view, furnished with a collection of local antiquities and, more important, inhabited by Mr Kirkman, the official archaeologist, who has been in charge of the operation.

At five o'clock that evening the fort was at its rosiest under the full blaze of the westering sun when, through the kindness of my new sapper friend, I had an appointment with Mr Kirkman. Few people in Mombasa had had the chance to see the work in progress and a privileged party of six or seven assembled at the gate and were led up to the ramparts. There is nothing of the dry and solemn official scholar in Mr Kirkman. He is an exuberant enthusiast for the comic as well as for the scientific aspects of his works.

The Public Works Department had built over the old structure a shoddy conglomeration of guard rooms, cells, latrines, barrack rooms, wash houses and exercise yard. All these were being demolished and the original levels were being restored. The Arabs had left a few finely carved inscriptions, but what emerges from the excavation is essentially a Portuguese Government House of the seventeenth century.

That evening I dined with the Provincial Commissioner. Like everyone I met in Mombasa that day and later, he was in a daze of gratification at the Queen Mother's visit. On every occasion she had done more than was asked of her. Unflagging in the steam-heat, she had completely defeated the boycott the politicians had tried to impose. In particular, she had made a conquest of the Arab sailors whose dhows fill the old port at this season. Nasser's wireless had been denouncing her as the symbol of Western imperialism. Dhows came sailing in from Zanzibar and all the little ports of the coast. The Queen Mother went to the waterfront and paid them a long, happy call which will be talked of for years in the Hadramaut and in the Persian Gulf.

Politics do not seem to be a major concern in Mombasa. Much of our conversation that evening was about the prospects of developing the Kenya coast as a holiday resort. There are sands, surf, coral reefs, deep-sea fishing for marlin, tunny and shark, an almost unexplored sea bed for goggle divers, everything in fact that draws tourists to the West Indies. At present Mombasa is used mainly as a port and rail-head; rich sportsmen go straight to Nairobi and set out on safari from there into the game reserves. The Commissioner hopes to see his province become a pleasure coast, not only for visitors from Europe and America but for families from the highlands of Kenya and Rhodesia . . . .

February 19. Zanzibar . . . To elderly Englishmen Zanzibar is most famous for the great Bloomsbury rag, when Virginia Woolf and her friends inspected an English man-of-war at Portsmouth in the guise of the Sultan and his entourage, and for Bishop Weston's occupation of the Anglican see. Weston was the hero of many sermons in Lancing chapel and his cathedral, built on the site of the old slave market, is the symbol of British beneficence in East Africa. Weston it was who, just before the First World War, threatened a schism in the Church of England by delating his neighbouring bishops for collaboration with nonconformists. Readers of Ronald Knox's *A Spiritual Aeneid* will remember the intense excitement of his coterie about the incident which, he said, the Lambeth committee found 'eminently pleasing to God and on no account to be repeated.'

The Cathedral has a rather forlorn appearance today. One clergyman presides where there was a 'mess' of six. The main activities of the mission are now on the mainland and the historic little edifice has, with its brass plates commemorating British officials, the air of a Riviera chaplaincy. No church has made much progress in this last of the Arab sultanates. Eighty years ago it was hoped that a province was being added to Christendom. British rule has merely created an Indian settlement.

It was ironic, too, to find notices in the ship and on the quay requesting European ladies to respect local susceptibilities by dressing modestly. Shades of Mrs Jellyby and of all the sewing parties who used to make 'Mother-Hubbard' gowns to clothe the naked heathen! The French are said to be the most shameless tourists. Unless turned back by the police they parade the bazaar in bikini bathing dresses.

There are no beggars or touts in Zanzibar. The narrow lanes are clean and fragrant and shaded. I saw no changes except that the fort has been tidied and made public. It is a very pretty town. Few buildings are more than 150 years old but all are built in the traditional fashion of plastered rubble, painted and repainted, with here and there delicate blue washes relieving the mottled white, with carved doors and hidden gardens, and the streets wander along the paths first traced by pack animals. Besides the usual trash for tourists there are genuine Arab and African antiquities to be found in the shops. The money-changers have vanished, who used to produce from their leather bags gold pieces struck all over the world and still current, priced by weight, whenever the Arab dhows put in port. A few trousered figures flick wads of escudos under the noses of passengers bound for Mozambique, where venerable, turbaned obesities once squatted by their scales. There is still no tourists' hotel. Magicians still frequent the north island of Pemba – coming from as far as the lakes for their final schools in the black art. The reigning Sultan succeeded in 1911 and has been on his throne longer than any living ruler. His subjects have no nationality, part Arab, part Indian, part Swahili; British administration is pure, effective and benevolent. No doubt we shall soon read in the papers about 'Zanzibar Nationalism' and colonial tyranny. . . .

February 23 [Tanganyika]. I do not regret my insincere expression of interest in mediaeval Arab ruins. It has taken me to some delightful places and introduced me to delightful people. Today I booked to fly to Kilwa. My resolution to eschew aeroplanes – like Belloc's to eschew trains on the *Path to Rome* – has had to be broken. The road is impassable at this season; a steamship plies from Mombasa, but to take that would have extended the expedition by some three weeks and inflicted a visit of unbearable length on my kind hosts – for there is no hotel. Visitors must either bivouac or impose themselves as guests on the District Commissioner. So prejudice, now and later, had to be put aside and at noon I stepped into the suffocating little machine (which of course was late) bearing what I was told would be acceptable, a leg of mutton frozen, when I put it in the rack, to the consistency of granite but soft as putty when I presented it to my hostess.

My destination is some 200 miles down the coast from Dar-es-Salaam. There are three Kilwas – the island of Kilwa Kisiwani, all ruins now and a few huts; the sleepy little nineteenth-century town of Kilwa Kivinje, Arab and German built, eighteen miles to the north on the mainland; and Kilwa Masoko, the new boma, or administrative station, to which I was bound. The aeroplane stopped at Mafia Island, a flat grove of coconut and mangrove which attracts deep-sea fishermen. We passed the Rufigi delta where the wreck of a German warship has lain visible for forty years. The Kilwa airstrip is near the boma. Here I was met by the District Commissioner and his wife and carried off to their house. His isolated position gives him a larger measure of freedom from bureaucratic interference than is enjoyed by any of his colleagues in Tanganyika. With the help of two young district officers he governs 3,000 square miles of territory. Inland, it is said, there are more elephants than taxpayers; the few villages are visited on foot in the old colonial style. There are three European bungalows at Kilwa Masoko, an office, a school, two Indian shops and a pier. It is to this pier that the boma owes its existence for in the heady days of the 'Groundnuts Scheme' it was designed to be the railhead for the produce of the still virgin bush. The DC himself is one of the few benefits of that scheme; the 'ground-nutters' have a low reputation, largely I gather deserved, but there was among them an appreciable number of zealous and efficient officers from the army who came out full of the faith that they would be doing something to help feed the victims of the war. These were the first to realise that the scheme was fatuous; some returned to England, others, of whom my host was one, remained in Tanganyika to do valuable work in other services. His wife and he are an exhilarating couple, both devoted to their large, lonely territory, without any regrets for the social amenities of the towns.

February 24. A narrow channel separates the boma from the island of Kilwa Kisiwani. We crossed early in the morning by motor-launch, embarking at the pier and wading ashore up the sandy beach. Once the Sultan of Kilwa ruled from Mafia in the north to Sofala (near the modern Beira) 900 miles to the south. It was by far the greatest of the East African sultanates. Now, with its neighbouring islands of Songo Mnara and Sanji ya Kati, it is inhabited by a few families of fishermen. The Persians probably came here first and set up a dynasty in the tenth century. It was under the Arabs of Oman that the place became great. The Portuguese came there at the beginning of the sixteenth century. In 1589 the Zimba ate all the inhabitants and left a waste that was irregularly reoccupied. Once, in the eighteenth century, it recovered some prosperity, again under the Oman Arabs. It then declined steadily until the last sultan was deported by the Sultan of Zanzibar in the middle of the last century.

Archaeologists, notably Sir Mortimer Wheeler and Fr Gervase Matthew, have lately paid professional attention to the district. There is plenty to delight the mere sightseer.

A very faint, inexpungible tinge of luxury lingers in this desolate island. The goats and the few tiny cows which pasture there have made glades and open spaces of parkland between the trees whose flowers scent the steamy air as though in a Rothschild's greenhouse; gaudy little birds flash and call as they used in the aviary at Hackwood. Phrases from Tennyson's Alcaics come uncertainly and not entirely aptly to mind. 'Me, rather, all that bowery loveliness'; there are no 'brooks of Eden mazily murmuring' on Kilwa, nor 'cedar arches'; but 'rich ambrosial ocean isle' and 'the stately palm woods whisper in odorous heights of even' are exact and might have been written here.

The only man of importance is a nonagenarian dervish, on whom I was taken to call by the DC. He looked like a black Father Christmas. His chief possession is a large, carved bed which is coveted by the museum at Dar. He was not using it that morning, but was recumbent in a low chair, unable to rise to greet us, but attended by a pretty girl who carried a baby he assured us proudly was his own. I once supposed that dervishes employed themselves either in spinning like tops or in breaking British Squares, but I have since looked them up in the encyclopaedia and learned that the term is so wide as to be almost meaningless; they can be orthodox, pantheistic, mystical, political, ascetic, orgiastic, magical, ecstatic; they can live as members of strict communities or as hermits or nomads, mendicants, scholars, revivalists – almost anything, it seems.

While the DC was exchanging politenesses in Kiswahili I noticed over our host's head a framed picture of King George VI with an inscription signed by a former Governor in the name of His Majesty 'as a record of the valuable services rendered by him to his own Country and People and to the British Government in advancing the Moslem religion.' It seemed an odd tribute from the Defender of the Faith.

On saying goodbye the genial old man produced from his bosom a hen's egg and presented it to me. That afternoon the DC's wife had a sewing class on her verandah for the few native girls of the station.

February 25. Drove to Kilwa Kivinje – well laid out, well planted, picturesque, decaying. There are no European inhabitants. An Englishman sometimes visits an office where he transacts business in mangrove bark.

He was in fact my fellow passenger from Dar and returned there with me on the next flight. An aged Swahili magistrate sat in the old German court-house. In the ramshackle little German hospital Indian doctors rather ironically displayed their meagre equipment. A few youths squatted on their door steps playing the endless and unintelligible gambling game of dropping nuts very swiftly and earnestly on a board hollowed out for them as for marbles in solitaire. No crafts survive in the town except, among the women, very simple grass matting; the ancient woodcarvers are represented by a single clumsy joiner. There are a few Indian grocers and a pleasant little market of fish and vegetables. Meat is almost unprocurable; hence my offering of frozen mutton. It was a regrettable and much regretted decision to move the boma to Masoko. Anyone having business at headquarters has a walk of nearly forty miles. There is, I think, no unofficial wheeled vehicle in the district. The DC and his wife knew everyone in the place and were plainly welcome at every door. He had lately on his own initiative repaired the sea wall, thus preserving a promenade dear to Arab social tradition.

February 26. The aeroplane came in the morning to take me back to Dar. There was in it a copy of that day's *East African Standard* containing this paragraph: 'Bishop Homer A. Tomlinson of New York, self styled "King of the World," flew into Dar-es-Salaam last night from Salisbury. He is to crown himself King of Tanganyika today. He intends to leave the New Africa Hotel at 10 a.m. and walk around the town for two hours crowning himself on a suitable site at noon.'

This seemed a happy confirmation of the theme of Eric Rosenthal's *Stars and Stripes in Africa*, which had beguiled my voyage out.

We landed at eleven o'clock. Mr Thompson met me at the aerodrome. He had not heard of Bishop Homer A. Tomlinson's assumption of sovereignty. We drove up and down the main streets of the city looking for him and making inquiries. His progress, if it had occurred, had been unobserved. At noon we came to the New Africa Hotel. This, the leading hotel, is near the Club, separated from the water-front by a little public garden and a war memorial. In the tropic noon the place was quite empty except for half a dozen policemen and two journalists. They were waiting for the Bishop and we joined them in the scanty shade.

I expected a flamboyant figure from Harlem. Instead there presently emerged from the hotel an elderly white man dressed in a blue kimono. He was unattended and somewhat encumbered by paraphernalia. He gave no indication of expecting any kind of ovation. As purposeful and recollected as a priest going to his altar to say Mass, the Bishop shuffled across under the blazing sun, opened a folding chair and sat down in the garden. The police, the two journalists, Mr Thompson and I collected round him. A representative of the local broadcasting organisation appeared with a tape recorder. The Bishop ignored him and like a priest or rather, perhaps, like a conjuror, began arranging his properties. He had a bible, a crown which seemed to be light and inexpensive, a flag, not – shade of Rosenthal! – the Stars and Stripes but something simple but unidentifiable of his own design of blue and white stars, and a bladder. The stuff of his little chair was slightly regal, a pattern of red and gold with ornamental tassels. He dropped the flag over his head as though preparing for a nap. Then he blew noisily into the bladder which proved to be an inflatable, plastic terrestrial globe. He blew hard and strong but there was a puncture somewhere. It took the form of a wizened apple but not a full sphere. After a few more puffs he despaired and laid it on the ground at his feet. Then he removed the flag from his head and began to address us in calm nasal tones.

He was, he said, the acknowledged leader of the largest religious body in the world, about 100,000,000 strong to date. In 1923 he had received the call to be a bishop; in 1953 to be a king. He was the sovereign of fifty-two realms and proposed to complete his vocation by crowning himself in every State in the world including Russia. Under his simple autarchy peace would be assured to all his subjects. He then prayed for the prosperity of Tanganyika, placed the crown on his head, collected his impedimenta and retired to the New Africa Hotel.

The temperature that day was 90°, humidity 100.

From time to time in the next few weeks I had news of him. The Sultan of Zanzibar did not welcome a rival in his dominions. He was forbidden to crown himself there. He got to Nairobi by air but the immigration authorities of Kenya suspected him of subversive activities and would not let him leave the aerodrome. They would not even let him crown himself in the waiting room.

Saturday, February 28 [After Morogoro] . . . We drove on refreshed, and late in the afternoon came to a huge clearing in the bush, 90,000 acres of grassland. This is all that remains of the Kongwa groundnuts plantation which twelve years ago was a topic of furious debate in London and of bitter recrimination in Africa. The Overseas Food Corporation ceased to exist in March, 1955. The Tanganyika Agricultural Corporation is now engaged in saving what it can from the wreck. Some 9,000 head of cattle, in herds of 300, have been put in the care of Gogo families. These tribesmen have reverted to their former scanty dress and rebuilt their houses on the ancestral model, very low rectangles of mud, with flat roofs of turf. Three veterinary and administrative officials are the only white population. The cattle are healthy and may multiply. But the Sodom apple threatens to overrun the pasture if not constantly resisted. If the experts go, the grass will go with them.

At my request R diverged from the main road to visit the once populous site. It was not easy to find. The roads of Kongwa are breaking up, the railway lines have been removed, the airstrip is overgrown. Few buildings remain and those are up for sale. As we drove to the only inhabited bungalow an Englishman came out to ask if we had come to buy the school hall, for the final failure on this disastrous scene has been that of a secondary boarding school, the only one in Tanganyika, which that month was reopening (in the Southern Highlands) after some scandalous goings-on at Kongwa.

On a slight rise stand the empty bungalows which were once called 'Millionaires' Row' and 'Easy Street' where the high officials lived in the intervals of flying to Dar and London; sad sheds with the weed growing high in their gardens. We made our way through the growth and peered through the windows at the empty little rooms. It was hard to conceive that they had ever been the object of derisive envy.

There are two excellent documents. *The Groundnut Affair* by the late Alan Wood, written in 1950, and a brief retrospective paper by Mr A. T. P. Seabrook, the Chief Administrative Officer of the Tanganyika Agricultural Corporation, written in 1957. Wood was a loyal socialist and Public Relations Officer in the early stages of the scheme. When he wrote there still seemed a chance of growing some nuts. When Mr Seabrook wrote, he counted the secondary school which was now being dismantled under our eyes, as one of the positive gains to the Territory.

There was no injustice in treating the fiasco as a matter of party politics. The scheme was conceived in an ideological haze, prematurely advertised as a specifically socialist achievement and unscrupulously defended in London when everyone in Africa knew it was indefensible. No one at the top made a penny out of it. The officials were underpaid and had in some cases given up better jobs to come. I well remember the indignation, some twenty years ago, of a foreign art expert who recounted to me in great detail the transaction by which the National Gallery had acquired a painting of doubtful authenticity. 'And all of them,' he concluded in disgust, 'the Director and his committee are gentlemen of private fortune. Not one of them received even a commission. It could not have happened in any other country.'

Africa has seen many great financial swindles. This was not one of them. The aim was benevolent; the provision of margarine for the undernourished people of Great Britain. The fault was pride; the hubris which

leads elected persons to believe that a majority at the polls endues them
with inordinate abilities.

Mr Strachey's plan was to clear 5,210,000 acres of virgin bush in 1947
which in 1950 would produce 600,000 tons of groundnuts. The total
expenditure, spread over six years, was to be £24,000,000. The estimated
profit was £10,000,000 a year. It does not require acute hindsight to dis-
cern something improbable in this calculation. In September, 1948, the
administrative heads of departments in Kongwa submitted a report
expressing dismay at the progress of the venture. This was ignored. At
the end of that year £18,000,000 had been spent and current expenses
were £1,000,000 a month. No considerable quantity of groundnuts was
ever produced; nor was there a need for them – they were piling up in
mountains in West Africa needing only transport to make them available. Altogether I believe some £40,000,000 were squandered by the
Overseas Food Corporation. Rival politicians had every reason to make a
row about it.

But the imagination is moved by the human elements of the story. The
Labour Government conceived it as their duty as trustees of the native
races to institute trades unions and sent salaried officials to teach them
how to strike for higher pay. In the first year their efforts were rewarded.
The Europeans working at Kongwa had to be enrolled as special con-
stables and organised in armed patrols for the protection of themselves
and their servants. Bands of African spearmen blocked the roads. The
railway stopped running. The tractors lay idle. Police had to be brought in
from Dodoma. The union leaders were taken to prison and the strikers'
demands remained unsatisfied.

Frantic supply officials saw enormous quantities of derelict army
stores accumulate at Dar from the Philippine Islands, brought in unlisted
lots, the useful and the useless inextricably confused.

The site at Kongwa had been selected for its emptiness. It was empty
because it was waterless. The encampment at Kongwa housed some
2,000 men and women from Great Britain and some 30,000 natives.
Their presence among the simple Wagogo came near to dissolving tribal
loyalties. Their high wages put up the price of food so that natives not
employed by the scheme went hungry. Many of the natives who were
attracted by the high wages left their own small holdings uncultivated, so
that less food was grown in the Territory than ever before. Large
quantities were imported to feed those who were supposed to be export-
ers. It was even proposed to import bees into an area where bees were the
principal natural terror, in order to pollinate the sunflowers (which died
of drought anyway). A half of all the liquor imported into Tanganyika

was consumed at Kongwa. It was a new experience for most natives to see Englishmen demonstratively drunk. It was new, also, to see them convicted of theft. Villages of prostitutes, who charged stupendous fees of five shillings or more, sprang up round the encampment. The hospital orderlies did an illicit trade in injections which they pretended cured syphilis. Thieves infested the stores and workshops. A firm official promise that first priority would be given to the erection of 1,000 African married quarters resulted by the end of 1948 in 200, and those inferior to what were provided by the Greek sisal planters; respectable Africans refused to move their families into them on the grounds that Kongwa was a bad address. The equalitarian ideas of the home government found no sympathy in Africa. The infinitely graded social distinctions among the workers (there are seven recognised classes of Mauritians alone) came as a surprise to the English socialists. By the end of 1948 there was a turnover in the labour force of 20 per cent per month.

The pity of it is that many of the original 'groundnutters', like my host at Kilwa, had come out to Africa with high, altruistic motives. These mostly left Kongwa in the first two years. It is ironical now to read what Alan Wood (who himself resigned in protest at the obliquity of public utterances in London) wrote in 1950: 'I believe that in Africa, as in Europe, the only real reply to Communism will be Socialism. The best answer to the Africans who dream of Soviet Russia is to boast that the groundnut scheme can be as remarkable an experiment as anything done under the Five-Year plans; that it is based on some of the same principles, something new in Colonial development, a huge co-operative venture not run for private profit, which will eventually be run by the people who are working for it; but which represents an advance on anything in Russia, in that large-scale economic planning is combined with political freedom.'

We turned back to the main road past traditional villages of the Wagogo. The inhabitants waved cheerfully at us. The immigrants have all departed leaving them much as they were when Livingstone passed through, but the richer for some fine cattle.

March 21. . . . One does not see many Africans in Salisbury; fewer it seemed than in London. There are black porters in the larger shops and the white shop-girls are abominably rude to them. They are also rather rude to their white customers, for they are at pains to demonstrate that under God all white men were created equal. The well-paid plumber who comes out to work in a private house expects to sit down in the dining-room with the family. He has a black, ill-paid assistant who squats outside. Here, as in England, the champions of the colour bar are the classes whose modest skills many negroes can master.

Southern Rhodesia differs historically from, say, Uganda and Nyasaland. Here the whites came as conquerors: there the natives voluntarily put themselves under the protection of the English Crown. The conquest was not a feast of arms to be remembered with pride, but it was an exercise of high chivalry compared with the occupation of Australia, where the settlers regularly put out poisoned food for the aborigines. The tribes which were conquered were, in many cases, themselves recent conquerors. Force of arms had always been recognised in Africa as giving right of possession.

The visitor to Rhodesia sees as little of the natives as a visitor in the United States sees of the very poor. (But in Rhodesia the natives are proportionately more numerous than the destitute in America). They have no obvious tribal characteristics. They are not beautiful like the Masai or buoyant like the Wachagga or picturesquely prehistoric like the Wagogo. All wear a drab uniform of shirt and shorts. They have the hang-dog air of the defeated people, which indeed they are.

What is known of Mashona history is ignominious; they were the prey of the Matabele before white men appeared in the country. Like the slum-dwellers of industrial England in the last century, they get very drunk rather often. They clearly enjoy football and splashing in the water. The missionaries say they have some enthusiasm in religious exercises. But on the superficial observer – or on me at any rate – they cast a gloom not easily dispelled. . . .

March 22. A last tourist trip, to the Matopos. These famous hills are second only to the Eastern Highlands in natural beauty and they are much odder. At Leopard Rock there were comparisons to be made with other scenery in other parts of the world. There is nothing I know at all like the Matopos. They comprise some fifty by thirty miles of bare granite and green valleys. The district caught the particular fancy of Cecil Rhodes and it is here by his wish that he is buried on a spot which he named 'the View of the World', which he designated as a 'Valhalla' for the heroes of the country. It is therefore a region of particular sanctity to patriotic Rhodesians. Also to the Matabele, who first chose it as a burial place for their king, Mzilikazi, who led them here out of Zululand in 1838. When pioneers rifled this royal cave, Rhodes had it walled up and made formal reparation for the sacrilege with the sacrifice of black oxen. But there are older associations than the Matabele. The rock clefts are covered with bushmen drawings of men, animals and unidentified shapes, categorised by archeologists into periods of varying skill, from, perhaps, before the beginning of the Christian era until shortly before the arrival of the Matabele.

Most modern Rhodesians seem to be morbidly incurious about native customs and beliefs. Their predecessors fought the natives, stole their cattle, tricked them into making concessions, but they perforce studied them in a rough and ready way and mixed with them. Dr Jameson was sworn as a member of Lobengula's bodyguard and, in violation of his oath, led the attack against him. Selous, the most famous hunter and explorer of Rhodesia, had a black wife; a mulatto daughter of his lives in the outskirts of Salisbury today. The Afrikaan conception of *apartheid* would have been alien and (I think) outrageous to most of the early adventurers.

Next day, **March 23**, we left at dawn and took the aeroplane to Bulawayo. A car was waiting there to take us to breakfast at Government House. This is the house built by Rhodes for his own use on the site of Lobengula's kraal. It is a charming, low, shady building in the Dutch-colonial style. In an outbuilding there is the model of a reconstruction of the kraal as it stood in Lobengula's day, part cantonment, part cattle ranch. In the trim garden stands a surprisingly paltry tree which is pointed out as the one under which he held court. There is nothing else at Government House or anywhere in his kingdom to awake his memory; his grave is unknown, his treasure stolen or lost, his posterity unrecognised. But he haunts it yet, a deeply tragic figure from Shakespearian rather than from classical drama; Lear, Macbeth, Richard II, he has a touch of them all. What a part for Mr Paul Robeson could be written of his doom. He was the victim of history. The Matabele kingdom was a military institution aptly organised to survive and prosper in any age before Lobengula's. He inherited a superb army and war was the condition of his authority. The young warriors had to blood their spears. If the white men had not entered Central Africa his dynasty might have lasted centuries. He was personally brave, majestic, intelligent and honourable. The curious thing is that he genuinely liked white men, protected them when it was in his power to annihilate, kept his word when he might have tricked them. The white men he met were mostly scoundrels. It is generally supposed that it was their avarice alone which overthrew him.

Mashonaland proved a disappointment to the prospectors. Driven by the hope of finding another Rand or another Kimberley they clamoured for Matabeleland. Contemporary accounts of Lobengula's last decade make shameful reading. The white concession-hunters camped all round him; they brought him champagne and rifles; Dr Jameson treated him with morphia; a squadron of Life Guards paraded before him in full dress; the Jesuits designed a coat of arms for his carriage door. And all the time his regiments watched their huge naked monarch grow fat and muddled. He wrote personally to Queen Victoria for guidance. He sent ambassadors to Cape Town who were kidnapped or murdered. And the young warriors grew mutinous.

It was not only the fortune-hunters who welcomed his fall. Before attacking, Rhodes sought the sanction of the missionaries, and got it. It is hard to realise now that at the time of the Diamond Jubilee many men of good will and intelligence thought the *Pax Victoriana* a reality. The bloody little forays of the Matabele seemed to them a shocking anachronism. Even now you will find people of some good will and some intelligence who speak of Europeans as having 'pacified' Africa. Tribal wars and slavery were endemic before they came; no doubt they will break out again when they leave. Meantime under European rule in the first forty years of this century there have been three long wars in Africa on a far larger scale than anything perpetrated by marauding spearmen, waged by white men against white, and a generation which has seen the Nazi regime in the heart of Europe had best stand silent when civilised and uncivilised notions are contrasted. But the missionaries genuinely believed that the autocrats, their fierce aristocracies and their witches were the only grave impediments to the establishment of the sign of charity. Fr Prestage, SJ, who gave his whole life to natives of Rhodesia wrote: 'If ever there was a just war, the Matabele War was just.'

Lobengula's flight after defeat, aged and half stupefied; his pathetic attempts to make peace by giving a bag of sovereigns to two troopers (who stole it); his wagon of treasure – carrying what? the rubbishy gifts of his European courtiers? ivory? gold? – driven into some cleft in the rocks, hidden, perhaps pilfered, perhaps still there; his disappearance across the river and death, it is said, from smallpox, in an unknown spot; all this comprises the very stuff of poetic drama.

After breakfast we drove back to Bulawayo. It has a quiet, old-fashioned air which, I am told, the inhabitants do not particularly relish. Not long ago it was the commercial capital of Rhodesia. Now Salisbury has cut it out. There are no skyscrapers here. The shops have a sombre, provincial respectability like those of the Scottish Lowlands. The chemist has a panelled window surmounted by the traditional glass bottles of coloured water and, inside, the drawers and jars with the Latin labels that used to delight one's childhood. Salisbury chemists are ablaze with advertisements of patent medicines, cosmetics and baby-foods.

Rhodes's original estate, which he left in trust to the colony, consists of 95,700 acres, the agricultural and arable part divided into fifteen farms let to tenants, and the rocky remainder, which is laid out and maintained as a pleasure ground. This is the Matopo Park, entered through gates presented by a member of the Beit family, which encloses Rhodes's grave on his View of the World. Beyond this there are some quarter of a million acres added by proclamation in 1953.

These do not come under the control of the Rhodes Trustees but of the National Parks Department, who have laid out roads and generally set out to make the place attractive to white tourists by reducing the number of native families. The natives had no wish to move. Many of them had quite clear memories of Rhodes's funeral, and of Colonel Rhodes's subsequent speech in which, with undisguised emotion, he had said: 'As a proof that I know the white man and the Matabele will be brothers and friends for ever, I leave my brother's grave in your hands. I charge you to hand down this sacred trust to your sons that come after you and from generation to generation and I know if you do this my brother will be pleased.'

Would the Great White Chief be pleased, they asked, to see them turned out in under fifty years to make way for picnic parties from the cities? Eventually the decision was modified; some 700 families with ten head of cattle apiece have been allowed to remain.

One can now drive to the foot of the hill called 'the View of the World' and an easy climb takes one to the summit. The panorama is indeed stupendous and worthy of all that has been written and said of it. Rhodes in naming it did not claim it was the finest 'view' in the world; he meant rather that from this quite modest eminence one does in that clear light and unbroken horizon get, as the guide-book says, 'a strange impression of looking out over the uttermost parts of the earth'. It is a curious fact that aeroplanes have added nothing to our enjoyment of height. The human eye still receives the most intense images when the observer's feet are planted on the ground or on a building. The aeroplane belittles all it discloses.

At Rhodes's funeral the Bishop of Mashonaland read a poem of four stanzas composed by Kipling for the occasion. The theme was Vision:

> Dreamer devout by vision led
> beyond our guess and reach.

The terms of panegyric amount almost to apotheosis:

> There till the vision he foresaw
> Splendid and whole arise
> And unimagined Empires draw
> To council 'neath his skies,
> The immense and brooding Spirit still,
> Shall quicken and control.

That was written only fifty-seven years ago and already every prediction has been belied.

In his own lifetime, and largely by his own imprudence and dishonesty, he had seen Afrikaaners and British in South Africa hopelessly embittered. Today his great project of the all-British Cape to Cairo route has lost all meaning; the personal, honourable ascendency of Great White Chiefs has degenerated into *apartheid*. One is tempted to the trite contrast of the achievements of the politician and of the artist; the one talking about generations yet unborn, the other engrossed in the technical problems of the task at hand; the one fading into a mist of disappointment and controversy, the other leaving a few objects of permanent value that were not there before him and would not have been there but for him. But Rhodes was not a politician; or rather he was a minor one. He was a visionary and almost all he saw was hallucination.

He was not, as Jameson disastrously was, a man of action. He was neither a soldier nor an explorer. Much has been made of the incident of his going out almost alone into the Matopos to make peace with the dissident Matabele. It was a courageous act, admirably performed, but in fact it was precisely what Fr Prestage had done with another group of Matabele chiefs four months earlier. The Matabele were then hopeless and leaderless. The promised immunity to rifle fire had proved to be an illusion. They could have been a considerable nuisance if they had continued to sulk with their spears in the inaccessible hills; but they were a defeated people. The significant feature of the celebrated Indabas was the personal effect Rhodes made. He was known to the Matabele only by repute. There can be no doubt that after those meetings they looked to him with something of the awe they had accorded their kings. African politicians who are now idolised, might with profit remember how capriciously these emotions can be aroused among their people.

Rhodes was a financier. He made a huge fortune very young at a time when other huge fortunes were being made. But the Kimberley millionaires were few and they were not lucky prospectors but assiduous businessmen. Rhodes's predominant skill was in the market, in negotiating combinations, monopolies and loans, in beguiling shareholders, in keeping up the price of Chartered Company stock when it never paid a dividend, in using first-hand information to buy and sell, in creating, imposing and preserving a legend of himself that calmed the stock market. And money for him was not an end; it was not the means to pleasure or even to personal power; it was the substance of his dreams.

There is an attractive side to Rhodes's character: his experimental farms; his taste in the houses he chose to live in; his respect for native pieties. The scholarships he founded at Oxford set a model which has been followed in other countries, whose confidence in their 'way of life' is so strong that they believe they must only be known to be loved. It is noteworthy that his scholarships were for Americans, colonials and Germans. The Latin countries were excluded. For his obsessive imagination was essentially puerile. His first Will, made before he had much to leave, provided for the foundation of a kind of secret society dedicated to the supremacy of the Anglo-Saxon race. He had a schoolboy's silly contempt for 'dagoes'; for the whole Mediterranean-Latin culture. He set out quite deliberately to provoke war with the Portuguese and was only stopped by Lord Salisbury. He saw in his fantastic visions of the future a world State of English, Germans and North Americans. But his most important associates both in South Africa and in Europe were nearly all Jews. That is the point, so often missed, of Belloc's 'Verses to a Lord'. There was no conceivable reason why Jews as much as Gentiles should not make fortunes in the diamond and gold fields, or why they should not welcome an exercise of force to facilitate their business. What was absurd was Rhodes's promoting their interests with idiotic cries of Anglo-Saxon racialism. . . .

March 26. The anniversary of Cecil Rhodes's death. Public notices had been inviting the citizens to commemorate the event at his statue in the main square of the town. The Governor was there, some police and some schoolchildren, but it was not an imposing gathering. Rhodes's picture hangs in all public places and in some private ones, but the cultus seems tepid. He is as much revered by the new generation of Salisbury as, perhaps, is Abel Janszoon Tasman in Hobart. The 'immense and brooding Spirit' no longer 'quickens and controls'.

Early that afternoon I took the aeroplane for Cape Town. . . .

March 27. Good Friday. We do not sail until evening, but I do not go ashore. It is pleasanter now to see from the decks the famous view of Table Mountain and the decent old city.

Anyone who travelled by troopship to the Middle East in the days when the Mediterranean was impassable, must have grateful – some, I believe, have tender – memories of the hospitality of Cape Town. After weeks at sea with blackened port-holes we found a town all alight, but much more than this we found what seemed to be the whole population extended to welcome us, the whole quay lined with cars to take us into the country. I remember the scene at night with the men returning to the ship, some drunk, some sober, all happy, laden, many of them, with great bunches of grapes like the illustrations in old bibles of the scouts returning to the Israelites in the desert with evidence of the Land of Promise flowing with milk and honey. It is a memory I prefer to maintain intact. Few peoples anywhere, I suppose, deserve the government they get. Too many English voices are at the moment raised to reproach the South Africans for me to join the clamour.

Comfortable, uneventful days succeed one another; a sense of well-being and repose after not very arduous travel. A half-day's stop at Las Palmas to refuel; a morning pottering round the streets of that charming town. Then on again punctually and smoothly.

April 10. Southampton in the early morning; effortless disembarkation. Nothing to record except appreciation of a happy fortnight. When last I returned from Africa it was by air and I landed, like everyone else, cramped and sleepless and fit only for days of recuperation. Today I came ashore buoyantly, very different from the old fellow who crept into the train south two months ago. That was the object of the trip.

I came abroad, as I noted at the time, with the intention of eschewing 'problems' and of seeking only the diverting and the picturesque. Alas, that is not possible. 'Problems' obtrude. There was in my youth a film which opened superbly with Buster Keaton as an invalid millionaire landing from his yacht in a Central American Republic. He is enjoying a rest-cure. The people of the country are enjoying a revolution. He progresses, if I remember rightly, in a bath-chair, up the main street, totally unaware of the battle raging round him. As the dead and wounded double up before him he raises his hat in acknowledgment of what he takes to be their bows of welcome. One cannot long travel in that way. From Algeria to Cape Town the whole African continent is afflicted by political activities which it is fatuous to ignore and as fatuous to dub complacently an 'awakening'. Men who have given their lives to the continent can do no more to predict the future than can the superficial tourist. All know that there is no solution in parliamentary democracy. But, ironically enough, the British Empire is being dissolved on the alien principles which we ourselves imported, of nineteenth-century Liberalism.

The foundations of Empire are often occasions of woe; their dismemberment, always. . . .

22/29 July and 19 August, 1960

William Harcourt

THE NORTHCLIFFE OF THE NILE

It is very difficult to buy a round of drinks for an Arab, and Sayed Mekkawi was standing me a cup of whisky on the red-tiled terrace of the Cultural Centre, formerly the Junior British Officials' Club, Khartoum.

'You are unemployed at the moment, Your Excellency?' Mekkawi asked.

'I am, Sheikh of Sheikhs,' I replied. The use of these fancy titles is one of those double-take jokes which show that both parties are free from imperialism and anti-imperialistic prejudice.

'Oh,' said Mekkawi. 'Tell me, can you spell?'

'English?'

'Naturally.'

'As well as the next man,' I said. 'Why?'

Mekkawi slid a massive brown paw into the pocket of his white night-shirt-like gellibya and brought out a limp letter.

'Honour me by reading this,' he said.

As I read, he signalled for two more cups of whisky. The letter was from the Ministry of the Interior, informing Mekkawi that unless the standard of the English edition of the *Khartoum Times* improved forthwith, his licence to publish would be withdrawn.

'Standard?' I echoed from the letter.

'The spelling,' Mekkawi explained. He waved his hand wearily over his damp face; it was a matter he was loath to dwell on.

'As you know, we do not distinguish your English "p" and "b" in Arabic.' He dipped into his pocket again and brought out a crumpled copy of his paper.

The banner headline read, 'WELCOME TO BANDIT NEHRU.'

'There have been other unfortunate typographical errors,' said Mekkawi in his cultured Oxford accent. 'Last week we had Khrushchev's 'massage' and a 'litter' from your Mr Macmillan. There have been complaints. The Minister doesn't appear to believe there is room for honest error. Or perhaps,' he sighed resignedly, 'he doesn't want to believe it.'

We sat in silence for a moment. Mekkawi seemed half asleep, sprawled in a deckchair, almost buried beneath his own belly. Then he roused himself. 'Do me the honour of taking employment in my establishment,' he said. 'Forty Egyptian pounds per month for three hours' work each evening, except Fridays, and all the latest scandal thrown in buckshee.'

As jobs don't grow on date palms around Khartoum I agreed – and then, feeling the need to make some generous gesture, I said meditatively, 'One changes with the times.'

Mekkawi closed his eyes again. He knew what was coming.

'New Establishments are sensitive,' I said. 'The Old Civil Secretary seemed to rather enjoy your exposures of the more intimate side of his life but now things are different. Perhaps the Minister's attitude might change if you stopped hinting about his relatives being mixed up in the vice trade in Egypt. Perhaps you should let it be known that you've destroyed those photostats of Egyptian police records you have in that safe in your office.'

Mekkawi sat bolt upright and made a sweeping gesture with his arm. 'It's all gone,' he said. 'Swept away. Colonialism and all its spawn has disappeared. No more corruption, no more nepotism, no more degeneration.' He made a rude Arab sound with his lips and called for two more cups of whisky.

The next evening, as the sun dropped into the Nile, I walked to the *Times* offices for the first time; through Khartoum's old brothel quarter – down dusty unpaved streets and narrow, furtive, mud-walled alleyways. As I passed, the Ethiopian and Arab girls, in European and Arab dress squatting in their doorways, discreetly dropped their veils and whispered '*tali hena*' ('come here'). Further on Ethiopian girls, clad only in semi-transparent cotton frocks, blatantly rolled their bellies and screamed enticements in Arabic. I heard one old-fashioned call in English, 'I am a virgin, Tommee.' Each street-corner café was a masculine oasis of yellow light and blaring Arab music.

Mekkawi's offices were in a broken-down red brick house squeezed in between a brothel and a street-corner café. He greeted me at the door and showed me over the building. In the front room stood his 'foreign correspondent', a radio from which he filched the BBC news. In the former harem part of the house stood the press, not too firmly attached to a concrete base. Stamped on it was 'Hamburg 1898', the year of Kitchener's reconquest of Khartoum.

As we watched at the door the operator switched the press on and bolted past us like a powder-monkey. The whole house started to vibrate as it groaned and clashed into movement like a steam-engine on slippery rails. No one was allowed in the room while the press was in motion,

Mekkawi explained. When the pressure was too great, blocks were liable to fly out and embed themselves in the walls.

The compositors were working on the back verandah, ankle-deep in a mess of discarded paper and printer's ink. Here I met other members of the staff: the foreman, a brown Buddha of a man on the run from Gamal Abdel Nasser; and a mournful, seven-foot-tall Christian Dinka from the Southern Sudan who could read and write English quite fluently, when sober.

On the third night of my new job I was working away, more or less happily, when Nafissa, the madame from next door, stuck her head over the wall. Things were slack, she explained, and perhaps we might like to pop over for a bit of relaxation. Mekkawi was out filling up with whisky and gossip at the Grand Hotel, so the staff downed tools to a man and invited me to follow them over the wall.

The sitting-room of Nafissa's house was dominated by a large portrait of Queen Victoria. Nafissa herself was a walking treasure chest of gold bracelets stretching from her wrists to her elbows, and necklaces of Maria Theresa gold sovereigns stretching from her waist to her neck. The Arabs called her 'arrousat et Nil' ('the beauty of the Nile'). Her fat cheeks were marked with wide vertical cicatrices and her massive bulk was always wrapped in yards of spotless white muslin. Sometimes she would allow her veil to slip from her head exposing her hair, set in hundreds of straight, tiny plaits, greased with animal fat.

We passed the time gossiping with Nafissa's favourite girls and supping on hamaam, young pigeons lightly grilled on a charcoal fire, washed down with aragi, a fiery liquor distilled from dates, with a kick like a racing camel.

About 11 p.m. Mekkawi burst in full of whisky and abused us, invoking the aid of the Prophet against us for wasting office time in a brothel. I learnt later this happened at least once a week.

I got on well enough with Mekkawi until the dry season, when tempers rose with the temperature. Some days it was 120 in the shade and Khartoum was like the stoke-hole of a coal-burning tramp steamer. News was slack, circulation was falling, and as there is no circulation-booster like British imperialism, Mekkawi started on a series of editorials.

We had a difference of opinion, for example, over the editorial on malaria which started, 'We have many insects in the Sudan due to fifty years of British Imperialism.' Quite logical, Mekkawi argued; the British had been in control for fifty years and they should have done something about the mosquitoes.

I also remember ineffectually objecting to his 'cocoa colonialism' campaign. Pepsi-Cola was already well established in the Sudan while Coca-

Cola was just moving in. Mekkawi approached the Coca-Cola company with a proposition. He would produce a Coca-Cola supplement along with an editorial implying that the essence of Pepsi-Cola was made from 'pepsin' which is made from the intestines of pigs. The company refused, so Mekkawi launched his campaign against 'cocoa colonialism.'

Now while there is no harm, and perhaps some advantage, in whipping the tired old lion in the Middle East, the new Establishments are a different matter and Mekkawi could not let sleeping dogs lie. One night, about six months after I had started on the *Times*, Mekkawi burst into the office, grabbed the Leica and beckoned me to follow him. His old enemy, the Minister, was whooping it up in the Kitchener Cabaret. Sure enough, when we entered the cabaret, we saw the Minister sitting at a table behind a potted palm with a cup of whisky in one hand and a cabaret girl in the other. We waited until the lights were dimmed for the floor show. Then, as I held the cabaret door open, Mekkawi crept up behind the potted palm, took a flash of the Minister and ran back through the door.

Back in the office once again Mekkawi sought the advice of his foreman on the Sharia (Moslem) law penalty for a man found guilty of drinking wine.

Next morning the *Times* came out with a full front-page picture of the Minister, glass in hand, cabaret girl beside him, with the caption 'This man deserves forty lashes.'

From then on Mekkawi was a marked man. A few weeks later, in an editorial, he mentioned that the Government party had accepted money from Egypt before the last elections – a fact that was common knowledge anyhow. He was arrested, charged with sedition, released on bail and the *Times* was ordered to cease publication as from noon the next day. It was also hinted that a deportation order might be awaiting a certain *inglesi*, so I booked a seat on the next plane for Cairo and returned to my hotel to pack my bags.

At about 2 a.m. an explosion rocked the city. A few minutes later Mekkawi burst into my room like a bull elephant in season. His gellibya was blackened and he was trembling with rage. Someone had planted a bomb in the *Times* offices, blowing off the roof and destroying the press beyond repair. Fortunately the building had been empty at the time. Would I help him with one last issue of the *Times* before its suppression?

We worked furiously through the night in the offices of a neighbouring newspaper and the last issue of the *Times* came out at noon with the banner headline, 'IMPERIALISM STRIKES' and the leader, 'We will fight on the beaches. We will fight in the towns and country. We will never surrender to Imperialism.'

Mekkawi saw me off on the plane that night. Later I learned the

Government had dropped the charge because of public sympathy for Mekkawi – and no one was unpatriotic enough to believe the suk rumour, spread by the Establishment no doubt, that Mekkawi had insured his offices for ten thousand pounds with an Egyptian insurance company shortly after his story about the Minister and the cabaret girl; and planted the bomb himself.

Since I left the Sudan there have been one successful revolution and several attempted coups, but as far as I know the *Times* is still being published – and on a brand-new press, imported from Germany.

6 January, 1961

Simon Raven

THE SERPENT IN HAPPY VALLEY

Many qualities are commonly imputed to colonial settlers, among them industry, greed, courage and obstinacy; but during the ten months odd which I spent as a soldier in Kenya I found that by far the most interesting was *guilt*. Guilt of a specialised and oddly slanted kind, certainly, but all the more fascinating for that. My own dealings with settlers were mostly social, so that it was on a social level – a level of eating and drinking – that I observed this phenomenon. But a man's attitudes in his pleasures are, if anything, more revealing than those he displays in business or official functions, and I therefore make no apology for treating the matter against a background of frivolity.

Let us, then, consider that most significant of Kenyan institutions, the Muthaiga Club. Situated in a wealthy suburb of Nairobi, the Muthaiga Club is the summit of the settlers' social aspiration. As a serving British officer, I was automatically an honorary member and I was therefore inclined to treat the privilege lightly; but I soon discovered that the waiting list for membership proper was almost endless, that fees and subscriptions were portentous, that the process of election was grudging to the point of inquisition. To admit junior British officers to the club was, in truth, a notable act of hospitality, for colonial officials and locally-born young bucks of comparable standing would not be elected for many years, not until they became formidable in rank or estate. To belong to the Muthaiga, to sleep there when you visited Nairobi for a weekend, was to have obtained, as it were, the letters patent of Kenyan nobility. And for this reason men who seldom came to Nairobi more than once a year, men from the coastal plains of the distant borderlands of Uganda, jostled and intrigued and paid heavy sums in money for a place. Nor, having done so, were they denied amenity: the bar, the longest in the colony, was stocked to meet the most *outré* or extravagant request; the service, provided by squads of white-robed Africans, was immaculate; the rooms, public or private, were comfortable, spacious; even, if you discounted the ubiquitous trophies of the chase, elegant; and the food was various and exquisitely prepared.

All of which was balm to the souls and bodies of exiled Europeans, such as I counted myself. One could eat, drink, sleep as civilised men understood the functions. But here lies the point. Most of the Kenyan members, the farmers and settlers, did not care for these refinements; having paid enormous fees to belong and being on one of his rare visits to Nairobi, the average settler misused this magnificent place of entertainment in order to do just what he did every day at home – to drink gin or whisky from six till ten p.m. and then to go drunk to a plain dinner accompanied by water ('No oysters or fal-de-rols for me, old man; just steak and veg.'). Every effort had been made by the committee to provide a club that would have done credit to London itself: and no pains were spared by the members to assert themselves, constantly and aggressively, as simple men of pioneering tastes who would have none of such decadence.

And yet they were proud of the Muthaiga and wished it to remain exactly as it was. The elaborate dishes and fine wines were untouched save by 'foreigners' (e.g., visiting Englishmen) and the soft-living city-dwellers of Nairobi itself; nevertheless the whisky-swilling 'pioneer' contingent, wholly contemptuous of such luxury, boasted of it all over East Africa ('Why, man, some of them even eat snails'). Nor is the clue to such equivocation far to seek. For on the one hand the settlers were terrified of being looked down on as 'colonials', as ignorant, unmannered bumpkins who knew nothing of the world, and they were therefore anxious to exhibit luxuries and refinements to match any in the West: but on the other hand they despised those who valued such delicacies.

The whole affair finally resolved itself into four simple propositions. First, a settler was as good as any of your Europeans and could meet them on their own ground (i.e., the Muthaiga Club). Second, a settler was much better than any of your Europeans, because he was contemptuous (though not ignorant) of their effete habits and cultures, and preferred a rough, tough, adventurous life and a cuisine consisting of convenient essentials, such as whisky followed by tinned luncheon meat. Third, he was fortified by such customs and sustenance to maintain a firm and unsentimental attitude toward the native African, who was himself a simple man and respected unsophisticated usage. Last, it was the European's over-elaborate and over-leisured habits of entertainment and, by extension, of thought that led them to take up uncalled-for liberal attitudes toward African questions.

A compact view, one might think, and consistent after its fashion. But the essential flaw in these propositions reveals the curious brand of 'settler' guilt. For if pioneer ways were the purest and the best, then why erect – and *covet* – the ultra-smart Muthaiga Club in direct contradiction of those ways? Clearly, there was a guilty doubt lest the 'European' might, after all, be right – and right about African questions as well as about food and drink. And equally clearly, guilt might be temporarily and in part assuaged by entering the halls of luxury and false enlightenment and there defying the tutelary Lares – by wearing tattered drill trousers and insisting on raw spirit and coarse food.

One inevitable result of the Mau Mau emergency in Kenya was an increase in government organisations of every kind, some of which did an excellent job. But all of these still centred round the two oldest – the Colonial Service and the Kenya Police.

Before the emergency, both bodies had been held in esteem; but by the time the Mau Mau revolt was running down, while the Colonial Service remained more or less reputable, the Police had attracted odium and contempt. It was all a matter of recruitment. The Colonial Service, compelled by ever-increasing commitments to make temporary appointments and to advertise short-term contracts, was nevertheless careful to offer these either to old 'Africa hands' or the more presentable of their sons; with the result that their new auxiliaries had some knowledge of Africa and were disposed, provided their authority went unquestioned, to treat Africans fairly. The Police bestowed their contracts altogether less discriminately and attracted some of the riffraff of England and the Colony. Young men turned up as 'Inspectors' (to receive generous salaries and to command large bodies of native policemen) who had often never been out of England – and, what was far worse, the sort of young men who had been kicked out of their university for drunken driving or were in trouble in their home town for cashing bad cheques. In common with 'white trash' everywhere, they were eager to find someone – anyone – over whom they could claim superiority. The native African was the ideal victim for this purpose. Africans were wrongfully arrested, prisoners and suspects were beaten up.

In 1956 I was attached to a company of English soldiers which was stationed near a village in the foothills of the Aberdare Mountains. It was an important village, the seat both of the local District Officer, an old and unusually civilised Kenya number with an emergency Colonial appointment, and of the local Chief Inspector of Police, an Irishman called Lynn Flynn, who was of the 'old' and regular school of policeman and was liked by us well enough. I should explain the 'Chief Inspector' was the lowest 'commissioned' rank in the Kenya Police. 'Inspectors', of whom Lynn Flynn had several under him (all of them 'short contract' men), scattered round the locality, were considered as being on probation as Lynn Flynn made very plain, to be reckoned only as the equals of our own sergeants. He therefore suggested that any of his Inspectors who had business with us (information about Mau Mau and the like) should be entertained, if at all, in the Sergeants' Mess. This did not at all suit the temporary Inspectors' *amour propre*. In their dealings with other units of the army they had often contrived to bluff their way into Officers' Messes and they did not like being excluded here.

Now, the pride of our Officers' Mess at this time was an African cook, whom we paid out of our own pockets and who had once cooked in Government House itself. Thence he had been dismissed by some busybody for being discovered drunk; but we had argued that any good cook must be expected to drink, and since he carried the recommendation and the security clearance of our own District Officer, we had engaged him. And had no cause to regret it. He could improvise a *bouillabaisse* out of the dreariest tins, he knew all about the use of cream, brandy and wine, and he had a knack of making even the skinny local chickens seem plump and tender. True, he not only got drunk at night but also behaved louchely with the village women; but artists of his calibre, we said, must be allowed some moral licence – and in any case (this rather inconsequentially) he was a great favourite with the men, who called him 'Randy Dad'.

So no one was at all pleased when Lynn Flynn went off on a course and the morning after his departure an Inspector – his stand-in – drew up in a Land-Rover and said that he had come to arrest our African cook. On what charges? we asked. Charges, he said, need not be specified – under Emergency Regulation So-and-So. What about a warrant? Not needed – under Emergency Regulation So-and-So. But – this was Army ground, WD property, and unless he could show a warrant authorising him to enter and make his arrest, then he should now leave at once before he was thrown off . . . First round to us. The Inspector drove away radiating high-frequency malevolence, while Randy Dad beamed and started to prepare an extra-special lunch.

The next day the Inspector was back, armed with a warrant apparently signed by everyone from the Provincial Commissioner downward; and

Randy Dad was taken away, a sad little figure in the back of the police Land-Rover, to be charged, so the Inspector in his triumph was indiscreet enough to tell us, with raping a girl in the village.

That night the District Officer was to come to dinner. He had especially asked for Randy Dad's Suprême of Chicken cooked in *pâté de foie* and was vexed when given a corn-beef hash. We explained what had happened, but he sulkily refused bridge and left at once. The next morning he reappeared: he had been questioning the local men and women, it seemed, and discovered that the Inspector had been badgering them for any information such as would make our poor old cook suspect of complicity with the Mau Mau. They hadn't given it, for they had none; but after the fashion of Africans being questioned by a white man they had politely agreed that the Bwana was no doubt right. This had given the Inspector his excuse for his first attempt at arrest. Thwarted, he had then used bribes and threats to induce a black girl who was known to have granted her favours to Randy Dad to say that she had in fact been raped: hence the high-powered warrant.

What the Inspector did not know, and what could hardly have occurred to anyone so ignorant and so base, was that the local Africans held their District Officer in some reverence and affection, if only because he spoke their language fluently, and fell over themselves to tell him any news they thought he would be grateful to hear. So the Inspector's attempt to revenge himself on us through our stomachs was speedily squashed. What became of him I have no idea, as I left the district a few days later. But it was just this combination of malice, stupidity and bad dealing on the part of 'short-contract men' which afflicted the Kenya Police throughout the Emergency.

The 'new' racecourse in Nairobi is some two miles out of the city proper, up the Ngong Road and beyond the cemetery. The surroundings are attractive, the course itself is well laid out, and the arrangements for eating and drinking compare more than favourably with those at the Ally Pally or Hurst Park. The racing itself, however, gives less cause for satisfaction. Despite a positively Augean clean-up in 1954, despite the unquestionable integrity of the stewards, there remains an impression, so strong as almost to amount to physical presence, that there is something about Nairobi races incurably and inalienably *wrong*.

There could, of course, be several very simple reasons for this. The horses are none of the finest, and African stable boys are no more scrupulous than any other kind. The wealthy settlers who predominate among the owners, having spent their youth and maturity in a rough and ready 'frontier' atmosphere inimical to moral or financial refinement, are often less delicate in their 'arrangements' than the stewards might wish. And then there is the matter of the jockeys. For professional jockeys, Kenya can be very near the end of the line; they may have been warned off in England, Australia, India and Hongkong before arrival, and be somewhat less than predictable. But none of this entirely accounts for the leprous state of racing in Nairobi.

Late in the summer of 1955 I attended Nairobi races with an advertising manager from the city, famous for his poker and his knowledge of form. But the form, as always in Nairobi, was totally unreliable, and so, being heavily down after the first five of the seven races, I selected a horse for the sixth by the ancient pagan method of waiting to see which was the last to defecate before they left the paddock. This animal duly obliged at long odds, cleared my previous losses, and left me a nice sum of 'up-money', all of which I decided to risk on the last race. Feeling that the old gods, by so kindly arranging the omen for me, had done all that could be expected of them for one day, I reverted to the Christian faith and chose a horse called Holy Roller. My advertising chum was sceptical and remarked that Holy Roller's jockey, whom I'll call Addy Bates, had only just recovered from a terrific bout of DTs. Not to mention, he added, that he was thought to be wanted on charges of fraud and bigamy in Lourenço Marques.

From the start of the race a horse called Naivasha Boy took up and maintained a lead of some five lengths; Holy Roller never got within three lengths of him and at the post he was a clear second to Naivasha Boy – who was cheered in with some enthusiasm since his jockey, a cheeky little African, was a favourite with spectators both black and white.

'Well,' I said, 'it was worth a try.' And started towards the car park.

'I shouldn't go just yet,' my chum said. 'There might be an objection. Addy Bates is a great one for objecting.'

'He can't object,' I said, 'the black boy went right ahead at the start and neither Addy nor anyone else got within a mile of him.'

'All the same . . . ,' my friend said. And at that moment the loudspeaker announced an objection.

'They won't allow it,' I said. 'They can't. Addy must be warming up for another go of DTs.'

'He could always say something happened at the start,' my friend said. 'It was a bit of a mess. And in any case I rather *think* you'll find that Addy will now get the race.'

And so it was. Naivasha Boy was disqualified (the alleged reason for this being obscured by a sharp cackle from the loudspeaker), Holy Roller was declared the winner and I had picked up a very pleasing sum.

'And now,' I said, 'perhaps you'll explain?'

'People here are rather keen on keeping the blacks in their place.'

'Meaning no black jockey can ever win a race?'

'Oh no. It's quite all right for black jockeys to beat white ones. But if a white one raises an objection . . . that means a white man is accusing a black of cheating. And if a white man does that, he *must* be upheld as a mere matter of face. In this case, I expect Addy cooked up some story about the start of the race – and he just had to be believed. There's still a few jockeys, mostly amateurs of course, who are too sporting . . . But with a man like Addy Bates, to object is standard procedure – unless he'd happened to back the African himself . . . But what the hell are you moaning about? You won money, didn't you?'

And there was a lot, of course, in that.

24 March, 1961

Shiva Naipaul

MASTERS, SLAVES AND UHURU

It was my last day in the small lakeside town and the Kenyan couple with whom I had been staying suggested that it would be a good idea for me, a traveller from distant regions, to introduce myself to the District Commissioner of the area. It would, they implied, be not only a courteous gesture but a modest act of homage rendered to the new Kenya whose virtues had been sung loudly to me during the previous weekend, 'You will like the DC,' my friend's wife assured me. 'He is one of the kindest, most honest men I know. You won't meet a more straightforward person anywhere.'

If the DC's proclaimed honesty, straightforwardness and kindness were surprising qualities (in black Africa power, whether exercised by a President for Life or a petty bureaucrat, is a raw, untamed force), no less so was the revelation that he was a Masai. A Masai . . . Like the mountain tribesmen of the North-West Frontier and the Arabs of the deep desert, the Masai – a condensation of the dark heart of Africa – have consistently fed the sex-based fantasies of many Europeans. To such they have seemed (borrowing the language of Joseph Conrad) 'savage and superb, wild-eyed and magnificent.' Karen Blixen gives perhaps the classic summary of this European reaction to the Masai in her well-known book *Out of Africa.* 'A Masai warrior is a fine sight . . . daring, and wildly fantastical as they seem, they are still unswervingly true to their own nature, and to an immanent ideal . . . The muscles of their necks swell in a particularly sinister fashion, like the neck of the angry cobra, the male leopard or the fighting bull, and the thickness is so plainly an indication of virility that it stands for a declaration of war to all the world with the exception of the woman.' The sexual appeal is overt in this bizarre passage which, I believe, tells us rather more about Karen Blixen – and cobras; and leopards; and fighting bulls – than it does about the Masai.

The sedentary Kikuyu (like the Bengali babu, like the town Arab) suffered by comparison. He was condemned for his cunning, his laziness, his pretensions, his restiveness. On the other hand, almost every trait of the Masai lent itself to fantasy: their physique (tall and slim); the Hamitic regularity of their features; their nomadism; their militaristic code; their history of conquest and their predatory relationship with neighbouring tribes; their resistance to the arts and habits of modern civilisation; even their diet (milk and blood) was a contributing factor. Alas, all things change. Today, the sexual pull between black and white, broadened and cheapened by package tourism, embraces anything that looks suitably black and suitably primitive – even the level-headed Swiss have been known to go native. The wheel has turned full circle for the maligned Kikuyu whose political ascendency is now firmly established over Kenya; it is now *de rigueur* to heap praise on his cleverness. As for the Masai, they have become a worry to the men from the World Bank and UNESCO. Resistant as ever to the necessities of contemporary existence, they continue – when they are not selling their Masaihood to the tourists – to roam the sere plains of their reservations, trailing after their herds of under-nourished, under-productive cattle, turning the land over which they pass into desert. All in all, the man I was about to meet – a humane Masai bureaucrat – could be considered something of a phenomenon.

We were welcomed with subdued official graciousness. The hand that I shook was fleshy, moist and femininely limp; the voice that spoke was fluting and petulant. The DC, swollen rather than plump, moved with pained slowness. All that remained to him of his Masai ancestry were the narrow nomad eyes; eyes born to the searching scrutiny of luminous plains. They possessed a curiously goat-like intensity and their gaze seemed disturbingly out of place in a domestic setting. I could detect nothing in him of the angry cobra, the male leopard or the fighting bull. Civilisation had had a bad effect on the DC.

We were taken upstairs to the sitting-room. The house, overlooking the grey lake, was full of swirling, water-cooled breezes. The official photograph of Kenyatta (to be found even in brothels), Father of the nation, First President of the Republic – known to one and all as Mzee, the Old Man – was prominently displayed. Grouped about it were a number of reproductions of paintings with religious themes. A neatly printed placard informed us that Jesus Christ was the head of the DC's household. He was the 'Silent Guest,' the 'Unseen Listener.' The twin pieties of Heaven and Earth, of Christ and the Mzee, hung heavy in that lake-cooled room. Coca-Cola and cake were offered by the DC's wife. The DC, in a piping drawl, asked if I was enjoying my visit to Kenya.

I said I was and, for a while, extolled the physical beauties of the country.

'Uhmmm . . . uhmmm . . . uhmmm . . .' The distracting, goat-like noise faded away only gradually.

I sipped my Coca-Cola and nibbled at my slice of cake.

'Uhmmm . . . uhmmm . . . uhmmm . . .'

I looked from Jesus to the Mzee. Silent Guests. Unseen Listeners.

The DC inquired next about the state of education in Trinidad. He wanted to know if the literacy rate was high. I said I did not know the precise figure but believed it was quite high.

'Higher than in Kenya?'

'I think it is. But . . .', I added quickly, anxious not to appear too boastful,' . . . but you have a much bigger population to cope with. For us it's relatively easy. For you . . .'

'What's the population of Trinidad?'

'We are only one million.'

'That is *very* small. Here we are over twelve million.'

I nodded humbly. 'So,' I said, perhaps a little too eagerly, 'your problems are twelve times as difficult.'

The DC brought his palms together. 'Uhmmm . . . uhmmm . . .' He seemed not to be listening. 'Tell me, is Fiji independent as yet?'

I was not prepared for this. I washed down the last of the cake with the last of the Coca-Cola. 'Did you say Fiji?'

'Yes. Fiji. Has it got its independence as yet?'

'I believe they've been independent for some time,' I said. 'But I don't know too much about Fiji. That's in the South Pacific. A long way from Trinidad.' I smiled apologetically.

The DC paid no attention to this disclaimer. He went on rubbing his palms. 'What's the situation over there nowadays?'

I looked at him questioningly, wondering what 'situation' he might be referring to. 'Do you mean the education situation in Fiji? I'm afraid I . . .'

The goat's eyes wandered dreamily about the room. 'Somebody told me that the Asians over there began to outnumber the local people. Is that true?'

Of course! How foolish of me not to have guessed. There was silence in the room as we each, in our own way, contemplated the racial nightmare. It was a truly malevolent moment. I was not an individual any more. The racial nightmare had, in the twinkling of an eye, transformed me into a spokesman for my race; one more specimen of a dangerous breed. (Later, in Tanzania, I met a man on a train who, when I told him I had been born in Trinidad, leaned forward and whispered in a sickening mockery of intimacy, 'Tell me something. How is it that *you people* get everywhere?')

To the DC I murmured something about constitutional arrangements which ensured etc . . . etc . . .

'Uhmmm . . . uhmmm . . .' He did not seem convinced.

More Coca-Cola, more cake was offered. The talk became general. And when the DC heard that I was planning to leave for the Highlands later that day, he offered to arrange my transport. He levered himself up carefully from his armchair and went out of the room.

My friend's wife inclined her head towards me. 'Isn't it kind of the DC to take such trouble on your behalf! I told you he was a nice man.'

The DC returned. Everything, he announced, had been arranged. I had nothing to worry about.

'It really is kind of you to take so much trouble,' my friend's wife said aloud.

The DC was deprecatory.

It was time to go: our host had clearly run out of small talk. We rose and made our farewells, my friend's wife continuing to exude loud gratitude for the cake, the Coca-Cola, the trouble that had been taken on my account. As we drove down the gravelled drive, she said, 'In the colonial days we could never have gone to the DC's house for a drink. Such a thing could never have happened.' Her eyes glowed, radiant with an inner delight.

Ah . . . the joys of Uhuru!

From a letter in the *Daily Nation*, 7 September, 1976:

'. . . it is incredible that an Asian who has been living in Kenya for at least the last ten years . . . is ignorant of the true reasons why the Kenya African still has a deep resentment towards citizens of Asian origin . . . He not only remains the same bigot he was fifty years ago but has also become a master of pretence and a firm believer in the philosophy of eating his cake and having it . . . sooner than later he will (like Rhodesian Smiths) live to regret . . . he must discard his bigotry and pretence. Then, and only then, should he demand that the African recognise him as an equal human being . . .'

Not many days after I had arrived in Nairobi I was treated to a modest display of the African's 'deep resentment' of the Asian. Someone – an 'Asian' as it happened – came for me in his car which he parked in the vicinity of a taxi rank. As I was stepping in, one of the drivers, put out at being deprived of a fare, came rushing over and banged on the window. 'That's the trouble with you Asian coolies,' he shouted. 'You want to keep Africans poor. You don't want us to have anything.' Coolie – as a term of racial abuse – is well-known in Trinidad. It was many years since I had last been so addressed: the Nairobi taxi driver's use of the term provoked a flood of nostalgic memories.

Why is the Asian so much disliked in East Africa? The question is an interesting one. Kenya's Europeans have not inherited this burden of resentment. On the contrary. They continue to prosper and seem daily to grow more secure and confident. In fact, their confidence is such that an ex-settler politician like Sir Michael Blundell could declare in a recent interview published in *Newsweek* that he could foresee the day when Africans would be electing Europeans as their representatives in the National Assembly. I have no doubt that he will be proved right; having a white MP can easily become a sort of status symbol. On the face of it the situation is a peculiar one. Who, after all, did more 'harm' to the African? Was it not the settler who banished him from the Highlands? Was it not the settler who consistently denied him – and the Asian – an effective political voice? Was it not the settler who was the direct cause of the brutal Mau Mau campaign? Yet much of this is forgiven and even forgotten – except, of course, on sacred occasions like Kenyatta Day when the tired old rhetoric of anti-colonialism is dutifully wheeled out by politicians in three-piece pin stripe suits.

In Kenya history has been rewritten and falsified. Thus, in the *Newsweek* interview already referred to, Sir Michael Blundell can say this: 'In Kenya the Africans got to know the settlers and understand them. Settlers and Africans would help one another when they were ill . . . out of this grew the present very friendly atmosphere.' Very touching. But is it the whole truth and nothing but the truth? Did whites and blacks really go rushing over to each other's sick beds? It is both sad and amusing to see Kenya's grim colonial past being reduced to such frivolous maunderings. On the other hand the Asian is now portrayed as a miserly dukawallah (small shopkeeper) who ceaselessly exploited and cheated the innocent African. Is *that* the whole truth and nothing but the truth?

'It is the Indian trader who, penetrating and maintaining himself in all sorts of places to which no white man would go or in which no white man could earn a living, has more than anyone else developed the early beginnings of trade and opened up the first slender means of communication. It was by Indian labour that the one vital railway on which everything else depends was constructed. It is the Indian banker who supplies the larger part of the capital yet available . . .' The writer is Winston Churchill, reporting on his visit to the East African territories in the early years of this century.

Typically, it takes a European eye to see the Asian achievement; to point out the heroism – even the romance – of their activities in East Africa. The traders and bankers and navvies about whom he writes would never have perceived the larger significance of their labours. They would never have thought of themselves as 'pioneers' opening up a continent. In their peculiar Indian way, they would have been myopically chained to their particular vocations, cocooned in the claustrophobic world of caste and community loyalty, and hence utterly incapable of the Churchillian vision. Few people are more prosaic and have so fractional a perception of the world. Other men – and they have been few and far between – have had to sing on their behalf. This near-total absence of imagination has played no small part in the downfall of the East African Asian. It has led to him losing his case by default; to his pathetic reliance on his British passport; to the lies and caricatures that now imprison him. A people without vision must inevitably perish. The Asian, blind at the beginning and blind to the point of idiocy at the end ('We are very Western,' they tell you in their lilting Gujerati accents, 'we like opera') is doomed to further suffering. And not only in Africa.

But the European knew – and still knows – how to sing his own songs. More importantly, he knows *what* songs he must sing. He starts with an immense advantage: the African's longing to be absorbed, to lose himself, in the white man's world. Out of this has been forged the black-white dalliance in independent Kenya; the forgiving and the forgetting. Between oppressor and oppressed, master and slave, there exist profound psychological bonds. (Never come between a man and his slave: the slave will surely kill *you* first!) Beyond all else, the slave yearns to be *like* the master. His hatred, so full of cruelty, is often no more than a perverted adoration turned inside out. It is because of this yearning for the oppressor that slaves are never genuine rebels. The history of Jomo Kenyatta following the heady days of Mau Mau furnishes ample evidence of that; as do the European MPs predicted by Sir Michael. The slave is a born conservative.

The Asian could offer the African none of the psychological satisfaction which the European had at his disposal. Alien, hermetic and lacking in the prestige that only power can confer, the Asian universe is not attractive to the African. The Asian is a nowhere man in the eyes of the

latter; an obvious victim. The African wants his shop. Beyond that he has
no further use for him. He also wants, it goes without saying, the rich
Highland farms. Both these things, for the most part, he has obtained. But
from the European he wants something more than mere land: he wants to
be told by him and him alone that he is a man.

1 *January, 1977*

Shiva Naipaul

JOURNEY TO THE KENYAN HIGHLANDS

The taxi which had been arranged for me by the District Commissioner
was already more than fifteen minutes late. However, I did not worry
unduly. 'You will get royal treatment,' my friend's wife had assured me.
'Remember it's the DC himself who fixed it up for you. If anything goes
wrong and *he* makes a complaint, you can be sure that somebody somewhere will be out of a job. Just one word from *him* and . . .' She paused,
smiled broadly and patted my wrist, 'Don't you worry about a thing. You
will be treated like a king.' She laughed pleasantly.

I glanced at my watch (the taxi was now over twenty minutes late),
thought of my kingly powers and was comforted. One telephone call
from me to the DC and somebody somewhere . . . The prospect, as the
minutes ticked by and no taxi showed up, of throwing someone somewhere out of a job became increasingly alluring. But I decided to exercise
restraint. In any case, I was not at all certain that my complaint would
be well received. I harboured grave reservations about the DC's goodwill towards me. Across the road from the wide glass-louvred veranda
of the hotel red roofs showed through the dark green foliage of what I
took to be mango trees. Further on, I could see a colourless arm of the
lake. A canoe, hugging the line of the shore, was being poled slowly along
it. Beyond the lake an olive-green plain faded into a rampart of bare
hills. A wide-winged bird of prey soared through the blue depths of
the sky. The iron silence of early afternoon had closed in over the
land.

Looking at the lake, the hills, the sky, one sensed the vastness and emptiness of the continent. Africa is not built on a human scale: stand on the

edge of a plateau whose sides rise sheer from a plain some three thousand feet below; gaze out over a tawny ocean of land dissolving in the misty distance to barely discernible mountain ranges, mere emanations of colour and line, that float mirage-like against a luminous sky; realise that in all that vertiginous expanse of space and light there is no sign of human habitation or handiwork. The beauty is awesome.

'Sit straight! Just look at the mess you are making! Your table manners really are a disgrace!'

I emerged from my reverie with a start. The English voice, clear, precise, confident, travelled down the length of the veranda. Turning, I saw its source: a handsome, sun-browned woman, most of whose face was hidden behind a pair of dark glasses. Sitting beside her were two children. A benignly smiling man – presumably Daddy – completed the party. I listened as the woman, oblivious to everything, fussed, scolded and corrected. I had been in Africa for only a month but already such echoes from Western suburbia rang strangely in the ear, possessing an almost surreal quality. These lessons in table manners were touching – and faintly ridiculous; as touching and ridiculous as dressing for dinner in the middle of the jungle.

A motor-car horn blared in jarring, semi-musical notes. I looked out and on the road below saw an ancient Peugeot station-wagon. Blazoned across its rear windscreen in garish lettering was the legend, 'Love You Baby.'

'Your taxi,' a waiter said.

I looked at him doubtfully. 'There must be some mistake,' I said. 'The DC himself arranged . . .'

He regarded me coldly. The horn blared again.

'That is your taxi,' the waiter said.

Surely the DC could not have had a vehicle like this in mind. That thing standing outside the hotel was nothing but a *matatu* – a pirate taxi – of the lowest order. They were notorious for their gross overloading; their mechanical defects; their unlicensed drivers. Scores of people were killed annually by matatus. Surely . . . Once again the horn blared. The driver screeched impatiently from the roadway. I gathered up my bags and hurried out of the hotel. My kingly status had melted away with alarming suddenness. High up in the blue sky the bird of prey soared with serene confidence.

The driver seized my bags and tossed them into the rear of the station-wagon without ceremony. Raucous music raged from a cassette machine ensconced in the dashboard. By now my ear could recognise without difficulty the deadly harmonies of Zairean pop music – then enjoying a great vogue in Kenya.

'Listen,' I said, trying to make myself heard above the uproar. 'Listen . . . Did the DC arrange for this car?'

He stared at me with sullen incomprehension.

'The DC,' I shouted. 'The *District Commissioner*. Are you sure this was the car he arranged for?'

He continued to stare at me, sullenness turning to irritation. Finally, he muttered words in a strange language and, shrugging, got into his seat and slammed the door. It was an ultimatum.

'Can't you speak English?' I shouted.

He started the engine. I got in. He indicated that I was to sit in the back row. I climbed over the middle seat and huddled despairingly against a window.

Africans tend to drive either dangerously fast – or dangerously slowly. This one drove dangerously fast, horn ceaselessly sounding; and, all the while, the Zairean music poured forth at top volume. It was the noisiest vehicle I had ever travelled in. Driving in Africa is high adventure. It is impossible to tell what your driver or the driver of the car ahead – or behind – will, from moment to moment, decide to do: for no apparent reason any or all of these might take it into their heads to switch lanes; or stop without warning in the middle of the road to have a chat with a friend; or suddenly accelerate and overtake on an inside lane or blind corner or steep rise where the oncoming traffic is an unknown quantity. (Pedestrians too are unpredictable. Without even a cursory glance to right or left, they will turn and walk calmly across the road.) The roadsides of East Africa are littered with the rusting remains of motorcars, buses and lorries. On a recent drive from Mombasa to Nairobi I counted no fewer than four freshly overturned lorries.

The African's relationship to modern technology is a problematical one. He falls on it with childish, uncaring zest – no bank clerk will deign to perform the simplest arithmetic without resort to his little electronic calculator which lights up so prettily whenever he presses one of its buttons. The world represented by that electronic calculator is a magical one; little understood, but greatly – oh so greatly! – desired. In its essence, the nature of the ties linking the African with the European has not really changed since the first Portuguese ships went sailing down the west coast of the continent; the sophisticated magic of the white man remains irresistibly alluring to the black. The African did not, in any fundamental sense, want to know how to make the glittering baubles which the white man dangled before him during the early centuries of contact. He was content with simple possession. To achieve that end he was prepared to sell anything on which the Europeans cared to put a price. One aspect of the contemporary black tragedy is that the desire simply to possess remains uppermost in the mind of the African. He is content to *appear* modern rather than *be* modern; he opts for the shadow and not the substance. The skyscrapers of Nairobi symbolise nothing more than the power of self-delusion. Between black and white the gap of civilisation has, if anything, widened over the centuries. No aid project devised on earth – or in heaven – can ever lessen the terrifying gap of intellect between a race of men who can land on the moon and another who, if left entirely to themselves, would, in all probability, be unable to manufacture a bicycle pump.

'But what can you expect from people who have just emerged from the jungle?' The Nairobi-based entrepreneur spread his arms wide and smiled resignedly. 'Be realistic. Some of our friends here are less than a generation removed from the jungle. What *can* you expect from them?' From the story he had just told me I knew he had personal reasons for bitterness. Not all that long ago his engineering firm had been awarded a contract by one of the major state-owned organisations. To begin with he had had an Asian workforce. The job had been completed in record time; the workmanship was of a high standard; everyone had been full of praise. As a result, he had been given a new contract. But then had come the first expulsions of the Asians. Virtually overnight his workforce evaporated. To keep in line with the policy of Kenyanisation he was forced to employ Africans in their place; and virtually overnight the quality of the work dropped drastically. Their laziness was the least of their faults.

The entrepreneur shook his head. 'You can take it from me that Africans don't know about straight lines. They just don't seem able to grasp the concept of a straight line.' Metal plates were bent and twisted one on top the other; every screw was awry. 'You must understand these weren't people I had picked up off the street. They were "qualified." They could show you their certificates.' He had sacked them all and had himself physically completed the job, working day and night. 'Look at me. I'm not a young man. My hair is grey. Do you know they wanted to give me another such contract? "Thank you very much," I said, "but you can keep your contract. I've had enough. You can get in touch with my competitors." The only thing you can do with our friends is to give them a nice chair, give them a nice-sounding title and put them in a position where they can do least harm.' Beyond the windows of the restaurant where we were sitting the lights of Nairobi twinkled with Manhattanesque self-assurance.

Was he exaggerating? Perhaps. Stories of African conceptual incapacity have acquired something of the abstract quality of fable. There is a famous one about wheelbarrows. One version of the story goes something like this. Some Africans are building a road. Their European adviser watches them running to and fro carrying basketsful of stone on their heads. They are quickly exhausted and have to take frequent rests. He goes away and returns with a wheelbarrow. He explains its advantages – the physical effort required is considerably less, the load that can be carried much greater and so on. Do they understand? 'Yes sah! Yes sah!' Dozens of wheelbarrows are supplied. Some days later his foreman comes to him in a state of great agitation. The workers, he reports, are on the verge of complete physical collapse. Naturally enough, the European adviser is astonished. 'But that is impossible. I gave them wheelbarrows!' He rushes off to the site to see what is happening. And what does he find when he gets there? (At this point the eyes of the storyteller usually light up merrily.) He finds that the African workers have been trying to carry the fully loaded wheelbarrows on their heads. Get that? *On their heads!* Imagine all those darkies (they never managed to invent the wheel, you know) lifting up their wheelbarrows and . . . and . . . There follows explosion after explosion of helpless laughter.

This story, varying in its detail, was told to me by a number of people each of whom swore that it was absolutely true. One even claimed to be a good friend of the 'European adviser' involved. All I can say is that I have seen Africans handling wheelbarrows in a perfectly normal manner. I consigned the story to the realms of racist apocrypha. Nevertheless, not many weeks ago a small news item on the back page of the *Daily Nation* made me pause. It told the tale of three African workers who had incinerated themselves while attempting to weld a petrol tank that was full of petrol.

'People [from Europe] go to Africa,' Elspeth Huxley wrote in 1943, 'and they see Africans living in a way which appears to them . . . shocking in its lack of scope, its ignorance and simplicity. They do not always stop to consider that you can't convert in the space of forty years a people living at an early Iron Age level of culture . . . to a level achieved after two thousand years of civilisation, and after the Industrial Revolution.' Elspeth Huxley is not a 'liberal' in the current sense of that term. But in this passage she espouses a type of argument commonly to be met with among those Europeans in Africa – mainly expatriates on two- or three-year contracts – who, out of blind ideological or sentimental conviction, and despite all evidence to the contrary, refuse to despair about the future of the dark continent. There are two points I would like to make; and make, alas, all too briefly. The first is that Africans – not all certainly, but a significant number – have been exposed to European influences for almost four centuries; and, on the East Coast, they have had contacts with the great civilisations of the Middle East and India for a thousand years or more. Challenge has not provoked response – as it did, say, in the case of the Japanese when they were confronted by the superior technical skills of the West. The second point, not unconnected with the first, is the near-magical transforming qualities the liberal attributes to 'Time.' 'Give them time' is the phrase one hears again and again in Africa. But Time is an entirely neutral element. By itself it guarantees nothing. It is the actions of men that matter. Neither Time nor the most altruistic breed of expatriates will ever be able to 'convert' the underdeveloped peoples of the earth; or instil into them the passionate energies that result in creation. How do you teach a man to cling to the substance and not the shadow? Conversion can only come from within. Without the will to create, without the lifesaving vision of his own autonomous manhood, the African will never find his way.

We drove to the bus-station which was crowded, dirty, noisy and hot. The driver moved energetically among the throng touting for custom. A young girl with a baby settled beside me; the place next to her was taken by a man in bright yellow trousers carrying an enormous transistor radio – the type of transistor radio one only sees in the underdeveloped world. Gradually the middle row filled up. A fat, voluble woman took possession of the seat beside the driver. Pumpkins, bags of grain, live poultry, a mattress, were stowed away on the roof and behind the back seat. Already we had exceeded the legal quota by two, but the driver continued to tout for more passengers. The middle row emptied, the seat was pushed forward. I watched with alarm as, somehow, a woman managed to squeeze in next to the man with yellow trousers. That meant there were nine of us. Another passenger was found for the middle row. Ten. A slim girl joined the fat woman sitting up front. Eleven. The middle row emptied again. A boy dressed in short khaki trousers and a green shirt appeared out of nowhere. Without a word or a glance he placed himself on my lap. Twelve. When next I looked a third passenger had been able to insinuate himself up front. Thirteen – or fourteen if the baby was included. I examined the boy who sat very still and tranquil on my lap. He was very black, with the bloom of grape on his black skin. The man in the yellow trousers began tuning up his transistor; the Zairean music raged unabated from the dashboard. Somewhere a hen fluttered and squawked. I could hardly breathe.

'Look here,' I shouted when the driver reappeared. 'What's this damned boy doing on my lap?'

The boy turned to look at me. I glared at him ferociously. His large, black eyes regarded me with a kind of bewildered wonder. I wilted under their gaze, embarrassed and a little ashamed of myself.

'You want to throw him out?' someone inquired from the middle row.
There was accusation in the tone.
I was aware of the boy's eyes fixed on me. He was very still.
'You want to throw him out?'
I shook my head.
'Now we go,' the driver said in an unexpected burst of English. We
lurched out of the bus-station, horn blaring.
I was on my way to the Highlands.

                                                                    8 January, 1977

Richard West

STEAMING TO THE CAPE

One of the pleasures (if sometimes not unmixed) of travel by train in
South Africa is the chance it gives of meeting the Afrikaner half of the
white population. When the former Boer General Botha won power after
the First World War, backed by the smaller English Labour Party, one of
the first things he did was to nationalise the railways and make them into
a job reserve for the then underprivileged Afrikaners. Today the whites
in the quarter-million-strong work force of South African Railways (the
figure includes ports and airways) are overwhelmingly Afrikaans in their
first language. Largely because of this, train travel seems to be much
more popular with the Afrikaans- than with the English-speaking public.

Therefore, on boarding the Trans-Karoo train from Johannesburg to
Cape Town, I was not surprised to see as the complement of the sleeping
car: 'Mnr J. H. van der Graaff. Mnr R. de Lange. Mr R. West' – the clerk
notes in which language you booked your reservation. The second of
these gentlemen did not appear; perhaps he was that Mnr de Lange I had
read about recently in newspapers who, when charged under the Immor-
ality Act after being found stark naked in his car with a black girl, told the
police and judge (who were not impressed) that he had been working late
with fibreglass, which made him itchy, and so had stripped before getting
into the driver's seat. But Mnr van der Graaff, as I have called him here,
was conspicuous by his presence.

He was a big, heavy sallow man with a touch of bronze on his balding
scalp, a lowering, hot-eyed frown and prognathous jaw. He was wearing a

short-sleeved, short-trousered safari suit that tended to emphasise the fact that one of his legs was covered in bandages and one of his arms was missing. These had not been the only casualties in van der Graaff's life of some fifty-five years. His throat was a mass of scars as though several enemies had attacked him at once with broken bottles, and his scalp was gouged and criss-crossed with the remains of old wounds. 'I was bad once, when I was boy,' van der Graaff explained, pointing towards his cranium, 'I stole almost everything I saw and I was always fighting the Cape Coloureds.'

At 10.30 a.m. the train started its journey of almost a thousand miles south, and van der Graaff rose to his foot with the help of his crutch and then unlocked a metal case that lay on the floor of the compartment. 'The hospital said I should take things easy,' he explained, 'but I like to smoke and I like to booze.' Saying which he took from the case a litre bottle of brandy and one of Coca-Cola to match. When our drinks were fixed van der Graaff started to point out the wonders of what he called 'the most beautiful country in the world,' which may be true of the rest of South Africa but is hardly so of the industrial Transvaal. 'Look, Mr Waysht, there are the largest man-made mountains in the world,' he said, indicating the tips from some disused gold mines, '. . . and there is our steel industry. We have everything here, Mr Waysht, except oil, and when we get that we can say fuck off to the rest of Africa,' he said, giving a two-finger sign northward. Later we passed great fields of mealies or maize, some of them miles long, and van der Graaff said, 'Take a look, Mr Waysht, but I tell you those fields are small compared to the Orange Free State. Take a look at those cows, Mr Waysht. You're not looking. Mr Waysht, put that book away. Reading is the most unsociable habit.'

To get away from van der Graaff and from his brandy-and-coke, I walked to the observation car where you can watch the passing scenery from an armchair. Here I read up the notes I had made of Johannesburg station's Railway Museum, a rich horde of artefacts. Here can be found brass ash trays, early typewriters, a Gecophone (whatever that may be), a Boyd Plunger Fire Extinguisher, bilingual brass badges for staff, such as 'Bedding/Beddingoed, Ticket Examiner/Kaartje sondersoeke,' and a silver plaque saying that 'meals and refreshments were served by the staff of the South African Railway and Harbours in this dining car at the British Empire Exhibition held at Wembley, England, 1924–1925.'

There are memorial programmes decorated with nosegays and maidens in honour of Lord Milner and Field-Marshal Roberts and even a 'Souvenir of the Visit to Natal of the Royal Commission on Martial Law.' One of the oldest exhibits shows the 'Bye-laws and rules for workers' enforced by the original Cape Town Railway and Dock Company Locomotive and Carriage Department Salt River Works (1862), notably Rule 18: 'Any workman having grievances or complaint who leaves or neglects his work for the purposes of enforcing or advocating his views . . . through the medium of "a strike" will not be allowed to be employed in any way.' This, and a rule to prevent the closed shop, were drawn up 'as a protection to the honest, industrious and intelligent mechanic against dissatisfied and inferior workmen.'

There are no strikes today on South African Railways, which may be regrettable, but at least there are plenty of jobs. For example Peter Best, the chief horticulturist for the 1,053 railway gardens, employs a staff of 150 whites and 1,000 blacks on the eleven nurseries and one greenhouse-on-wheels. Service rather than speed is the attraction of South African trains, which never seem to run at more than about 35 mph. At lunch on this Trans-Karoo express, which does not try to compete with the luxury Blue Train, there were clean blue tablecloths and silver cutlery for the four very good, very cheap courses. The head steward was attentive, too attentive; he made sure that I sat with 'my friend' van der Graaff, who had come swaying down the corridor to show me a few more 'beautiful things Mr Waysht,' and to drink four double brandies and several beers in the observation car. At lunch we shared a bottle of South African Riesling.

After lunch I escaped back to the compartment to read and doze for a few hours until I heard the approaching slow thump of van der Graaff's ever more lurching progression along the corridor. The narrow-gauge train sways wildly in spite of its slow speed, and van der Graaff would not accept a supporting hand. I went back to the observation car where the barman was talking about his recent national service on the Angolan border: 'My friend was shot dead just next to me. He was my friend but all I felt at the time was, thank goodness it got him and not me.' He spoke with a heavy Afrikaans accent yet it transpired that both his father and grandfather had served in the British army here. 'I'm the first to fight for South Africa, instead of against her,' he said.

We came to Kimberley, the site of Rhodes's diamond mine. 'It's the biggest man-made hole in the world, Mr Waysht,' said van der Graaff, who had once more rocked down the corridor to reprove me: 'Mr Waysht, you should not be reading. How often again will you have this chance to look at South Africa?' He dropped his crutch on sitting down to dinner, then went to sleep with the fish. After dinner the head steward, a waiter and myself dragged and pushed van der Graaff back to his sleeping berth, hoping to catch him if he fell.

In the observation car later I noticed two young men who had got on at Kimberley and talked ever since about trains. 'They're railway freaks,' the barman explained. 'We get a lot on this line.' It turned out that both men were employees of De Beers, the diamond mines, and were not so much railway freaks as steam freaks, because South Africa is almost the only place in the southern hemisphere where steam is used. One of the steam freaks is an Englishman with an army moustache and public-school manner to match, who had been only a few weeks in South Africa but could tell me all about it:

'I've been sent out to South Africa and I'm delighted to go to the country with the largest steam transport system in the world. This train starts electric, changes to steam at Kimberley and then to diesel at De Aar. Can't you tell how smooth it is now we're on steam? [I could not.] We get to De Aar at about 11.10 p.m. but I'm going to be up at five in the morning to see the sun rising over the largest steam sheds in the southern hemisphere. People say I'm weird. My contemporaries say so, who have no other intellectual views. I'd rather be weird than use plastic cups. This is a really civilised country. I'm amazed to see what they do to find employment for the blacks. When you write your article, say that we hate diesel, say that we hate electricity but say that we love steam and South Africa.'

The bar was about to close at 10.30 p.m. when, to my dismay, I heard the by now familiar approach of van der Graaff, his whole huge weight resting perilously on the tip of one crutch. He drank several large brandies and shrugged off all offers of help on the way to our compartment. There he took out what was left of his brandy and stripped down to his underwear. 'Do you know Mr Waysht that I used to be a tennis player, a golfer, a cricketer and a boxer. I can still ripple my muscles.' Here the fat on his belly started to undulate. 'You know what I'd really like from England, Mr Waysht? That's three or four good dirty books. I expect everyone asks you that but you see the only way we can get them is to know a ship's captain.'

He started to jabber to himself, partly in English partly in Afrikaans, about his father, and Western Cape, his cricket team. It was midnight and I switched off the light on my side of the compartment. At two in the morning all the lights went on again and I woke to see van der Graaff staring reproachfully. 'What sort of mate are you? I went to the toilet and fell over in the corridor and I've been lying there for an hour. You know, Mr Waysht, I feel thirsty.' He finished off the bottle of brandy and then said, 'Mr Waysht?' I grunted. 'Mr Waysht, in the morning you must give me your address so I can write to you for those dirty books.'

16 April, 1977

Shiva Naipaul

VICTIM OF RAMADAN

The idea was simple enough and, on the face of it, harmless: to spend a few days in Fez and write a short piece about it. Idly, I set off for Morocco. But I would not have gone if, beforehand, I had received this letter which I found awaiting me on my return to London. '. . . I want [the New York editor wrote to me] . . . that sense of place which the great travel writers of the past so wonderfully evoked and which I hope to restore, albeit in a more modern idiom . . . photographically, I see this as a dramatic, riveting story which should provide wonderful contrast to a piece such as the English Lake Country or trekking through New Zealand. In words and pictures, the redolence of spices, the ceaseless counterpoint of languages in the market; the silence of the Arab mosque, the clamorous and enveloping crowds of the street – all that should be conveyed by both words and pictures . . .' Really, there is no need for me or anyone else to have actually been sent to Fez. The dramatic and riveting story could and should have been composed in Manhattan. It would have been far more convincing, far more convenient and much cheaper.

Nor, perhaps, would I have gone if I had known it was the holy month of Ramadan and been forewarned of the privations and dangers to which I would be exposing myself during this season of austerity and exacerbated religious sensibility. In Morocco, as I was soon to discover, the dietary strictures of Ramadan are enforced on the Faithful by state power: Muslims caught eating, drinking or smoking between the hours of sunrise and sunset can be jailed for six months. But, as Royal Air Maroc bore me swiftly over the brown coast of Christian Spain, traversed the wrinkled neck of the Mediterranean and swooped low over the beaches of Islamic North Africa, I had no conception of what lay ahead. Tribulation began almost immediately: while waiting for my luggage to be disgorged from the aircraft a policeman bore down on me, grasped my arm and ordered me to extinguish the cigarette I was smoking. Other, more obvious foreigners were smoking too but they were not troubled by his zeal. It was my misfortune to look as if I ought to have been a Muslim and, therefore, to be treated like one. Argument was useless – and, possibly, full of potential peril. Most Moroccans had never heard of Hindus; and the few who had seemed to think that my ancient religion was merely an eccentric form of Islam.

At my hotel I was told that the restaurant would not be open until 8.30 in deference to the nutritional needs of the staff who would be eating for the first time that day. I went into the bar. The barman looked askance at me. Out on the terrace I could see French and German tourists drinking tall, icy glasses of beer. I ordered a Scotch. He frowned at me. I showed him my room key, showed him my passport. The waiters watched and whispered. Reluctantly, I was served.

As I crossed the market square of the Grand Socco, my shoulder bag lightly brushed the arm of a young man. It was nearing noon and extremely hot. He stopped, turning back towards me, his face sullen with rage as he pointed at his arm. I apologised. He did not, however, seem to want a peaceful solution, but continued to advance on me. I apologised a second time – a little more profusely. This appeared to mollify him slightly. Muttering curses, he went on his way. 'It is Ramadan,' I was assured again and again whenever I sought from my Moroccan acquaintances an explanation for some display of enigmatic brutishness. Under a blazing sun, men deprived of food and drink operate on short fuses. The Faithful become unpredictable, liable to explode at any moment, to reach for their knives. Ramadan may bring men closer to Allah and Paradise but not, it would seem, to tolerance and compassion. It is a scarifying – not a softening – experience; it must entrench the association of religious purity with suffering and violence.

Ramadan alters the rhythms of life. By day, lethargy reigns, all effort directed towards the conservation of energy. Inert bodies lie sprawled in parks and pools of shade. In field and factory men slow down waiting for the sun to disappear. After dusk and the break of the fast they return to life. At night, the streets of downtown Tangier swarmed with sated and voluble promenaders. Hordes of men crowded bright cafés and restaurants, drinking sweet coffee and mineral water. The atmosphere would become almost festive. Until the small hours of the morning there poured through the open windows of my un-airconditioned room the babble and roar of human activity – for there was a second meal to be eaten at two or three o'clock in the morning. In Fez, almost the whole town, it seemed, would migrate by car and bus to the resort oasis of Sidi Harazem. There, under a nearly full moon floating above the encircling hills, the smoke of kebab fires hazed the air, plump Berber tribeswomen sang and danced in concrete pavilions, pious beggars recited sutras from the Koran. In the swimming baths which have been built there, bikini-clad women splashed unaffectedly in close proximity to strange men – a reminder of the comparative mildness of Morocco's Islamic regime; a mildness which, I sensed, may be under threat. Over all of them, on chanting beggars as well as bikini-clad girls, there arched the enforced rhythms of Ramadan, regulating metabolism and mood. Islam, especially during this holy month, is an inescapable reality clamped down on everyone and everything. The unstable cycle of torpor and release, of denial and satiety, induces a kind of claustrophobia. I recall seeing from a train a peasant clad in coarse robes making his obeisance towards Mecca in a bleak, sunburnt field. When the world becomes a mosque, there is nowhere to seek refuge.

The package tourists who sweep in and out of towns like Fez are a fortunate breed. Sealed off by their air-conditioned coaches from the dusty anarchy through which they move, protected from its assaults and treacheries by their well-trained handlers, they are immune from reality. They come, they take their photographs, they go away. It is a splendid way to travel. I returned from Fez to Tangier, exhausted, after four days. During that time, I had been harried by cheating merchants, felled by a bad stomach and threatened with grievous bodily harm by my guide because I refused to allow his rapacity. The congested alleys and lanes of the medina had quickly lost their charm. I recoiled from the ceaseless counterpoint of language in the marketplace and the clamorous, enveloping crowds. I brought back with me on the long train ride not the redolence of spices but the stench of animal droppings, of heaps of rotting vegetables, of dripping, uncured hides destined for the tanneries. The cloying sourness of the medina seemed to cling to my clothes, to exude from the pores of my skin. Mostly, though, as the train crawled through sunlit, semi-arid dereliction, there hovered before me the feral cunning that had darkened the face of my guide as he sought to terrorise me. It had been a pitiless performance. I thought I would rest for a day or two in Tangier before setting out in search of further adventure.

The hotel I chose was pleasant and sedate – washed in white and green-shuttered. From its terraced garden, planted with bougainvillea and oleander, pines and palms, there was a view of the town and, beyond, the Mediterranean. When there was no mist I could see the mountains of Christian Spain. They were a comforting sight.

Even my guide book, which usually made mountains out of molehills, admitted that there was nothing much to see in Tangier. I had seen what there was to see – the Kasbah, the medina, a palace, a few heavy old guns. Freed from guilt, I felt I could stick to the hotel. Within its high walls my alien status was accepted and I could do much as I pleased. Grateful for the opportunity to recuperate from Fez, I sat by the swimming pool and watched the sunbathers. My attention came to rest on two men with dark glasses and a little girl. This was not only because the child was making a nuisance of herself. I was intrigued by the language they were speaking, not French or Spanish or German or Dutch. From what exotic corner of Europe did that guttural sing-song emanate? With a slow start of surprise, I found myself able to pick up the occasional English word. Gradually, it dawned on me that they were, in fact, speaking English; that they were from Liverpool. When the older of the two men, both of whom seemed mildly drunk, knocked over his glass of beer into an ashtray filled with stubs, the girl shrieked with joy. She held the ashtray close to his lips. 'Drink it! Drink it!' The man demurred, but without force. She insisted, joy turning to rage. 'I want you to drink it! I want you to drink it!' The high-pitched voice cut like a knife through the peace of the afternoon. I could only wonder at the childish desire to inflict public humiliation.

Later, I went down to the palm-lined sea front. The sun was low, colouring the tops of the apartment blocks whose roofs bristled with television antennae. In Tangier they consider themselves triply blessed: they can receive, in addition to the local service, Spanish and Gibraltar television. I rested on a decaying concrete bench facing the sea, my skin irritated by the prickly heat of late afternoon. Armed policemen paraded in pairs, on the lookout for any signs of impiety. The day's fast was drawing to an end and the vendors of kebabs were stoking their fires. Young French and German vagrants, bohemianly rough, struggled by under the weight of backpacks. There wandered by a barefooted girl of European provenance. She was wrapped, sarong-style, in a strip of green cloth, exposing shoulders flayed by over-exposure to the sun. Meandering at a snail's pace along the corridor of palms, she murmured to herself frequently stopping to stare vacantly about her, plucking distractedly at the pages of what looked like a passport. Hers was a stylish delinquency, a studied throwback to vanquished hippiedom. A ragged youth circled about me. He offered hashish, he offered boys, he offered girls. Night was falling. I walked uphill through nearly empty streets: at this hour of impending release Tangier retired indoors. As I neared the hotel, a gun boomed through the dusk, muezzins wailed. Another day of abstinence was over. Fearlessly, I lit a cigarette.

The Liverpudlians dominated breakfast, the shrieks of the little girl now joined to the penetrating voice of her American mother – who was dilating on her feminist views. At the table next to mine a demure English couple exchanged scandalised whispers.

'They drink like fish,' the lady said. 'They make a real spectacle of themselves. When they get drunk, they even begin to sing . . .'

After breakfast I went out on the terrace overlooking the garden. The morning was clouded and humid; the town was quiescent. A sea mist obscured the mountains of Spain. Tranquillity was shattered by the arrival of the Liverpudlians. They were quarreling about money.

'I try to ask a straight question,' the American was saying, 'and I get bullshit.'

'Calm yourself,' urged the man who had almost been compelled to drink out of the ashtray.

The American would not calm herself. 'I don't like this fucking space at all, let me tell you. This trip is my bag. I want to know what's going for what . . . I'm not that spaced out. But this whole scene's too far out . . . too fucking far out. I can't relate to it. It bugs my head, man . . .'

The little girl shrieked. He of the ashtray started to sob, laying his head on the shoulder of his friend.

On the street below, a group of veiled women walked slowly downhill, carrying clanking milk churns.

'I don't want to be bugged,' the American shouted. 'I wanna keep my head straight, relate to my own space. I don't want no fucking MCP to lay some heavy sexist trip on me . . .'

The veiled women disappeared around a corner. But I could still hear the clanking of their milk churns.

'You know,' the writer said, 'I believe in the Islamic identité.'

He was Moroccan, he lived in Paris, but returned home four or five times a year so that he could keep in touch with his 'roots'. We were sitting in an open-air restaurant in the small, white-washed town of Asilah on the Atlantic coast of Morocco, about an hour's drive from Tangier. The restaurant lay in the shadow of a fifteenth century Portuguese fort. Atlantic waves exploded against the remnants of a sea-wall. Asilah had had a turbulent past. Octavius had deported its people to Spain because they had supported Mark Antony. In 1578 King Sebastian of Portugal had landed here in a disastrous attempt to conquer Morocco. It had formed part of the Spanish zone during Morocco's colonial period and was restored to it only in 1956 when the country regained its independence. (The Spanish still hold the enclave of Ceuta.) It seemed a peculiar place to be talking about identité.

'The strict enforcement of Ramadan might seem harsh to you,' he said, 'but it helps to remind the people of who and what they are. Ramadan brings us back to ourselves. It renews our sense of being Muslim.'

I suggested that *identité*, in the sense in which he understood it, strangled rather than liberated men; that it took no account of the historical process and was a sad and overheated reaction to Western dominance.

He laughed. 'We are dealing with eternal truth,' he said. France was a decaying country, a cemetery. Would I deny that the West was riddled with moral and spiritual disorder?

Disagreement was silenced by the memory of the American woman. Between him and her, I felt lost.

The mountains of Spain beckoned: it would be pleasant, I thought, to traverse the Mediterranean, to escape Ramadan for a few hours. I decided to make a day trip to Algeciras. There was confusion on the dock. My first attempt to board the ferry was repulsed: my exit card had not been properly stamped. I returned to the long, slow-moving queue.

A German voice spoke close to my ear. 'Is it possible to ask where to get one of those?' He pointed at my exit card. I told him; he ran off.

Some minutes later, the voice spoke again. This time it was tinged with panic. 'Why do they all have blue cards? I do not have a blue card. What does the blue card mean? Is it possible for you to explain?'

It was not possible for me to explain because I myself was not in possession of a blue card. Looking around, I saw what he meant. Blue cards everywhere. We both ran off. It seemed likely that I might miss the ferry.

'Writer?' the immigration officer asked. 'What do you write?'

'Books . . .' I hazarded.

'Books? You are a writer of books? What kind of books? Please tell.'

I could not grasp what this might have to do with a day trip to Algeciras. Nor did it seem the appropriate place or time to embark on a literary discussion.

'I write stories,' I said.

'You are a journalist, perhaps?' He scrutinised my face, comparing it with the photograph in the passport. With deliberation, he studied the official record of my travels.

'You are a great voyager,' he said. It was not intended as a compliment. 'What have you been doing in Morocco?'

'Nothing,' I replied truthfully. 'Tourist,' I added, also with considerable truth.

He scowled, grudgingly applied his stamp and flung the passport unceremoniously in my direction. I headed for the good ship *Ibn Batouta*.

'Passport . . .'

By the gaping jaws of the ferry I submitted to another cross-examination. The officer fingered my shoulder bag. 'Open . . . open . . .'

I opened it up. He examined my guide book, thumbed the novel (*A Passage to India*) I was reading, sniffed my cigarettes, explored every pocket and niche of the bag. At last, I was allowed on board. But already I was exhausted. My day trip between Islam and Christianity, between Africa and Europe, had gone sour on me.

The white huddle of Tangier receded. A sign above the bar declared that it was forbidden to serve alcohol to Muslims. Not wishing to provoke a jihad, I contented myself with coffee. Going up on deck, I stared at the corrugated Spanish coast. In the distance loomed the rectangular, misty mass of Gibraltar. Dolphins frolicked close to the bows of the ship. To cross from the Spanish enclave of Ceuta into Morocco was, by all accounts, a murderous business; to cross from the British enclave of Gibraltar into Spain could, by all accounts, be a murderous business; and, as I was now discovering, to cross from Tangier to Algeciras was no joy ride – not, at least, for those who called themselves writers. How much nicer to be a dolphin.

'That is the Rock.' I turned to find a wizened American dowager, incandescently clad in an emerald green trouser suit, standing beside me. 'That is what the Brits call Gibraltar,' she added.

I thanked her for the information.

'Where are you going to in Spain?' she asked.

'Only as far as Algeciras.' I pronounced it with a 'g'.

'Al*h*eciras,' she corrected. 'It's a Spanish name, you know.'

I thanked her for the information and sidled away. How much nicer to be a dolphin.

The Spanish let me in. There was little to do in Algeciras. I drank some wine in a café not far from the ferry terminal, deafened by a churning cement mixer. At five, I returned to the ferry terminal. The Spanish let me out. Morocco, however, had other ideas. The boatride was a nightmare. Orders to submit to immigration control were ceaselessly relayed on the Public Address system. Islamic righteousness had turned it into a prison ship.

'You're a writer . . . what do you write? . . . are you a journalist? . . . what have you been doing in Morocco . . . you need a visa to enter our country . . .'

'But I have a visa.'

'It is expired. It is suitable for only one entry. You cannot enter Morocco. You will return to Spain.'

'But I have all my luggage in a Tangier hotel . . . I have a plane ticket, a passage booked . . .'

Silence.

'Let me at least make a phone call.'

'Stand back!' Oriental despotism had spoken and I was shoved away.

'It is Ramadan,' said a Belgian lady who lived in Tangier – and who had befriended me. It was from her, with the mountains of North Africa hard and high in the afternoon light, that I learned of the death of the Shah of Iran.

'Such a shame,' she said, 'that only Sadat should have had the courage to attend his funeral.'

I had been in Iran; I had written about the Shah; I had judged harshly. But now I could sympathise. He must have known about that *identité* which, one day, would eat Iranians alive. Against that hard and high North African skyline, he became a little easier to understand. That *identité* had proved itself locust-like in its voracity: it was even trying to eat me up. I was sad that only Sadat had had the courage to attend his funeral.

We docked; the passengers disembarked. 'Hope to see you again,' intoned the PA. On came the cleaners. The Belgian lady promised to get in touch with my Moroccan acquaintances, but she was nervous and would commit neither names nor addresses to writing. Two hours later, I began my third crossing of the Mediterranean. If the Spanish were surprised to see me back so soon, they did not show it. At two o'clock in the morning I set out to look for a hotel. Ragged and luggageless, I did not rate my chances very high. But the four star Reina Christina took me in without a murmur. How dreadful it was to wake up the next morning. Unshaven, my head swimming with fatigue, my clothes crumpled, I considered my position. I decided I would call on the British Consulate. They were courteous but completely unhelpful.

'It is your problem,' I was told. The man smiled charmingly and shrugged. It was Ramadan. The Moroccans were always difficult during Ramadan. They could exercise no influence over them.

I wandered around the streets of Algeciras, unable to face the Moroccan consulate, feeling and looking like a tramp, reflecting wistfully on the failure of the Christian Reconquest of Spain to extend itself to the shores of North Africa. I drank glasses of Fundador and cups of black coffee. Resolution returned and I went in search of the Moroccans. I submitted to the same old questions, filled out forms in triplicate, tried to remember the names of my grandfathers and grandmothers, had to decide who in London I could use as 'references'. When I lit a cigarette, officials screamed at me and pointed at a portrait of King Hassan. In the end, I was given a visa valid for five days. It occurred to me that I should avoid the ferry and take the hydrofoil which goes from Tarifa. Late that afternoon, I crossed the Mediterranean for the fourth time.

Policemen in brown robes and yellow slippers shepherded us off the hydrofoil, barking orders. I had begun to detest these under-developed Moroccan faces, trapped, it seemed to me, in a perpetual adolescence; a perpetual puberty.

My passport was seized and put away. 'Stand aside!'

I was too stunned to protest. I was made to wait until all the other passengers were processed. Files were searched. Eventually, it was agreed that I could re-enter Morocco. I found a taxi.

At the gate of the dock a policeman halted us.

'Where's passport . . . where's luggage . . . where you stay in Tangier . . . where's airplane ticket . . . what you do here? Eh? Eh?' In due course, I was allowed to proceed.

'I seen you in Tangier,' the taxi-driver said. 'I seen you walking around. Tourist?'

I did not answer. The world was becoming too small, too dangerous. Early the next morning, I went to the airport.

More shouting. More barked orders. My luggage was searched once, twice, a third time. I appeared to be running a gauntlet. The immigration officer demanded that I write down the titles of my books.

'What magazine you write for? You journalist? Give name of magazine . . . give name . . .'

But I did not give any names. To lie seemed the safest course. I continued down the gauntlet. Just when I thought I had made it to the relative safety of the departure lounge, a policeman waved me aside. I was taken away into a room full of other policemen. My mouth went dry. I realised that anything could happen among the lesser breeds without the Law. My shoulder bag was opened up; my books were leafed through; hands crept up my trouser legs, were inserted into my shirt.

'You like hashish . . . ' said one of the grinning policemen.

'Where you keep the hashish?' asked another with an adolescent leer. 'Where? Suppose we find a little hashish on you . . . what then? Moroccan jail not good, no?'

Miraculously, I got out of there. Half an hour later, high over Spain, my mouth was still dry.

Two days afterwards, I had a nightmare: I was dreaming I was in Libya.

13 September, 1980

Alexander Chancellor

NOTEBOOK

After five days I was fed up with Salisbury. I had read that many, many miles away in the mysterious valley of the Zambesi River there lurked a nomadic tribe called the Doma who lived by hunting and eating honey and who had yet to be informed that their country was now called Zimbabwe and had a black government. I thought I should go and tell them the exciting news, but I never had the chance. When I arrived in the bush – flying low up the Zambesi in a private plane, frightening herds of elephants and buffaloes, sending crocodiles slithering into the water – I found no nomadic tribesmen but the elegant figure of the *Spectator*'s proprietor, Algy Cluff, sitting in front of a tent on the river bank and gazing at yawning hippopotami over the top of a leatherbound volume of Livingstone's Letters. Here there were none of the shortages complained of in Salisbury. There was plenty of excellent cheese and chilled South African wine (though still no Marmite). Delicious meals were served under a huge acacia tree, cooked by Africans who could not have been Doma for they were clearly trained in Paris. We went out walking behind a white hunter and found some elephants. I slept in a luxurious tent to the night sounds of the jungle. For hundreds of miles around there were no human beings – only the invisible Doma eating their honey. This is probably the nicest sort of holiday in the world, and I am told it can be yours for only £10,000 a fortnight.

24 October, 1981

Andrew Brown

FANTASTIC INVASION

Banjul, Senegambia

The queue of quietly melting tourists does not move forwards for minutes at a time. One man is still wearing a black leather overcoat from Stockholm, 6,000 kilometres north and 105 degrees colder. He nudges me, and points with suppressed excitement to the bullet-hole in the glass-walled office behind the Gambian passport clerk. We must have come to the real Africa at last. A burly Senegalese officer padded from his office when my landing card was passed through to him and greeted me. 'Are you a journalist? Then I hope that you haven't come here to write something about this country.'

Through the glass walls of the departure lounge we could see black teenagers hustling last week's Swedes like tropical fish darting among a shoal of cod. They seemed suddenly far too close. I shrugged and smiled, and was allowed to sidle past the passport desk. Later, it seemed obvious that the officer, like the bullet-hole, was only acting his part. That is the reception one expects in an African country, and this is a place where the tourists can have anything they want (and from which journalists are expelled from time to time). But what the tourists want is not the Gambia that works – that's far too complicated – but a sort of Bongoville-on-Sea: dirt, flies, and poverty as a backdrop for a cast of little weeping piccaninnies whose lives would be empty but for the interest we take in them and the money that we pay to watch them.

And this is what they get, too, though they can always retreat from it to their hotels. The walls of the hotel compound are raw brown concrete topped with broken glass. Within them, everything is Swedish: even the sun-hats sold there are flown in from Stockholm. The lizards seem ready to turn back into European sparrows at any moment. Outside the compound walls Bongoville pressed round us like a cloud of flies, noisy and inescapable but yielding freely to every movement. The pimps, touts, beggars, and male prostitutes who line the road to the town of Bakau address every European whom they see in fluent Swedish first, then in English. The ruthless, disciplined and unattractively corrupted traders are black, the feckless and corrupting savages are white. The traders sell the tourists anything but solitude; this can only be found in the national library, which is the saddest place in the whole country, for it is the home of a god that has almost failed. Ambitious Gambian parents now pull their children out of school, and tell them to work the tourists instead, since this is the more promising career.

It takes some days before they will even allow a tourist to climb into a taxi by himself. One night I met a Swedish farmer at the gates of the compound. We had shared a taxi from the airport, and on the strength of this acquaintance Birger greeted me as an old friend: 'I had a Gambian bint last night. It was really nice, because the curfew caught us, and I had to spend the night there . . . she wasn't much in bed, though,' he added as we walked towards the duty-free bottle in his room. The friendly night, the whisky, and the prospect of another 'bint' later in the evening combined to fill him with morose and undirected melancholy. He told me of his failed marriage, and of his unhappy passion for a girl who taught him English in evening classes: 'I feel so funny here [clutching his heart with one hand] every time she talks to me. I don't know where to put my hands. I don't dare make a pass at her, because she might laugh at me if I did. She's only 23, and I am 40.' This was his third visit to the Gambia. He had a friend in the President's office who was trying to encourage him to move down here for good, but he had the sense to see that this would destroy him very quickly. He knew that if he were not expected to work, he would not be able to work at all.

When we left for a night-club, we had not walked ten feet from the compound towards the waiting taxis before two young pimps fell into step beside us. They were dressed in Swedish working-class party clothes. Their sunglasses glinted in the light from the street-lamp as they greeted Birger as an old friend. He didn't recognise them, and he certainly wanted nothing to do with them. But by the time we had climbed into the taxi, they were there too, asking tenderly after our names and professions, and directing the driver to 'the Swedish disco, full of nice Gambian girls' before we had a chance to speak. As we walked up a dirt path at our destination, in the grounds of another hotel, Birger paused and urinated in a flower-bed. After a brief hesitation, the Gambians followed his example.

We refused to pay their entrance fees, as they confidently demanded that we should, but they had somehow reached the bar and ordered drinks all round (we paid) while we were still examining the room. The Swedish disco was dark, spacious, comfortable and quite deserted but for two unhappy white couples, three waiting ponces, and a Gambian girl who slipped away from the bar as we arrived. Vast speakers swept the dance floor clean with Abba's music. Birger grew increasingly morose. He told me that he was going to hit one of the pimps soon, and then disappeared, followed, of course, by his 'friend'. I told the other 'friend' for the fifth time in 20 minutes that I didn't want a girl, so he put his hand on my thigh. Birger was sitting in the dark with the girl from the bar. I made my inaudible excuses and left, though not without being asked for money by the pawing pimp.

'Of course, you can't really blame them,' said the girl from Thompson's, 'I mean, look at them and look at us. We'd do the same in their place, wouldn't we?' She was discussing the attempted coup last summer, which she regarded as a Gambian revolt against white affluence – which it wasn't at all. But her words should be carved above the entrances of all the tourist hotels. The tourists and their shepherds are at all times excruciatingly conscious of their colour. They see the Gambia through a mist of complacent pity, with just a tinge of fear to darken the view. They damn all Gambians by refusing to blame any of them for anything, and then they believe that this is tolerance. So it was natural enough for a tourist guide (who was not there at the time) to believe that the rebels had sacked the hotel in which we stayed. They hadn't. The attempted coup remains a mysterious affair, but the one thing certain about it was that it was a purely Gambian quarrel, and not a very bloody one. Most of the killings occurred when the rebels started handing out guns to the mob. This led to a spree of drunken looting and murder, but popular resentment was directed against the Gambian upper classes, and not against the foreigners.

The President has built himself an enormous house just down the road from the corrugated iron town of Bakau. The President's family were held hostage in this monstrous building, which is exactly the sort of thing that a newly rich German millionaire would have built to announce that he had arrived. But the house next door, which is owned by a British engineer who was out of the country at the time, was left quite alone and unlooted in the fighting. The government claims that Libya and, ultimately, Russia were behind the coup attempt. This may well be true, but it is in an important sense irrelevant. This remains a civilised country, not one to which power politics travel well.

Everything seems as the prurient traveller would expect: the curfew enforced by an army of occupation; the opposition exiled or in jail; the roads emptying for the presidential motorcade. But all these things are modified in practice, either by incompetence, corruption or that lively popular sense of the ridiculous which distinguishes civilised countries. Curfew runs from one to six, and is rigorously enforced for a while every night, to the astonishment and subsequent discomfort of six or a dozen tourists every week. But in the small hours no one seems to care about it very much. I was driven back to my hotel at three in the morning past the President's villa and the depot where the Senegalese are quartered. The driver had a Senegalese *laissez passer*, so the ride was quite legal, but he had no occasion to prove this on a ride of six or seven miles that passed by the prime targets for any revolution.

The Senegalese army is everywhere to be seen in daylight, and its occupation is very unpopular. But the troops themselves are not. At night, you will find them in all the cheap bars (the Gambian police seem to prefer marijuana), where they sit quietly nursing their beers, etiolated, lithe and black as shadows cast by moonlight. Of course, their presence here is a serious matter. They are all that can prevent another coup (though not the rumours of one). The fighting last summer frightened away four fifths of the expected tourists from England, and the confederation with Senegal has put an end to smuggling, which used to be more important to the economy than tourism. Peanuts are doing well, but they make money only for the government, so the tourists must somehow be lured back. The government's dislike of journalists can only be explained by the assumption that increasing repression will be necessary to keep the country sufficiently calm to attract the package trade. Bongoville sells, so they will build a Bongoville in this otherwise delightful country.

His excellency Sir Dawda Jawara, the President whom the Senegalese have reinstated, grows more and more unpopular. When first elected, he could travel alone around the country. Nowadays security men surround him even when he plays a round of golf, and when he drives out to the course all other traffic must pull in to the side of the road and wait while the motorcade goes by. It sounds impressively tyrannical, but the motorcade consists only of four dusty cars and three weaving motorcyclists. This lack of ostentation cannot be because he can't afford to travel in more style: the first aid loan that the country received after the coup attempt paid for a fleet of air-conditioned Mercedes limousines.

This sort of thing horrifies the Scandinavians if they get to hear of it. If only they were as venal, coarse and disgusting as the English tourists, they would do less harm. But most of them have come here to sympathise and to understand for 14 days, not to behave like pigs inside the hotel compound. Even the middle-aged women who come down here winter after winter, because no one will sleep with them at home, want romance as much as they want jig-a-jig. But romance in the tropics is a seller's market. The working Gambians despise the ponces, and the ponces in their turn despise their customers, who despise themselves. The younger tourists, who have come here for drugs rather than for sex, want another sort of romance. They corrupt because they cannot be corrupted. Everything they say is vague, indefinite, elastic. The Gambia they have come to understand recedes from them through the clouds of ganja smoke which rise from these meetings. Gambian marijuana is cheap, strong and very popular, but the Europeans have brought with them the idea that only Jamaicans and those who pretend to be Jamaicans can really understand the drug.

One of the guests at the hotel was a Gambian Rastafari who had returned to his roots after five years as a student in Sweden in order to apply for a Swedish work permit, which can only be obtained from outside the country. I saw him on the beach one morning collecting the address of one of the tourists: the black man stood with his head bowed in front of the white, who rested his pad of paper on the Rasta's shoulders while he wrote. One must suppose that he was delighted that such a genuine African would want him as a friend.

13 March, 1982

Shiva Naipaul

ISLANDS IN THE SUN

Through a grey half-light I had my first glimpse of the islands, disposed like dreams in a grey sea. The aircraft's ultimate destination was the rounded volcanic rump of Réunion, another thousand miles or so to the south of the Seychelles. Réunion, still firmly French, was a reminder of the inchoate political geography of the Indian Ocean; an ocean whose waves washed the shores of India, South Africa, Australia, Madagascar . . . its waters patrolled by the great navies of the world, none of whom could claim a special primacy.

It was not a quest for the exotic which was taking me to the Seychelles: those scattered islands, islets and rocks of granite – the remains, some say, of a submerged continent – interspersed with reefs of coral, spread across several hundred thousand square miles of ocean, offering refuge of a kind to a population reckoned with rough optimism to be approaching eighty thousand. I was going there because the Seychelles, on a Disneyland scale and in a Disneyland atmosphere, had succeeded in reproducing in an astonishingly short period (ten years) so many of the dismal features of the post-colonial world. Coup d'état, mercenary invasion, army mutiny – in the space of a few years the islands had lived through an accelerated cycle of political temptation and folly. For me, following these remote events, the islands gradually acquired a fascination comparable to that exercised on geneticists by *Drosophila*, the fast-breeding fruit-fly.

It would not be altogether untrue to say that between 1502 – when, it seems probable, they were sighted by Vasco da Gama on his way to India – and 1964 – when political parties first made their appearance – not much of moment had occurred. In 1756, the French, for want of anything better to do, laid claim to them; and in 1814, along with Mauritius, they passed from France to Britain. In between there had been settlement by a few French planters each equipped with a modest entourage of slaves and by assorted piratical adventurers.

I emerged into a vaporous, windless morning. Beyond the roof of the terminal building rose the mountainous spine of Mahé. I stared at the striated cliff-faces of elephant-coloured rock crowned with forest, surprised by the scale, by the splendour. The man from the Seychelles News Bureau was there to meet me. If you call him Gilbert and pronounce it in the French way that will do. He was youthful and smiling, with eyes narrowed by the tropical glare, with skin the complexion of tinned butter. He was one of the beneficiaries of the Revolution of 5 June 1977: a member of the youthful 'parastatal' aristocracy that had been created by it. We walked out to the car under the indolent gaze of a group of undeniably black, undeniably African soldiers dressed in camouflage uniforms.

'Tanzanians?'

Gilbert glanced at the soldiers. 'Seychellois,' he replied.

No one denies, so far as I am aware, the presence of Tanzanian soldiers in the Seychelles. They are the official guardians of the Revolution – which, in effect, means that they are there to guard the airport and the radio station. Yet Gilbert was always quick to negate any particular sighting, always perversely insistent that the soldiery we saw were of purely Seychellois origin. The Tanzanians did not appear to fraternise a great deal with the locals and looked queerly out of place and ill at ease.

We took the narrow main road winding along beside a blue, blue sea to Victoria, the toy-town capital of the islands. Across the water I could see the Air France jet shimmering on the runway, that eerie expanse of whiteness projecting like an oversized domino into the ocean. Built a mere ten years before, it had unleashed competing visions of late 20th-century reality on an unsuspecting and unprepared people.

Light-headed, somewhat unhinged by the nightmarish journey from

Paris, I continued to be stupidly surprised by the height of the hills. It was easy to imagine that I was back in Trinidad and not on the Western fringes of an unfamiliar ocean. Everything – the racial mixtures of the faces I saw at bus-stops, the small shops with glass cases and fly-blown jars of confectionery, the wooden shacks half-hidden among luxuriant bush, the more modern brick-built bungalows with louvres instead of windows, the flapping fowls narrowly escaping the wheels of the car – everything was touched with an odd intimacy. We went past a brewery, the first modest indication I had of industrial activity. Ahead of us glinted harbour installations, cranes, fuel tanks. We were entering the outskirts of Victoria. A handout from the Seychelles News Bureau called it the Queen City of the Indian Ocean, '. . . so prettily pint-sized [the writer went on to say] it could easily form the frontierspiece [sic] of a colourful storybook'. We passed the white-painted offices of Cable and Wireless – another focus of drama in the recent history of the Seychelles – the dark-interiored stores of Indian and Chinese merchants, the colonial Court House, the silvery clock-tower, said to be a replica of one on Vauxhall Bridge Road.

We left the sea and town behind, the road looping and climbing into the hills, threading its way to the western side of the island, towards the beach at Beau Vallon – where Adnan Khashoggi, an intimate of James Mancham, the deposed President, had once owned land. The vegetation was rich and wild. I stared at pawpaws drooping like elongated breasts, at the breadfruit and jack-fruit and dark green mango trees, at the tangled vines and orchids and big-leaved epiphytes; at the bougainvillea and hibiscus, croton and marigolds and oleanders growing in untidy yards. Descending, we came in sight of the sea again. The hotel to which I was being taken had, not long before, passed into the hands of the government, brought under the protection of yet another 'parastatal' enterprise – COSPROH (Compagnie Seychelloise de Promotion Hotelière). In a few days I was to become quite used to the pseudo-acrostic plague created by these bodies. I think – without particular effort – of SEYCOM (Seychelles National Commodity Company), SADECO (Seychelles Agricultural Development Corporation), NAIL (National Agro Industries Limited).

But not even COSPROH could spoil the tourist-brochure loveliness of it all. The room in which I found myself that afternoon would have fulfilled the paradisal fantasies of most people. My veranda overlooked a sequestered cove screened by coconut palms and banks of yellow hibiscus. Farther out, the wind-blown water shone. I slept uneasily through the afternoon, startled into intermittent wakefulness by a louder crash of waves or by sudden gusts lashing through the palms. Towards dusk I made my way down to the terrace. Smooth, wave-sculpted rocks were disposed along the shore, coconut palms decorated the slope of a green hill. I sat in the shade of a waxy-leaved frangipani studded with voluptuous outbursts of orange-white blossom. Seychelles cardinals fluttered like flames among the bushes. 'Don't you find,' an acquaintance remarked some days later, 'that there is an over-ripeness about everything here? A faint lasciviousness? It's almost embarrassing.'

Some boys were decorating the bar with coconut leaves: there was going to be a discothèque later that evening. The voice of Bob Marley complained from a pair of powerful speakers, hysterically sombre amid the green gaiety. The manager of the hotel, a Seychellois Chinese, introduced himself to me. Our conversation turned to the tourist trade: in the Seychelles, it is an obsessive topic. Not even socialist revolution could alter that. It was the government's aim (he said) to attract 150,000 visitors a year to the islands. At the moment they were getting less than half of that number. Obviously, some of the shortfall could be explained by the recession in Europe. But the recession alone was not to be blamed. The foreign press, he implied, was frightening people away by painting too dark a picture of post-coup Seychelles. Still (he sighed, staring out across the twilit water) it could not be denied that mercenary attack and an army mutiny that had led to the seizure of tourists as hostages were not the best possible inducements. Tourism was a sensitive industry. A very sensitive industry indeed!

The omens were not good. In happier times British Airways had operated three flights a week from London. Now rumour had it that they were threatening to withdraw altogether. Rumour also had it that Lufthansa was clearing out. To compound the tragedy, the South Africans were keeping away. Lately, they had been feeling unloved. After the mercenary invasion of November 1981 – financed and armed by certain circles in Pretoria – the Government had retaliated by withholding landing rights from South African Airways. (Other trade continued to flourish – socialist Seychelles remains heavily dependent on the food grown by their meddlesome southern neighbours.) As we talked, an enlarged sun sank with bloody splendour.

After dinner I returned to the thump-thump-thump of the discothèque on the terrace. Down there, on the edge of the ocean, the night was being danced away. It was a sad, half-realised scene, a pale reflection of the gaieties of the Mancham era when native and tourist connived at each other's fantasies. Mancham had had some intriguing ideas about cultural enhancement. For instance, a law was passed forbidding the erection of hotels taller than the surrounding palm trees. These hotels of palm height were also instructed to allow unhindered access to any Seychellois who wished to make use of their 'facilities' – provided (for even in so liberal a dispensation standards had to be maintained) they were decently dressed and behaved themselves; and, less romantically, could pay the bill. No fee was to be exacted for dancing. 'In that way [Mancham has written] our pleasure-minded people were made to see tourism for what it should be – an industry which could bring untold fun and happiness . . .'

His approach was rooted in an older tradition of Seychellois hospitality. He refers to a 50-rupee note adorned with a group of emblematic coconut trees. When examined from a certain angle, the fronds patterned themselves into the letters S-E-X. (I was given a tie adorned with the same motif.) 'This,' Mancham has written, 'admirably suited the island of love image which Seychelles had acquired during the second world war when travellers had turned up to find that much of the male population was absent and the women friendly'. Under his guidance, the brothel-state was to hand. I sat out under the frangipani, breathing in the fragrance of the blossom, looking at the gyrating bodies on the dance floor. Cockroaches whirred out of the darkness and the waves broke white among the rocks.

But during the period other frailties, other temptations were maturing. That night, before falling asleep, I read a poem (composed in 1976, at the height of fun-time) dedicated to Albert René, leader of the Seychelles People's United Party.

> Hail SPUP, spearhead of the people's cause
> Which in its long march never did pause
> Bearing the banner of the rising sun
> To find our rightful place under the sun
> From a past bleak and dreary
> To a future full of promise and glory!

Until 1964 politics as such could hardly be said to have existed in the Seychelles. The franchise was restricted, confined to the landowners and professional elite. Assisted by a handpicked Executive Council and a tame Legislative Assembly, the Governor led a peaceful life. The Seychelles floated in a sunny and aimless isolation, as anachronistic as the slumberous tortoises on Aldabra atoll. Mombasa, the nearest worthwhile landfall, was over a thousand miles away, a three or four day journey by boat. And the boats didn't come all that often. The islands' isolation, their removal from the realities of the 20th century, was underscored when the Seychelles were chosen as a suitable place of exile for that troublesome Cypriot, Archbishop Makarios.

Reality, when it did belatedly begin to intrude in the middle Sixties, did so with vengeful rapidity. First there came the Seychelles People's United Party, the creation of France Albert René, a London University-trained lawyer. The SPUP announced that it had consecrated itself to the unceasing struggle 'for the total liberation of the people of Seychelles from colonialism and neo-colonialism'. It promised to create a socialist state purged of all forms of discrimination and exploitation. The Organisation of African Unity granted its imprimatur. René was no slouch when it came to rabble-rousing. 'The people of Seychelles,' he declaimed, '. . . will one day, somehow or other, kick out the British, kick out the Indians and kick out all those who have not . . .' etc, etc. Under the guidance of SPUP, the Seychelles would be identified with all 'progressive' forces wherever these might happen to exist.

In response to all this frightening talk, there arose another lawyer, James Mancham, the handsome son of a local businessman. He set up the Seychelles Democratic Party and possessed the not unrare facility for mixing sex with politics. His fantasies were rather different from those of Albert René. 'My dream for the Seychelles,' he wrote in mournful exile, 'was a place of smiles and laughter with, under each coconut tree, a young man with a guitar.' Where the young women would be he did not say. In his mind's eye (Mancham cannot be accused of having had a political programme) he saw the Seychelles transformed into a sort of tropical Switzerland; it would provide a safe mooring for the ocean-going yachts of the seafaring rich. His party turned its face against the independence being clamoured for by René, suggesting instead some form of associate status with the United Kingdom. Mancham's party won every election that has ever been held in the Seychelles. Ominously, the losers murmured about corruption.

In 1971 there occurred a momentous event – the opening of the International Airport on Mahé, the main island of the group. Physical isolation was broken. Previously, perhaps a thousand visitors had arrived on the islands each year. A few years later, on the eve of Independence, their numbers would have climbed to nearly eighty thousand. Assorted celebrities and adventurers, in search of rest, recreation and lucrative investment, swooped down out of the skies. The Seychelles, perceived as a sexual and financial paradise, had become the place to go. Peter Sellers turned up with someone called Titi Wachmeister – in the fun time, the islands were overrun by women whose bodies were lovely but whose names were hard to pronounce.

The Seychelles began to be courted. Mancham was invited to France by President Giscard d'Estaing. In proper statesmanlike fashion they discussed the development of fishing and agriculture. But Mancham, to his credit, was also interested in the development of closer cultural ties with the French. Accordingly, it was agreed that a pornographic film (*Goodbye Emmanuelle*) should be shot in the Seychelles. As if that were not glory enough, Roman Polanski was also persuaded to come out to the islands to make a film about 'high fashion'. As Mancham observed, the trip augured well for 'Franco-Seychelles friendship'. Alas, there would soon come a time when he would not be so sanguine about the French connection. Polanski duly arrived with one of his pubescent mistresses. On the night of their departure a policeman discovered the couple making love on the edge of the runway. The matter was reported to Mancham who was at the airport to see his new friends off. A charge of indecency was possible. Nothing, however, was done. The future President was amused rather than outraged: it was a suitably public affirmation of the new Seychelles style he was working so tirelessly to promote.

The economy, previously dependent on the slender resources of the coconut tree, was booming. Hotels were springing up among the palms; there were traffic jams on the narrow roads. In faraway cities Seychelles land was being bought and sold in a frenzy of speculation. Real estate values soared. Everyone, it seemed, wanted a share of paradise. A nephew of the Shah of Iran turned up. He wanted to acquire an island on behalf of the Shah and his Empress, a retreat to which they could retire when in need of 'rest and meditation'. In the event, the Prince didn't buy just one island – he bought three.

The British, nevertheless, continued to baulk at the idea of associate status. Despite the stagnation of his hopes, Mancham was triumphant in a third general election in 1974, winning all but two of the fifteen seats. The Opposition voiced the by now standard charges of corruption and gerrymandering. With Independence looking more and more inevitable, the two parties, under pressure from London, were blandished into an unlikely coalition in June 1975. Their reward was internal self-government. Mancham was installed as Prime Minister while René was appointed to the less glamorous – but powerful – Ministry of Works and Land Development. Both men, in a sense, had got what they wanted. Mancham was now able to travel out of his spanking new international airport with enhanced style and prestige, attracting to himself queues of fair women; the more dour René, the favoured son of the Liberation Committee of the Organisation of African Unity, could consolidate his power and await his opportunity.

In June 1976, the improbable coalition holding, the Seychelles was invested with full independence. Mancham metamorphosed from Prime Minister to President.

On 5 June 1977, with Mancham, Honorary Knight of the Most Excellent Order of the British Empire, Officer of the Légion d'Honneur, absent in London to attend the Commonwealth Conference of that year, Albert René, voicing fears that Mancham was plotting the subversion of the democratic process, carried out his coup d'état with the help of Tanzanian soldiery. A policeman guarding the Armoury was shot dead. Political murder had at last come to the islands. Suitably enough, when his bedside telephone rang at 3.45 a.m., the ex-president was companioned by a 'guest' who was 'sleeping prettily' beside him. Suitably enough too, the caller with the bad news was his good friend, Adnan Khashoggi.

France Albert René, '. . . freedom fighter, kingpin of our liberation struggle and father of the Seychellois nation', had become Head of State.

Reality, African style, had caught up with the islands.

'If some of our people cannot see that they are being hoodwinked into submission,' Albert René wrote in his party newspaper in 1971, 'then it is the duty of those of us who can see the light to show them the way.'

Ogilvy Berlouis was one of those who had seen the light; one of the small band of insurrectionists – dressed to kill in flashy combat fatigues – who in the early hours of 5 June 1977 seized various key installations in the capital. He had his reward. Nowadays he runs the Ministry of Youth and Development and lives in a well-appointed house on the hills overlooking Victoria. I met him in his office. A small, lightly bearded man, he affects a Guevarist informality.

'We joined the coalition because we believed in *unity*. From 1964 we were advocating Independence. Mancham was very much against Independence. Then in 1974 Mancham changed his mind. Once he accepted the idea we thought we could work together.'

– Despite your ideological differences?

'We thought we could *educate* them.'

– But you couldn't . . .

'Unfortunately we could not. The difference in ideology remained. They didn't have any interest in the welfare of the people in general. Mancham was only for the foreigners investing in this country. They didn't mind if the poor remained poor while the rich got richer. So the coalition wasn't working and the people, as you know, decided there should be a change and all that.'

– The *people* decided?

'It was the *people* who reacted on 5 June 1977 and decided to change the government because they could see that the President was not fulfilling his promises and that the next general election would be postponed. The people were wondering – "What is happening? What is *really* happening?" The people felt that their interests were not being looked after. We were still a colony a year after Independence.'

– You say the people decided and thought all those thoughts. But wasn't the coup carried out by a small group in the dead of night . . . while, in fact, the people were asleep?

'As you know, not *everybody* can be involved in such a matter. What you have is a small group of people doing it on *behalf* of the rest of the population.'

– If you were so worried about the subversion of democracy, why then did you decide to set up a One-Party state?

'Well, we found out that the One-Party state was *exactly* what was convenient for the people of this country.'

– How did you find that out?

'We did not believe that there was any point in continuing to have more than one political party in the Seychelles.'

– But why? You confuse me.

'It is not convenient for the Seychellois people to have too many parties.'

– But why?

'If the people of this country agree to the policy of our Party . . .'

– Do they agree? How do you know they agree?

'If the people of this country agree to the policy of our Party, why should they be bothered by another political group? It is not that we are afraid of having another party. If we have a One-Party state that is only because it is what *they* want. And, let me say, we still have general elections in this country. We had one in 1978 and we plan to have another. Because there's only one candidate for President it doesn't necessarily mean that this candidate will be elected.'

– It doesn't?

'The procedure in *this* One-Party state is that everyone can vote either yes or no. If the candidate is rejected then we have another election.'

– Why not have two candidates? Mightn't that be simpler and more logical?

'To some people, yes, But *not* to the Seychellois.' (Pause. His voice when he started to speak again took on a note of stridency.) 'What outsiders will say about our One-Party state being wrong . . . *we will not listen to outsiders*. I would regard it as *external interference* in the affairs of Seychelles. We have our own system whereby the people can voice their criticism – they can criticise at their branch meeting. They are free to come to this office and complain. But, if the government is doing right, why should there be any criticism against it?'

12 November, 1983

Shiva Naipaul

A SEYCHELLOIS IDENTITY

Along Independence Avenue, Victoria's main thoroughfare, one sees the developing modern profile of the Seychelles capital. Here you will find a couple of newish office blocks, the Ministry of Youth and Defence and, nearing completion while I was there, the building designed to house the State Monetary Authority – which, I was told, would be faced in black marble. At the eastern end of Independence Avenue, towards the harbour, there rises a piece of monumental sculpture, glowing white in the heat, commissioned to mark the 200th anniversary of the town. It took me a while to realise that it was a representation of three birds with soaring, sail-like wings. They symbolised Africa, Asia and Europe (l'Afrik, l'Azi e l'Erop – as the Creole would have it), the three continents that had contributed towards the making of the Seychellois people. Going north from this monument, along the Avenue of 5th June – commemorating the date of the coup – you pass a patch of waste ground called Freedom Square and come, eventually, to the radio station. Security here is strict. Tanzanian soldiers lounge at the entrance, lazily suspicious of everyone who comes near. On the hill above the radio station is the Union Vale army camp, protected from intrusion by a fence of barbed wire. According to some, it has been used as a detention centre.

South of the avian monument is another centre of the town's social life, the Yacht Club – by no means so fearsome an institution as the name would imply. From the Yacht Club you can see at the top of a hill called La Misère the installations of the American satellite station, its great white globe floating like a moon against the sky. The tracking station, set up in the dying days of colonial rule, was the result of semi-secret negotiations between the British and Americans. Seychellois sensibilities had not been consulted. Mancham, exhibiting traces of a nascent national feeling, was a little hurt by this, though he had no objection in principle to the deal. Injured pride was tempered by schoolboy exuberance. 'At a stroke the Seychelles had gone from the 18th to the 21st century.' René was less welcoming, interpreting the deal as yet another imperialist imposition, a harbinger of every kind of evil. All the same, the tracking station was to survive the Socialist coup without apparent difficulty. It remains on its hill, scanning the southern skies, its great moon exuding a cosmic indifference to the fates of those below.

Victoria is a singularly characterless town. It betrays the emptiness and cultural isolation of the Seychellois past. One hundred and fifty years of British rule have made remarkably little impact. English, of course, is spoken but most Seychellois are not entirely at ease with it. It remains a formal language. French continues to be the more natural medium of expression for the élite; the less educated speak Creole. British dominion cut the Seychelles off from the living root of the French connection and never really replaced it with anything except the superficialities of colonial administration. The islands were too small, too far away, too deficient in the attributes that might have attracted settlers. One or two Englishmen may have acquired coconut estates. A handful of Indian and Chinese merchants ventured out. Their numbers were too small and their activities too minor to make any significant difference. The Seychellois lack not only a history (the islands must be one of the few colonial possessions not to have a fort) but a style. The 'planter's punch' ambience cultivated by the hotels is wholly derived from the Caribbean. Unblessed are the unexploited and unremembered! Mancham – perhaps unconsciously – sought to overcome this characterlessness by transforming the islands into a paradisal garden of sexual adventure. His efforts could, in their bizarre way, be considered an attempt at nation-building. Better a brothel state than nothing at all. Albert René also recognised that there was a problem and embarked on his own search for a Seychellois 'identity' that would make sense to the Liberation Committee of the Organisation of African Unity.

Socialism requires a past as well as a future. In the Seychelles the former had to be invented; or, at any rate, be subjected to a fundamental reinterpretation. For René to make himself and his party credible (if only to each other and the Liberation Committee), it was necessary to concoct visions of oppression and suffering; to stimulate dystopic fantasies. Historical resentment had to be manufactured, the void had to be filled somehow. With so little to hand, the urge to 'revolution', to coup d'état, had to invent itself. 'For hundreds of years,' René proclaimed to the first Congress of his Party, 'the Seychellois people have depended on others – employees on employers – consumers on merchants – the whole population on foreigners.' They had been crushed by a 'system of religion which attributes all responsibility to God . . . .' These abstractions are almost Buddhist in their mantric vacuity. In that airy dystopia, white had brutalised black, class had warred ceaselessly with class. Life, in other words, had been hell.

The picture painted was like a child's drawing of a house – recognisable but lacking in the particularity and concreteness of truth. Out of bloodless invocations such as these, a Seychellois identity, a national purpose, was to be forged. So there descended on the Seychelles the lethal abstractions which were to lead to 'Party Congresses' and, eventually, to coup d'état, political murder and the One Party State. Consider the language once more: '. . . the patience of the people ran out and in the early morning of 5 June 1977, a group of dedicated and courageous men . . . took up arms and overthrew the corrupt regime then in power . . . hand in hand the entire people, under the banner of freedom . . . march on towards true liberty, equality and fraternity . . . .' The event described is hardly real to its perpetrators. It is hardly real because they are telling lies. But lies, reduced to the language of fashionable fable, become a marketable commodity and make those who tell them acceptable to themselves and to a world ready to believe anything.

The search for a Seychellois identity has led in other directions. Not surprisingly, it has assumed a linguistic complexion. Creole, the language of the street, of the market-place, has been endowed with official status, taking its place alongside English and French. The government newspaper uses all three. They call this trilingualism. Indeed, Creole may be regarded – it being the tongue of the 'people' – as *primus inter pares*. It has been designated the 'first national language', and will be employed as the medium of instruction during the first two years of schooling. Its adoption has not been without problems. Not only have new textbooks had to be written, but other predictable difficulties have arisen – Creole having led a mainly oral existence – over its spelling and pronunciation.

'Everybody says Creole is a dialect and not a language,' the Director of Information said to me. 'But what does that mean?' He glowered across the width of his desk. 'How did French begin? Wasn't it a dialect of Latin or something?' A faint air of triumph livened his austere countenance. After 200 years, Creole had established its right to exist; it had come of age. Naturally, they would have to invent new words for certain scientific terms and so on. But why was that ridiculous? Which language didn't have to do that? The Seychellois were now a *nation* and Creole was an essential element of the national culture. On whose authority was it to be decided that Creole was a mere dialect? The Director of Information leaned towards me, 'Does God only hear you when you speak in English or in French? Doesn't he hear you when you speak in Creole?' I tried to suggest that it was not a question of communication with the Almighty, but rather, of communication with other men whose languages afforded wider access to worlds of intellect and spirit than that allowed by Seychellois Creole. The objection was waved aside.

The Minister of Education and Communication was a no less ardent advocate of the cause. It was, he pointed out, a well-known tactic of colonialism to fool the colonised into believing that their way of speech was not the 'correct' one. That deception was known as 'cultural alienation'. It was clear that I myself had suffered deep cultural alienation. Did I know what was being done to a Creole-speaking child when he went to school for the first time and was taught in French or English? 'I will tell you. That child is being *traumatised*. You are destroying his whole means of self-expression. You are destroying his whole means of understanding.'

My mind went back to my own schooldays in Trinidad where there was a clear distinction between the language of the street and the language of the classroom. Street talk played havoc with conventional grammar and pronunciation. It could easily be phoneticised into a semblance of autonomy. You moved, as the situation demanded, from one to the other. It was no good, for instance, walking into a rum-shop and using the Queen's English. You would have been laughed out of the place. But I do not believe that I – or any of my contemporaries – was traumatised by our linguistic acrobatics. It all seemed perfectly natural. No doubt part of the explanation lies in the fact that the requisite 'political consciousness' did not exist in the 1950s. If you don't know you are supposed to be traumatised you tend not to be. It is an acquired habit. Nowadays, it is altogether different. It is beyond argument, an influential Jamaican intellectual says, that the first language of the Jamaican child is Creole – English-style of course. The phrases of discontent leap from his pages – 'cultural bombardment', 'mental dependency', 'deculturation' . . . and so on. To render these notions in Creolised English – or French – would, I imagine, require considerable ingenuity. Needless to say, no serious attempt is ever made to do so. Standard English is used to vilify Standard English.

'Identity' is an addictive notion. As a member state of the Organisation of African Unity, as clients of Tanzanian military might, the Socialist regime likes to stress its African credentials. This too has not gone down well with everyone.

'Do I look African?' asked a young woman I met. 'I'm not African. We are not African.' She waved at the people sitting round the table; she gestured towards the ocean glittering below us. 'Africa is somewhere over there. More than a thousand miles away. What have we got to do with Africa?'

'Well – what do you belong to if not Africa?'

'Seychelles . . . what else? We're Seychellois, not Africans.'

'And what does it mean to be Seychellois?'

She laughed. 'That is a more difficult question.' Her ancestry was typically confused. At the turn of the century, her grandparents – they were traders – had emigrated from India. They had become converts to Christianity. At some point, Ethiopian blood (so she put it) had crept into their veins. Their ties with India were severed; the sub-continent was forgotten. To say you are Seychellois is one way of saying you are nothing in particular: a waifish confection, out of touch with Africa, out of touch with Asia, out of touch with Europe. Those who are afflicted by this malady or un-belonging all, to a greater or lesser degree, become unhinged.

L'Afrik, l'Azi (for the proletariat) – e (for the Francophile Creole aristocracy) l'Erop. 'Our cultural reality,' the avuncular Foreign Minister – Dr Maxime Ferrari – says, 'is also very related to Europe, above all to France.' Latterly, there can be no doubt that France has tried to instil new life into that moribund cultural reality. As is well known, the French and British have different ideas about these matters. The British do not have that sense of cultural mission felt by the French. 'Anglophone' does not pack the same messianic punch as 'Francophone'. Whatever the status accorded to English, whatever the communal rivalries between Creole and French, *la créolophonie* remains a sub-species of *la francophonie*. Mancham goes so far as to suggest that his overthrow was connived at by extremist Francophones in the Quai d'Orsay who saw the would-be rebels as possible conduits of a resurgent French pre-eminence. Certainly, France was one of the first countries to accord legitimacy to the coup. In addition, it quickly filled the manpower shortage caused by the expulsion of British officials and advisers. René, despite his University of London education, is not a card-carrying Anglophile. He once accused Mancham of wanting '. . . to adopt everything British – British language, British prostitution, British homosexuality and all'. To a leading light of the new regime the Chef du Service de la Francophonie is alleged to have said: 'Thank you, dear friend, for chasing out the British and for having returned Seychelles to its family.'

The Seychelles, in its quest for an 'identity', twists first this way and then that. But in no one direction is there a consummate satisfaction to be had. The people are confused and distracted.

> . . . the National Youth Service has . . . made me a true and good militant . . . Before I joined the NYS I was a good for nothing who didn't know how to plant and do other work, but now I feel I am prepared to do anything that I know will benefit others as well as myself' (NYS student).

The National Youth Service remains the most fundamental and contro-

versial innovation introduced by the new regime: an attempt to flesh out
with substance the image of New Seychellois Man. Next to it, the patronage of Creole pales into eccentricity. To take children away from their
families, to confine them in camps (with minimal interludes of release)
for two years, to put them into quasi-military uniform and subject them
to all the rigours of barrack-room discipline, to attempt to instil all the
ardours of collective egalitarianism, adumbrates totalitarian urges out of
all proportion to the scale of Seychellois existence. As is so often the case,
home-spun Third World 'socialism' collapses into unreflective cultism.

After some effort a guided tour to a National Youth Service camp had
at last been arranged for me. Early one morning Gilbert and I set off on
our little excursion. 'Would you,' I asked him, as we drove through jungly
verdancy, 'would you have liked to have gone to one of these camps?' He
narrowed his eyes evasively – he with his fondness for double Camparis,
his leisurely working habits, his devotion to his expense account . . . he
who, a day or two before, had told me that the people were 'stupid' and,
consequently, had to be herded and goaded . . . Gilbert, brother to a minister, whose job bordered perilously on that of informer, one of the more
novel vocations introduced into the islands by the Revolution.

'Yes,' he replied. 'I think I would have liked to go to a camp.'

No one was more in need of reconstruction. But I did not believe him.

The tarmac road came to an end. We bumped and shuddered along a
rutted track, crossing narrow bridges spanning still, black-watered
lagoons. Gilbert, who seemed unfamiliar with the area, questioned some
labourers. Apparently we couldn't miss the fence: and we didn't. A
wooden barrier blocked the access road. Two uniformed young women
emerged out of a guard-house. Gilbert stated our business, the barrier
was raised. We went past a plot of vegetable cultivation being watered by
a revolving sprinkler. Ahead of us were low buildings of unpainted grey
brick. We reported our intrusion to the main office. Our guides had not
arrived. We sat outside in the shade of an almond tree, gazing out at the
loveliest of coves, its waters calm and fringed by dense greenery. Under
another dispensation there would have been colourful umbrellas here;
bodies, hungry for the sun, littering the sand.

Our guides arrived – a middle-aged woman (she was called the 'village
co-ordinator') and a younger man of Chinese extraction. We returned to
the office, furnished in the dour, minimalist style characteristic of
collectivist endeavour. A printed exhortation was affixed to the rough
wall facing me. 'Washing One's Hands Of The Conflict Between The
Powerful And The Powerless Means To Side With The Powerful'. This
particular village – so the camp was referred to – contained over 800 children. Boys and girls were separated, though all shared equally in the com-

mon labours and duties. Both the sexes were organised in 'clusters'. Each cluster was further divided into three 'units'. This arrangement found visual expression in the star-shaped design of the buildings accommodating each cluster, the wings housing each unit radiating out of a central communal area like the spokes of a wheel.

Each unit had an *animateur*, an older student of settled progressive outlook, who provided ideological as well as practical inspiration to those under his care. Once a month the students might be briefly let out to visit their families; at Christmas they were given four days' leave. But, for most of the year, they remained confined within the fenced compound. Everything possible was done to promote the spirit of egalitarianism. The students were permitted only the most elementary of personal possessions. Pocket money was strictly forbidden. Instead, vouchers were provided, equivalent to about 25 rupees (under £3) a month. These vouchers they could spend as they pleased in the village shop.

Transgressors were dealt with by 'persuasion' and the techniques of 're-education'. If persuasion and re-education proved ineffective the authorities could resort to 'necessary punishment' – the infliction of a heavier burden of communal duty and the withdrawal of certain privileges. An especially grave offence could lead to expulsion. (Expulsion was no blessing in disguise: those who had not completed their two years in the camps were debarred from all further education.) To date, there had been some 50 expulsions from the village. The girls appeared to be particularly at risk. They were given pregnancy tests every three months – expulsion was automatic if the result was positive.

The village was not as neat as I had half-expected it to be. The sandy soil had a wasted look. Already, the cleared bush was reclaiming its own, subverting and satirising the aims of those who had only unexamined and reflexive notions of individual and social redemption. We stopped at a small clinic. Three lethargic boys were stretched out on cots. The presence of authority appeared to rob them of the powers of speech. One had cut his foot. Another, according to the nurse on duty, claimed that his eyes were hurting him. The third complained of recurrent headaches. Returned outside, I gazed at the ragged vistas of the compound. Here and there uniformed students moved slowly along the sandy lanes winding through the camp. The scene, despite the sunshine, was enervatingly colourless.

I looked into a girls' dormitory, a long room partitioned into cubicles by screens. Within each cubicle were two cots. Here a military precision and austerity prevailed. On each cot was arrayed the spartan equipment of its occupant. A tin plate. A mug. A spoon. Next to these – a beret, a brown shirt, a red scarf, a towel.

All the same. All equal.

From behind one of the partitions came a creaking of bed-springs accompanied by a spasm of coughing. One more, I assumed, was about to be added to the sick list. We inspected the communal kitchen. Hordes of flies had settled over the concrete work surfaces, feeding on the remains of vegetables that had not been cleared away. I looked askance at my companions. The village co-ordinator was apologetic. Unfortunately, the *animateur* had fallen ill a couple of days before. How fragile a thing is revolution: one sick *animateur* and the flies move in.

We paused by a playing field, a neglected rectangle of bare, beaten earth and wild grasses.

I remarked on the quietness of the place.

'It's the time of day,' the village co-ordinator said.

I remarked on the sombreness of the faces I saw.

'What makes you think they are sad?' she asked. 'They lead very fulfilling lives here.'

Even Gilbert seemed thoughtful as the barrier at the entrance to the camp was raised and we returned to the outside world.

North-east of Mahé, a 15-minute plane-ride away, lies Praslin, the second largest island in the Seychelles group. I went there to attend the opening of a new hotel which just so happened to be owned by a brother of the Foreign Minister. The scale of the enterprise was modest; but since anything to do with the tourist trade is big news it was a well-publicised event. What was more, the occasion was to be graced by the presence of the Minister himself. Palm fronds bedecked with flowers ornamented the pillars of the open-air lounge. Tables were set out under the coconut palms bordering a sugar-coloured beach washed by a placid sea.

Assembled there in the descending dusk was a collection of travel agents and travel writers, each a courted prince of power and patronage, each come to reassess a paradise once suddenly found, then as suddenly lost, and which now yearned to see itself regained. For, after all the treason, all the empty words, all the killing, one humble truth still survived: without tourists, the Seychelles had no reason to be; without tourists the island would die. The Minister, easefully tropical in dress, cut a ribbon and made a speech. Many people, he observed with benign incredulity, seemed to have been infected by the idea that Socialist Seychelles did not want tourists. He was a little flabbergasted by that – because nothing could be further from the truth. Seychelles wanted all the tourists it could get. The President himself was as committed as anyone to the revival and expansion of the trade. *Le Président lui-même!* He was prepared to concede that some mistakes had been made . . .

My attention drifted. Cameras flashed. The travel agents and travel writers showed polite interest and offered polite applause. Rather incongruously, a church bell tolled somewhere in the distance. The ghost of Jimmy Mancham haunted that Socialist twilight. Through the coconut groves came the strains of a hymn. Later that night I walked back to my hotel along the deserted beach. Moonlight gleamed on the leaves of the bushes and the palms. The dark sea was calm. Blackened garlands of seaweed striped the pale beach which lay stretched out under the moon like an outsized zebra's hide put out to dry. Stray dogs shadowed my progress, now approaching, now retreating. The silence of the blue night, broken only by the splashing waves and the barking of the pursuing dogs, was unsettling. A primal immediacy imbued the scene.

It was here, on Praslin, in the last quarter of the 18th century, that the coco-de-mer palm was discovered. The macabre suggestiveness of this peculiar palm has always encouraged speculation. General Gordon – who visited the islands in 1881 – decided that Praslin was the site of the Garden of Eden. 'Surely,' he wrote, his mind obsessed by the errant Eve, 'if curiosity could be excited by any tree, it would be by this.' He concluded that the coco-de-mer – whose nut mimics the female genitalia and whose male inflorescence mimics the phallus – must be the Tree of Knowledge. Less convincingly (for it is not a native of the islands) he argued that breadfruit was the Tree of Life.

The Seychelles have never fully recovered from this exegetic exercise. Gordon took it upon himself to devise a coat of arms for the colony. It showed the coco-de-mer supported on the back of a tortoise. Around the trunk of the palm is entwined a snake. The contemporary coat of arms is remarkably similar: the coco-de-mer and the tortoise are still there. Only the snake is missing.

19 November, 1983

Edward Theberton

CHAMELEONS

Tanzania

We went down to our regional capital last week. Fortunately, a break in the rains had made the road passable, at least to a Land-Rover. At the height of the rains it can take up to two weeks to drive the 60 miles or so.

We gave a lift to a colonel and three of his men, two of whom carried Uzi sub-machine guns. (Although Teacher Nyerere officially supports the PLO and swears eternal solidarity with Yasser Arafat in the hope of handouts from the oil states of the Middle East, he evidently prefers Uzis to Kalashnikovs.) The colonel and his men were accompanying a prisoner on a charge of armed robbery, a slightly crestfallen youth who belonged to a notorious local gang of criminals who usually bought their immunity from prosecution by sharing the booty with the police. For some reason, which the youth did not understand, the system had broken down, and he, a minor member of the gang, had been captured.

About halfway to our destination, I noticed a bright green chameleon crossing the deeply rutted red mud road. It crossed hesitantly, each step preceded by a series of ambivalent rocking movements. I stopped the vehicle, thinking the chameleon would make a nice gift for a small expatriate boy I knew who had recently been devastated by the loss of his white rabbit, which had escaped the hutch and wandered into the African bush, where he might be presumed not to have survived very long.

I picked up the chameleon, a splendid prehistoric monster in miniature, with swivelling turret eyes, a scaly ruff around his neck which he flapped when handled, and a gaping mouth with a lower row of teeth that would have been formidable had he been the size of *Tyrannosaurus*. I put my brave little monster on to a copy of the *Times Literary Supplement* which I happened to have with me, and he changed almost at once from his emerald green to the black and white of newsprint, with a few faint yellow stripes. His tail curled into a tight coil.

As I approached the Land-Rover with my captive, the colonel jumped out and ran 50 yards down the road though he was, by African standards, no longer young. The men with their machine guns drew back and cowered, terrified of the small creature, the whites of their eyes standing out against their dark skins, beads of sweat appearing on their brows.

I coaxed the colonel back into the waiting vehicle, though he came only after an assurance that I would keep the chameleon safe by me. As we continued on our journey, I asked my assistant why Africans were so afraid of these harmless reptiles.

'Me, I am not afraiding,' he said proudly, though I later observed that he refused to touch the chameleon, or even to come near it.

At first, they all denied their self-evident terrors; but gradually they revealed their reasons. Each had his own.

'If a chameleon gets in your hair,' said one, 'it never gets out again.'

'The tongue of the chameleon is poison,' said another. 'Otherwise, how could it catch flies?'

'The bite of the chameleon never heals.'

'If a chameleon grips your skin it can never let go, unless the sister of your father does magic.'

I demonstrated the falseness of some of these propositions by allowing the chameleon to crawl all over me. My companions looked on with horrified fascination, but their terrors were too deep-rooted to be removed by my naively rationalist gesture. I felt they were concealing the true, possibly magical significance of chameleons from me, but I was not anthropologist enough to discover it.

A discussion of snakes not surprisingly followed, and I was given a useful hint about what to do in the event of being encoiled by a python. I must take several bamboo poles, and while the snake wraps itself around me I must break the poles with a sharp snap. This will lead the python to suppose that my ribs are cracking, and consequently he will relax his grip to eat me.

I pointed out a few objections to the theory – for instance, that snakes cannot hear, that constrictors do not crush their prey but merely prevent them from inhaling, and that in any case no one had ever been attacked by a python – but what could I be expected to know of Africa after a few months' residence, compared with people whose ancestors had lived there since the beginning of the world?

It was then that one of my companions had the clever idea of putting irrational fear to good use. He suggested that we place the chameleon on the prisoner to make him squeal. The prisoner did not much care for this idea, a form of torture that would leave no traces. He was saved from his ordeal by the fear the guards themselves had of the chameleon, which prevented them from lifting it on to him.

We reached our destination safely, in spite of our accursed passenger. The mother of the little boy for whom I had intended it was playing bridge with three other expatriate ladies, over tea.

'I don't want it in the house,' she said. 'The Africans regard them as unlucky, and there must be something in it.'

'I saw a more beautiful one this morning,' said another of the ladies. 'It was green all over.'

'They go black whenever they're angry or afraid,' said the third.

'And if you put them on a patch of blue,' said the last, 'they get so confused they lie down and die.'

5 January, 1985

Colin Welch

CHAOS AND LAUGHTER IN NKRUMAH'S GOLD COAST

On what would have been Klemperer's 100th birthday, BBC2 re-broad-cast a film of him, already 78, conducting Beethoven's choral symphony. For the most part Klemperer sat impassively beating time, bringing in new sections of the orchestra as unemphatically as one might pick a jar of jam off a shelf. The results throughout were stupendous. At times his gaze would rise far above the orchestra, as if he were seeing visions, exploring for the first time a virgin land of unimaginable splendours and beauty.

I found it all terribly moving, though well aware of the perils of build-ing fantasies on facial expressions. Pater and others have concocted pages of purple prose out of what the Mona Lisa was thinking about. Veal for supper, D. B. Wyndham Lewis irreverently suggested, or fish?

I was once badly misled by the face of Geoffrey Bing – you remember, 'left-wing' MP from Hornchurch, later Nkrumah's 'attorney-general', a sort of dilute Vishinsky, half Ulster by origin, half, I think, Vietnamese, in which case his name were perhaps better spelt Binh than Bing, with its sturdy English associations – Douglas ('put a rose in your hair, Mavis –. there's a cabload of sailors at the door') and the Admiral shot *pour encourager les autres* (though he was Byng). 'You mean,' said Kingsley Amis, 'that he might just as well have been called, say, Bong?' Just so.

I was in the Gold Coast, as I still prefer to call it, for the *Daily Telegraph*, one of a series of correspondents each greeted with fiery denunciations of his predecessor, each to be denounced in his turn. My predecessor, Ian Colvin, had characterised the Asantahene's 'palace' at Kumasi as built of mud and corrugated iron, an observation which, true or not, gave no pleasure. I was denounced for having confirmed that a senior expatriate police officer had gone to Switzerland to investigate ministers' bank accounts.

Nkrumah was already Prime Minister. Above him presided like a cere-monial fig-leaf a British governor, whose relations with Nkrumah re-sembled Lafayette's indulgent subservience to the mob. Lafayette, said Heine, was like a tutor who accompanies his charge to dram shops lest he gamble, to gaming houses lest he whore, to brothels lest he duel and, when it comes to a duel, jumps up to second.

I stayed at the rambling ramshackle one-storey Seaview Hotel in Accra. Ghana's hotels were not then of the faceless inter-continental variety, but of rich individuality. At the Kingsway in Kumasi I had a room with shower. This last consisted of a cold tap on the fungus-stained wall, from which a rusty pipe ran up to and across the ceiling. I turned the tap. Distant gurgling, knocking and coughing sounds ensued, then silence. A large weird insect emerged from the pipe and peered irritably around, plainly annoyed at being disturbed. Of water no sign, and the insect huffily withdrew.

A welcome fellow-guest at the Seaview was Kingsley Martin, editor of the *New Statesman*, as ever friendly, bright, bird-like, 'progressive' and optimistic. Our rooms all opened, through half-doors like those of stables or school lavatories, onto a rough courtyard filled with rusting tricycles, débris of a failed ice-cream venture. Kingsley's bed was positioned diagonally in the middle of the room, like a battleship in the paper game Jutland. Against my advice, he moved it tidily into a corner. That night there was a terrific storm, with rain bouncing six feet and fireballs hurtling like flaming onions in all directions. Kingsley was drenched; before it was moved, his bed had been in the one dry area. Moral for radicals: respect what seems irrational; it may serve some deep but hidden purpose.

The next night Kingsley had Geoffrey Bing to dinner, and kindly invited me. The meal itself was memorable. The menu announced 'Fish No.1' and 'Fish No.3'. These were monsters with eyes on stalks and vestigial legs, dredged up by the Colonial Development Corporation from depths hitherto unplumbed, for which no name had been found. They ate like lumps of coarse kapok, full of needles, on which a fish had expired and decayed, leaving behind a ghostly taste and noisome fragrance. Kingsley asked for the wine list. 'We have two waines, sah,' the waiter beamed: 'whaite and black.'

Even more unexpected were the affability and humour of Mr Bing. He talked mostly absolute nonsense about the African consciousness, Western exploitation and oppression, negritude, Ghana bled white by the British (actually it had been bled by the Cocoa Marketing Board, which Nkrumah, also partial to a drop of blood, gratefully retained) and the 'hopeful experiment in democracy' which was taking place there. Mr Bing had a guttural German 'r', so that 'democracy' turned out something like 'demochrrracy'. Each tirade concluded with a broad grin, as if in self-mockery.

Not a bad chap after all, I thought: at least he can laugh at himself. I grinned too. Ever wilder grew Mr Bing's self-parodies, ever broader the grins. I laughed out loud. Kingsley laid a warning hand on my knee. Bing exploded. It dawned on me that they weren't grins at all, but a fearful involuntary rictus, containing no trace of mirth. A fragile solemnity was with difficulty restored.

My first call in Accra had been on our Liberian stringer, proprietor and editor of the local paper, so lavishly inked that, after reading it, one's fingers and bedclothes were black. As in Peter Simple's *Nerdley Clarion*, the same block could readily have served to depict a smart wedding, a road smash or a massacre. The office, in a maze of open-drained side streets, was held aloft on seven-foot pillars, approachable only by a ladder which could be withdrawn against creditors, government narks and those who fancied themselves wronged. Against one of the pillars reposed a blind man – the ace parliamentary reporter, I was told, who, with that total recall which God sometimes confers on the blind and illiterate, could reproduce *verbatim* hours of rhetoric: 'And Mr Gbedemah, he say . . .' The editor was at first reserved, thinking I had come to sack him. As it became clear I had no such intent or power, he cheered up and produced beer. He confided that he had had a real scoop for the *Telegraph* the other day, but, alas the damn goat had abstracted the copy from the out-tray below and eaten it. Primitive and eccentric as his printing plant was, it must have been powered by electricity. Rumour had it that he had once run the whole lot off a lead plugged into the nearest street-lamp.

Kingsley Martin had to fly to Lagos. I went to see him off. West African airways pilots were then mostly 'Wasps'. Towards the cockpit of Kingsley's aircraft, however, strode a gigantic Paul Robeson-like figure, covered in gold braid. Kingsley blenched and fell silent. A test of egalitarian nerve was at hand. 'Hang it,' he cried, 'I've left my tickets at the Seaview. I'll have to take a later flight.' As he turned, his jacket swung open, revealing a BOAC wallet. 'They're in your pocket.' 'Thank God,' he sighed, without conviction. Remembering the three or four horrendous pile-ups we'd passed on our way to the airport, I could have bitten my tongue off.

29 June, 1985

Zenga Longmore

LONG ENOUGH IN JO'BURG

Whenever a white person deigned to speak to me in Harare, I knew he or she must be South African and not Zimbabwean. The Zimbabwe whites treated me with utter disgust, and refused to speak, even when I patted one of their numerous pomeranians. They felt very bitter that '*they*' (the blacks) had taken over, and I was one of '*them*'.

The white South Africans, however, on hearing my English accent, forced drinks down my throat at an alarming rate, begging me to see the light concerning the glories of apartheid. When they found out I'd actually been to Johannesburg, they preened themselves in ecstasy.

'How did you like it? Isn't it a wonderful town!'

'Well, apart from not being allowed in the buses, restaurants, hotels, shops and practically everywhere else, yes, it's wonderful.'

'Oh, but it's got to be like that, don't you see! Before we came there, the blecks had nothing, just huts, then we came and gave them houses to live in – OK, slightly far out from where they work, but still they have free electricity. We've done everything for them. Everything, and what have they done in return? Thrown it all back in our faces. Don't laugh! The average bleck is at its happiest when leading a simple life, leaving the politics to us !'

'Personally speaking, I'm at my happiest when leading a complicated life, full of steamy intrigue.'

'You! You're different. You're from a superior culture to them. You're nothing like the blecks back home. You should come over to my father's farm and see what they've done to the toilets there! If these people can't even use a loo without making a hash of the whole thing, imagine the mess they'd make of running a country!'

'You racialist, you!'

'No I'm not! I'm talking to *you*, aren't I! And what's so funny?'

The more they talked, the more I drank, so the more I laughed. At the end of the conversation I would be rocking in my seat, cackling and wiping my eyes, as I was told how the 'blecks' are the lowest form of animal life.

The white Zimbabweans would sniff disdainfully. They must have thought I was being amused by witty repartee, and humorous one-liners.

All this took place in Zimbabwe, where I could talk to the whites with ease, and laugh at them safely without fear of being bashed over the head with a truncheon. Actually being in Johannesburg was another story altogether.

May this year saw my white step-brother, Fabian, and I step off the plane in a blaze of sunshine at Johannesburg airport. My heart was in my mouth. I felt that anything could happen in this, the world's most controversial country. Would people mistake Fabian and me for man and wife and arrest us? Fabian, who had been there before, assured me that we would be safe.

Queueing for immigration was lengthy and slow; I suppose we were all being checked to see if we were subversives in any way. I smiled toothily at the officer, and used my best English accent on him, but he eyed me suspiciously, and only after a five minute gaze into a computer did he reluctantly let me through.

The airbus is the only form of mixed public transport in Johannesburg, so luckily Fabian and I could sit together as we whizzed through the Jo'burg suburbs. Large bungalows line the streets, interspersed with dinky little shops. Worn-looking African women, laden with shopping, plodded slowly in ones and twos, sulky white babies slumped on their backs. Men crowded around the shops, smoking and drinking beer out of cans. Few whites walked the streets, no Africans drove the cars.

As soon as we approached the town centre, diamonds seemed to fall from the sky. Jo'burg glittered. Buildings shone in a haze of concrete and glass. Exquisite parks were dotted here and there, shops were filled with designer clothes, gold and precious gems, opulence radiated.

We alighted from the bus and picked up the heavy luggage. 'The hotel's a ten minute walk away,' said Fabian. 'I usually walk through the station, but I'm afraid we can't today.' 'Why not?' The station was an enormous stretch of polished wood and glass, but completely devoid of passengers. Then I looked up at a huge sign above the station, and almost dropped the luggage in shock. 'WHITES ONLY.' The letters were huge and belligerent. I have read and read about such things, but actually seeing them there in front of me, and knowing they actually meant business, shook me to the hilt. To think there is a law which says Fabian can walk in that station, but his sister can't . . . I was lost for words, and could only nod my head and pick up my bags.

A little way up I saw the sign: 'BLACKS, ASIANS, COLOUREDS.' A small, dark room crammed with people, arms and legs flailing, yet no one seemed to be talking. No noise, just an ominous silence.

'The white station's ten times the size of the black, yet it's always empty because all the whites have cars,' Fabian pointed out, rather unnecessarily.

So at last we reached the President Hotel, a towering skyscraper gleaming with power and strength. I began to feel a deep pang of guilt. A black man and white woman stood at the reception. I wondered if they got paid the same wage. They were both friendly and chatty, and soon a porter was showing us up to our rooms.

'Give my sister the nicest room.'

'Your *sister*!' The porter began to laugh. When Fabian knocked on my door, half an hour later, we ordered a pot of tea from room service. 'Either you or I will have to disappear into the bathroom when the waiter arrives.' 'Why?' 'Because there'll be trouble if we're caught in the same room.' 'But we're brother and sister.' 'But still, one of us ought to stay out of the way, just in case.' 'Shame on you! How can you deny your own sister just because of some ridiculous law they've cooked up here.'

A knock on the door, and a black waiter stepped into the room, balancing a tea tray. The shock of seeing me sprawled on the bed, and Fabian lounged on a chair, almost caused him to lose his balance. He stared from me to Fabian in utter disbelief, then, with trembling hands, clattered the tray on the side table, and darted out. 'Wait,' I cried. 'Your tip!' But he was gone, some dreadful crime was being committed almost before his very eyes. 'Tea, Fabian?'

That evening we ventured out into town. The streets were wide and sumptuous. Fabian told me there was only one restaurant where we could safely eat together, and that was an Indian restaurant in the back streets of town. Walking through the streets, I began to feel numb. The whites all seemed to have stepped off a Dallas film set. Women strolled in designer dresses, crowned with Dynasty hair styles, arm in arm with men in immaculate suits and somewhat loud ties. Black vagrants were *everywhere*: lying asleep in parks, disused cars, and pavements, sitting in classic poses of despair on benches and the sides of streets. Often, a Joan Collins look-alike would step daintily over a sprawling figure without a glance, and continue to chatter to her beau. As we walked along, we received such outraged stares from one and all as to make my heart's blood freeze. People stopped in their tracks to stare, and mumble loudly. A group of African men, standing around a takeaway café, spat at us in one accord, as we walked quickly past. Two white men, well into middle age, pushed into me, causing me to trip over, and ran on without an apology.

The Indian restaurant was small and dark, with excellent food and service, but somehow I found that my appetite had gone. There were many mixed couples, hidden away in the darkness, chatting and laughing.

On the way back we passed a long cinema queue of whites dressed up to the nines, creamy faces heavy with disdain. At the end of the queue was an African man, a young man, maybe in his late teens, picking his way through a rubbish bin. The cinema was showing *Beverly Hills Cop*. That night I had terrible nightmares, interrupted by two massive explosions at two in the morning.

Next day we met Tandie Klaason, South Africa's number one jazz singer, a small lively woman, full of laughter and fighting spirit. 'That's where my brother was tried to be hung.' She pointed to an imposing High Court building. 'Then the man who had actually committed the offence confessed a year later, and my mother died of the shock. I also lost my sister around that time when she was beaten to death by thugs coming out of Soweto. It may have been the same thugs who threw petrol on me and set me alight – I don't know.' Her face was tragically scarred. 'Let's go and see my friend. He's Indian, so he's not really allowed to live in Jo'burg, but he does. He's a very brave man!'

Walking to his flat with Tandie was like walking with Michael Jackson. Every black person we passed stopped and gaped in awe. 'Hi sis Tandie! How wonderful to see you!' People shouted and waved from every direction. 'Hi sis Tandie! Hi sis Tandie.' 'Wow! you're a film star,' I gasped. Tandie laughed and squeezed my hand.

The Indian's flat was gaudy to say the least. An orange carpet with purple blotches, green vinyl sofa and gilt cocktail cabinets that played music when opened. 'Come in, come in!' He was a small wiry man, with a constantly amused expression. Tandie looked at him proudly, and seated herself. 'Oh, so you're from London, I see. What's it like? Is it true you have West Indians there? It must be dreadful. They're frightfully violent, aren't they.' Fabian was too shocked to reply, leaving me to murmur a raspy 'No.'

'I'm not allowed to live here, but what I say to the police is: "I'm coloured, and we have coloureds in Parliament now, so I have a right to live where I please – it's not as if I'm black." ' And an amused chuckle rippled forth.

'Er – who's that baby in the photo?' I asked quickly to change the subject. 'Oh, that's my son. Would you like to see him? Sarah!' he bellowed, in so savage a roar that I laughed, thinking he was joking. 'Bring in my boy!'

Next minute: 'Here, master.' A bowed black woman of middle years padded in, head bent, eyes averted, holding in her arms a fat, grey slug of a child.

'Ah! You see, my son! OK Sarah, a pot of tea for four.' 'Yes, master.' 'And take my son *back*!' 'Yes, master.' And she padded out again. I looked at Tandie, who beamed back.

As soon as we left the flat, Tandie, who had kept up a respectful silence, burst into talk. 'Oh, isn't he nice! Although he's coloured, and I'm black, he lets me come into his flat to chat, and sometimes gives me a meal. Colour doesn't make any difference to him.' 'Oh,' I said, thinking of Sarah.

Huge empty 'WHITE ONLY' buses sped past us, occasionally followed by tiny 'BLACK ONLY' coaches, crammed to bursting point.

'There's a club where we can all go tonight. Can you imagine! A black, a coloured, and a white – but it won't matter,' she chortled.

In the taxi, I suddenly began to feel tingly and strange. Then I began to shake and sweat, and found it difficult to breathe. 'Fabian, take me back to the hotel, I think I'm going to black out.' 'Ell tek you to the hospital if you lek', came the cabbie's Afrikaans tones. 'There's a non-white hespital just up the road.' 'No, just go back to the hotel, please.' A doctor was called and told me over the phone that it was an anxiety attack. 'A lot of visitors from the UK suffer from such symptoms. Just rest.' I felt tired and miserable, so I took his advice.

Fabian and Tandie went out to a night-club, while I lay in bed. I ordered a cup of tea. The waiter arrived, looking nervously right and left, and plonked the tray down. 'He's not even allowed to buy property here,' I thought. 'He's probably got a wife working in one place as a maid, and kids living in another with not enough to eat.' 'How can you stand it here?' I asked, ludicrously overtipping him with Fabian's money. He hurried silently from the room.

Next day we boarded the plane, Lesotho bound. Freedom! 'Bye Jo'burg!' I said, and stuck my two fingers up at the plane window.

Two weeks later, when I had arrived in Zimbabwe, a blonde bespectacled South African said: 'But you were only there for two days! How can you say you didn't like it? You weren't there for long enough!'

Not long enough! I spluttered into my double G and T.

21/28 December, 1985

Anthony Daniels

NOT AS BLACK AS IT'S PAINTED

Ex Africa semper aliquid novi – except, of course, good news.

For the last 20 years the news from Africa has been unremittingly bad. It is the playground of the Four Horsemen, the continent where Malthus may yet be proved right. It is the only region of the globe where *per capita* food production has declined over the last two decades. Desertification is advancing more rapidly than industrialisation. Forests are being hacked down with no thought of replanting, the population is doubling relentlessly every 25 years (unless checked, that is, by the spread of Aids). In some countries, there is hardly an animal, except a goat, to be seen. Perhaps most depressing of all, one is now grateful for a president who, however dictatorial, does not actually *eat* his opponents.

Expressing pessimism about Africa is therefore the order of the day. Another fashionable pastime, righteous indignation being what it is, the most gratifying of emotions, is finding someone, or something, to blame for the present lamentable state of Africa's affairs.

Africans themselves tend to blame the World Economic System which, they say, also brought them colonialism. They point out that, in general, the terms of trade have moved consistently against them: it now takes much more of their produce to buy a tractor (or a Mercedes) than it once did. They forget the world has moved on while they have not. Besides, it is less than luminously clear what is the 'just' price of, say, a personal computer, calculated in pineapples or peanuts.

They are no doubt right when they allude to the nefarious practices, such as transfer pricing, of multinational companies. However, as several nations have found to their cost, there is only one thing worse for an African country than being exploited by a multinational, and that is *not* being exploited by a multinational. And even if it were true the World Economic System were entirely to blame for the present mess in Africa, it would be a sterile discovery. As I remarked, no doubt cruelly, to several young African radicals, even if Africa were to unite economically, it would still scarcely amount to Switzerland. Politics is, or should be, the art of the possible.

Visitors to and foreign residents of Africa, on the other hand, tend to blame the Africans themselves: indeed, African incompetence is to their small talk what the weather is to English conversation. Certainly, there is no shortage of grounds for castigating the collective laziness, rapacity, stupidity and corruption of African officialdom, from the highest to the lowest. It makes little difference whether the leader of the country is a cheap plaster saint like Nyerere or an out-and-out villain like Mobutu. Almost the only way to assure oneself of a decent standard of living in Africa – at least, one which allows the consumption of western goods – is by joining the pigs at the trough.

Governments have consistently favoured the urban, parasitic classes at the expense of the rural, productive ones. The reason for this is quite simple. If the modern history of Africa teaches anything, it teaches that he who controls the capital controls the country. Maintaining its own power has, not surprisingly, been the chief preoccupation of every national élite (and explains, incidentally, the Organisation of African Unity's principle of non-interference in the internal affairs of member states).

An overvalued currency, that has disastrous economic effects which are then *not* automatically corrected by the imperative IMF devaluation, has been one of the elite's favourite mechanisms. No less an authority than Nyerere admitted as much when asked why he refused to devalue the Tanzanian shilling. 'There would be riots on the street,' he said, 'and I would lose everything I have.' In response, the peasants tore up their coffee bushes – at a time of record world prices – and grew maize for their own consumption. Meanwhile, there was no money to pay for the *shipment* of oil, let alone for the oil itself, while the Central Bank resorted to filching private accounts.

There are, no doubt, purely economic constraints on Africa's advance. If all of Africa were to produce tropical commodities as efficiently as possible, supply would so far exceed demand that prices would fall catastrophically. And there is little hope of industrialisation. Africa is so technically backward that it would be cheaper to ship things from Mars than to produce them on the continent. An arms embargo on South Africa has produced an arms industry; an arms embargo on the rest of Africa would produce bows and arrows.

It is above all the cultural condition of Africa that prevents economic expansion. There is little in traditional African culture that is compatible with a modern economy, and much that is inimical to it. The early missionaries, who wanted to change Africa, understood this. They may have been intolerant, but they were surely not wrong. They merely underestimated grossly the power of formal education to change deep-rooted patterns of thought. No doubt the award of the Nobel prize for literature to Wole Soyinka is a legitimate cause for pride: but an award to an African in physics or chemistry would have been of far greater import.

The cultural impact of the West on Africa has been, in the main, disastrous. It has caused confusion and disarray, and awakened aspirations that cannot be met. Chinua Achebe, with regard to Nigeria, has written of a cargo cult mentality, in which Nigerians believe that one day, without any creative effort on their own part, all the good things of the world can and will be theirs. In one form or another, this mentality is present throughout Africa and is by no means discouraged by Western efforts at assistance.

Very few Africans have – can have – the faintest notion of the depth of the cultural and scientific tradition necessary to produce a Mercedes, or even a simple light bulb. For them, education is simply an obstacle course to a government post, from which they will be able to extort happily for the rest of their lives. (Failure to do so would be regarded as both foolish and reprehensible, insofar as it would be a failure to do the best for one's family, village, clan etc.) The idea of trade exists in Africa, but the idea of developing products does not. Industry, except of a very second-rate kind, will not be possible in Africa for a long time to come. The trouble is, Africa does not have a long time.

Yet all this is profoundly misleading if it is taken to mean that Africa is a continent of unrelieved gloom and misery. To that extent, the proponents of the New World Information Order, who want the world's press rendered safe for dictators, have a point.

The picture I have painted of Africa – surely by now a commonplace one – may injure the *amour propre* of the deracinated African elite, but it is far from capturing the whole of African life. We too easily assume that poverty, even increasing poverty, equals misery. We also assume too easily that what would make *us* unhappy must make African peasants unhappy.

But two years in an African village, and thousands of miles of travel through Africa, during which I reported, for obvious reasons, under the pseudonym of Edward Theberton, have convinced me this is not so. Within very wide (but not infinitely wide) limits of governmental incompetence and mismanagement, people in Africa are capable of leading lives whose major concerns are not the large questions of economic or political philosophy, but the small change of everyday existence. Perhaps I can best illustrate what I mean by reference to the life of Alice, my housegirl in Tanzania.

Alice was very poor. Before she came to work for me she had no monetary income of any description. She lived with her aged mother in a mud hut through the cracks in whose walls daylight was visible. Alice was . . . well, receptive to the charms of men, all of whom left her the moment she became pregnant. She had four children, all by different fathers. The first child was called *Bahati*, which means Luck or Fortune; the fourth was called *Matatizo*, which means Problem. The six of them lived off a little piece of land, growing maize, beans and bananas, and with a chicken or two. As soon as the children were able, they worked; they fetched water from a stream half an hour away and weeded the fields.

Alice was a charming woman and completely honest. She laughed whenever she caught your eye. Simple things delighted her: she once spent a week's wages on Polaroid pictures of herself and her family. On returning from England I brought her a stereophonic headset. I have never seen anyone derive such pleasure from a material object: she went round the house squealing with happiness. The batteries were exhausted in a day and she was devastated, until I gave her some more. Thenceforth, she wore her headphones even when she had no batteries, just to increase her status in the village. Chocolates made her laugh for joy. She asked me for a loan to buy fertiliser but, discovering it had sold out, used the money for a *kanga*, a piece of cloth the Tanzanian women use for a skirt, instead. How could I be angry? When there was fertiliser again in the village shop, I gave her more money.

One day she brought little Matatizo to me. He had stepped on a puff adder and it had bitten him. His leg had swelled and she was worried he would die. I put him to bed, gave him a paracetamol, and in a few days he was better. She was convinced I had saved his life.

Not long afterwards, I found her deep in acrimonious discussion with a man whom I discovered to be her current lover. (In two years she had two pregnancies aborted by a village wise woman, resulting in horrible infections.) She was in the process of breaking with him. Two days later she came to me in a state of great agitation: her erstwhile lover had planted some stolen goods in her fields and had denounced her to the police. She was soon to be arrested.

I rushed off to the police station with her and testified to her honesty. Looking back on it, it seems extraordinary that the police should have dropped the matter merely because I told them to. However, in Tanzania police cases are rarely decided by strict evidence, so I had no hesitation in using my prestige as a doctor in defence of someone I knew to be innocent.

Her lover, however, took his revenge. While she was at work, he went to her hut and in full view of the children cleared it out of her few possessions, even taking from the walls the pictures she had gleaned from advertisements in my magazines. Naturally, she was very upset: her lover decamped for another part of the country and personal identity being a very fluid thing in Tanzania, there was no hope of catching him.

Still, she soon recovered and was even able to laugh about it. I visited her some time after I had left the area when once more she had no monetary income. I found her with her children shelling beans outside the hut. They were talking and laughing when I arrived. She seemed very pleased to see me and ordered Matatizo to fetch their only chair for me to sit on. Then the children came one by one to touch the top of my head as a gesture of respect. Alice gave me a chicken (a considerable gift in the circumstances) and I gave her some money, which she would have spent at once on some conspicuous trifle.

The simple point of this banal story is that while Alice's life was far from easy, it was by no means miserable. It had its ups and downs, but these were not related to the operation of the London commodities market. She was a simple woman who could barely read, but this did not deprive her life of meaning. I think her lot was on the whole more tolerable than that of the unemployed in the north of England.

So I am both pessimistic about Africa in the sense I believe it is unlikely to develop economically fast or far, and optimistic about it in the sense this does not necessarily entail utter wretchedness for the great mass of the African population. There is as much misery in Geneva as in Kinshasa. Life in Africa, as everywhere else, is more complex than the schemata of intellectuals, or even of political journalists, would have us believe.

31 January. 1987

Jeffrey Bernard

OUT TO LUNCH

Towards the end of my stay in Kerkenna the hotel manager, who is also the mayor of the island, seemed to think that I was a VIP. God knows why, since I am so shy and retiring, not to say comatose. He drove me to the ferry – he half owns the shipping line too – and took me up to the bridge for the crossing, away from the well of the ship teeming with Arab fishermen and farmers who take their wares to Sfax most days. The crew of the ferry don't bother with uniforms. The captain wore a leather jacket, chewed on a cigar, looked like Pedro Armendariz, and the crew too looked as though they had been leased by Warner Brothers c. 1946. When we docked I was surprised to find that the hotel manager had laid on a car for me with driver to take me all the way to Monastir airport. He had put both car and driver at my disposal for the entire day. The driver, called Sfaxi, said, 'You are to do with me what you will.' We stopped at a few bars on the way to lunch at Sousse and although he was a Moslem he said it was all right for him to have just the one because he felt sure that God was looking the other way that day. We had a pretty hefty lunch in Sousse which set me back all of £4. There is a very good salad in Tunisia called *mechouia* which is a mixture of tomatoes, mild green peppers, chillies, onions and garlic all grilled then peeled and *minced* with caraway seeds, olive oil and lemon juice. But I didn't like their wine much although good manners forced me to persevere with it.

The hotel manager gave me an odd guide book. Under the heading 'Helpful Hints' it says, 'Never lose your temper with the hotel staff, always smile, always look as if you need help – result, instant affection.' Tunisian understatement. I did venture to smile at a waiter one evening and I always need help. Result? He spent half an hour brushing a breadcrumb from one of my succulent thighs. He turned out to be mad. He told me, in French of course, that he had once spent ten days in Liverpool, and that he thought it a very wonderful city. He probably would simply adore Belfast. And speaking of Liverpool it is extraordinary how that name or the name Ian Rush can open doors for you abroad. As Tom Baker pointed out to me when I came home you can work your way across Europe by simply smiling and saying things like, 'Manchester United. Very good, yes?' It is best done with a silly Italian accent like Chico Marx's. Then they'll do anything for you.

Anyway it's been all go. As soon as I got back I went to Berlin the following day. Yes, a day trip to Berlin. I know people who used to make frequent trips to Berlin some 40-odd years ago but it does seem rather a long way to go for lunch. I don't agree with this business of us and the Germans being so alike. I find their addiction to sausages, beer and transvestism to be very foreign. They are also very keen on 'gay' jokes and I don't see that homosexuality is any funnier than heterosexuality. They probably do though because there is slightly more chance of being humiliated if you happen to be queer. But after Berlin I shall never again go on a freebie in a group of journalists. It is essential to be a snob about some things and I simply cannot afford to be seen with teenage girls who work for women's magazines or grown men who report for the *Sun* and who should know better. What do they *report* for the *Sun*? Also, gay readers of *The Spectator* will be pleased to know that they were well and fairly represented in Berlin by four correspondents from two gay magazines or papers. Also, there was a man I think from *Time Out* to represent the pot-smoking, Marxist, puritan ethic. I was representing you, whatever that means, and what a bunch of absolute sweeties you are. Home after ten days and I find so many lovely letters from you concerning my legal trials and tribulations. Sitting here with Monica, the dreaded typewriter, I feel as though I'm writing to friends. And it's like old times again. This morning I had to wipe some cauliflower cheese off Monica's keys. Another home-life mystery.

8 November, 1986

5 THE MIDDLE EAST

J. H. Morris

CHANGE OF STATUS

Just a year ago, when I was working as a journalist in the Cairo office of a news agency, I announced that I was going to end my contract and spend the next two years as an undergraduate at Oxford. My announcement was greeted by my Egyptian colleagues with profound consternation; not because my services would be particularly missed – indeed, I was rather out of favour at the time because of some things I had written about the Imam of the Yemen – but because it was considered highly undignified and in doubtful taste to exchange the high calling of a journalist for the menial status of a student. I noticed a definite cooling off of the atmosphere. Our translators no longer introduced me quite so fulsomely to their friends; no longer, I fancied, did the messenger boys spring quite so smartly to their feet to open the door for me.

For I had insulted a well-established order of social precedence that gives the journalist in the Middle East a quite unique and highly enviable position among his fellow-beings. On the Continent, I am told, though for the life of me I failed to find any signs of it, the Englishman enjoys a certain hereditary respect, partly for his own honesty and decency, chiefly for his father's money. In the Middle East rather the same kind of mystical adulation is accorded the European journalist, whatever his newspaper, whatever his politics. He is considered a figure of mystery and glamour, part spy, part politician, part scholar; nobody can afford to displease him, and yet nobody is in a position to get anything very positive out of him. He is the representative of a foreign Power; and yet he has those attributes of individualism and self-dependence that every man of Arab stock instinctively admires.

The result is that while not all European journalists are sincerely welcomed at the Embassies of the Middle East, they are treated as honoured guests by the mass of the Arab population. Cairo's futuristic new Press Club, a marvellous glass and concrete thing on stilts, has opened its influential arms to British and American journalists in the area; and a strangely assorted company has taken advantage of the gesture. A curious collection of people they may seem to us. But to the ordinary Egyptian every one of them is, if not a king, at least a power behind some throne or other. And this was the status I was to abandon in favour of the rags and revelries of student life! Clearly the whole affair jarred on the sensibilities of my Egyptian confrères.

One very senior member of our staff found cause for satisfaction in my decision. He assured me that I was doing the right thing, since the University of Oxford would undoubtedly benefit from my experience as a newspaperman. He was an expert in both fields; for he enjoyed, in the coffee-houses of the city, the reputation as a sage, with a knowledge of the stars and the universe as well as of the prosaic techniques of newspaper life. Sages could very well be reporters, for all reporters were potential sages; and it was not in the least fanciful to suggest that a newspaperman could teach that old University of Oxford a thing or two.

But, of course, this aspect of the case occurred only to the most penetrating brains of the office; and I was still pestered by incredulous subeditors crying 'You, Mr Morris! You going back to school!' And at twelve o'clock each morning, when the cinemas opened and swarms of young men from Fouad I University fought for tickets – then, as often as not, I would catch a glimpse of somebody in the office looking first out of the window at the seething queue, and then, with a rather bewildered air of disappointment and reproach, across to me in my swivel chair. It would be, they felt, an altogether unworthy exchange of occupation; and, upon my soul, there have been times in the bar of the Union when I have been inclined to agree with them.

And the situation was, perhaps, rather aggravated when I decided, shortly before the end of my contract, to spend a week-end in Beirut – and to travel there, for reasons which will be familiar enough in this heart of an Empire, as a deck passenger on a Turkish steamer. A celebrated Egyptian reporter volunteered to see me on board; and I shall never forget the look of utter shame that blushed over his face when, at the top of the gang-plank, the purser took one look at my ticket and contemptuously handed me over to the care of the dirtiest and nastiest-looking sailor in sight.

I am glad, for their sakes, that members of the Cairo Press Club did not see me on the journey. The word 'deck' in 'deck passage' does not apparently mean the kind of deck that has given its name to those comfortable garden-chairs. Far from being ushered into the airy sunlight of the ship's upper parts, I was guided deeper and yet deeper into its dark and unpleasant bowels, until at last, bruised from the steel ladders, soaked from the water which flooded the passages, daunted by the oily smell and scared stiff by the great thug in whose charge I was, I found myself in a vast and filthy cavern with my fellow-passengers. The first looked, to me, identical with a girl reporter I had known in Bristol; but she indignantly denied it, and as she only spoke Rumanian I was forced to believe her. The second was an elderly American in a hand-painted tie, quite the most prosperous-looking person on the ship, who told me he was in the oil trade; it would not surprise me to discover that he owned the entire oil industry of the Middle East, and it surprised me even less when he unaccountably won most of my money from me at poker. The third was a likable Chinese dwarf whose wizened face was notable for its air of inconsolable melancholy. There were probably others too; but so gloomy were the corners of the huge metal room that, although from time to time I thought I heard muffled cries and baby noises, I could see no one.

Let me be frank with you. I did not enjoy the journey, and I was glad when, having been kicked upstairs by the purser's assistant, I found myself, at Beirut, the subject of an entirely different kind of attention. My friends in Egypt, deeply disturbed by the circumstances of my embarkation, had done their best to ensure that I was treated with due courtesy at the other end of the voyage. Waiting on the quayside for me was a Lebanese dignitary of high importance; on board to usher me through the formalities was a smooth and courteous aide; the purser's face was a picture of baffled scorn as I was taken to the head of the first-class queue and, with a whispered word to the customs officers, swept ashore.

'But come now, Mr Morris,' said the high Lebanese dignitary as I waved goodbye to the Chinese dwarf, 'there's a political purpose behind your voyage, isn't there? Travelling on deck, indeed – you, a *journalist*! You can't expect me to accept that so easily!'

For it was as unthinkable that a British journalist should be hard up as it was to imagine him hurrying in cap and gown down the High to the Examination Schools; and it was shocking to my good Arab friends to imagine me in either situation. Let me assure them now that I am comfortably established on a generous Government grant; that I am much too busy at twelve o'clock in the morning to join the cinema queues; that I am doing my best to give Oxford the benefit of my special knowledge; that I have no political purpose in becoming an undergraduate; and that as the editor of the undergraduate magazine, *Cherwell*, I enjoy, if not quite the same status as the one accorded me in Cairo, at least a certain notoriety all its own. And let me thank the anonymous official who, by plastering the word 'Journalist' all over my embarkation card, allowed me to take so many delectable things through the customs on my way home.

28 July, 1950

Evelyn Waugh

TOURIST IN AFRICA

February 4. Port Said at dawn. Over a hundred dauntless passengers left for the gruelling dash to the Sphinx and to Suez. I did not land. The officials who came on board wore khaki service dress and Brodrick caps. No tarbouches to be seen. The touts have discarded their white gowns for shoddy western suits, exemplifying the almost universal rule that 'Nationals' obliterate national idiosyncrasies. Even the 'gully-gully' man wore trousers.

I have often wondered about the history of these performers, more comedians than conjurors, who, as far as I know, are peculiar to the Canal. Few tourists in these days go shopping in Port Said or sit in its cafés. (I remember the days when everyone going out, male and female, bought a topee at the quayside and those returning to Europe from the tropics threw them overboard in the basin to be scavenged by Arab boatmen.) So nowadays the 'gully-gully' men ply between Port Said and Suez, boarding the ships and giving performances on deck at advertised times. I first saw them in February, 1929, when perforce I spent some weeks in the port. Their repertoire is as immutable as the D'Oyly Carte's. The craft, I have been told, is hereditary. The man who squatted on the deck of the Rhodesia Castle must be the son of one of those whose attentions in 1929 became rather tedious after long repetition; or perhaps he was one of those tiny children whom I mentioned in a book called *Labels*. 'There was a little Arab girl,' I noted, 'who had taught herself to imitate them perfectly, only, with a rare instinct for the elimination of essentials, she used not to bother about the conjuring at all, but would scramble from table to table in cafés, saying "Gully Gully" and taking a chicken in and out of a little cloth bag. She was every bit as amusing as the grownups and made just as much money.'

There is a distinctly military tinge about the gully-gully ritual, which dates perhaps from 1915, much facetious saluting and the address: 'Oh you, officer, sir,' when chickens are produced from waistcoat pockets. There is also the invocation of the name of Mrs Cornwallis-West derived from a remote and forgotten scandal. But who began the art, when? Most

Oriental and African conjurors assume converse with the supernatural. No doubt Egyptian conjurors did a hundred years ago. Some unrecorded Charlie Chaplin or Grock of the waterfront must at about the time of *Aida* have first hit on the idea of introducing farce; perhaps the literal progenitor of all gully-gully men. I wish I knew.

All day in the Canal drifting past the dullest landscape in the world, while the passengers hang fascinated on the taffrails and take spools of snapshots.

I remember once seeing a soldier of the French Foreign Legion desert, jump overboard just before luncheon, and stand rather stupidly in the sand watching the ship sail on without him. Once, much later, during the last war, I remember a happy evening on the Canal dining with two sailors whose task was to employ numberless Arab bomb-watchers. When they reported an enemy aeroplane and a splash, traffic was stopped until the missile was found. The clever Italians, I was told, dropped blocks of salt which dissolved, leaving no trace. Divers worked for days in vain searching for them and the Canal was blocked as effectively as by high explosive. But there was nothing of interest during this day's journey. All one could see was a line of behinds as the passengers gazed and photographed nothing.

The Captain tells me he finds the Canal the most interesting part of his voyage.

The weather grows pleasantly warm; not warm enough to justify the outbreak of shorts which both sexes, from now on, inelegantly assume.

February 6. A cool, fresh breeze down the Red Sea. For an Englishman the English make ideal travelling companions. I have been accosted twice only; once by a woman who took me for my brother, Alec, and again by a man who mysteriously claimed to have been at Cambridge with Ronald Knox.

The constant music, I suppose, caused genuine pleasure to 5 per cent of the passengers; pain to 1 per cent; a vague sense of well-being to 50 per cent; the rest do not notice it.

February 8. Anchored off Steamer Point, Aden, after luncheon. The ship stays until midnight. A bazaar is set up on a raft below the gangway. Launches ply to and from the quay.

Since I was last here Aden has grown green; not very green, but there are distinct patches of foliage where there was only dust. We originally occupied Berbera, in Somaliland across the straits, in order to have somewhere to grow cabbages and fruit for the garrison of Aden. Water has at last been struck and piped. The continuous trains of shabby camels no longer pad along the road from Crater Town. There are taps and water closets now in the settlement. I saw only one camel and that was a sleek riding animal from up-country, sitting beside its master at an Arab café feeding on a hamper of green vegetables.

Most of the passengers drove off to see the water-tanks ascribed to King Solomon. In a thousand years' time will Central African guides show tourists the mighty ruin of the Kariba dam as one of the works of Solomon? I wish I could think so.

I took a taxi to Crater Town and walked its narrow streets for an hour looking for remembered landmarks and finding none. Not that there has been much modernisation, but things have disappeared. I could find no trace of the 'Padre Sahib's Bungalow' where I once spent a week. Nor of Mr Besse's emporium. I was Mr Besse's guest on several occasions in his rooms above his offices and warehouse. I also went with him on an appalling climb to the edge of the crater and across the burning volcanic debris to his shark-infested bathing beach on the far side of the little peninsula. He was an enchanting man. I described him in a book called *Remote People* as 'Mr Leblanc,' and was told later that he greatly relished the portrait. I wish he had shown his gratification by leaving me something. He was a rich man then. His great fortune came later, and I was astounded ten years ago to read that he left £2,000,000 to Oxford University, an institution which can never have caused him a moment's pleasure. I do not know what he was by race or religion. They named the college he founded St Antony's, but when I inquired here, no one knew or had troubled to conjecture which, if any, of the twelve canonised Anthonies they were commemorating.

The smells of Crater Town are unchanged – spices, wood smoke, coffee, incense, goats, delicious Arab and Indian kitchen smells, garlic and curry, sewage and hair oil. It is always a wonder to me that the English who cheerfully endure the reek of their own country – silage, spaniels, cabbages, diesel fumes, deodorisers, fish and chips, gaspers, ice-cream – fight shy of 'native' streets.

Back to Steamer Point. Here there has settled all the tourist trade which used to flourish in Port Said, but in a sadly standardised form. Simon Arzt's in the 1920s was richly cosmopolitan. You could find most of the luxuries of Europe there. At Aden the shops are all kept by Indians and each has an identical stock of Japanese counterfeits – 'American' fountain pens, 'Swiss' watches, 'French' scent, 'German' binoculars. I searched for cigars but found none. There used to be two hotels at the extremes of the crescent. Their verandahs were haunted by touts and money-changers and shirt-tailors and each possessed a 'mermaid' – a stuffed manatee, I think – which was kept in a chest and exhibited on payment. Now one of these hotels has gone and in its place has arisen a large, modern, air-conditioned building; no place for a mermaid. The other is its old shabby self.

I had a personal interest in the mermaids, because six years ago I suffered briefly from hallucinations in the course of which I imagined myself to be in communication with a girl in Aden. She complained of having nothing to do there. I went into some detail (which I omitted from the account I wrote of the experience) about the rather limited diversions of the settlement. Among them I mentioned the mermaid. 'It's gone, Evelyn, it's gone,' she said later, in tones of reproach as though I had maliciously sought to raise false hopes of pleasure, 'it isn't here any more.'

I was curious to discover whether in this particular as in all others my 'voices' had been deceiving me. But here she spoke the plain truth. The first servant I addressed at the hotel looked blank and shrugged, supposing I was demanding some exotic drink. But a much older man came forward. 'Mermaid finish,' he said.

'How?'

'One man came finish mermaid.'

'When?'

'Not so long.'

The curse of Babel frustrated further inquiries. I should have liked to know how the mermaid was finished – bought, stolen, destroyed by a drunk? – and particularly when it disappeared – before or after or even during my conversations with my forlorn confidante?

February 9. In the Gulf of Suez we lost the breeze which kept us cool in the Red Sea. Once round Cape Guardafui we are in the steam-bath of a New York heat-wave. It is more agreeable and, surely, healthier to come to the tropics gradually than to be deposited there suddenly by an aeroplane in the clothes one wore shivering a few hours before in London.

A great stripping of clothes among the passengers. Cortes marched from Vera Cruz in armour; Stanley crossed Africa in knicker-bockers and a braided tunic; I in my humble way have suffered for decency. I have worn starched shirts at Christmas dinners in both Zanzibar and Georgetown, British Guiana; but these young people must be almost naked in order to lie in deck chairs in the shade. The thighs of middle-aged women quiver horribly at the library steward's table. How different the three Arabs we have taken on board at Aden, who are travelling to Zanzibar. They wear the light cotton robes of their people and always look cool and elegant and clean. They sit playing dominoes in the smoking-room and three times a day spread little mats on deck, take off their sandals and prostrate themselves in prayer.

I have found a diverting book named *Stars and Stripes in Africa; Being a History of American Achievements in Africa by Explorers, Missionaries, Pirates, Adventurers, Hunters, Miners, Merchants, Scientists, Soldiers, Showmen, Engineers and others with some account of Africans who have played a part in American affairs*, by Eric Rosenthal, 1938.

It begins rather surprisingly with Columbus, who once put in to the Gold Coast. Some Americans believe he discovered the United States, but can many, I wonder, suppose he flew the Stars and Stripes? Mr Rosenthal was injudicious only in his choice of title; perhaps his publishers chose it for him; American publishers are more presumptuous than European in these ways; anyway the sub-title fully explains his achievement. He rejoices to trace every connection however tenuous between the two continents and has produced a fascinating collection of uncommon information. In fact, I think, the only time that the Stars and Stripes were taken into Africa was at the head of Stanley's expedition to Livingstone (who appears here among American worthies on the grounds that one of his sons died after the battle of Gettysburg: he had enlisted in the Federal army under an assumed name, was wounded and taken prisoner. It is not quite clear from Mr Rosenthal's account whether he fought in the battle).

Americans have every excuse for claiming Stanley as a compatriot. He claimed it vehemently himself and was at one brief period a naturalised citizen. But he was born and died a Briton. He was the illegitimate son of Welsh parents, jumped his ship at New Orleans, enlisted in and deserted from both sides in the Civil War. When he became widely advertised and was invited to explain his origins, he hesitated between the embarrassments of admitting his illegitimate birth and his illegal entry. He then formally abjured his country. When he became respectable, rich and married he re-naturalised himself British, sat in Parliament and was knighted.

It is interesting to learn from Mr Rosenthal of the enthusiasm of individual Americans for the establishment of the 'colonialism' in Africa which their grandchildren reprobate. At the time of the Boer War, he tells us – I was about to write in the manner of a book review, 'he reminds us'; I had no idea of this or of most of the facts he adduces – Theodore Roosevelt wrote to Selous: 'the most melancholy element in the problem is what you bring out [in *The Spectator*] about Englishmen no longer colonising in the way Boers do.'

In the invasion of Matabeleland in 1893 it was a young American trooper, Burnham, who hoisted the Union Jack over Lobengula's Kraal.

There were eight American members of the Reform Committee in Johannesburg who first invited and then repudiated the Jameson Raid.

One of them, Hammond, was condemned to death but later with his fellows was bought off for £25,000 a head.

A Philadelphian built the first synagogue in Rhodesia.

These and many other facts I have learned from Mr Rosenthal. The most moving narration is of the efforts made in 1900 to solve the problem of the Boers by wholesale evacuation. The Governor of Arkansas offered 5,000,000 acres of his State as a free gift. Colorado followed suit. In Wyoming 300,000 acres were actually irrigated and planted for the Boer immigrants. If these farsighted and generous policies had been realised much annoyance would have been spared Her Majesty's loyal subjects.

15/22 July, 1960

Simon Raven

ON THE ROAD TO BYZANTIUM

'Tomorrow,' said the second-class steward of the SS Mustapha Kemal, 'we come Iskenderu. Iskenderu is first port of call in Turkey. There will be the formalities.' He pronounced the word with a heavy, whining accent on the penultimate syllable. 'Turkey formaleeties,' he said, and giggled rather wildly. 'Turkey formaleeties take all day, gentlemans, take all night. So long as customs mans on ship, they eat ship's food, see? So they stay long time – eat breakfast, lunch, tea, dinner, supper. They so stupid with eating, gentlemans, they find nothing.'

He went into his cubby hole and came out with an armful of skirts, blouses and assorted lingerie. He spread it all carefully and evenly over the five tables; he then covered it with a layer of newspaper, the newspaper again with tablecloths, and proceeded to lay the breakfast things for the next morning.

'You see, gentlemans? These things I buy in Cyprus for my wife. Customs mans want much money – is no good. So I hide here. Customs mans, policemans, always eating. So no one look under tablecloth.'

At first we were sceptical about this strategem, but the next morning we saw how sound it was. There were about ten customs officers of varying grades, some fifteen uniformed security men and a fair-sized platoon of hangers-on. From the moment they came aboard, they started eating in

relays in the Second-Class Dining Room. At any given moment of the
day, half the officials on board would be consuming one meal while the
other half was champing for the next. There could be no question of lifting the tablecloths. Our steward, winking and giggling, hurtled in and
out of his cubby hole with unending replacements of crocks and proven-
der, while the officials gorged and belched like happy schoolboys at a picnic, as ignorant as Medea's husband of the enormity which underlay
their feast.

At Mersin, the second port of consequence as one sails up the west coast
of Turkey, we disembarked ourselves and our car for the drive to Istanbul.

'Formaleeties,' said a man on the quayside.
'But,' we said, 'we went through all the formalities at Iskenderu.'
'Here,' he said, 'only ver' *leetle* formaleeties.'
Now, the secret of Turkish formalities is this. A document, which is
regarded as a symbol of enlightenment and progressive administration, is
a thing to be reverenced rather than understood. No one really knows
whether it is in order or even what it applies to; but reverence for a certain time it must and will receive, and therefore the fewer documents
you produce, the sooner you get away. On the other hand, if you produce
too few you are suspect, not so much as a potential lawbreaker, but rather
as though you were a religious apostate of some kind, lacking in the
proper respect for sacred matters. So a nice balance must be struck –
enough documents to reassure people, not enough to occasion serious
delay. For the 'ver' leetle formaleeties' at Mersin we decided to submit
passports, an out-of-date insurance policy for the car (this to test the
acumen of our persecutor), and one international driving certificate.
The out-of-date insurance policy, being on thin and expensive paper,
was a great success. The official hopefully asked for more like it, was
denied, took his revenge by charging five Turkish lire (three shillings)
to stamp the driving certificate, and waved us (not without courtesy) on
our way.

It would seem from their history that the three basic elements in the Turkish national character are cruelty, courage and inefficiency. This
impression is confirmed by the dress and the physical features of the
ubiquitous soldiers. In Konya, a famous inland resort where we spent our
first night, the Sunday streets were full of them – little men with trailing
khaki greatcoats, filthy boots, hatchet faces and beady eyes, wandering
aimlessly round the town without a *kuru* in their pockets, some of them
hand in hand. They appear as tough as they do amiable; and I am told that

although they are badly led by corrupt officers, in close combat at least they are very effective.

This was explained to me by a schoolmaster in Dinar (a nasty little town apparently built in a marsh), where we spent the following night. The Turkish landscape, he said, is alternately savage and boring. It does not compromise or apologise; mountains are all sheer, lakes treacherous (and often salt), deserts merciless and plains vast. It follows that the men who come from most of this country must be brave and resourceful; to have survived at all they must have developed a remarkable talent for survival, which stands them well under arms. By being a harsh and ungenerous parent, the country has endowed her sons with the virtues necessary to defend her. Or so my schoolmaster informant would have had me believe.

But however brave or cunning they may be, I cannot believe in the Turks' capacity to carry through any enterprise, even that of self-defence, until something is done about that mixture of fatalism and *laissez-faire* which we should call their inefficiency. Yet what can be done about it? Ataturk tried hard enough, Heaven knows; as a result of his efforts, it now takes only an hour and a half to cash a traveller's cheque in a large provincial town, there are only a hundred or so potholes to every hundred yards of road, and even the smallest village seems to have at least one shop devoted solely to the sale of busts and photographs of Ataturk. But for all these blessings, he has really changed nothing fundamental. For the point is, of course, that the Turks are Moslems – unenthusiastic Moslems, for the most part, but Moslems nevertheless – and they are therefore prepared, indeed grateful, to leave the entire direction of affairs to Allah.

Consider the following incident. A small bridge had collapsed on the main – ie., the only – road between Selçuk and Ismir (Smyrna). On either side of the bridge there were vast queues of traffic. There was not a single policeman in sight, but a gang of lorry drivers was attempting, in an aimless and amateur manner, to construct a temporary road of stones, shrub and earth down the bank, over five yards of stream and up the bank on the other side. Plainly only Allah knew what would come of this, so we drove away to camp the night in the nearby ruins of Efes.

In the middle of these ruins was a small restaurant-bar, which, although the ruins were seldom visited so early in the year, was luckily open. At the bar were two imposing gentlemen, who greeted us because we were foreigners, allowed us to buy them drinks for the same reason, and announced that they were, respectively, the Mayor and the Chief of Police of Selçuk. They had taken refuge in the ruins, they explained, because otherwise people would come and pester them about the bridge and the traffic. (The disaster had occurred just inside their area.) This kind of thing was always happening after the spring floods; it was doubtless very annoying for a lot of people; but what could they do about it? The traffic police would be very angry if called out for extra night duty; the official in charge of repairs had gone to see his brother in Antalya that morning; his men were useless without his direction and almost useless with it. Then when, we asked, did he think we would get to Smyrna? He shrugged his shoulders as if we were talking about Peking. The only thing to do he said, was to let matters take their ordained course: one day was as good as another for seeing Smyrna, which was a noisy city full of dirty and expensive whores. Yes, another raki would be acceptable . . .

Without much hope, we returned next morning to the bridge. By some miracle, it seemed, the temporary road was nearing completion, and the yoghurt vendors, who had done a brisk night's business, were already leaving. And indeed, after an hour more, the traffic began to move – only one way at a time, but palpably to move. Then, at the high moment of victory ten traffic policemen, magnificent in blue uniforms and white caps, appeared to take charge of the situation they had ignored all night; a moment or two later, the Mayor and the Chief of Police took their stand by the temporary road, bowing and raising their hats to each newly released vehicle as it passed.

'Good morning, gentlemen,' said the mayor with smiling effrontery when it was our turn. 'It is all as I said, you see. All our arrangements have gone smoothly, and you will be in our beautiful city of Smyrna in good time for your lunch.'

31 May, 1963

Shiva Naipaul

THE IRANIAN DISEASE

Teheran

The house, as is usual in Persia, was hidden behind high walls. Its style was vaguely Iberian – facade washed in white, red-tiled roof, a ground floor veranda framed by arches. The proportions were those of a small palace. A swimming pool gleamed in a corner of the twilit garden. My host, a lawyer, was rumoured to have made his money only within the last ten years; the house, a tangible expression of that success, was less than a year old. Northwards the lights of Teheran were spread like a rash up the lower slopes of the Elburz mountains. Snow streaked the higher summits. Beyond that black mountain wall lay the Caspian, sea of sturgeon and caviar. A majordomo waited on the pillared porch. I was led through a hall adorned with Persian miniatures, across a parquet floor strewn with rugs of intricate design. My host and his wife were in the library. A bell summoned a manservant. He approached soft-footedly and, bending low over me, took my drink order. I gazed at the books.

'Over five thousand volumes,' my host said.

The books were ranged on two floors, the upper, bordered by a wrought-iron balcony, housing, my host explained, his collection of Persiana; the lower, books of a more general nature. A spiral staircase connected the two. The house, in fact, had been designed around the library.

'We ran out of space,' my host's wife said. 'In the end we decided that the only thing to do was to build a new house.'

A girl of about fifteen – the daughter of the house – appeared. She put on a jazz record. Both she and her brother attended American boarding schools. My gaze strayed to a group of teracotta animal figures arrayed on a sideboard.

'3000 BC,' my host said.

Other guests began to arrive. Abdul and Manny; Ali and Leila; Xerxes and Fatima. The women glittered with jewels, sparkling on fingers, necks, bosoms. Their fat husbands were more casually dressed, T-shirts sleekly stretched over bulging stomachs. A servant passed round caviar on thin slices of toast.

My host's wife fingered Manny's soft white dress.

'It's exquisite, Manny. Really fabulous. Where did you find it?'

'I picked it up the other day in a little shop in Soho.'

'Is it Indian?'

'Afghan, I think. Abdul insisted I buy it. "That's you, Manny," he said. You know what Abdul's like.'

But now it was Manny's turn to praise. 'What a beautiful emerald that is! I don't think I've seen you wearing it before.'

'I got it on our last trip to New York. I can't resist Sachs. Every time I'm in New York I just *have* to buy something at Sachs.'

'I know the feeling,' Manny said. 'Abdul and I were in Chicago not long ago.'

'What was Chicago like?'

'Very windy,' Manny said.

'They say it's a windy city,' my host's wife confirmed. 'Did you buy anything there?'

'I picked up quite a nice diamond . . . but, you know, I prefer to get my jewels in Paris.'

'It's *ages* since we've been to Paris,' my host's wife said. 'Darius is getting lazy in his old age.'

'So is Abdul,' Manny said. 'Lazy and fat. Last year I literally had to drag him to that health farm in Sussex.'

'Darius won't hear me talk about health farms.' My host's wife looked martyred.

Manny smiled sweetly at me. 'Do you know Paris well?'

'Not very.'

'Do you know,' Manny said, 'I spend sleepless nights worrying that Paris might change, that one day they might pull down Notre Dame and build a supermarket. I must see Notre Dame at least once a year. I would die if I didn't.'

The ladies drifted away. More caviar was passed around. Dinner was announced. Two candle-lit tables had been set up in the dining room. A manservant filled our crystal goblets with a rosé wine. I was sitting next to Leila, a pretty, scented creature. She smiled at me. 'Do you come from Tahiti?' she asked.

'What makes you think that?'

'Ali and I were there a few weeks ago.'

The line of deduction was not easy to follow. 'What were you doing in Tahiti?'

'Ali *loves* islands. We've been to Jamaica, Barbados, Mauritius, the Seychelles, Fiji . . . Ali's really into islands.'

I looked at Ali (he was sitting at the other table), the man who loved islands. He was masticating slowly, majestically, his eyes half-closed, sunk in satiated repose.

'If you don't come from Tahiti, where do you come from?' Leila asked.

'I come from Trinidad.'

'Is that an island?'

'I'm afraid so.'

The news excited Leila. 'Ali! Ali! This man comes from a place called Trinidad. An island! Have you heard of it?'

Ali blinked. He studied me with inert, saurian voracity. Would he devour me on the spot?

'I must write it down,' Leila said. She called for a pen. The manservant offered his. Leila stared critically, disapprovingly, at the instrument – an expensive Parker ballpoint.

'Look.' She showed it to my host's wife.

My host's wife shrugged. 'What can one do?'

'I would keep my eyes on that fellow,' Xerxes said.

The pen was passed around the company. Obviously, the man was getting above himself. A peasant with a Parker. What next?

Liqueurs were served in the library. I had cognac mixed with Grand Marnier.

The story is told of the lady – the wife of a man who had speculated wisely in real estate – who wished to decorate her house in the style of the Louis XIV period. But then she was advised by a cruel friend that the style of Louis XXX was much more chic. So she went to Paris and began asking around in the shops for Louis XXX furniture. 'That,' the man who told the joke said, 'sums up the nouveau riche of our country. Ignorant and West-mad.' Teheran is rife with rags-to-riches stories – tales of street-corner hawkers who have become millionaires, of building contractors who have become multi-millionaires, of chauffeurs who have become property tycoons. The Shah himself is, of course, something of an arriviste. Despite his strong sense of imperial grandeur and his frequent invocations of Cyrus the Great, his dynasty – the creation of his rough soldier father – is barely fifty years old. His chief worshippers are to be found among the 'West-mad' elite. He is *their* Shah. They are *his* people.

The money is new. Very new. Nearly all of it has been conjured up within the last ten glorious years of OPEC. It is these new rich who give Teheran its tinselly glamour, whose buying power, whose taste, is reflected in the shops crammed with costly foreign goods; whose cars flood the broad avenues and make a journey at any time of the day a torment; whose imported cultural aspirations find fulfilment in the opera and ballet performances that are put on in the Rudaki Hall; whose lusts are catered for in opulent brothels where mere entry might cost fifty thousand ryals – almost four hundred pounds; who fill to capacity the Iran Air jumbos flying West: last year two hundred thousand Iranians visited London, spending, on average, nearly two thousand pounds per head; whose sons and daughters wear faded jeans, chew gum, play guitars and speak bad English in rank American accents; for whom the 'International' channel of National Iranian Radio and Television fills its broadcasting hours with *I Love Lucy* type programmes and whose presenters are brought over direct from the United States – 'Good evening. This is Teheran. Here is the noos . . . .' And everywhere there are the spivs, the young men in tight trousers who call you 'Meestah' and who, in the later afternoon, loiter outside the cinemas, gawking at the near-naked, lasciviously posed women festooning the posters advertising Western films.

The boom town atmosphere is oppressive. Fifteen years ago Teheran had a population of about three million. Today, it is approaching five million. This seems to cause neither alarm nor misgiving: Iranians are proud of their burgeoning megalopolis. They regard it as indispensable, a necessary attribute of modernity. One can almost literally see the city taking shape day by day. Everywhere cranes rise into the sky. Everywhere there are excavators spewing up clouds of dust. To combat the menace of the traffic a Metro is being constructed – by the French – at a cost of untold millions: whatever Iran wants, Iran gets. Dense clusters of apartment blocks are being built on the outskirts of the city to meet the housing shortage. But, despite the spate of building, the cost of accommodation remains exorbitant. A perfectly ordinary two-bedroomed flat can easily cost five hundred pounds a month. Often a man must have more than one job if he is to meet his commitments. Landlords are reaping a rich harvest. But, as in all boom towns, little attention is paid to engineering proprieties. For Teheran, this negligence spells future catastrophe. The city is in a high-risk earthquake zone. On the fateful day of its destruction, it will be a death-trap. The flimsy towers of concrete and steel will collapse like packs of cards.

However, no one gives much thought to earthquakes: the present will do. So, the population continues to grow, money continues to be made, money continues to be spent. Unemployment is virtually unknown. The factories that line the western reaches of the city have to compete with each other for labour. 'Here,' the PRO of a firm making domestic appliances said, 'the simplest worker can get 1000 ryals (£8) a day.' A technician would earn 100,000 ryals a month. He himself earned 140,000 ryals a month. As for the directors, their salaries were anybody's guess. In fact, salaries of a million ryals a year are not all that uncommon: Iran has one of the most skewed income distribution curves in the world. The PRO was a happy man. A Jew of Iranian birth, he had been lured back from Israel by the government. He told of the bonuses, the low taxes, the 49 per cent of the shares owned by the workers – this last one of the edicts of the Shah's 'white' revolution. 'Very nice policies,' he murmured. 'It is very nice for all of us.' Did the workers have a union? 'They have a very nice union. For your surprise we even have strikes! One of them lasted three days.' He grinned delightedly at me.

The factories are devoted to the assembly of consumer goods. They cannot satisfy the hunger for their products. The 150,000 washing machines (all parts imported from Italy) turned out every year by the Arj works comes nowhere near meeting existing domestic demand. At the Paykan car plant the story is much the same: they make four hundred Hillman-type cars a week, but the waiting lists grow longer. Iran's revolution is founded on affluence, on consumption. It requires no austerity and no sacrifice. The process of development has been turned on its head. Money buys everything; and the money is there in quantity. 'We're running,' the pessimistic economist conceded, 'before we've learnt how to walk. The balloon's bound to burst. What a bang that will be!'

Agriculture has suffered because the farmers cannot always compete with the wages offered in the factories and on the building sites. Some land has actually gone out of use. Many of the villages round and about Teheran are half-deserted. Neglected orchards line the roadsides. It is a rare sight to see anyone actually at work in the fields. One of the consequences is that Iran has to import more and more of its food. Subsidies are used to keep prices down – meat, for example, brought in from France, is generously subsidised; so is wheat. The chances are that if you order tea in a restaurant you will be provided with a cup of boiling water, an English teabag and an English packet of dried milk.

So acute is the scarcity of labour – and skill – that Iran now has one million foreign workers, mainly Turks, Indians and Pakistanis. Large numbers of Indian and Pakistani doctors staff the Medical Corps who work in the countryside. A dearth of doctors is not the only cause of this: the fact is that not many Iranians show any keenness for the idea. They prefer to stay in the towns – or emigrate to the United States. For the expatriate, Iran is paradise.

One afternoon I ran into a cheerful Indian working (illegally) in a smallish, family-run hotel. He had come to Iran 'touristing', but had found the pickings so good he had stayed on: indeed, the owner of the hotel (at which he had originally turned up as a bona fide client) had become so dependent on his electrical know-how that he would not hear of his leaving. 'I am making too much money,' he said happily, 'too much money. These people can do nothing. They want me to do all their work for them. If a light-bulb goes wrong, they cannot fix it. They call me. If the air-conditioning stops working, again it is me they call. They can do nothing at all for themselves.' He wagged his head in gleeful despair. 'I cannot respect these people. They have too much money but they seem to have no wish to learn. Too much money has made them stupid. They do not know what to do with themselves.'

He cited as a typical example of Iranian idleness and decadence the son of the hotel owner. 'That boy cannot sit still. He's always travelling somewhere, wasting his father's money. Europe, UK, America. Always going somewhere. He says he is studying. But what can he be studying? If you ask him something, he knows nothing. He is always only boasting of fucking the foreign girls. No, I cannot respect these people.' All the same, he was going to stay – the money was too good. Wasn't he afraid of the police catching up with him?' 'Maybe they will ask me to fix locks in their jail for them. They too might want me to do their work.' He laughed fearlessly.

Proud dependence, aggressive helplessness – these are the chief symptoms of the Iranian disease. 'Iranians really believe they are God's gift to mankind,' the expatriate complained. 'One of them said to me the other day, "We are not human beings. We are *Iranians*". So you laugh or cry?' One cries, I suppose. Take computers, very fashionable but also very troublesome. In one office I visited a sophisticated machine had been installed a couple of years previously. Every time it broke down an Israeli had to be flown in to do the repairs. The breakdowns became so frequent (its operators were bewildered by the thing) that, in the end, the Israeli had to be invited to take up permanent residence in Teheran. Often though, sophisticated machinery is simply abandoned. An American technician who had been in the country for some years was sunk in gloom. He had no faith in his Iranian assistant, a man equipped with all the paper qualifications. 'Put that guy in front of a machine and he goes dumb. But you should see the fancy digital watch he wears. Never stops playing with it. The guy isn't stupid – he's quite good mathematically. But to translate that mathematics into practice . . .' He sighed. 'I can't figure it out. If all the foreigners cleared out tomorrow, there'd be ruins everywhere. This place would be a twentieth-century Persepolis.'

There are Iranians who understand – such as the well-heeled but melancholy businessman I met at a dinner party. 'Industrial revolution? What industrial revolution? Listen. The other day I was looking at a catalogue from South Korea. I suddenly thought – why, we couldn't even make the goddamned catalogue. We couldn't even make the staples that hold the pages together. All this talk about industry is a fraud. What's going to happen to us when the oil runs out in twenty-five years? Are we going to live off pistachios and carpets? An oil-less Iran is going to be worse off than Bangladesh – at least, they still know how to grow food. We would have forgotten even how to do that.'

He raised his brandy-filled glass. 'Cheers!'

Intellectual life in Iran is dead, a death symbolised by the knots of soldiery, bayonetted rifles at the ready, who keep guard outside the gates of Teheran University; by the censored, sycophantic newspapers; by the paid ideologues of the regime who compare the Shah to Napoleon and call him the saviour of mankind. 'I don't like the word *intellectual*,' the lady with courtly connections observed, 'because that usually means anti-establishment.'

'It's bad,' the poet said. 'I sometimes think it can't possibly get any worse, that we can't sink any lower than we have already done.' He had given up trying to write. The atmosphere did not lend itself to creation. Who, in any case, would publish his work? Who, outside a tiny coterie of friends, would read it? Writers cannot survive without an audience and in Iran there was no audience left. 'I'm just standing still, doing nothing, trying to preserve my mental balance, to keep sane.'

Yet (he went on) Iran was no trumped-up country. It wasn't like Kuwait or, even, Saudi Arabia – oil-rich deserts peopled by nomads. Thousands of years of culture could not be abolished just like that. 'They're cramming this so-called Western culture down our throats, force-feeding us with all kinds of rubbish and bad dreams. But I know in my heart that our people won't accept it. Maybe this generation is lost. But in the end we'll reject the bad dreams they're ramming down our throats.'

But, if Iran rejected the West, what would it put in its place? Was it possible – or desirable – to go back to a fundamentalist Islam that lopped off the hands of thieves, locked women out of sight and attacked banks because they charged interest? Did he approve of those young men who called themselves Islamic Marxists, who, in one breath, called for radical social and economic reform and, in the next, threatened to throw acid in the faces of women who had taken the road to 'liberation'?

No, of course he did not believe in anything like that. Islamic Marxism was merely one of the symptoms of confusion, of mental disturbance. That kind of reactionary past was dead – or ought to be dead. The *mullahs* were as undesirable in one direction as the Shah and his 'clique' were in another. 'We're not Arabs, you know. We are Persians, descendants of Cyrus and Darius and Xerxes. The Arabs may have conquered us, but it was *we* who civilised them.'

I had been in Iran long enough not to be surprised at this sudden eruption of national fervour; it was often there, just below the surface, tempering the decadence and the West-made inanity.

'We are a people with thousands of years of civilisation behind us, do not forget that.' He spoke with rising warmth. Iranians were possessed of a profound national sense, a profound sense of their identity, of who they were. 'They' were doing their best to destroy it. But *it* would destroy them. 'Iran will reassert itself. It may take fifty years for this madness to work itself out. It may even take a century. But we will come back to ourselves. We will win out.' Iran had always absorbed its conquerors. It had absorbed Alexander's Greeks, it had absorbed the Arabs and the Mongols. Ultimately, it would absorb the West too, it would create something quite new, something uniquely Iranian. What that something would be, what shape it would take, he could not say. But if the Japanese could absorb the West and survive, so could the Iranians. It was to Japan he looked for comfort.

I felt he was whistling in the dark.

27 May, 1978

Jan Morris

NOTES FROM A DYING CITY

Istanbul

Hardly had I unpacked my bags in the clear old Pera Palace (still faintly fragrant, I was glad to note, of Ottoman cigars and ancient omelettes) – hardly had I unpacked and taken the funicular down to the Galata Bridge, than I got mixed up with a protest parade clambering noisily up the other side of the Golden Horn.

It was, in its way, a stately demonstration, for its movement was given a deceptive dignity by the steepness of the hill. With gasps and heavy breathing the dissidents bawled their slogans, male and female in antiphony, and with thickly heaving chests their powerful escort of soldiers, guns across their chests, helmets over their glazed eyes, laboured alongside. An armoured car brought up the rear, turret light flashing blue and white, but even it seemed to be having trouble with its gears.

What were they protesting about, as they disappeared over the ridge towards that shrine of all protesters, Constantine's blood-soaked Hippodrome? What did those wheezy slogans signify? Were they, as Istanbul parlance has it, Leftists or Idealists? I never discovered. They were simply angry people, disturbed people – inescapable familiars nowadays, I was presently to realise, of this always difficult and sometimes alarming city. Wherever I went I found them. Whatever I said, they answered back.

Istanbul is difficult, of course, by its very nature. Ataturk's attempts to wish logic and modernity upon it have failed, and it is as obscurantist, as devious and as stubborn today as ever it was in the days of the Sultans. It is clogged by the accumulated filth of the centuries, layered generation by generation upon the original defecations of Byzantium. It is entramelled equally by age and change, unravellable labyrinths of bazaars, desolate abortions of progressive planning. The Golden Horn stirs but sluggishly, viscous with oil and ordure: ever and ever and again the city staggers into immobility, jammed by some unseen and never-to-be-explained calamity round the corner.

There are several cities in the world where the forecasts of the demographic Cassandras do seem visibly to be coming true. One is Calcutta of course, another is Cairo, and a third is Istanbul. After two and a half millennia of civic existence, it is distinctly past its best. They can never clear that rubbish now. They can never, it often seems to me, get the traffic moving again. And how can all those ferry-boats survive, inextricably thrashing beside the mooring stages, desperately wailing their sirens, or apparently totally out of control in mid-stream?

I was in Istanbul only to pursue the footsteps of the Venetians, commanded by that blind old rascal Doge Enrico Dandalo, who led the criminal assault on Constantinople in 1204, and were the most perspicacious of its looters. My task was altogether agreeable, and entailed a good deal of hanging around waterfronts and coffee-shops, looking at Stamboul through half-closed eyes and imagining historic escapades. But preoccupied though I was by the past, I was mercilessly nagged by the present.

Nobody would let me be. The retired sea-captain who accompanied me from the Pantokrator to the Chora compared the city ominously with his memories of Shanghai, and frequently drew my attention to piles of garbage which were, he said, breeding-grounds of choleric rats. The bank manager who was my kind cicerone at S. S. Sergius and Bacchus believed Istanbul to be on the brink of Leftist-inspired, or it may have been Idealist-motivated, anarchy. The foreign financier talked darkly of pulling out. The colonel at the Hilton party only wanted to discuss Cyprus.

It is hard to be a hedonist by the Golden Horn these days, to sit and meditate as Pierre Loti used to, romantically on his belvedere above the minarets. Istanbul is obsessed with its own anxieties, its inflation rate, its political hazards, or the ever-present and imminent probability of being knocked down by a No 11 trolley-bus.

Even inside Santa Sophia I was harshly reminded of the municipal antagonisms. There I chanced to meet an eminent Byzantine specialist from Oxford, loitering in a scholarly way in the Narthex (itself longer, he told me incidentally, than the nave of Tewkesbury Abbey). I mentioned to him the now empty tomb of the desecrator Dandalo, up in the gallery, and remarked that nobody seemed to visit it these days.

'I do', said the sage fiercely. 'I go to spit on it.'

*

'Why did Constantinople get the works?
That's nobody's business but the Turks.'

So went a popular song I used to like, and for myself, despite those varied warnings and intrusions, I was perfectly happy to let the Turks, who have always been kind to me, mind their own business.

Every day I ate on one or other of the restaurant-boats on the Stamboul side of the Galata Bridge, where I could watch the cavalcade of the streets go by. Down there one sees more bucolic figures than in most parts of town, clumpier, goatier, and one gets a powerful sense of the organic, not to say elemental nature of the place.

I love it there, but I have to admit that something fairly awful happened before my eyes almost every day. Once a man collapsed apparently dead upon the bridge. Once a dazed deserter was pounced upon by two of the implacable military policemen who haunt the quaysides there. Once an elderly man carrying a tyre over his shoulder was abruptly frog-marched away, limply protesting, by a couple of thugs whom I took to be detectives.

But the fish was delicious, and anyway there was always the dear old Pera Palace to return to at the end of the day. There, after soaking the Byzantine effluvium off me, I could relax to the music of the palm court trio.

One night though, I think it must have been a Saturday, something upsetting happened even there. The fiddler had just played the last haunting notes of a waltz, was just making his bow to the *hausfraus*, when suddenly the place of the trio on their platform among the potted plants was usurped by two wild young men, dressed Anatolially I would assume, playing a crackled and frenzied rhythm upon a reedy trumpet and a drum.

A moment later there burst into the room a phalanx of six swathed and turbanned girls, apparently welded together, and exuding a savage fury. They shrieked, they stamped, they waved handkerchiefs about, they whirled and leapt and pranced and shrieked again, while all the time the trumpet blared behind them, and the drum thundered on.

They left the room as suddenly as they had arrived, and in the shattered peace that ensued we were left to contemplate the nature of the Turks. 'My God', I said to the Americans at the next table, when I got my breath back, 'I'm glad they're on our side!'

'Ah but *are* they?' the man replied. 'Why, I was talking to some of our people in Ankara yesterday . . .'

28 October, 1978

Jeffrey Bernard

CHECKING

I've had two weeks on the road stopping overnight twice at Copenhagen, looking in at Stockholm airport once, but staying in Moscow, Leningrad, Beirut and Cairo. As far as low life is concerned Beirut is definitely the place I'd prefer to live in of all of them if I had to, and in many ways it's my favourite city of all. I stayed there ten years ago for a couple of weeks, thanks to Lord Thompson, and in those days, before you got shot at, it was a real delight. Apart from the fact that I got raped in a telephone kiosk in a nightclub by a quite charming girl there are other things which might seem unimportant to you but that stick in my mind about the Lebanon. The fertility of the land there is quite amazing. Tomatoes are the size of grapefruits, lettuces the size of cabbages, and the whole place runneth over with fresh orange juice.

On this visit I was driven about 50 miles along the Damascus road, up into the mountains near the Syrian border, for lunch. It was my birthday and my Lebanese host, a racehorse trainer of all things, really laid it on for me. For starters there were no less than 22 plates of different hors d'oeuvres on the table and that lot was washed down with two bottles of arak. Then followed another eight courses accompanied by champagne – French, not rubbish – and we finished with strawberries the size of your fist.

After lunch we drove to my host's racing stables. The driving isn't a lot of fun these days since you have to pass through innumerable checkpoints manned by various factions armed with machine guns and even Sami, my host, carried no less a weapon than a magnum special in his trouser belt. We did the rounds of evening stables and then there was a happening I'd like to see adopted by racehorse trainers in this country. Sami snapped his fingers and two stable lads brought a table and several chairs and set them down in the middle of the tatty but charming Arabian-style yard. We sat down and were given Turkish coffee, mineral water and ice-cold lager. Then Sami gave one of the lads some money. He ran off, came back three minutes later and presented us with cakes of hash. We ate that and then the lad rolled us all our own joints. A far cry from proceedings at Newmarket or my own Lambourn but the only sad thing was that it must have been very poor quality stuff since the only buzz I got was from the few lagers I drank.

After all that, I went back to my hotel and sat by the edge of the swimming-pool with a lizard who glanced at me every time we heard a rifle-shot or machine-gun in the distance. It's an extraordinary city and a mad situation. American newspapermen drifted in and out of the bar and the pool, all of them talking about the 'situation' and muttering a lot of 'oh my ghad's and then Sami came back with his brother – also armed to the teeth – to take us on a motor tour of the front of the city by the sea. I've always cherished those two weeks I'd spent in the Saint George Hotel and now there it was, a burnt out shell. The Holiday Inn, the Old English Club, in fact the entire seafront is smashed, shelled and burnt out and it's very, very sad.

But it hasn't stopped what's the Lebanese cottage industry, which is making money. As far as I could see, apart from street traders, hoteliers and shop keepers, no one seems to be actually a professional anything; they are just money makers. They're extremely friendly though when they're not trying to blow you up. The second morning I was there I took my insomnia out for a stroll at about 5.30 am and I passed a bakery where three lads were hard at work. I stopped to look at them shoving pancake-like bread into the gas oven and they beckoned me in and sat me down by a fridge full of canned lager which we dipped into for the next hour. We conversed in mime and it wasn't the first time I've been abroad and thanked Joan Littlewood in my mind for having once employed me in her theatre.

Later that morning, Sami drove me to the airport to get the Cairo flight and I felt quite miserable at having to leave. Then the mortars started to go off and some rockets too. It was the day 25 people got killed, 28 May, and it was one of the worst days for the past few years. The airport was immediately closed and we went back to the hotel. Sami now started checking his vicious-looking automatic every few minutes and, as I sat once again at the edge of the swimming pool, I kept checking my vodkas and orange juices every few minutes, just in case one of them might signal final orders from the big barman in the sky.

7 June, 1980

Daniel Farson

TWO GUIDES TO TURKEY

'I am number one man in Istanbul,' Yusuf informed me when we left the tourist office after he had been chosen as my guide. 'Twenty per cent of Istanbul knows me. I do not know them. Funny! My mother was a countess, my father was a count, I am son-of-a-gun.'

'You certainly are,' I agreed.

Wiry and swarthy, with the penetrating eyes of an experienced interrogator, Yusuf exuded intrigue like a character from a bad film about the Casbah or the Grand Bazaar in Cairo, and I became a sweaty Sidney Greenstreet following in the wake of his Peter Lorre. He claimed he had lost his voice on the new Orient Express, which was hard to believe for he never stopped talking. To Yusuf, interruption was the spice of conversation. This was the first time that a guide had been laid on especially for myself and I began to realise how delicate this relationship can be. If the guide is too strident, overwhelming the ignorant traveller with his superior knowledge, moving at a breathless pace with no time on the schedule to sit down and drink, it could ruin a visit. Fortunately, Yusuf and I developed a sardonic understanding and though this was built on mutual suspicion it avoided the risk of an all-out row. Also, it must be admitted that Yusuf knew Istanbul backwards, at home in the hustle of this tough, vibrant city, a fusion of east and west, with the marvellous, hovering skyline of mosques and minarets, and dark, desperate alleys. It seemed a pity that my briefing was so respectable: old wooden houses and tourist attractions. Yusuf descended with such authority that I wondered if he belonged to a secret international police, and at one exasperated moment I asked him, 'How many men have you killed?'

'I prefer to make crime,' he replied mysteriously. To show he was joking, he added: 'My wish is for the advancement of humankind and world culture.' He came out with many phrases like that.

Nothing was beyond his intelligence, no human experience had been denied him. But even Yusuf was only permitted to hint at the proof in his possession of visitors from space. His reticence implied that he had been involved personally in this close encounter; had they landed, listened to

Yusuf, and gone away again? Disconcertingly, his wildest claims proved true. Allegedly fluent in sixteen languages, he really had written a guidebook to Istanbul in Japanese.

'You did not realise?' he rebuked me when I expressed surprise. 'I *am* part-Japanese.'

When a Turkish girl who works in the architectural department of the government brought me a magnificent poster of the wooden houses she is trying to preserve, Yusuf nodded his approval: 'Yes, I took that photograph myself.'

'*You* did!' the girl and I exclaimed simultaneously, and sounded so incredulous that Yusuf modified his claim: 'I held the camera for the photographer.' But I discovered that he had taken several of the colour shots for the glossy brochure of the venerable Pera Palas Hotel where I was given further proof of Yusuf's versatility as he sketched me on a pink piece of paper in the ornate Middle Hall.

'I did not realise you were an artist, too.'

'My pictures are everywhere in Spain.'

'The Prado?'

'No,' he corrected me indignantly. 'All in private houses.'

He signed the portrait with a flourish, *El Turco*, presumably the equivalent of *El Greco*, and I have kept it in case any twinge of vanity should ever rise in me again: the rosebud lips of Oscar Wilde, the mirthless eyes of Edward Heath, and a look of horror all my own.

'Lifelike,' I remarked wanly, with the awful suspicion that it was.

'But of course', he smiled, accepting the compliment. 'No problem.' As a guide, Yusuf could not be faulted. He protected me from beggars with volleys of abuse, shook his fist alarmingly at small boys who wanted to ask about my camera, bullied the courteous staff of a fashionable restaurant into serving me a banquet on the Bosphorus. He never let me down, until my last evening, when he disappeared. As I waited for him, sipping a beer in that splendid hall in the Pera Palas, I thought I had caught him out at last. In my anxiety when the time of my flight drew closer, I was hardly aware of the discordant music coming from a distant room until it grew so strange that I stopped to listen – someone was playing the piano very badly indeed. *El Beethoven*? It had to be, and was.

'You did not know I am musician?' Yusuf looked up proudly as I hurried in.

'No, but I recognised your touch.'

There was plenty of time to wait at the airport, there always is, and I felt that Yusuf was bracing himself to ask a question. Should one tip guides I wondered, and discovered later that indeed one should, but this request had nothing to do with money. Yusuf is in love with an English girl who worked in our embassy at Ankara – 'now she has returned home and there are no letters.' If 'Lorraine' should read this he hopes to hear from you again. Presumably she will recognise the description, there can be only one Yusuf.

It was disappointing to realise that behind the bluster he was vulnerable just like the rest of us, and it ill became him. My flight was called and I was relieved by the return of arrogance as he shook me clammily by the hand with the firm instruction to ask for him should I return to Istanbul: 'I will be happy to have the happiness to be your guide-friend, and be sure I'll be the best in Turkey.'

My second guide to Turkey proved the perfect antidote. Ibrahim was a gentle man. He met me at Antalya airport advancing with the waddle of a jovial penguin, due to a crooked foot after a fall from his horse at the age of seven. Ibrahim's association with animals has a terrible irony as I discovered over dinner that first night on the prow-like balcony of the Talya Hotel.

A few months earlier he had been told of an abandoned dog whose neck was twisted horribly by a coil of wire. Probably this had been used to tie it up as a puppy, but now the wire was strangling the animal slowly as it grew larger. Ibrahim hired a car, fetched the local vet, and set out for the village where everyone denied knowledge of the dog until a boy whispered that he might find it in a ruined house on the outskirts.

Sure enough he glimpsed a flash of frightened eyes in a corner before the dog made a dash for it, but Ibrahim managed to seize it by the ears. The vet moved in quickly and gave it an injection; they cut the wire, cleaned it up, and when the dog recovered it was free. Before they left the village Ibrahim gave some money to a family to feed the dog, but the vet refused his fee saying, 'If you're mad enough to do all this for some strange dog, I haven't got the heart to charge you.'

Ibrahim was rewarded. On that same day of my arrival a man from the village had called at his office to tell him some good news: 'The dog has had five puppies and all are well.'

A nice enough story but Ibrahim's courage in seizing a wild dog by the ears was beyond a natural reaction from someone who is fond of animals – Ibrahim is *allergic* to dogs.

It started with that fall from his horse which left him with an upturned foot which convinces every dog that he is about to be kicked and had better act first. A bulldog on the boat to Istanbul where young Ibrahim was sent to hospital was restrained with difficulty from attacking him and this has been a penalty of Ibrahim's life ever since. Even so, when he saw a stray mongrel sleeping in front of the wheels of a jeep near his office in Antalya, he did not hesitate to lift it out of harm's way. In the panic of being woken, the dog scratched his hand accidentally but deeply enough for Ibrahim to go to the doctor who told him that unless he traced the dog within four days and found it free from disease, he would have to be given injections.

For the next four days Ibrahim and his friends searched every corner of Antalya but the strange dog had disappeared. So Ibrahim started a course of injections. After the fourteenth his body became paralysed while another man died from the same drug. Ibrahim recovered but he had to spend the next five months at home convalescing. At last he was able to return to work and as he approached his office saw the same stray mongrel trotting along the edge of the pavement – perfectly healthy. His year of pain had been pointless. Today he remains as fond of dogs as ever, but he cannot even bring himself to stroke them. This is why he was so courageous in seizing the wild dog by the ears.

Though Ibrahim could be sentimental, he revealed unexpected passions. When we stopped at the lagoon of Olu-Deniz, I noticed an older man with an attractive woman and wondered about their relationship.

'Eighty-five!' cried Ibrahim in my ear.

'What?' The man did not look that old.

'You stare at her breasts?'

'Well . . . as a matter of fact . . .'

He interrupted me proudly. 'I can always tell measurement of ladies breasts – I am expert.' For a moment it could have been Yusuf.

Ibrahim's knowledge was remarkable, for his education came to an end with the fall from his horse. When he was nineteen he worked for an American firm laying diesel pipes across the country, and this was how he learned English and became a guide though the lack of a formal education has kept him in a low grade with a monthly salary of £60, even now on the verge of retirement. Yet Ibrahim is the doyen of guides, a master of his art, advising ten Presidents and the Aga Khan family for the last 20 years. Taking his work as seriously as an ambassador, he regards a rapport with his clients as vital: 'People are like envelopes – until you open them up you don't understand them.' He refuses to be rushed but proceeds at his own leisurely pace: 'I don't like to be robotic guide.' When a party asked him to 'do' the ruined city of Termossos in an hour, squeezed into their schedule, he declined: 'I have some feeling. I do not accept their programme.' But when he led me there, climbing to the necropolis where ten thousand tombs tumble down the mountainside much as the earthquakes left them nearly 2,000 years ago, he showed the agility of a goat in spite of his crooked foot, resting every hundred yards or so to give me the historical background to this extraordinary place where the people defied Alexander in 333 BC.

It was Ibrahim who was sent for when Prince Rainier and Princess Grace came to Antalya for Jacques Cousteau's conference on pollution in the Mediterranean. First grade guides and top officials flew in from Ankara especially, but when they were unable to answer the questions from Princess Grace the whisper went out to fetch the lowly Ibrahim who had been banished from this special occasion.

'But I am nothing,' he protested, savouring every second of his power, 'I am only eighth-grade guide.'

'That doesn't matter,' they told him impatiently. 'We need you. Today you can be first-grade guide.'

When Princess Grace heard his replies and sensed his intelligence, she insisted on Ibrahim as her personal guide for the rest of the visit, refusing to start her cocktail party on the last evening without him. Ibrahim had not been invited due to protocol, so they hurried to his house again.

'Princess Grace wants *me*?' he asked with humility. 'Are you sure you have the right man?' But Princess Grace waved to him when he arrived, so he waddled through 500 glittering guests to sit beside her at the top table. With her particular interest in the mythology of this part of Turkey, they talked for an hour until Ibrahim sensed the glares of the protocol officials and made his excuses: 'Princess, you are very important person and I do not like to prevent others from seeing you. It is time I go back to my home.'

The next day Prince Rainier presented Ibrahim with a medal, a family album of photographs, and a final compliment: 'If you ever come to Monaco, *we* shall be your guide.'

Ibrahim in Monte Carlo is not an image that springs trippingly to the mind. If he should present himself at the castle gates, mopping his brow and wiping his spectacles, I should not be surprised if the guards turn him away, but I think that Princess Grace would have spied him from her window in the best tradition of fairy tales as he limped down the road, and called him back as she remembered his wisdom and courtesy.

This is how I felt about him when we ended our journey at Marmaris, and when we parted on the quayside I embraced him suddenly in the Turkish style for I knew I was saying goodbye to a friend, as well as a valued guide.

23 October, 1982

· Gerda Cohen

SEEING A NEW LIGHT

Jerusalem on Friday night had the rigour of an English Sunday, locked into the family, the dry velvet night smelling of dust and resin, indigo at the zenith, reddish towards the unseen sea, an infinite severity of dark towards the Judean desert. 'We can't take the car out,' said my host, 'or we'll get stoned.' 'But why take the car out?' demanded his wife. 'I'm dishing out the soup.'

They live in a tall block in north Jerusalem, a citadel. From the slit windows arose a scent of chicken soup. 'Everyone has chicken soup on Friday night,' said my host bitterly, 'even the pagans.' He did a chat show on Israel television and tried hard to find pagans to appear on it. 'The trouble is, pagans don't exist here. Everyone must be in a category: Arab Christian, vegetarian Jew – ' 'What?' demanded his wife, 'vegetarian Jew – why not Buddhist Arab?' They love argument. After a bout, suddenly tired, they went onto the balcony. A dry desert wind fanned the night. It had a desolate beauty, trembling with neon from the citadel blocks of Jerusalem. 'Do you think,' began my host, 'we could find a flat in Wembley?' 'Wembley has blacks,' objected his wife. 'Camden Town we can't afford,' he told her sternly. 'So . . . Wembley.' He turned his large lustrous eyes towards me, pleading, 'Can we find a three-room there?' The cicadas shrilled and shrilled.

His wife cried from the kitchen, 'If not Camden Town, we move to the Bethlehem road. I can't stand these Jews any more. Black beetles!' She meant the orthodox, explained my host, and the new orthodox. 'They're destroying the country – no joke.' Downstairs, he imparted gravely, the Joyful Light Movement had converted some of their nicest neighbours to Judaism. But weren't they Jews already? 'Not *that* kind,' he said, gloomily watching the news. Outside came the muezzin call to prayer, very high and loud in the dark. 'Exotic, eh? I had a muezzin on my chat show.' After dessert we sat arguing whether they could afford a flat on the Bethlehem road. South Jerusalem cost – God knows what! But fewer zealots, definitely fewer zealots.

Behind the tattered palm trees on the Bethlehem road stood leftover

Arab villas built of Judean stone, rosy burnt umber, inhabited now by oriental immigrant families, taxi-drivers, poets. Some media people had moved in. 'How lucky you are,' they told me, 'staying on the Bethlehem road.' In the dark red villa opposite a large Iranian family had taken up residence. Their menfolk swayed in the courtyard, chanting under their wavy striped prayer shawls. A fat red pillar box looked comfortable on the pavement. Going to post a card, one found the slit gagged; a piece of red steel nailed across. It must have been there since the British Mandate. On Saturday morning at eight, a bucketing roar awoke the street, like Liverpool scoring a goal. 'I am ancient Persian,' said the neat man opposite, 'driven from my country.' He folded his prayer shawl into a blue velvet bag and wished me a happy Sabbath. 'I have fine selection of carpets near the King David Hotel' – he gave me a card – 'discount for you ten per cent.' His dark oval face disappeared into a taxi. The dazzling winter sky stretched overhead, taut as satin. Magenta morning glories turned their calyxes to the east, twined around the courtyard where the Persians prayed. In the winter light, every detail shone with arid brilliance.

The Arab bus to Bethlehem shook with eyes, painted eyes hung over the windscreen to bring good luck. A dry desert wind pummelled the bus, which could hardly make the ascent to Manger Square. Milling and noisy, it smelt of fried chick-peas. Tripper coaches jammed the square; yet all around, silent, the naked desolate beauty of the Judean hills. Into the dark nave of the Nativity church went the endless reverent tread. Minnesota Baptists, Utah interfaith, Tokyo united holyland tours, everyone on tiptoe, expectant. The noise was awful. 'It hadn't *occurred* to us,' a couple from Guildford sat behind a column, 'quite how – well, it hadn't occurred to us quite how *universal* it is,' they smiled bravely, 'the Christian Communion.' They got up bravely. 'Must see the cave, dear.' 'You mean the grotto.'

They were being taken round by a tall, handsome youth. 'Ibrahim is Moslem, but he knows everything,' the Guildford couple smiled up at him, 'ecumenical approach, you know it's *natural* to Islam.' They gathered themselves up. 'You game?' We went down a rock stair to the grotto where Jesus was born, the dry smoky cave filled to choking with candle grease, Utah interfaith, Minnesota Baptists, reverent Japanese. 'It never occurred to us,' the Guildford couple tried to smile, 'quite how *universal* . . . the Christian communion . . .' The handsome youth propelled them out, 'I find you a better cave, a nice cave, where Saint Jerome did first translation of the Bible into English.' They are amazed. 'English?' 'English, Greek – what does it matter?' His beautiful eyes blazed. 'The same word of God!' Outside, an exquisite pure light shone from the desert.

Away from Manger Square, the hubbub stilled. Abu George the Tailor invited us in to admire the view from his balcony. Not the landscape exactly, but the posh new villas, coloured emerald and tangerine, with television aerials in the shape of an Eiffel tower. 'You see,' Abu George went on ironing a trouser leg, 'most belong to Moslems.' Abu George, sad though genial, said business was fine. 'We are doing fine; also, we are occupied. Occupied Palestine.' Abu George's son will go to college abroad. 'Most Christians go away,' he ironed with a smooth definitive stroke, 'Moslems have moved in.' Abu George hung up his trousers. 'Now they are the majority. Before, Bethlehem was Christian.' He trod up and down the rail of dark suits, examining them with silent appreciation. 'Funeral wear is our speciality. We have too many customers. Jews come from Tel Aviv, even from Haifa. Jews know the best tailor.' Over his door hung a calendar of Saint George plunging a dart into a very small vermilion dragon. 'Your saint of England.' Abu George invested the words with particular intensity. 'My cousin lives in England, in Wembley. You know Wembley?' He did not wait for an answer. 'My cousin is doing fine in Wembley,' Abu George said in a tone of dismissal; 'here in Bethlehem, what future? What future?'

On the edge of town lay pyramids of gravel and rosy quarried stone for building. Contractors have made a fortune out of building. Along the entire north-south axis of Judea and Samaria, a kind of citadel suburbia has sprung up. On the high places of Judah, supermarkets; and on the mountains of Ephraim, commuter developments. North, south and east of Jerusalem, even to the verge of the wilderness, the bare heights dazzle with citadel suburbia. It's well built. In contrast, the Arab towns look archaic. They too have solar heaters and indoor lavatories, but they seem irrelevant. On the heights beyond Bethlehem, a garden city is going up. The first select maisonettes dominate the Hebron highway like a palatial fort. Every home at Ephrat will have its own garden. 'Our own garden,' Dave and Marilyn told me, exultant, 'that's why we're moving to Ephrat.' Their future home was unbuilt, but it was worth waiting. 'That's right,' Dave and Marilyn agreed, 'that's right!'

A handsome young couple, they scrambled over the crags to point out the exact site. 'Somewhere for the kids to play, clean air.' 'Fantastic air.' Dave and Marilyn breathed it in. 'Not so good as Hove,' Marilyn giggled. 'Nicer view,' Dave said. Beyond the new maisonettes dropped a desolation of stone, a few Arab women with goats, and an earth-mover, ramming the next terrace hard. Hebron Arabs do all the building. Ephrat will have 30,000 people, 'a nice size, about the same as Hove'. Marilyn and Dave sounded a bit nostalgic, having grown up there. 'We never thought seriously about Judaism. Just medium *frum*, you know, till we Saw the Light.' They held hands, such a good-looking couple, he a computer analyst, she a dental technician. 'Marilyn will work till we have our fourth.' Her fair curly hair was pinned under a kerchief and she wore opaque knee hose. 'You know, we didn't think of kids *positively*, till we Saw the Light.' Ephrat would be ideal for children. 'That's right,' Dave bounded over the rocks, 'our own garden, no cars on the Sabbath; we could have a daily to do the cleaning.' Most people at Ephrat have an Arab daily. 'I don't know,' Marilyn said, her jubilation dulled, 'I don't know about that.'

22 December, 1984

Hilary Mantel

LAST MONTHS IN AL HAMRA

There are children, frail and moribund, who live inside plastic bubbles; their immune systems have not developed, and so they have to be protected from the outside world, their air specially filtered, and their nourishment – you cannot call it food – passed to them through special ducts, by gloved and sterile hands.

Professional expatriates live like that. Real travellers are vulnerable creatures, at once attracted and repelled by the cultures they move amongst, but expatriates are hard to reach, hard to impress, they carry about with them the plastic bubble of their own culture, and nothing touches them until it has been filtered through the protective membrane of prejudice, the life-support system that forms their invisible excess baggage when they move on, from one contract to the next, to another country and another set of complaints.

Still, expats do travel sometimes. Their journeys can be very small; a chance word, a look. It needs only a pinprick of event, a chance germ, and the outside world has breached the defences. You know what you have avoided knowing; it is not the country that is foreign, it is not the climate or the people, it is you.

When I went to Saudi Arabia, three years ago, I was driven from King Abdul Aziz International Airport to an apartment block off Jeddah's Medina Road; it was night, and I could not make sense of the city, and the next day produced no enlightenment. When you arrive in Saudi Arabia you cease to travel, in the ordinary sense. To move between cities you need letters from a higher authority, a sort of internal passport, and these are not granted without good reason; women, also, need written permission from their husbands if they want to make a journey. Within the city the situation is not much easier. Women may not drive, and they don't walk in the streets either, if they know what's good for them. Nor do men, except under pressure of extreme poverty; these streets are not made for walking. They are made for the car, and the cars eat up the people. Someone told me that every year more people are killed on the roads of the Kingdom than are born there; it seems a dubious statistic, but it may have poetic truth.

The city is cut up into its ghettos; palaces for the rich Hejazi merchant families, and for the princelings of the House of Saud; compounds behind walls for the *khawajahs*, the light-haired ones, the managers and experts; pre-fab work camps for the Asiatics, the labour force, the people the Saudi newspapers call Third Country Nationals. It is not easy to move between these ghettos. Still, there are the small, telling, journeys that no regime can prohibit; I went upstairs to meet my neighbour.

Our first flat was uptown, spacious, none too salubrious. It was what people called 'very Saudi'; there was frosted glass in all the windows, to preserve the privacy of the inhabitants and the modesty of their women. Downstairs was a noisy Sudanese family, whose visitors rang our gatebell at all hours. Their dinner, a goat, was often tethered below my window, and I could see it if I went out onto the balcony; different dinners, some perhaps more succulent than others, but with the same way of twisting about at the end of the ropes, like people already hanged. Sometimes I thought of sneaking downstairs and cutting the dinner free, but where would it run? Only to death on the adjacent six-lane highway.

The cities of Arabia are all alike today; skyscrapers, fast roads, municipal greenery nourished at vast expense; a seafront called the Corniche, Al Kournaich, the Cornish Road. The joyless, oily sea is lined by vast amusement parks, where grave sheikhs and their male offspring test their nerve on the rollercoasters; the women, in chaperoned parties, shop for furs and diamonds in vast glittering malls, in the Schönbrunns and Winter Palaces of the consumer's art. There is a pervading smell of sewage, a burning, used-up wind. Petrol is paid for out of small change. At the sliproad by the Marriot Hotel, negro children dash into the traffic and trail rags across your windscreen, tapping on the glass and holding out their hands for money. Sometimes you might see an old man sitting on the sidewalk, his thobe dirty, his knees pulled up to his ears, staring out at the stream of traffic. The pace of life is murderous. Each intersection has its little massacre.

The frosted glass seemed to be cutting me off from real life; one day drifted into the next. If I went out onto the balcony men congregated in the street to stare at me and make easy-to-understand gestures, multi-cultural invitations, monoglot expressions of contempt. We moved down-town then, to another flat in Al Hamra; this is the city's best district, where the embassies congregate. It was a newish block of four flats; some Sri Lankan Christians, a well-connected Pakistani couple, and a Saudi accountant, his wife, his baby. The last occupant of our flat had been moved out forcibly; a lonely and garrulous American bachelor, an innocent sort of man, not young, he had got himself into trouble because he had spoken to the Saudi lady; he had met her on the stairs, she in her veil, going out to a waiting car, and he hanging around, hoping for company; he had harassed her by passing the time of day. His company had moved him into a hotel now, waiting to see if he would be deported; it seemed likely.

So we had to go very carefully, approach our neighbours with caution. We had our expatriate bubble-world to live in. We would eat hamburgers with friends, sit around talking, and watch illicit videos. We would buy *The Times* at £1.50 the copy, and read the bits that the censors had left for us. At weekends you could drive along the coast looking for beaches; the Saudis have most of their sand in less than useful places, but they have come to like the seaside life, and have imported some from Bahrain. What else is there to do? There is a choral society. Home brewing occupies many hours. The Brits play cricket against the Pakistanis, though matches may be regarded as unlawful assemblies, and broken up by the police. Ladies hold coffee mornings, where they sell craftwork to each other; and dinner parties, too, are a competitive sport.

All this time I was conscious that there was another sort of life going on, just above my head. I hardly ever saw my neighbour. We shared a communal hallway with a marble floor; it was no one's particular territory, no one hung around there. Sometimes – suitably garbed, long-sleeved, perhaps ankles showing – I would be taking out the trash, or sweeping out the grey dust that banked up incessantly on the hall floor; my neighbour's husband would come striding down the stairs. A hesitant half-smile would be met with an opaque look, nothing that could be construed as acknowledgement from one human being to another. He might have been looking straight through me, to the paintwork and the brick wall.

The woman herself was just a shape, glimpsed sometimes in the early evenings, bundled into her concealing black *abaya* and the Saudi version of the veil – which covers the face completely, even the eyes. Clutching her small baby, she swayed from the front door to the car, and into the back seat. Family cars in the Kingdom are furnished not only with fringed mats, and boxes of Kleenex, and dangle-dollies, but with curtains; so that once she is safely in the back seat, the woman can lift her veil. She cannot be seen, she cannot see; but what does she want with the view?

The girl upstairs was 19, my Pakistani neighbour told me. And she wanted to meet me. My Pakistani neighbour was a good Muslim, who concealed her limbs, and always covered her head, but she had a wardrobe of Western clothes for trips abroad, and she had, she said, lived for 18 months in Hampstead. She explained to me that our neighbours were a more than averagely traditional family, more than averagely religious, and she hinted, but she did not say, that the accountant might frown on his wife making the acquaintance of a Westerner. It might be true. None of the women I knew had any Saudi friends.

The newspapers, especially the Friday religious columns, would spell the situation out. They would quote the Holy Koran, and especially the favourite Surah, 'Al-Nisa', verse 34: 'Men are in charge of women, for Allah hath made one of them to excel the other . . . '. Such notions are not to be corrupted. 'Why can't they accept the fact,' the letter-writers grumble, 'that the male has been created superior to the female? God meant it to be this way.' There was a day when my Pakistani neighbours called unexpectedly, and found my husband ironing a shirt. The meeting was set back a little, I felt. Meanwhile she went between us, like a good marriage-broker, whetting our appetites, and talking about one to the other.

Then one day when I was hanging out some washing in the high-walled enclosure by my back door, I heard voices above my head. Jamila, my Saudi neighbour, had opened a balcony door; hidden, she was gossiping with a woman in the next block. Wrapped in their curtains, they called to each other. Her voice surprised me, up there in the air; harsh, guttural, uninhibited. For a moment she stepped out onto the balcony, holding a wisp of cloth over her nose and mouth; her neighbour, then, must have drawn her attention to my presence and she glanced down. Both of them laughed. I did a servant's jobs about the place; this, I thought, was what caused the merriment.

In the end I went upstairs because Jamila wanted help in reading poetry. She was taking an English literature course at the Women's University, attending evening lectures, and she couldn't understand her set books. I was afraid that I wouldn't understand them either, but I sent a message that perhaps I could help. So on that first visit she ordered Pepsi-Cola for us; the accountant had just gone out to work. A huge black and white photograph of him, ten times life size and framed in gilt, dominated the living-room; the individual features were a blur of dots, the definition gone. On the empty bookshelves was a model clipper ship, which lit up and cast a soft reddish glow into the room. Daylight came uncertainly, greenish-grey, filtered through the broad dusty leaves of the tree outside the window. I had been watching this tree; it never budded, never lost a leaf. It might have been made of plastic. Jamila's living-room, higher than mine, looked out over the same vacant lot; commanded a wider view of desolation, where mosquitos bred in standing pools.

Jamila set out her textbooks. She was a vigorous square-jawed woman, who looked strong; her long hair had a rippling wave, and a coarse black sheen. Her face, unveiled, was very white, unnaturally so, slightly pitted from recently cleared acne; I thought of women in Europe, not long ago, whitening and poisoning their skins with lead. Later she told me that one's marital fortunes could depend on the colour of the skin, although the man must take it on trust, because it is still not the custom in good families for the veil to be lifted before the ceremony. She had been lucky; her small daughter, however, had an unforgivably flat nose, and hair like wire. It doesn't, she told the accountant, come from my side of the family.

At the Women's University they do have male lecturers, but only on closed-circuit televisions. *Absalom and Achitophel* was what she had to read. 'I don't know anything about Dryden,' I said. I read the notes at the back of the book. It said the poem was all about political manoeuvres in the reign of James II. I thought we might get on with it, on that basis. Jamila was charmingly inattentive. She played with the gold bracelets which ran up her arm. 'Where did you meet your husband?' she said. 'Was it arranged by your family? Did you meet him in a discotheque?'

It's good for a girl to be educated, but not to be educated too much. After marriage, she may do courses as a hobby. If her family are very liberal, she may work, perhaps in a primary school, just for a year or two; or in a women's hospital. She may work anywhere, really, where she knows that she will not, on her daily journey, or in the course of events, come across a man. There's a whole sealed-off floor at the Ministry of Planning, where women economists sit at their desks, and communicate with their male colleagues by telephone. They send each other, not *billets doux*, but computer disks.

It is apartheid: stringent, absolute. The cafés are segregated, the buses. Allah has laid a duty on both men and women to seek knowledge, but, says one of the letter-writers crossly, 'They can read books and do researches at home.' Education is an ornament. It makes one a better mother. The girls have a chilling saying: 'We will hang our certificates in the kitchen.'

Now her voice, rasping, confident, would be on the phone in the mornings. 'We are going to Mecca. Do you want anything?' When the coast was clear she would come downstairs, veiled for the minute's journey, and drink coffee with me. She would throw off her *abaya* inside the front door, and reveal her Levis and tight T-shirt underneath. 'You ought to get one of these,' she would say, dropping the black cloak on the sofa. 'Lots of English women wear them. You can just throw them on over any old things that you're wearing.' But she wanted to know, very much she wanted to know: what is it like to sit and talk to your husband's friends? What is it like to drink alcohol? What is it like to sit and drink alcohol and talk to your husband's friends?

We did not seem to progress with the Dryden. Her teachers wanted her to know about metre, they didn't care about the meaning. We sat at the dinner table, polished by her maid with some lavender wax spray, the smell of which seemed to scour the inside of my nose; I would turn my head away, sniffing, counting for her the stresses on my fingers. Jamila reeked delicately of 'Joy'. She would push across the table to me one delicate counter, of envy; and then on top of it place, with her shaped polished nails, another counter, of pity. Saudi women believe that their sisters in the West have been the victims of a confidence trick. They believe that men have lured them, with promises of freedom, from the security of their homes, and made them slaves in offices and factories. Their proper domain has been taken away from them, and with it the respect and protection to which their sex entitles them. Their honour has been sold; their bodies are common property. Liberation, say the Saudi women, is a creed for fools.

Her friend S'na came. It seemed that I might as well teach two people, and S'na was taking the course, but she was not married. This made a difference. She was 20 perhaps, but she seemed younger than Jamila. Marriage had given status to my neighbour, maternity had given her command. Within her limits she was free. S'na dressed more soberly, ankle-length dresses even beneath her *abaya*. She had a pretty lemon-coloured face, and because she was so pliant, by training and disposition, her tall thin body seemed to bend and sway in all sorts of unexpected places, as if she had no proper joints. When she took off her veil, unwinding the cloth, it seemed that her arms became water. It was some days before her voice rose above a whisper. When we sat side by side over our texts her eyes would slide away, and her little mouse hands would flurry and contract with fear, and if I asked her a question she would tremble. She had other burdens, beside the Dryden. She had to read *Huckleberry Finn*. 'Last year,' she mouthed, 'we did *The Nigger of the Nurses*, by Joseph Conrad. I didn't understand it.'

There was a second living-room in Jamila's flat, a stuffy chaotic room, with big comfortable cushions on the floor, and the baby's toys strewn around. Jamila spent her mornings there, entertaining any acquaintances who might be conveyed there by their drivers; but if I was the one who turned up I would see her scrambling up hastily as the maid let me in, ready to show me into the grand salon with the proper chairs. I wanted to say, I would rather sit in there with you; I hinted it, but she only smiled. She didn't get dressed till 11 o'clock, perhaps noon; she had a repertoire of flimsy nightdresses, of silky housecoats that swirled out behind her as she brought in our coffee. A good deal of the morning she spent on the phone, laughing with her friends; the rest, watching television.

Television in the Kingdom is mostly 'Prayer Call from Mecca', 'Islam in Perspective' and 'A Reading from the Holy Koran'; then in the late afternoon there are cartoons for the children and for the men returning from their offices. But during the morning there are Egyptian soap operas. Large-bosomed women fill the screen, rolling their eyes, wringing their hands: each Mater Dolorosa in a dozen domestic dilemmas familiar to the viewer. Sometimes Jamila pretended to study. I saw her anthology of English poetry tossed aside on one of the cushions, the thin pages fanning over in the draught from the air-conditioner: 'The Burial of Sir John Moore', 'Sea Fever', 'Sailing to Byzantium'. Jamila said, 'What do you and your husband talk about, when you are alone?'

While we were chatting and construing our verse, Jamila's Malaysian servant crept about the house. The export of female servants is a big industry for the world's poorer Muslim populations. Sometimes Jamila would break off the Dryden for a tirade on the girl's shortcomings. She didn't come when she was called, didn't seem to understand any Arabic or the simplest word of English. Her name was hard to pronounce, and she had resisted Jamila's efforts to rename her something simpler. 'She's just an internal servant,' Jamila said, 'I want her just for the house. Just for the washing and ironing, for the cleaning and looking after the baby and helping me with the cooking. I don't want her going out gossiping and bringing gangs of thieves to the house.' Housemaids are regarded as fair game by Saudi husbands. Sometimes they run away, or commit suicide. The authorities in Sri Lanka (or so the *Saudi Gazette* reports) have made it compulsory for maids to undertake martial arts courses before taking posts in the Middle East.

'I hope you are not studying Shelley,' my Pakistani neighbour said. 'Shelley was an immoralist.'

'You can come to my house,' S'na said in her usual whisper. 'Not to teach me. Just to talk.' Her eyes travelled to my legs, dubiously. 'Do you ever wear long skirts? That would be better.'

But I never went. I was resisting them. 'You should put on more make-up,' Jamila advised me. 'It makes you nice.' She gave me a blue opal on a thin gold chain. They could make me feel callow, unloved, a drudge. I saw Jamila dress for an evening party, in a modest gown of grey chiffon, pearls in her hair. When the oil price fell, my husband's job was under threat; there were cut-backs. Jamila telephoned. 'I'm sure,' she added, 'that we can do something about this. Tell us. My husband will fix it.' I was constrained and polite. Tears – of humiliation? – stood in my eyes. I felt I was becoming a worse human being; a recipient of favours.

There is no crime in Saudi Arabia, the newspapers say. There is no corruption. All women are chaste. All families are happy. The Indian clerks at the office tell a different story. In a shabby block of flats by the waterfront, a Third Country National is found raped and strangled on her bed; her infants, decapitated, are in the kitchen. The system is cracking up from the inside. Jamila tells me how it cracks, her voice low and thrilled. 'Some bad types of women go to the Jeddah International Market to buy jewellery. They let these men touch them. They put out their hands from their *abaya*, with their nails painted red, and the men try bracelets on them.'

Patrols walk the shopping malls, vigilantes armed with canes; they are the delegates of the Committee for the Propagation of Virtue and the Elimination of Vice. 'Some girls,' says Jamila, 'go to the shops with their telephone numbers on a paper, and give it to any man they meet. Then they ring up and have a relationship, they plan to deceive their parents and to marry.'

There are no crimes, but there are punishments. A woman is stoned to death. Amputations are carried out, after Friday prayers. We could never talk about these things. I felt, by the end of that interesting year, an increasing sense of oppression. I no longer wanted to spend the mornings with my two Muslim friends. We took a villa on an expatriate compound, and then a few months later we moved out of the city altogether, to one of the company 'villages' which resembled an English housing estate. It was only in the narrowest sense that you were abroad; only the heat told you, and your own tetchy bouts of homesickness. I knew that the journey upstairs to my neighbour's flat had been, for me, a significant one. I had been offered a friendship I could not accept. It was a chance to build a bridge; but I thought, no, you swim to my side. My values were changing. When I travelled at first I used to ask what I could get out of it, and what I could give back. What could I teach, and what could I learn? I saw the world as some sort of exchange scheme for my ideals, but the world deserves better than this. When you come across an alien culture you must not automatically respect it. You must sometimes pay it the compliment of hating it.

During my last months in Al Hamra I used to feel stifled, desperate for the open air. Sometimes I would continue my journey upstairs, past Jamila's apartment, and up to the flat roof. Hot winds, as if from convection ducts, pulled at my clothes, and plastic bags from Al Safeway Supermarket would blow past my head and tangle in the television aerials. The city lay below its dust-haze, its grid plan scarred by construction sites, derricks and cranes spiking the sky. To the left was a strip of grey, the coast road, where miles of street lamps arched, like the bare ribs of some giant animal whose time has come. Beyond that was another grey strip, without lights, and I used to watch it hopefully, thinking of the months crossed off on the calendar, and knowing that it was the open sea.

24 January, 1987

Jeffrey Bernard

PHARAOH-NOIA

To stand hatless in the Valley of the Kings in a temperature of 115°F while afflicted with very serious diarrhoea is faintly ridiculous and rather frightening. You daren't move. I stood there staring at the mountains wondering what does it all mean and that is a subject only fit for contemplation when alone in bed at night. The sun was drilling my skull for blood. There was some sand in my mouth and the colonic spasms made me drip sweat. *That* is what I remember most vividly of Egypt. That and the river Nile itself. Temples, tombs and ruins are strictly for tourists gazing in groups and I prefer to be alone and find my own sights.

I never meant to get sucked into a group and it was foolish of me to imagine I wouldn't be when we set sail from Aswan to go downstream to Luxor. Groups hellbent on 'sightseeing' shuffle along in a slow-moving queue avaricious for anything of antiquity and quick on the draw with a camera. And I wonder how well Kodak do out of the film wasted on the other obsession of the tourist – the *views*. You really need something a little special other than a Pentax to take pictures of views and local postcards are best. But the group from the boat seemed to think I was an oddball sloping off to find my own views which didn't register with any of them. In a refreshment bar near King Tutankhamun's tomb, where I found a lavatory with as much wonder as Carter experienced in 1922 on opening that tomb, I watched dried-up old Arabs smoking their pipes and drinking coffee over endless games of backgammon. I drank very cold beer and liked it for the first time in years.

When the group came in at last after having seen the tombs of generations of kings they immediately got into line for Coca-Colas and 7-Ups and they seemed to look disturbed at my drinking beer. After all, wasn't I about the only person of about 300 on the boat who drank alcohol in the lounge bar? It was the same sort of hostility tempered with curiosity that I felt steaming up the Mississippi from New Orleans to Memphis and cruising around the fjords of Norway between Oslo and the North Cape. On the Nile it occurred to me that if travel broadens the mind then Australians and Americans set out with precious little of it.

But there was a strange atmosphere in both the Valley of the Kings and the Valley of the Queens. Perhaps I am romancing or letting my imagination run away with me but the feeling of time and an age going back 4,000 years made me feel as though I was being watched. The desert and the mountains had, after all, soaked up so many people over the years and the old Egyptian preoccupation with death and the dead somehow lingered in those scorched and blistered rocks and sand. Fanciful maybe, but that it how it was to me. On the way back to the banks of the Nile where a ramshackle ferry waited to take us back to our luxury boat our coach stopped to allow the group to photograph an old pillar and to buy some papyrus. Watching people barter bores me. Trying to do it myself embarrasses me but it seems to be obligatory. They actually like being knocked down, these street traders. We had stopped on a muddy land in the fertile sugar-cane fields that accompany the river from Aswan to Luxor. The camera buffs didn't see the dog lying in a puddle and panting from the heat or the open-doored tin sheds with old women inside seated at tables and emulating the miracle of the loaves and fishes. A small boy drove a flock of goats with expertise but the Canons and Nikons, aimed at the old pillar, chattered away like castanets.

Back on the boat I witnessed the largest order for Coca-Cola the world has ever known. Into mine I poured some vodka out of my duty-free bottle and was spotted doing so by an Australian teacher in charge of a revolting crocodile – the only one on the Nile – of 26 schoolgirls. She turned to her companion, an overweight PE teacher, and said, 'That isn't allowed. Should we report him?' A combination of heat and impatience with middle-class Australian priggishness prompted me to lean forward and suggest she mind her own f – – – ing business.

I had hoped to meet the lovable Sir Les Patterson or some of the wonderful drunken wits who jeer at the English from the Hill at Sydney cricket ground but no such luck. But I did make one little friend on the boat – and American 14-year-old boy called Philip who is an amalgam of

Huckleberry Finn and Portnoy. He deserves to be laid very soon by a discerning and sympathetic woman. When we disembarked at Luxor to fly back to Cairo my bar bill was £E102. His was £E80. His father was not pleased but being a professor of genetics probably managed to rationalise it. My daughter Isabel's bar bill was £E32 for four days' Coca-Cola which struck me as being fairly revolting. I don't think she liked the holiday much and she is not yet sufficiently streetwise not to be intimidated by waiters, hotel porters and taxi drivers. Anyway, for her, anyone over 21 is geriatric, although she told me she made some 'pen friends' from the group of Australian schoolgirls. It remains to be seen whether anyone can actually write. At least Isabel has learned the wonder of signing bar bills.

On our last day we went to see the pyramids and the Sphinx and took pictures of each other standing in front of them. An Arab insisted on taking a picture of me holding on to his camel. Disgusting animals. All the while our own personal guide spouted history lessons. All I wanted to know was how Egyptians live *today*. After all, can they have so much regard for archaeology who kept Egyptian railways running for a ten-year period using no other fuel than mummies? But I shall remember the Nile especially during its brief sunsets. The heat of the day makes the sky white and not blue and when the sun does go down over those angry orange carbuncles of mountains, it is also pale and yellow. Then the colour of the river changes too and it becomes as gunmetal. The distant chanting of calls to prayer are only interrupted by calls for Coca-Cola on the boat. I hope the ghosts of the old kings get angry one day.

18 July, 1987

6 THE FAR EAST
AND AUSTRALIA

Graham Greene

BEFORE THE ATTACK

January 5. At the military airport at Hanoi at 7 a.m. to wait for a plane on the shuttle service to Dien Bien Phu, the great entrenched camp on the Laos border, which is meant to guard the road to Luang Prabang, the capital of Laos. There is a daily fog over the camp which lies in a plain surrounded by Viet-held mountains. At 11 a.m. we got away. Among the passengers two photographers in camouflaged uniforms. They seem to me comparable to those men who go hunting big game with cameras alone.

I always have a sense of guilt when I am a civilian tourist in the regions of death: after all one does not visit a disaster except to give aid – one feels a *voyeur* of violence, as I felt during the attack two years ago on Phat Diem. There violence had already arrived: it was there in the burning market, the smashed houses, the long street empty for fear of snipers. It was very present in the canal so laden with bodies that they overlapped and a punt of parachutists stuck on a reef of them: and it came suddenly home on patrol when two shots killed a mother and child who found themselves between the opposing forces. What panic had they felt? I felt a little of it myself when for a few moments I lost my companions and found myself stumbling between the Viet Minh and the Foreign Legion. I told myself then that I hated war, and yet here I was back – an old *voyeur* at his tricks again.

Violence had not yet come to Dien Bien Phu, except in the smashed and bulldozed plain which three weeks ago had been a Thai village and a forest of trees and ricefields among the stilted houses. Giap's men were known to be all round, perhaps two divisions strong, and heavier artillery and anti-aircraft than they had yet employed were on the way. With coolie labour it was being brought down from the Chinese frontier. The French are waiting and hoping for an attack, the air is noisy with planes building up supplies, and primrose parachutes come wavering down like the seeds of some wild plant on a windy day.

In the mess at lunch there was a big blonde woman over for the day to see whether the Social Services could be of assistance to the camp. Colonel de Castries (his neat dark histrionic features reminded me of Mr

Ernest Milton in *King John*) teased her unmercifully. The time, he told her, had not yet come for sweets. He had '*autres objectifs.*' She became angry and rather pitiful, this big woman with her desire to help among a lot of amused and uninterested men who did not want her feminine care.

Then the Colonel in turn lost his temper with two of his brother officers who insisted on discussing Na-Sam, the strong defensive post in the north evacuated last year by the French. He said he would not have another word spoken about Na-Sam. Na-Sam had nothing in common with Dien Bien Phu. 'This is not a defensive post, this is a post from which to counter-attack. I will not have Na-Sam mentioned in the mess.' His chief of staff hastily asked me if I had seen Claudel's *Christophe Colombe* when I was last in Paris.

Before dark fell the mortars tried out their range. The evening star came out to the noise of the shells. I had a sense of unreality. There the Viet Minh were, able to observe the arrival of every plane, every movement in the camp from the encircling hills. They knew our strength better than we knew theirs. We were like actors in an arena.

The French had so planned their defences that if the Viet attacked – and the most likely hours were between four and ten in the morning when the heavy morning fog began to lift – they would have to pass down between three small fortified hills that stood like sentries at the entrance to the plain. They would be enfiladed here, they would be enfiladed there, but I just couldn't believe that anything was even going to happen.

Slept after an admirable dinner in a dug-out shared with the Intelligence officer.

January 6. Before lunch visited the camp of the Thai partisans. A delightful domestic scene. Up to the present they had been allowed to keep their families with them. Small boys were playing in and out of the emplacements and dug-outs. A woman suckled her baby while her husband in a steel helmet stood admiringly by; a small girl returned with green vegetables from market; a group of women gathered round a cooking pot. War momentarily seemed charming and domestic, but if a shell were to burst here, how far worse than any man's war.

After the camp a Thai village outside the lines. The Thai women, from the moment they walk, wear the same elegant close-buttoned costume, the same hat like an elaborately folded napkin; in the same dress they toddle beside their mother and stumble as an old woman towards the grave. They have more open faces than the Vietnamese: in old age their features are almost European, so that you could easily mistake them for weather-worn Breton women in their national costume. In one village lived the mission priest in a hut that was chapel and dispensary as well as home. He had a long sharp nose and a long narrow beard and eyes full of the amusement of life. One hand was bent and crooked – he had been tortured by the Japanese, and he carried also the scar of a Viet Minh wound. His business was not conversion, there were practically no Catholics among the Thais: he was there to serve the mass for himself and to serve the Thais with medicine and friendship.

In the afternoon caught a military plane back to Hanoi in time to wash and dine with an old friend. It was good to lie down and relax after dinner and smoke and talk as two years ago. His opium was the best I had smoked since I was in Hanoi last.

16 April, 1954

John Wells

PLUS ÇA CHANGE

One of the most fundamental mistakes made by travel writers, it seems to me, is that they still believe we are interested in reading about something 'different.' In spite of the fact that every modern traveller experiences the opposite, they still persist in giving the impression that everything beyond the horizon is 'strange' or 'foreign,' 'typical' of some ancient and exotic culture that is quite alien to our own. Their attitude recalls the old travellers' tales, when brave men brought back news of bizarre customs beyond the seas, stories of dog-headed men, and accounts of pygmies who bounced along on their bottoms emitting little whoops of pleasure.

In the past this was no doubt all well and good: our forefathers drew comparisons, satirical or otherwise, with their own condition, and were able to renew their sense of wonder and delight at the strangeness of their environment. In our own age, however, it is obviously absurd to suggest that anywhere is different, let alone more different than anywhere else. Guests at the Hilton Hotel are frequently reduced to dialling room service to find out which country they are in. The more we change, the more we become the same.

This sameness has long been a source of distress to the old-fashioned traveller. Noting the similarity between the Kebabburger served in Jerusalem and the ordinary American Hamburger found in Hamburg, old-fashioned travellers have been known to poison themselves eating 'authentic' local food. Similarly, many old-fashioned travellers have had their holidays poisoned for them by a fruitless search for the authentically 'different' atmosphere promised by the travel writer. Far better for the travel writers to accept reality as it is, and to enthuse instead about the wonderful sameness awaiting the traveller abroad.

I stumbled on this truth some years ago when I was travelling in Japan. All the traditional shrines of Japanese culture, theatres, baths, brothels and temples, seemed to be thronged with European visitors, and as I was anyway short of money and had been away from England for almost a year it struck me, sitting among the guidebooks in Tokyo, that the ideal place to go would be a pub in Kobe called 'The Red Lion.' The guidebook also mentioned a place called the Kobe Club, where English colonels could be seen drinking pink gin and playing dominoes. I cabled my bank in London to transfer a meagre sum to Kobe, and set off immediately by train.

The journey itself was uneventful, except for the arrival in the doorway of the compartment of a sales girl, apparently selling boxes of chocolate. I selected a rather nice-looking box with a picture of some mountains and a lake on the front, showed the sales girl some coins, a few of which she took, and settled back in my seat to unwrap the goodies. I was aware almost immediately of those opposite looking at me with their impassive almond eyes, but paid no attention and went on trying to undo the tight cellophane wrapping. The packet seemed to be made of light tin, and when the lid finally came off I was surprised to find it contained only flat strips of fried seaweed. I looked up at the four pairs of attentive and still impassive almond eyes, affected a quietly triumphant smirk to suggest that the packet contained after all what I expected, shut the lid, put it into a paper bag with the rest of my belongings, and looked out of the window.

I was not surprised after that to find when I arrived in Kobe that it was the Emperor's birthday and that all the banks were shut. I was also not entirely certain where the English bank had transferred the money to, but after a walk through the colourful streets, where the soldiers mutilated in the war had been brought out in hundreds in yellow uniforms with the red star in the cap to beg in the gutter, I found a bank with a plate beside the door saying that they were agents for my own bank in England. The front doors were shut, but a door round the side had been left open, and I went in, hoping to meet someone who might be able to speak English. It was deserted. I was some way in among the clutter of little desks behind the main counter, innocently searching for some list or notice that might give me the name of the British representative, when I heard a sharp exclamation, presumably in Japanese, from behind me in the doorway. I looked round and found a man in semi-military uniform pointing a gun at me.

After some moments of misunderstanding it emerged that he spoke pidgin English, and he immediately became most charming. He put his gun away, explained that he had learned English while working as a pirate in Hong Kong, and insisted that I should come up to his nightwatchman's room for a drink. He had just bought an electric mixer, and he poured in a tin of orange juice and a bottle of saki and turned it on. He showed me a piece of his pirate boat, which he had been blown up in by the Japanese air force during the war, and a Union Jack-draped portrait of King George VI, for whom he apparently had great affection. We then drank the saki and orange – he prefaced each glass by remarking 'God Save the Queen' – I thanked him, and found my way out into the street.

'The Red Lion' was shut. I had a look through the keyhole at all the English chairs and tables, and then set off rather extravagantly in a taxi for the Kobe Club. True to life, they were all sitting there playing dominoes and drinking pink gin. I ordered the same, and settled down contentedly to listen to the familiar cadences and the restful click of the dominoes. After a few moments one of the colonels got up from his game and came over. I explained that I was in the army, had got a lift from Seoul on an American aeroplane, had left my uniform with friends in Tokyo and come down to Kobe in my only suit of civilian clothes with a paper bag containing, among other things, a tin of seaweed, to visit the British pub.

He listened to my story about the bank, seemed sympathetic, and suggested very helpfully that I might like to stay in one of the guest rooms of the club until the money came through. He would, however, have to confer with the committee. The committee, six or seven kindly old men in blazers and silk squares, then literally went into a huddle over by the window, from time to time casting a glance in my direction, and I sat as nonchalantly as possible at the bar looking into space. In the end, one of them came back and said he'd never heard such nonsense in his life and would I get out immediately. You couldn't get much samer than that.

15 September, 1967

Alexander Chancellor

INDIAN NOTEBOOK

One of E. M. Forster's characters in *A Passage to India* finds that the Indians remind him of the Italians. I was surprised to have the same feeling. It was the natural gaiety of the Indians which struck me. They like fairs and excitements of any sort and have a weakness for fairy lights with which they deck their public buildings and temples. Despite the poverty, you are seldom infected by that gloom which attaches to Indians in mackintoshes when you see them shopping in Oxford Street. Even Calcutta, that ultimate sewer of a city, is not really depressing. The problems there are enormous and apparently insoluble. Of its nine million inhabitants, about three million live in slums. Slums are defined as shacks built by their occupants out of mud, corrugated iron, or whatever else comes to hand. Their walls are decorated with little round cow pats which are used as fuel. You cannot stand up in them. Each minute shack contains six people or so. They have no light, drainage or water. The narrow paths between the shacks are littered with human excrement. When the monsoon comes, this washes indoors. There is no suggestion that the slum dwellers should ever be re-housed. The most that the authorities dream of doing is to supply one light, one tap, and one lavatory for each slum containing several hundred people. Yet the underfed children continue to smile. It is hard to understand it.

17 March, 1979

Shiva Naipaul

AN INDIAN ENCOUNTER

I knew she was extremely rich, I knew she was held in awe by those whose lives she controlled, and I knew she was approaching a vigorous, undaunted middle-age. So much Mr Chaudhuri – the astrologer who had effected the introduction – had told me. Her voice crackled faintly on the bad telephone line.

'I should be delighted to meet you,' she said. 'Mr Chaudhuri has told me so much about you. You sound a most interesting person.'

I laughed lightly, but volunteered no comment.

'Have you ever seen an Indian country house?' she asked. I said I had not. 'Then, in that case, you positively must come. I'll send a car and a driver to pick you up.'

I put the receiver down and looked at Mr Chaudhuri. He was standing next to me, smiling and rubbing his hands.

'So,' he said, 'It is all fixed up.'

'I'm afraid so.'

He shook his head. 'Nothing to be afraid of. She is a most extraordinary lady. You will not regret it.'

Mr Chaudhuri was a darkly handsome, happy and prosperous man. Of late, his business had been booming to such an extent that he had been able to alter his rates from 180 rupees for a 45-minute consultation to 180 rupees for a 30-minute consultation. 'You can tell these Germans anything,' Mr Chaudhuri said, 'and charge them anything.' (Germany seems to provide the bulk of India's well-heeled tourists.) He had, so to speak, adopted me. Exactly why, I was not sure. But I had no reason to complain. Astrologers get around in India and Mr Chaudhuri seemed to know everyone of consequence. He talked familiarly of cabinet ministers and industrialists and film stars: all seemed to have need of his services.

'What did you tell the lady about me?' I asked. Mr Chaudhuri giggled but would not say. I had first encountered him in a heavily curtained cubicle he rented in the basement of the hotel where I was staying. He was sitting on a low stool, surrounded by magazines and newspapers. On a bookshelf behind him were arrayed his celestial charts, treatises and almanacs. He had taken my right hand. 'Oh God,' he exclaimed, kneading the tender flesh. This outburst, naturally enough, had aroused both curiosity and alarm. However, all was well. It so happened, Mr Chaudhuri explained when he had calmed down, that mine was one of the most astonishing palms he had ever had to interpret. Its configurations heralded a future resplendent with honour and fame. So impressive was his perspicacity that we became friends. He had insinuated me into the presence of one of his cabinet ministers, he had manoeuvred my way an industrialist or two, and now there was this woman, a legend in Delhi's high society, fabled for her riches, who, at his prompting, had invited me to her country house. Could anyone expect more from his astrologer?

Car and driver arrived at precisely the appointed hour. The chauffeur oozed an odd mixture of deference and hauteur as he hurried before me, opening and closing doors.

'I hope I did not keep you waiting, Sahib.'

'Not at all. It was I who kept you.'

My answer appeared to pain him. 'Of course not, Sahib. If I waited for you that is my job.'

He ushered me into the car. Was the Sahib perfectly comfortable? Would he like the windows down? Half up? Closed?

'What do you think would be best?' I asked.

He offered the shadow of a smile. 'That is not for me to say, Sahib.'

Eventually, it was decided that I should have them rolled up half way. We set off, moving smoothly along empty avenues. It was easy – traversing these broad roads lined with lovely old trees, catching glimpses of mansions protected by solid walls, circling roundabouts planted with beds of flowers, looking out into a cool night bathed in a blue electric glow . . . it was easy to put aside the poverty of India, to slip into the mood required by a country house evening. The sensation of opulence was enhanced by our transition to a multi-laned highway. On our right, necklaces of multi-coloured lights patterned the runways of Delhi's airport. Then we were out of the city, driving along narrower roads bordered by dusty trees and invisible fields, flashing past bullock carts piled high with hay. After about an hour, we slowed at a pair of heavy, wrought-iron gates supported on stone pillars surmounted by illuminated globes. A guard inspected us. He saluted. The gates swung open. We entered a broad drive flanked with shrubs and palm trees. Landscaped grounds stretched away into a leafy darkness punctuated by carefully dispersed spotlights.

I was let off at a flight of steps leading to the main entrance of a large house of modernistic design. To my left, on a lower terrace, was a swimming pool. This was screened on one side by a hedge of illuminated shrubbery which cast an eerily perfect reflection of itself in the still water. Beyond this oddly unsettling aquatic fantasia was another house similar in design to the one outside which I had been deposited. It too might have been an eerily perfect reflection. The front door opened, framing a strangely attired figure. I saw an elderly man of dwarfish stature – he was some inches less than five foot – with creased mongoloid features. He wore a loose crimson robe, a furry hat whose edges were twisted upwards like the eaves of a pagoda and a pair of outsized leather boots the tips of which narrowed to a wrinkled apex. It was difficult to decide what to make of this apparition, how to react. My sense of hallucination deepened as, standing there in the lighted doorway, he wordlessly beckoned me within.

As I entered, he presented the guest book. I signed my name. This ritual completed, he led me into a spacious reception room. Immediately on my left was gathered a group of perhaps half a dozen men dressed in white kurta pyjamas, occupying a cluster of sofas and armchairs arrayed around a low, glass-topped table. They were talking in low voices. My irruption caused their conversation to die away altogether. Assuming they were fellow guests, I began to move in their direction. However, my crimson-robed manikin nudged me away from them, guiding me across the room to another, but untenanted, cluster of sofas and armchairs. The room was heavy with silence, the voices across from me not having been reactivated. Only the subdued hum of the air conditioners disturbed the sepulchral gravity. Another attendant appeared. This one, perhaps in deliberate contrast to the former, was a tall, fine-featured Rajput. He was dressed in white – white, starched tunic, close-fitting white trousers, white turban cascading in a stylish flourish down to the nape of his neck. He carried a silver tray. Bending low, he elicited my choice of drink. Within half a minute a generous measure of Scotch had been set down on a silver coaster on the immaculately polished glass table in front of me. Gliding behind the sofa where I was sitting, he put on a record: discotheque pop. I noticed the strange group of men were not drinking anything. Their manner suggested unease and patient submission. Obviously, they were not guests like myself. I examined my surroundings more closely. Every surface was spotless, every ornament that could glitter glittered. A tapestry of abstract design covered one wall. Around the rails of a balcony overlooking the room were draped garlands of marigold. I sipped my Scotch, awaiting developments. Voices sounded. An elderly man in a navy-blue blazer and a plump, sari-clad woman, pale neck and arms glinting with jewellery, entered the room. The manikin guided them over to where I was sitting.

'Where's Bubbly?' asked the woman. 'Bubbly' was the name by which our hostess was familiarly known. I said I had yet to set eyes on her.

'Bubbly,' shouted the woman. 'Where are you hiding yourself?' An answering cry came from a distant room. It summoned her to its presence. The woman disappeared, leaving in her wake a trail of sweet perfume. Silver tray clutched at his side, the Rajput bent low over the man with the blazer. A whisky and soda was requested. We introduced ourselves. He was, he revealed, in business, the chairman of 'two, three companies'.

'What do your companies trade in?'

'We manufacture things, you can say.' He stared vaguely, taking his drink from the hovering Rajput. He appeared not to want to talk about his business activities. 'Actually,' he said after a short silence, 'my number one love is flying. Before I took up business I used to be a fighter pilot.' He paused. 'I was given the highest award after the last war with Pakistan.'

I congratulated him.

'The highest award.' He patted his right leg. 'There's metal everywhere inside of there. Got shot up during the bombing of Karachi. You must remember the bombing of Karachi.' He took a gulp of whisky.

How could I say I did not?

'I also served with the RAF during World War Two,' he expanded. 'I bombed France. I bombed Germany. I bombed Holland. I bombed everywhere.' A nostalgic smile overspread his face as he caressed his injured leg.

A hoarse voice resonated through the room. The enigmatic group of men stood up. Our hostess had arrived.

'You must think I'm very rude,' she began, making straight for me. 'But I have delegations of people coming to see me all the time. It's difficult to turn them away. Many have travelled a great distance just to come and see me. Being rich is hard work . . .'

She spoke breathlessly, her round, dark eyes darting about the room. She was of medium height and voluptuous build – a voluptuousness which, here and there, had begun to melt into mere fleshiness. Coarse, extravagantly black hair flailed like a horse's tail as she restlessly tossed and twisted her head, taking in the scene.

She was dressed in the conventional Punjabi style – clinging trousers, smock, loose hanging scarf. Her full, furrowed lips were painted scarlet, her cheeks were rouged, her eyes were lined with kohl. She clapped her hands. The Rajput and the manikin came hurrying up to her. 'Drinks, drinks for my guests.' She seized my nearly empty glass, placing it on the Rajput's tray. She addressed the room. 'You can have French wine, champagne . . . anything . . . anything . . . Lama, Lama . . .' She grasped the manikin by the shoulder. 'Bring food . . . khanna . . .' The grinning Lama scurried off. She looked at me. 'Mr Chaudhuri has already told me all about you. He's a most remarkable man in his way . . . what did he tell you about me?'

'That you were a most remarkable woman in your way.' Her hoarse laughter resounded, her hair flailed. 'That is good. I like that very much.' She signalled to the enigmatic group of men, still standing in poses of submission. 'Tonight you see me in my role as patroness of the arts. Those men you see over there are singers, dancers and musicians, unknowns who have been brought to my attention. If they are talented, I may be able to do something for them.'

'Do you patronise the arts a great deal?'

'The rich have their duties . . .'

'I suppose so.'

'Especially in a country like India. I do a lot of social work. Half of my time is devoted to helping the villages around here. I'm very keen on birth control – you might say it is one of my passions.' She adjusted her scarf. 'Most people believe I'm a hard, unscrupulous woman. Would you say that is all I am? Would you wipe me out when the revolution comes?'

'Are you expecting a revolution?'

She laughed and moved off towards the troupe of unknowns, chattering to them in Punjabi.

The war hero had drifted away, his place taken by a bony, black American girl whose skull was draped by a beaded curtain of pendent ringlets. I discovered that she lived in Sweden, was a dress designer and travelled regularly to India in search of fabrics. The sofa opposite was occupied by a big, barrel-shaped man costumed in the traditional regalia of a Congress Party wallah – peaked white cap, white tunic and close-fitting white trousers. Two minions were perched deferentially on either side of him.

The Congress man boomed his name.

'I expect you have heard of me,' he said. I hesitated. 'Surely you have heard of him,' one of the minions put in, gazing reproachfully at me.

Then I remembered: he was one of those politicians now considered closest to Indira Gandhi, a man of consequence, suddenly reaping the rewards of an alsatian-like fidelity to his mistress – a fidelity which had never once wavered even during her darkest days.

Without prompting, he embarked on a catalogue of his more memorable exploits. His egocentricity was so unabashed, so child-like in its naiveté, that it was almost captivating. I heard how he had been detained during the Janata era, how nobly he had conducted himself while in captivity, how 'the people', outraged, had taken to the streets in their thousands to protest the injustice of his incarceration.

'I was never afraid,' he said.

'Correct,' the second minion said. 'Fear was never known to him during that time.'

'Never,' confirmed the first minion.

Lama was circulating kebabs. The great man paused while he helped himself, washing it all down with draughts of whisky. 'In fact,' he said, resuming his narrative, massaging his belly, 'in fact it was police who were afraid. Can you imagine such a thing? Why should police be afraid of me?' He spluttered with amusement.

'Police were quaking in their boots,' the second minion said. He talked about his involvement in the recent outbreak of communal rioting between Muslims and Hindus – how he had gone to one of the affected towns and how, single-handedly, he had restored the errant citizenry to their senses.

'Who gets hurt in riots?' he asked.

'Yes,' said the first minion, looking sternly at the Swedish resident and myself. 'Who? That is the question you must both ask yourselves.'

'It is the poor who get hurt,' answered the great man, smiling contentedly at his wisdom. 'Not Hindus or Muslims or Christians – but poor people. That is what I told them. Poor people, I told them, have only one true religion – their tummy.'

Lama circulated more kebabs, the Rajput poured more drinks. The great man chewed, swallowed, gurgled and massaged his belly.

'That is so,' the second minion said. 'Tummy is only religion of poor people.' He too, perhaps empathising with their misery, began to massage his belly.

Bubbly was clapping, calling us to attention: the evening's entertainment was about to begin. Lama and the Rajput guided us upstairs to a terrace festooned with garlands of marigolds. Rugs were spread on the floor of the terrace. A dance, performed by a teenage boy, opened the evening's entertainment. Bubbly, crouched beside me, clapped softly, body swaying to the rhythms the boy tapped out with his feet. He moved with confidence and grace, smiling girlishly at us. There were oohs and aahs of appreciation. While he danced, more food, more drink, was offered. 'Do you like my house?' Bubbly asked, eyes fixed on the dancer. I said I did.

It was, she pointed out, simplicity itself. 'I told the architect to give me four walls, four windows and a roof. And that is what he did. Isn't that what a house is supposed to be?' I enquired about the other house I had seen beyond the swimming pool.

That, she said, belonged to her husband. It had occurred to them that having separate houses was the best way to preserve their marriage. 'If he wishes, he can have a bird in there and I don't have to know about it. I can have a lover in here and he doesn't have to know about it. It is a good arrangement.'

It suddenly struck me that she was not altogether sober. This was something of a mystery. I had not seen her drinking all that much – only, every now and again, swallowing tiny crystalline pellets stored in a bottle kept by Lama.

'You know,' she said, 'I was always stinking, stinking rich. Our family were zamindars. We are stinking, stinking rich . . .'

The boy finished his dance. Everyone applauded: he was adjudged a promising prospect. Bubbly, propelling herself with her hands, sped across the floor to congratulate him. A sequence of love songs – ghazals – followed. Bubbly exclaimed, clapped her hands, sighed.

'The singer is serenading me,' she explained, crouching down once more beside me.

'What is he saying?'

'He says my face is pale like the moon, my cheeks are like peaches, my teeth are like pearls and my lips are the colour of pomegranates. He says all men pine for me as I wander through my walled garden, green after the monsoon, feeding my peacocks . . . it is not so good in English . . .' She pounded on the floor. 'Lama, Lama.' Lama came running. He supplied her with another pellet. She drank it down with wine. She took off across the room, propelling herself with her hands, clapping, shouting encouragement at the singer, flailing her hair. 'Yah, yah, yah.' She came back. 'Stinking, stinking rich,' she murmured to herself, gulping more wine, swallowing another crystal. 'Stinking, stinking rich . . .' Energised, she circumnavigated the terrace. 'Yah, yah, yah.' She came back. 'What they sing is to me like Shakespeare, Shelley, Keating, Kant and Hegel all rolled into one.' She grasped a clump of her hair and stared cock-eyed at it. 'Only Mr Chaudhuri knows what a great romantic I am. Only Mr Chaudhuri knows the secrets of my soul . . .'

She resumed her roaming, clapping, shouting, flailing her hair. I noticed that one of the great man's minions had cradled his head on the lap of the American girl.

'Yah, yah, yah . . . Lama.' Another crystal. More wine. The entertainment ceased. She was back beside me. 'Stinking, stinking rich . . . .' She stared at me with reddened eyes. There was something wild about her now. Her head lolled. 'Mr Chaudhuri told me you were very passionate, very full of emotion. Is that true?'

I cannot remember what I answered.

'If you stay with me this one night you can kiss these lips like pomegranates, you can stroke these cheeks soft as peaches. Let us wake together in my walled garden and listen to the song of the peacocks at dawn.'

'You have peacocks?'

'Hundreds.' Her head lolled. The guests were making their way downstairs. The Rajput watched us. 'I'm frightened,' she said. 'I cannot stand straight. I shall fall if I stand. I feel as if I'm falling into a black hole, as if I'm dying . . . Lama, Lama.' He came running. The Rajput watched. I too went downstairs.

'What are you doing in India?' asked the wife of the war hero, on our way back to Delhi.

'Collecting material for some articles,' I said.

'What kind of materials are you interested in? Cottons? Silks?'

'Cottons,' I said.

20 December, 1980

Auberon Waugh

TRAVELLER'S TALES

Chiang Mai, North Thailand

There comes a moment in the life of most travellers, I imagine, when they ask themselves: 'What on earth am I doing here?' Such a moment of doubt came to me a few days ago when I found myself alone and stranded beside a car stuck on an unmarked, unsurfaced mountain track in the region of the Golden Triangle between Laos, Burma and Thailand whose only inhabitants – primitive, opium growing tribesmen – were said to shoot at any *farang* or Caucasian on sight.

The reason for their hostility is quite understandable. The only white faces they ever see belong to people who are trying to stop them growing opium – whether directly employed by the dreaded Drug Enforcement Agency, whose highly paid American employees and vast network of spies give the impression of running an alternative, vastly richer and less accountable administration holding their government in suspicion and ill-disguised contempt – or Western journalists anxious to write an *exposé* of this Trade in Misery and Death for their miserable, boring colour supplements. Thai poppy growers – and no doubt their Laotian and

Burmese colleagues in this delightful corner of the world where national frontiers do not seem to possess the *magisterium* attributed to them in the chancelleries of the West – see their occupation as an honourable one. The activities of the Thai government and DEA are seen rather as small businessmen and farmers in England regard the VAT inspectors, health inspectors, cruelty inspectors, fire inspectors, planning and child welfare inspectors who batten on their labours and try to prevent them doing any work – except that here the welfare gang is liable to arrive in armoured helicopters with flame-throwers and medium machine guns.

The explanation for my presence in Chiang Mai dates back to a conversation of two years ago with Richard West, the celebrated traveller, philosopher and visionary, in a Soho pub. I had just returned from a visit to Bangkok and was feeling generally sick of England. He said the only place to go was Chiang Mai. When pressed to explain its advantages over Bangkok, the one thing he could think of was that it had an English pub. He looked benignly around the bar where we stood, with its dingy, furtive inhabitants, its revolting beer, its abiding smell of stale cigarettes and cats' piss and the permanent, haunting presence of Jeffrey Bernard. Oh yes, he said, and there were also the most beautiful girls in the world and opium dens.

All my life – or at any rate, ever since reading Ernest Bramah's Kai Lung stories and discovering Graham Greene at the age of 15 – it had seemed to me that an English writer who had not smoked opium was like a soldier who had never seen active service, a politician who had never been down a coal mine, a female contraceptive guidance welfare health counsellor who had never been . . . anyway, I wanted to do it.

And so I did, although those who wish to discover how will have to buy the February issue of *Business Traveller*. That admirable publication, one of the very few remaining outposts of free journalism, paid for my tickets and arranged my luxurious accommodation in Chiang Mai's Rincome Hotel, although it did not actually pay for the opium. But when on my first visit to the town's famous English pub – a strange and marvellous institution, not at all like the model which inspired it – I mentioned the purpose of my visit, I noticed that a chill descended on the company. The pub, which is in fact an elegant, well-appointed restaurant situated just round the corner from the Rincome Hotel, admits Americans too. Several of the overpaid boy scouts who work for the US Drug Enforcement Agency use it as their local. And it was an American who reacted most violently.

Was I aware that I would almost certainly be shopped, if not shot, by the traffickers, he asked. The penalty for opium possession was 30 years, he said. Did I know that their gaols provided no food for prisoners, and there was no longer a British consulate in Chiang Mai to look after them? No, I was not aware of any of these things, but it seemed rather a long way to have come if I was going to abandon my quest now. Then he became emotional. He was tremendously opposed to drugs, he said, and he would tell me why. He had told nobody this before. He once had a little niece in Florida who was nine years old. A bad man started giving her drugs – it was quite normal, this, in Florida – so that she would become addicted and, when she was grown up, buy his wares. Then, by accident, he put too much dope in a pretzel he was giving her one day, and she died. Snuffle, snuffle. We all looked into our beer. I suggested he tell his story to the Pulitzer Prize committee. There might be some money in it. He said he wasn't interested in money, just the facts. The atmosphere was becoming rather heavy so I left, having an early morning appointment.

No doubt he thought he remembered losing a niece in this way. But what sort of businessman is going to give away good dope for seven or eight years on the off-chance of a paying customer at the end of that time? The story's literary origins will be familiar to many from Tom Lehrer's song, *The Old Dope Pedlar*:

> He gives the kids free samples, because he knows full well
> That today's young innocent faces are tomorrow's clientele.

But nobody has suggested that Mr Lehrer was offering a serious contribution to any study of the subject. He was making a grisly joke about the irrational fears of parents. Another example of how the Drug Enforcement Agency sustains its morale as it sets about destroying the livelihood of the poppy farmers was suggested by a picture in Bangkok's *The Nation*. This showed a former American employee of the Drug Enforcement Agency posing with the corpse of his wife who had been shot in the head by a lone kidnapper, himself shot by police. But all this happened in Chiang Mai last October. The reason the sad picture was being reprinted was that the American government, unsatisfied by the Thai police conclusion that robbery was the motive for the kidnapping, had demanded a second police enquiry to establish that a drug trafficking syndicate was involved. Terrified of offending the Americans, the Thai government has set up a new commission, under two generals of the police force, to revive the enquiry and reach a different conclusion.

At the same time, a report by Thailand's Narcotics Control Board reveals that Thai addicts, denied their usual opium and heroin, are being forced to look for substitutes in petrol, paraffin, volatile lacquer and insecticides. Although heroin can be a powerful toxic agent, the effect of these substitutes on the nervous system and blood corpuscles is almost instantaneous. But then nobody supposed the DEA was concerned about the welfare of Thai addicts. It is purely concerned with the law and order problems created by the illicit trade in the United States. That this illicit trade is entirely of its own creation is a thought best suppressed by preposterous tales about nine-year-old girls caught in the flower of their innocence.

Obviously, heroin is a hideously dangerous substance, and the extreme libertarian position – that if adult human beings wish to destroy themselves, it offers the most agreeable means – is not tenable in a 'responsible' democracy largely dominated by strident social busybodies. But when these same busybodies start visiting their own problems on peaceful corners like the Golden Triangle between Laos, Thailand and Burma, then the time has surely come to put insecticide in their beer and tell them to go home.

28 November, 1981

Alan Ross

GOODBYE TO CALCUTTA

The temperature is 105 degrees, humidity 100 per cent. Between now and the monsoon in two months' time both will get worse. Power cuts remain lengthy and unpredictable; the Japanese-built telephone system rarely works, and that vast trench running like a banked sewer through the centre of the city and allegedly to become a metro has not only made travel virtually impossible, but Calcutta hideous. As a child in the 1930s I thought Calcutta, that 'village of palaces', a heaven on earth, and on each of four visits during the last 20 years there appeared to be mitigating circumstances for evidence of decline: the Bangladesh war, refugees, a Marxist government. The metro, unlikely ever to be finished, a permanent disfigurement, seems the last straw.

It was the Russians a decade ago who foisted this folly, a central government not a state project, on Mrs Gandhi, then at her most susceptible. The advice of British, American, Japanese and various European traffic experts to go for roads or flyovers, easily constructed at a fraction of the cost, was rejected. No one in Calcutta that I spoke to held out much hope for its successful completion or operation. Most believe that it would even now – despite the large waste of money and effort – be safer and more sensible simply to fill it in. Instead, because of political pride and bureaucratic intransigency, spasmodic digging will probably continue year after year, until Calcutta grinds finally to a halt. No work can be done in the rains, and only a quarter of every rupee spent contributes to the construction. The idea of trains actually operating under ground in Calcutta – prey to subsidence, flooding, loss of power, extremes of heat, to say nothing of an inevitable invasion of pavement-dwellers – is even more appalling than the desecration of the city and the waste.

Meanwhile trams, buses, rickshaws, cows, cyclists, taxis, and old beat-up Ambassador cars jostle along what little remains of the streets. The public and private buses, carrying double their proper loads, frequently lose or squash their protruding passengers or overturn. In the suburbs or upcountry, pedestrians, who rarely look in either direction when crossing the road, are regularly knocked down, though in surprisingly few numbers, and when this occurs the offending bus, taxi or car is immediately surrounded and set on fire. The driver runs for his life and the passengers, too, if they are lucky.

Of course, Calcutta, that Brechtian city of the imagination – a metropolis beyond invention – has been, in the eyes of most people, in decline for over a century. Five generations of my family have lived there off and on, probably contributing to that, and a number of them have died there. The British cemeteries, in fact, are one of the few things that flourish. Though no longer a growth industry in the same way, their ghosts bloom under revived conservationist interest, pampered as few living things are in Calcutta.

One of my earliest memories of Calcutta is the race-course, the most centrally situated of any major city in the world. That, at least, has not changed. A couple of minutes from the colliery-like inferno of Chowringhee and lying between the Victoria Memorial and the Hooghly, its track, paddocks and turreted stands form the same fine flourish to the southern end of the maidan. There may no longer be palatial residences at Garden Reach, the handsome colonial houses of Alipore are mostly company flats or taken over by Marwaris – those shrewd Rajastani entrepreneurs who have become the affluent scapegoats for all Bengal's economic injustices – and Kidderpore docks are only a shadow of their former glory, but the race-course, with its flags flying, its crisply-suited men and dazzling women, is as splendid as ever. From the boxes on the members' stand, with Chowringhee only discernible at roof level, it might still be as I used to dream of it through a decade of adolescent separation. Satyajit Ray, to whom I delivered a viewing-filter and who lives in the next street – huge shabby houses among palms and banana trees – where I used to visit my grandmother, says he could not imagine living anywhere else, so the dream must still be real for someone.

One thing the Bengal government learned from the Bangladesh war was that Calcutta can afford no more refugees. Accordingly, during the Assam atrocities, camps were set up in the frontier areas, and approaches to Calcutta sealed. Although criticism of Mrs Gandhi for persisting with the elections in Assam remains fairly general, tea-planters who have spent their whole lives there do not support it. According to them, there was little reason to predict butchery, certainly not on the scale that took place. Plainly, government advisers underestimated the real or contrived ferocity of local feeling, but if it was a misjudgment there was no precedent for acting otherwise.

In general it is impossible not to be amazed at the good humour and gentleness with which Indians, and the people of Calcutta especially, support the trials of their existence. Yet the violence when it erupts is horrifying. Large-scale demonstrations are no problem. Thousands mass on the maidan under local banners, the haranguing goes on all day, and then, when everyone is worn out, they disperse peacefully and return to their homes. It is the individual violence that shocks. Hardly a day passes without reports of an unwanted wife or daughter-in-law being set fire to and burned to death; last week, in a change of roles, a wife set fire to her husband.

There is no green quite like the green of Bengal. And once you are out of Calcutta the landscape assumes the timeless quality and serene beauty that haunt for ever those who fall prey to it: the raised, ruler-straight road lined with tamarind, peepul, bamboo, mango, gol mohur, ashoka; wheat and rice stretching away to the horizon; water buffaloes, only heads visible, motionless in hyacinth-filled lakes; the occasional cyclist under a black umbrella and, at the hour of the cowdust, creaking bullock carts. The villages are mere scatters of thatched huts and markets, rivers curve under coconut palms, women in turquoise, lemon or pink saris stride in their marvellous way under pitchers or copper bowls. Within half an hour Calcutta simply seems an aberration. The empty battlefield of Plassey, recorded by a single monument, or the Residency ruins at Lucknow have more immediacy than the broken sewage-pipe washing facilities and lightless suburbs of Calcutta.

No matter whom you ask, 'corruption' is always the answer when you try to assess responsibility for inefficiency and chaos; corruption among politicians, civil servants, petty officials, businessmen. Nothing proceeds without bribery, to such an extent that the inhabitants of Calcutta are disinclined to believe that this is not standard practice everywhere for everything. At the same time West Bengal, under its Marxist govern-ment, has one of the most honest and civilised administrations in India. Unfortunately, it is also a power-conscious one and investment in Bengal has as a consequence dried up. J. R. D. Tata, the 70-year-old head of the Tata empire and one of the shrewdest men in India, recently gave an interview to Calcutta's new newspaper the *Telegraph* (better written and printed than any of its older rivals) in which he laid much of the blame for India's present plight on Nehru's adherence to the Soviet pattern of industrial development and neglect of agriculture. According to Tata, the dismantling of bureaucracy, as recently achieved by Jayewardene in Sri Lanka, and a change from a parliamentary to an Indian-adapted presi-dential system offer the only hope of reversing the present slide into dis-order and bankruptcy.

Affection for a city can blind one to almost anything. I don't think, all the same, that I shall ever want to return to Calcutta; not only because of its unsightliness and the relentless degradation of human life there, but because, for the first time, I felt it as a faintly hostile place. It was to be expected that all monuments to the Raj should be disposed of, but the painting out or removal of every single road sign in English and the replacement of familiarly named childhood streets by Lenin Sarani and Karl Marx Sarani etc. give one a strange feeling. It is as if the past had been rearranged to create not only confusion but a sense of alienation and dispossession.

Bengalis, for all their bureaucratic obstructiveness, can be marvellous people and occasionally, at sunset or dawn, with the air sweet off the Hooghly, the old ties seemed to be re-establishing themselves. But if I ever had to live in India again it would certainly be Bombay or Bangalore, even Delhi, that I would choose, not Calcutta, and that is an admission I never expected I would have to make.

30 April, 1983

Alexander Chancellor

NOTEBOOK

'No legs at *all*, no legs at *all*.' I heard the words wafting up from the pave-ment behind me as I supervised the unloading of my luggage from the car which had delivered me to Calcutta airport. The words were correctly pronounced in almost BBC English and sounded detached and rather quizzical. But they were no less than the truth, for I turned round to see a pathetic, legless youth stretching out his hand towards me. 'No legs at all' were clearly the only words in English he knew and I felt he might have picked them up over the years from departing British tourists – 'Oh look, my dear. Isn't it *ghastly*. No legs at *all*.' So I gave him a couple of rupees and went to catch the aeroplane for London. Having spent a week in Calcutta brushing beggars aside, I spend my last morning there handing out minute sums of money to the regulars as a reward for their persistence. Most people, particularly foreigners, advise one strongly against giving anything to beggars. They enjoy a reputation similar to that in Britain of the social security scrounger. One is encouraged to regard them as thoroughly undeserving and probably rather rich. It is put about that they mutilate themselves on purpose in order to attract sympathy. But I don't believe that people cut off both their legs for fun. And if it is the case, as it appears to be, that they are not among the lowest earners in the city, this can only mean that a lot of Indians feel genuine pity for them. In the slums of Calcutta, which are inhabited by one quarter of the city's 10 million people, the average wage is 107 rupees (about £7) a month. In one slum I visited, however, I was told that the beggars earned 10 to 12 rupees a day (about £22 a month).

16 July, 1983

Patrick Leigh Fermor

DIALOGUE IN BALI

Three languages are in use in the island, an arcane priestly tongue which is unknown to the laity, the language of the High Caste and the language of the Low Caste. The High Caste language is high-flown, elaborate, and full of compliments, the Low Caste familiar and colloquial. But it is beneath the dignity of a high-caste Balinese to address a low-caste Balinese in anything but the lower-caste language and when a Balinese of the lower caste addresses a high-caste Balinese, decorum enjoins the exalted idiom of the higher. As it is not etiquette for the lower caste to look at the other directly, he fixes his glance no higher than his interlocutor's leg

below the knee, and addresses his words to it. Here is a transposition of
this unique conversational punctilio.

*Scene: a bamboo-grove by the sea at sunset. Enter, right, a high-caste and,
left, a low-cast Balinese.*

High-caste Balinese: 'Ow yer blowin', cock?

Low-caste Balinese: It is indeed gracious of your Legship to deign to
address his servant.

HCB: Not 'alf! 'Ow are all the Missises and the nippers?

LCB: Prosperity, which is both the hand-maid and the guerdon of dili-
gence, encloses the brows of the former like a fragrant wreath, your
Legship, and the artless innocence of the latter bespeaks a burgeoning
virtue which kindles a glow in the breast of their begetters.

HCB: 'Alf a mo, though! One of them little bleeders needs a clip on the
ear. Blow me if 'e wasn't pinchin' mangoes last night from my
backyard! The blinking branch bust and your Young 'Opeful comes
arse over tip in a cow-pat. Proper pickle 'e looked. Larf – I nearly split
meself! But I'd tan 'is bum for 'im.

LCB: Retribution, your Legship, shall visit iniquity with tribulation.

HCB: That's the ticket. You give the little perisher wot for. 'Ow's the rice
comin' on?

LCB: Ripe rice-grains, your Legship, are as pearls unto the people and a
moiety thereof as the treasures of the deep.

HCB: 'Ear, 'Ear! But 'ow's it doin'?

LCB: The green ear betokens a white granary.

HCB: Go on? So we're sittin' pretty, like?

LCB: The burning eye of the sun may shrivel the young stalk, your
Legship, and the pinions of aspiration, moulting beneath its parching
glance, fling our fledgling hopes prostrate in the paddy-field.

HCB: (gloomily) Then we'd be up the creek.

LCB: Even so. But may the Merciful Ones on high cast a ray of partiality
on your Legship and on his servant.

HCB: Keep our fingers crossed, like? 'Ere! Crikey! It's time for me nosh! I
won't 'alf catch it from my better 'alves if I show up late for me evenin'
blow-out! So I'll be sayin' so long.

LCB: May digestion entwine satiety with a garland of poppies!

HCB: Mine's something chronic.

LCB: Half a spoonful of brine from the ocean, your Legship, scourges
wind from the abdomen and smòoths the puckered brow.

HCB: Go on? I'll 'ave a bash at it, blow me if I don't! Well, I'll be shoving
off. All the best, cock, and toodle-oo.

LCB: Heaven shower its lustre on your Legship! May it endow his thews with the strength of the trunk of Ganesh and scatter the path of his spouses with frangipani and marigolds. May it grant them the benison of fecundity, and to his concubines, eyelids like the violet, cheeks like the lotus-petal, waists as sinuous as Naga, hips like water-melons in the season of water-melons and embraces as tender as those of the holy Apsaras. Let the fruit of his loins be manifold as the stems of the banyan-tree, straight as the arrow of Arjuna, swift as Garuda – that noble bird! – valiant as Rama, nimble as Hanuman and as tuneful upon the flute as the Lord Krishna himself!

HCB: Thanks, cock. Keep smiling!

(*Exeunt on opposite sides*)

As the sun disappears beyond the volcano, the moon rises beyond Lombok, Borneo and the Wallace line.

17 December, 1987

A. M. Daniels

THE LAND OF THE FAT

Landing in Nauru after having flown over seemingly endless miles of glistening blue Pacific, one feels like congratulating the pilot for having found so small an island in so vast an expanse. Nauru has an area of only eight square miles, and would be of no significance whatever to the rest of the world were it not for one rather curious circumstance: it has the highest per capita income of the world.

The basis of its wealth is fossilised bird droppings, now valuable phosphate rock, which have been deposited over millions of years to a depth in some places of 80 feet. Phosphate has been mined in Nauru since the turn of the century, but only since 1968, when it gained its independence from Australia, has Nauru controlled its own enormous wealth.

The Nauruans do not do much of the mining themselves, of course. They import helots from other parts of the Pacific to do it for them, who live in a segregated area called *the Location*. Like all migrant labourers they are kept in a state of insecurity by an all-powerful and capricious employer. The Nauruans work, if they wish to work at all, for the government.

By no means all Nauruans are rich, however. Land is held privately, and only families with holdings in the area mined since independence (about a fifth of the population) have received royalties of up to $150,000 an acre. But every Nauruan receives a pension from the government, together with free housing and electricity. Imported goods are free of duty (whisky, for example, costs $3 a bottle), so work is a luxury rather than a necessity.

The social effects of this easy money have been precisely what moralists might have predicted. Deprived of any foreseeable need to earn a living, children do not see the point of education, and refuse to learn at school. Boredom and disgruntlement are rife. Delinquency and drunkenness have become almost universal among the very young. (The Co-operative Store, incidentally, carried a large supply of Château d'Yquem to cater simultaneously to the Nauruan taste for sweet things and alcohol.) But above all, the Nauruans indulge in their national pastime: eating.

On average, the Nauruans consume twice as much as Canadian lumberjacks at the height of winter. Their culinary tastes have not undergone refinement since their accession to wealth, their favourite meal still being a mountain of glutinous boiled rice crowned with a large tin of Australian corned beef. People eat this up to six times a day. They wash it down with a carton of 24 tins of soft drink or beer.

It is hardly surprising, then, that Nauruans are rather fat. When they travel by air, they frequently have to take two seats. More than half of them are diabetic, and their life expectancy is about 50, not greater than that of impoverished Pacific islanders. The dangers of their way of life are perfectly well understood by them, but they cannot conceive of an alternative.

Nauruans certainly do not use their wealth to beautify their homes. It is impossible to tell from the outside whether the owner is a millionaire or a mere pensioner. Rusting shells of cars, piles of empty beer cans, flowering hibiscus bushes, pigs and chickens seem to surround all the houses.

Waste in Nauru makes California look parsimonious by comparison. A man ordered a Ferrari, but discovered when it arrived that he was far too fat to drive it, so it now sits abandoned outside his house. Another man, having bought a new car, was angered when it ran out of petrol. He and a friend set it alight, and next day bought another one. In order to impress a visitor with his wealth, one Nauruan used $20 notes as lavatory paper.

The supply of phosphate rock is not limitless, however. Within about ten years it will have been mined out, and Nauru will be left an inhospitable moonscape of bare coral pinnacles. Very few Nauruans individually have prepared for this apocalyptic future, but the government, led by President Hammer de Roburt, who is a close friend of President Marcos, is negotiating the purchase of an island in the Philippines to which the Nauruans will be able to move when Nauru is utterly uninhabitable.

The government is completely dominated by the President who, by force of personality combined with the prevailing Nauruan inertia, has become virtual dictator of the island. He has been President almost continuously since the island became independent, and few decisions are made without his approval. He spends as much time out of the country as in it, and each of his many departures and arrivals is marked by a ceremony at the airport.

Nauru has very considerable overseas investments (including the largest office building in Melbourne, known locally as Birdshit Tower) but the exact state of Nauru's finances is not known except to the President, who does not believe it is in the interest of Nauru to reveal it.

But the most conspicuous of Nauru's investments is undoubtedly its airline, Air Nauru. A nation of 4,000 people has a fleet of five passenger jets, which operate at a loss generally thought to be staggering (the airline does not publish accounts) on routes unlikely ever to be profitable. Planes are sent 5,000 miles with two passengers. They have also been used as private taxis for the President, leaving would-be passengers stranded for days.

The state of Nauru's finances is the most important question facing the country, for when the phosphate runs out the Nauruans will have to live on investment income alone. The life of joyless ease to which they have become accustomed will not readily be exchanged for something more satisfying or productive. Unless they undergo a change of heart, they are destined to remain parasites for ever.

Nauru has a singularly unfortunate history. It was first colonised by the Germans, who were cruel and harsh. After the First War it was administered by the Australians, who were not too particular about their method of exploiting it. During the Second War it was occupied by the Japanese, who deported the Nauruans to Truk in the Carolines, where they allowed half of them to die of starvation. But its greatest misfortune of all has been, paradoxically, its great good fortune.

17 December, 1983

Richard West

SHANGHAI'D

Shanghai

The old Shanghai of the Twenties and Thirties has always been, after St Petersburg, the city I most wanted to visit except in the sense that, like most addicts of cheap fiction and Hollywood films, I have countless times been to Shanghai in imagination. I am familiar with those murky alleys where opium smugglers clash with White Russian princes, and secret agents with indescribably evil faces are found with daggers of an intricate oriental design stuck in their backs. I must long ago have seen *The Shanghai Gesture*, complete with gambling den, brothel and sad policeman, where Gene Tierney, the prostitute, says: 'It has a ghastly familiarity, like a half-forgotten dream. Anything could happen here.'

I have quite recently seen again *Shanghai Express*, where Marlene Dietrich, asked if she has a husband, drawls the immortal line: 'It took more than one man to change my name to Shanghai Lily.' I know such buildings on the Bund as the Cathay Hotel, where Noel Coward wrote *Private Lives*, and the British Club, with the longest bar in the world. 'The long bar's like the Café de Paris. Stay there long enough and you'll meet everybody you know,' says Major Brabazon-Biggar, a Far East bore in one of the P. G. Wodehouse books, who goes on to tell a hilarious story, a pastiche of Somerset Maugham, of being approached at the long bar by a dishevelled Englishman, gone to the bad through drink, drugs and native women. Of course he turns out to be Sycamore, who went to the old school and once made 146 before going out to a googly.

Having just witnessed what had been done to Peking, I sadly imagined that every building and artefact of the old Shanghai would have disappeared along with the gangsters, the whores and the White Russians – thousands of whom were returned to Russia in 1949 and there shot or enslaved in the Siberian Arctic. But I found to my surprise and delight that modern Shanghai has scarcely changed, physically, from the Shanghai of my daydreams, and may not have altered much in its character. If appointment is the opposite of disappointment, Shanghai is the biggest appointment in my travels.

In two days of incessant walking, with taxi drives to the outer suburbs,

I was amazed to find so much of the old city not only still there but well-maintained. In the French Quarter you pass under a canopy of leaves from the plane trees lining the street, past villas, apartment blocks, shops and restaurants in good condition. I thought at first that Shanghai must be one of those 'Potemkin villages' that were built to deceive the Empress of Russia on tours of the provinces – but you cannot build a Potemkin village of ten million people and then let strangers wander about it at will.

The Chinese city, which once was an enclave of crime, wretchedness and depravity in the European Quarter, is still a warren of alleys but now is devoted to honest trade rather than brothels, grog shops and opium dens. The municipality employs wardens with arm-bands and loudspeakers to regulate the pedestrian traffic of shoppers for every kind of food, and goods as various as TV sets and fish-hooks.

The British Club is now a hotel for Chinese only, and little remains of its ancient grandeur except for the 'Doulton and Co, Lambeth and London' porcelain in the gents and, yes, the long bar, in what is now the restaurant. The physical bar has been cut in three and you cannot sit at it, but we were able to pose there for photographs after our lunch. The shrimps and beef in oyster and chicken legs, with Tsing Tao beer, cost just over a pound a head and tasted better than what I should guess was the old club fare of overcooked beef and sour claret. The Cathay Hotel still flourishes under the name of the Peace Hotel. In its coffee-house each evening, a band, composed mainly of saxophones, blares out American hits from the Thirties and Forties like 'Time Goes By', 'Chattanooga Choo-Choo' and 'Melancholy Baby', still further giving one the sense of having strayed into an ancient Hollywood movie about Shanghai.

The bookshop of the Peace Hotel has most of my own favourites, from *Scoop* to *Heart of Darkness*, as well as Pan Ling's *In Search of Old Shanghai*, the wisest and most enjoyable book of its kind I have ever read. That would merit two articles just to itself. Among other things, Miss Ling observes that the old restaurants have now reappeared, most of them under their former names, to satisfy the hunger for spiced beans, Nanxiang steamed buns and fermented glutinous rice soup. She says that the Shanghai dialect has survived the efforts to replace it with Peking speech: 'Nor have the slangy expressions thrown up by the preoccupations of the old society – gambling, whoring, European-bashing and ripping people off – been totally blotted out by . . . a socialist and straitlaced society.' She reminds us that 'Shanghai's vocation has not been government, or art or religion – it has been money-making.'

It still is. One of the weirdest buildings in Shanghai is the yellow and brown mock-Tudor mansion, with lawns, cedars, cypresses and Surrey pines, that once belonged to the Sassoon family. So rich were the

Sassoons in their time that their name was used by the Chinese for all the
Jews, as in the story recounted by Evelyn Waugh of a Chinese servant
explaining Good Friday to a friend: 'Number one Sassoon gets nailed to a
cross and other Sassoons get angry.'

When Shanghai fell to the Communists in May 1949, the last of the
Shanghai Sassoons, who had got his money out, said in New York: 'Well,
there it is, I gave up India and China gave up me.' The stock-broker Tudor
house survived the Cultural Revolution and indeed was used as the HQ
and residence of the Maoist Gang of Four. When the gang was disgraced
and jailed, the mansion was leased to the British Petroleum Company,
whose representatives, when I called there, had much enjoyed their stay,
although they were moving to Canton.

The Chinese Central Committee has just published its plan for drastic
liberalisation of trade and industry and the encouragement of the profit
motive: Shanghai appears to have jumped the gun. The shops in Nanking
Road are packed with merchandise and shoppers, like Oxford Street in
the sales – it is a sight inconceivable in the Soviet Union or one of its
colonies such as Poland, whose wretched people – those not in the boss
class – must queue for hours each week, even for the essentials of life.
The factories of Shanghai make this the largest industrial city in China.
An ever-increasing number of firms have some sort of link with foreigners, especially the 'overseas Chinese', who enjoy privileged status.

On my first day in Shanghai I was approached by a young man who told
me in English that he was an economics graduate, a worker who wanted
to be a businessman. All he needed, he said, was a foreign partner who
could provide the capital. Delighted to find that Shanghai had restored
one of its ancient professions, that of the con man, I asked him what sort
of business he had in mind. 'Import-export,' he said. 'We would sell tea
from sources I have in the provinces, and in return we would import pho-
tographic equipment. We could sell it legally in the shops. The government encourages private enterprise because the state system doesn't
work. And foreigners get a tax concession.' Regretfully, I told him I had
no capital – or, as the Irish say, on the contrary.

An Englishman in our group made the comparison between Shanghai
and Liverpool. Both were great ports, centres of shipbuilding, with splendid edifices of banking, insurance and commerce, world-famous hotels,
racecourses and sleazy redlight districts. Both have Anglican cathedrals
built by the architect Scott. Shanghai had a large European quarter –
Liverpool had a large Chinatown.

Who would have thought in 1949 that Shanghai would now be pros-
pering, while Liverpool has deteriorated into a vast slum of misery, crime
and idleness, its port almost defunct, its shipyards and factories closed by

the trade unions, its old buildings decayed or knocked down, its population addicted to drugs and race riots, or shoved into still more horrible new towns like Kirkby?

In Shanghai, in one year in the Thirties, 20,000 people were picked up dead in the streets. Liverpool MPs such as Mr Heffer were outraged when Norman Tebbit, the Cabinet minister, suggested that people who wanted a job should 'hop on a bike'. Almost the whole population of Shanghai hops on a bike to go to work.

The Roman Catholic Archbishop of Liverpool Derek Worlock and his friend the Anglican Bishop David Sheppard, who joined in the protest over the bikes, and often support the fashionable left-wing causes at home and abroad, should study the churches in Shanghai. The Scott cathedral is closed. The Jesuit church of St Ignatius is open and well kept. I noticed that the Stations of the Cross are here represented by sacred paintings and not, as in Liverpool's Catholic cathedral, by photographs of Vietnam war victims and 'underprivileged kids'. The garden is bright with roses, chrysanthemums, salvias and Michaelmas daisies, in contrast to Liverpool's Catholic cathedral, surrounded by weeds and empty beer bottles.

All that was lacking at St Ignatius's was any sign of a priest. The doorman was evasive. Some English language students next door lost all their fluency when taxed with this matter. An aged Catholic fled when some bystanders started to listen in to our conversation. This may be one of the 'national churches' that have renounced allegiance to the Pope. Most of the real priests and their congregations were among the 30 million or so Chinese who were murdered shortly after the 'liberation' or during the Cultural Revolution, when Red Guards destroyed two of the spires of St Ignatius. According to Amnesty International, the Roman Catholic Archbishop of Shanghai, the 84-year-old Ignatius Pinmei, has been in prison for 30 years. Ten Roman Catholic priests and monks in Shanghai were jailed in November 1981, and the 76-year-old Bishop Peter Joseph Fan Xueyan, who had been in prison 15 years, was given a further ten-year sentence. Perhaps these men did not have the enlightened, left-wing views of the clergy in Liverpool.

3 November, 1984

Nicholas Coleridge

SRI LANKAN IMPRISONMENT

Since I have never been inside a British jail, it is difficult to draw comparisons with a Sri Lankan one. But for hilarious bedlam I do not suppose that anywhere begins to match Welikade Prison, Colombo, where I have just spent ten days under suspicion of being an international terrorist and Communist agitator. Welikade Jail (or 'lock-up' in local parlance) is a vast and austere compound containing 1,500 prisoners on the outskirts of Colombo. Attached to it is a prison hospital, designed like a series of cricket pavilions, and it was here that I and my two journalist companions were remanded. This was regarded as a 'luxury' billet, though luxury is relative; it allowed us access to a draughts board with 17 of its 24 pieces extant.

Since we had not been charged with anything, beyond being journalists reporting the Tamil war, we relied heavily on the local press for information. The quality newspaper in Sri Lanka is the Colombo *Daily News*: a curious publication, partly written in Edwardian English, rich in conjunctions, and partly in pidgin. The *Daily News* was very excited by our predicament and revelled in rumour. It was amusing, though eerie, to read that 'Nicholas David Coleridge, a Briton, is known to have been trained in Moscow'; the following day he had developed Palestinian connections: a reference, I deduced, to my first book being published by Naim Attallah, the Palestinian entrepreneur of Poland Street. Later in the week, for no good reason, Nicholas David Coleridge was transformed by the press into Roger Coleridge, and then Roger Coleman, to the bemusement of readers.

For the new boy in a Sri Lankan jail the first task is to establish which are one's fellow prisoners and which are the guards. Both dress alike and stare in a half-witted manner when you pass by. Several times I was praising the beautiful Sri Lankan climate, with intent to subvert a prison officer, only to discover this was a double murderer. Conversely one would be swapping a little facetious badinage about conditions, only to learn this was the prison governor.

My cell, which was large, was decorated with three pictures: of the

Buddha, Jesus Christ and Miss Sri Lanka 1964. Of the three, Miss Sri Lanka drew the most comment. The double murderer, our tea boy, has plans to seduce her when he is released in 18 years' time. By then Miss Sri Lanka will be aged 61.

When you are checking in at a prison most of your belongings are taken away and meticulously listed in a ledger. Since I do not always unpack to the bottom of my suitcase between holidays, some peculiar items had travelled with me. These included a plastic ice cream spoon from a tub at the Haymarket Theatre, a book of matches from the Caprice restaurant and a *Daily Express* Millionaires Club card. The Millionaires Club card excited particular interest, since it was believed to be an executive credit card, like gold American Express, allowing instant credit of a million pounds. Despite the painstaking inventory of my things, nobody thought to frisk our suit pockets, so we were still in happy possession of 2,000 American dollars. This is a fortune in Sri Lanka. Prison guards earn three dollars a week, so we felt rather like Noël Coward in the opening scenes of *The Italian Job*, strutting about in silk pyjamas in Wormwood Scrubs. The dollars afforded us a constant supply of king coconuts, tinned salmon and Pepsi-Cola. There was great rivalry between the guards for the spent bottles, for the money back on the empties.

Most afternoons we were visited by Sri Lankan CID to help them with their enquiries. With the exception of a fiendishly cunning Assistant Superintendent, Sri Lankan policemen seemed genial but dozy. We were never interviewed by fewer than six of them at a time and all were determined to get their fair share of questions. Our replies were tape-recorded on a cassette which ran out half way through each interrogation. Many of the questions were surreal and rarely followed each other in any logical way. 'How much money have the Tamil Tiger terrorists bribed you?' we would be asked. And then: 'Mr Nicholas, how much does your watch cost at duty-free prices?' (A peculiar trait of Sri Lankan CID was to address me as 'Mr Nicholas' in the manner of a 19th-century housemaid.)

In between these interviews some kind of detective work was going on behind the scenes. One afternoon I was informed that the *Standard*, for whom I had filed a report, had been 'checked up' and found to be a subversive newspaper. Later a copy of the *Daily Telegraph*, which happened to be in my luggage, was also deemed subversive. 'Where did you get this newspaper?' I was asked. 'A newsagent,' I replied. 'Which newsagent?' 'W. H. Smith.' 'Please spell Smith.'

My passport, which is a full one, was regularly fingered. A 1976 package holiday to Russia was thought highly compromising. 'Where did you go in Russia?' 'Moscow and Leningrad.' 'How did you travel?' 'By train.' 'Aha, so you confess you were trained in Russia.'

The tone of these interrogations was volatile. One moment it was self-effacing: 'We are a simple and peaceful nation, Mr Nicholas. Look out of the window, do you see any terrorists?' (From CID headquarters all you could see was sky.) But it could change in seconds: 'Don't you realise that we're at war, Mr Nicholas? There is a state of emergency. We have extraordinary powers. We're fighting for our survival against these terrorists.'

Something that I like about journalism is its limited attention span. The journalist concentrates his mind on a story for a few days or weeks, then forgets most of it as soon as it's filed and moves on to a new article. The Sri Lankan CID do not share my journalistic outlook, and it became rather tiresome, as time went by, to persist in flogging a dead Tamil horse. Even my dexterous demonstration of American break dancing failed to distract them for long.

One of the prison officers was a particularly agreeable chap. His English was perfect and we lent him Agatha Christie novels. Like all senior officers at Welikade he apologised several times a day for our being there at all, and said he did not know what the country was coming to. We, being well mannered prisoners, said: 'Honestly, it doesn't matter at all, don't worry, ten days in your delightful prison is no inconvenience.' Another guard showed us photographs of his father, a civil servant under British rule, who had made the crucial century in an inter-departmental cricket match. In the evening we set up coconut shies, using upturned king coconut shells, and pelted them with rolled-up socks. This event was keenly enjoyed by everyone at Welikade and promises to become an established prison pastime.

One night, on our way back from a particularly abstruse interrogation at police headquarters, we were taken to a Chinese restaurant. This was a peculiar episode. First the road around the restaurant, the Nanking, was cleared of all vehicles and sealed by jeeps and guards brandishing Kalashnikov machine guns. Then the poor waiter, shivering with fright, was escorted outside to take our order through the car window (we were not allowed to leave the back seat). Presently several bowls of shark's fin and crab soup were carried out, having first been dragged for secret messages, followed by Chinese fish and chips. The final scene of this comic meal was the waiter bawling after the jeep as we sped away: 'No tips! Why, oh why, do policemen never leave no tips?'

After ten days in Welikade it was eventually conceded that evidence for our being international terrorists was rather limp, so the airport was indicated instead. An ominous development in Sri Lanka at the moment is an allergy to journalists; two French reporters were being deported on the same flight as us. Nevertheless, despite the daft clowning of the Government, I greatly look forward to returning to Ceylon; it is a delightfully sultry island for a spot of winter sun.

23 February, 1985

Colin Welch

AUSTRALIA'S CHARM, REFINEMENT AND HP SAUCE

'I have greatly enjoyed my first visit to Australia,' the earnest man from *The Times* declared. 'I hope it will not be my last. Meanwhile, I would like to take back some souvenir or memento, something wholly characteristic of, ahem, "down under", which will recall to me and suggest to my wife, unable alas to be with us here, Australia's unique and gracious charm. Now what, Mr Watson, would you suggest?'

More than 30 years ago, it was my first intercontinental freebie. BP had very kindly invited a party of hacks from London to witness the opening of its new refinery at Kwinana, Westralia. At Sydney we were reinforced by antipodean hacks, including Mr Kingston ('King' to his friends, of course) Watson, then editor of the Sydney *Daily Telegraph*. King's humorous face was as wrinkled as a walnut, a bit like a sun-baked Sid James. Long and carefully he pondered the *Times* man's request. At last he spoke: 'What about a bottle of HP sauce?'

His wise counsel came back to me when I read a recent headline, 'Reagan lifts US ban on HP sauce'. A kindly President had noted that the ban had brought 'unanticipated consequences' and 'severe hardships' to 'users' of the sauce, not only Britons but presumably Australians too, whose national symbol King had pronounced it to be. Good on yer, Ron! King's pronouncement was indeed a symbol perhaps of Australia's coming of age, marked by an ability to laugh at herself, as also by a heartening eagerness to absorb and learn from hitherto shunned swarthy Mediterranean immoes: already then pavement cafés proliferated at King's Cross.

Our party was in the charge of a delightfully avuncular BP boffin, his converse liberally spiked with self-parody, lemon juice and Tabasco. Even at Heathrow he had introduced me to a fantastic refinement of U and non-U behaviour. A gorgeous Qantas hostess came with a box of cigarettes. She innocently enquired, 'Do you smoake?' 'Damn cheek, these interrogations,' he burbled as she wiggled off up the aisle. 'What's it matter to her whether we smoke or not? Why doesn't she just offer us a cigarette and have done with it?' True courtesy would have left us free to smoke it, chew it or install it over the ear.

The boffin had been in Abadan during the crisis. Of Dr Mossadeq he took a more jaundiced view than that propounded by Brian Lapping in the *End of Empire* television series. So far from thinking him 'well-connected, incorruptible and dedicated to the principles of liberal democracy', he compared the Doctor unfavourably with hatters, fruitcakes, coots and other symbols of insanity. 'Trouble is, we never bribed them properly. They expect it, you know. The Yanks told us to butter them up, but we were too grand and stuffy. Don't ask them if they drink or smoke – causes offence. Just slip 'em Havanas and the Widow – that's the drill.'

Mr Dick Stokes had flown to Teheran to impress upon Dr Mossadeq the dire consequences of seizing the Abadan refinery. Frustrated, Mr Stokes reported back to the Cabinet: Dr Mossadeq's only response to every threat had been, *'N'importe, n'importe!'* 'Namport, namport,' Mr Attlee broke in : 'a Persian term, I take it?' 'I ask you!' the boffin wailed. 'Rotten school, Haileybury. Hope you weren't there?'

Memories crowd back. At a Perth barbecue I was introduced to a tall, voluptuous girl: 'Shirl, meet Collen, Collen, meet Shirl, and this is Kevven.' Shirl's opening gambit was unexpected, though highly topical in view of her attire. 'When I sit on a wickerwork chair in short shorts, Collen, I get a criss-cross pattern on my bum. Look!' I left her with Kevven and sought advice. Provocative her remark certainly was. Was it meant to be? Was it a 'come-on'? Or was it the fruit of innocent naivety? 'Certainly the last,' my host judged, 'make no mistake. Just take the conversation straight on from there.' 'Another sort of damn cheek,' the boffin mused. I returned, disappointed.

We were driven in a Holden limousine to a nature park. The driver stopped abruptly and pointed: 'a kookaburra!' There it sat in solemn silence on a nearby branch about six feet off the ground. *The Times* and the *Economist* conscientiously tiptoed across and stopped beneath it, ears cocked attentively, as if expecting delicate flute-like tweets, trills and melodies and eager not to miss a limpid note. King, familiar with the bird's utterances, stayed in the car, surveying the music lovers with a saurian eye. 'Look at those two drongoes. If that baastard issues a statement, it's like an engine whistle. You can hear it five miles off.' Taciturn as Coolidge, the bird had no message for the nation.

Two wild New Zealanders left Perth early. We took a bottle of Corio dry gin to the airport to soothe the pain of parting. Farewells were effusive and boisterous, with much back-slapping and embracing, culminating in the wilder of the two snatching the gin with a triumphant guffaw and charging off zigzag across the tarmac like an All Black wing three-quarter. We only gave up the chase when, appalled, we saw the thief's head pass unscathed between the revolving blades of the propeller.

Fate brought us all together in Sydney – the New Zealanders, a luxuriant Australian who'd served in the Brigade, or so he said ('No, not the fire brigade, Collen, the f——ing Grenadiers'), a couple of nurses. Drinking hours in Sydney were then restricted, so we adjourned to my bedroom for room service. At about three in the morning Peter Kirk, not yet an MP, insisted on ringing up his (I think) godfather, E. W. Swanton, in Brisbane. 'He'll never forgive me if I don't.' 'He'll never forgive you if you do' – but the genial old boy did. He took it well.

Waking hesitantly and with forebodings the next morning, I found myself lying stark naked on the bed-cover. A 'don't disturb' card had been thoughtfully hung on a – well – convenient projection. I looked around with mounting horror. Debris of last night's knees-up: only to be expected. Less reassuring a cup of cold tea, white-filmed, beside the bed, and a huge breakfast congealing on a tray; a suit back from the cleaners hung on the door hook; on the stool a parcel of clean shirts; on the floor, the day's *Sydney Morning Herald*. My shame must have been witnessed by half the staff (and who knew who else besides? The *nurses*? Well, at least they must have seen it all before) of a hotel so respectable that it couldn't tolerate shirt-sleeves at 100 in the shade!

Yes, yes, but what about the refinery? Ah, the refinery . . . Did I ever get to it? I dutifully wrote an article for the *Daily Telegraph*, but lavish press kits may have sufficed for that. Memory is a perverse sieve, retaining curious trifles, allowing to escape what is 'important' and 'serious'. Enthusiastic Israeli government press officers showed me on a later trip a potash works. What do I recall of that save that it was at Sodom?

15 June, 1985

Richard Bassett

TIBET'S BARBARIC CONQUERORS

Lhasa

A crowd of hundreds gathers in front of the Jo-kang temple. For once they are not prostrating themselves in front of their cathedral. Instead they form a crowded human corridor several rows deep stretching from the Jo-kang to the end of the square 100 yards away. As they attempt to narrow the gap between them, furious bald monks race up and down the space between whipping them back with the tattered ends of their heavy claret-coloured robes. From the golden roof of the temple, a primitive and slightly sinister noise is blasted from long horns by more yellow-hatted monks. From almost everywhere rises the unforgettable asphyxiating smell of rancid butter.

Most of the crowd sitting and standing in the sun are Tibetans. Prayer-wheels, beads, handsome but filthy grinning faces dressed in green headscarves or black woollen coats. Many are Khambas, traditionally fond of a roughhouse, who in the 1960s shattered the myth that the Tibetans were not a warlike race by massacring several Chinese garrisons. Their jet-black hair is trussed up in black or red strings of cotton and as a score of Mao-coated Chinese rush up to help keep the crowds apart, they easily push these sullen midgets aside.

At the far end of the square, from a white car, alights the rotund bespectacled figure of His Celestial Holiness, the 10th Panchen Lama. As he makes for the temple, he is forced to run a gauntlet of honorific *kushna la* greetings as a hail of white scarves descends about him. Eventually dragged by harassed Chinese soldiers, His Holiness finally makes it to the temple whose vast wooden doors slam shut in front of the hysterical mob. For the Tibetans, returning to their prostrations and twirling prayer-wheels, this was the climax of China's sophisticated 20th anniversary celebrations of the founding of the 'autonomous region of Tibet'.

It was also a reminder that despite years of communist rule, the Tibetans' traditional religious fervour had in no way been diminished. The 10th Panchen Lama is very much second best for the Tibetans, most of whom revere their god-king, the 14th Dalai Lama who has lived in exile since Chinese troops attempted to spirit him away in 1959. But despite the widespread feeling that the Panchen Lama is too pro-Chinese – he spends much of his time in Peking and toes that city's line on the Tibetan question – he is the closest Tibetans living in Lhasa are likely ever to come to their god-king.

Also, of all the events organised for the celebrations, this alone had a distinctly spiritual character, free from the heavily armed motor-cycle outriders and ranks of machine-gun-toting Chinese troops. Earlier the same morning, a mass rally had been held during which several Chinese politicians had extolled to a bewildered Tibetan audience confused by their refined mandarin rhetoric the virtues of Chinese rule. The Tibetans who attended this rally had been shipped in trucks from all around Lhasa. Those who refused to attend risked fines of 400 yuan. Those who refused to disperse afterwards in the same trucks were warned by the heavily armed troops of a similar punishment.

In the evening, the Tibetans were invited to gaze at that most colourful of Chinese arts, a display of pyrotechnics. Hour after hour the Potala Palace was silhouetted against a barrage of red and green rockets as thousands of fireworks shot up into the sky from what sounded like dustbins. The green-coated Chinese soldiers, if implausible as a fighting force, showed themselves spectacular exponents of this noisy art, lighting the blue touch-paper and scrambling for cover at a speed which would have impressed a Gurkha. The Tibetans, however, not forced to attend this spectacle, preferred to prostrate themselves or remain at home away from the cordite-filled air and fall-out of scraps of cardboard which rained down on pedestrians and cyclists.

The fireworks, like the mass rally in the morning, had been celebrations for the Chinese not the Tibetans. It is perhaps important to stress for those who have only a hazy notion of Tibet the differences between the Tibetans and the Chinese. Tibetans do not look, talk or build like Chinese. They even spit in a different way, their art of silent expectoration being completely unknown to the Chinese.

Since taking over the Tibetan capital by force of arms in 1959, the Chinese have done their best to wipe out Tibet's culture. In the 1960s the Maoists destroyed monasteries, killing hundreds and imprisoning thousands of Tibetans who refused to embrace their Marxist creed.

Today the Chinese acknowledge that this mailed fist approach was 'a mistake'. They are overtly contrite and say they are pouring money into Tibet to restore temples and atone for earlier misdeeds. No longer are their Red Guards eager to test some lama's supernatural powers by making him and countless others walk off the roof of the Sera monastery. Tibetan culture, says Peking, can flourish as Chinese culture under Chinese communist rule, liberated from serfdom, freed from despotism. Thus has marble been fashioned from straw.

True, the days when to speak Tibetan to a Chinese official was enough to merit a spell in a concentration camp are over, but Peking's policy, if not her methods, remains the same: to convince the Tibetans that they are first and foremost Chinese. To achieve this, all the tactics of assimilation familiar to observers of Romanisation practised by the Ceausescu regime in Transylvania are relentlessly employed. There are already 500,000 Chinese in Lhasa encouraged to marry and 'convert' Tibetan women. Prayer stones which once proclaimed the ubiquitous *om mani padme hung* still form paving stones in Chinese barracks. Where they once stood, alien characters command 'Forward with the Chinese Party'. Nor has this vandalism been confined to Tibetan monuments. At Gyantse, fragments of the tombstones of the 23 British officers who were killed on the Younghusband expedition of 1904 lay strewn around one army barracks-cum-resthouse.

Chinese cinemas, Chinese television – a particularly potent weapon in Tibet – Chinese hotels, customs houses, theatres, all these, if not in the course of construction already, will envelop Lhasa within the next two years, leaving only pockets of the city with any distinctive Tibetan character. Last year, 80,000 Chinese workers were imported into the city. Many Tibetans had to move out of their houses to accommodate them. Their arrival meant that some 80,000 Tibetans employed in construction lost their jobs overnight. Those who resist this rosy Chinese path of improvement can still find themselves marched off at bayonet point to a concentration camp behind the Sera monastery.

As the new buildings go up, old Tibetan architecture comes down, demolished by bulldozers rather than artillery, though during one afternoon before the celebrations it was possible to see and hear howitzers playing upon a distant hillside outside Lhasa. Those buildings which are restored, such as the magnificent Potala Palace, are often given gaudy colours to emphasise any Chinese elements. The old distinctive battered façades, which emphasised the converging verticals, giving the impression of architecture rising like waterfalls from the ground, have been lost.

Even more distressing is the attempt to 'educate' Tibetan youth. On the one hand, this involves an appeal to material instincts through cassette-recorders and televisions, on the other, the barbaric practice of removing children from their families for several years at a Han Chinese school. The Tibetan parents rarely have any say in this and several Tibetan mothers in Lhasa described how they watch their sons day and night in case they, too, disappear. This may be fanciful superstition, but there are few Tibetans between the ages of 15 and 21 on the streets of Lhasa.

In the face of all this, it is perhaps remarkable that the Tibetan culture has managed to survive at all in its homeland. Monasteries which once boasted several thousand monks barely muster today a few hundred. The deserted Sera monastery is a depressing place to visit. The Chinese guide will insist that there are 400 monks there, but one of these '400', asked in Tibetan, gave the more plausible answer of 70. Like many Tibetans, the monks have learnt to live with the Chinese. In the dark silk-strewn chanting-rooms of the temples, they smile at the Chinese soldiers who snap away like tourists, holding their noses as their delicate sense of smell is overwhelmed by the all-pervasive smell of butter-tea.

In their cells, however, they will quickly frown at the mention of the despised *gyanak* (Chinese). Nearly every monk's cell is a shrine to the Dalai Lama. Production of his image even on something as flimsy as the air edition of *The Times* evokes instant reverence. They cannot understand the text of his recent interviews, published last month, but the paper is blessed, touching a dozen heads before taking its place among other photographs of the god-king. The monks believe that the thousands of Chinese troops stationed around Lhasa will one day march away. It is a characteristically optimistic and unrealistic hope. Although it would only take a nod from their god-king for them to rise up and wage guerrilla war in ideal conditions against the intruders, the amount of blood spilt in the process would cripple the Tibetans, for Tibet would stand alone against the Chinese hordes.

Twenty-six years ago, the free world stood and watched a unique culture being crushed by a communist state towards which both Britain and America believed it was in their interests to behave in a manner little short of obsequious co-operation. It is unlikely that the free world will stand by Tibet in the future. Nonetheless it could and should exert some pressure on Peking to improve human rights in Tibet and to insist that Tibetans and their culture are not watered down by the flood of Chinese manpower and propaganda which fills their cities. Only then will the Chinese have any justification in calling Tibet 'an autonomous region'.

14 September, 1985

A. M. Daniels

BANGKOK GIRLS

Bangkok is celebrated for its Buddhas and brothels, not necessarily in that order.

On the aircraft from Rangoon I met an American ambulance salesman who spoke Thai. He had a Thai wife back home whom he had met on a previous trip. South-East Asia was his sales patch. By coincidence, he and I were staying in the same hotel, the Oriental.

'Joseph Conrad and Somerset Maugham stayed there too,' I said.

'Who?'

'Just some famous writers.'

'Oh. The only trouble with the Oriental is they don't allow women – hookers – in there.'

'I don't think that would have troubled Somerset Maugham much.'

My companion, as he now was, had an air of middle-aged frustration about him, though he was only 30. His sandy hair was thinning and receding, and he was running to fat. He had a silky fair moustache which he kept tugging.

As soon as he learnt that I was a doctor he pointed to the left side of his chest, where he thought his heart was. 'I get these pains,' he said. 'Like little stabs. Do you think it's my heart?' I told him it was not his heart. All the same, he should lose weight and give up smoking.

'I know. Maybe I'll do some exercise – jogging. What do you think?' I thought it was most unlikely he would ever take any exercise. After a few minutes' silent rumination he said: 'Maybe I'll get it checked out anyway.'

'What?'

'My heart.'

We reached the hotel. The old Oriental had been dwarfed by a luxurious new block, and reduced to what was now called 'The Writers' Wing'. Inside, it was full of hothouse plants, as though writers were an exotic tropical species in danger of extinction. The ambulance salesman and I were going out on the town together.

'I'll just take a quick shower,' I said.

'No need. Bangkok is full of people who'll give you a shower. In fact,' he added, rubbing his hands together, 'if you're dirty to start with, it takes more time.'

We left the hotel. Before we started on our erotic adventures, however, my companion wanted to find a pharmacy. He had haemorrhoids. 'They're hurting like hell,' he said. 'I want pills, not suppositories.' I was unaware that there were any pills for haemorrhoids.

We found a street pharmacist where every medicament was freely available over the counter, even powerful anti-cancer drugs. These were for when people felt they had a touch of leukaemia. My monopolist professional feelings were outraged. If people could buy any medicine they liked, what need of doctors?

My companion was offered two kinds of pill, both from Germany. The latest thing, said the pharmacist, for whom the latest thing was obviously synonymous with the best. 'Which do you recommend?' my companion asked me. I had seen neither of them before. 'This one,' I said firmly.

His purchase completed, he rubbed his moist hands together and said: 'Let's get ourselves a piece of the action.'

The action he was seeking was about 200 yards away, but he insisted on taking a bus because he hadn't his walking shoes on. The bus was more tightly packed than a tin of sardines, and as soon as we got on we had to prepare to get off, by pushing our way through a dense mass of passengers to the exit door.

'Phew!' he said, mopping his brow after we had alighted. Even the greenhouse heat of the Bangkok night seemed balmy by comparison with the bus. 'Do you realise we didn't pay for that bus ride?' He grinned triumphantly.

The action was down an alleyway of brothels. We entered one of them. It was a narrow, barely lit room with a one-way window through which we could see but not be seen. Behind the window was an amphitheatre, on which sat a hundred naked Thai girls, waiting to be picked by customers like trout in a tank. Businessmen – West Germans mostly – in expensive suits lingered over their choice, leaning on a railing close to the window.

'Jeeze, look at that one,' exclaimed my companion, sweating profusely in spite of the icy air-conditioning. 'She's nice.' He put his elbows into my ribs. 'Don't you agree?' It was difficult to know about whom he was talking. 'The one with big tits!' He pointed frantically.

The businessmen looked at him angrily, as though this were the reading room of a club. My companion's eye was caught by another girl. 'Christ, look at *her*! They must be made of silicon, or something.' I thought he was going to faint, or have an attack of angina. I whispered that I didn't much care for the place. 'You don't fancy any of these girls, huh? I guess they're not really all that great. One or two are not bad. But there are plenty more places in Bangkok.'

He rolled out into the alleyway. I mentioned that the girls had been utterly expressionless. 'You mean you prefer something with a little more personality?'

We went in search of something with a little more personality, down a street of garishly illuminated bars. We entered one of them. Four girls immediately hung round our necks. 'Only two!' shouted my companion, dismissing the others with a practised flick of his hand, as though he were used to fighting off women. The girls sat on our laps. Mine was rather plump for a Thai and my leg went to sleep. I had to ask her to sit on the other.

'She's kinda cute,' said my companion. The sweat glistened through her make-up. Through his translation I learnt that she was a secretary by day, a prostitute by night. She had an illegitimate child. 'The Thais are very relaxed about that kind of thing,' he said, absentmindedly fondling her breasts. 'But they're also very puritanical.' He didn't explain the apparent contradiction further; instead, he said: 'Come on. Let's go someplace else.'

We pushed the girls off our laps. In the street he looked around him like a glutton who cannot decide which chocolate to take from a box. 'By the way,' he said, 'I invited your girl to lunch with you tomorrow at the hotel.'

'What?'

'It's all right. If you don't want to, just don't be there, or tell her to go away. She was very impressed you were staying at the Oriental.'

We spent the next two hours roaming the bars. Once, we entered a homosexual bar, and my companion beat a hasty retreat. Out in the street he karate-chopped the air. 'I'd kill them if any of them came near me!'

In yet another bar, with a girl fawning on his neck, he made a sudden announcement. 'I don't think I'll get laid tonight.'

We decided to have dinner. He said it would be fun if we invited some girls he met on his last visit to come with us.

'We'll just take them out to dinner,' he said. 'Nothing more. Doing something like that sets you up for next time. You take them out to dinner, next time you fuck them free.'

'Really?'

'Sure. Money isn't everything. Sometimes you need finesse.'

But finding them was a problem. They no longer worked in the same bar.

'They never stay in the same place long,' he complained.

'Perhaps they found a better pension scheme elsewhere.'

He looked at me hard. 'We better go check out their homes.'

He led us to a labyrinthine slum of shacks, with whose topography he was admirably conversant. A wooden path between the shacks had been laid directly on to the underlying mud, which seeped through the planks and made the way treacherous. The occasional street lights threw long black shadows. It was late, and we saw the unsuccessful prostitutes walking home in their flimsy dresses, suddenly passing from brilliant light into utter darkness, and back again.

He found the shack for which he was looking. He knocked on the door several times, but there was no answer. Eventually a girl in a translucent gown from a neighbouring shack opened her door and asked us what we wanted. A heated conversation in Thai ensued, and we entered her room. It was five feet wide and eight long. It was impossible to stand without stooping. There was a bed, an electric fan, a radio and a profusion of cosmetics. Hanging on a peg on the door were several tissue-thin dresses. My companion translated.

'She says Silent Blossom' – the girl whom we were seeking – 'is ill, malaria or something. It's only an excuse. She doesn't want to come.' I couldn't blame her. It was late, and even prostitutes need sleep. This girl wouldn't come either.

'She says she's already eaten.'

'Most people have.'

'That's not the point.'

He tried once more to persuade her to accompany us, but to no avail. We left her to go back to bed, but my companion was terribly angry. 'It's an insult,' he said. 'They insulted us!'

'It's very late,' I said, trying to calm him. 'And one of them was ill.'

'Ill! Ha! Goddamn bitches! I'm never going to see them again.'

We had dinner in a cheap café which was about to close for the night, and returned to our hotel. My companion was leaving for Seoul early next morning; in the afternoon, I was leaving for Cairo.

He spotted a woman – a hooker – in the entrance lobby. 'I thought they weren't allowed in here,' he said. 'I wish I'd known.'

We shook hands in the lift. His hands were drier now. 'Let me know how your lunch date goes,' he said, getting out. How could I? I didn't know his name, let alone his address.

18 January, 1986

Colin Thubron

FLYING TO CHINA

After the short night, the sun rose upon a country of such desolate strangeness that the woman sitting beside me leaned forward with her hands tensed over her stomach and let out a constricted 'Ohhh!' For three hours we sat craning at the aeroplane window while the snow-peaks of the Karakoram and the western Himalaya glimmered and died among camel-coloured mountains, the mountains merged into hills, and the hills burrowed at last into the Taklimakan Depression, the deepest waterless region on earth. For a while to the north the blades of the Tian Shan range erupted from cushions of cloud, turned pink and harmless by the climbing sun. Then these too vanished, and we were flying along the southern fringes of Mongolia and the Gobi desert. And still, in this country of a quarter of mankind, we saw no sign of life.

Her nation's vastness seemed slightly to have appalled the woman. She said: 'Are you travelling *alone?*'

She was young, conventionally pretty. Only her stained teeth suggested some history poorer than her dress. She wondered where I was going in China, and – covertly – why.

But I could scarcely answer why. The opening-up of China had stirred me unbearably. It was like discovering a new room in a house in which you'd lived all your life. Five years ago the country had been almost inaccessible. Today nearly the whole land could be penetrated by a traveller going alone. More than two hundred and fifty different regions and cities had fallen suddenly open, and the traffic of trains, boats and buses between them offered ways of vanishing into the wilds. I dreamed of criss-crossing classical China (no Tibet, no Manchuria) almost at random, of penetrating the tribal regions abutting Burma along the Mekong river, of reaching the eastern Himalaya and following the Great Wall to its end in the far north-west.

But to the woman I only said, a little ashamed (since no Chinese could see so much of her country): 'I want to visit Peking and Shanghai, and maybe I'll go up the Yangtse, then to Canton and . . .'

She smiled her set smile. Perhaps she was wondering what the foreigner could ever understand of her nation – this Westerner with his boorish rucksack (I'd dropped it on her feet) and his failure to travel in a group. What could he ever learn?

Even in childhood – the time of intense, isolated images – my ideas of China had been contradictory and distorted. Its colours then were cold and subtle. It lay embalmed in distance and exotic etiquette. Chinese atrocities were chattered about at my prep school, during the Korean War. 'Have you heard the latest Chinese torture?' my classmates would demand, before twisting somebody's arm or neck in a novel direction. The Chinese, after all, were stunted and yellow and looked alike. Their multitudinous numbers lent them anonymity. They weren't quite human. Yet for me their landscape resolved into a mist of waterfalls and twisted pines – the Shangri-la of the scroll-paintings – and the idea of a Chinaman harboured a paradoxical element of the ridiculous (something to do with pigtails and The Nutcracker Suite, I think). In any case, China was too distant to be threatening. It was – and remained – a luminous puzzle.

People's images of countries are rich in such buried sediment, which goes on haunting long after experience or common sense has diluted it. And by now – as we floated above the wrung-out steppes of the Gobi – other strata had overlaid the first. In the anarchy of the Cultural Revolution, between 1966 and 1976, the Chinese people had not merely been terrorised from above but had themselves – tens of millions of them – become the instruments of their own torture. The land had sunk into a peculiar horror. A million were killed; some 30 million more were brutally persecuted, and unknown millions starved to death. Yet it was less the numbers which appalled than the refinements of cruelty practised – in one province alone 75 different methods of torture were instituted – and I never thought of the country now without being dogged by a tragic question mark.

The woman was rummaging in her handbag. In the seats behind us a conclave of Peking businessmen sprawled, their shirt-collars open, their eyes closed. I was seized by the foolish idea that each one of them was withholding some secret from me – some simple, perfect illumination. Because that is the foreigner's obsession in this country. At every moment, round every corner, the question 'Who are they?' erupts and nags. How could they be so led? How could they do what they had done? And had they ever changed – this people of exquisite poetry and refined brush-strokes, and pitilessness? A billion uncomprehended people.

Beneath us now, where the last hills tilted south-eastward out of Inner Mongolia into the huge alluvial basin of the Yellow River, I could see the divide between plateau and plain, agricultural hardship and sufficiency, drawn vertically down the earth's atlas with the precision of a pencil-line. To the west brown, to the east green.

Within half an hour we would be landing in Peking, and as if these last airborne minutes might liberate us from inhibitions I started talking with the woman about the Cultural Revolution. She turned quizzically to me and asked: 'What do you think of Mao Tse-tung in the West?' I said we thought him a remarkable leader, but inhumane. She said coldly: 'Yes. He made mistakes.'

Mistakes! He had caused more than 20 million deaths. Sometimes he had acted and talked about people as if they were mere disposable counters on an ideological gameboard. And she talked of mistakes! It was how the Russians spoke of Stalin. I said tightly – I felt this might be my last (and first) chance to vent anger in China: 'Mistakes! All that suffering inflicted on your people! How can you forgive that?' Then I added: 'I think he became a monster.'

She went quiet and stared somewhere beyond me. The fact did not seem to have occurred to her before. Then she said simply: 'Yes.'

For some reason I felt ashamed. Whatever she meant by her 'Yes', its tone – distant, as if admitting something irrelevant – signalled that I did not understand. She fastened her seat-belt. I said: 'Of course it's hard for us in the West to imagine . . .'

Us in the West. We must seem outlandish, I thought, with our garish self-centredness, our coarse opulence, our sentimentality. Somebody had told me that the Chinese found our big feet and noses preposterous, and that to them we smelt. The next moment I had asked the woman penitently: 'Do we smell?'

Her fragile face smiled back at me. 'Yes, of course.'

I baulked. 'Very much?'

'Oh yes. All the time.'

I supposed that her bemused smile was there to cover embarrassment. But I asked finally, edging a little away: 'Do I smell?'

'Yes.'

It was too late to go back now. 'What of?'

'What?'

'What of? What do I smell of?'

'Oh!' She plunged her face into her hands in a sudden paroxysm of giggles. 'Smell. I thought you said smile!' The tinkle and confusion of her laughter sabotaged the next few sentences, then she said: 'Only in the summer. Westerners sweat more than Chinese. That's all, that's all. No, you don't . . . smell. No, really . . . no.'

We were coming in to land.

25 January, 1986

7 NORTH AMERICA

Kenneth Tynan

KEEPING WARM

New York, Winter, 1951

My room overlooks Central Park, and the trees, as I write, are shrieking in silhouette against a smoke-coloured afternoon sky. The temperature outside is well below freezing point. This is my first visit to New York, as the taxi-driver who drove me to the hotel guessed when I tipped him ten cents instead of the now obligatory quarter-dollar. I rectified the mistake, and he wished me well, adding a kindly hope that I should enjoy myself 'viewing duh many jewels wid which this great city is encrusted wid.' A Polish immigrant of 40 years' standing, he said he could remember the time when 'not a boddle of champagne but wasn't bein' imbibed out of some lady's sleeper.' Nowadays, he suggested, this and similar profligacies had vanished from the Avenues.

He may be right. All the same there is prosperity here evident and uproarious enough to deafen English ears. It extends a hand to you; you cannot help noticing it any more than you can help noticing the mica that winks and glitters in the pavements. An office-boy in the Radio Corporation of America earns, they say, more than a departmental chief in the BBC; the President, to fill vacancies in his Cabinet, must seek among the dwindling ranks of men who are willing to work for the slim increment of 15,000 dollars a year; and, to come nearer home, few literary agents will consider disposing of a thousand words of reportage for less than the price of a small car.

There is no denying that New York is a wonderfully accessible city, and one garrulous about its secrets. The people make a point of wearing their hearts pinned to their sleeves, almost as if they were campaign buttons. Socially their arms are open for you, in a gesture of sincere rhetorical hospitality. European drawing-rooms are wont to hold the intruder guilty until, by his deft negotiation of a series of conversational hurdles, he proves his innocence: here, unfairly almost, one is deprived of the fun of this intricate game. To the visitor all doors are unlocked (though I am not sure that all burglar-alarms are disconnected); and more women remove their shoes within the first half-hour of a cocktail party than one would have thought possible. One sighs briefly for the loss of pattern, poise and artifice, and learns to accept in their stead a kind of artless benevolence, a suave chumminess, and a clear understanding on the part of your host that nobody will object if you put your feet up on the *chaise-longue* and take a nap.

The talk at such Christmas gatherings as I attended was more assured and generally better informed than its English counterpart. But one must remember always that in New York there is small-talk and there is large-talk, light conversation and heavy, and few people bother to mix the breeds. As a plausible generalisation I would hazard that Americans discuss serious subjects as if reading from a book held up just behind your right shoulder, and comic subjects as if unable to read at all.

The abiding social rule is based on the importance of feeling and keeping warm. Radio and television reflect it. Its exemplars are the followers of one Norman Brokenshire, who first popularised, twenty years ago, that glowing, ripe, nothing-up-my-sleeve style of commercial oratory which we tend to accept as the Voice of America – the breezy, button-holing, falsely intimate tones which can switch, without a pause or a change of inflection, from the fact that Italy has blown up to the fact that its beer is Rheingold, the dry beer. The first radio-set I turned on hit the note squarely enough: 'And now, folks, this is Vic Marcella, who loves his mother and thinks everybody's swell, signing off until tomorrow night, same time . . .'

A touch of the dial, and I heard this, a tribute from the Voice to a colleague who had just died penniless: 'In a time when friends were hard to come by, he made me feel warm and welcome. For me, as for so many others, it's goodbye, Harry, and God bless you. And now I want to tell you all about the life-span of a seagull. You'll wonder what that has to do with Schlitz beer, but wait a moment: tests show that the time taken to mature the barley that goes to the making of . . .' Warm and welcome: these are key words, together with the phrase about 'All you lovely people who've been so sweet to me,' and the other one: 'Joe's kind of *dear*, don't you think?'

The warmth of the welcome and the degree of dearness or loveliness are naturally intended to bless him that takes; and failure to register a proper delight will quickly stamp you an outcast. I heard one flourishing manufacturer explaining how he had dealt with one of his employees, who had enquired why the staff Christmas party had this year been cancelled. 'I said to him like this,' the manufacturer said: ' "A guy gives parties and so on to such people as he would wish to break bread with, and in whose company he feels welcome." I said, "But I'm afraid, Eddie, that subsequent on the strike last May there ain't above twelve guys in this whole entire plant as I feel in this way about, and in these circumstances what do you expect?" ' He spread his hands. Somebody mentioned that word of this exchange had probably caused alarm throughout the factory. The manufacturer smiled broadly. 'That's what I figured,' he said.

Even today it is indisputable that in Europe – at least, in its literate strata – the rich man, however obsessed by his profits and however independent of the claims of culture, retains a traditional regard for the artist; and this tacit recognition of status, though it frequently indulges and flatters bad artists, always helps to preserve the self-respect of good ones. In New York, by a process of iron financial logic, it has all but disappeared: the artist has no standing at all outside Hollywood or best-sellerdom. The effect on what one might call the unmarketable intelligentsia has been unhealthy, and even shocking. They enrol you, from first acquaintance, as an honorary member in a sort of outlaws' republic. In this furtive freemasonry anyone who writes, paints or sculpts is treated at once as confidant and automatic equal; as a brother in tolerated crime. There is no accepted hierarchy of letters, no yardstick of a writer's skill, no native voice strong enough to command his respectful attention. In the resulting state of affairs there is much fecklessness and more than a seed of chaos.

The reading public, on the other hand, is receiving elaborate attention at the hands of such people as Mrs Yoder, the founder and head of the Yoder Reading Clinic on East 46th Street. By means of psychological tests and ophthalmographs Mrs Yoder teaches her patients, quite blankly, to read more rapidly, or, as she puts it, 'to increase their visual intake with maximum comprehension.' Her pains are bearing some interesting fruit; the clinic already has nearly 200 clients, one of whom is an editor of *Collier's*.

She specialises in people suffering from 'blockages,' and her star pupil is a stammering physicist whose intake, under her care, was increased in ten days from 500 to 1,500 words a minute. During a slack period, when nobody was coming to the school, Mrs Yoder buckled down and put her secretary, a simple girl who did not want to read at all, through *Paradise Lost* in two afternoons with 45 per cent comprehension. (Mrs Yoder, of course, is the judge of what constitutes comprehension.) I infer that she looks askance at those misfits who prefer to read in their own time at their own pace. She may well, however, start a vogue, in which case the whole world of letters will be available for consumption to anyone with a month's vacation and no fixed plans.

There is much in New York this winter about which to be legitimately quizzical, but there is a good deal more to like and admire. The wakefulness of the place, for instance; I find myself sleepless and energetic if my eyes open at dawn. The tang in the dry air forbids shiftlessness. There is vagrant electricity everywhere, and the door-knobs transmit sharp and often painful shocks to the fingers, for New York is the most gigantic lightning conductor in existence, almost per-suading one to hold, with James Thurber's aunt, that electricity leaks. The neon signs on Broadway ripple, glare, rotate, leap, quiver and blow smoke rings at you, instead of (as in Piccadilly) merely blinking; and any-thing from a chiropodist to a television set is instantly obtainable from room service in any good hotel.

And there is, lastly, a unique characteristic of this cubist monolith of a town which strikes me with the same force whenever I cross a traffic-light. Being built in a web of right-angles, with streets for the most part arrow-straight, New York is the only city in the world where, from all cross-roads, you can see four uninterrupted horizons. All roads led to Rome (as Mr Robert Taylor remarks in the new film *Quo Vadis*: 'You can get to Rome *via* Brundisium'), but all roads lead out of New York, and, in spite of the ferocious and oppressive overcrowding, one never quite loses contact with the width, the openness and the space of the unfolded coun-try outside. One feels like a pioneer with a compass, and gets the sensa-tion, possibly illusory, of being one's own master.

11 January, 1952

Ludovic Kennedy

FOREST LAWN

Readers of Mr Evelyn Waugh's *The Loved One* must sometimes have wondered how far his fantastic Californian cemetery of Whispering Glades corresponds to the real thing. The other day I visited the Memo-rial Park of Forest Lawn in the Los Angeles suburb of Glendale. This con-sists of three hundred acres of artificially-cultivated lawns, laid out on the sides of several sloping hills and enclosed by an eight-foot fence. A three-hundred page *Art Guide* says that there are twenty-eight buildings in the park, 20,000 trees and shrubs, eighty miles of underground water-systems and drains and nine miles of paved roads. The organisation employs 750 people. 100,000 persons lie buried here, and the present burial-rate is between six and seven thousand annually.

One enters, fittingly, through the largest wrought-iron gates in the world ('twice as wide and five feet higher than at Buckingham Palace'). To the left is a large pond on which ducks and swans paddle contentedly; to the right an improbable edifice which Mr Lancaster might call California Tudor. This is the administration and mortuary building. It is modelled, says the *Art Guide*, on the historic old manor-house of Compton Wynyates in Warwickshire, and is the only Class A, steel and reinforced concrete mortuary building in Los Angeles. Here are the air-conditioned 'Slumber Rooms' where, before the funeral service, 'Bereaved Ones' take farewell of 'Loved Ones.'

Beyond the administration building the vista of green-turfed hills, spotted with shrubbery, statuary and wreaths, stretches away into the distance. The park is divided into sections bearing such names as 'Vesperland,' 'Brotherly Love,' 'Benediction Slope,' and these vary in price according to situation and size. 'Lullabyland' and 'Babyland' are reserved for children. Some plots have been bought outright, under the 'Before Need' arrangement, both by private individuals and public organisations; the largest is that owned by the Brotherhood of Railroad Trainmen.

As one drives about the park one is struck by the number of dead-white statues which, like seagulls, lie dotted over the grass. There are nearly four hundred of these, having such diverse titles as 'Elevation of the Soul,' 'Little Duck Mother,' 'Rudyard Kipling,' 'Bronco Buster,' 'Joan of Arc,' 'Three Old Pals,' 'Ship Ahoy,' 'George Washington,' 'Baby's Bath,' 'Moses,' 'Baboons,' 'Look, Mommy' and 'John Ruskin.' Beneath each statue is a facsimile in stone of an open book, in which the statue is explained. Under 'Baby's Bath' we read, 'Baby leans forward confidently as his tiny toes touch the water.' Another novel idea is amplifiers concealed in the bushes, relaying sacred music.

The two largest buildings in the park are the Mausoleum-Columbarium and the Hall of the Crucifixion. The former is 'fire-and-earthquake-proof, and contains enough steel and concrete for a seventy-story building.' Here, in such unlikely places as Gardenia Terrace and Daisy Corridor, 'Loved Ones' lie in caskets, or, having been cremated, in urns, set in recesses in the walls. The show-piece here is the Memorial Court of Honour – 'a New-World Westminster Abbey' – where beneath a stained-glass reproduction of Leonardo's 'The Last Supper' are special crypts for 'those famous Americans who have contributed a service to humanity so outstanding that future generations will recognise it as unusual and enduring.' So far only Mr Gutzon Borglum and Mrs Carrie Jacobs-Bond have been found worthy of this honour. The Hall of the Crucifixion contains the 'largest religious painting in the world,' Jan Styka's uninspired *Crucifixion*. It is '195 feet long, 44 feet high, and portrays nearly 1,000 human figures.' Outside the building a huge notice-board, entitled 'The Reason,' explains the ideals and purpose of Forest Lawn. The last sentence reads, 'A dollar at Forest Lawn has greater purchasing-power than anywhere else.'

Finally there are the three 'regularly-dedicated Old World churches'; the Little Church of the Flowers, the Church of the Recessional and the Wee Kirk o' the Heather. The first is a miniature reproduction of the church at Stoke Poges where Gray wrote the 'Elegy,' the second of St Margaret's, Rottingdean, where Rudyard Kipling worshipped, and the third of the church at Glencairn, Dumfriesshire, where Annie Laurie is buried. Marriage, as well as funeral, services are held here; in fact there have been more marriages (38,000) in these churches than in any other church in America.

Outside the Church of the Recessional is a small courtyard. At one end is carved Kipling's 'If'; at the other a plaque says, 'This alcove has been set apart for the youth of America where they may dream their dreams and find a guide for their to-morrow.' It was occupied, when I visited it, by two elderly gentlemen. In the Wee Kirk o' the Heather eight stained-glass windows depict the love-story of Annie Laurie and Douglas of Fingland; and among some odd relics in the vestry is a letter from Sir Harry Lauder saying that the Church is 'a wee bit o' dear auld Scotland in California.' Outside in the shrubbery some heather sprouts sadly. Near-by is a wishing chair, 'built of the very stones which formed part of the original kirk at Glencairn.' Here newly-wed couples hold hands and recite this verse, carved in stone at their feet:

> 'Busk't i' braws, an' a' oor lane,
> We're doupit i' the wissin chair,
> Wilk spaes bien fairn tae ilka ane
> Wha gies a bridal hansel there.'

Forest Lawn is nothing if not thorough. Some minutes after I had passed through the wrought-iron gates and was bowling back towards the world of Jumbo Malts and King-sized Gas Buys, I saw, at the far edge of the park, an Elizabethan cottage. 'Forest Lawn Life Insurance,' said a notice; and an arrow pointed the way in.

3 October, 1952

John Betjeman

CITY AND SUBURBAN

I have been for a month in Cincinnati, Ohio, Queen City of the West, lecturing to breathless sophomores, striding round the maple-studded campus, listening to Louis Armstrong, drinking Bourbon, seeing the old river towns, those Cheltenhams in white wood, visiting Kentucky, the home of horse-worship, seeing the houses of millionaires in the generously laid-out suburbs of Cincinnati, suburbs which stretch for miles over wooded and grassy hills, looking at much really fine modern architecture, glass and stone interpretations of the teahouses of Japan, hearing about the Cincinnati house of the Wurlitzers of cinema organ fame, whose dining-room floor very slowly revolves so that at the beginning of a meal you are facing a wall and by the end of it you are looking out of the window to the winding Ohio, visiting too some of the worst slums I have seen which are mercifully being pulled down – all this I have done on the eastern borders of the Middle West, and 1860 over there seemed as old to me as Perpendicular does here, and Red Indians seemed as long ago as Anglo-Saxons, and what is time anyway? – all this I have done and learned one thing, which all who have been to America know, that the Americans care for their old buildings and look after those which have beauty far more reverently and conservatively than we look after ours.

12 April, 1957

William Golding

THE GLASS DOOR

Hollins, VA

I don't know how far the Alleghenies stretch. They are the small patch of brown, half-way up the map of America on the right-hand side. They consist of parallel ranges, and cover, I suppose, more area than the British Isles. They are not very distinguished as mountains go. They are relatively low, and tree-clad. They have no violence, but abundant charm. How should they not? They pass through Virginia, where charm is laid on so thick you could saw it off in chunks and export it.

Here, in Virginia, is none of the restless energy, the determined modernity, the revolutionary fervour, which in retrospect I see to have characterised my own country. I crossed the Atlantic from the passionate antagonisms of Salisbury traffic on a market day, to the controlled silence of New York in a rush hour. New York traffic flows in a tide too full for sound or foam, and is peaceful by comparison. I thought then that the allegedly horrifying pace of American life was a European invention; and when I got to Virginia I was certain of it. Shout at Virginia, shake it, slap its face, jump on it – Virginia will open one eye, smile vaguely, and go to sleep again.

Our base of operations is Hollins, a rich girls' college, lapped about by fields, and set down in a fold of the Alleghenies. It is ineffably peaceful. Wherever you look, there are hills looped along the skyline. Every circumstance pleases, woos, soothes, and makes comprehension difficult. We arrived during the Indian summer, when every blade of grass, every leaf, was loaded down with cicadas, each of which seemed to be operating a small dentist's drill. Eagles and buzzards floated a thousand feet up in the hot air. Blue jays played in the fields and a delicately built mockingbird balanced on the white fence by our window like a lady with a parasol on a tightrope. On the day of our arrival, a mountain bear – probably walking in his sleep – wandered into the nearby town, saw himself in the glass door of a drug store, panicked, woke up the neighbourhood, was anaesthetised and taken home again.

Hollins sits among its mountains and fields, remembering the eighteenth century. There is a sulphur spring in the grounds, surrounded by a sort of bandstand. In the old days, mammas would take pallid or spotty daughters here to have them cleared up; and the place became a spa. Judging by the pictures of strolling ladies and young bloods driving curricles, it must have been a thriving marriage market – an activity which it has never wholly lost. But in the 1840s the mammas left, social rooms and dormitories were built, and the place became a college.

Hollins, set in its estate of several hundred acres, grew to be an enclave of colonial architecture, all white pillars and porches, grouped round a quadrangle of grass and splendid trees. Lately, a most expensive chapel has taken the place of the old one. A magnificent library building has been added, modern to the last air-conditioned, glass-fronted detail, where the bookstacks have a most generous expanse of working space round them. It is typical of the almost parody southernism of the place that the laboratories are still inadequate. But I have to admit that this choice of what things come first seems splendidly liberal to me, who have suffered from the contrary conception.

Here, then, we work gently, with cushions under us, and plate glass between us and the rest of the world. It is pleasant to contemplate the clock on the administration buildings, by which we regulate our affairs. For the clock is a Virginian clock. The minute hand toils up, lifting the heavy weight of the hour until it totters upright. Then, as if that effort had exhausted the mechanism, the hand falls down to half past three and stays there, collapsed. Long may it continue so to make a mock of the arbitrary, enslaving time-stream! It is as useless and decorative as the carillon which tinkles out Mozart minuets, or hymns, or snatches of old song, from the chapel spire.

Under the trees, along the cemented paths, go the drifts of girls, pathetic and charming, giggling or absorbed, shy of the bearded foreigner behind his plate glass, but courteous to the helplessness of old age. Some of them are northerners, but the most part southern, and some are from the deep South. Like all women students, they are inveterate, comically obsessive note-takers, who hope by this method to avoid the sheer agony of having to think for themselves. Often they have an earnestness before the shrine of this unknown god Education, which seems at odds with their careful make-up and predatory scent. They will propose a scheme of studies which leaves them no time to eat in the middle of the day; but 40 per cent of them leave to get married before they reach the end of their studies. They are intimidating, ingenuous, and delightful; and about the realities of life in the world at large they know absolutely nothing at all.

Yet how should they? Problems are smoothed over, and have the sharp edges blunted for them by space, prosperity, and the American capacity for presenting any situation in a series of ready-made phrases. Even that problem in the South which has made such a stir in the world does not occur here so acutely, since the coloured population in this neighbourhood is only about 10 per cent of the whole. Certainly it exists; and an Englishman, who sees everything at one remove, understands not only the discourtesy of meddling with it, but the difficulty of dealing with the problem precisely because it is *not* acute. Hollins is an enclave, an educated and liberal one. It has preserved almost as an archaeological relic what was inoffensive in the white/black pattern, without perhaps noticing what was going on.

Across the field outside our window is a wood, under Tinker Mountain. In the wood, and partly visible, is a hamlet, a red church with a white, clapboard spire. This is a negro village. In the old days, when girls came to Hollins, they brought their body slaves with them, and sometimes these slaves stayed on. They settled in the hamlet, and now provide the servants for the college. I see them every afternoon, making their dignified way across the field, large, comfortable women in bright clothes, young men who go whistling and with a dancing step. As your eyes grow accustomed to the light of this ancient country, you begin to see that the man who empties your ashcan is coloured; so are the men who sweep your road or work in the power-house, so are the girls who clean or wash or sew, or serve in the canteen. Yet at Hollins, because of its isolation, the relationship is a historical relic. What keeps a girl out of Hollins is not a colour bar but an economic one. It costs more than £1,000 a year to keep a girl there.

For the problem is smoothed over, is down out of sight. The servants, like college servants everywhere, have a long tradition of service. They seem proud of the college and the college is proud of them. Here, embalmed, is a tiny section, a left-over bit of history, which loyalty, education and kindliness have minimised until it has a sort of willow-pattern charm. Yet north of us is an area where the public schools have shut down to avoid integration. South of us, the railway has segregated waiting rooms.

The problem is at once too foreign, too vast, and too muted for my comprehension. At least there is a fund of human goodwill here, which makes the cheap jibes flung from outside seem blunted weapons. Let me do no more, therefore, than record a scene, before the adjustments, the manoeuvres, the shrugs of history have taken it away for ever. I emerged the other day from a book-lined room to the shock of autumn's air on the campus. A dozen coloured men stood by leaf-piles, with brooms and rakes in their hands. Some of them talked, and pushed the leaves about. Others stood motionless, leaning on rakes. They wore bright blue and red, rich brown. They worked, when they worked, with inspired slowness, under the Virginian clock. Silhouetted against the white columns, among thick trunks and clattering leaves, standing among drifts of girls who tinkled here and there with laughter, the dark men seemed a still life. They seemed happy to do this, as the girls seemed happy to do that. Passing among them in the brisker air, some obscure compulsion made me speak to the oldest man of all. He was small and gnarled, dressed in bright blue, his black face startling under a stubble of white hair. I made some inane remark about the weather, which woke him up. He laughed and crowed, and his body jerked. 'Yas-suh!' he said; and we both knew, with one of those psychic flashes that are so often wrong, that we were taking part in some ripe old comedy of the South – 'Yas-suh!'

I reeled on, conscious at last of my solid presence in this mild, foreign land, and struck myself a shattering blow on the invisible glass door of the library. I tottered inside as the carillon tinkled out a minuet by Mozart; and sank into a seat among the girls who were studying the mythological sources of Oedipus and Hamlet, or surveying Spanish Literature, or reading *The Rights of Man*.

For the problem has not yet come consciously to Hollins. Perhaps it never will, but be by-passed. Yet the enclave is not secure. As the town expands, the value of the Hollins land goes up and presently there will be pressure to sell. Moreover, now that America has inherited an ancient mantle, exotic students are coming to Hollins; Indian and Korean, like the business interests pressing south into Virginia, they are a sign of things to come. They are a colourful sight, in the national costume which is their only defence against the ancient intolerance of the countryside. Moreover, an inter-State highway is advancing across the land, majestically shouldering hills out of its way; and like it or not, that road will divide the estate not half a mile from the campus.

Yet for today, preserved, there stands the pattern; the friendly faculty, the girls, the tall, colonial columns, the dark servants and the quiet sun.

24 November, 1961

Peter Ackroyd

LIVING AT THE CHELSEA

New York

The lobby resembles some vast junk-shop; the paintings are coated in a layer of dust, and portable sculptures have been placed in odd corners and then forgotten. A very old lady is sitting on a sofa, staring into her handbag; a young couple are squatting on the floor near her, engaged in what seems to be a difficult conversation; a fat man with a black eye patch wanders past and waits for the lift. He may wait for hours. This is the Chelsea Hotel, perhaps the most famous and certainly once the most notorious hotel in New York. It has been designated a 'national landmark': it cannot be torn down, and survives in the middle of a slow decay. Outside, on West 23rd Street, there are vagrants asking for money and mad people gesticulating into the air – as there always are in this part of New York – but the hotel will remain the same, crumbling a little, filled with what Nelson Algren called 'lonesome monsters'. In a recent novel, survivors of a nuclear attack come and live here – an appropriate setting since the Chelsea has always seemed a refuge for the embattled or the insecure, what New Yorkers like to call 'artists'.

Brendan Behan and Arthur Miller stayed here. It was from here that Dylan Thomas, according to the bronze plaque outside, 'sailed out to die'. Sid Vicious met a similar fate, and he did not have to leave the hotel. It is as if all the desperation were somehow being kept in the family and this quality of strung-out, ironic doominess survives in Andy Warhol's *Chelsea Girls*, a film made in several of its apartments. One of the stars of that film, Viva, still lives here. Stanley Bard, the manager of the hotel, was ecstatic about her; she was, he told me, 'brilliant and beautiful'.

Stanley – as everyone calls him – has several good words for all of his guests. I first saw him by the lift, trying to placate an elderly man who was shouting at him. 'Forty years I've been telling you to get that ceiling fixed, and now some plaster fell down again.' Stanley did a nervous two-step around him, trying to speak. 'Chelsea chicken shit Hotel.' 'Let me take a look at it,' Stanley pleaded. 'I'm not letting you in, Stanley. I am not letting you in that apartment.' They got into the lift together, and I rode up with them. By the time they reached the seventh floor, the man was smiling. Stanley is devoted to his residents, and they know it. 'He's a great artist,' Stanley told me later of the complainant. 'Look at this press-cutting. I think he's a genius.'

His father, David Bard, bought the place in 1940 and Stanley has been around ever since; now his son is studying hotel management. 'They all come to me with their problems,' Stanley was saying. 'Moral problems, financial problems, you name it.' Certainly the Chelsea has a reputation for being one of the least stuffy hotels in New York: strange and difficult creatures live here, and it has coped with people who, like Brendan Behan, have been thrown out of everywhere else. Stanley cannot sit still; he jumped up from his desk and beckoned me into an adjoining office. 'Look at all the books written here.' And there was a row of them in the bookcase – *The Naked Lunch, You Can't Go Home Again*, something by Yevtushenko but, before I could see what it was, Stanley took down an engraving of Shakespeare from the wall. 'Peter Brook gave me this. He always stays here. Do you know Peter?'

The walls of the office were covered with paintings. 'This was done by Paul Hogarth, this is by a German. I'm known all over the world. See this one is signed to me also.' A gentleman known as Milton was sitting in the corner, looking benignly at Stanley. 'Wouldn't you say this was the greatest concentration of creative talent in America?' Stanley asked. Milton smiled and nodded. Now Stanley was on the telephone, talking very quickly. I was just admiring some begrimed cupids, scantily clad in green and gold and disporting themselves across the ceiling, when Stanley grabbed my arm. 'Yes, this used to be a ladies' lounge. But I want to give you something before you leave, Peter.' He handed me two or three yellowing articles. 'Read this, take it away and read it. It's about the hotel.'

The clippings told me all I wanted to know. How the building was erected in 1883 as a number of apartments for artists and how, at 11 storeys, it was the tallest building in New York. Mark Twain and Sarah Bernhardt stayed here. How its somewhat raffish reputation continued throughout the century and how, in the Sixties, it became the haven for the 'beats'. The *jeunesse dorée* have gone, now; one of the Chelsea's residents is 107, and many of the others have lived here for 30 or 40 years. Like all great hotels it reflects the life of its occupants and now it, too, has grown somewhat tired and old with them. But when visitors come, they still want to stay: most of them rent rooms from three months to a year.

I was an exception. I was just passing through. It is cheap, at $45 a night, and although it is not particularly comfortable it has a grim splendour of its own. The ceiling of my room was high, very high, and the size of the room was enhanced by the few articles of furniture within it. At night the radiator murmured like a senile creature talking to itself.

Outside, on the window ledge, there were butts of old cigarettes which seemed to have floated down from the upper floors. Beyond them was the view of an area past its best, a once fashionable street which was now dirty and wasted by noise, giving off that faint sour smell which is characteristic of New York. The corridors of the hotel seemed deserted; they were quiet except, on occasions, for the echo of footsteps on the ornate iron staircase which rises to the top of the building.

Edgar Lee Masters wrote a poem while staying here which, strangely, he called 'The Hotel Chelsea':

> Today will pass as currents of the air
> That veer and die. Tell me how souls can be
> Such flames of suffering and of ecstasy
> That fare as the winds fare.

It is not a good poem (poems written in hotels rarely are) but it captures the tacky grandeur, the comfortable sadness, of this large and lonely place, where the paintings are dirty and the residents old but where they are still, ever hopeful, 'artists' and where Stanley Bard sits and reassures them.

19 February, 1983

Peter Ackroyd

CALIFORNIA DREAMING

Los Angeles

The screen-writer, one of 'the fifteen best in Hollywood', was getting nervous. We were lunching in La Dome, a Hollywood restaurant apparently carved out of green ice-cream, with an Englishman, a 'mini-mogul'. The mini-mogul stared distractedly out of the window whenever talk of the writer's project came up; he jumped up and went out to the lavatory when a 'pilot' was mentioned. The screen-writer began to shake visibly, and took a handful of pills out of his wallet: blue ones, pink ones, yellow ones, enough to kill an elephant. The mini-mogul cackled ecstatically and called to the waiter: 'Can we have a glass of water for Mr Frankenthaler's pills, please?' He was beginning to enjoy himself; I swam into view. 'And so is that all you do, then, sit in London and write *books*?'

'Well, I work for a magazine called *The Spectator* as well.' 'Oh, *The Spectator*. I came out here to get away from all that crap'. The screen-writer began to relax; the mini-mogul was having a good time. 'Come on, let's go shopping. I want to buy you something American.' I now have a silk cowboy shirt, bearing a legend of fearsome obscenity. But I was a late arrival; Nathanael West had discovered Hollywood much earlier, in *The Day of the Locust*: 'It is hard to laugh at the need for beauty and romance, no matter how tasteless, even horrible, the results of that are. But it is easy to sigh. Few things are sadder than the truly monstrous'.

The people who come to Hollywood are pursuing an idea – of money, of power, of 'stardom'. 'Yes,' a young man said to me at a party, 'the people who are interested in the future come to California. We create the fantasies for 98 per cent of the planet'. He was an executive, he was a success, he was 'into psychic technology'. As we spoke, a cabaret magician was performing to disco music; the guests – relatively incurious about each other – stamped and whistled as red and blue doves appeared and disappeared. Even when these people relax, they need to keep their illusions. And the need runs very deep. At a beach club in Santa Monica, two elderly couples were sitting in their cabin; there was a large mirror on the far wall and, with their backs turned away from the beach, through that mirror the four of them looked at the reflection of the sea. It was exotic and it was also chilling, another reminder of why it is that Disneyland is the Holy City of California. Among the plastic trees and the humanoid dogs and ducks, a new world is being created: 'We are now entering Tomorrowland. The world of the future where man's anxieties have passed'. And the ride only cost fifty cents.

In this process, this striving toward illusion, the human personality becomes a blurred thing, something to be instantly transformed – a kind of television image. It has been said that nothing is real in Los Angeles until your agent and your psychiatrist have agreed that it is so. For certain reasons, which remained curious and inexplicable to me, the apartment in which I was staying was also being used as a film set. An artificial moon had been created, by lighting, above my bed. The setting was Boston in the early Sixties; an actor and actress were locked in an embrace. It was like a new 'Ecstasy':

> Our hands were firmly cimented
>   With a fast balme, which thence did spring,
> Our eye-beames twisted, and did thred
>   Our eyes, upon one double string . . .
> . . . And while our soules negotiate there,
>   Wee like sepulchrall statues lay;

> All day, the same our postures were,
> And wee said nothing, all the day.

The silence was intense; the technicians stared; the moon's heat was like a furnace. And then the director came up to the pair, their lips still firmly sealed each to each, and swivelled them around. They remained locked together as the cameras rolled.

In such a context, to look for any ordinary reality would be as absurd as looking for Martin Buber in Disneyland. From the air, all one can see of Los Angeles are the swimming pools – like some blue jigsaw puzzle with the pieces scattered slightly. As Gertrude Stein said of another place, there is no there there. The city has no observable identity of its own, and so each inhabitant has imported his own style from whatever corner of America he came in search of the dream. Everything is amorphous, irreconcilable. A house in the style of a Chinese pagoda nestles beside a mock-Gothic department store, a Versailles mansion has been jammed up against a pink bungalow. The only feature indigenous to Los Angeles is the pavements: they are all encrusted with stars.

A city with no identity is also, of course, a city without a history; it acquires its character from whomever happens to be most successful at that moment, and so it is appropriate that the oldest artefacts in Los Angeles are the homes of the legendary movie-stars. Here is Shirley Temple's house, and just next door lived Joan Crawford – this is the lawn where her butler used to beat up any children who came to her door on Halloween. And just round the corner is the house where Johnny Weismuller lives – the garden is full of ropes and foliage. The new stars have moved here too, in an implicit act of homage. Hugh Hefner's palace is surrounded by guards and cameras. The son of the unlucky Shah of Iran has bought a house here, too; unfortunately he shocked his neighbours by painting all the statues green and gracing them with pubic hair. Close by, Getty's house is crumbling over the side of an artificial cliff. The whole area is utterly quiet, deserted except for the occasional security patrol and guard dog. The silence is so intense that the petals fall off the mimosa with an audible crunch. Beverly Hills is one of the most terrifying places in the world.

And, without a history, there can be no sense of a viable culture. Anthony Hopkins was playing Prospero in a local performance of *The Tempest*; the songs had been turned into advertising jingles, Miranda was clearly waiting for her first film part, and Anthony Hopkins mumbled and meandered through the lines to rapt applause:

> 'O brave new world, that has such people in't!'
> ''Tis new to thee.'

The whole audience laughed out loud, as though they had heard the line for the first time. Most of them had. 'Wasn't that the greatest show?' one rather gaudy American matron asked me. She looked like a Christmas tree on an acid trip; she turned out to be in 'the industry'. The industry, is, of course, the film industry; or, rather, the industry *is* the town. Los Angeles must be the only city in the world where the audience watch the film credits with more attention than they watch the film.

By courtesy of my new friend, the mini-mogul, I was transported to a large party at Paramount Studios. It was a 'wrap-up' party for seven 'major motion pictures', and it was held among the sets of the studio; here, at last, were the real inhabitants of those mock-Western saloons, the nineteenth century New York street scenes, the facade of an early twentieth century cinema. The directors, agents, producers, financiers, stars seethed around – looking as if they had just emerged from small nooks and crannies of these cunning replicas, and were still slightly ill at ease in the real air.

'Dustin got all the credit, but he was off the wall on that one'.

'I wanted to put Barbra against Dolly, it would have looked good aesthetically but it was just unreal. Really unreal.'

'What happened to your agent's girl-friend? She was with the wrong group last night.'

'Well she's into a real voyeur trip. She's in a bad space. I don't know where she's coming from'.

Everyone was 'working the party', as the strobe lights flashed, the Paramount extras doubled as nineteenth century French chefs in order to serve elaborate food on plastic plates, as video-cameras recorded the party live on large screens above the party itself. The dream may change its form, but it never ends. There had been an article the next day in the *Los Angeles Herald Examiner*: 'The lights are the symbol . . . They signify the limitless potential for achievement and creativity in this city. The lights go on for ever, and so do the opportunities'.

It so happened that, that night, I was taken to Terminal Island Prison to watch a play written and acted by the inmates themselves. The energy and enthusiasm here, in an old-fashioned theatrical setting, were powerful and real. At the end, the inmates presented their 'outside' producer with a small wooden box, perfectly crafted and enamelled. The refrain of the production had been an insistent one: 'I am my own man. I am not to be bought and sold'.

Outside, in the city of lights, the cars went zooming past bearing their solitary occupants. All over Los Angeles people were talking to each other on the telephone.

*

San Francisco, to the north of Los Angeles, is a city that invites platitudes: the cable-cars, the gentle people, the possibility of 'liberation'. A young man was talking to me in a bar. He was feeling very 'mellow', he told me, he was 'in his own space'. He had been dealing with his energies, and had decided to relate to their changes. 'I look at it this way: you can either be happy or be miserable'. He was from Idaho. He had a rather vacant smile.

Similar young men and women have come from all over America to this place, in order to discover their 'liberation'. This is still the last frontier: but now the people come to escape from themselves. The easiest way of achieving this, the method which requires the least moral and social effort, is to attach yourself to a group and thereby acquire a new identity: to become a 'feminist', a 'gay' or a 'moonie' – sometimes all three at once. San Francisco is a city of cults and religions, a city of strident white minorities, a city of people who wear their respective uniforms and who wield the impersonal vocabulary of liberation. They have done what they came such a long way to do: they have lost themselves. But what exactly is it that they have found instead?

In the fairy story, the two children have gone astray in the wood; they wander on through the foliage until, finally, they see a hill. This will be their way out, they will be able to see where they are. And so they climb the hill laboriously – only to see more hills stretching toward the horizon, as night begins to fall. It is well known that San Francisco is a city of hills – even here, liberation is not to be readily acquired or easily sustained. The gay community, for example, is finding its dream of sexual and social freedom slowly turning sour; after the riots last month, as a result of the virtual acquittal of Harvey Milk's killer (Mr Milk was a homosexual politician, now in the process of being beatified), the slogan on the wall read GAY BULLETS WILL KILL PIGS. A gay bullet is, as yet, an unknown quantity. But the paradox of the language reflects the paradox of the situation itself: a minority is oppressing itself, is dehumanising itself, with its own rhetoric.

For, again paradoxically, the more people who travel to California lured by the myths of freedom and endless balmy days, the less those myths can be realised. When homosexuals, for example, moved into certain neighbourhoods of San Francisco, they invaded those areas which had been predominantly Mexican and Chicano. They pushed up the rents; they even became the landlords of the previous native inhabitants. It is now common to see young homosexuals and young Mexicans confronting each other on the streets, with equal aggression on both sides. The pursuit of the Californian dream has actually set minority against minority. 'Liberation' is not a human or individual activity; it has to do with sheer weight of numbers and with an external, sometimes aggressive, style. Minorities are not freer here; there are simply more of them.

And what is it, anyway, that such people are being liberated into? As a city, San Francisco exists in a kind of vacuum; it is a pleasant but essentially uninteresting place, a rather more respectable and quainter version of Disneyland. There is a great deal of narcissism in the air – 'How could this happen here, in San Francisco?' one newspaper asked after the riots – but it is the aggressive narcissism of a city which knows itself to be provincial. Boredom has become a habit. I was taken to an elaborate studio where a laser and hologram show was being painstakingly constructed; across the television monitor, a thousand intricate shapes and tones were formed and re-formed. It was beautiful, but it was empty. The shapes were elaborate, but they were quite without resonance.

Nevertheless, there is a quite rare and attractive mysticism in the Californian temperament – it has to do with slowness, with their affinity with this peculiarly exotic land – and in people of great intelligence or even great beauty the effect is astonishing. It is like coming upon some new race of men, some wondrous species who have been able to empty their heads of anything the rest of us have ever learned. At dinner with an eminent academic, I was being rather rude about the work of a certain poet. 'I don't think,' the academic said quite calmly, 'that we need make judgmental values about anything.' After dinner, I drove across the Golden Gate bridge; beyond it, there is nothing but the Pacific. And, when you realise that this is all there is left of the land, you realise also that this is the visible, definite limit of the West.

16 June, 1979

Peter Ackroyd

THREE DAYS IN GREENLAND

Narssarssuaq

First day
The first sight of Greenland, from the air, is of a vast and ancient wedding-cake; as though the sea had turned white with age. As the plane moves over the ice-cap, some of the passengers begin to clap. This wasteland is their home. The woman next to me has the features of an Eskimo.

I ask her if she is from Greenland. 'Yes. I am born here.' 'You are an Eskimo?' 'No. This is not the word. I am inouit.' She writes it down for me; it means 'human being'. The inouits are the natives of this place. 'What are the inouits like, in character?' 'They are hard.' She giggles. Below us, the mountains are like motionless black waves. The ice is cracked, and blue rivers are flowing through it.

When we land on the small air-strip at Narssarssuaq, a middle-aged Irishman comes up to me. 'It's a godforsaken place this, isn't it? But I've got a little bottle of Irish whiskey in my case here.' He is carrying a Penguin edition of the Vinland Sagas. When we arrive at the hotel, which is in reality a converted American air base and the only building in sight, there seems very little to do. The Irishman persuades me to take a boat with him across the adjacent fjord, to view the remains of the first Viking settlement in Greenland. 'Did you see the programme on the television about the Vikings, by that fellow Magnus Magnusson? Well that got me interested. I'm a bachelor by trade, and I have the time for the reading.'

We start walking towards the small harbour. 'It was settled by Eric the Red. He left Iceland after killing a man, he was a terrible fierce character. They were like the old Irish, a lot of drinking and trading and whoring around. Well let's see now if we can talk to these people.' A group of inouits are standing around the harbour, their speedboats parked closely together like motorbikes. The Irishman points to the far shore, and shows them his Penguin paperback. He writes down 'Viking' and 'Eric the Red'. The faces of the youths are bland and inexpressive but, eventually, one of them agrees to take us across the fjord for a small fee.

On the other side, we see nothing but a few sheep and some relatively modern dwellings. A young woman is squatting upon the ground. The Irishman goes up to her; characteristically, she keeps her eyes averted, staring into the distance, until he actually addresses her. 'Eric the Red? Viking?' He shows her a map in his book. She points along the coast, and mutters something unintelligible. 'Thank you, miss.' He turns to me when we have walked a few paces, and whispers. 'Did you smell the drink on that poor woman? She was half-plastered. These poor people.' He sighs, and shakes his head. To our side, the fjord is as bright and as blue as a Hockney swimming pool. The mountains rise in the distance, their summits covered with snow, but all round us the green hills slope toward the water. Two young inouits ride past on ponies. 'Look,' the Irishman says and grabs my arm. 'They must be growing vegetables here. Is it potatoes, I'm wondering? The poor souls probably pay their taxes to Denmark. You know in the old days the Irish had to pay tax to the English for their windows. It was a terrible time. But we won't go into it just now.'

We reach an area of levelled ground, with pieces of broken stone in rough circles. 'This must be it,' I say. 'Well,' he says, 'I'm going to take a little leak for a minute. Keep a look-out for small ditches.' With this enigmatic piece of advice, he retreats behind a boulder. When he comes back, the two young men on ponies are riding towards us. They stop and watch. The Irishman waves his hands around the area. 'Viking? Eric the Red?' They stare, in that curiously inexpressive way, and then ride off. 'Well,' he says, 'they didn't seem to know much did they? They're saying to themselves, we kicked the fuckers out. We don't care.' He is right, of course. This was the first European settlement in Greenland, an object of research, a tourist attraction, but the natives, who inhabited this land before and after the Vikings, are scarcely interested in the remains of a brief colonisation. The settlement lasted for 500 years and then suddenly disappeared. Some say it was destroyed by inouit attacks; some say by a change in climate which literally froze the Europeans to death.

The Irishman spots a man building some kind of wooden structure – I imagine it to be a museum under construction. It turns out, however, that the man is building his own house and that this is his land. We have been walking the wrong way. The builder points in the opposite direction, and raises four fingers. 'He must mean four kilometres. Well, Peter, what's the old saying? Send a fool on his way happy'. And so we walk back, passing a small inouit settlement with some 20 houses, a school, and one store. 'This,' the Irishman says, 'must be the Company store. What's that old song about it? Another day older, and deeper in debt.' He sings it, but forgets the tune.

And then we see it. On a stone outcrop, there are some green hieroglyphics, one of them a cross. They are clearly of modern manufacture, but around them are stones forming large square shapes. There are the tracings of three houses, a small church and what appears to have been a barn. 'Hang on a minute. Just let me check this.' He consults his book and, yes, this is definitely it. This is the earliest settlement, the home of the man who named the island 'Green Land'. Around the ruins small white birds are whistling, darting from stone to stone. After a few minutes staring at the remains, I suggest that there is very little to detain us. 'Well, Peter, don't think of that. It's the sense of place you need here.' When we eventually return to the other shore, two or three young inouits are diving into the waters of the harbour. They look like young seals. The early Europeans may have vanished, but these people have survived.

We walk slowly back to the Arctic Hotel. 'What you would need here, Peter, is a life of the mind. It would be a grand place to write poetry and to read, wouldn't it now?' I mention the long winter evenings, as everyone does. 'Yes,' he says, 'now what's that old song? It's a long time from May to September.' He sings it as we walk back. That night, I go out into the air. One long cloud hangs across the sky, like a raised fist, the hand of some old god.

Second day

An excursion to the ice-cap has been arranged, to see that vast frozen field which covers most of the country's surface, and is said to contain one third of the world's fresh water. My Irish friend tells me that his back is playing up and, alas, he cannot make the trip. And so I join a band of German tourists, a large proportion of whom are, apparently, lesbians.

The first part of the journey is by coach, until the road runs out – stopping, literally, on the edge of the wilderness. At first we find ourselves walking through a small valley, with birch and willow growing along its stony sides. I am in front, with the Norwegian guide. 'These Germans,' he mutters to me, 'are wasting too much energy singing and talking. It is not good.' We climb steadily upwards now, stumbling over rocks and across streams. One woman falls, and lets out a high-pitched scream. She is given some cognac, and revives. And then we reach a plateau, with a large natural lake. The Germans reach for their cameras, and take pictures of each other. 'Wunderbar!' We rest here, and drink the cold water from the lake. 'But what is an Englishman without his Guinness?' an old German asks me in a hearty manner. 'Nothing,' I reply. He laughs.

We walk on, the Germans by now in single file and chanting some kind of marching song. And suddenly there, in the middle distance, is the enormous whiteness. I can hear the sound of rushing waters somewhere to my left but there, ahead, lie only stillness and hardness. A cold wind blows off the ice. As we come closer to it, I see that it is not the flat, white plain of my imagination. It is broken, striated, with white and grey mottled patches, stretching hundreds of miles into the distance.

The more hardy, or foolhardy, of us follow the guide as he scrambles down a steep slope towards the edge of the ice. Two of the more masculine German ladies go ahead of me, and help me down. The air is appreciably colder now. Tiny white and blue flowers are concealed beneath the rocks. The sky is much lighter immediately above the ice, as though it has turned pale with fright. After ten or 15 minutes, we are beside the ice-cap. It towers some 20 feet above us, a cold wall. Its interior is filled with caverns, where the water runs in torrents. It is unkempt, dishevelled. It freezes the air around itself, despite the bright sun. Small pieces come tumbling off the side. The voices of the Germans echo across it, as though we were in an empty cathedral. And then we all start breaking off pieces of ice and eating them. It is a strange gesture, almost an instinctive one. Like a savage tribe coming across some mysterious and unnameable material. We have to feel it, and taste it, to tame it perhaps.

That night, I meet my Irish friend in the hotel bar. We are both clutching our ration cards, which are arranged in 72 tiny squares – one square for each drink. The Irishman keeps on tearing off two at a time, for a double whisky. It turns out that he went to the same school as James Joyce. He tells me of his days as a travel agent, as a hotel-keeper in Donegal, of the exploits of priests and dairymen.

As we talk, the inouits are getting quickly, and extraordinarily, drunk. Their Danish employers are also the worse for wear: they roll over each other like fat cattle. Some inouits are standing in the middle of the room, transfixed, staring at the wall. One or two come over to us, shake our hands, and stand above us smiling. 'They're all langers drunk,' the Irishman observes in a good-humoured way. He is obviously used to such behaviour. 'The poor souls will soon be all over the floor.'

He had been talking to me about Catholicism, conscience, and the 'absolute duty' of man towards his fellow human beings. And here were the inouits, in all but name still a colonised people, wearing Western clothes in a rather ungainly fashion, unable to cope with the drink which they now seem to need so badly. One inouit comes up, rather furtively, and asks if he could buy some ration 'points' from us. The Irishman turns to me. 'We'll give them to them, Peter. We'll share them out equally, so that some poor man doesn't get pissed stupid on the lot.' And then, with great tact and courtesy, he does so.

Third day

The mist rolls in during the morning. It is like the breath of the ice itself, dark and heavy and oppressive. I sit down to read about this bewildering place. There are 50,000 people living in Greenland, the largest island on the earth, of whom some 40,000 are inouit. There are approximately 80 settlements scattered around the shores. The country is ruled by Denmark, which has granted limited self-government to the native inhabitants. Many inouits, however, are pressing for complete independence, to complete that process which began when the first Viking settlers mysteriously disappeared off the face of the wilderness. One Danish poet wrote of Narssarssuaq, 'If you have loved it, you will be lost.'

The pictures in my book were of old engravings of the inouits; they looked like monks with cowls, sitting upright in their small boats, unsmiling, staring into the distance. They had a kind of emblematic force; they had been depersonalised by the European artists and turned into a symbol – of what? Fortitude? Endurance? Hardness, like the hardness of the ice and the granite which surround them? Or strangeness, perhaps, the strangeness of the unknowable.

13 September, 1980

John Stewart Collis

AN UNINHABITED EMPIRE

There are two routes by which we should approach the Grand Canyon: from the Painted Desert and the Petrified Forest; or from Phoenix, Flagstaff, and Sedona. If we choose the former we will be amazed enough to be prepared for anything. We see a 300 mile desert that does not seem a desert; a rainbow laid upon the lap of earth, not arched above it; a green prairie in the distance that is not made of grass, but of stones; the predominant hue a rusty pink fuelled by the iron in the sediments that stained the flowing flint 300 million years ago. Yet not a constant picture, this Painted Desert. For, standing on high ground above the badlands of the plain, the light aloft affects the earth below in ceaseless change of aspect: a forbidding moor under black rain clouds; shifting colours caught on the ribbed surface as the summer clouds pass over; while with the rising and the setting of the sun the prevailing rust is turned to red.

Adjacent to this desert is the Petrified Forest. We come upon logs, sometimes a landslide of them in a gully. We cannot pick them up, they are much too heavy. For they are not made of wood. Once there had been a great forest here, which, sinking under encroaching sediment, was swathed in clay, until, after 150 million years' erosion, that cover was taken off and the trees were seen again. But they were no longer trees or trunks. Not one atom of wood remained. Yet their facsimile, their fossiled script, their photographs, are here. No one really quite understands how this was done; by what combination of forces in the forge and turmoil of time, by what secretions and additions in the cauldron of re-creation, the likeness has been preserved and the substance changed. But the likeness is here for all to see. That which was destroyed is restored in outward semblance. That which was lost is found. We see the replicas in many sizes. There are logs, not composed of coal as we might expect, but of quartz and iron, of manganese and silica, so that a smooth sliced stump glows with yellow, orange, and white, with black, blue, and purple shades; there are small twigs perfectly recorded; there are massive trunks still rooted in the rock-matrix like unfinished sculptures, and many lie prostrate on the ground – prostration, true gauge and image of eternal rest, beyond even the calendar of Nature to disturb.

Clearly this makes a good approach to the Grand Canyon. Yet I favour a more prosaic route which has the advantage that you eventually arrive at the most impressive point of the Canyon with precipitative immediacy. That is to say you go from Tucson, Phoenix, Flagstaff and Sedona.

When flying across America I have often been impressed by how few people seem to live there. A faulty view, no doubt, but excusable seeing the amount of wild open spaces uninhabited. At least this seems true of Arizona. Driving along, I have never seen so much of nothing. Neither to the right nor left of the long ribbon of road is there anything to behold – save the petrol stations. These places have names, though terribly incongruous with the startlingly characterless nature of their appearance: Horse Thief Basin, Deadman's Wash, Desert Hills, Badger Springs, Bloody Basin Road, General Crook Trail, Skunk Creek, Happy Valley, Pioneers Road, Thundering Road. In that order. Evocative enough of settlers who had failed to settle. Nor had many people settled yet, it seems, except the owners of petrol stations. However, when we reach Sedona a change occurs. Great gorges appear and huge isolated rocks looking from afar like vast cathedrals built with red stone. Monumental rock-faces in the shadow of which in a Western a Lee Marvin pursued by a John Wayne is finally brought down. And if we mount to a town in the vicinity, called Jerome, high on a hill, the enormous stadium of Arizona becomes apparent because of the sight of the long high rim of a mountain range that serves as background to the mighty plain.

Presently we reach the Grand Canyon. We come upon it suddenly at one of its most impressive points. Indeed, stepping from the car for only a few yards I was able to lean against a railing and see the Canyon.

An eagle flew below me. People in the gorge would see it flying high above them in the heavens; yet I, with my feet upon the flinty earth, looked *down* upon the bird that winged it in the sky.

It was with some consternation that I gazed into the awful abyss: my mind was not attuned to such silence; such terror; and such beauty. It was one mile in depth; eight miles across to the other side; and 217 miles in length. I had been unaware of these dimensions.

Then for the chief surprise. There is always a chief surprise when we visit famous places. Something unexpected. I found myself looking across at – Ancient Egypt! True, I looked down upon a gorge, every inch representing a million years cleavage of the hard substance of rock by the soft substance of water, so that at the bottom two thousand million years are writ upon the deepest rocks. But that was not what surprised me. I was also gazing across a *land*, an empire with gigantic pyramids, towers, temples, sculptures.

This was no idle fancy of my own. When I came to the most popular view-point of the Canyon, I found there a focusing 'telescope' by means of which you could concentrate upon various aspects of the scene; and special focusing places on the dial were marked as Pyramid I; Pyramid II; Cheops; Zoroaster; Aztec Temple; Buddha; Sphinx – and so forth.

But it was not like other lands, other empires. Though gloriously englamoured by every species of shape and colour, and receiving the conflagration of the sunset, light adding to light, earthly hues multiplied by heavenly rays – it was yet *unpeopled*. No one lived in that country. No one worshipped at those shrines. No one entered in at those temples, nor gazed at those pyramids. When night came on, no lights began to appear across the land, for there were no houses as there were no streets, and no vehicles, and no citizens. It was fearful to watch the darkness absorb it into speechless night. All was blotted out as if it had never been . . . But, at every dawn, when the sun rises the lost land emerges again; at first entangled in vapour, then gradually declared, until at last the terraces and towers, the monuments and pyramids and temples are wholly established; and this empire, without kings or commoners, unconquered and unconquerable, resumes its supremacy.

8 August, 1981

Jeffrey Bernard

GOING WEST

I'm still smarting a little over a totally inaccurate line in a recent copy of this journal which said 'Jeffrey Bernard is on holiday'. Now, I ask you, who would choose a place for a holiday where you can get shot, stabbed or raped or all three at any time after dusk or where, during the waking hours, they talk of nothing but money, success, position and money again? So I got a free ticket and the generous blessings of *The Spectator*, but you wouldn't call it a holiday. These people who have voted for two consecutive presidents, one originally a peanut vendor and the other a geriatric cowboy, have to be seen and then disbelieved. Their values are quite extraordinary, and observing the smart set in the trendy Hollywood restaurant, Ma Maison, I found myself missing the squalor of Old Compton Street and almost longing for a boring conversation with a few of the old lags. I'd been kindly taken to lunch by Jeff Silverman, the William Hickey of Los Angeles, to watch the Hollywood set with their feet in the trough. We sat at a table on the fringe of the room against a wall. Apparently it was the only place to sit. 'The people in the middle of the room', Silverman told me, 'are dead.' It seems that where you sit in America is of paramount importance and I made a mental note never to be seen drinking again at the Greek Street end of the Coach and Horses. This sort of nonsense got up my nose a little after a few days in Los Angeles and it pleased me not a little to irritate those Americans who asked me rather patronisingly about the state of England. 'It's marvellous,' I told them, 'you're allowed to fail in England. You can be nobody, have nothing and have friends.' I think they thought I was sending them up.

In the beginning I flew to Louisville, Kentucky, and then got the Greyhound bus to Lexington. The highways in and out of Lexington are lined with stupendously laid out stud farms. The paddocks are as well kept as billiard tables but why they call it the Blue Grass country, God only knows. It looked green enough to me. I fell off the bus in a parched condition and fell into the first bar I saw. The action started almost at once. As I raised the foaming and pathetically weak beer to my lips a man at the end of the bar was arrested, handcuffed, pushed up against the wall outside and questioned at gun point. It was much better than watching television, as was the argument which ensued between a barman called Fabulous Kelly and a customer called Hot Horse Harry. Truly sparkling dialogue: 'Give me a tip you bastard and I don't mean one for one of your goddam horses.' Of such banter is America made and you get to feel that everyone learns their script before they come out in the morning. The scripts in Hollywood are not so gentle. A few days later, I was walking round the corner of Hollywood Boulevard and Vine Street and bumped into a nasty little confrontation. A respectable nonentity of a middle-aged housewife was being verbally assaulted by a very small boy who couldn't have been a month more than eight years of age. 'What are you fuckin' starin' at?' he screamed at her. She looked startled and took a step back. Then the boy threw a paper cup of Coca-Cola in her face and screaming again said, 'Go and fuck yourself.' In London I might have kicked him up the arse. There, I felt as alarmed as the woman. Later, I was told it was par for the course.

In Hollywood, and elsewhere in Los Angeles, I was always aware of the undercurrent of violence. That and the fact that I was 'nobody', with less than a million dollars in my current account, had me brooding between bars. But the ridiculous image they try to put over is a 24-hour acting job. One morning I decided to have my heart starter in the Polo Room bar of the Beverly Hills Hotel. I'd heard it was 'real posh' and positively crawling with stars. I sat at the bar with my back to another version of Fabulous Kelly and watched them at it. At the nearest table a silver-haired, middle-aged tycoon was lunching with a pretty, young woman who was all tits and legs and apparently not on the expense account for her conversation. In the hour I sat there tippling I didn't see him address a single word to the poor cow. He ate two courses and drank a bottle of wine with a telephone wedged between his shoulder and ear and didn't remove it once. Perhaps I'm a little old fashioned but it did strike me as being an appalling way to treat even a young girl trying to screw her way to the top. I boldly said as much to the barman. He simply shrugged and said a man had to make deals when he could. Yet again I thought of Soho and smiled with pleasure at the thought that no one had made a deal since 1949 when Greek Tony lost his café to the cook after a game of poker.

The girl in the Beverly Hills Hotel reminds me that American ladies, by and large, are very well packaged indeed. The vast majority of them are intent on being regarded as sex objects and, as Philip Marlowe said, are easy on the eye, unlike our own dear sisters on the *Guardian*. Yes, I'm afraid they have *them* there too. What's more you can see them at the crack of dawn on television. Now that was one thing I did like about the States, being prone as I am to insomnia and waking at five o'clock. You can sit up in bed and watch the box, and what a box of tricks it is. The early morning commercials concerned the big American problem, which is having a problem – pronounced 'prahblum'. The major prahblums involve drinking, divorce, child battering, unhappy marriages, cancer, diabetes, getting married, going mad, constipation, diarrhoea, not being married and for three New York lady novelists I watched being interviewed, *being taken seriously*. Yes, apparently writing is a very serious business and if you don't get taken seriously then you've got a serious prahblum. Having listened to these three ladies talking crap I thumbed through a couple of their novels in a bookshop and found myself reading soft porn – sex between very rich beautiful people who telephone at the lunch table. But I liked the way the television told me how to organise my day. One morning I had to go and have a cervical smear *immediately* and the next morning I was told that God had missed me recently and that I was to contact him *at once* on 436-236-7070.

It was when leaving Los Angeles airport for New York that I stood next to a woman with an elastic prahblum. As she was checking-in, her knickers fell down and came to rest around her ankles. Not having seen a pair of knickers for at least ten days I was considerably cheered and thought it augured well for New York, a city I dearly love. The bars and the restaurants are a delight, I could sit in them all day and probably did. What gave my small mind the greatest joy there was to meet and spend a day with a man who has been my hero since I was a schoolboy in 1947. I speak of Rocky Graziano who was the middleweight champion of the world, 1947–48, and is a remarkable bloke. From the East Side, via reform school, prison in the army, a dishonourable discharge to three of the most exciting fights in boxing history with Tony Zale, this extraordinary man has captivated New Yorkers as well as this English fan. It may be ridiculous to have a hero, but there it is. A delightful man called Jim Harelson and Bradley Cunningham who has a bar in Greenwich Village fixed up for me to meet the Rock and, as luck would have it, we hit it off (film stars are usually frightfully disappointing in the flesh).

The first thing I noticed about one of the hardest punchers of all time was his hands. Delicate, not gnarled and with the most vulgar ring I've ever seen on the fifth finger of the famous left. It consisted of an enormous diamond set in platinum. 'I suppose you bought that after you won the title,' I said. No, it was given to him by a fan who summoned him from Chicago, one Al Capone. After lunch – thanks to Harleson – Rocky took me on a rather smart pub crawl with Freddy Russo, a one time featherweight who beat four world champions, and a heavyweight who hadn't been a success but who was a friend. I've said it before but must reiterate that boxers are the nicest of all sportsmen. I assume that no one who can *really* do it has to be nasty. So now there's a picture of Rocky Graziano knocking someone out of the ring on my kitchen wall, a New York hangover that just won't go away and a deep hole in my pocket caused by an outlet of dollars. Skint again. A nobody who hasn't done a deal on the phone for ages. Never mind. Apart from the absence of Graziano, London is lovely. I think I even prefer the Coach to P. J. Clark's.

                                                          10 October, 1981

Peter Ackroyd

SACRED BLANKNESS

Austin, Texas

When I arrived here, they told me it was different. It wasn't like Houston – well Houston was just too big and too rich, they were taking so much oil out of the ground that it was sinking; it wasn't like Dallas – people in Dallas were mean and hard and straight. Austin was the real Texas. It was just a small town. It was clean. It was old. It was safe. It was liberal.

And indeed it does retain in part the atmosphere of a small town – friendly but slightly eccentric, slightly closed in. But it is growing now and, like every city in Texas, spreading into the desert and the hills so that from the air the whole state resembles one vast city. Mrs Williams, the owner of the Williams Hotel, was telling me about the redevelopment. 'They're knocking down the old buildings and planting a lot of *trees*. Who wants to go and sit down under a *tree*?' Across the road from the hotel, there is a barn filled with old pianos: no one comes in or goes out. Downtown, on Sixth Street, across the road from the Hotel Alamo, there are still standing the bars and stores built in the 1880s. They do not resemble the knock-about props of Western films: they are lavishly decorated and finely built, covered with subtle colours. Mrs Williams warned me not to walk there at night: 'A lot of *street people* around there. Go get a taxi. They just come in from other states and *wander*. All those little children, too. Why don't they stay in their own state?' Everyone is coming here, however. Texas is the new good place, the richest state in the union and conveniently close to the South American Empire when it arises.

If you walk one mile from Sixth Street, from the old saloons where country music blares out and from the restaurants where the men still wear stetsons at breakfast, you will find something quite extraordinary. Here is the campus of the University of Texas, what has been called 'the imperial university', with an annual income of 1.9 billion dollars. Huge limestone buildings are scattered across the campus, like Rubik cubes dropped by the gods. There are three rare books libraries here, two art galleries, a complex devoted to the teaching of film and television, a stadium so large that from the top seats the field is the size of a television screen: if you want to play squash, you have to take the elevator to the ninth floor.

This is the real Texas, the Texas not of legend but the one established upon oil and banks. You can smell the money, feel the money in the buildings: oil converted into stone, oil converted into 'culture'. Everything is glass, limestone, marble and piped music: a kind of sacred blankness covers everything, as light and as airy as the affability of the people themselves.

In one corner of the campus stands the LBJ Library. As you enter, you are ushered into an 'orientation movie'. Here is little LBJ in a prospect of cotton fields and wooden shacks, a child with a preternaturally old face as if he had already seen the future and been blasted by it. You leave the cinema and there, close to the First Lady Theatre, is a vast display area devoted 'To the Moon and Beyond'. In a vast portico of marble, and behind hermetically sealed glass, are the presidential archives. From wooden shacks to marble porticos, from cotton-picking to the Moon: this is the history of Texas. A sign dominates one of the university buildings: 'O Earth, What Changes Thou Hast Seen'.

O Texas, what changes you have wrought. It has all happened so quickly that no one seems to know quite how or why it has happened. The imperial spirit of Texas derives solely from the power of money, and so that spirit itself seems curiously impersonal and characterless. Other places have an ethic, or at least an atmosphere, of their own – whether it be the aggressive 'calm' of California or the innocent ferocity of New York. Texas has no atmosphere, unless the blithe acceptance of affluence counts as one; it has no ethic save that of acquisition. Perhaps all empires seem like that during the period of their growth – perhaps they all seem dead, suffocated by the power which they wield. Texas bears the weight of acquisition for the sake of acquisition, the piling up of money and of buildings for no other reason than that they should be piled up. There is nothing here for the imagination to hold on to, and to make its own. On a hill above Austin, a see-through church has been constructed; would it be too crass to assume that it represents a see-through culture?

11 December, 1982

P. J. Kavanagh

GOD'S COUNTRY

'You English? You like New York?' said the taxi-driver, a thin, humorous-looking man. 'Very much,' I replied, adding, because I knew it was expected, 'but it frightens me a little.' 'It sure scares the hell out of me,' he said. 'It's a hard town. You've got to get your hit in first or they walk right over you.'

We were on the way to the airport, and soon we came to a tunnel that took two lines of traffic while five lines tried to get into it. The resulting jam gave me time to ponder my polite untruth: I had not found central New York frightening. On the contrary, it had seemed less hostile and hurried than central London. Sure, you had to know what you wanted and ask for it clearly. Sure, you couldn't stop anyone to ask the way because they walked past you, glazed, as though you had not addressed them. (Often they were then observed to be wearing head-sets and were presumably wrapped in their own cloud of sound.) But on the whole you were welcomed, however brusquely, as a fellow human. There was none of that wearying sense of being 'placed' socially and economically, to be flattered as a possible target for a rip-off, or rejected as an unlikely prospect.

It was a hot afternoon. The five lines of cars came closer together as each driver fought to enter the tunnel, and tempers shortened. Nevertheless, what happened next was shocking. The occupant of our neighbour car, a cultivated-looking man in an expensive machine, turned slowly, Shane-like, to my taxi-driver, and said quietly: 'If you scrape my fender I'll knock your fucking head off.'

I gaped, there was no danger of such a thing, but my driver, deprived of his chance to get his hit in first, began his reply before the other had finished speaking and Escalated the Conflict. He announced that it would give him the greatest satisfaction, not only to grapple the other's fender clear away, but to demolish his whole car and then its occupant. Our neighbour then replied in kind. It was violence of the tongue, at a chilling, conversational level, on the grand scale. It was also profoundly unpleasant, a kind of generalised hatred, but my anxiety was brief, that they would have to settle it with jacks and wheelbraces (as they would have had to in England, never mind one of the Latin European countries) and I would thereby miss my flight. They meant it all right, but it was not intended to come to that; it was, perhaps, part of the image of the 'tough' city that New Yorkers seem to cherish (even if with a shudder) that, carried through, would make the place uninhabitable – which clearly it is not.

I thought of this incident when I read President Reagan's recent vilification of the Soviet Union; violence of the tongue for which any referee would have to send him off. I hope Russia realises it is a normal American mode and, though meant, is not meant to lead to anything else, as it would in Europe. This is what makes Mrs Thatcher's abuse, presumably intended to please her host the President ('megaphone diplomacy' in Lord Carrington's phrase), much sillier. The way she spoke is not the way European nations speak about each other in public, unless they mean business.

It has been pleasant to note a minor furore that has broken out on Radio 4's *PM* programme. A listener wrote in to say what a pleasant place Russia was to visit, and the jolly presenter, Susannah Simons, commented that he must have been wearing his rose-coloured spectacles. Since then their postbag has burst with passionate defence of Russia and Russians which, at the present time, is cheering. Few indeed of those who write to the BBC sound like Party Members . . .

And if I'm pleased to hear people standing up for Russia let me put in a word for the USA. At the time of the taxi/fender confrontation I was returning from a trip into Virginia, one of the most beautiful places on earth – no wonder the early settlers called it 'God's country' – and shamingly friendly and pro-British. Shamingly, because we seldom say a good word about the US. In one of those superb ice-cream places that line the highway my Yankee companion became convinced that the beautiful girl behind the shining sundae machines was of English descent. He asked her, and she blushed. 'Why, *thank you!*' she cried, and had to decline the distinction. Thanks – and delight – at being mistaken for British . . . May we have the grace to blush ourselves and labour to deserve such a reaction.

22 October, 1983

Roy Kerridge

IT MUST HAVE BEEN A MULE

Down in Cleveland, Tennessee, at the Church of God convention, preacher after Southern preacher shouted, sang, prayed and prophesied. By the time my stay in the Bible Belt was over, I felt I had enjoyed a rare peep into the soul of the white Southerner, and liked what I saw. The very first sermon I heard was an attack on Darwin, and although this high standard was not always maintained, nearly every preacher had something to say.

'Oh my friends, I was at a little church meeting once, when the folks was all praying, talking in tongues an' ever'thang, and one of the sisters gets into a *mood*.

' "I see God!" she cries.

' "Well, what's He like then?" one o' the congregation inquires, kind of interested, y'know.

' "He's got long ears! An' a long face! An' big eyes!"

'Straight away someone sings out, "It must have been a mule! 'Cause God don't look like that." '

The vast auditorium rang with applause, and the preacher warmed to his work, every now and then returning to his theme and crying out, 'It must have been a mule!'

Until the coming of the motor car and tarmacked road, mules must have been very useful in the Appalachians. Clearly they have left a deep impression on all who knew them and many who didn't. Another speaker quoted the Church founder, A. J. Tomlinson, who likened the Church of God to a mule that fell down a well and was taken for dead. The bereaved farmer shovelled earth on top of the unfortunate animal, but instead of being buried alive the mule shook off each load and climbed up on it, rising higher and higher until soon it was grazing safely on solid ground. So would the Church of God overcome its critics, given time.

Outside in secular Cleveland, old farmers from the hills of Cherokee County sat in the 'Shopping Mall' and told stories to each other, with many pauses, while their wives bought the week's supplies. The original centre of Cleveland seemed to have dwindled away to nothing, its pavements deserted, as everybody did their shopping along the roads outside, from low garage-like buildings with enormous parking spaces. Farmers and others seemed to have grown *more* peasant-like, not less, for instead of their going to town, the town, in the form of shops, had moved to the country. Even the Mall was too metropolitan for some farmers, and as soon as their wives were ready they ran back to their 'pick-up trucks' with wild shouts of 'I'm gettin' the heck *outa* this town!'

To me, however, the Mall seemed a delightful place to spend a lazy day. If empty, it would have resembled one of the shiny new shopping precincts that disfigure so many of our ancient towns. However, I never saw it empty, since air-conditioning had made it a mecca for heat-struck Southerners, who walked up and down greeting one another ('How ya perkin', Uncle John?' 'Rela-tivvily well, sir!') or playing music on the stage provided, or sitting on the edge of the stage and talking about mules.

Big men with wrinkled faces and blue dungarees would sit staring forward silently, huge hands on their knees, until an acquaintance came along and sat nearby. After 20 minutes or so, one of the two would say, 'Way back yonder in 1955 when we had that dry spell . . . ' and begin a monologue that would last until the wife appeared.

'Hey, Nat, got any *mule* jokes?' a young man called out on one occasion.

Nat hadn't, but trotted out a hoary collection of mountain chestnuts with great simplicity. I never heard a swear word or saw a 'teenage-cultist' all the time I was in Cleveland. Nor did I hear any jargon, surely unusual for America. All was innocence, as the punch-lines to various jokes testified.

' "I'm driving?" he says, "I thought *you* were driving!" ' 'I thought I saw him, and he thought he saw me, and when we got nearer, it was neither of us.'

Ignorant of the outside world they may have been, but in a way this was their good fortune. All knew their Bible, King James version, which together with an outdoor life seemed all that they needed to know. White Southerners are blessed with no interest in ecology, psychoanalysis, the women's movement or any movement they can't shoot down and bake in a pie. To me they represent the Hope of America. Against this background of kindly philistinism, great writers have emerged, while California or New York have yet to produce a Mark Twain, an Erskine Caldwell or a Chandler Harris. Or, for that matter, a Richard Wright, or a Frederick Douglas, for negro authors who hated the South were yet its children, and wrote better than anyone in the East European-influenced North.

Tall, gangling negroes in jeans, evidently farm workers, also sat around in different parts of the Mall, looking rather stunned at the big city. Some riffled among cheap blues records by B. B. King, on sale in cellophane packs, while others clapped hands to the hillbilly music played by local groups on the stage. This music, outwardly cheerful, showed something of the dark undercurrent of the Southern soul. Typical musicians and fans were young married couples, all pink cheeks, blond hair, smiles and teeth. Yet the lyrics they warbled to a toe-tapping beat owed much to Scottish morbidity or the fatalism of pioneer days.

As opposed to blues singers, who are always waking up this morning, country musicians are always going somewhere, whether up on the mountain to drag the devil down (wrestle with sin) or down to celebration river to lay this dead man in his water grave (be baptised).

'You can take me to the graveyard, lay my body down,' one trio of guitar-pickers proposed blithely. One of the strangest songs I heard was the macabre 'Conversation with Death', which borrowed many verses from 18th-century tombstones I had seen in English country churchyards. Other lines went as follows:

> 'O Death, look how you're treating me.
> You've closed my eyes so I can't see.'
> 'I'll lock your jaw so you can't talk,
> I'll fix your feet, so you can't walk.'
> 'Too late, too late, my friends farewell.
> I know my soul will burn in Hell.'

In our yellow school bus, the party of English West Indians I had set out with, led by the intrepid Pastor McCalla, explored the American South. Up in the mountains of North Carolina, set among thick forests of loblolly pines with spreading boughs, white oak trees, Southern beech, ash, birch and maple, we found wooden plank cabins where fat, genial smallholders waved to us from their porches, where they sat in rocking chairs. I was as surprised to see them as I would have been to see Chinamen with pigtails in modern Peking. Once we stopped at one of the roadside stalls where hillbilly farmers sold their produce from ramshackle shanty-stores: great orange pumpkins, barrels of peaches and 'Sourwood Mountain Honey' in jars, complete with combs. Tree frogs dropped from the maple leaves into puddles, like tropical leeches, and brilliant blue jays flashed their plumage among the trees. The dove-shooting season was just over, and long-tailed mourning doves with pink-washed breasts sat on telegraph wires. A little skinny Irish-looking woman with freckled hands and a doughty, earnest expression served us, while her huge laconic husband leaned on a vine-twined fence speaking. A square 'corn patch' had been hacked from the forest, and rows of golden maize stood five feet high, flittered over by large blue and black butterflies.

Other stalls, further along the road, sold tame animals that had been trapped nearby, 'polecats and wildcat kittens', which in England we would call skunks and lynx cubs. Early settlers tended to call new-world animals by old-world names. 'Turkey shoots' were advertised, as turkeys are game birds in Appalachia, and notices proclaimed that hunting dogs and (wait for it) mules were for hire. I was told of bear-hunting clubs, where the beasts were tracked on foot, tackled by hounds, shot and then cut up on the spot. Old values of 'game for the pot' prevailed, and most white Southerners hunted deer, one lady declaring venison to be healthier than beef, as it had 'no chemicals'. When I told her of safari parks in Britain, she imagined lions were let loose for sportsmen to shoot.

On 'Labor Day', when no one worked, tobacco-spitting contests and catch-the-greasy-pig competitions were held. Our coach travelled south, to Fort Oglethorpe, Georgia, a town where beautiful Southern houses, each one a mansion, stood around a village green. Some of these houses were of stone, and probably not unlike the slave-owners' dwellings that had been razed to the ground during the Civil War. Memorials to decimated regiments stood by the roadside against grassy banks and luxurious driveways. The vernacular architecture of the South must be one of the glories of America, and suburbia in Cleveland, Fort Oglethorpe and elsewhere is a pleasure to explore. Nearly all the houses are of planks, some in Gothic styles, others in English Georgian, but all with porches and rocking chairs. Obviously the ideal is the plantation owner's mansion, with marble columns and mint juleps. There is no division between the hillbilly and the rich man, for the farmer's cabin, with its porch and wooden posts supporting a shingle roof, is a humble, home-made version of Colonel Beauregard's verandah. Few flowers bloom in Southern gardens, but instead baskets of ferns hang over the porches, looking delightfully cool.

On the green at Fort Oglethorpe, yet another country music group, the Gentry Family, sang high sweet harmonies and urged everyone to go to church on Sunday. Three dollars bought a hot picnic lunch on a tray, and one dollar locked the person of your choice in a model jail from whence it would cost him two dollars to get out. Looking very dark among the friendly white crowds, the West Indians spread out and began to enjoy themselves. From a stage, an announcer greeted 'our visitors from England' and then began drawing numbers from a hat for the cake walk.

'What's a cake walk?' asked a tall young man in our party, and a friendly cake-walker showed him the ropes. To a shuffling rhythm from a loudspeaker, people walk round and round a giant ludo-board painted

on the ground, every square having a number. When the music stops, so
do you, and the judge pulls a number out of a hat. If you are lucky, you are
handed an enormous chocolate cake by a woman who stands in the
middle of the ring. Then you leave, smacking your lips, and the music
begins again.

On a hill above our Holiday Inn stood a lorry drivers' café, or 'truck
stop' as the Americans term such places. I walked up to it along the verge
of the forest, where giant butterflies, red, gold and black, settled on leaves
broader and more jungly-looking than those of beech or oak in England.
Inside the café I met with stony looks and was served without comment.

'My name's written on the tail of my shirt, I'm a Tennessee hustler and
I don't have to work,' sang the juke box.

I left a copy of the English rock newspaper, *New Musical Express*,
behind as a parting gift. This was a mistake, for when I returned that
evening I was barred by the lean, tough-looking girl assistant, who stood
in the doorway regarding me through narrowed eyes. Walking along the
road was a suspicious act in itself, I discovered, while the *NME*, with its
letters page dotted with obscenities, put the lid on it. I tried to explain
that I only read it as a barometer of our times, but the girl wasn't interested.

'You caint come in with that sack!' she declared, pointing at my plastic
bag. 'What are you, a hitch-hiker?' Sack indeed! Too affronted for words, I
walked away.

As a climax to the week of preaching in Cleveland's Tavernacle, the
town's leading citizens, the mayor, the owner of the insurance company
and the head of the merchant bank, all arrived to do honour to the head of
the Church of God of Prophecy. This was the Bishop Tomlinson, son of
the original founder. All addressed our worthy leader, a venerable old
man, as 'Bishop' in friendly tones, and the Church was praised for its high
moral standards.

A postman in a big peaked cap struggled to the rostrum with an enormous letter, about four feet square.

'Why, here's the mailman!' said the mayor. 'What have you got for me?'

'It's a letter from Bishop Tomlinson, but I'm a bit embarrassed as
there's 20 cents to pay on it.'

'I knew the Church of God was cutting down on its costs, but that's
ridiculous!'

Inside was a giant card, 'Good luck, Mayor Dethero.'

When the banker's turn came, he began with a homily on the beneficial effects of Christianity and then handed the Bishop a pencil.

'D'ye remember, Bishop, how in the 1930s you sold 30,000 pencils for a
church?'

'I sure do.'

'Well, here's a pencil for ye, and now I'm gonna ask for it back. I'm an Indian giver, I think they call it. No, wait, I'm gonna buy that there pencil offen you, Bishop, for ten thousand dollars, and here's my cheque!'

To thunderous applause, the Bishop took the cheque, which was made out to the Church. The banker looked around, beaming.

'I feel like dancing like David before the presence of the Lord!' the Bishop exclaimed. And so he did, uttering war whoops as he ran from one end of the stage to the other, hopping up and down and waving the cheque triumphantly in the air.

29 October, 1983

Jeffrey Bernard

ROCKY

Boulder, Colorado

Boulder City lies at the foot of the Rockies 25 miles from the state capital, Denver. It is just over 5,000 feet above sea level and there is very little humidity and not too much oxygen. It is a campus town full of charm, Victorian and clap-board houses, tree-lined streets and, as far as I can tell, there doesn't seem to be a mugger in the place. Last week, on election day, Boulder was the only town in the county that came out for Walter Mondale and it gave him 24,160 shoulders to cry on. As my American friend and hostess said, 'Doesn't that say it all, why I live here?' It is indeed a very liberal town and there is some sort of protest almost every time President Reagan opens his mouth. On the night of the election there were two parties going on at the Boulderado Hotel. Upstairs some fairly staid Republicans were slowly warming up to their celebration party while downstairs in the bar they were chanting, 'Fuck you, Mr President.' The Republican persona is more evident among the rednecks than it is among the middle classes. Rednecks, unpopular with local residents, are the ranchers, cowboys and farmers who live out of town. They still drive American cars, stick cigars in their mouths, wear cowboy boots and like to look tough. They probably are. Their obsession – and most other men's too for that matter – is football. The female obsession is psychology and psychoanalysis.

One day last week we drove up into the mountains to look at an old mining town called Gold Hill. There was a town store with a pot-belly stove in the middle of the shop just as Hollywood would have it, but this store was typically run by a middle-class, semi-hippie, semi-dropout couple. When I walked into the store I was thinking, this is it, the real old West, and to my horror the first words I heard coming from a woman leaning against the counter were, 'I've just got the results of my personality test and it says that stress makes me nervous.' John Wayne must be turning in his grave. Such people spend $100 a week to garner such obvious and silly information. Americans are terribly serious in spite of such ghastly frivolities as having a compulsion to smother their food with melted cheese. Television breakfast-time chat shows bear witness to their deep sincerity and Colorado watches discussions on infidelity, euthanasia and alcoholism while they eat their pancakes and syrup at the crack of dawn.

Of course, I've been searching for any signs of low life but there aren't any. Neither is there high life. Boulder City is still life, but a nice enough one for residents, I imagine. The abundance of bookshops, the slow pace and the campus atmosphere is catching. Any feelings of mania have deserted me by teatime and I have retired to our cabin in the foothills to read and to watch the picture-postcard sunsets. Yesterday, reading a biography of Ulysses S. Grant, I came across a good piece of Americana. During his post-presidential world tour he stopped off at Venice and remarked, 'It would be a great town if they drained it.' Americans love draining places and sooner or later they'll probably get around to the Everglades.

In spite of this strange penchant they are very good at filling glasses. The measures in most bars here are quite ridiculous by our standards. Most of the barmen are what they call free pourers, which is to say that the actual measure is redundant. Tumblers are filled to the top. And most barmen like most of the other people here are very friendly. Even crossing the street someone will pass you and say, 'Hi there, how you doin'?' It is a far cry and in some ways a happy one from New York. Only once have I been reminded of that city and that was when I went into town one evening to see Larry Holmes defend his heavyweight title against 'Bonecrusher' Smith. They show fights and football games on a big screen in the bars and there I was watching the referee stop the fight because of a horrendous cut over Smith's eye when a man behind me shouted out, 'Hey ref, what's the matter, he's still got his eyeball in, hasn't he?' Such loud asides grate in a town like Boulder and it's something of a paradox that these people still shoulder a load of guilt about having wiped out the entire Arapaho tribe.

But the women are something else. The two words that I hear bouncing off the walls and ceilings more than any other are 'relate' and 'relationship'. As I say, the seriousness here is of gargantuan *Guardian* proportions and you could read the *New York Times* every day for a year without smiling once. Yesterday I heard a girl tell her friend, 'I find it almost impossible to relate because I go for looks.' Later her friend said, 'I want a meaningful relationship but how the hell can you relate with a man?' Seething as it is with stunning-looking girls it would take a brave Englishman or a sociologist to take one on in Boulder. Mind you, it must have taken pretty serious men to drive wagons all the way from the east to come here to dig holes in the sides of these amazing snow-covered Rockies. I see them now through the window and wonder at the initial explosion which threw up a range that stretches from Canada to South America. It must have been like Earth splitting her pants.

And now, on my last day in Boulder City before setting out for New Orleans and the Mississippi, I shall go into town in our truck and try to relate to a couple of barmen. There's no escape and yesterday a barman in the Boulderado Hotel told me that he'd worked in the Plough Tavern in Museum Street while he was studying at the LSE. It sounds even worse than digging holes in the mountain sides. Doubtless I'll meet someone in New Orleans who once worked in the Coach and Horses. And how is that dreadful place?

17 November, 1984

Jeffrey Bernard

YANKS

Natchez, Mississippi

All Americans are tourists in their own country. The Russians can't afford to be and in the second biggest country in the world, Canada, they are far too parochial to shift far, although they occasionally emigrate – escape? – permanently. Horace Greeley exhorted the Americans to go West, and having done so they have now embraced North, South and East and have done so armed with cameras, Hawaiian shirts, fortissimo voices, jewel-encrusted fingers, wads of the almighty dollar, a short memory for history and the narrow-minded certainty that they are the chosen race:

the peacemakers with one finger on the button and a tongue in the cheek at the conference table. They certainly disarm me. Forthright, politically naive, charming and forthcoming as a well-oiled teenager, they are a mass of contradictions. At once hospitable and friendly, they are ruthless about money and do not suffer paupers gladly. I like them tremendously and yet I find their values stink. Without money and fame or either you are dead. They worship more gods in more churches than any other race, and yet they invented lynching. They inherited Abraham Lincoln and lumbered themselves with Richard Nixon. America was born under the sign of Gemini. You can get oysters in New Orleans for a mere ten cents each and yet the American brain is a hamburger. Is the American dream becoming a nightmare? It is certainly an introverted dream. Americans display little interest in much beyond their own front doors except for a great fear of Russia. Tell them that the Russians are just as or more frightened of them and your words will fall on deaf ears. Fear rules.

All these things preoccupy me, surrounded as I am by them as I steam up the Mississippi towards Memphis. The river is as thick and brown as gravy. At dawn and at sunset it is a sepia photograph with a vein of twisting gold that runs through the surrounding forests and marshes. Ulysses Grant fought the Confederate army here and like most Unionists claimed that the Civil War was all about the business of the abolition of slavery. Slaves – literate ones – must have been a little bewildered. Lincoln said that the direct cause of the war was to do with the question of whether a minority in a democratic country could or should have the right to defy a democratically elected majority. Shades of Arthur Scargill. But Lincoln and his supporters and colleagues never thought that black slaves were actually *equal* to white men, repugnant as they thought slavery to be. Americans are still trying to be nice to blacks and it is still an uphill struggle. For a race that attaches more importance to what state a man comes from than the Manchester United supporter attaches to whether a man is a City or United supporter, race and colour is almost an insurmountable hurdle. It certainly is for blacks I have met, not as aggressive as the London West Indian population, but seemingly indigenously stunned into a partial apathy by their history. They may even be losers yet without the compensating factor of being promoted to the survivor division.

But anyway, here I am, sitting by the rails on the veranda outside my cabin looking at Natchez where we've just docked. My socks and shirt are flapping in the Mississippi breeze. There is no laundry on this boat, but I have with me a pre-frozen glass of vodka martini. The barmaid on the boat tells me that her father has a pet alligator which has eaten two dogs belonging to his neighbours and at the 13th hole of the local golf course the hazard is a 12-foot alligator which waits for players in the bunker. Poisonous snakes abound and magnificent hawks soar above the 'Big Muddy'. Americans are conservation-conscious and yet compulsive hunters and shooters of almost anything that moves: a man in the bar at lunch-time told me that his hobby is killing bats with a tennis racquet. But I can't concentrate yet on the Mississippi. I am still brooding on New Orleans and its trellised verandas, fountained patios, palms, jazz, mad and crazy gay clubs, seafood, and the fact that I'd rather live in the old French quarter outside of anything I know apart from London, with the possible exceptions of Granada, Brighton and Barcelona. I think it was the seminar about lesbians over 60 that finally convinced me that New Orleans was quite as mad as you could wish to be. We stop at Vicksburg tomorrow and I shall study the terrain over which the most important southern battle of the Civil War was fought. The river goes on and on.

24 November, 1984

P. J. Kavanagh

REFLECTIONS IN KAMLOOPS

In his sermon this Sunday the Irish priest continually muddled up 'emigrant' and 'immigrant' – while exhorting us to understand the troubles in our midst. What did the distinction matter? At some point the one is bound to become the other, if the traveller survives. In Ford Madox Brown's 'The Last of England' the couple are staring back, they are emigrating, and the young man is ill-looking and fearful, as well he might be. When they arrive the verb will change, but in the St Lawrence River is an island where they detained the dying Irish who had contracted cholera on the way; these never 'immigrated'.

A few days before, I had been in Kamloops, a town in British Columbia built, as was everything in Canada, by immigrants. Perhaps everything, everywhere, is the result of some form of migration, but in Canada you feel this.

I was with an old friend, Patrick Lyndon, an Anglo-Irishman who has become a Canadian: he had driven me there from Vancouver. He is a man of an almost shuddering and humorous refinement and as we paced the empty streets I could feel this dread that I was going to say something obviously dismissive and Old World about Kamloops. I said nothing because I did not know what I thought, I was only surprised and disturbed by what I felt.

Kamloops is five or six hundred miles from any major settlement of people. The distances in Canada are what everyone knows about it, but they are extraordinarily difficult to take in. They accounted for my surprise, that the place should be there at all among so much emptiness, and a European dread of what it must be like to live there.

The downtown part, where the shops and banks are, few of them more than three storeys high, and all new, is a grid of possibly eight blocks. Then the tarmac declines into gravel and then into bare, infinite hills.

It was six in the evening and Patrick, for my sake, suddenly announced he would do something he had not done in 20 years in Canada – go into a Canadian pub. Sure enough, above a blank wooden door flush with the street was the word 'PUB' in letters two inches high. The door opened outwards, like a cupboard, and precisely as he pulled it a friendly-looking man half-fell out and continued across the street at an angle of 30°, one arm stuck out in front of him, one stuck out behind, exactly like a drunk in a music-hall sketch. Still smiling at this, we surveyed the interior, which was dark and windowless, so we left. Outside, the drunk was now on the pavement, bloody. He had clearly continued on his way till he had met an immovable object with his face. He was being tended by four Indian boys (it is usually the Indians, alas, who have to be tended) and we heard the ambulance already on its way.

We stopped outside a photographer's window and looked at the local groups. They were all magnificent human specimens. They made me remember a remark by Harold Robbins, who told of earning cents an hour in New York shovelling snow. Asked about the agony of his creative process he replied, 'It knocks the hell out of shovelling snow!' So must Kamloops knock the hell out of what their forebears left – Ireland starving, Highland evictions, miseries in the Ukraine. They came in search of a better life and the photographs show that their children have found it.

Also, their town has a history. 'Kahmolops' in Indian means 'meeting of the waters' and at the junction of the North and South Thomson rivers a fur-trading post was built in 1812. It is still a trading post for all sorts of things – grain, agricultural machinery, timber – on the motor-highway now, and this is littered with vast motels. We sat in the bar of one of these, subtle Patrick amused to see me silenced by his New World, I preoccupied by the deserts it sat among: I was dismayed too, for I had discovered that I, the son of an immigrant, whose great-grandfather had emigrated, was hopelessly wedded to the frowsty, stale, overcrowded, Old one. Whereas these, the Kamloops of the world, that a breath of wind could blow away, were probably the future, as the photographs in the window showed, in the glowing cheeks, the superb dentition. Nor could I forget the drunk; now possibly toothless.

19 October, 1985

Nicholas Coleridge

DIARY

A good story is going the rounds in New York at the moment. An English girl in her twenties was sent over for a business meeting by her merchant bank. It was her first time in the city, and she was apprehensive about being mugged. On the last night of her three-day visit she returned to her hotel in the early hours. (Opinion is divided over whether it was the Pierre or the Helmsley Palace she was staying in.) In any event, the lobby was deserted. While she waited for the lift to arrive, a tall black man came and stood next to her. He wore dark glasses and a leather coat and had a giant German sheepdog on a leash. The English girl found him sinister. When the lift arrived, and they had both got in, the girl pressed her floor number but the black man pressed nothing; he stood there watching her. The lift began its ascent and the girl was convinced she was going to be mugged. As the lift approached her floor the man grunted: 'Down! Down on the floor.' The girl complied at once and, trembling, fell onto all fours. Just then the doors opened and she made a dash for it, followed by the black man who unlocked the next-door room. Only then did she realise that, of course, he'd been addressing not her but the dog. The following morning she checked out. To her surprise, the bill had already been paid and a message left for her. It said: 'I haven't laughed so much for ages. Regards, Lionel Richie.' Lionel Richie is the multi-millionaire American entertainer who sang the mawkish song 'Hello' and performed at the closing ceremony of the Olympic Games, and people are describing this as the perfect New York anecdote. It has all the elements: fear, black men in dark glasses, paranoia in a lift, a smart hotel, money, show biz and something for nothing. In two weeks I must have been told the story five separate times. I've told it several times myself since getting back, and here lies the disappointment. The editor of *Cosmopolitan* insists that she heard exactly the same anecdote ten years ago, set in Chicago and featuring two old ladies and Harry Belafonte.

18 January, 1986

John Mortimer

MY VOYAGE ROUND REAGAN'S AMERICA

New York

We got into the stretch limo on Central Park South for the purpose of going to a dinner of television executives. The motor car was long enough to have held half a dozen coffins placed end to end and an appropriate crowd of mourners. In the private living room, in the shade of the black glass windows, armchairs were set at casual angles round the bar. We had just passed the Plaza Hotel when one of the two telephones bleeped to tell his wife that American bombs had fallen on Tripoli. We switched on the television as we crossed Third Avenue. Soon the country would receive what its critics now say is its most popular form of entertainment, a small war going on somewhere at the other end of the world which it cannot lose. So a Victorian gentleman sitting in his club in St James's might have turned the pages of the *Illustrated London News* and enjoyed drawings of another punitive raid by the army on the North-West Frontier. Her enemies have thus described America, but I have to report that the atmosphere in the stretch became truly funereal and at the large dinner party in 'Laurent' we heard no word of approval for the Reagan adventure. Such joy as there was seemed confined to taxi drivers, lift men and newspaper editorials.

Speaking of terrorism, which I suppose we were, the news pictures, before Tripoli, were of a motor car blown up on a New York street and the murder of a certain Frank De Ciccio. When John Gotti, De Ciccio's superior in the Gambino family and now on trial for racketeering in a Brooklyn Federal Court, was asked to comment on this extreme manner of settling the problems of power, he said, 'It's hard to be a gentleman around here.'

The administration's defence of the Tripoli bombardment seemed, when it came, to express much the same sentiment.

It was our last day in America when President Reagan ordered his F-111 bombers to leave the peaceful reaches of Lakenheath and Upper Heyford and go out and kill Libyan families. We had arrived ten days earlier in a New York glittering in the sunshine, with the cherry blossom and magnolias out with the depressed joggers, cheerful muggers and yelling paranoiacs in Central Park. Beefy girls wearing top hats and bits of dinner jackets were driving out-of-town tourists in hansom cabs. The traffic moved almost imperceptibly. Moments of danger were caused by the brutal cyclists who wear crash helmets and mount the pavements blowing whistles and mowing down pedestrians. In the marvellous Fifth Avenue book stores I kept my ears open for scraps of dialogue. 'She left Treve City and went to live on Riverside Drive with a 90-year-old man. Of course, she threw herself out of a 15th storey window.' And, 'When I saw him last year his nose had gone *completely*.' In the quiet Frick mansion the Rembrandts testified to eternal human values and the discernment of the great American collectors. For me the most important ritual of a visit to New York is to pay a call on Calvin Trillin, a hugely talented humorist, food writer and expert on murder and groceries, who lives in the Village. Together we sample the Italian delicatessens and Cantonese restaurants, find the best beanshoots and mushrooms grown in New Jersey and end with a ceremonial game of Noughts and Crosses (known to the natives as 'Tick Tack Do') with a live chicken in a Chinese amusement arcade. This malign bird, squawking and ruffling its feathers, pecks viciously at a series of buttons in its cage, its human opponent pushes a button and a nought or a cross appears on the patterned screen. Every game ends in the same way; the screen lights up with the simple legend 'Bird Wins'. We went with those well known American intellectuals, Joan Didion and John Gregory Dunn, who were somewhat miffed to find that they were quite unable to conquer a common and presumably uneducated fowl. At long last aggrieved Miss Didion suggested that the victor's button might have the assistance of 'a computer. Calvin Trillin professed himself profoundly shocked at this suggestion, having always, it seemed, believed that the bird had learnt the art of Tick Tack Do from years of long practice in some Chinese gambling den. Whatever the truth of the matter it gives a proper sense of humility to a visiting Brit author to find himself not even able to force a Sino-American hen to draw.

As important as the visit to Chinatown, is the first lunch in the Oyster

Bar at Grand Central Station, a huge art deco room, as brilliantly lit as La Coupole in Paris. Bringing the blue points and sword fish with Californian Chardonnay, the Cuban-Jewish waiter said we had lost a great Englishman. When I asked, 'Who?' he said, 'Peter Pears. Britten wrote *Death in Venice* to suit his character exactly, didn't he? I love that opera. I'm not doing badly at the Met. I just got tickets for *Parsifal* and *Don Carlos*.' The joys of America are a perpetual surprise. Who has ever eaten a dozen oysters in the buffet at Paddington Station, washed them down with an excellent white wine and discussed the Britten operas with the waiter?

Up the coast of Connecticut the Yale students are concentrated on law, business methods or accountancy and there are few revolts. The Reagan intervention in Nicaragua and the funding of Contra terrorists, who have nothing to learn from the appalling Colonel Gaddafi, have few supporters, even among taxi drivers and lift attendants. Nicaragua is not Vietnam and it produces no student marches. The American resumption of nuclear testing seems to have passed without a single demonstration. However, apartheid is the protest flavour of the month and some students have built a small shanty Soweto on the campus outside the principal's office in protest against the Yale shareholding in South Africa. Right-wing alumni came by night and knocked Soweto down with sledgehammers. Then the police were called in to remove the demonstrators. Now the voice of the youth seems to be silent as they sit behind the ivy-clad walls engrossed in computer studies.

Our hosts in New Haven told us that their friends were cancelling all holidays to Europe except to safe spots such as Budapest. They take the view that behind the Iron Curtain law and order prevail, the airports are ruthlessly guarded and cars rarely explode in the streets. Perhaps this provides a glimmer of hope for the world. A new Disneyland and Miami Beach might be developed on the shores of the Black Sea and the way be opened for an era of East-West understanding.

The Boston journalist was a plump and maternal-looking lady and an expert on British crime writers. She told me that she had been determined to join the Sherlock Holmes Society but that that chauvinist organisation prohibits women members. She had an uncle in the theatre who had a gentleman's suit made for her, advised her to sound like a high-voiced man and not a low-voiced woman, never to move too far because her walk would betray her and to mend bicycles and then wash the oil off her hands to open the pores of her skin. Her disguise was so effective that she not only penetrated the meetings of the Baker Street regulars but a number of gay Holmes experts made passes at her. I was left to wonder at the American attention to detail and to consider that no amount of reading crime stories produces competent detectives.

We were too late to catch a regular airline so we flew People's Express, affectionately known as 'People's Distress', from Newark. This company, owned by its employees, provides extraordinarily cheap flights which leave from a basic building which looks like a vast, uncarpeted garage. Out of the night crowds of young people came in shorts and sweaters, extremely overweight and carrying bags of tennis equipment. They lay on the ground or sat in chairs to the arms of which were fixed tiny, quarter-in-the-slot televisions which they peered at until the money ran out. Posters at the airport carried slogans such as 'Support Star Wars or Start Learning Russian' and 'Nuke Jane Fonda'. Carrying these messages were pale and depressed looking volunteers, as ignored as the missionaries of some extremely unattractive religion. It seems that they are the adherents of a Mr Lyndon LaRouche, a new politician who believes that Walter Mondale is an influential KGB agent and that the Queen of England is the centre of an international league of drug-peddlers. LaRouche leads a nomadic life, sheltered by his disciples, in order, as he says, to avoid death at the hands of communists and Zionists. Incredibly two LaRouche supporters won nominations as the Democratic lieutenant-governor and secretary of state in Chicago. This astonishing choice seems to have been made because the LaRouche candidates had Anglo-Saxon names and weren't known as machine politicians. Perhaps the event proves little except the amazing inefficiency of the Democrats, who weren't aware that a couple of loonies had been chosen to run with Adlai Stevenson. Meanwhile the LaRouche fans at the airport seem only slightly more embarrassing than those who used to offer us flowers, and the fat-thighed, open-necked, silent army of tennis players goes on its way, unperturbed by the news that the White House chief of staff, Mr Donald Regan, has, according to LaRouche, joined the Queen of England in the drug trade.

In Cleveland we met our first completely dedicated Reagan enthusiast, a defecting Polish diplomat. Romuald Spasowski, a tall man in his sixties with gold glasses and a grey goatee, looked like a professor in a Chekhov play. He had been ambassador to India and to the United States and Poland's deputy foreign minister. His father, whom he clearly admired, was a Marxist philosopher and an atheist, but since his defection Spasowski has been received into the Catholic Church and sentenced to death by General Jaruzelski. I asked him if he wasn't depressed by the apparent reluctance of the Great Powers to attempt an agreement on disarmament. Why did the Americans have to go on testing? 'You can never trust the Russians. They always cheat.' 'Perhaps they think the same thing about the Americans?' I wondered, and the ex-ambassador replied, 'I know Mr Reagan. He is a very simple man. A very emotional man. I don't think he'd cheat.' Spasowski said he felt that his death sentence, pronounced in his absence, had lightened his guilt after years of supporting communism. We sat in a television studio before breakfast, making small jokes about the rigours of a book tour, and I wondered how hard it would be to reject the beliefs and preoccupations of a lifetime and give such a warm welcome to a sentence of death.

The city we were in had been devastated by the collapse of the steel industry. Although it has its slums it also has a remarkable orchestra and an art gallery. Snow was falling on the grey building and another Polish dissident, a sailor who jumped his ship at the port on the lake, turned up at the literary lunch. 'Welcome,' the chairman said to him. 'And thank you for choosing Cleveland.'

'Chicago,' said the girl who worked on the *Sun-Times*, 'is the one place where, whenever I vote, I feel sordid. I've got a friend who hasn't lived here for 20 years and she says that she knows that her name is still put down as a voter for someone at every election.' Even the judiciary participate in the city's cheerful but dubious way of life. In an operation called 'Graylord', attorneys from another state penetrated the courtrooms and alleged that a considerable number of judges were bribable. A public lawyer who represented children in trouble said that rich parents could even pay not to have their abused offspring ordered into care. It seems an unbelievable situation in a court which has to deal, not only with child drug-pushers, but child prostitutes and child ponces. Behind the tall lakeside buildings the slums are sullen with racial tension, and yet the city is bursting with life, there are packed theatres and a new generation of important playwrights. It also has Studs Terkel, a small, grey-haired man who wears an old open mac, an open-necked shirt and sneakers, chews a cigar, talks in the gravelly accents of *The Front Page* and writes splendidly. Studs Terkel seems to have met everyone, from Al Capone to Ivy Compton-Burnett. Born in the year the *Titanic* sank, he spent his youth playing gangsters in radio soap operas. 'I only had two lines,' he said: ' "Get in the car!" and "My God, they've got me!" I used to act with Nancy Reagan's mother. Now Clint Eastwood's been elected Mayor of Carmel it seems you have to be an actor in politics, preferably an actor that's performed with apes. What are we doing round the world? Trying to recover from losing in Vietnam. Were you surprised we managed to beat Grenada? Would you be surprised if Mohammed Ali managed to knock out Woody Allen?' Studs Terkel professes himself proud to come from a city which has produced some extremely patriotic gangsters. 'Momo Giancano,' he says, 'one of the jewels in our city's crown, was called by the CIA when they wanted to do in Fidel Castro. And who can ever forget the moving plea of Al Capone, dying in Alcatraz? "Set me free and I'll help you fight the Bolsheviks." '

We sat at dinner looking down on the string of lights by the waves on the lakeside beach, the jewelled necklace, they call it, on Chicago's dirty neck. Our host was a psychiatrist who had made a study of the traumatic mental effects of severe burns, having travelled to England to meet those young servicemen horribly disfigured in the Falklands campaign. I asked him what nervous disease brought the most patients to his couch in the Windy City. He answered with a single word, 'Greed'.

In Minneapolis a local Supreme Court judge told me that a play had been written about one of the strangest of courtroom gambits, the so-called 'Twinky defence'. Students of recent American crime will recall the unfortunate Harvey Milk who, together with the Mayor of San Francisco, was shot by a fellow council member named Dan White. Mr White received a lenient sentence for manslaughter. It was suggested that his victim's homosexuality may have had something to do with the result, but part of his defence was that he lived on junk food and a diet of 'Twinkies' had addled his brain. It almost tempted me to go back to the bar and try it on at the Old Bailey. 'It wasn't insufficient weaning, my Lord, or the pressure of life in the inner city. Blame it on the Wimpy Bar.'

Back in New York I stood in a room at the top of a huge oil corporation tower looking out over the Statue of Liberty. On one of the roof tops below us a track had been built for the shapeless employees of a neighbouring publisher condemned to jog during their lunch hours. The oil men seemed nervous about the consequences of the American treatment of Libya, although the theory was gaining ground of some sort of tacit Russian agreement. The Russians must have tracked American ships in the Gulf of Sidra as well as the F-111 bombers and yet they clearly failed to warn Gaddafi. Is it possible that, when it comes to matters of war, the world's two greatest powers understand each other better than anyone thinks?

In a short stay in America, meeting publishers, journalists, bookshop owners, even readers, we were bound to encounter the opposition to Mr Reagan. What was surprising was its extent and its bewilderment at his continuing support. All the mistakes, the speeches loaded with misinformation about every subject from the distance of Nicaragua to Russian nuclear testing leave the old boy apparently unstained, so he has become known as the 'Teflon' President. Nothing, it seems, can impair the actor's essential lovability in the eyes of a great part of the public who fear, for instance, his interference in South America. On the whole, journalists fail to cross-examine his spokesmen and a television news editor said that he'd stopped pointing out the mistakes in the President's speeches as to do so might be unpopular. The myth that has grown up seems to be, not that what Reagan does is right, but that he is too nice a chap to be blamed for being wrong. It doesn't seem to be a belief we have to share, however much we love America.

Most of the people I have met asked about the television version of *Brideshead Revisited*. I remembered that Evelyn Waugh had written that he didn't think that more than eight Americans would ever enjoy *Brideshead*. Now they have Lord Sebastian Flyte look-alike contests in the streets of San Francisco. Even old Horace Rumpole, that most British of barristers, has American restaurants named after him and societies on the West Coast which meet to study his cases. I would advise Mrs Thatcher, in all friendliness, to be as British as possible if she really wants the Americans to like her. It's no good ruining our reputation for political wisdom and common sense, falling over ourselves to become the American aircraft carrier or rushing to join President Reagan's somewhat doubting constituency. Apart from the deaths in Europe and Tripoli, the tragedy of the last ten days is that Britain has lost its identity and is in danger of becoming a tasteless mid-Atlantic mess, like the food in an international airport hotel.

26 April, 1986

8 CENTRAL AND SOUTH AMERICA

Ian Fleming

AUTOMOBILIA

One man who is even more childishly vain than myself is Noël Coward. Last year, in Jamaica, he took delivery of a sky-blue Chevrolet Belair Convertible which he immediately drove round to show off to me. We went for a long ride to *épater la bourgeoisie*. Our passage along the coast road was as triumphal as, a year before, Princess Margaret's had been. As we swept through a tiny village, a Negro lounger, galvanised by the glorious vision, threw his hands up to heaven and cried, 'Cheesus-Kerist!'

'How did he know?' said Coward.

Our pride was to have a fall. We stopped for petrol.

'Fill her up,' said Coward.

There was a prolonged pause, followed by some quiet tinkering and jabbering from behind the car.

'What's going on, Coley?'

'They can't find the hole,' said Cole Lesley from the rear seat.

Coley got out. There was more and louder argumentation. A crowd gathered. I got out and, while Coward stared loftily, patiently at the sky, went over the car front and back with a tooth-comb. There was no hole. I told Coward so.

'Don't be silly, dear boy. The Americans are very clever at making motor-cars. They wouldn't forget a thing like that. In fact, they probably started with the hole and then built the car round it.'

'Come and look for yourself.'

'I wouldn't think of demeaning myself before the natives.'

'Well, have you got an instruction book?'

'How should I know? Don't ask silly questions.'

The crowd gazed earnestly at us, trying to fathom whether we were ignorant or playing some white man's game. I found the trick catch of the glove compartment and took out the instruction book. The secret was on the last page. You had to unscrew the stop-light. The filler cap was behind it.

'Anyone could have told you that,' commented Coward airily.

I looked at him coldly. 'It's interesting,' I said. 'When you sweat with embarrassment the sweat runs down your face and drops off your first chin on to your second.'

'Don't be childish.'

4 April, 1958

Ian Fleming

PLEASURE ISLANDS?

It seems that a middle-aged couple who received a lot of publicity in a recent court case have just sailed for Jamaica 'to start a new life.' When I read this I felt sorry for them, because I had a sudden vision of that splendid tear-jerker, *The Last of England*, by Ford Madox Brown, and I continued to feel sorry for them after the picture had faded from my mind. I thought of the other seekers after a new life that have crossed my path, and particularly of those I have met in Jamaica, where I built a small house after the war and where I spend all my holidays.

Each year there are new arrivals and new departures. Three years ago an extra bathroom was installed in 'Bonaventure,' and Major Jones and his nice wife (But will she stand the heat? What's he going to do all day?) gave a house-warming. Loving dusky fingers had moulded the sausage-meat canapés and decorated each with a little squirt of Heinz mayonnaise (My dear, she only costs me sixteen shillings a week!), and everyone was given a paper doily for the warmish rum cocktails so as not to spoil the new furniture. Two years later the MacNaughts were installed, and 'Dunlookin' was inscribed on the gate. The Joneses had gone back to an aunt at Cheltenham £5,000 the poorer.

The trouble is that after forty it is difficult to start a new life without a new psyche, and perhaps a new envelope for it. If one can't settle down at home, one is unlikely to settle down abroad. The only true geographical misfits are people with asthma or tuberculosis who *have* to seek a new climate in order to exist. For the rest of us, however difficult life may be 'at home,' the roots are too many and too deep. Emigration is for the under-thirties, and for them there are wonderful and promising futures in the young continents and islands of the Commonwealth. Even in the West Indies, which I know fairly well, you have only to study the merchant adventuring of the Dominions Colonial and Overseas branch of

Barclays Bank to see how much exciting development is going on in all the various islands of this young 'dominion' – citrus, bananas, coconut-products, essential oils, fisheries, minerals (Jamaica has the largest baux-ite deposits in the world; being exploited by Americans, of course), dia-monds, hardwoods, tourism, oil, tobacco and so forth, all with openings for men who are patient and sober.

They must be patient, because without patience you cannot live and work with coloured people, and they must be sober because alcohol ruins your health in the tropics. It goes straight to your liver and stays there. The Scots are naturally patient and sober, and that is why they make such wonderful colonisers. And they have another virtue which is important in the tropics: they have a hardy and absorbing inner life which they take with them wherever they go and which makes them very undemanding of their surroundings. The provincialism and intellectual apathy of the tropics do not irk them. They get all the mental exercise they need from the constant battle to maintain sanity and symmetry in their immediate neighbourhood and to keep tropical chaos at bay. Other peoples also have these virtues, but in the case of the Germans, for instance, they are part of a disciplined way of life, a self-imposed carapace, which is all too apt in the hot sun to become nothing but a pressure-cooker for the neuroses it conceals.

Melancholia, bile and *accidie*, or noonday sloth, are man's deadly enemies in the tropics, and they can only be cured by the obvious remedies, creative work, physical exercise, mental stimulation, and by such spiritual resources as may be present in the afflicted. But, above all, if the settler or visitor is to be happy, he must really *embrace* the tropics. It is easy to enjoy the orchids and the humming birds. They are exotic extensions of things we know; but there is much that is very strange in the tropical flora and fauna, and to many people 'strange' means 'inimi-cal.' The sixth sense of the vultures and their hideous heads, the blood-thirst of shark and barracuda, the huge hawk moths, the praying mantis (Nature's 'mobile'), the fruits which are sometimes deadly poison until ripe and thereafter delicious, the obscene banana flower, the zany riot of the cannon-ball tree, the ants' nests like brown goitres on the trees, the sharp and poisonous coral, the forest of black needles on the sea-eggs – all these can become bogeys if they are not seen with something of the natu-ralist's marvelling eye.

One must, of course, also like the sun and take pleasure in the sudden thrashing rain. One's senses must not be offended by a world of very strong primary colours, blues, reds, yellows and greens, nor by the deep texture of the night with its piercing zing of crickets and plaintive tinkle of tree-frogs. One must get used to the deep hush which underlines these

insect noises, and to the knowledge that there will be few people abroad
after dark for fear, in Jamaica, of the rolling calf, that terrible phantom, its
legs bound with chains and its nostrils flaming, which comes rolling
towards you in the glare of the moon. Because of him and of other fearful
'duppies' you need also not pay too much heed to the tales of naked black
men, their bodies glistening with coconut oil, who roam abroad at night
to thieve and rape. In fact, I believe that most black races have more fears
than the whites. They are timid experimenters and inept or unwilling
rationalisers of their fears and superstitions. For instance, in Jamaica
they insist on believing that the common lizard will bite, and a popular
maxim of the country is: 'When you see old lady run, no axe wha' de matter, run too.'

They have other characteristics which are strange to us, but again not
necessarily inimical, and they and their peculiarities must also be
'embraced' if you decide to live among them. I find that their organs of
sight and hearing are keener than ours, and that their extra-sensory perception, their sixth sense, is more highly developed. On the other hand, I
think their physical strength is often undermined by weak nerves, and
this makes them an easy prey to sickness or fear. Their tempo is their
own and cannot be altered, but they are full of goodwill and cheerfulness
and humour. They are loyal to good employers and sober and honest
unless sorely tempted, but when they fall they fall heavily and far.

These miscellaneous thoughts on life in the Caribbean may seem
rather flimsy, but the major pros and cons are so obvious that they will
have been already weighed by prospective visitors and settlers or can be
gleaned from the *West Indies Handbook*. The Caribbean is very beautiful,
very healthy, very 'safe'; and the cost of living is medium to very low. But
it is expensive to get there, and the territory is remote from the stream of
history, and, for many reasons besides those I have mentioned, to settle
there is more of a gamble than in territories less tropical or nearer home.

I can only hope that the couple whose departure brought all this to my
mind were quite clear that 'no ebery ting wha' got sugar a sweet' when
they chose the pleasure islands of the West Indies in their search for a
new life.

4 July, 1952

Shiva Naipaul

NOWHERE IN PARTICULAR

'Welcome to Puerto Rico, USA' said the handout in my hotel room. I was being greeted by the Puerto Rican Manufacturers Association. They told me they were confident I would enjoy their 'Caribbean island paradise'. Manufacturing, I was then informed, had transformed the island into one of the foremost industrial centres in the Western world. There were over 2,000 factories in operation. These had created approximately 150,000 jobs.

It seemed an odd introduction to a paradise. Through plate-glass doors I stared out at hibiscus, at oleander, at wind-ruffled coconut palms, at a turquoise sea breaking over a line of rocks. I could have been almost anywhere in the Caribbean. But, as the message from the Manufacturers Association had hinted, this was not just another beach-ringed 'paradise'. I had come to an island which had managed to elude many of the maelstroms of Caribbean history; whose failure to wrest an independent existence for itself appeared to have paid handsome dividends.

From afar I have watched Jamaica set itself up as a leader of the Third World, propel itself into economic chaos – and teeter on the brink of civil war; I have watched Guyana succumb to a deadly megalomania fuelled by corruptions that defy reason – a state of affairs which reached an apocalyptic climax in the massacre at Jonestown; I have watched Grenada free itself from a Duvalieresque dictatorship only to fall into the hands of a group of men who look to Cuba for inspiration; I have watched the sandspit of Anguilla make a unilateral declaration of independence; I have witnessed an attempted coup by the army in Trinidad; I have heard rumours of secession in Tobago; I am told that Barbuda has no desire to be associated with Antigua; and, most recently of all, the deposed Prime Minister of Dominica attempted to reinstate himself with the aid of mercenaries recruited from the Ku Klux Klan, hoping to set up on his island a sort of kingdom of the underworld.

Puerto Rico is an anomalous sort of place. Not quite a colony, not quite a state of the American Union; at one and the same time proudly autonomous and hopelessly dependent. In English the paradox is expressed by

the somewhat enigmatic term 'Commonwealth'. In Spanish, this puzzl-
ing condition is rendered as 'Estado Libre Asociado' – free associated
state. The island's hybrid status is, it seems to me, admirably expressed by
this mildly oxymoronic description. Puerto Ricans are American citizens. As such, no restrictions are imposed on movement to and from the
United States (the million or more Puerto Ricans who live on the mainland show just how popular a privilege this is) and, as a quid pro quo, they
can be drafted for military service. On the other hand, they do not pay
Federal taxes and cannot vote in Federal elections.

The situation is hopelessly blurred. It has been so ever since the Americans – chary of imperialism in the old-fashioned sense of the word – took
over from the Spanish in 1898. But the perplexity was not a wholly novel
one for the Puerto Ricans: 'status' has been the one abiding political question for the last 150 years. It was the dominant theme during the dying
decades of Spanish control; and it has remained so under the American
dispensation. Puerto Rican flexibility is well illustrated by the fact that,
within a year of the annexation, a political party was formed to clamour
for complete absorption. Today, the island's two main parties owe their
existence to the differing views they have adopted on the status issue:
one advocates statehood, the other the indefinite perpetuation of the
ambiguities of the Commonwealth.

'Puerto Rico, USA' can be regarded as the slogan of the former. At a certain level the assertion rings true. The transition from New York to San
Juan involves no 'culture shock'. Driving along the superhighway linking the capital to Ponce on the south coast is a purely American experience. Only the lush tropical vegetation greening the hillsides and the
occasional glimpse of some remote hovel strike an errant note. Miami
(they say with pride) is recreated in the Condado section of San Juan. Suburban life finds its confirmation in stylish shopping centres replete with
air-conditioned banks and gaudy temples dedicated to fast-food. Puerto
Rico, USA exists when you flick from television channel to television
channel and from radio station to radio station. Unbelievably, in Ponce's
art museum you can look at paintings by Rubens, Constable, Courbet,
the Pre-Raphaelites. America exists in the one million motor-cars shared
among the island's three million inhabitants, in the paucity of public
transport, in the basketball courts you see everywhere, in the fat policemen with hands poised on bulging gun-holsters, in the smoking chimneys of oil refineries and petrochemical plants. You will be told again and
again that, with the exception of the United States proper and Canada,
Puerto Ricans enjoy the highest standard of living in the western hemisphere. Pitying, contemptuous shrugs accompany references to the
Dominican Republic, to Cuba, to Haiti, to Jamaica. Ah . . . the miseries of

Independence! How blessed, how fortunate is Puerto Rico! 'We are *American* now,' a Ponce city official insisted. For him, statehood was the only legitimate aspiration. Its realisation would confer a proper dignity. It was no good carrying on indefinitely as quasi-Americans. Puerto Ricans, he assured me, were impatient to assume the full responsibilities of citizenship. Also, as a passionate believer in 'democracy' he could see no other way of guaranteeing its survival in Puerto Rico. Unfettered Hispanic culture, he seemed to suggest, was inimical to it.

The Commonwealth faction is more cautious. They worry about the additional taxation burden which statehood would bring; they wonder if most Puerto Ricans really understand the rigours it would involve. These anxieties fade off into trepidation about the cultural fate of the island – still 'Hispanic' after all, still Spanish-speaking – if it were to be entirely absorbed. Look at what had happened to Hawaii . . . Would Spanish, for instance, be driven into the wilderness? The Ponce city official laughed at these fears. 'What is wrong with learning English?' he asked. 'If we have to learn English, we'll just have to. That's all. Learning English isn't going to make Puerto Rico disappear.' The fears of those who oppose him may be exaggerated. But they are not completely unfounded. While I was there, the Puerto Rican Bar Association was driven to protest when a US Army major decided that all personnel at the Armed Forces Entrance and Examining Station must cease using Spanish even in private conversation. For some, incidents like these are portentous; for the ardent advocates of statehood – such as the Ponce official – they are no more than tea-cup typhoons.

But the advocates of statehood and Commonwealth share one feeling. They both react with horror to the idea of Independence, a dying dream stained by terrorism and undercut by hard-headed realities. Puerto Rico, despite its industrial revolution, despite those 150,000 jobs created by the manufacturers, remains a basket-case: more than half of the population depends on food stamps and other Federal handouts. Puerto Rico knows it will never make it on its own; it knows that it needs to be protected from itself.

Sixty miles to the west the Union Jack flaps limply over those scattered crumbs of the Empire known as the British Virgin Islands. Area: fifty-nine square miles. Population: approximately 11,000. 'Tortola,' said a 19th century writer, 'is well nigh the most miserable, worst inhabited spot in all the British possessions'. I wouldn't go as far as that. I can think of at least a dozen more miserable spots.

Like Puerto Rico, the islands have an internally autonomous political life and no one seems to care much for the idea of Independence –

though, one gathers, the British would be only too happy to oblige. 'Give we Independence,' said one canny local, 'and you give we a dictator. No, man! We doing fine just as we is.' After which, he offered me some marijuana. The Governor sits in his house up on the hill and interferes little. Faint rumours of corruption surround the administration. The Chief Minister, it is alleged, has a fondness for acquiring property. But if the locals have their doubts about the propriety of his real-estate transactions, the expatriates have none. To a man, they lavish praise on his wisdom and devotion to duty. If, I was told by one of them, he has done well for himself, that was only because he was a tremendously hard worker and an extremely clever man. Which, I am sure, is true.

Away from the water not much happens. Road Town is one narrow, winding main street. Its chief architectural monument is a white-walled jail crowned by barbed wire. What else can one say? There are no forts to look at; there is no visible sign of agricultural effort. Liquor is extraordinarily cheap and, apparently, is one of the hazards of expatriate life on the islands. There is talk of drilling for oil. During my stay an art gallery was opened and a Society of the Blind founded. The sea shines. Yachts move dreamily. At night, jolly loads of 'boat-people' descend on Stanley's Beach Bar and jive to the steelband under the watchful gaze of hungry-eyed blacks in dark glasses. Placid expatriates draw word pictures of their contentment. The most dramatic happening on the islands occurred about 150 years ago when an Englishman was hanged for mistreating his slaves. Nothing of consequence happened after that. The islands sit amid their shining seas, awaiting nothing in particular.

3 October, 1981

Patrick Marnham

FROM CARTAGO TO LIMON

Costa Rica

Irazu is a live volcano. At dawn, as the light steals down into the crater, the colours slowly seep through its uneven surface. There are gashes of yellow and, in one area where the rain has collected, it is livid green. It is 15 years since Irazu last erupted. On that occasion the lava poured down the northern slopes and blew out over the central Costa Rican plateau covering the fields and towns in a fine grey ash. The eruption lasted for two years. The northern slopes are still black and dead, but the rest of the mountain is planted with trees. The muck that pours out of a volcano makes good fertiliser, eventually.

Twenty minutes after sunrise you can look down on the redder patches of cloud to the east that appear to hide the sun somewhere over the invisible Atlantic. Then the real sun shows, silver and much higher than it had seemed. The peak of Irazu is 11,260 feet. Even at this chilly altitude there are doves, sparrows and plump black birds with long tails flocking in the juniper bushes. They have come up from the thickly wooded southern slopes. They avoid the lava runs on the north side, though even there some plants grow. Between the red lava and gritty black sand, tree trunks are twisted into fantastic shapes. They look dead from a distance. Closer one can see that they bear scrappy green shoots pushing directly out from the thick trunks, without benefit of branches. And below the lip of the crater rubbery plants with swollen circular leaves grow directly out of the rock.

At this altitude one has to catch one's breath suddenly, sometimes after a slight movement such as turning round. The lack of air can cause dizziness. Looking down into the crater there are no signs of life. The level of its surface varies by hundreds of feet: in some places deep rain gorges have cut down into the mountain, in others there is a smooth expanse of flat sand that looks firm enough to drive a lorry across. Although the volcano has been quiet for 15 years this interior surface changes all the time. The sand levels collapse into deep chasms and the rocky gorges are covered over in their turn. The father of my guide was once actually in the crater of Irazu when it went up without warning. He and his party scrambled for the sides and tried to climb to safety, but their feet slipped back a step for every two paces they took. Fortunately it was a minor event: the wind carried the poisonous fumes away from them and only one man was killed. The neighbouring volcano, Turrialba, is also live and smokes away steadily most of the time.

The highest peak on the opposite side of the plateau is called Sierra de la Muerte, but it is unwise to count on any of these volcanoes being dead. Some years ago another volcano, Arenal, which had long been thought extinct, went up with such force that it blew its cone off and many of the people living on its slopes were killed by gas and ash. A few days before, parties had been camping overnight on the floor of Arenal's crater. And a few days after I ascended Irazu the volcano rumbled back to life again. Seismologists recorded 137 tremors from the crater in a period of 34 hours.

By half past six on the morning of my visit the clouds in the sky over the Atlantic, deceptive maps, have been replaced by a real coastline. It is clear enough to see an island in the sea. Behind us the Pacific is also now clearly visible, though from this distance it looks no larger than a lake. Balboa, silent on a peak in Darien, with his first sight of the Pacific, must have been an optimist or a man with a theory.

Descending from Irazu one passes through some of the richest farmland in Costa Rica. The thick black soil is skilfully carved along its contour lines by ploughmen using oxen. The oxen wear embroidered leather head-dresses. The ploughmen wear velvet cowboy hats and carry short swords in leather scabbards. One might think that living on the slopes of a live volcano would add a little zip to daily life, but these men seem as peaceful as their beasts. There is something of Somerset in the wet grassy banks and deep combes that divide their plots. They are probably doped by the soft, warm rain that falls on them for most of the year. Historically they seem to suffer more from earthquakes than from volcanoes. Cartago, which is their nearest town, was originally the capital city but it was destroyed by earthquakes in 1841, and again in 1910, so the government moved to San José. The last time it was so bad that only three houses were left standing.

Even today there are few houses in Cartago higher than two storeys, and most houses are built of wood, which seems rather fatalistic. The town contains one magnificent stone ruin, which is the old parish church and must have been as large as many cathedrals. A notice outside says that it was totally destroyed in the earthquake of Saint Antolon and then totally destroyed again in the earthquake of Saint Monica. You have to have a certain familiarity with earthquakes before you start naming them after saints. It may seem surprising that a stone building of such strength should have been shaken to the ground by Saint Monica, but the people of Cartago know what happened. They say that they once had a parish priest whose brother married a very beautiful girl. The priest then seduced his sister-in-law and from that day on the church was cursed. They have not tried to build it on that spot a third time. The Gothic ruins now surround a beautiful garden. The enclosure is popular with courting couples who are kept under general observation by the guardian of the site. He walked up and down in the rain holding his furled umbrella by his side. There were quite a lot of men in Cartago who walked in the rain with their umbrellas furled.

While I had lunch in a bar a traveller carried a large cardboard box into the room and opened it. It was full of live crayfish. The fat girl who was sweeping the floor was frightened into squealing like a puppy. The crayfish were not at all frightened. They spread out across the floor of the bar and it was some time before they were all recaptured. In an adjoining room there was some sort of engagement party. At one table a girl was sitting with two men. The older man, much older, seemed to be her fiancé. They were surrounded by an all-male band – three trumpeters, three guitarists and a singer. The bandsmen wore tight trousers with three rows of brass studs down the outside seam. The singer stood directly behind the girl's chair and gave it full volume. There was an expression of restrained happiness on every face except that of the girl who looked thoroughly embarrassed. Round the sides of the room there were several other bands in different uniforms waiting their turn to serenade her. There was a rack for guitars by the door; she was the only woman in the room.

I wanted to spend the night in Cartago and I went to a hotel which was said to be clean and welcoming. A surly man took my money in advance and led me to a room overlooking the railway track. I sat on the bed and the fleas rose in a cloud. It is one thing to be bitten by the occasional flea; it is altogether different to see the little fellows lining up and applauding your arrival.

Forced to choose between the fleas of the mountains and the mosquitoes of the coast I chose the coast. There is something less personal about mosquitoes. One doesn't care where they have been before. I had a long argument with a taxi driver about the fare to Puerto Limon, a three-hour drive, which he won. He stopped on the way beside a small shack where he was greeted ecstatically by his children and by his contented wife who was sitting in the crumbling porch sewing buttons on his shirts. The ecstasy was apparently caused by the news of the fare. I felt less bitter about losing the argument. Next stop was the garage. This man must have been completely broke before he picked me up, because he filled up with petrol, changed the oil and bought a new tyre. Eventually the car was in reasonable condition to continue. 'Now we are safe,' he said. Just then the rain came down so hard that the wipers were quite unable to penetrate the curtain of water on the windshield. Somewhere ahead of us the tail-lights of a lorry disappeared into the storm. The taxi driver accelerated happily. 'Now you can sleep,' he said. Remembering the happiness of his children I realised that this man was not going to have a crash, so I went to sleep.

In Central America the people of the Atlantic coast are mainly of African descent, hired originally in the West Indies to work on the banana plantations. They speak Spanish and English, and in Puerto Limon they speak a sing-song Jamaican English, which is pleasant to hear. When I arrived the African receptionist at my hotel was being gently persuaded by three Cubans, two men, one woman, to let them share a double room.

After a while one of the men made her giggle and then she gave in. It was hard to say whether the Cubans were trying to save money or have a good time. Maybe in Cuba you can do both.

Aware of the need to recover her dignity she told me, when I asked to see a room, that I could see two rooms, but that if I wanted a towel I would have to sign for it. It was three days before I saw her smile again. She told me that her great grandparents had come over from Jamaica nearly a hundred years ago and that I would find most people in the town were bilingual even now. I noticed, however, that the older people spoke better English than their children.

Slowly the community is changing its English culture for a Spanish one. On Sunday evening these African people gather in families and make a formal *paseo* through the streets and round the park, something which one rarely sees today in Spain. The people of the coast are the poorest people in Costa Rica. There is little work apart from the docks and the banana farms which are owned by American fruit companies and are frequently the scene of violent strikes, violently put down. It is this part of the country that the government intends to develop as a tourist paradise.

On Sunday, while the town slept in the afternoon heat, I walked out onto the wooden quays to watch the bananas being loaded onto a boat owned by the Del Monte fruit company. The banana trains go right out onto the rotting wooden piles and shunt up and down in the glaring heat. You have to keep a sharp lookout for loose wagons. If there is a signalling procedure they keep it to themselves.

The dock foreman was lying on a crate resting. He was a vast man with a blue-black skin and pouring with sweat. I have never seen a man look so peaceful and so hot. He declined to have his photograph taken. After resting for a few minutes he stood under a water pipe to cool off. His day's food was a yard of raw sugar cane and three cobs of sweet corn. He said his wife was living on an abandoned banana plantation beyond the swamps; that meant she was squatting. The owners call such families who work abandoned banana farms for their own profit *parasitos*. The profits to be made from the tropical fruit business are very acceptable.

Walking round to the stern of the Del Monte banana boat, I noticed that this American company had registered the boat in Panama, thereby taking advantage of less stringent safety and labour regulations. That night I came across the following passage in *Nostromo*, where Conrad's character, Charles Gould, the owner of a Central American silver mine, speaks: 'What is wanted here is law, good faith, order, security . . . that's how your money-making is justified here in the face of lawlessness and disorder. It is justified because the security which it demands must be

shared with an oppressed people. A better justice will come afterwards.
That's your ray of hope.'

19 June, 1982

Patrick Marnham

WAITING FOR TROTSKY

Mexico City

We are sitting in a booth in Tenampa, a bar in the Plaza Garibaldi. A man
is singing to us. He has a face like a rubber monkey and the most mischie-
vous eyes in Mexico.

'So, farewell,' he sings. We remain. 'Oh, what drinking took place during this night of sentiment.' This is more like it. 'There can be no other
land like mine,' he sings. 'Where you find men who are pure *macho*, and
where you find the real drunks.' The song is most affecting. The noise is
unbelievable. He is not singing alone. He is accompanied by three guitars,
two violins, a double bass and two heart-rending, ear-splitting trumpets.
All these musicians, who are clustered around our booth, are dressed in
skin-tight black trousers and short waistcoats and they are dripping in
silver embroidery and silver ornaments. The singer's voice soars above
the general racket. We are drowning in the sound and sentiment. We
gaze deeply into his eyes. I think I am about to burst into tears, overwhelmed by the beauty of this musical philosopher.

The situation is saved by the arrival of another man, holding a contrap-
tion. It looks like surplus police stock, from the interrogation room.
Edward says that this man's middle name is 'Annihilation'. Annihilation
invites me to attach myself to his electric shock machine. I agree to do so.
He has a grey track running through his hair, like a lightning flash. He
says that 'the maximum strength of the machine is 90'. Ninety what?

'Ten,' he says, moving his little dial. 'Twenty.' Edward and Stella look
on with interest. 'Thirty.' Can these be my hands gripping two metal barrels which are attached to wires, which run back to Annihilation's
machine? I feel an agreeable tingling sensation in my arms. It must be the
tequila, or maybe the mescal. Edward says that at the altitude of Mexico
City tequila does not make you drunk. He says that you must never drink
it at sea level. 'Fifty.' Annihilation is observing me closely. 'Sixty.' But it is

all right at 7,300 feet. At 'Seventy' I let out a scream and manage to drop the electrodes. Annihilation beams with pleasure. He was beginning to think there was something wrong with his machine.

'Why don't you all hold hands?' says Annihilation. Edward and I can each hold an electrode, and Stella can sit in the middle and be electro-cuted. What a good idea. It is also highly scientific. It is a repetition of one of the earliest electrical experiments. In France in the 17th century some alchemist persuaded two dozen friars to lock themselves to an iron chain along which an electrical current was passed. It was possible to trace the progress of the electrical charge as the friars hopped up and down. This kept the audience happy for hours. But we are in 20th-century Mexico, not 17th-century France. As we form a human power cable and gaze trustingly up at Annihilation I wonder why we have such confidence in amateur Mexican technology. Professional Mexican technology does not support this confidence. Already a bottle of Pedro Domecq's *Los Reyes blanco* has exploded in the waiter's hands, powdering my food and my left eye with glass. And while munching from a can of peanuts supplied by Industrias Mafer I heard a crackling noise and discovered that a pea-nut-sized lump of glass had been included with the peanuts.

It is when Annihilation says 'Fifty' that we realise something has gone wrong with the experiment. Stella and I feel nothing. We are just sitting there holding hands. My electrode is apparently dead. But Edward, whose hair is at the best of times arranged in a rather spiky and electrical style, is another matter. He is jerking up and down like a yoyo, twisting from side to side, going red in the face and seems set to give out sparks at any moment. 'Stop playing the fool,' I say, just as Edward's feet jerk off the steel bar on which he has inadvertently placed them. The short-circuit is thereby bridged, and the three of us are fused for one unforgettable moment at 'One hundred and twenty'. Annihilation, unaware of the short-circuit, had flicked a switch and doubled the charge.

The Plaza Garibaldi is a small square near the centre of Mexico City. It is the gathering point for all the *mariachi* bands who have nothing better to do. In the centre of the square there is a glass-fronted shrine contain-ing the image of the Virgin of the *mariachis*. All around, beneath the trees and far into the night, stand groups of trumpeters, accordionists and guitarists, playing to each other or to any passer-by who will pay for a song. The floor of the shrine is covered with notes and coins offered by those who hope that their visit to the musicians will change their luck or the course of their lives. Around the square are various bars and cafés, some of which do not admit women. *Mariachi* songs seem to be more con-cerned with drink and manhood than with love. The Mexicans make a distinction here. The atmosphere of the Plaza Garibaldi, formed by the noise, the dashing style of the bands and the cheerfully insulting words of the songs, is relentlessly Mexican.

To recover from the attentions of Annihilation we order another round of tequila. *Porque non?* By now our band has been taken over by two young porters on a night out from the food market. In Mexican fashion they join in the singing. They have to support each other as they stand up to do so. Moved by an uncharacteristic benevolence towards foreigners, they dedicate their song to us.

'You do not know,' they sing, 'You can *never* know, how drunk we are. Or how happy we are. Oh, how many times have I been thrown out of this bar. And so I have walked in the streets, singing my songs, with a lump in my throat, and my *mariachis* at my heels.' The porters sway in harmony by our table, their limpid brown eyes moving gently in and out of focus. One of them is clutching a photograph of himself looking fierce in an enormous sombrero. The other is clutching something far more valuable: a new tube of toothpaste. There has been no toothpaste in the shops of Mexico City for the past three weeks. The rumour is that the factories have plenty of paste and many empty tubes but there are no caps for the tubes. The caps have to be imported from the United States and there is a national shortage of foreign currency. We are being advised to use a mixture of salt and bicarbonate of soda instead. The porter puts his toothpaste on the table behind him. Two of the *mariachis*, taking advantage of his preoccupation with the song, start to nudge the tube towards the edge of the table with their violin bows.

A waiter approaches with more tequila. He murmurs something in Edward's ear. Edward says that the waiter is called 'Gigantically'. This is hardly likely. What is his second name? 'Sexual.' The waiter is by now making smoochy noises at Edward. Behind his back the *macho* refrains clang together from several parts of the hall. Gigantically Sexual has dyed black hair and looks about 70. We find his interest in Edward diverting, but he is a cunning old fox and when we eventually leave the bar Gigantically abruptly alters course and it is Stella who gets kissed. I forget to ask her what he tasted like. She may not be aware of the toothpaste crisis.

In Mexico City it is possible to while away many happy hours in bars like Tenampa. But should one do so? Should one travel for a month and 6,000 miles in order to drink tequila at this crazy altitude and munch glass chippings and volunteer for electric shocks? Surely the answer is – Yes, one should do it as frequently as possible. But for those who disagree I have an explanation. I did not wish to leave Mexico City without visiting the house of Trotsky, and I could not visit the house of Trotsky because it was closed for Holy Week.

Only after the doomed Christs had been processed around every town in Mexico, and the dead Christs had been taken from their crosses and laid in crystal biers, and the risen Christs had been nailed back in triumph on thousands of altars, and only after all the penitents and flagellants had scourged themselves to shreds with cactus thorns and changed their shirts and gone back to work, only then did the steel doors of the house where Trotsky was murdered reopen for visitors.

23 April, 1983

John Stewart Collis

THE AQUA EYE

Recently I found myself on the South Cay, which is the smallest island, and furthest from the shore, out from Port Royal at Kingston in Jamaica. It contained one mangrove tree and a few bushes. It was about the size of three tennis courts. Its beach was chiefly composed of coral chippings. There can be smaller islands than this dotted in the oceans of the world. Sometimes they can be illusions and sink when you land on them. Thus, Theobald, author of *Physiologus de Naturus XII*, mentions how sailors landed on a certain island which was rather small, and lit a fire. But they had made a mistake. It was not an island. It was composed of some basking whales. The lighting of the fire caused them to submerge at once, and the sailors were drowned. However, this shoal of earth on which I stood in the Caribbean was no illusion, and it served as a good base from which to swim out with a snorkel. It certainly goes against the grain to use so ugly a word as snorkel in reference to so wonderful an experience. I wish we could do away with it and use instead a term such as 'the Aqua Eye'. Anyway, thus equipped we can explore the submarine world of coral.

I wonder if there is anything in Nature more wonderful than coral. It appears to be rock, and it is hard enough and sharp enough to pierce the hulls of ships, and to serve as a barrier to affright the fiercest sharks. But it is not made of rocks. It is made of skeletons. Yet its top layer is *alive*, consisting of millions of tiny creatures called polyps. They are rather like jellyfish, but they possess rudimentary bones which by virtue of lime in the sea water become very hard. We call the final product coral, and we can truly say of polyps that their bones are of coral made, for they have suffered a sea change into something rich and strange. How does the coral reef grow, how does it increase? We think of another little creature called the hydra. Its manner of giving birth to new hydras is by growing them on its person like buds on a tree. After a certain period they break off to live a life of their own. The losing of a head is no problem to a hydra: it simply grows another. Thus we speak of the hydra-headed monster. A polyp has the same organisation as the hydra, the same method of budding its offspring – with one difference. The hydra breaks off from the parent body, the polyp continues to remain attached, thus increasing the body of which it forms a part.

One polyp is seemingly a poor thing. But the multiplication of polyps in their millions, clinging together to form a whole which grows and swells and marches, is a very great thing. There is no term to their existence, nor limit to their empire. The Great Barrier Reef along the north-eastern coast of Australia stretches for a length of one thousand miles. In the construction of this coral there is a remarkable exchange between the living and the dead. When a polyp dies, all the soft parts of its body perish and are washed away, while its skeleton is left to make a further contribution to the strength and size of the polypary. The skeletons are broken but not lost: the alchemy of lime works upon the fallen bones and cements them to the whole. In summary, we have the living creatures reaching upward, and the dead creatures, while their fleeting flesh decays, casting down their remnants to reinforce the pedestal upon which the others stand. The living reef arrayed with many colours is based upon the congregation of the dead.

. . . I take my Aqua Eye and swim out. My head is practically on the surface, but my eye could be fathoms deep. As I pass along I see miniature mountain ranges, crags and cliffs and caves and secret recesses, and valleys winding through hills. I see coral in so many colours and shapes: some like huge green leaves, others like battered tables, like a group of stags' antlers, like tapestried cannon-balls, like sponges, like hedgehogs: some as thin as ferns, others in the form of boulders with marks upon them as hieroglyphics of the first scripture traced upon the foundations of the world.

As I pass through this element I am struck by the extraordinary purity of it – the extremity of its cleanliness. Here there is no dust, no dirt. Not a thing here needs to be sent to the wash. In this kingdom nothing is rusty or in need of a coat of paint; there is never any smoke or fog or fumes or foul smells or dreadful noises or shameful sights. It was not till life had pushed its way from the water to dry land that the earth was *stained*.

The fishes seem unaware of my presence, they take no notice of me. They do not appear to be in any hurry or in search of anything particular;

they twist here and there, examine a recess, look into a corner then pass on unconcerned, they are not troubled. I marvel at the versatility of their designs; that neat one over there, a bright yellow; that larger one in stripes, that long one looking like a translucent snake: here a shoal, there a lone ranger. Clearly they are superior beings. They do not fear the Monster that rules our movements. Every creature on dry land is obliged to keep its feet upon it or perish. If we go over the edge of a cliff we are instantly pulled to the bottom and killed. We call it falling. There is no fall of fishes. Unimpressed by gravitation they survey their world with equanimity. Never do we see a fish bruising itself by ignoring the law which governs us. They are supported on all sides in an element which unfailingly evens itself out. No need of arms or legs: with a flick of a tail they can mount their Matterhorn or descend their Everest in perfect equilibrium. Exempt from our bondage and freed from our fears, they live in so democratic an element that no monarch among fishes, with the indifference of princes, is ever in a position to say – *Après moi le déluge.*

20 August, 1983

Jeffrey Bernard

HEAVENLY

Last Sunday the Fisherman's Pub in Speightstown was closed. I was very disappointed. Outside on the beach, sitting under the tree where the fishermen play dominoes, there was an old man who I saw at once had had his right hand chopped off at the wrist. I asked him where could I get a drink in Speightstown on a Sunday. He said he'd show me and bade me follow him. As we walked along a dusty backstreet in almost suffocating heat he asked me about myself and emphasised every question by prodding me gently with his stump. I wondered what on earth he was leading me to and began to wonder whether I shouldn't have better stayed with the Four Horsewomen of the Apocalypse, Irma Kurtz, Anne Leslie, Sally Vincent and Suzanne Lowry, who were either wandering through botanical gardens or lounging by pools.

Eventually we arrived at a typically seedy and rather dilapidated Bajan bar. Three or four men were sitting on a bench arguing and another sat on a stool in front of a fruit machine feeding it relentlessly with 25 cent coins. Behind the bar an enormous fat woman was cutting up pork with an electric saw and with her was the boss man. My guide hadn't come along for the ride and I asked him what he would like. He ordered a rum and Pepsi-Cola and 20 cigarettes. I asked for a vodka, bottle of soda and a half of a lime. The boss put two half-bottles on the bar and that was 16 measures each. He introduced himself as Robert and came round and introduced me to his customers. We all shook hands and I was all right, I gathered, because I was English and not American. The man at the fruit machine was drunk already. He asked me if I knew Richard in London. I told him there were lots of Richards in London. The boss said, 'Take no notice. We have a word for people like him in Barbados but you probably wouldn't understand it. He is what we call a wanker.' I told him we had that word too and that seemed to please him. The stump, my guide, poured himself a rum to the very top of his glass and it slid down his throat like something going home where it belonged. He chased it with a minute quantity of Pepsi which made his face wrinkle. Then we poured ourselves another and the three of us went outside to stand on the pavement.

Opposite the bar was the Church of Christ. It was a blindingly white church in the sun and the windows were open as the morning service was in progress. I could hear the murmur of prayer. Suddenly there was cacophony. Wonderful cacophony. The church broke out with the most hair-raising hallelujah chorus. Cymbals, hand-clapping, drums and the chanting almost wailing, with a mild hysteria that was incredible. In the middle of all this, as we sipped in the sun relishing the sounds, the fruit machine suddenly vomited the jackpot. It spewed all over the floor and the idiot operating the horrid machine was by then too drunk to pick up his loot. It was really rather amazing. I had God to my left, nuts to my right, the sun in heaven and a bottle of vodka that was condensing on the outside – beautifully cold – and begging for friendship. The stump was swaying and reeling to the church music. The boss man said that business was looking up and the fat wife came out from behind the bar and handed me a lump of fried chicken. Who needs Claridges?

And, further down the beach from our splendid luxury hotel, the Treasure Beach, the day before had involved a visit to a nice little beach bar called – aptly – Kisses. This was and is run by a beautiful piece of long-legged, ebony machinery called Diana. It always amazes me that my colleagues think I'm asleep. I'm so aware it hurts. I can't swim which is a nuisance but while others snorkel I'm not entirely without other sporting resources. I come to life in the sun. The grey-haired skeleton comes to life and nearly death. I had a very mild touch of sunstroke one afternoon and had to be swathed in ice packs. Anne Leslie administered and cured.

Everyone was marvellous and the PR who arranged the trip, Geoff Fleming, has to be the only PR in England who isn't a bore and who knows what he's doing. Decent people deserve plugs. Not that many *Spectator* readers will sensibly avail themselves of Barbados, but if you are loaded it's well worth a call. The English racing fraternity invade it to such an extent in January and February they call it Newmarket-by-the-Sea. But it's very jolly, hot and fairly friendly. The only person who might disagree with that was the prostitute who threw a glass of beer in my face when she propositioned me and I asked her to give me time to think.

Today is the Arc de Triomphe so it's away again to Paris. Rainbow Quest might do it for England but I've a hunch a French horse will win. They'll stop at nothing to avenge Waterloo. Too late, thank God. In Bridgetown there's a statue of Nelson erected 85 years before our Trafalgar Square version. Shame.

6 October, 1984

Matthew Parris

UP THE AIRY MOUNTAIN

Peru

There were three of us: Louisa (an Italian lady interpretess from Luxembourg), a male friend, and myself. I could guarantee my friend's anonymity by revealing only that he was the SDP Euro-candidate for Hampshire Central, but as he emerges from the episode with credit, he can be named: Francis Jacobs.

We had had a long day's march. Following the little Rio Tigre towards its source, and gaining altitude all the time, loaded down with tents and stoves and sleeping bags, we had passed through many tiny Andean villages, been mobbed by swarms of Indian children, but finally sensed, as the air grew thinner and the villages scarcer, cares lifting from our shoulders and a pleasant weariness descending.

Before dusk we reached a rather strange Indian settlement called Jajachaca. Its mud huts were mean and nobody approached but three hideous old men. They blocked our path, more than usually far-gone on coca, remnants of the leaves of which were hanging from their teeth, and begged for money. We noticed that the llamas looked in better condition than their owners. 'Probably llama-rustlers,' joked Francis.

It was getting dark so, with the village behind us and our path clinging to the edge of a high, steep gorge, we clambered down the side to the banks of the river, a hundred feet beneath. It felt enclosed, safe; and the tents were soon up, and supper on the boil.

In the fading light we thought we saw a man halted on the path above us, staring for some minutes and then moving off: but we were not much disconcerted.

Louisa was tired but by now quite thrilled with camping. Francis had offered assistance with her bedroll in that 'Happy, darling?' way they do in the movies. I could ruin his prospects in the Alliance by saying that he planned to share her tent . . . or rescue my career in the Conservative Party by saying she planned to share mine . . . but I shall say nothing.

Louisa retired to the tent. Francis and I stayed up a little, talking. After an argument about the financing of London Transport, he started telling me a funny story about his last trip to Haiti. We laughed together, lapsed into silence. Suddenly, there was a man's voice shouting. It seemed to come from the path above – high and hysterical and in no language we could understand.

I shouted back in Spanish, 'What do you want?' The response was immediate, unintelligible but enraged.

'Come down,' Francis shouted, 'and talk to us.'

That was no doubt the SDP training: a call for dialogue. For myself I asked myself (as one always does) 'What would Mrs Thatcher do?' The answer was clear. 'Let's go for them with our penknife!' I said to Francis. He must mentally have consulted Shirley Williams: 'No. We'd better find out how many of them there are, and whether they're armed.' I'm glad it is to the SDP side of the Alliance, and not the Liberal, that Francis inclines. Had David Steel been his mentor, he would have been off joining the bandits before Louisa and I had time to run.

The shouting only got worse, and we realised it was in Quechua – the Indian language. We shouted back. Then it gave way to singing – of a strange, wild kind: it filled us with unease. 'We mustn't show we're worried,' Francis said. 'Let's try John Brown's Body in reply.' So we did – a lusty rendering.

A great rock whistled past my ear, missing me by inches and thudding into my tent. It would have put me right out of action. I shouted angrily back. More rocks and stones rained down as we ran for the cover of the undergrowth.

Louisa was out of the tent by now, and terrified. We all were. There was something nightmarish about being trapped in a gorge, beneath your enemy and unable to see him. We crouched behind boulders and bushes, the river rushing behind us and rocks hailing down from the mountain-face before us.

I saw that the moon was about to rise and remembered that it was a full moon. All my life I have been a little afraid of darkness. Now it seemed to be our friend. 'Quickly,' I said, 'let's get out of here. Not all together or we'll be an easy target. You go one way, Francis: you take off your white windcheater, Louisa – it's too easy to see – and follow me.'

She did. We crept from bush to bush, zig-zagging out of the moonlight, up towards a stretch of path away from the shouting. We got separated from Francis and dared not call. Reaching the path, I handed Louisa the penknife and torch. 'Run back to the village. Stay there or bring help.' She hesitated, then ran.

Freed from a feeling of responsibility for anyone else, I began to enjoy myself. I wanted to size up our enemy, so scrambled a little above the path, then slid along the mountainside, in the direction of the shouting, until I reached a cockpit of boulders perched just above the source of the noise.

It was only one man! He seemed to be wearing a light-coloured poncho and was standing with his back to me, screaming at the tents and loosing off rocks. From time to time he would dance a swaying dance, holding a stone in each hand and clicking them together violently. Then he would hurl them, with some accuracy, at the campsite. He thought we were still in it. I could have surprised him by leaping on him from behind but I am not a good grappler and Louisa had the knife. I remember contemplating this and then chuckling to myself at the recollection of a correspondence I had left unfinished in England. It was with Edward Du Cann about my wish to assemble an All Party Civil Liberties Group.

Abruptly, and to my dismay, the man stopped his noise and loped off – in the direction of the village where I had sent Louisa. Francis emerged. Should we go after her? Before we could decide we heard her coming back. She was sobbing. Her face and arms were grazed.

She had been locked out of every hut. The village had barred its doors and extinguished its lamps. She had set out back to us. Then, on the path, she had run into our enemy, who knocked her down and dragged her along the path. She had struggled free, shouting intercessions to Jesus and the Virgin Mary (which seemed to frighten him), and escaped. He had not followed.

After a hasty conference we decided we could not stay in our tents. The site was too vulnerable: what if he should come back with reinforce-ments? Nor could we break camp in the dark and move on. Along the path we would be an easy target. We decided to leave our tents and move our belongings up to the cockpit of boulders I had discovered, above the path. There we could see without being seen. One could keep watch while the others slept. We would have the advantage of height over any assailant.

I helped Francis and Louisa with their rucksacks and sleeping bags, and installed them in our new lookout. Then I prepared to clamber back down to the tents to fetch my own things. Just as I started, I saw something moving in the moonlight, 300 yards away. It was six men approaching silently along the path from the village. I knew they could not see me and dropped back into the bushes. Louisa and Francis were in the boulders behind me. I hissed to them: 'He's coming back. Hide! There are six. They're spreading out along the path.' (silence) 'They're throwing rocks!' (silence) 'They're shouting at us. They think we're in there.' (silence) 'Fire! They're setting fire to the bushes around the camp. Let's go!'

Instinctively we ran, clambering, under cover, up the mountain. We stopped to re-form, panting. At 12,000 feet, oxygen is short, and we lay there gasping for breath. In the panic Louisa had left her rucksack at the boulders. 'Hide, and wait with Francis,' I said. 'I'll get it.' I clambered down, back to our old hideout. Flames were leaping up from the campsite towards me and I could hear shouting and see men running. Afraid of being seen, I grabbed Louisa's things and scrambled back towards the others. Where were they? At last hissed whispers brought a response from a large bush, and the three of us huddled down together.

It was no good going back to the path. One way led back to the enemy village, the other led farther into the mountains with no return. The only way was up – straight up our mountainside. What we did not know was that the mountain rose to 17,000 feet. Yet the top never seemed more than 500 feet above us. So we just kept climbing.

By now, the altitude was affecting us badly. The slope could only be tackled on all fours and sometimes on our stomachs. Our handholds were sharp rocks and vicious cacti which cut our hands badly. We grew shorter and shorter of breath. Louisa was the weakest so I carried her shoulder-bags and Francis's rucksack, leaving Francis to help pull her up the worst parts.

We were spurred on by the sound of distant, thin whistles and shouts, coming up from the valley far below. Once we looked back and saw the opposite side of the valley lit by a great red flickering glow. We realised with horror that it was the reflection of bush fires around our campsite. We heard more whistles and they seemed closer. Louisa's nerve cracked momentarily and she started to cry. I tried to comfort her.

Up and up we scrambled, breathless to the point of nausea. We didn't know it, but we had climbed nearly 3,000 feet and it was by now many hours since we had left our campsite. What was worse, the rocks were becoming steeper and what appeared to be a cliff face rose before us. To left and right was impossibly precipitous. Behind and beneath us lay the valley of bandits. Upwards was still the only way.

We caught our breath as Louisa screamed. She had momentarily lost her footing. Quickly she regained control. But in the silence that followed we heard something from the valley below. It seemed to answer Louisa's scream. It was a thin, high song played on the Quena – the Indian flute – distant but clear on the mountain air. We seemed to hear in it the chilling message: 'We know where you are. We have heard you. We are in no hurry.' Louisa started crying again. She and Francis were exhausted.

'You stay here,' I said, 'and look after all our stuff. I'll go on and see if I can find a way round or up this cliff.' There did seem to be a way round. I was soon alone, out of sight of the others, and climbing. Without luggage and without dependent companions, all my fear dropped away from me again, as it had while I had been shadowing the man in the poncho. I felt exhilarated and free, climbed quickly, gaining some 500 feet among the broken, rocky cliffs, dogged only by the thought that it would be hard for the others to follow. Then I came to a rock face which seemed impossible. I stared at it for a while and at the precipices to each side: then tried a couple of footholds.

There was a way up. I reckoned I had a good chance of doing it without falling, though a fall would have been fatal: but I knew the others could not make it. It was one of those ethical choices that my Moral Sciences tutor at Cambridge had told me do not occur in real life. I looked at it from all sides and followed each possible choice through to its range of possible outcomes. The last of these reflections was: 'What will I say to Francis's mother?' That was what clinched it. I have always suspected she is a Conservative. 'No,' I decided. 'Back you go.'

Francis and Louisa were huddled under a rock. 'We're more or less trapped,' I told them. There seemed to be little choice: we would try to sleep until first light, then spy out the land and consider whether and how to return. A bitter wind had got up. It was too steep, and we were too tired to find anywhere sheltered or level, but I wedged myself against a cactus, wrapped in a llama-wool blanket (a souvenir), and slept. The others couldn't. They lay there, listening for sounds of attack – but all noise from the valley had ceased.

Before dawn, we clambered down the mountain. Headstrong as ever, I led Francis and Louisa over a small cliff. We managed a controlled tumble. No one was hurt, but Francis ripped his trousers in a rather final way, at the back. Perched a thousand feet above our campsite, we waited for sunrise.

Agonisingly slowly, the light crept over the snowy ridge of the Andes. It appeared that our campsite was deserted. The hillside was blackened and smouldering, but the tents were still there. With sunrise, our confidence returned. We could bypass the campsite and return to the homeward track but we could not avoid the enemy village. It seemed such a waste to leave the tents behind – but what if an ambush awaited us? I decided to go down alone, ready to run at the first hint of danger. Louisa handed me the penknife!

It was difficult descending into that valley. When I reached the campsite I had to stop, momentarily, to summon the courage to search it. The rushing river drowned all other noise, so no approach could be heard. I tried to keep watch in all directions at once, while searching. The hardest thing was to go into the tents which they had tried, unsuccessfully, to burn. There was nothing and no one there. Everything had gone. Luckily we had kept money and documents with us. Francis and Louisa had lost little, but my rucksack was gone – sentimental value at least – with all its contents, including a book, *Cases on Civil Liberties*. I hope the bandits find it useful.

Personally I would gladly have razed their little straw huts to the ground, careless of their civil liberties.

As I called the others down, I thought I saw the disappearing silhouette of an old woman on the skyline. Anxiously, we packed the tents. There was nothing for it but to go back, and we could not avoid passing the village. I would go through first, unladen, ready to sprint, while the others observed my fate from the path.

People withdrew into their houses as I approached but nobody challenged me. Two snowy-white llamas, shampooed and back-combed, with scarlet tassels in their ears, raised their heads and stared at me with ill-grace as I passed. I signalled to the others that all was well. As they left the village, an old crone, looking like one of the witches in Macbeth, stepped out of the shadows and hailed them in broken Spanish:

'How are you today?' she cackled. Francis and Louisa answered that they were in less than fine spirits. 'Oh dear! What a shame! Tell me, which side of the mountain did you go up? We were wondering . . . .' They made no reply. 'Oh well – the night is past. You are safe now. Goodbye!'

When I got to Lake Titicaca, I sent the Chief Whip a postcard. Francis has not told David Owen. He does not think he would be interested. Francis is very modest. Louisa has not told her father as he would be angry. He lives in Milan. I hope they don't take *The Spectator* there.

22 December, 1984

A. M. Daniels

THE GRINGO PRISONERS

La Paz

The gringo prisoners in San Pedro jail in La Paz, says *The South American Handbook*, would appreciate a visit from anyone with a few minutes to spare.

I went with two friends, Richard and Frances, both of them doctors. The guards at the gate in the implacably featureless wall of the prison that faced the Plaza San Pedro signalled us to enter by a wave of their guns. Frances filed off to the right, to be frisked with the prisoners' wives; Richard and I to the left. We each emerged with a plastic card warning us that if we lost it we would not be allowed out of the jail.

Four prisoners *de habla inglés* were waiting for us in a courtyard. News travels fast in prisons. They crowded round us, laughing and expostulating like puppets controlled by puppetmasters with St Vitus's dance: they had so much to say that it came out in an excited, unintelligible babble. One of them managed to ask us whether we would buy them a meal in one of the prison canteens, and we agreed.

'Boy, this is our lucky day!'

On the way they explained the prison system. Everything could be bought in San Pedro. For rich prisoners it was like a luxury hotel with a few minor restrictions which could usually be circumvented. Colour televisions, guns, liquor, prostitutes – all were available from the warders. The cocaine in San Pedro was said to be the finest in the world. Sixty per cent of the prisoners, and all of the gringos, were drug smugglers.

Life was very different for those without money. They lived in the catacombs. Any cell larger than a coffin sized hole in the wall had to be rented from the warders. If a cell possessed a light, the warders were paid for the electricity. They were exacting landlords: eviction to the catacombs occurred at the first non-payment of rent.

The canteen had a few greasy tables near a steaming serving hatch. The prisoners ordered their food, and we heard the squelch of the anticipatory saliva in their mouths. The meal was a plate of dishwater in whose centre swam a large chunk of grey meat on a bone.

We had never seen people eat so ravenously. All social inhibitions were abandoned. A spoon proved too slow for one of them, who picked up the soup and poured it down his gullet, losing half of it in the process. But the meat was the real prize: they tore at it like hyenas.

The meal was over in 30 seconds. They sat back and patted their stomachs contentedly.

'Boy, was that good!'

Frances gave them cigarettes and they started to talk.

'We're not exactly innocents in here,' said one of them.

'We hadn't supposed you were,' said Richard.

The first was a 22-year-old Norwegian who had learnt English in the outback of Australia. He was tall and lean, and his hair was already thinning. When we passed a mirror he glanced at himself and said, 'Christ, I've aged!' and tears came to his eyes.

But his mood was otherwise buoyant. His three-year sentence would be completed in only a month's time. The others shook their heads at his naive belief that he would be released at the end of his sentence. They had seen such hopes dashed before.

He thought that, unlike the others, his capture had been merely bad luck. He had all but boarded the aircraft at La Paz airport when he was pulled back. Several kilos of cocaine were found strapped to his body.

'What is this white powder?' asked the man who searched him.

'You know what it is, you bastard.'

He was taken to another room where a crowd of policemen gathered. The chief took over the interrogation.

'Is this cocaine, gringo?'

'You know it is.'

'We had better make sure.'

He took out a chemical testing kit.

'If this test turns blue, gringo, it's cocaine.'

'I know it's cocaine, you bastard, there's no need to test it.'

The policemen enjoyed the mock-suspense. When the test-tube turned blue they crowed in triumph.

'It's cocaine, gringo. Tut-tut.'

The chief put some on his palm and took a deep sniff.

'It's very good, gringo. Where did you get it?'

'I'm not telling you, you bastard.'

All the policemen took a turn at sniffing the cocaine, and then the chief dismissed them from the room.

'You're in trouble, gringo. You could go to prison for 20 years. That's a long time.' He paused. 'Unless you give me $20,000.'

'I don't have $20,000.'

'Come on, gringo, cocaine like this is worth a lot of money.'

He lowered his demand to $10,000, but the Norwegian was unable to pay even this. In any case, there was no reason why, having taken the money, the policeman should have released him. Bribes in Bolivia achieve their end only often enough to keep the institution of bribery alive. The Norwegian received a comparatively short sentence on account of his youth.

We asked him whether he would resume drug smuggling after his release. He said no; but he added that one successful trip could set up a man for life.

The second of the prisoners was a young blond Canadian who would have been handsome had he not been so obviously racked with disease. The others whispered that he was an alcoholic: if he didn't find alcohol by ten in the morning he grew desperate, and even had fits.

He had been caught not by the Bolivian police but by the American Drug Enforcement Agency (DEA). Acting on a tip-off, the Bolivian police had searched his hotel room (the hotel in which we were staying) but found nothing. The day before his departure three American agents broke into his room, pushed him into the bathroom and held a gun to his head.

'We have no authority here in this country,' they said. 'But you are going to tell us everything you know.'

Before long, they had found the cocaine, stuffed into a pair of aqualungs (he had told the Bolivians he used them for diving in Lake Titicaca).

He had been in San Pedro three years before he was sentenced. He paid lawyer after lawyer, who said: 'Don't worry, it'll be all right, but we have to wait until the appeal comes up in Sucre'; and then they disappeared with the fee. In three years he had appeared in court 35 times, without ever speaking in his own defence.

The only purpose, he said, of having a lawyer in Bolivia was to act as a conduit for your bribe to the judge. But the bribe often failed to reach the judge; or it if reached the judge, he took no notice of it; or if he took notice of it, political turmoil ensured that by the time your case came to judgement he was no longer a judge. Besides, there was every incentive for a conviction. The DEA paid the authorities a bounty for each smuggler convicted; the prisoner went on bribing; and finally, they got the cocaine.

The blond Canadian had lost $30,000 in this way. But he was sentenced all the same to 15 years in jail, with a $2,000 fine to pay before he was allowed to leave the country.

The third prisoner was another Canadian who looked physically at the end of his tether. His hair was unkempt, his spindly arms were covered with sores and scars from injections with dirty needles, and he told us, not without a certain gallows pride, that he now weighed less than 70 pounds.

He was a drug-addicted, habitually violent criminal. His first conviction for armed robbery was in Montreal at the age of 16. Having eaten his free meal and procured a packet of cigarettes, he drifted off, no longer interested in us.

The last of the four was a French-Canadian with no cause to love the third. He came from a small, economically-depressed village in Quebec where there was no work. After his father drank himself to death he moved to Montreal where, being completely unskilled, he found no work either. Eventually someone offered him $5,000 to bring some cocaine from Bolivia, with the third of the prisoners as companion in the enterprise. The French-Canadian made it safely through customs, but his companion was caught and immediately grassed on him, since he did not relish the thought of languishing in a Bolivian jail alone while the other collected his $5,000. Each of them was sentenced to 10 years and an $8,000 fine at the end of it.

We asked him whether he did not wish to kill the man who had betrayed him thus.

He replied that at first he had been subject to murderous inclinations, but his Catholic faith helped him to overcome them, and now he merely pitied him.

All of them, with the exception of the Norwegian, half-expected to die in San Pedro. Not long before, a warder had been found upside down with his head in a latrine. A Colombian prisoner had hanged himself after murdering a compatriot over a quarrel during a game of cards. Two prisoners had needed operations, one for appendicitis, the other for a broken ankle: both died under the anaesthetic.

They wanted to show us their cells, and we walked through the prison with them. We saw the kitchen where the gruel for those prisoners who could afford no other food was prepared. In the centre of the kitchen was a boiling cauldron, large enough for a man to drown in. The walls, the floor and the ceiling were thickly caked with dried gruel that had turned black with age.

The 'cook' stirred the contents of the cauldron with a crowbar and gave us an evil, sweaty grin.

We crossed the main courtyard where the prisoners spent much of their time, day after day, year after year. Old lags stood exchanging stale prison gossip. Various prison characters were pointed out to us: notorious homosexuals, the controller of the illicit still, a prostitute whose boast it was to have had intercourse with every prisoner in San Pedro, including the 85-year-old doyen.

We saw the prison mascot, a mongrel bitch.

'That bitch has pups every six months,' said the blond Canadian.

'I suppose they're half-human,' I said.

'Don't joke,' he replied. 'That bitch is the most fucked bitch in Bolivia.'

He told me the Quechua word for one who find dogs attractive.

'That's the kind of Quechua I speak,' he said.

We went to his cell, a dark room five feet by eight up a rickety ladder in a neglected part of the roof. We had bought him a bottle of spirits – oleaginous and industrial-tasting. He drank half a bottle at a gulp.

'You've made me happy for a day,' he said.

He showed us his sketches, portraits of other prisoners mostly. He was a talented draughtsman but had run out of paper and pencils. He hoped his mother would send him some for Christmas in six months' time.

Six months! The mention of time stirred his emotions and his voice cracked. He would be more than 40 when he left San Pedro, if ever he did, his youth gone, his life in ruins. He finished the bottle.

The French-Canadian showed us his cell too. It was a kind of penthouse, he said, for no cell was higher up. We noticed a crucifix hanging above his bed, and noticing that we noticed he said:

'I still say my prayers.'

Suddenly ashamed, he added:

'My prayer says, God get me out of here.'

He laughed, but there was a plaster statuette of the Virgin by his bed as well.

'I'm just about keeping it together,' he said, referring to his sanity.

If ever he left prison he intended to go straight: work as a labourer in the Canadian North, where the wages were good and temptations few. After four years of existence at the outer edges of experience, his ambitions were entirely ordinary: to be married, to have a son, to own a house.

Before we left his cell he showed us his special treasure, folded in a tobacco tin under his bed. It was a doggerel epic of prison life, bequeathed by a former inmate of San Pedro.

A kind of ceremonial attached itself to the reading of this epic, performed only on special occasions. Each line was greeted as an old friend; they laughed in anticipation of the jokes. When the poem was over, it was folded away sadly.

We returned to the prison gates via a catwalk from which there was an unimpaired view of Illimani, the mountain of 21,000 feet that towers over La Paz. It was silent, calm, majestic, and they looked at it almost with reverence. To them it symbolised the outside world, freedom. They said they never failed to gather there to watch it as the sun went down.

'If they really wanted to punish us,' said the French-Canadian, 'they would build a wall to blot it out.'

The three of them strained at the gate to catch a last glimpse of us. 'Boy, was this our lucky day!'

21/28 December, 1985

Alexander Chancellor

TWO ETONIANS IN JAMAICA

I was 16 years old when the Suez crisis took place. Although at that age I had almost no knowledge of or interest in politics or world affairs, an awareness of Suez was forced upon me by the excitement it seemed to arouse in my father. We had just acquired our first television set, a thrilling event, and the earliest images I can remember seeing on it were of the Prime Minister, Anthony Eden, looking very grave.

Perhaps it was only for Mr Eden's appearances that my father turned the thing on, but I don't recall ever seeing anything else on television at that time apart from his gloomy face going on about putting out forest fires in the Middle East and saying that our quarrel was not with the Egyptian people but with a man called Nasser. For some reason this infuriated my father, who on one occasion threw a glass of whisky at the screen and stamped out of the room. It was quite clear to me from this that Eden was a bad man, that whatever he was planning to do to Egypt was not only a serious mistake but also – as my father assured me – in contravention of a very important principle known as the 'rule of law'. The custodian of this principle was an august and possibly even sacred body called the United Nations to which Mr Eden showed a deeply culpable indifference.

When I went back to my boarding school at Eton, I was surprised to find that his attitude towards Mr Eden's Middle Eastern policy was by no means universally shared. The other boys had fathers too, and these had trained their similarly impressionable offspring to adopt the precisely opposite position. So far as I remember, I was about the only boy in my boarding house who was not baying for Johnny Gippo's blood. None of the other boys seemed to have heard of 'the rule of law' or to comprehend the inequity of defying the United Nations. I was ignorant, self-righteous and alone. To my good fortune, I was then a regular reader of the *Daily Mirror*, which in its coverage of public affairs reflected the depth of my own interest in them. On Suez the *Mirror* was splendidly sound. Its comments read almost as if my father had written them. It furnished me with ever more pious arguments to deploy against my fellows, thereby increasing my glorious isolation.

Virtue of this quality does not go unrewarded. After the Suez expedition and our humiliating retreat, the Prime Minister, feeling ill and exhausted, went off to Jamaica to recover. Imaginative newspaper as it then was, the *Daily Mirror* responded instantly by announcing a readers' competition. It asked for no more than 200 words on how to solve the Suez crisis. The prize for the author of the best contribution was a fortnight's holiday for two in Montego Bay, Jamaica, 'home of ex-kings, press lords etc'. It was the beginning of winter in England and the weather was miserable. Lacking the confidence to enter the competition myself, I mentioned it to my sister Susanna, who is four years older than I and was then working in London in some sort of secretarial job. Having received the same paternal guidance as myself, she duly wrote a vigorous 200 words about the United Nations, 'the rule of law', and the shortcomings of Mr Eden. It was one of 7,000 entries. Unanimously the judges declared her the winner.

When her identity was discovered it was an embarrassing moment. My father was then general manager of Reuters news agency. The chairman of the *Daily Mirror*, Mr Cecil King, was a Reuters director. It was rumoured that Mr King tried to get the judges to award the prize to someone else, but they were immovable. Susanna's was the entry they liked best. So the *Mirror* accepted the inevitable and announced that a 20-year-old London typist called Susanna Chancellor was the lucky winner of a once-in-a-lifetime holiday.

The publicity began at once, with daily front page stories of Susanna's preparations for her departure, including a moving account with photograph of her saying goodbye to 'her dog' (a dalmation belonging to my parents for which she had little affection).

If the selection of her as winner was embarrassing to the *Mirror*, there was worse to come. The prize was a holiday for two. Who was Susanna to take with her? The *Mirror* hoped she would take a boyfriend, to give the story a bit of romantic interest. Her nearest thing to a boyfriend at the time was Jock Bruce-Gardyne. But good sport that she was, she announced that she was taking me. She could hardly have made a less satisfactory choice. Not only was I a dreary younger brother. I was an

Etonian, like the despised Mr Eden. This unpalatable fact resulted in a crisis meeting of the *Mirror*'s senior editors. They concluded there was nothing to be done. Under the circumstances, they might as well go the full hog. When my moment to leave for Jamaica arrived, there appeared on the *Mirror*'s front page a photograph of a pale, heavily wrapped up youth waving goodbye through the mist at London airport – and above it an enormous headline: 'Another Etonian leaves for Jamaica'. I arrived in the island a week after my sister because I had had to wait until the end of school term before I could go. The *Mirror* generously extended Susanna's prize to three weeks so that we could be a fortnight there together. By the time I got there she was already a celebrity. Her photograph had appeared in the *Mirror* every day. She had been shown in a bikini drinking rum out of a pineapple. She had been entertained by the governor, Sir Hugh Foot. She had even been shown exchanging smiles with the Prime Minister on the tarmac at Kingston airport under the cheeky headline: 'Susanna sees Eden off.' She had become 'Susanna' to the nation.

The man responsible for making her a star was the first real journalist I had ever met. I still remember him with affection. He was called Barry, though I can't recall the rest of his name, and had been sent down from New York to make the most of this unpromising story. He was a good-natured, cynical fellow, blasé about his luxury assignment and completely unscrupulous about what he chose to write. After a final burst of twaddle, in which he sought to establish that my reunion with my sister was a moment of high emotion for both of us, Barry decided he had done his stuff, deposited a large sum of money in the bank of the Sunset Lodge Hotel and flew back to New York.

For a week we were alone in this luxury hotel by the edge of the sea, learning what it was like to live like millionaires. Lord Beaverbrook was staying in the hotel. Marilyn Monroe passed through. We were taken up by the late Adele Astaire, Fred Astaire's sister and dancing partner, who had us over to meals at her hotel nearby. When we were asked to a New Year's party in Kingston, we hired our own aeroplane. We had come to find the 100 mile taxi drive too gruelling.

Although the time was not long, by the end we were bored and eager to get home. Everybody else seemed immensely old. We had spent Christmas alone together in Jamaica. Then came my birthday, for which Susanna had organised an agonising surprise – the singing of 'happy birthday to you' by a calypso band. Lord Beaverbrook, dining at the next table, looked extremely sour.

It had been, all in all, a slightly disappointing experience. But there was one good thing about it. Throughout all the time we were in Jamaica, I don't think we mentioned Suez once.

8 November, 1986

Zenga Longmore

NO REFUGE FOR RASTAS

After a week in Jamaica, I was so convinced I was in hell that I found myself wondering when I had died and what I had done to deserve such terrible retribution.

The scorching heat was to me the flames of Hades, the inflamed mosquito bites were the plague of boils, and the misery on the faces of the poverty-stricken people was surely the mark of souls in torment.

I was not dead, however. I was alive and well and staying in a small Clarendon town, for a month's holiday, with my sister, brother-in-law and his family. The house in which we were living was a huge bedraggled bungalow, home for armies of ants, cockroaches, giant spiders, rats, bats, nine children, and eight adults.

I would escape into the towns occasionally, but this was difficult, owing to the lack of transport. There is no public transport in Jamaica, only privately owned minibuses, with such fierce competition that the drivers grab you, shouting: 'Kingston! Mandeville! Spanish Town!' The strongest of the lot will seize you and frogmarch you towards a tiny minibus, packed solid with people. 'B-but I don't want to go to Kingston!' you protest as you are wedged in between a tight-lipped old lady and a basket of green bananas. 'Is where you a-go?' 'May Pen!' But it's too late. The bus boggles down the road at breakneck speed. Evil Knievel is the idol of the Jamaican driver. The bus finally deposits you at a remote town, leaving you almost too dazed to inquire how to get to where you first wanted to go.

The towns are crumbling away in a heap of decay. Every Jamaican between 16 and 50 feels that Jamaica is merely a transit land, which one has to put up with until one can get to England or America. Because of this, Jamaica is unloved. No one bothers to make a go of the good life there: instead of building up a better Jamaica, Jamaicans merely save up every penny they can earn, and shoot off to England or the States, leaving bitter wives, husbands and children behind. Buildings that were once grand and gleaming, stand peeling and filthy, surrounded by foul refuse.

The shops, such as they are, sell the barest utility foods. Dead dogs lie in the gutter, their insides strewn on the pavements.

People just stand, waiting for nothing. They stared at my sister and me with blank, shuttered faces, muttering, 'Foreigners,' as we passed. It took me a while to realise that we were not being insulted. It is a statement; we are not Jamaican (although black), so we come from 'foreign'.

Everywhere I went I saw children: children who don't play, children who stand or sit motionless. Families are large, and yet there are very few facilities for children. I saw no playgrounds, and few toyshops. The school I visited was a swarming mass of impeccably dressed children standing three to a desk, copying off the blackboard. The teacher stood at the front of the class glaring, strap in hand. When I asked to see a ten-year-old's book he showed me a page of beautiful Victorian italic writing, all about the English Queen.

'What does it say?' I asked.

He looked at me blankly.

'Read some out to me.'

'Me nar read,' he said.

Jamaican schools appeared to be a showcase of immaculate uniforms and copying, but no teaching. I came across no child under the age of 14 who had the first clue concerning reading and writing. The adults didn't blame the schools. They blamed Jamaica itself. 'It jus' dat foreign pickney dem is clever,' I was often told.

The people had a touching love of England. The grannies, who dominate Jamaican life, sat around telling their families that England is the mother country, and Jamaica her daughter. My sister and I were treated as English duchesses. We were not allowed to do our own washing or washing up. 'You's a lady, so you mustn't get your hands dirty,' we were told, as we were dragged away from the sink. Our accents and 'high gold' complexions were a passport to having first place in any queue, and a seat on the buses. It felt most odd to be treated like English royalty in Jamaica after a lifetime of not being considered English in England.

White people were neither here nor there, but 'fair-skinned' black people were guaranteed posh jobs and affected snobby mannerisms. I was considered inordinately rich, and received more offers of marriage in my first week than ever before in my life. Once I was taken to see a prospective mother-in-law, an old lady living in the Blue Mountains in a one-roomed wooden shack, along with six grandchildren and a frail old husband. There was no gas or electricity, only kerosene lamps and a firewood cooker. The water was supplied by a stream half a mile away.

'Please marry my son, ma'am. Tek him to Englan' and mak him rich.' I glanced at the gormless young man, and told her I'd have to think it over. Then I took a long, pensive walk back to the nearest town.

The scenery was the most beautiful I have ever laid eyes upon. Lush palms and banana trees, and exotic flowers, all in vivid colours. Fabulous mountains, rivers, gorges and lakes. Sitting on a rock by a waterfall in the Blue Mountains, I realised that what I had mistaken for hell was in fact paradise.

Then I began to notice the implicit honesty of the people. No one ever swindled, mistrusted, or cheated me. Market traders left their wares unattended, and shoppers would pick up the goods, and leave the right amount of money by the side of the stalls. Even in Kingston, that great sprawling town of incomparable ugliness, I never felt unsafe, even when alone at night. Because of Kingston's violent reputation, nobody walked the streets, so there wasn't anyone around to be violent. Just street after street of dilapidated houses, empty shops, and vile refuse. Festering on the outskirts of Kingston were forlorn shanty shacks, lying higgledy-piggledy in muddy pathways. They are built of wood, corrugated iron, barrel lids – anything that will keep out the tropical rainstorms. The goats and dogs of these shanty towns seem as miserable and apathetic as the people.

On my last day in Jamaica, my relations finally succeeded in dragging me to a church. The family members who didn't come were bowed down with guilt and apologies. Everyone goes to church in Jamaica; only the 'quashie dem' don't go. ('Quashie' are the lumpenproletariat, the hoi polloi; 'dem' being the plural. Plurals and tenses are few and far between in Jamaica.)

The church was an enormous hall, crammed with hundreds of people, grannies, grandads, mums, dads, and kids. Our party could get a seat by virtue of 'coming from foreign', but hundreds of others stood round the hall, packed solid against the walls. White hats and lace dresses sparkled in the sunshine. The singing was lovely, sweet voices harmonising soulful gospel music. Then the preacher began her sermon, shouting into a microphone about the Devil and his cunning ways. I am afraid I am unable to elaborate on the speech, because I promptly nodded off to sleep.

I was awoken with a jerk by a sharp nudge in the ribs. 'Wake! Wake! Preacher she say would foreign lady stand up.' I stood up, swaying slightly on my feet. The preacher smiled at me. 'It nice to have English miss in our congregation. Welcome.' I smiled goofily back, and the service went on. Thousands of people singing and banging tambourines.

Church services sprang up impromptu wherever I went. In busy market places a spontaneous preacher would leap up and begin to declaim the Bible to the masses. Shoppers crowded around, and listened avidly to his sermon. Amens rent the air. Then singing of pure beauty filled the thronging market, and I found myself swept along with the religious fervour, shouting and clapping.

> Steal away, steal away, steal away to Jesus
> Steal away, steal away home, I ain't got long to stay here.

All the energy in Jamaica seems to have gone into the churches, the creation of the slaves, a force much stronger than materialism. Maybe this has something to do with the honesty and humility which radiate from the people, especially the young people. There are no 'teenagers' in Jamaica. People under the age of 18 are children, and anyone over is an adult. This means that, thank goodness, there are no gangs of youths in Jamaica, who stand on street corners, smoking and shouting abuse at passers-by. I was amazed to find that reggae is hardly heard. It is looked down upon as a rough music, like punk rock, music of the quashie dem. Any self-respecting Jamaican will listen to Jim Reeves, and Sixties ballads. Rastas are a rare sight. They are considered godless backsliders, who are prayed for in church by their weeping relatives.

When I told a middle-aged lady that London is simply stuffed with reggae and Rastas, she shuddered and gasped: 'And I allowed my Errol to live in that wicked place!' I didn't tell her that I had imagined Jamaica to be a Rasta haven, with reggae parties blaring from every house. Far from it; Jamaica is not a young person's country. Night-clubs are empty, save for a handful of middle-aged men, and young men keep well in the background. The image of violent Jamaican youth is instantly dispelled on seeing the somewhat gauche young men who are too much in awe of the bossy old grannies to speak.

The young girls were more assertive, relentlessly begging me to send for them when I returned to England. Because they would not take no for an answer, I ummed and ahhed until my last day.

I left Jamaica with a feeling that it is heaven and hell combined. As I sped through Kingston's ruinous streets for the last time, I had a conviction that something must be done fast, but what? Somebody has to do something to make Jamaicans love Jamaica, land of the world's most exquisite scenery and of careworn, religious people.

22 November, 1986

NOTES ON CONTRIBUTORS

PETER ACKROYD. Novelist and biographer. Literary editor of *The Spectator* 1973-77. Joint managing editor of *The Spectator* 1978-82. Cinema critic for *The Spectator* 1982-87. Books include *The Last Testament of Oscar Wilde, Hawksmoor* and a biography of T. S. Eliot.

KINGSLEY AMIS. Novelist and winner of the Booker Prize for *The Old Devils* in 1986.

DIGBY ANDERSON. Director of the Social Affairs Unit, journalist and 'Imperative Cooking' columnist of *The Spectator* since 1983.

E. ARNOT ROBERTSON 1903-61. Novelist, broadcaster, lecturer and film critic. Her novels include *Four Frightened People* and *Ordinary Families*.

RICHARD BASSETT. *The Times* correspondent in Warsaw. Frequent contributor to *The Spectator* since 1983 on Eastern Europe.

JEFFREY BERNARD. Writer of *The Spectator*'s 'Low Life' column since 1978.

JOHN BETJEMAN 1906-84. Poet Laureate 1972-84. City and Suburban correspondent in *The Spectator* during the 1950s.

DHIREN BHAGAT. Frequent contributor to *The Spectator*, usually about India, since 1983.

ANDREW BROWN. Regular contributor to *The Spectator* 1980-87. Now religious affairs correspondent of *The Independent*.

ROWLINSON CARTER. Roving foreign correspondent. Contributor to *The Spectator* since 1986.

JOHN CASEY. Fellow in English of Gonville and Caius College, Cambridge. Author of *The Language of Criticism*. Former editor of the *Cambridge Review*.

ALEXANDER CHANCELLOR. Editor of *The Spectator* 1974-83. Currently Washington correspondent for *The Independent*.

HUGO CHARTERIS 1922-70. Writer and journalist. Wrote regularly for the *Daily Mail* and the *Daily Telegraph*.

GERDA COHEN. Journalist and frequent contributor to *The Spectator* since 1978. Formerly based in Israel.

NICHOLAS COLERIDGE. Editor of *Harpers & Queen* since 1987 and contributor to *The Spectator* since 1983.

JOHN STEWART COLLIS 1900-84. Wrote many columns and reviews for *The Spectator*. His most famous book, *The Worm Forgives the Plough*, came out of his experience of working on the land during the war. Both Richard Ingrams in a memoir and A. N. Wilson in an appreciation published after his death spoke of his 'genius'.

ANTHONY DANIELS. A doctor who has practised in five continents. Frequent contributor to *The Spectator* since 1983 (including under the name of Edward Theberton). Author of *Coups and Cocaine* and *Fool or Physician*.

ELIZABETH DAVID. Cookery writer and regular contributor to *The Spectator* throughout the 1950s. Her books include *French Provincial Cooking, Italian Food* and *An Omelette and a Glass of Wine*.

ALICE THOMAS ELLIS. Novelist and regular contributor to *The Spectator* with a column called 'Home Life'. Her novels include *Birds of the Air* and *Unexplained Laughter*.

DANIEL FARSON. Journalist and author. His most recent book is *Soho in the Fifties*.

IAN FLEMING 1908-64. Journalist and author. Creator of James Bond. Brother of Peter Fleming.

PETER FLEMING 1907-71. Regular columnist in *The Spectator* throughout the 1950s as Strix. A well-known traveller whose most famous books are *Brazilian Adventure, One's Company* and *News from Tartary*. Brother of Ian Fleming.

TIMOTHY GARTON ASH. Eastern European correspondent of *The Spectator* since 1982, *The Spectator*'s foreign editor since 1983. Author of *The Polish Revolution: 1980-1982*.

WILLIAM GOLDING. Novelist and winner of the Nobel Prize for Literature in 1983. Books include *Lord of the Flies* and *Rites of Passage*.

GRAHAM GREENE. Novelist. Literary editor of *The Spectator* 1940-41, and cinema critic during the late 1930s.

DENIS HILLS. Speaks Polish, German, Russian and Swahili. He has been thrown out of Poland twice and condemned to death by Idi Amin. Among his books are *My Travels in Turkey, The Last Days of White Rhodesia, The White Pumpkin* and *Return to Poland*.

ALISTAIR HORNE. Historian and journalist. Books include *A Savage War of Peace: Algeria*.

BARRY HUMPHRIES. Music-hall artiste and author; his most famous creation is Dame Edna Everage.

P. J. KAVANAGH. Poet and writer. Poetry editor of *The Spectator* since 1985 and regular contributor with his 'Life and Letters' column. Books include *The Perfect Stranger*.

LUDOVIC KENNEDY. Writer and broadcaster. Books include *10 Rillington Place*.

ROY KERRIDGE. Journalist and regular contributor on social and racial matters to *The Spectator*. Brother of Zenga Longmore.

PATRICK LEIGH FERMOR. Traveller and travel writer. Publications include *Mani, A Time of Gifts*, and *Between the Woods and the Water*.

ZENGA LONGMORE. Occasional contributor to *The Spectator* since 1986. Sister of Roy Kerridge.

ROSE MACAULAY, 1881-1958. Travel writer and novelist. Frequent contributor to *The Spectator* in the 1930s and 1940s. Her works include *They Went to Portugal* and *The Towers of Trebizond*.

NOEL MALCOLM. Political editor of *The Spectator* since October 1987.

HILARY MANTEL. Winner of the 1986 Shiva Naipaul Memorial Prize. Novelist and *The Spectator*'s film critic since 1987.

PATRICK MARNHAM. Twice literary editor of *The Spectator* and regular contributor. Now Paris correspondent for *The Independent*. Books include *The Private Eye Story, Fantastic Invasion* and *So Far From God*.

PETER MAYNE 1908-79. Born in England, but lived and worked in India and Pakistan until he retired to Morocco, where he wrote *A Year in Marrakesh*.

NANCY MITFORD 1904-73. Novelist and historical biographer who contributed frequently to *The Spectator*. Her books include *The Pursuit of Love, Don't Tell Alfred* and

The Sun King.

CHARLES MOORE. Editor of *The Spectator* from 1983.

JAMES MORRIS (see below)

JAN MORRIS. Travel writer and historian whose works include the 'Pax Britannica' trilogy and *Venice*. Regular contributor to *The Spectator* during the late 1950s as James Morris.

JOHN MORTIMER. Barrister, playwright, author and journalist. Contributor to *The Spectator* since 1985.

SHIVA NAIPAUL 1945–85. Travel writer, novelist and regular contributor to *The Spectator* 1975–85. Books include *Fireflies*, *The Chip-Chip Gatherers* and *Beyond the Dragon's Mouth*. Brother of V. S. Naipaul.

V. S. NAIPAUL. Novelist and winner of the Booker Prize in 1971 for *In a Free State*. Novels include *A Bend in the River* and travel books include *Among the Believers*. Brother of Shiva Naipaul.

HAROLD NICOLSON 1886–1968. Politician, writer, critic and diarist. Wrote 'Marginal Comment' column in *The Spectator* throughout the 1950s.

MATTHEW PARRIS. One-time Conservative MP, now broadcaster.

SIMON RAVEN. *The Spectator's* fiction reviewer during the late 1950s. His own novels include the *Alms for Oblivion* series.

CYRIL RAY. Regular contributor to *The Spectator* throughout the 1950s on wine and food. Author of many books on these subjects.

ALAN ROSS. Author, publisher and journalist. Editor of *London Magazine* since 1965.

JOHN RALSTON SAUL. Canadian novelist who has lived in France and Thailand. His books include *Birds of Prey*, *Baraka* and *The Paradise Eater*.

GAVIN STAMP. Architectural historian and journalist. Frequent contributor to *The Spectator* since 1981 on architectural matters.

DAME FREYA STARK. Well-known traveller and travel writer. Her books, mainly about Arabia, include *A Winter in Arabia*, *Beyond Euphrates* and *Riding to the Tigris*.

EDWARD THEBERTON (see Anthony Daniels)

TAKI THEODORACOPULOS. Weekly 'High Life' columnist in *The Spectator* since 1977.

COLIN THUBRON. Travel writer. Books include *Among the Russians* and *Behind the Wall: a Journey in China*.

KENNETH TYNAN 1927–80. Critic, producer and author. Theatre critic of *The Spectator* in 1951.

AUBERON WAUGH. Journalist and columnist. His regular column 'Another Voice' has appeared in *The Spectator* since 1976.

EVELYN WAUGH 1903–66. Novelist, travel writer and frequent contributor to *The Spectator* throughout his writing life. His travel books include *Labels*, *Remote People* and *Waugh in Abyssinia*.

COLIN WELCH. Journalist, political correspondent of *The Spectator* 1982–83. Lead book reviewer of *The Spectator* since 1983. Deputy editor of the *Daily Telegraph* 1950–80.

JOHN WELLS. Founding member of *Private Eye*. Frequent columnist in *The Spectator* during the late 1970s.

RICHARD WEST. War correspondent in Vietnam, traveller and journalist. Regular contributor to *The Spectator* since 1975.

SAM WHITE. Legendary Paris correspondent for the *Evening Standard* and regular contributor to *The Spectator* since 1975.

THE SHIVA NAIPAUL MEMORIAL PRIZE

Shiva Naipaul was one of the most gifted and accomplished writers of our time. When he died in August 1985 at the age of 40, *The Spectator* announced that it was setting up a fund to establish an annual prize in his memory.

On the first page of a recent notebook, Shiva Naipaul wrote: 'All journeys begin the same way. All travel is a form of self-extinction.' As a man outside every tribe, Shiva Naipaul saw himself as a traveller of the world, observing curiously the loyalties of men which he could not share. It was from this observation that he derived his greatest insights. He also wrote:

> A journey, one hopes, will become its own justification, will assume patterns, reveal its possibilities – reveal, even, its layers of meaning – as one goes along, trusting to chance, to instinct, to hunch. Journeys undertaken in this spirit – acknowledging, that is, the obscurity of the impulses that have provoked them – resemble a work of the imagination; a piece of fiction, say. Sometimes when we set out to write a novel all we have to begin with are stray, enigmatic images, evanescent scraps of feeling and intuition, which unite to create an intimation of possibility. Our literary labours delve after that possibility and seek to bring it to the surface and give it form. When you start off you do not necessarily know where you are going or why.

The Shiva Naipaul Memorial Prize is awarded to the writer best able to describe a visit to a foreign place or people. The award is not for travel writing in the conventional sense, but for the most acute and profound observation of cultures and/or scenes evidently alien to the writer. Such scenes and/or cultures might be found as easily within the writer's native country as outside it.

For full details of the award please write to: The Shiva Naipaul Memorial Prize, The Spectator, 56 Doughty Street, London WC1N 2LL.

INDEX

Names set in small capitals denote contributors